Beyond the Nass Valley

National Implications of the Supreme Court's *Delgamuukw* Decision

EDITED BY OWEN LIPPERT

The Fraser Institute

Vancouver   British Columbia   Canada

2000

Printed in Canada.

Canadian Cataloguing in Publication Data

Main entry under title:
Beyond the Nass Valley

Includes bibliographical references.
ISBN 0-88975-206-0

1. Indians of North America--Land tenure--Canada. 2. Indians of North America--Legal status, laws, etc.--Canada. 3. Land tenure--Law and legislation--Canada. 4. Natural resources--Law and legislation--Canada. 5. Indian land transfers--Canada. I. Lippert, Owen. II. Fraser Institute (Vancouver, B.C.)

KE7739.L3B49 2000   346.7104'32'08997   C00-910729-0
KF5660.A75B49 2000

Contents

About the Authors

CLAUDE BACHAND is a Member of the House of Commons, where he has represented the riding of Saint-Jean, Québec, since he was first elected in October 1993. He is currently the Bloc Québécois Indian Affairs and Northern Development Critic. From 1993 to 1997, he was the Official Opposition critic in this area. Born in Saint-Jean-sur-Richelieu in 1951, Claude Bachand, before being elected to the House of Commons, was actively involved in his community, in particular as president and spokesman for the Confédération des syndicats nationaux [Confederation of National Trade Unions] for the Haut-Richelieu region.

DARRELL BRICKER is the Executive Vice President, Angus Reid Polling Group, Toronto, Ontario.

DON CAYO was serving a two-year term as president of the Atlantic Institute for Market Studies (Halifax and Saint John, N.B.) at the time his chapter in this book was written. He is currently editorial page editor of the *Vancouver Sun*. He previously worked as a writer and editor for newspapers in Saskatchewan, British Columbia, Newfoundland and New Brunswick, as well as *The Canadian Press* in Halifax and Saint John. He was a reporter, commentator and producer for *CBC Radio and Television* in Newfoundland, and he taught journalism at Holland College in Prince Edward Island.

He has won 14 prizes for writing, including a B'nai Brith human rights award and a Canadian Policy Research citation for reporting on native issues across the country. This book-length 1997 series was published over four weeks in the New Brunswick Telegraph-Journal, where he was editorial page editor at the time.

THOMAS FLANAGAN is perhaps the only person ever to have lived in both Ottawa, Ontario, and Ottawa, Illinois. Born in Ottawa, Illinois, he studied political science at Notre Dame University, the Free University of West Berlin, and Duke University, where he received his Ph.D. He has taught political science at the University of Calgary since 1968.

Dr. Flanagan's research interests include political philosophy, Canadian politics, and aboriginal rights. He is best known for his books on Louis Riel and the Metis, including *Louis "David" Riel: "Prophet of the*

New World" (1979); *Riel and the Rebellion: 1885 Reconsidered* (1983); and *Metis Land Claims in Manitoba* (1991). His *Introduction to Government and Politics* (with Mark Dickerson) is widely used in Canadian colleges and universities as a textbook.

During 1991/1992, Dr. Flanagan took partial leave from the University of Calgary to act as Director of Research for the Reform Party of Canada. In 1995, Stoddart published his book *Waiting for the Wave: The Reform Party and Preston Manning*, which was partially based on that experience.

Dr. Flanagan was elected to the Royal Society of Canada in 1996. The University of Toronto Press published his *Game Theory and Canadian Politics* in 1998. His most recent book is *First Nations? Second Thoughts*, published by McGill-Queen's University Press in April 2000.

GORDON F. GIBSON was born in Vancouver in 1937. He attended the University of British Columbia (B.A. Honours Mathematics and Physics '59), Harvard Business School (M.B.A. Distinction '61). He has been involved in a number of businesses including pre-fabricated buildings, hotel and real estate development, and has served on the boards of several public companies.

In politics, he served as Assistant to the Prime Minister (1968–1972) and ran in three federal elections. He was elected to the Legislature of British Columbia in 1974 and served as both MLA and Leader of the British Columbia Liberal Party (1975–1979). Since then he has been active in both business and public affairs in Western Canada, including 12 years on the Canada West Council. With Canada West, he co-authored "Regional Representation" (1981), authored "What if the Wheels Fall Off?: the Case for a Constituent Assembly" (1992) and served on the Task Force on National Unity (1991–1993).

In 1993, he joined the Fraser Institute as Senior Fellow in Canadian Studies, specializing in research on Federalism. He has published two books through the Institute entitled *Plan B: the Future of the Rest of Canada* (1994) and *Thirty Million Musketeers: One Canada for All Canadians* (1995) and has written numerous papers on the topic, many of which have been published in *Fraser Forum*. He regularly releases the setting of the Canada Clock, a measure of the probability of Canada's survival in its present form.

Over the years he has been a regular columnist with (successively) *The Financial Post*, *The Vancouver Sun* and, currently, *The Globe and Mail*.

Mr. Gibson has produced a major public discussion document of British Columbia's position on the restructuring of federalism and other issues, commissioned by the Province of British Columbia and released in August 1997.

JOHN L. HOWARD, QC was Senior Vice-President, Law and Corporate Affairs, MacMillan Bloedel Limited until his retirement October 1996. He obtained degrees in law and business administration from the University of British Columbia and Harvard, was appointed a federal QC in 1977, is a former member of the Bar of Quebec and continues to be a member of the Bar of British Columbia.

In addition to his business and law practice experience, he has spent some 12 years as a federal public servant administering regulatory programs related to labour unions, corporations, securities markets and bankruptcies. During some eight of those years, he was an Assistant Deputy Minister in Consumer and Corporate Affairs Canada and, as such, indirectly involved a well in programs relating to consumer protection, competition law and patent and trademark law. He has also participated actively in the process of setting accounting standards in Canada as a member and chairman of an advisory board of the Canadian Institute of Chartered Accountants.

He has participated as author or consultant in the publication of several major policy studies relating to the regulation of corporations, bankrupt estates, mutual funds and securities markets and was a co-draftsman of federal bills or proposed bills relating to these subjects.

In 1979, he joined MacMillan Bloedel Limited as Vice-Preside t and General Counsel. In 1981, he was appointed Senior Vice-President with responsibility for administration of legal and government affairs, as well as other internal support services. He is presently retired and living in Sooke, British Columbia.

PAUL JOFFE is a member of the Québec and Ontario bars. Since 1974, he has specialized in aboriginal, constitutional, international and human rights issues. As legal counsel, he headed negotiations for Inuit on environment and development issues in relation to the James Bay and Northern Québec Agreement (1975). More recently, he was part of the legal team acting on behalf of the Intervener Grand Council of the Crees in the Supreme Court of Canada *Reference re Secession of Québec* (1996).

OWEN LIPPERT directs the Law and Markets Project at the Fraser Institute, Canada's largest independent economic think-tank. He writes and researches on intellectual property, aboriginal, legal and trade issues. Previously, he served as a policy advisor to the federal Minister of Science, the Attorney General of Canada and to the Premier of British Columbia. He holds a Ph.D. in European History from the University of Notre Dame, Indiana and a B.A. from Carleton College, Minnesota. He has most recently edited and contributed to *Competitive Strategies for*

Intellectual Property Protection (Fraser Institute, February 2000). His articles have appeared in the *Wall Street Journal, National Post, Globe and Mail* and many regional papers in Canada and the United States. He writes the Law and Economics column for *Canadian Lawyer* magazine.

J. KEITH LOWES is a Vancouver lawyer who represents natural resource businesses involved in claims to aboriginal rights and title. In court, he appeared as counsel for forestry, mining, ranching, tourism and other businesses in *Delgamuukw* and as counsel for the major fish processors in most of the leading aboriginal rights cases including *Sparrow, Van der Peet, Gladstone,* and *Nikal.* He advises the Business Caucus on Aboriginal Issues, a broad based coalition of resource industries, on aboriginal issues arising in the context of treaty negotiations and government policy as well as litigation.

THOMAS LUTES is an associate in the Vancouver office of the national law firm, Fraser Milner Casgrain. He practises in the area of aboriginal law, with an emphasis on resource and consultation issues for aboriginal, industry, and government clients.

MICHAEL J. MCDONALD is a consultant lawyer of Fraser Milner Casgrain and co-chair of that firm's Aboriginal Practice Group in the Vancouver offices. He is also a member of the Peguis First Nation and has extensive experience in the field of aboriginal law and development. Mr. McDonald is the former chair of the Aboriginal Law Subsection of the Canadian Bar Association (BC) and is currently a board member of World Vision Canada, Canada's largest non-profit humanitarian aid, relief, and development organization.

DAVID T. MCNAB is an Adjunct Professor in the department of Native Studies, Trent University, Ontario. He is a public historian who has worked for over two decades on Aboriginal land and treaty rights issues in Canada. He is currently a claims advisor for Nin.Da.Waab.Jig., Walpole Island Heritage Centre, Bkejwanong First Nations, and an Honorary External Associate in the Frost Centre for Canadian Studies and Native Studies at Trent University.

KENT MCNEIL is a graduate of the University of Saskatchewan (B.A., LL.B.) and Oxford University (D. Phil.). He has been a faculty member at Osgoode Hall Law School in Toronto since 1987. He is the author of numerous publications on the rights of indigenous peoples in Canada, Australia, and the United States. These works have been influential in the development of the law in relation to these rights. In particular, his book, *Common Law Aboriginal Title*, has been used by the Supreme Court of Canada and the High Court of Australia in landmark decisions on indigenous land rights.

PATRICK MONAHAN is a Professor of Law at Osgoode Hall Law School and an Affiliated Scholar at the law firm, Davies, Ward & Beck, in Toronto. He has written extensively on constitutional issues relating to aboriginal rights and has advised both governments and aboriginal organizations on these matters.

GEOFF PLANT was called to the Bar in British Columbia in 1982 and in the Yukon in 1984. He practiced with Vancouver law firm of Russell & DuMoulin from 1982 to 1996; was counsel for the Province at trial in *Delgamuukw*; appeared as counsel in other aboriginal rights cases including the Meares Island case and *R. v. Alphonse and Dick*. He was elected as member of the British Columbia Legislative Assembly in 1996. Mr. Plant has written and presented papers on various legal topics, principally in the area of aboriginal rights and education law. He is the Official Opposition Critic for the British Columbia Attorney General.

ALEC C. ROBERTSON received his Bachelor of Commerce and Bachelor of Laws from the University of British Columbia in 1955 and 1957 respectively. In 1958, he received his Master of Laws degree from Harvard Law School. He returned to British Columbia and in 1959 was admitted to practice law in the province.

Mr. Robertson left private practice in 1995 to become the full-time chief Commissioner of the British Columbia Treaty Commission. The Treaty Commission is the independent body that monitors and facilitates treaty negotiations between First Nations in British Columbia and the governments of Canada and British Columbia.

Prior to becoming Chief Commissioner, Mr. Robertson practised general business law and administrative law as a partner in the Vancouver law firm of Davis & Company. The business law practice included commercial development on Indian lands, a number of forestry related projects, and business acquisitions and dispositions. The administrative law practice focused on professional governing bodies, principally the Registered Nurses Association of British Columbia, for whom he was general counsel for many years.

In the past, Alec Robertson donated his time to several associations, including the Canadian Bar Association, of which he was President of the BC Branch, a member of the National Task Force on Gender Equality in the Legal Profession, and a co-author of its report entitled "Touchstones for Change."

Mr. Robertson's term as Chief Commissioner expired in May, 1998 and he has returned to practice with Davis & Company.

SÁKÉJ (JAMES YOUNGBLOOD HENDERSON) was born to the Bear Clan of the Chickasaw Nation and Cheyenne Tribe in Oklahoma and has become one of the leading Aboriginal philosophers, advocates and strategists of North American peoples. In 1974, he was one of the first American Indians to receive a Juris doctorate in law from Harvard Law School. During the constitutional process (1978 to 1993), Professor Henderson served as a constitutional advisors for the Mikmaq Nation and the Assembly of First Nations. He is a co-author of *Aboriginal Tenure in the Constitution of Canada* (Carswell, 2000) *and Protecting Indigenous Knowledge and Heritage* (Parish, 2000). He is a member of the College of Law. He is also a noted international human rights lawyer and a member of the Advisory Council to the Minister of Foreign Affairs that identifies strategic and emerging foreign policy issues. He currently pursues justice for Aboriginal Peoples of Canada through all the activities of the Native Law Centre as its senior administrator and Research Director.

SATSAN (HERB GEORGE) is a Wet'suwet'en Hereditary Chief. He is a member of the Frog Clan. Satsan is currently Vice-Chief for the BC Region of the Assembly of First Nations. He has been a long-time Speaker for the Wet'suwet'en Nation. He is an Adjunct Associate Professor in the School of Public Administrations at the University of Victoria and he has taught for several years in the University's Administration of Aboriginal Governments Program. Satsan was a key figure and strategist in the *Delgamuukw-Gisday Wa* case, which was the subject of a successful judgement before the Supreme Court of Canada in December 1997. He has extensive experience with regard to Aboriginal rights and title, in general, as well as Aboriginal self-government and education.

Satsan is trained in law and education. He attended Simon Fraser University and the University of British Columbia.

BRIAN SLATTERY is a Professor of Law at Osgoode Hall Law School, York University, Toronto, where he teaches and writes in the areas of Constitutional Law, Indigenous Rights, Criminal Law and Legal Theory. Dr. Slattery is a graduate of Loyola College, Montreal, (B.A., Honours English), McGill University (Bachelor of Civil Law) and Oxford University (Doctorate in Law). Before coming to Osgoode Hall in 1981, he worked for some years in Tanzania, East Africa, initially as a CUSO volunteer assisting political refugees from Southern Africa, and later teaching at the Law Faculty of the University of Dar es Salaam. He also served for several years as Research Director of the Native Law Centre at the University of Saskatchewan. More recently, he acted as a Senior Advisor to the federal Royal Commission on Aboriginal Peoples, headed by Chief Georges Erasmus and Justice René Dussault. He was elected to the Royal Society of Canada in 1995 for his contributions to the development of the law relating to aboriginal rights.

BUD SMITH, QC, is a businessman and former practising lawyer who has served in public office as MLA for Kamloops as Regional Economic Development Minister and as Attorney General of British Columbia. Mr. Smith was born in Kamloops in May of 1946. He received his B.A. from the University of Victoria in 1970 and his L.L.B. from the University of British Columbia in 1974. He has been a member of the Law Society of British Columbia since May, 1975. He was Principal Secretary to the Premier of British Columbia (1983–1986). He was MLA for Kamloops (1986–1991) and a Cabinet Minister (1988–1991). Mr Smith is currently president of Mejia Property Inc. and YKA Travelwise Kamloops Ltd., Chairman of christopher James gold Corp., and director of Urban systems Ltd. He has served as a Director of the BC Development Corporation, Canada Post Corporation, and several private-sector reporting companies.

MELVIN H. SMITH, QC spent 31 years in the public service of British Columbia. A lawyer by profession, from 1967 until 1997 he was the ranking official on constitutional law and constitutional reform issues for four successive provincial administrations. He was a key player in the Patriation of the Constitution in 1981 and also served as a Deputy Minister for 13 years in various Ministries until his early retirement in 1991. A leader in the "No" campaign on the Charlottetown Accord, he now spends his time as a consultant, commentator on public issues, columnist and university lecturer. He is the author of the Canadian best seller, *Our Home or Native Land?* He lives in Victoria, British Columbia.

ROBERT C. STROTHER was a tax partner at Davis & Company, Vancouver, British Columbia when his chapter in this book was written. A Sir James Dunn Scholar, Mr. Strother graduated as the Gold Medallist in Law from Dalhousie Law School in 1974 and obtained a Masters of Law from Harvard Law School in 1975. Thereafter, he practiced tax law in Houston, Texas and London, England. He practiced as a tax partner with two large Vancouver firms before joining Davis & Company in November, 1990.

Mr. Strother was called to the bar in Alberta in 1978, in British Columbia in 1981, and in the Yukon in 1992. Mr. Strother practises law in the areas of Taxation, Aboriginal Law and Corporate/Commercial law.

Mr. Strother has taught as an adjunct professor of law at UBC Law School and at the University of Alberta. He has lectured extensively for the Canadian Tax Foundation, the Continuing Legal Education Society for British Columbia, the Canadian Institute, and Insight Educational Services. He has written numerous nationally published articles on taxation and has addressed the general session of the Annual Conference of the Canadian Tax Foundation.

Mr. Strother has been the tax and financial advisor in three northern land claims and is counsel to the Union of New Brunswick Indians in respect of a challenge to the provincial sales tax law and also in respect of comprehensive land claim matters.

Mr. Strother professional activities are as follows: Member, Canadian Bar Association, B.C. Tax Section, Vancouver Bar Association, Canadian Tax Foundation, Member, Law Societies of Alberta, British Columbia and the Yukon, Adjunct Professor of Law (Taxation 1), University of British Columbia Faculty of Law, 1981–1985, Sessional Lecturer (Commercial Law), University of Alberta Faculty of Law, 1978, Course Conductor—Taxation, Bar Admission Course, Alberta, 1979. He is also a member of the Vancouver Board of Trade and a Member of the Pacific Corridor Enterprise Council.

KENNETH MICHAEL SUMANIK received his B.Sc. (1963), his Teaching Certificate (1964) and his M.Sc., Biology (1966) from the University of Alberta. He was a member of many committees and organizations such as Clayoquot Sound Sustainable Development Strategy Committee, Standing Committee on Environmental Control and Reclamation, Ministry of Aboriginal Affairs, Third Party Advisory Group, Cross Sectoral Committee, Business Coalition, Third Party Interest Group involved in the *Delgamuukw* (Gitksan) Appeal, and the Nisga Update Committee. He was director of the British Columbia Conservation Foundation (1987–1990). Mr. Sumanik was also a Director for British Columbia Forestry Association and the Director of Environment and Land Use for the Mining Association of British Columbia.

ADRIAN TANNER has been teaching at Memorial University in St. John's, Newfoundland since 1972. His first encounter with aboriginal people was in 1957 to 1959 when, while working on various arctic weather stations, he got to know several Inuit families of self-sufficient hunters. He obtained his B.A. and M.A. from the University of British Columbia and a Ph.D. from the University of Toronto. Starting in 1964, he has conducted research among a variety of northern aboriginal groups, including the Tutchone of Yukon Territory, the Ojibwa of northern Ontario, the Cree and the Naskapi Innu of northern Quebec, the

Innu of Labrador and the Mi'kmaq of Newfoundland. He has published two books and numerous articles on various subjects, including Cree rituals associated with hunting, aboriginal rights and land claims, the political development of Canadian Indians, indigenous healing movements and Cree opposition to the Great Whale hydroelectric development. He has also worked on a number of practical issues, including aboriginal land claims, community relocation projects and social impact assessment of development projects. He gave expert court testimony in the injunction against the James Bay hydroelectric development and several more recent cases involving aboriginal rights. He is the main author of a report on aboriginal governance in Newfoundland and Labrador, prepared for the Royal Commission on Aboriginal Peoples. He lives with his wife, the Cree linguist Marguerite MacKenzie, and his two daughters Megan and Nailisa, in Petty Harbour, Newfoundland, where he is on the board of directors of the East Coast Trail Association.

PAUL TENNANT was born in Saskatchewan and raised in Kamloops. After graduating from the University of British Columbia, he obtained his M.A. and Ph.D. from the University of Chicago as a Woodrow Wilson National Fellow. He then spent a year in the United States Congress as the first Canadian to hold a Congressional Fellowship. He has taught at the University of British Columbia since 1966, specializing in local government, British Columbia government and politics, and the politics of aboriginal peoples. He has been adviser to First Nations and municipalities in Alberta, the Yukon, and British Columbia, to the British Columbia, Yukon, and federal governments, to the British Columbia Claims Task Force, the British Columbia Treaty Commission, the Council for Yukon First Nations, and to aboriginal land councils in Australia. He is author of *Aboriginal Peoples and Politics: The Indian Land Question in British Columbia* (UBC Press, 1990).

KENNETH J. TYLER, Barrister and Solicitor, Borden Ladner Gervais LLP, Vancouver, is an associate lawyer in the Litigation Branch, responsible for cases relating to Aboriginal and Treaty rights, the Division of Powers between the federal and provincial legislatures, and the Canadian Charter of Rights and Freedoms. Formerly: Counsel, Constitutional Law Branch, Manitoba Department of Justice Counsel, Constitutional Law Branch, Saskatchewan Department of Justice. Defended against challenges to provincial legislation and the Criminal Code based upon the Canadian *Charter of Rights and Freedoms*, the division of powers and Aboriginal or Treaty rights. Provided legal and policy advice to government departments on constitutional and Aboriginal issues; assisted in the drafting of legislation relevant to constitutional issues; provided advice in relation to constitutional reform initiatives. Manager, Constitutional Law Unit, Department of Justice, Government of Newfoundland. Provided advice to the Premier and Minister of Justice on the Charlottetown constitutional reform process. Co-ordinator of Constitutional Relations, Constitutional Branch, Saskatchewan Justice.

Provided advice to the Premier, the Minister of Justice, and the Department of Economic Development and Trade on the Meech Lake Accord and the Canada-U.S. Free Trade Agreement; member and legal advisor to the Saskatchewan Government's negotiating team to settle outstanding Treaty Land entitlement claims in Saskatchewan. Sessional Lecturer, Faculty of Law, University of Manitoba in Canadian Constitutional Law. President of Tyler, Wright & Daniel Ltd., a small research consulting firm specializing in historical research on native land claims.

Education: LLB., University of Manitoba, 1984. M.A. (History), University of Alberta, 1979. Thesis: "A Tax-Eating Proposition: The History of the Passpasstayo Reserve." Publications: "Indian Resource and Water Rights", [1982] 4 C.N.L.R. 1. "A Modest Proposal for Legislative Reform to Facilitate the Settlement of Specific Indian Claims," [1981] 3 C.N.L.R. 1. Biographies of Chiefs Pasquah, Cowessess and One Arrow in the Dictionary of Canadian Biography.

ALEXANDER VON GERNET is Professor of Anthropology at the University of Toronto at Mississauga where, for ten years, he has been teaching courses relating to Aboriginal studies. He is one of a few Canadian scholars who have published contributions in archaeology, ethnohistory, as well as oral historiography. His main interest is in reconstructing Aboriginal pasts by using various sources of evidence in methodological conjunction. He is in considerable demand as a consultant for both government and First Nations clients and has served as an academic advisor and expert witness in numerous Aboriginal litigations in Newfoundland, Québec, Ontario, Alberta, British Columbia and New York State. He was one of the contributing authors of the Report of the Royal Commission of Aboriginal Peoples and was the Editor-in-Chief of *Ontario Archaeology*. Professor von Gernet is currently writing a book on oral traditions as evidence in Aboriginal litigation.

KERRY WILKINS is a Toronto lawyer, called to the Ontario bar in 1992, whose practice has focused principally on issues in constitutional law, the Canadian law of aboriginal peoples, and more general issues of public law and justice policy. His publications include "The Person You're Supposed to Become: The Politics of the Law School Experience" (1987), 45 U.T. *Fac. L. Rev.* 98, "... But We Need the Eggs: The Royal Commission, the Charter of Rights, and the Inherent Right of

Aboriginal Self-Government" (1999), 49 *U.T.L.J.* 53 and "Of Provinces and Section 35 Rights" (1999) 22 Dalhousie L.J. 185. He is currently writing a series of articles on aboriginal peoples and provincial authority, and another series exploring how to situate aboriginal rights of self-government harmoniously within the mainstream legal system.

JACK WOODWARD is the author of *Native Law* and a leading legal authority on aboriginal rights in Canada. Mr Woodward represents Band Councils throughout British Columbia with respect to aboriginal rights, land claims, fiduciary concerns and business matters.

NORMAN K. ZLOTKIN, Professor, College of Law, University of Saskatchewan, LL.B. (Toronto), LL.M (London); Research Director, University of Saskatchewan Native Law Centre, 1982–1986. Practised law in Ontario, 1973 to 1981, specializing in the rights of Aboriginal Peoples. Advisor to the Assembly of First Nations and Nishnawbe-Aski Nation on Constitutional law, and a member of the legal team for the First Ministers' Conferences in 1983, 1984, 1985 and 1987.

Beyond the Nass Valley

Introduction

OWEN LIPPERT

About 10,000 years ago, humans started to walk cross the Bering Strait, pushing southward to populate the Americas. On December 11, 1997, the Supreme Court of Canada released its judgment in the case, *Delgamuukw* vs. *British Columbia*, defining the rights of those Aboriginal people vis-à-vis later arrivals who came by ship from another direction. The majority decision was written by Chief Justice Antonio Lamer, who retired two years later. Four judges concurred with him; two added their own finer points. Beyond the Art Deco marble walls of the courthouse, the media and public reaction at the time reflected no obvious consensus. Responses ranged from jubilant vindication to apocalyptic warnings. One might have expected as much, given the immense scope of Lamer's decision. At its core, the *Delgamuukw* decision judges what our long past shall now mean as Canadians decide upon serious issues of the ownership and use of land, economic development, governance and social relations—issues that will affect every Canadian, in every corner of the country.

The national significance of *Delgamuukw* case prompted the Fraser Institute to hold two conferences on the issue, the first in Vancouver in July 1998 and a second and larger one in Ottawa in April 1999. This book contains the papers and proceedings of those two events.

The Gitksan and Wet'suwet'en bands from Northwestern British Columbia initiated the case in 1984. (A direct predecessor of the case, *Calder vs. B.C.*, began even earlier, in 1968.) In brief, the Aboriginal plaintiffs argued for recognition of unextinguished Aboriginal title to land they claimed as traditional territory. (The case name, *Delgamuukw*, comes from the Aboriginal name of the first chief listed in the filing, Earl Muldoe.) B.C. Supreme Court Justice William MacEachern ruled against the plaintiffs in 1991. His verdict was appealed to the B.C. Court of Appeal, which in 1995 largely upheld his initial ruling. An appeal to Supreme Court followed.

In his reasons for judgment, Chief Justice Lamer addressed five questions:

(1) Can the appeal from the B.C. Appeal Court be considered by the Supreme Court of Canada?

(2) How may the facts of Aboriginal rights and title cases be interpreted?

(3) What is the content and requirements for proof of Aboriginal title?

(4) What can be made of the arguments for self-government?

(5) Can the Province extinguish Aboriginal title?

Lamer made relatively short work of the first and the last two points. On the first point, the appeal could not be considered because the appellants had changed their suit from one of "ownership" and "jurisdiction" to one of "Aboriginal rights" and "self government." Thus, the case was sent back to trial. That new trial has yet to commence. In his fourth point, Lamer reasoned that the claims made for self-government were too general, and thus could not be considered by the courts. On the fifth point, he cited several recent Supreme Court cases upholding that the Province did not have the jurisdiction to extinguish unilaterally Aboriginal title. The bulk of the decision examined the second and third questions.

I will not go any further in explanation of Lamer's decision. The first chapter of this book, *Basics of the Decision*, provides ample analysis of the judgment. Professor Brian Slattery of Osgoode Hall Law School provides a detailed legal background to Aboriginal title. John Howard, Q.C., a retired counsel to a major forestry company, gives a historical perspective to the issue. Kent McNeil, also of Osgoode Hall, more closely examines Aboriginal title from a constitutional perspective. Geoff Plant, Liberal MLA and former counsel to the B.C. provincial government when the case was before Justice MacEachern, and Mel Smith, Q.C., former constitutional advisor to the B.C. government, raise questions as to the consistency and creativity of Lamer's ruling. Professor Jack Woodward of the University of British Columbia traces the influence of Lamer's decision in several important cases since 1997. Alexander von Gernet, a professor of Anthropology with the University of Toronto at Mississauga, gives a social scientist's perspective on a key part of the decision, namely the use of oral testimony in determining Aboriginal title.

When the Court released *Delgamuukw*, the reaction, both pro and con, came mostly from British Columbia. The case, after all, originated in B.C. The issue of Aboriginal title has provoked great debate in that province since the middle of the last century. Unlike most of Canada (though as you will learn, not all), the Crown in B.C. had not settled treaties with Aboriginal people, other than in parts of southern Vancouver Island and on the narrow strip of land between the Rockies and the Alberta border in the lower eastern part of the province. From entry into Confederation onward, successive provincial governments maintained that Aboriginal title had been extinguished or, if it had not been, whatever claims put forward were the sole responsibility of the federal government. The province's position did not, and did not have to, change when the Supreme Court in 1973 delivered a deadlocked three-to-three (one abstention) verdict in the *Calder* case. At the time, Prime Minister Pierre Trudeau, less than certain of how the Court would rule in future, began negotiations with one of the most persistent of the B.C. bands, the Nisga'a, without the province's participation.

The mid-1980s brought a change. Even as the Gitksan and Wet'suwet'en bands prepared to launch the *Delgamuukw* case, a new and popular Premier, Bill Vander Zalm, signaled a change in policy in British Columbia. The province would negotiate land claims, if perhaps not Aboriginal title, starting with the Nisga'a, who were already in discussions with the federal government. The relationship of *Delgamuukw* to the B.C. Treaty negotiations is complex and ever shifting. To try to make some sense of it, we are pleased to start Chapter 2, *Impact in British Columbia*, with an overview by Alec Robertson, Q.C. who served as the first Commissioner of the B.C. Treaty Commission. As treaty negotiations have advanced in the wake of *Delgamuukw*, new participants have emerged. Professor Paul Tennant, a leading authority on the history of Aboriginal land claims in B.C., provides a view on the diplomacy between Aboriginal bands and the municipalities. Bud Smith, the Attorney General in Premier Vander Zalm's government at the time of the decision to negotiate, further explores the theme of community involvement, linking it to B.C.'s constitutional role through a discussion of possible changes in the disposition of resource rents. Further to the question of who should pay for land claim settlements, we have a paper by Mel Smith Q.C., who in many ways brought the issue to light in his book, *Our Home or Native Land?*

A challenge at the outset of this project was to convince people outside of B.C. that *Delgamuukw* could, and surely will, have consequences across the country. Many Canadians thought the case applied only to B.C., where treaties had not been signed. Someone who grasped the national implications of *Delgamuukw* from the start was political scientist Tom Flanagan of the University of Calgary. As he shows clearly in his paper, the introduction of oral history to determine Aboriginal title will likely have a significant impact in Alberta, even though Treaty Eight covers that province. Professor Norman Zlotkin of the University of Saskatchewan Law School covers the legal interpretation of the Prairie Treaties (Six through Eight) in the new light of *Delgamuukw*. For a legal practitioner's view, we welcome the contribution of Ken Tyler, who for many years dealt with land claim issues in the Manitoba Ministry of the Attorney General.

Crossing over the Lakehead, we reach Ontario. Kerry Wilkins of the Ontario Ministry of the Attorney General provides a thoughtful discussion of how *Delgamuukw* will influence the emerging new forms of Aboriginal self-government. Professor of Native Studies at Trent University, David T. McNab, argues that Aboriginal oral traditions in Ontario may well open up discussions of land claims in Ontario as a result of *Delgamuukw*. It is instructive to note that in Ontario, as elsewhere, *Delgamuukw* has at least the potential to shift the ground in discussing existing treaty rights.

In Quebec, *Delgamuukw* has a unique significance in relationship to a possible Quebec secession as well as in its potential impact on the 1975 James Bay and Northern Quebec treaties between the Cree and Inuit people and the governments of Ottawa and Quebec City. Two differing but intersecting views are presented here. Claude Bachand, Bloc Quebecois MP for Saint-Jean, stresses the continuity of *Delgamuukw* with Quebec's approach to Aboriginal communities. Paul Joffe, a lawyer who has acted on behalf of the Cree Grand Council, asserts that the decision and Quebec's policies conflict.

Proof of the far-reaching significance of *Delgamuukw* was evident in the 1999 Supreme Court decision in the *Marshall* case concerning Aboriginal fishing rights. The Court's subsequent and highly unusual clarification suggests that it too has yet to comprehend its full meaning. *Marshall*, focused the Court's attention on the "real world consequences" (in the words of Justice Beverley McLachlin) of *Delgamuukw* in Atlantic Canada. James Youngblood Henderson (Sakej), research director the Native Law Centre at the University of Saskatchewan, examines the treaty evidence and argues forcefully that *Marshall* is merely the first of many cases yet to come in the Maritimes. Adrian Tanner, a professor of Anthropology at Memorial University, examines the situation in Newfoundland and Labrador, shedding considerable light on the extent of the Mi'kMaq people. Award-winning journalist, Don Cayo, rounds out the discussion of Atlantic Canada with a call to keep future discussions focused on improving the economic conditions of Aboriginal and non-Aboriginal individuals in the region.

In Chapter 7, we turn to the overall economic impact of *Delgamu-ukw*. In my own essay, I attempt to describe many of the decision's ulti-mate costs as transaction costs—the costs of measuring, implementing and enforcing agreements—and suggest ways to reduce them. Certainly, the major unknown cost is that of compensation. J. Keith Lowes, a Van-couver lawyer, reviews the range of economic impacts arising from com-pensation. Two other Vancouver lawyers, Michael J. McDonald and Thomas Lutes, provide a more detailed analysis. Robert Strother, who specializes in forestry law, examines in detail possible impacts on forest-ry, primarily in B.C. Also from a B.C. perspective, Ken Sumanik with the B.C. Mining Association does the same for mining.

One of the difficulties of making economic predictions about the consequences of *Delgamuukw* is that it remains uncertain how matters will proceed—by litigation or negotiation. The final chapter, *All Still Here and All Looking Ahead*, focuses on what may happen next. Darrell Bricker, a vice president of one of Canada's best-known public opinion research companies, Angus Reid, lays out Canadians' attitudes about the range of Aboriginal issues. His research shows clearly that Canadi-ans want to improve the economic prospects of Aboriginal people. Patrick Monahan, a well-respected constitutional law expert at Os-goode Hall Law School, examines the pros and cons of each approach, litigation and negotiation. Dene Chief Bill Eramus provides some com-mentary to Monahan's discussion. This volume ends with a conversa-tion between two people personally and intimately committed to finding answers to the challenges posed by Canada's past to its present. I speak of Gordon Gibson, Senior Fellow in Canadian Studies with the Fraser Institute, and Chief Herb George (Satsan), who as a hereditary chief of the Gitksan and Wet'suwet'en has lived and breathed the case and the ones before it for nearly thirty years. Both provide a human, ev-eryday perspective on the legal analysis.

This book departs from the usual Institute publication in that it does not present a focused set of public policy recommendations. In part, this is due to our goal in this instance of providing a wide spec-trum of views and opinions. It is also due to the fact that judges, not governments, may rule on many issues under discussion.

Still, from all the contributions contained within, some points emerge. The Canadian Parliament and the provincial legislatures have a responsibility to debate and resolve issues arising from Aboriginal rights and claims. They cannot simply abdicate their responsibility to the courts. Conversely, the courts, and in particular the Supreme Court, should refrain from translating their own public policy perspectives into jurisprudence, even if legislators prove reluctant to address critical areas. The legislature is far better able to assess what Justice McLachlin calls "real world consequences." Finally, the lasting value of *Delgamu-ukw*, if it is to have one, depends upon helping Aboriginal people break out of the *status quo*. A sense that something is terribly wrong with the structure of and strictures upon Aboriginal life as it now exists united all participants, Aboriginal and non-Aboriginal alike, at the two confer- ences. In that sense, Canada's past only has value for its future if it leads to greater material and social well being for all its citizens.

A few final thanks are most necessary. I would like to thank the Donner Foundation of Canada for its generous support. Thank you Lorena Baran and Danielle Smith for all your work in arranging and conducting the two conferences. Thank you E. Kaye Fulton for your ef- fort in helping to edit this book. Finally, thank you to all the contribu- tors for your time and effort.

1 Basics of the Decision

The Nature of Aboriginal Title

Brian Slattery

Introduction

The concept of aboriginal title is an autonomous concept of Canadian common law that bridges the gulf between aboriginal land systems and imported European land systems.[1] It does not stem from aboriginal customary law, English common law or French civil law. It coordinates the interaction between these systems, without forming part of them.[2] Aboriginal title is thus a *sui generis* concept—one that does not fit into pre-existing legal categories.[3]

The unique character of aboriginal title is explained by the distinctive history of aboriginal lands in North America during the formative era extending into the nineteenth century. This history can be divided into four phases:

(1) the period prior to European contact, when aboriginal peoples were independent political entities with international title to their territories;

(2) the period of contact, when European states launched exploratory voyages and issued Charters embodying territorial claims;

Notes will be found on pages 27–33.

(3) the period of initial settlement, when permanent European colonies were established and inter-European treaties were concluded, delimiting the boundaries of exclusive colonial spheres; and

(4) the period of imperial expansion, during which Crown suzerainty was gradually extended over aboriginal nations and a constitutional framework emerged that embraced both settler communities and aboriginal peoples.

Before Europeans came to North America, the indigenous peoples of the continent were independent entities, holding international title to the lands in their possession.[4] However, the map of North America, like that of Europe, was far from static. The boundaries between aboriginal groups shifted over time and groups migrated in response to such factors as war, epidemic, famine, dwindling game reserves, altered soil conditions, internal conflict and population pressure. Lands that were vacant at one period were later occupied. The identities of the groups themselves changed, as communities dissolved or coalesced and new ones emerged.[5]

Far from ending this fluidity, the arrival of Europeans often magnified it, as novel technologies, diseases, alliances and trade opportunities upset existing balances of power and stimulated fresh forms of competition and conflict. For example, the well-known wars of the Iroquois against their aboriginal neighbours in the seventeenth century were partly spurred by the European fur trade. The introduction of the horse and firearms to the Western plains gave rise to new and more mobile styles of life among the Western Indians, which ironically are often taken to exemplify traditional Indian culture.[6]

The early territorial claims launched by European powers had little basis in reality and had no impact on the territorial rights of indigenous American peoples. Nor did the advent of Europeans have the legal effect of confining aboriginal peoples to the lands they happened to possess at the time of contact, or prevent them from acquiring new lands in the future. Most of the continent remained an area open to movement and change, where the title of an aboriginal group rested on long-standing possession or agreement with other groups, and territory was gained and lost by appropriation, agreement or abandonment.

Nevertheless, the situation changed gradually as the colonial powers concluded treaties among themselves, sorting out their territorial claims *inter se*. While these treaties could not bind indigenous groups that were not parties, they had the effect of designating exclusive European spheres of influence in America and progressively reduced aboriginal opportunities for wider international contacts. This was particularly true in the period following the *Treaty of Paris* in 1763, when

France and Spain withdrew from the eastern and northern sectors of North America, leaving Britain free to pursue its imperial enterprises there. Henceforth, the British Crown and its successors, the United States and Canada, asserted exclusive rights to maintain relations with the aboriginal peoples occupying the territories in question: in particular to conclude treaties with them, to secure suzerainty over them and to obtain cessions of their lands.

Restrictions on the cession of aboriginal lands arose from another source. The English-style land systems prevailing in the colonies had one common characteristic. They were based on the premise that title to land, so far as the settlers were concerned, could only be secured by grant from the Crown or its deputies. It followed that private settlers could not gain title by simply settling on the land or purchasing it from the indigenous peoples. In theory, at least, this rule ensured that the Crown retained control over the pace and manner in which land was settled and that the Crown benefited from any revenues flowing from land grants. The restriction also helped to abate the fraudulent practices that often tainted private purchases of Indian lands.[7]

In various stages, the Crown made good its claims over the territories now making up Canada and brought aboriginal peoples under its protection. This process had several legal consequences for aboriginal land rights.[8] First, under British law, the Crown gained the ultimate title to the lands held by aboriginal peoples, as it did to all lands in newly acquired colonial territories. This effect flowed from the feudal character of the British constitution, whereby the Crown was not only sovereign of the realm but also supreme landlord.[9] Second, the territorial title of an aboriginal group became a communal title at common law that formed a burden on the Crown's ultimate title and gave the aboriginal group the right to the exclusive use and occupation of their lands for a broad range of purposes. Third, aboriginal title could not be transferred or sold to private individuals; it could only be ceded to the Crown. As just noted, this restriction stemmed largely from the feudal systems of tenure imported into the colonies and from a desire to prevent fraudulent land transactions.[10] Finally, under the shelter of aboriginal title, customary land systems remained in force within aboriginal communities and governed the relations of their members among themselves.

Character of Aboriginal Title

The basic attributes of aboriginal title were identified in the leading case of *Delgamuukw v. British Columbia*, decided by the Supreme Court of Canada in 1997.[11] The case involved a claim by hereditary chiefs of the Gitksan and Wet'suwet'en peoples to separate portions of a tract encompassing 58,000 square kilometres in northern British Columbia. Their claim was originally for "ownership" and "jurisdiction"; however by the time the case reached the Supreme Court of Canada, it had become mainly a claim for aboriginal title.[12]

Strikingly different conceptions of aboriginal title were advanced before the Court. The aboriginal parties argued that aboriginal title was equivalent to an inalienable fee simple. By contrast, the governments of Canada and British Columbia maintained that aboriginal title was simply a bundle of particular rights to engage in specific culture-based activities on the land, or alternately the right to exclusive use and occupation of the land in order to engage in such specific activities.[13] These differing approaches merit closer examination.

According to the aboriginal parties, aboriginal title was similar to a fee simple, which is the largest possible form of land title known to English common law.[14] Most lands held by private parties in Canada (outside Quebec) are held in fee simple. A person who holds a fee simple on land is for all practical purposes the absolute owner of the land, or at least as close to being absolute owner as English common law permits. In theory, under the English doctrine of tenures, all lands owned by private individuals are held of the Crown, which has the underlying and ultimate title to the land. The main practical significance of the Crown's ultimate title is that the land reverts to the Crown if the owner dies without leaving an heir to the estate (a process known as "escheat"). The aboriginal parties argued that a group holding aboriginal title was the effective "fee simple" owner of its lands, with the right to use them for any purpose it saw fit. However, aboriginal title differed from a fee simple in one major respect: it could not be transferred to private parties but could only be surrendered to the Crown.

The Canadian and British Columbia governments rejected this model and argued that aboriginal title was at best a bundle of particular aboriginal rights. This bundle would allow an aboriginal group to engage in a range of specific activities on the land, and it might also give the group the exclusive right to use and occupy the land for those specific purposes. However, aboriginal title would not enable the group to use the land for any purpose it saw fit. The group would be limited to performing the particular activities forming part of the bundle.[15] Moreover, the group would have to show that each activity in the bundle was itself an aboriginal right—that is, an element of a practice, custom or tradition that was integral to the group's distinctive society at the time of European contact.[16]

So, according to the governmental argument, the content of aboriginal title was *variable*. It differed from aboriginal group to aboriginal group, depending on the group's cultural practices at the time of European contact. By contrast, the aboriginal parties argued that the content of aboriginal title was *uniform* and did not depend on historical practices. If a group had aboriginal title, it could use the land as it wished, subject only to the rule prohibiting transfers to third parties.

In its judgment, the Supreme Court rejected the governmental argument and adopted a position close to that advocated by the aboriginal parties. The Court begins its analysis with the century-old *St. Catherine's Milling* case,[17] where the Privy Council famously characterized aboriginal title as a "personal and usufructuary right." This perplexing formula had bedeviled the case law ever since, spawning unhelpful analogies with the concept of usufruct in Roman, French and even Scottish law. The Supreme Court takes the opportunity to give the formula a decent burial, observing that the Privy Council's choice of terminology was "not particularly helpful to explain the various dimensions of aboriginal title."[18] So doing, the Court opens the way to a clearer and more accurate characterization of aboriginal title.

Following in the footsteps of Justice Dickson in the *Guerin* case,[19] the Supreme Court points out that aboriginal title is a *sui generis* land right. As such, it is a unique right that does not correspond to the categories known to English common law or French civil law. Neither can it be understood simply in terms of aboriginal legal systems. It has to be viewed from both aboriginal and non-aboriginal perspectives.[20]

Aboriginal title has three basic features that differentiate it from ordinary titles held under common or civil law. First, aboriginal title is inalienable. It cannot be sold or transferred directly to private third parties. It can only be surrendered to the Crown, which in turn may grant it to third parties. However, the fact that aboriginal title is inalienable (and so "personal" to the holding group) does not mean that it is a nonproprietary interest like a licence to use and occupy the land, which cannot compete on an equal footing with ordinary land rights under English or French law.[21] Aboriginal title is a true property right. In effect, then, the Court rejects the notion that alienability is a necessary feature of a property right. This notion stems from European property systems and has no application to aboriginal title.

The second distinctive feature of aboriginal title is its source. Under English property law, all lands in the hands of private parties are in principle held of the Crown either mediately or immediately, by virtue of a legal fiction positing that the Crown was the original owner of all lands in the realm.[22] Influenced perhaps by this conception, the Privy Council in *St. Catherine's* had suggested that the source of aboriginal title in Canada was the *Royal Proclamation* of 1763, issued following the cession of New France to Great Britain.[23] However, this approach implied that aboriginal land rights did not exist unless recognized by the

Crown. In *Delgamuukw*, the Supreme Court disclaims this approach and holds that, while the *Royal Proclamation* recognizes aboriginal title, it does not bring it into being. In the Court's view, aboriginal title arises from the prior occupation of Canada by aboriginal peoples, and from the interaction between the incoming common law and pre-existing systems of aboriginal law. In effect, aboriginal title stems from possession *before* the advent of the Crown. [24]

A third distinctive feature of aboriginal title is its communal nature. As Chief Justice Lamer explains:

> Aboriginal title cannot be held by individual aboriginal persons; it is a collective right to land held by all members of an aboriginal nation. Decisions with respect to that land are also made by that community.[25]

Although the Chief Justice does not elaborate on this point, it has several important ramifications. First, any decision to surrender aboriginal title to the Crown must be a communal one, made by the aboriginal group as a whole. It is not possible for a single individual or collection of individuals (such as a particular "chief" or "chiefs") to dispose of communal lands apart from group consent. The requirement of group consent is a uniform rule of Canadian common law that does not vary from group to group in accordance with local custom. This inference is supported by the *Royal Proclamation* of 1763, which provides that Indian lands shall be purchased only by the Crown "at some publick Meeting or Assembly of the said Indians." Moreover, as a matter of policy, it would be undesirable for the validity of a land surrender to depend on the vagaries of local customary law, which would often be unknown to the Crown parties and in any case might not contemplate land transfers.

The communal character of aboriginal title has a second ramification. The internal law of the group governs the manner in which group members share the land among themselves, unless this law has been modified by statute or other means. So, in effect, the concept of aboriginal title supplies a protective legal umbrella, in the shelter of which the customary law of an aboriginal group may develop and flourish.

A third ramification may be noted. Since decisions about the use and disposal of aboriginal lands must be made communally, there has to be some internal mechanism for communal decision-making. The need for such a mechanism is one of the cornerstones of the right of self-government. At a minimum, an aboriginal group has the inherent right to make communal decisions about how its lands are to be used and by whom. As the Supreme Court observes:

the common law should develop to recognize aboriginal rights (and title, when necessary) as they were recognized by either *de facto* practice or by the *aboriginal system of governance.*[26]

In particular, the group has the right to decide how the lands are to be shared among group members; to make grants and other dispositions of the communal property; to lay down laws and regulations governing use of the lands; to impose taxes relating to the land; and to determine how any land taxes and revenues are to be used and distributed.

Scope of Aboriginal Title

In *Delgamuukw*, the Supreme Court holds that the scope of aboriginal title is governed by two basic principles. First, aboriginal title confers a right to the exclusive use and occupation of the land for a broad range of purposes, which are not limited to the practices, customs and traditions of the group at the time of contact or any other historical period.[27] Nevertheless, under the second principle, the uses that an aboriginal group makes of its land must not be irreconcilable with the nature of the group's attachment to the land. On this point, aboriginal title differs from a fee simple, which allows the land to be used for any purpose whatsoever. Let us consider these principles more closely.

1. Exclusive use and occupation

Aboriginal title confers the right to the exclusive use and occupation of the land for a broad range of purposes. This explicit holding in *Delgamuukw* is the culmination of a series of observations made in previous Supreme Court rulings. Notably, in *Guerin*, Justice Dickson held that aboriginal title is "a unique interest in land" which encompasses "a legal right to occupy and possess certain lands,"[28] which implies a right to use the land for more than traditional or customary purposes. Justice Dickson also held that the interest of an Indian band in a reserve is the same as aboriginal title in traditional tribal lands.[29] So, the law governing reserve lands presumptively applies by extension to aboriginal title lands. Under s. 18 of the *Indian Act*,[30] reserve lands are held "for the use and benefit" of the band and may be used "for any other purpose for the general welfare of the band." Nothing in this section suggests that the band's "general welfare" should be defined narrowly in terms of aboriginal practices prior to European contact rather than the present-day needs of aboriginal communities.[31]

This conclusion is supported by the *Indian Oil and Gas Act*,[32] whose overall purpose is to provide for the exploitation of oil and gas on reserve lands that have been surrendered to the Crown.[33] In *Delgamuukw*, the Court holds that this statute presumes that title to reserve lands includes mineral rights.[34] Since aboriginal title is the same as reserve title, aboriginal title must also encompass mineral rights. In effect, lands held pursuant to aboriginal title may be exploited for their oil and gas in the same way as reserves--regardless whether or not this was a traditional use of those lands. The Court also quotes s. 6(2) of the *Indian Oil and Gas Act,* which provides:

> Nothing in this Act shall be deemed to abrogate the rights of Indian people or preclude them from negotiating for oil and gas benefits in those areas in which land claims have not been settled.

The Court observes that the areas referred to in this section must include lands held under aboriginal title, since by definition these lands have not been surrendered to the Crown under treaties or land claims settlements. So, s. 6(2) presumes that aboriginal title permits the development of oil and gas reserves.[35]

This conclusion is significant. It suggests that an aboriginal group may exploit the mineral resources on its lands without necessarily having to surrender the lands to the Crown, so long as the process does not involve the transfer of land to third parties or sever the group's original connection with the land (as discussed below). In other words, although the *Indian Oil and Gas Act* envisages the surrender of reserve lands in order to facilitate their exploitation for oil and gas, there appears to be no reason in principle why such a surrender is necessary under the common law of aboriginal title.

2. The inherent limit on uses

In *Delgamuukw,* the Supreme Court holds that lands held pursuant to aboriginal title cannot be used in a manner that is "irreconcilable with the nature of the attachment to the land that forms the basis of the particular group's aboriginal title."[36] If an aboriginal group wants to use its lands in a way that aboriginal title does not permit, it has to surrender the lands to the Crown and convert them into non-title lands.[37]

The scope of this limitation has to be understood in light of its rationale. Chief Justice Lamer explains that aboriginal peoples have a special bond with the land, as evidenced by the central place that the land typically occupies in their cultures. For most aboriginal groups, the land is more than just a fungible commodity; it has an inherent and unique value quite apart from its economic value. The law of aboriginal title gives effect to that special bond by recognizing the importance of continuity in the relationship between an aboriginal group and its land, and the need for that relationship to endure into the future. As a result, uses of the land that would jeopardize that relationship are ruled out.[38]

In other words, aboriginal title does not permit uses that would defeat the title's fundamental basis and rationale, which is to preserve the land for future generations. An aboriginal group has the responsibility to ensure that its basic bond with the land is maintained.

How can we determine which uses of the land are legitimate and which are illegitimate? The key lies in the nature of the aboriginal group's historic occupation of the land, as determined by the activities that have taken place on the land and the uses to which the land has been put, as well as by the group's traditional laws governing land.[39] The Court does not indicate what precise historical period is relevant in this context. However, since the Court later holds that aboriginal title arises at the time the Crown gains sovereignty, it seems to follow that the basic character of the relationship is established in the period succeeding sovereignty rather than at the time of European contact.[40] It bears remembering that a snapshot of aboriginal land uses at a single point in time is usually insufficient to capture the full range and depth of a group's ties with its land. A well-rounded account of that relationship will normally have to draw on a relatively lengthy historical period that embraces the full range of climatic, ecological and other conditions with which a group has to cope.

Unfortunately, the concept of an inherent limit on uses is open to misinterpretation. It could be read as reintroducing by the back door the concept of historically-based uses, which the Court has just rejected. The Chief Justice is clearly aware of this danger and goes out of his way to ward it off:

> This is not, I must emphasize, a limitation that restricts the use of the land to those activities that have traditionally been carried out on it. That would amount to a legal straitjacket on aboriginal peoples who have a legitimate legal claim to the land. The approach I have outlined above allows for a full range of uses of the land, subject only to an overarching limit, defined by the special nature of the aboriginal title in that land.[41]

The Chief Justice gives some concrete examples that help clarify his point. He notes that where an aboriginal group's historical occupation was based on hunting the group cannot now use the land in a way that destroys its value as a hunting-ground, such as by subjecting it to strip-mining. Again, if a group's bond with the land is basically ceremonial or cultural, the group may not use the land in such a way as to sever that bond, as for example by turning the land into a parking lot.[42] What these examples show is that the inherent limit precludes uses that are completely incompatible with the original relationship. However, the inherent limit does not rule out uses that are merely unfavourable to the relationship, so long as they do not destroy it. Moreover, the inherent limit does not prevent *part of the lands* from being devoted to inconsistent uses, so long as the original relationship can be maintained on other portions of the land. The inherent limit promotes an appropriate *balance* in the uses of the land rather than a rigid adherence to original uses. This interpretation is supported by the analogy that the Court draws with the English common law doctrine of "equitable waste." According to that doctrine, persons who hold a life estate in real property cannot commit "wanton or extravagant acts of destruction" or "ruin the property." The Chief Justice explains that these sorts of limits capture what he has in mind here.[43]

In effect then, the inherent limit operates only at a very basic level. In most cases, it would not prevent an aboriginal group from putting its lands to a full range of modern uses, so long as these uses do not destroy the land or prevent the group's elemental bond with the land from continuing. For example, a group that traditionally used its land exclusively for hunting, fishing and gathering might devote the land to a mix of residential, agricultural, dairy, commercial, industrial and resource-based uses, so long as these uses did not rule out the possibility of hunting, fishing and gathering *in some sectors of the territory*. It would not be necessary for hunting, fishing and gathering to be possible throughout the entire territory, for that would preclude most other uses. Nor would it be necessary for these traditional activities to be pursuable at the same level of intensity or with the same freedom as in former years. Clearly, the conversion of land to residential, agricultural or industrial purposes may reduce the opportunity for traditional pursuits, and conservation measures may reduce that opportunity even further. However, so long as an aboriginal group ensures that some reasonable opportunity is afforded for traditional pursuits, the criterion will be satisfied.

One important point emerges from the Court's two-fold analysis of aboriginal title. Under the first principle, aboriginal title is a *uniform right*, which does not vary from group to group. It gives aboriginal groups the right to the exclusive use and possession of their lands, regardless of differences among groups in their historical patterns of land use. In all cases, aboriginal groups are entitled to use the land for a broad range of contemporary purposes. Nevertheless, the second principle introduces an element of *historical particularity*. An aboriginal group cannot use its land in a way that is fundamentally irreconcilable with its original relationship with the land, a relationship that may differ from group to group.

Aboriginal Custom

What role does aboriginal custom play in this scheme? The answer lies in the fact that, while the doctrine of aboriginal title governs the rights of an aboriginal group considered as a collective unit, it does not regulate the rights of group members among themselves. The latter are governed by rules distinctive to the group, as originally laid down by custom.[44]

The doctrine of aboriginal title recognizes a communal title with certain general features. Apart from the inherent limit on uses, the character of this communal title is not governed by traditional conceptions or practices and so does not vary from group to group. However, the rights of individuals and corporate entities within the group are determined *inter se*, not by the doctrine of aboriginal title, but by internal rules originally grounded in custom. These rules dictate the extent to which any individual, family, lineage, clan or other sub-group has rights to possess and use lands vested in the entire group.[45] While the rules have a customary base, they are not necessarily static.[46] They are open to both formal and informal change, in accordance with shifting group attitudes, needs and practices.[47]

These considerations explain why a group may hold aboriginal title at Canadian common law even if traditionally it had no notion of private land ownership. So long as the group satisfies the common law criteria for aboriginal title, it has a communal title to its lands. The fact that group custom does not acknowledge private ownership may be relevant in determining the rights of individual group members, but it does not affect the title of the group as a whole. The same considerations support the conclusion that aboriginal title is not confined to "traditional" uses of land.[48] The doctrine of aboriginal title attributes to an aboriginal group a sphere of autonomy, whereby it can determine freely how to use its lands, so long as it does not sever its basic relationship with the land. Traditional conceptions may influence the group's decisions, but current needs and attitudes will likely play as strong a role.

Prior to the Supreme Court's decision in *Delgamuukw*, some courts had expressed the view that an aboriginal group is permanently limited in its use of aboriginal lands to customary practices followed at a distant historical period, such as the time the Crown first acquired sovereignty.[49] On this supposition, aboriginal title is like an historical diorama in an old-fashioned museum. Here, a smiling maiden strips birch-bark from a tree; there, a sturdy warrior aims bow and arrow at a mildewed deer; while in the corner, a youngster plucks plastic blueberries from a withered bush. We must, of course, disregard the next display, where a group of hunters plant their first crop of corn under the glassy eye of a black-robed missionary. If an aboriginal group did not practise agriculture traditionally, it is now forbidden. The difficulty with this conception, of course, is that aboriginal people are not waxen figures on display for tourists but living people who depend on the land for their livelihood. Any rule that would hold them in permanent bondage to outmoded practices must be viewed with skepticism.

The history-bound view apparently drew on English rules under which a party asserting a customary right must show that the custom has existed from "time immemorial" which, for curious reasons, is associated with the year 1189. However, the analogy is inappropriate. As we have seen, the doctrine of aboriginal rights is not based on English common law but arose in response to quite different historical conditions in North America. Indeed, it would have been contrary to imperial interests in America to confine aboriginal land uses to those existing at the time of contact. The European fur trade, which was central to the development of Canada, depended on the activities of aboriginal hunters and trappers whose practices had changed considerably since pre-European times.[50] When colonial officials, in other contexts, urged certain hunting groups to take up farming, they were not sanctioning an unlawful use of land.

We must guard against the notion that aboriginal societies are essentially static in nature, that the only true aboriginal land uses are those that were practised "aboriginally." In fact, of course, aboriginal societies have often been characterized by their ability to adapt to shifting circumstances in a highly flexible manner. Without this flexibility, they would often have had little chance of survival.[51] Significant changes in aboriginal life-styles occurred in pre-European times, and further changes took place in response to European contact. Such adaptations did not entail the abandonment of a group's essential identity, any more than Europeans lost their identity when they adopted federalism, took up lacrosse or started cultivating potatoes, corn and tomatoes.[52] The better view, then, is that taken by the Supreme Court in the *Delgamuukw* case. Aboriginal title gives a group the right to the exclusive use and occupation of their land and the right "to use it according to their own discretion,"[53] subject only to the need to maintain their basic link with the land.

Aboriginal Title as a Property Right

Aboriginal title is a true property right that may be maintained against the whole world, including the Crown. It is not held at the Crown's pleasure and it cannot be extinguished by a unilateral Crown act under the royal prerogative.[54] Where aboriginal title has been extinguished by valid legislation, it benefits from the common law rule requiring just compensation.

The royal prerogative consists of certain powers held by the Crown under the common law, which may be exercised apart from Parliament.[55] Prerogative powers should be distinguished from powers awarded to the Crown by statute. The legal character of a Crown act, such as an order-in-council or letters patent, depends on the source of the power to enact it. If the power stems from the common law, the act is a prerogative instrument. If the power is based on legislation, the act has the character of a statutory instrument.

Where the Crown issues a prerogative grant with respect to land burdened by aboriginal title, the grant does not extinguish aboriginal title. The Crown holds only an underlying title to aboriginal lands and cannot grant more than it possesses. To the extent that the grant purports to extinguish aboriginal title, it is ineffective.[56] Where the grant is based on statutory authority rather than the royal prerogative, its impact on aboriginal title depends on such factors as the competence of the enacting legislature; the clarity of the legislative provisions; the terms of the grant; and the effect of such constitutional instruments as the *Royal Proclamation* of 1763, s. 91(24) of the *Constitution Act, 1867* and s. 35(1) of the *Constitution Act, 1982*.[57]

At one time, the effect of prerogative acts was less certain than it is today.[58] In *St. Catherine's Milling and Lumber Co.* v. *The Queen*, the Privy Council said that Indian title held under the *Royal Proclamation* of 1763 was "dependent upon the good will of the Sovereign."[59] The statement was not explained and was not necessary to the decision. Nevertheless, it implied that Indian title was akin to a mere licence to use the land, which the Crown could unilaterally revoke at any time by prerogative act.[60] However, in the *Calder* case,[61] the Supreme Court moved in the direction of recognizing aboriginal title as a full legal right. Although Justice Judson merely repeated the Privy Council's statement,[62] Justice Hall adopted a well-defined position. He wrote:

> when the Nishga people came under British sovereignty ... they were entitled to assert, as a legal right, their Indian title. It being a legal right, it could not thereafter be extinguished except by surrender to the Crown or by competent legislative authority, and then only by specific legislation.[63]

According to this view, aboriginal title could only be extinguished by a voluntary surrender or by legislation. By implication, it could not be extinguished by a unilateral exercise of the prerogative.

This position was endorsed by the Supreme Court in the *Guerin* case. Justice Dickson stated that in *Calder* "this Court recognized aboriginal title *as a legal right* derived from the Indians' historic occupation and possession of their tribal lands," and he noted that "Judson and Hall JJ. were in agreement ... that aboriginal title existed in Canada (at least where it has not been extinguished *by appropriate legislative action*) ..."[64] Justice Dickson also adopted the view that the Indians were "the rightful occupants of the soil, with a legal as well as just claim to retain possession of it, and to use it according to their own discretion ..."[65] In her separate opinion, Justice Wilson explicitly held that the Indian interest "cannot be derogated from or interfered with by the Crown's utilization of the land for purposes incompatible with the Indian title unless, of course, the Indians agree."[66] In an important passage, she observed:

> It seems to me that the "political trust" line of authorities is clearly distinguishable from the present case because Indian title has an existence apart altogether from s. 18(1) of the *Indian Act. It would fly in the face of the clear wording of the section to treat that interest as terminable at will by the Crown without recourse by the Band.*[67]

It might be thought obvious that aboriginal title is a property right. Yet this conclusion has sometimes been doubted.[68] Once again, the confusion stems in part from the *St. Catherine's* case, where the Privy Council, in an unfortunate phrase, described Indian title as a "personal and usufructuary right."[69] This statement could be taken as suggesting that aboriginal title is a right held in some personal capacity against the Crown rather than a property right. However, the Privy Council subsequently disavowed this interpretation in the *Star Chrome* case, where it explained that Indian title is "a personal right in the sense that it is in its nature inalienable except by surrender to the Crown."[70] In other words, aboriginal title is a "personal" right only in the sense that it is exclusive to the group that holds it and cannot be transferred to private individuals.[71] Nevertheless, it could be argued that the restriction on the transfer of aboriginal title prevents it from being truly proprietary in nature, since a property right is characteristically alienable. However, the argument is misconceived. While there may be grounds in English law for associating property with alienability, the two are not necessarily linked.[72] In any case, aboriginal title is not a category of English land law but a *sui generis* right. As seen above, the restriction on alienability stemmed historically from the rule prevailing in settler communities that title to land flows from the Crown. This restriction is only partial, for aboriginal title may be ceded to the Crown and possibly also to other aboriginal groups.

Properly understood, the *St. Catherine's* case stands for the proposition that aboriginal title is a property right. The Privy Council held that Indian title is an "Interest other than that of the Province" in lands allotted to a Province by s. 109 of the *Constitution Act, 1867*.[73] Thus, the Crown in right of the Province holds only the underlying title to lands affected by aboriginal title until aboriginal title is surrendered to the Crown in right of the Federal Government, at which point the lands become available to the Province as a source of revenue. As the Privy Council later observed, the phrase an "Interest other than that of the Province" in s. 109 denotes "some right or interest in a third party, independent of and capable of being vindicated in competition with the beneficial interest of the old province."[74] It follows that Indian title is an interest in land, independent of and opposable to the Crown's underlying title, which it burdens.

In *Canadian Pacific Ltd. v. Paul*,[75] the Supreme Court removed any remaining doubts on the question. In a unanimous opinion, the Court stated:

> Before turning to the jurisprudence on what must be done in order to extinguish the Indian interest in land, the exact nature of that interest must be considered. Courts have generally taken as their starting point the case of *St. Catherine's Milling and Lumber Co. v. The Queen* (1888), 14 App. Cas. 46 (P.C.), in which Indian title was described at p. 54 as a "personal and usufructuary right." This has at times been interpreted as meaning that Indian title is merely a personal right which cannot be elevated to the status of a proprietary interest so as to compete on an equal footing with other proprietary interests. However, we are of the opinion that the right was characterized as purely personal for the sole purpose of emphasizing its generally inalienable nature; it could not be transferred, sold or surrendered to anyone other than the Crown.

The Court went on to quote, with approval, Justice Wilson's statement in the *Guerin* case that the Crown cannot derogate from the Indian interest in land unless the Indians agree.[76]

The fact that aboriginal title is an interest in land means that it benefits from the common law presumption favouring the payment of just compensation upon a compulsory taking. In the absence of clear words to the contrary, statutes that unilaterally extinguish aboriginal land rights should be interpreted as providing for compensation.[77] The concept that aboriginal title is a compensable right is not a refinement of modern jurisprudence. It is intrinsic to the characterization of aboriginal title in the *Royal Proclamation* of 1763. Indian lands are defined there as "such Parts of Our Dominions and Territories as, *not having been ceded to, or purchased by Us*, are reserved to them...." The Crown provides that "if, at any Time, any of the said Indians *should be inclined to dispose of* the said Lands, the same *shall be purchased* only for Us, in Our Name, at some publick Meeting or Assembly of the said Indians to be held for that Purpose..." These provisions portray aboriginal title as a valuable interest in land normally acquired by purchase, which involves the payment of a monetary consideration. It follows that, where the Crown does not buy Indian lands for a mutually agreed price but expropriates them, the act will be governed by the normal presumption requiring payment of just compensation.

In *Delgamuukw*, the Supreme Court explicitly confirms this viewpoint. In discussing the Crown's fiduciary duty under s. 35(1), *Constitution Act, 1982*, the Court holds that aboriginal title has an inescapable economic aspect. As such, fair compensation is normally required when aboriginal title is infringed, depending on such factors as the nature of the aboriginal title in question, the nature and severity of the infringement, and the extent to which aboriginal interests have been accommodated.[78] Although the Court is discussing the implications of the Crown's fiduciary duty under s. 35(1), it appears that s. 35(1) merely entrenches a common law duty that predated the enactment of the *Constitution Act, 1982*.[79]

In summary, the concept of aboriginal title is a distinctive concept of Canadian common law that coordinates the interaction between indigenous land systems and European-based land systems. Aboriginal title arises from the occupation of Canada by indigenous peoples prior to the advent of the Crown. It is a communal title and cannot be alienated except to the Crown. It gives a group the right to the exclusive use and occupation of the land for a broad range of purposes, so long as these are not irreconcilable with the group's original bond with the land. While the concept of aboriginal title is broadly uniform in nature, it allows for differing systems of land use and tenure to operate within aboriginal groups. Aboriginal title is a true property right, maintainable against the whole world, including the Crown. It is not held at the Crown's pleasure and it cannot be extinguished by a unilateral exercise of the Crown prerogative. Where aboriginal title has been extinguished by the act of a competent legislature, it benefits from the common law presumption ordaining the payment of just compensation.

Notes

1 This paper draws on material first published in B. Slattery, "Understanding Aboriginal Rights" (1987) 66 Can. Bar Rev. 727 at 741-53. For a range of theories regarding the origins and character of aboriginal title, see K. McNeil, *Common Law Aboriginal Title* (Oxford: Clarendon Press, 1989); B. Slattery, "The Legal Basis of Aboriginal Title," in *Aboriginal Title in British Columbia: Delgamuukw v. The Queen*, ed. F. Cassidy (Lantzville, B.C.: Oolichan Books, 1992); J. C. Smith, "The Concept of Native Title" (1974) 24 U.T.L.J. 1.

2 The point is elaborated in B. Slattery, "Making Sense of Aboriginal and Treaty Rights" (2000) 79 Can. Bar Rev. (forthcoming).

3 *Guerin v. The Queen* [1984] 2 S.C.R. 335 (S.C.C.) *per* Dickson J. at 379-82.

4 See J. D. Hurley, *Children or Brethren: Aboriginal Rights in Colonial Iroquoia* (Ph.D. Dissertation, Cambridge University, 1985; reprint, Saskatoon: University of Saskatchewan Native Law Centre, 1985); B. Slattery, "Aboriginal Sovereignty and Imperial Claims" (1991) 29 Osgoode Hall L.J. 681.

5 See, e.g., D. G. Mandelbaum, *The Plains Cree: An Ethnographic, Historical, and Comparative Study* (Regina: Canadian Plains Research Centre, 1979) at 7-46.

6 See C. G. Calloway, *New Worlds for All: Indians, Europeans, and the Remaking of Early America* (Baltimore, Md.: John Hopkins University Press, 1997) at 142-51, 183-87; G. T. Hunt, *The Wars of the Iroquois: A Study in Intertribal Trade Relations* (Madison: University of Wisconsin Press, 1960); F. Jennings, *The Ambiguous Iroquois Empire* (New York: Norton & Co., 1984); D. G. Mandelbaum, *The Plains Cree: An Ethnographic, Historical, and Comparative Study* (Regina: Canadian Plains Research Centre, 1979) at 7-46; R. White, *The Middle Ground: Indians, Empires, and Republics in the Great Lakes Region, 1650-1815* (Cambridge: Cambridge University Press, 1991).

7 In *Delgamuukw v. British Columbia* [1997] 3 S.C.R. 1010 (S.C.C.), Lamer C.J. observed at 1090: "... the inalienability of aboriginal lands is, at least in part, a function of the common law principle that settlers in colonies must derive their title from Crown grant and, therefore, cannot acquire title through purchase from aboriginal inhabitants. It is also, again only in part, a function of a general policy "to ensure that Indians are not dispossessed of their entitlements": see *Mitchell v. Peguis Indian Band*, [1990] 2 S.C.R. 85, at p. 133."

8 Cf. the analysis offered by Chief Justice Marshall in *Johnson v. M'Intosh*, 8 Wheaton 543 (U.S.S.C. 1823) and *Worcester v. Georgia*, 6 Peters 515 (U.S.S.C. 1832).

9 See *Johnson v. M'Intosh*, 8 Wheaton 543 (U.S.S.C. 1823); *Amodu Tijani v. Secretary of Southern Nigeria* [1921] 2 A.C. 399 (P.C.) at 407; St. *Catherine's Milling and Lumber Co. v. The Queen* (1888), 14 A.C. 46 (P.C.). For analysis, see K. McNeil, *Common Law Aboriginal Title* (Oxford: Clarendon Press, 1989); D. P. O'Connell, *International Law*, 2nd ed. (London: Stevens & Son, 1970) vol.1 at 403-05; K. Roberts-Wray, *Commonwealth and Colonial Law* (London: Stevens & Sons, 1966) at 625-36; J. Salmond, *Jurisprudence*, 7th ed. (London: Sweet & Maxwell, 1924) Appendix V at 554; B. Slattery, *The Land*

Rights of Indigenous Canadian Peoples (D.Phil. Thesis, Oxford University, 1979; reprint, Saskatoon: University of Saskatchewan Native Law Centre, 1979) at 45-62.

10 In some aboriginal groups, the sale or transfer of land outside the group may have been unknown or forbidden. To this extent, the restriction on alienation may coincide with traditional concepts.

11 *Delgamuukw v. British Columbia* [1997] 3 S.C.R. 1010 (S.C.C.). The majority opinion is written by Chief Justice Lamer, with the concurrence of Cory, McLachlin and Major JJ. Unless otherwise indicated, all references are to the majority opinion. La Forest J. writes a short separate opinion (with L'Heureux-Dubé J. concurring) in which he agrees with the Chief Justice's conclusions but disagrees with various aspects of his reasons. While McLachlin J. concurs with the Chief Justice, she also states at 1135 that she is "in substantial agreement with the comments of Justice La Forest." Since the views of the Chief Justice and La Forest J. are incompatible on some points, it appears that McLachlin J. agrees with La Forest J. only where the latter supplements rather than departs from the views of the Chief Justice.

12 *Ibid.* at 1028-29.

13 *Ibid.* at 1080.

14 See, e.g., B. Ziff, *Principles of Property Law* (Scarborough, Ont.: Carswell, 1993) at 38-39, 45, 118-120.

15 *Delgamuukw v. British Columbia* [1997] 3 S.C.R. 1010 (S.C.C.) at 1080-81.

16 Under the test governing specific aboriginal rights laid down in *R. v. Van der Peet* [1996] 2 S.C.R. 507 (S.C.C.) at 549, 554-55.

17 *St. Catherine's Milling and Lumber Co. v. The Queen* (1888), 14 A.C. 46 (P.C.) at 54.

18 *Delgamuukw v. British Columbia* [1997] 3 S.C.R. 1010 (S.C.C.) at 1081.

19 *Guerin v. The Queen* [1984] 2 S.C.R. 335 (S.C.C.) *per* Dickson J. at 379-82.

20 *Delgamuukw v. British Columbia* [1997] 3 S.C.R. 1010 (S.C.C.) at 1081.

21 *Ibid.* at 1081-82, citing *Canadian Pacific Ltd. v. Paul* [1988] 2 S.C.R. 654 (S.C.C.) at 677.

22 K. McNeil, *Common Law Aboriginal Title* (Oxford: Clarendon Press, 1989) at 79-93.

23 Royal Proclamation of 7 October 1763, in Clarence S. Brigham, ed., *British Royal Proclamations Relating to America* (Worcester, Mass.: American Antiquarian Society, 1911), 212.

24 *Delgamuukw v. British Columbia* [1997] 3 S.C.R. 1010 (S.C.C.) at 1082, 1098-99, citing *Guerin v. The Queen* [1984] 2 S.C.R. 335 (S.C.C.) at 376, 378; *Roberts v. Canada* [1989] 1 S.C.R. 322 (S.C.C.) at 340; K. McNeil, *Common Law Aboriginal Title* (Oxford: Clarendon Press, 1989) at 7; K. McNeil, "The Meaning of Aboriginal Title," in *Aboriginal and Treaty Rights in Canada*, ed. M. Asch (Vancouver: University of British Columbia Press, 1997) at 144.

25 *Delgamuukw v. British Columbia* [1997] 3 S.C.R. 1010 (S.C.C.) at 1082-83.

26 *Ibid.* at 1106; final emphasis added.

27 *Ibid.* at 1083. For a range of persuasive arguments supporting this conclusion, see K. McNeil, "The Meaning of Aboriginal Title," in *Aboriginal and Treaty Rights in Canada*, ed. M. Asch (Vancouver: University of British Colum-

bia Press, 1997). Justice La Forest disagrees with the Court on this point, arguing that the content of aboriginal title is determined by the traditional way of life of the specific aboriginal group at the time of Crown sovereignty, that is by the particular practices, customs and traditions that governed the way in which the specific group used the land to live (at 1128). He adds, nevertheless, that these uses, although confined to the aboriginal society's traditional way of life, may be exercised in a contemporary manner. In effect, then, La Forest J. holds that the contours of aboriginal title vary from group to group, depending on the group's traditional mode of life.

28 *Guerin v. The Queen* [1984] 2 S.C.R. 335 (S.C.C.) at 382. See also: *Canadian Pacific Ltd. v. Paul* [1988] 2 S.C.R. 654 (S.C.C.) at 677-78.

29 *Guerin v. The Queen* [1984] 2 S.C.R. 335 (S.C.C.) at 379.

30 Indian Act, R.S.C., 1985, c. I-5. For the genesis of this provision, see K. Mc-Neil, "The Meaning of Aboriginal Title," in *Aboriginal and Treaty Rights in Canada*, ed. M. Asch (Vancouver: University of British Columbia Press, 1997) at 148-49.

31 *Delgamuukw v. British Columbia* [1997] 3 S.C.R. 1010 (S.C.C.) at 1085-86.

32 Indian Oil and Gas Act, R.S.C., 1985, c. I-7.

33 Section 2 of the Act defines "Indian lands" as "lands reserved for the Indians, including any interests therein, surrendered in accordance with the *Indian Act* ...."

34 *Delgamuukw v. British Columbia* [1997] 3 S.C.R. 1010 (S.C.C.) at 1086-87. The Court invokes its earlier ruling in *Blueberry River Indian Band v. Canada (Department of Indian Affairs and Northern Development)* [1995] 4 S.C.R. 344 (S.C.C.).

35 *Delgamuukw v. British Columbia* [1997] 3 S.C.R. 1010 (S.C.C.) at 1087. For an argument to the same effect, see K. McNeil, "The Meaning of Aboriginal Title," in *Aboriginal and Treaty Rights in Canada*, ed. M. Asch (Vancouver: University of British Columbia Press, 1997) at 149-50.

36 *Delgamuukw v. British Columbia* [1997] 3 S.C.R. 1010 (S.C.C.) at 1080; see also heading at 1088. It is not clear whether this limit is also meant to apply to reserve lands. On the one hand, as just seen, the Court at 1085 reiterates the view expressed in *Guerin v. The Queen* [1984] 2 S.C.R. 335 (S.C.C.) that aboriginal title and reserve title are presumptively identical. On the other hand, the Court at 1085-86 quotes s. 18, Indian Act, R.S.C., 1985, c. I-5, which contemplates that reserve lands may be used for any purposes whatsoever.

37 *Delgamuukw v. British Columbia* [1997] 3 S.C.R. 1010 (S.C.C.) at 1091.

38 *Ibid.* at 1088-90.

39 *Ibid.* at 1088-89, 1099-1100.

40 *Ibid.* at 1097-99.

41 *Ibid.* at 1091.

42 *Ibid.* at 1089.

43 *Ibid.* at 1090-91, citing E. H. Burn, *Cheshire and Burn's Modern Law of Real Property*, 14th ed. (London: Butterworths, 1988) at 264; R. E. Megarry & H. W. R. Wade, *The Law of Real Property*, 4th ed. (London: Stevens, 1975) at 105.

44 Subject, as always, to valid legislation.

45 The position parallels that described by the Privy Council in *Amodu Tijani v. Secretary of Southern Nigeria* [1921] 2 A.C. 399 (P.C.) at 403-04: "In India, as in Southern Nigeria, there is yet another feature of the fundamental nature of the title to land which must be borne in mind. The title, such as it is, may not be that of the individual, as in this country it nearly always is in some form, but may be that of a community. Such a community may have the possessory title to the common enjoyment of a usufruct, with customs under which its individual members are admitted to enjoyment, and even to a right of transmitting the individual enjoyment as members by assignment inter vivos or by succession. To ascertain how far this latter development of right has progressed involves the study of the history of the particular community and its usages in each case. Abstract principles fashioned a priori are of but little assistance, and are as often as not misleading." This passage was cited by Hall J. in *Calder v. British Columbia (A.G.)* [1973] S.C.R. 313 (S.C.C.) at 355, and the decision itself was referred to with approval by Dickson J. in *Guerin v. The Queen* [1984] 2 S.C.R. 335 (S.C.C.) at 378.

46 On the mutability of aboriginal custom, see the remarks of Sissons J. in *Re Noah Estate* (1961), 32 D.L.R. 185 (N.W.T.T.C.) at 197.

47 We are speaking, as always, of the position at common law. The matter is now regulated in part by various statutes.

48 This also appears to be the position in United States law; see, e.g., *United States v. Shoshone Tribe of Indians*, 304 U.S. 111 (U.S.S.C. 1938); *United States v. Klamath Indians*, 304 U.S. 119 (U.S.S.C. 1938); F. S. Cohen, "Original Indian Title" (1947-48) 32 Minn. L. Rev. 28; F. S. Cohen, *Handbook of Federal Indian Law*, 1982 ed., ed. R. Strickland and others (Charlottesville, Va.: Michie Bobbs-Merrill, 1982) at 491.

49 See *Baker Lake (Hamlet of) v. Minister of Indian Affairs and Northern Development* [1980] 1 F.C. 518 (F.C.T.D.) at 559; *Attorney-General for Ontario v. Bear Island Foundation* (1984), 15 D.L.R. 321 (Ont. H.C.) at 354-61.

50 Thus, Mandelbaum writes: "The advent of the Hudson's Bay Company marked the opening of a new phase in tribal fortunes. ... Both the tribal culture and locale changed greatly under the influence of the English. The culture naturally altered with the influx of European goods and with the shift of occupational emphasis from food gathering to fur trapping during certain seasons of the year. The locale was enlarged because the traders sent the natives deeper and deeper into the back country to collect furs from the different tribes and to trap in virgin territory."; D. G. Mandelbaum, *The Plains Cree: An Ethnographic, Historical, and Comparative Study* (Regina: Canadian Plains Research Centre, 1979) at 20.

51 See H. Brody, *Maps and Dreams: Indians and the British Columbia Frontier* (Harmondsworth, Eng.: Penguin Books, 1983) at 21-30, 85-86, 247.

52 On the range of aboriginal contributions to modern European and North American cultures, see C. G. Calloway, *New Worlds for All: Indians, Europeans, and the Remaking of Early America* (Baltimore, Md.: John Hopkins University Press, 1997); J. Weatherford, *Indian Givers: How the Indians of America Transformed the World* (New York: Fawcett Columbine, 1988); J.

Weatherford, *Native Roots: How the Indians Enriched America* (New York: Fawcett Columbine, 1991).

53 *Guerin v. The Queen* [1984] 2 S.C.R. 335 (S.C.C.) *per* Dickson J. at 378, quoting a passage from *Johnson v. M'Intosh*, 8 Wheaton 543 (U.S.S.C. 1823) at 573-74. The same passage is quoted with approval by Hall J. in *Calder v. British Columbia (A.G.)* [1973] S.C.R. 313 (S.C.C.) at 381-82, who reiterates that "the aborigines of newly-found lands were conceded to be the rightful occupants of the soil with a legal as well as a just claim to retain possession of it and to use it according to their own discretion ..." (at 383). See also *Simon v. The Queen* [1985] 2 S.C.R. 387 (S.C.C.) at 402-03, where the Supreme Court of Canada rejected the argument that a right to hunt "as usual" embodied in an Indian treaty was limited to hunting for purposes and by methods usual in 1752, the date the treaty was concluded. Dickson C.J. stated that "the inclusion of the phrase 'as usual' appears to reflect a concern that the right to hunt be interpreted in a flexible way that is sensitive to the evolution of changes in normal hunting practices."

54 This rule holds true except in certain very unusual situations, such as in a conquered or ceded colony, where the Crown has the power to legislate under the royal prerogative prior to the summoning of a local assembly; see *Campbell v. Hall* (1774), Lofft 655 (K.B.); P. W. Hogg, *Constitutional Law of Canada*, 3rd ed. (Scarborough, Ont.: Carswell, 1992) at 14, 33; B. Slattery, *The Land Rights of Indigenous Canadian Peoples*, (D.Phil. Thesis, Oxford University, 1979; reprint, Saskatoon: University of Saskatchewan Native Law Centre, 1979) at 30-44. Of course, the Crown has the prerogative power to extinguish aboriginal title *bilaterally*, by accepting a voluntary cession from the relevant aboriginal group.

55 See P. W. Hogg, *Constitutional Law of Canada*, 3rd ed. (Scarborough, Ont.: Carswell, 1992) at 13-17.

56 The grant may not be entirely invalid but may give the grantee the right to possess the land once aboriginal title is extinguished.

57 The effect of statutory grants on Indian title was considered in *Canadian Pacific Ltd. v. Paul* [1988] 2 S.C.R. 654 (S.C.C.), with inconclusive results.

58 See, e.g., *R. v. Isaac* (1975), 13 N.S.R. 460 (N.S.S.C., App. Div.) *per* MacKeigan C.J. at 476, 479; G. V. La Forest, *Natural Resources and Public Property under the Canadian Constitution* (Toronto: University of Toronto Press, 1969) at 159-60.

59 *St. Catherine's Milling and Lumber Co. v. The Queen* (1888), 14 A.C. 46 (P.C.) at 54.

60 Other interpretations of the Privy Council's words have been adopted, notably that the Crown could express its will concerning aboriginal title only through legislation: see *Mathias v. Findlay* [1978] 4 W.W.R. 653 (B.C.S.C.). For discussion of the question whether the Proclamation of 1763 can be amended by the Crown under the royal prerogative, see B. Slattery, *The Land Rights of Indigenous Canadian Peoples* (D.Phil. Thesis, Oxford University, 1979; reprint, Saskatoon: University of Saskatchewan Native Law Centre, 1979) at 319-28.

61 *Calder v. British Columbia (A.G.)* [1973] S.C.R. 313 (S.C.C.).

62 *Ibid.* at 328, Martland and Ritchie JJ. concurring.

63 *Ibid.* at 402, Spence and Laskin JJ. concurring.

64 *Guerin v. The Queen* [1984] 2 S.C.R. 335 (S.C.C.) at 376-77 (emphasis added). It may be noted that this statement apparently does not take account of Justice Judson's ambiguity on the question of extinguishment.

65 *Ibid.* at 378, quoting from the judgment of Marshall C.J. in *Johnson v. M'Intosh*, 8 Wheaton 543 (U.S.S.C. 1823) at 573-74. The first portion of the quotation is italicized in Dickson J.'s judgment. At several other points, Dickson J. emphasizes that aboriginal title is "an independent legal right"; see, e.g., at 378.

66 *Guerin v. The Queen* [1984] 2 S.C.R. 335 (S.C.C.) at 349.

67 *Ibid.* at 352 (emphasis added).

68 See *Baker Lake (Hamlet of) v. Minister of Indian Affairs and Northern Development* [1980] 1 F.C. 518 (F.C.T.D.) at 577.

69 *St. Catherine's Milling and Lumber Co. v. The Queen* (1888), 14 A.C. 46 (P.C.) at 54. The usefulness of this phrase was doubted by Justice Judson in the *Calder* case, where he remarked with reference to the question of Indian title that "it does not help one in the solution of this problem to call it a 'personal or usufructuary right'": *Calder v. British Columbia (A.G.)* [1973] S.C.R. 313 (S.C.C.) at 328. Likewise, in *Delgamuukw v. British Columbia* [1997] 3 S.C.R. 1010 (S.C.C.) at 1081, the Supreme Court stated that "the Privy Council's choice of terminology is not particularly helpful to explain the various dimensions of aboriginal title." Significantly, the Privy Council itself disclaimed any intention of giving a comprehensive definition of Indian title (at 55): "There was a great deal of learned discussion at the Bar with respect to the precise quality of the Indian right, but their Lordships do not consider it necessary to express any opinion upon the point."

70 *Attorney-General for Quebec v. Attorney-General for Canada (The Star Chrome Case)* [1921] 1 A.C. 401 (P.C.) at 408.

71 In *Guerin v. The Queen* [1984] 2 S.C.R. 335 (S.C.C.) at 382, Dickson J. states: "the *sui generis* interest which the Indians have in the land is personal in the sense that it cannot be transferred to a grantee...." The Supreme Court confirms this view in *Delgamuukw v. British Columbia* [1997] 3 S.C.R. 1010 (S.C.C.) at 1081-82.

72 As noted in K. Lysyk, "The Indian Title Question in Canada: An Appraisal in the Light of Calder" (1973) 51 Can. Bar. Rev. 450 at 471: "restrictions on alienation are familiar to recognized interests in land at common law, for example, in leases or in estates in fee tail. As one writer has observed, at English common law there were times when most of the land in England could not be sold to anyone" (footnotes omitted).

73 *St. Catherine's Milling and Lumber Co. v. The Queen* (1888), 14 A.C. 46 (P.C.) at 58.

74 *Attorney-General for Canada v. Attorney-General for Ontario* [1897] A.C. 199 (P.C.) at 210-11.

75 *Canadian Pacific Ltd. v. Paul* [1988] 2 S.C.R. 654 (S.C.C.) at 677.

76 *Ibid.* at 677, quoting *Guerin v. The Queen* [1984] 2 S.C.R. 335 (S.C.C.) at 349. See also *Delgamuukw v. British Columbia* [1997] 3 S.C.R. 1010 (S.C.C.)

at 1081-82, citing *Canadian Pacific Ltd. v. Paul* [1988] 2 S.C.R. 654 (S.C.C.) at 677.

77 In *Paul v. Canadian Pacific Ltd.* (1983), 2 D.L.R. 22 (N.B.C.A.), La Forest, J.A. states at 34: "When a taking is, in fact, authorized by statute, it is presumed that compensation will be paid .... This, like the presumption against taking, must apply with additional force to the taking of Indian lands because this affects the honour and good faith of the Crown." For discussion, see B. Slattery, "The Constitutional Guarantee of Aboriginal and Treaty Rights" (1982-83) 8 Queen's L.J. 232 at 270-73.

78 *Delgamuukw v. British Columbia* [1997] 3 S.C.R. 1010 (S.C.C.) at 1113-14.

79 In his separate opinion, Justice La Forest notes that the treatment of aboriginal title as a compensable right is evident in the Royal Proclamation of 1763; *Delgamuukw v. British Columbia* [1997] 3 S.C.R. 1010 (S.C.C.) at 1133-34.

Probable Effects
Practical Construction
of New Legislation

JOHN L. HOWARD, QC

> The ideas of economists and philosophers, both when they are right and when they are wrong, are more powerful than is commonly understood. Indeed, the world is ruled by little else. Practical men, who believe themselves to be quite exempt from any intellectual influences, are usually the slaves of some defunct economist. ...But soon or late, it is ideas, not vested interests, which are dangerous for good or evil.
>
> J.M. Keynes, *The General Theory of Employment, Interest and Money* (383-84, Macmillan, London, paperback 1973)

> Ideas have a radiation and development, an ancestry and a posterity of their own, in which men play the part of godfathers and godmothers more than that of legitimate parents.
>
> Letters of Lord Acton to Mary Gladstone (1905), quoted in G. Himmelfarb, *On Looking into the Abyss: Untimely Thoughts on Culture and Society* 82, Vintage Paperback (1995).

Introduction

Speaking at a similar conference in 1997, I set out a quote from an essay on the novel by Lionel Trilling. In that essay, he argues that for at least the last 200 years, the novel has been the best means to exercise the liberal imagination, to examine in depth and to propose means to deal with moral issues that inhere in all societies. The central issue since the beginning of the industrial society has been social justice, now institu-

---

Notes will be found on pages 50–52.

tionalized as the difficult choice among government transfer payment programs. The essential issue is to achieve an effective balance between equality of opportunity and equality of result or, as Okun characterized it, between efficiency and equality.[1] The problem, always, is to get the incentives right,[2] to implement programs that give necessary support to those in need without reducing their will to help themselves. In contemporary economic jargon, the issue is to induce people to do productive work and to avoid the moral hazard of becoming dependent on government handouts, now euphemistically described as rent seeking.[3]

Although a persuasive supporter of the need for transfer payments to achieve a reasonable degree of social justice, Trilling was well aware of the pitfalls, reminding us that:[4]

> Some paradox of our nature leads us, when once we have made our fellow men the objects of our enlightened interest, to go on to make them the objects of our pity, then of our wisdom, ultimately of our coercion. It is to prevent this corruption, the most ironic and tragic that man knows, that we stand in need of the moral realism which is the product of the free play of the moral imagination.

What Trilling means by the moral imagination is an approach to social change that is, as far as possible, free of dogma; reviews the historical record of past successes and failures; projects probable outcomes; and considers feasible alternatives that can apply to the policy issue.

To date, Canadian policy concerning aboriginal peoples clearly has not been developed with Trilling's caution in mind. Instead of real analysis of the issues, we have created an atmosphere of guilt-ridden villains seeking atonement for the wrongs done to aboriginal victims. In this brief paper, I will attempt to demonstrate that even if there is some truth to the above characterization, it is irrelevant to the work at hand *if* one assumes that the policy end is not to compensate alleged victims of earlier policies now seen to be harmful, but to enable aboriginal individuals to lead challenging and productive lives in aboriginal communities or elsewhere as Canadian citizens.

The "Aboriginal Problem"

What is the work at hand? Policy analyses concerning the "aboriginal problem" in Canada have been so incomplete and so ambivalent that no one can state authoritatively what the policy of Canadian governments is beyond achieving a "deal" that will engender "peace in our time." Probably the best articulation of the sentiments (as distinct from ideas) implied in the statements of Canadian political leaders is to repeat US President Lyndon Johnson's declaration of purpose in the

Special Message to Congress on the Problems of the American Indian, part of his Great Society program:[5]

> A goal that ends the old debate about "termination" of Indian programs and stresses *self-determination*: a goal that erases old attitudes of paternalism and promotes *partnership* and *self-help*. An opportunity to remain in their homelands, if they choose, without surrendering their dignity: an opportunity to move to the towns and cities of North America, if they choose, equipped to live in equality and dignity. [Italics added.]

Even if diluted in strength by many of the "halo" words of the 1960s, such as "self-determination," "partnership" and "self-help," the intended effects of the policy were clear and have been vigorously pursued—at least by Congress—to the present date.[6] Based as they are on extensions of the *Indian Reorganization Act* of 1934, the self-governance programs remain subject to the power of federal bureaucrats to maintain oversight of expenditures and, as a corollary, to influence strongly the means proposed to achieve program goals. In sum, notwithstanding repeated pressure from Congress and even from the President,[7] a knowledgeable and sympathetic analyst concludes that, so far, self-determination or, in other words, the transfer of considerable decision-making powers from the federal bureaucracy to the tribes "... has come to little."[8]

That is not to say, however, that there is reason to despair. The social problems are never clear-cut, the legislated programs are necessarily complicated, and the implementation and *follow-up* costs are enormous. But such legislative experiments do demonstrate the central point of this paper: that policy choices are not between negotiation and litigation but instead range over a broad spectrum between those poles, as demonstrated by US experience.[9] Either negotiation or litigation is essentially an abdication by legislatures to bureaucrats or to the courts, which in the short-run broadly diffuses responsibility and renders focusing accountability virtually impossible. In the long-run, however, as an inherent feature of the parliamentary appropriation function, legislatures must implement follow-up procedures to determine the effectiveness of expenditures on aboriginal programs however characterized or implemented.

Transfer Payments: A Chronology

As Trilling points out, no matter how sincere the convictions of politicians and their constituents concerning transfer payments based on treating our fellow citizens as "objects of our enlightened interest," policy will degenerate inevitably from interest, to pity, to wisdom, and finally, to coercion if the original transfer program does not succeed. To avoid that, we must *get the incentives right*. It seems unlikely we can do so by way of backroom, negotiated "deals," as distinct from reasoned and well-administered programs that are consonant with our Parliamentary tradition. Even a summary review of the history of transfer payment programs, knowledge of which is implicit in Trilling's statement, demonstrates that they are complicated, prone to failure and, as a result, required to be subject to continual legislative scrutiny.[10]

(1)   During the mercantile period from 1536 to 1795, the *English Poor Law*, which was administered at the parish level, provided a safety net for all people in need, or indeed all the people if all were in need. This pattern was reinforced by the *Act of Settlement* of 1662, which largely precluded movement of people from one parish to another, effectively relegating the workers to a new form of serfdom.

(2)   In 1795, this provision of the *Act of Settlement* was abrogated in order to give workers the mobility to take jobs in the new industrial mills, paving the way to formulation of a relatively free labor market.

(3)   Concurrently, however, the *Speenhamland System* was implemented as a transition safety valve. But what it did was require the parish to supplement wages to maintain them at a fixed level. As a result all wages tended to fall below the minimum rate and the parish subsidized the difference. As a further result, labor productivity declined disastrously, reflecting the absence of any real incentive to work. The end result was a social and economic catastrophe.

In 1834, after enactment of the Reform Bill of 1832 (which largely eliminated the rotten boroughs to make Parliament more representative), the new Parliament in effect repealed the *Speenhamland System* and precipitately forced all workers into the unstructured, crudely operated labor market. Polanyi states that "Never in all modern history has a more ruthless act of social reform been perpetrated..."[11] The remarkable thing was that it did not engender a violent revolution.

The brutal shock of that event haunted for generations the daydreams of the British working class. And yet the success of this lacerating operation was due to the deep-seated convictions of the broad strata of the population, including the laborers themselves, that the system which to all appearances supported them was in truth despoiling them, and that the "right to live" [Speenhamland System] was the sickness unto death.[12]

Thus from the outset of industrial society, the thorniest policy problem has been the design, enactment, implementation and oversight of the effects of transfer payment programs. The *Poor Law* debate related to only the first and most traumatic of such policies. As reflected in Trilling's caution, similar and equally unsuccessful policies have frequently been implemented: the "pogey" system in the Canadian Atlantic provinces; the unemployment "insurance" system in Canada from roughly 1960 to 1992; the Great Society programs of President Johnson; and, of course, the welfare transfers to aboriginal people in North America since about 1950.

Aboriginal Policy: A Chronology

As if the central problem of designing incentives were not enough, to the aboriginal policy we add another equally difficult issue: the manner of governance of aboriginal communities. The issue has been simmering since the first Europeans arrived in the Americas. Again, the tortuous twists and turns of policy, which have been at least as traumatic to the aboriginal peoples as were *Speenhamland* and the *Poor Law* repeal to British workers in 1834, can be presented most emphatically in a brief chronology. The chronology touches on Spanish, American and Canadian policies. The issues are not only continent-wide but also universal. And, generally, the US has taken the lead in experimenting with new policies before they were introduced in Canada. As we shall see, these policies run the gamut, from recognition as "nations" through removal; reserves ("sanctuaries"); residential schools (assimilation by accretion); welfare transfers (block transfers to communities or specific transfers to individuals); termination (one-step assimilation); and self-governance.

(1) 1532-1579: Relying on legal advice, the Spanish Emperor concluded that since there was no war with any aboriginal peoples in the Americas, each distinctive community was entitled to be treated as a "nation."[13]

(2) 1778-1789: The US Continental Congress acknowledged Indian communities to be nations, even conceding by Treaty in 1785 to one nation, the Cherokees, the right to send a delegate to Congress.[14]

(3) 1789-1871: The era of the treaty making in the US was terminated by Congress because treaty-making was the sole prerogative of the Senate and thus precluded the House from exercising any decision-making power.[15] Treaty-making proceeded concurrently in Canada except most of British Columbia. The age of treaty making reopened with the *Alaska* settlement of 1971 and the proposed *Nisga'a* settlement of 1999.

(4) 1830-1879: In the US, this was the tragic period of Westward Removal, the forced emigration of the "civilized tribes" (Cherokee,

Choctaw, Chickasaw, Creek and Seminole) from the Eastern United States to Oklahoma.

(5) 1887-1934: Until 1879, both the US and the Canadian government, which tended to adopt US policy, treated the aboriginal communities as homogeneous, collectivist communities that had no concern for individual rights.[16]

(6) 1847: Congress authorized support payments to be made directly to households instead of block or earmarked payments to tribal leaders. The first objective was to undermine the authority of Indian leaders and so expedite assimilation; the second was to curb the growing bureaucracy of the Bureau of Indian Affairs.[17]

(7) 1887: Acceding to pressures from land-hungry homesteaders and, again, to accelerate assimilation, Congress enacted the *Allotment Act* (Dawes Act), which subdivided the reserve land into 360-acre blocks (twice the general homestead allotment), allotted one such block to each reserve Indian family and, in effect, confiscated any "surplus" Indian lands for distribution to non-aboriginals.[18] Each allotment to an Indian family was subject to bureaucratic trust constraints for 25 years, after which time the Indian title-holder could transfer ownership to any person. As a result, some 60 percent of Indian lands, the "surplus" lands and some Indian lands, were transferred to non-aboriginals. Canada did not adopt this policy—probably not because of Victorian virtue but because the Canadian reserves were not large enough to engender pressure for reduction.

(8) 1934: Congress enacted the *Indian Reorganization Act* ("IRA"), which repealed the 1887 allotment policy, reinforced the "nation" concept, encouraged economic development through tribal business corporations, and urged greater autonomy or self-determination. The major premise underlying the Act was that the Indian nations could prosper as collectivist societies and might even become a model for US society generally. The result was complete politicization—and hence bureaucratization—of all social and economic aspects, an approach that we know, with the benefit of hindsight, was doomed to economic failure.[19]

(9) 1953: Congress enacted a termination policy which, assuming specific standards were met, empowered a qualified tribe to vote to terminate and thus become immediately assimilated into the general population. This policy, too, failed. On seeing other tribes obtain further benefits from Indian status, terminated groups understandably reapplied for and, ultimately, regained that status.[20] Canada also toyed

with the policy but backed off, ostensibly because of its rejection by Canadian aboriginals but likely also because of the evolving bad experience in the US.[21]

(10) 1968: In light of President Johnson's Great Society declaration of 1964, building on the foundation of the *Indian Reorganization Act* of 1934, Congress has enacted several new, basic laws with a view to incrementally increasing autonomy at the tribal level and, as a result, increase tribal leadership, responsibility and accountability.[22]

(11) 1968: *Indian Civil Rights Act*

(12) 1974: *Indian Financing Act*

(13) 1975: *Indian Self-Determination and Education Assistance Act*

(14) 1998: Bill H.R. 1833 proposes to add to the 1975 Act two further titles: (1) Indian health services, and (2) a feasibility study of tribal self-governance compacts.[23]

(15) 1971: More than a century after the purchase of Alaska, the US Government entered into an agreement legitimated by the *Alaska Native Claims Settlement Act* of 1971 ("ANSCA"). Going beyond the admonitions of the 1934 IRA about encouraging business, the Agreement transferred about $1 billion and 40 million acres of land, some of it select timberland, to some 200 discrete community corporations, the shares of which were distributed among the approximately 50,000 aboriginal Alaskans.[24] Not surprisingly, depending on their initial resource endowment and level of management skill, some of these corporations succeeded and some failed.[25] It has been, however, a useful experiment and undoubtedly has influenced some Canadian settlements.

The foregoing chronology demonstrates that governments—and particularly the US Federal Government—have implemented, if not by design then at least impulsively, programs that almost cover the whole spectrum. In retrospect, it is easy to say mistakes were made. But when one attempts to read the historical record and to understand the action from the perspective of people advocating those programs, it is clear that more damage was done in attempting to do good than harm.

GAI/NIT Programs

One model missing from the spectrum is the guaranteed annual income/negative income tax (GAI/NIT). I proposed a trial program in a paper published in 1994, but the response was somewhat less than overwhelming, either for or against. Like all such programs, it entails great risk of moral hazard, that is, making recipients so dependent on such transfers that the transition to self-help becomes difficult, if not impossible.

Clearly, it has several advantages. First, it can be introduced concurrently on a trial basis in several different social environments and can be modified incrementally to fit any particular circumstance. Second, the transfers are effected under one program and are completely visible. Third, when coupled with NIT, the GAI permits the targeting of transfer payments, clawing back any transfers from individuals and households that are demonstrably not in need. Fourth, if designed well and continually adjusted, a GAI/NIT program can provide the appropriate incentives to induce individuals to enter the work force and remain continuously employed. Fifth, it obviates the large bureaucracy required to allocate discretionary payments. And finally, it focuses more responsibility for economic management on individuals and households. Upon reflection, it appears the last two factors elicit considerable resistance to any GAI/NIT program. The existing bureaucracy, both native and non-native, has a vested interest in the discretionary system. As well, the focus on individuals and households depoliticizes a very large part of the revenue flow to aboriginal communities, implying a substantial reduction of the power now exercised by the band political leaders.[26]

The Quintessential Political Problem

The purpose of this chronology is not to prove what was right or wrong about past policies. Rather, it is an attempt to evoke some new ideas and establish a means to demonstrate that the "aboriginal problem" is not unique. Indeed, like all transfer programs introduced since the *Tudor Poor Law*, it is a quintessential political problem. As Jouvenal forcefully states:

> A problem is compromised of precise and known facts and can therefore be solved: for any arithmetical problem there must be a solution. But a political situation is not of that order: what makes it political is "precisely the fact that the frame of reference in which it exists does not permit any solution in the exact sense of that term. A true political problem arises only when the given facts are contradictory, i.e., when it is insoluble."[27]

If the issue is quintessentially political, can it ever be cast as a legal problem that lends itself to judicial resolution? Before posing that question to *Delgamuukw*, one must consider the nature, function and limits of law. Conceptually, law is "... a dynamic process, a system of regularized, institutional procedures for the orderly decision of social questions, including the settlement of disputes."[28] That abstract concept embodies several essential elements of any legal system.[29]

(1) The rule of law, i.e. the impersonal universalized application of categories of substantive rules and standards to facts, largely ignoring particularities.

(2) The several sources of law, which include legislation, judge-made law and administrative rulings.

(3) Due process, meaning the right to reasonable notice of any legal proceedings and the right to submit a full defence before a competent, impartial tribunal in accordance with specified formal procedures.

(4) A first corollary of due process is that the tribunal admits only evidence that is considered credible.

5 A second corollary of due process arises in particular with respect to discretionary decisions made by public officials: they must be subject to a right of appeal or judicial review of administrative action, not just of the process but also of the correctness of the legal rule or standard applied, the adequacy of the evidence considered, the possibility of bias and even the fairness of the result relative to the treatment of other persons.

The first of these elements requires amplification, in particular the phrase "substantive rules and standards." In general, such rules and standards are the tests applied by the decision-maker to decide a legal question. Rules are straightforward. They are tests that, when applied, do not require the decision-maker to exercise any discretion, i.e. to make any judgment as to whether the law has been contravened. Standards are of an altogether different order: "The application of a standard requires the judge both to discover the facts of a particular situation and to assess them in terms of the *purposes or social values* embodied in the standard."[30] [Italics added.]

Typical standards are "due diligence," "good faith," "reasonable care," and "best efforts." Each leaves to the adjudicator considerable discretion to apply his or her subjective values to the specific case in the belief they reflect community values, the factor that legitimizes such decisions. It is this scope of standards that necessarily admits different applications and that, as a result, gives rise to sharp differences, depending on the political or social values of the critics. Although there are many other possible categories, in this century there have been four schools of legal thought.

1. Legal Formalism (Analytical Positivism)

By the end of the nineteenth-century positivism, the idea that any discipline[31]—law, history, sociology—could be, by thorough analysis, broken down into its constituent parts and reconstituted to prove a specific hypothesis just like any natural science, tended to dominate legal theory. By the 1920s, this somewhat ingenuous faith in the natural science analogue became discredited. A particularly sharp, recent critique merits reproduction, partly because it is so clear and partly because it applies in a haunting way to the *Delgamuukw* litigation:

> ... they [the social sciences] labour still under the burden of being false sciences. Their experiments do not provide any measurable progress in the manner of a real science. In place of real evidence they are obliged to pile up overwhelming weight of documentation relating to human action—none of which is proof, little of it even illustration. This sort of material carries the force of neither history nor creativity. What they are working on is circumstantial evidence. It is meant to create the impression of evidence by the force of weight.[32]

In sum, jurists came to understand well that broad, frequently used legal standards such as "reasonable," "good faith" and "due diligence" compelled a judge applying them "... to assess them in terms of the purposes or social values embodied in the standard."[33] Thus there can be no formula, however intricate, that can resolve legal issues.

2. Legal Realism (Pragmatic Positivism)

Responding to this insight, the doctrine of pragmatic positivism, or realism, evolved in the United States and, consciously or unconsciously, has influenced most legal thought since the 1930s.[34] The doctrine has best been summed up by its foremost advocate, Karl Llewellyn,[35] who emphasizes the dynamic nature of the law; the conception of law as an instrument, a means to an end and not an end in itself; skepticism of legal principles; standards and rules as pre-determining any decision a court makes; and evaluation of the law in terms of its practical effects.

3. Law & Economics

Although a topical theory, the law and economics approach to law has little relation to *Delgamuukw*, which basically concerns wealth transfers. Its approach is to test proposed legal policies by applying economic analytical tools such as cost-benefit analysis, risk analysis and efficiency measurement.[36] Had it been applied in *Delgamuukw* the focus would have been a cost-benefit analysis of similar policies in Canada and other countries, first to determine if it is likely to be effective (presumably to integrate aboriginal peoples in the contemporary economy), and second, to try to measure the efficiency of transfer payments in achieving that end.

4. *Critical Legal Studies (CLS or Post-Structuralism or Postmodernism)*

A fourth, current and very controversial school of legal theory, Critical Legal Studies (CLS), is difficult to relate to the previous three, for even though it does not disparage rational arguments, it does reject most of the premises on which they are based. In its extreme form, it is a "denial ... of the legitimacy of law itself, which is regarded as nothing more than an instrument of power."[37] Although sometimes nihilist in tone, for example in its rejection of liberal, realist theories, Turley states:[38]

> That is not to say CLS began as a negative movement. Far from it, CLS was, and continues to be, committed to shaping a society based on some substantive vision of the human personality, absent the hidden interests and class domination of legal institutions.

Reflecting its Marxist roots, CLS emphasizes a communitarian, class-less sense of altruism as opposed to liberal individualism, which has resulted in hierarchical class structures, alienation and exploitation of some by those in power. The CLS proponents are particularly hostile to liberal doctrine.

The liberal presents the "half a loaf" problem that relieves social pressure for change while basically retaining the original social structure and thereby preventing real social change. ... In this way liberal legislation can be strongly symbolic even though it may do little to alleviate class conflict and exploitation.[39]

Postmodernism and the Supreme Court of Canada

Although possible, given the long exposure of some members of the Supreme Canada bench to the academic tempest concerning CLS, it is improbable that the Court's decision in *Delgamuukw* was written with CLS or postmodernism in mind. More likely, to paraphrase Keynes, they are merely decision-makers in authority distilling their ideas "from some academic scribbler of a few years back."[40] Still, the Supreme Court's decision certainly reflects reliance on CLS ideas: it is radical in the sense of ignoring, and in effect even proposing to uproot, existing institutions; it is clearly conscious of class discrimination; is egalitarian; and is clearly biased toward communal governance.

Before 1980—that is, before the influence of postmodernism became pervasive and before the advent of decisions declaring Charter rights—the Supreme Court of Canada probably would have been more inclined (as was Chief Justice McEachern, the original trial court judge in *Delgamuukw)* to acknowledge that the policy decisions required cannot be articulated as conventional legal standards and, in any case, are far outside the inherent limits of any court's capacity to do social policy analysis.[41] Parliament, therefore, should deal with the issue. The judicial process is lacking in several respects. In general, truly representative parties are not present;[42] a court has no resources to conduct broad contextual social and economic analyses of costs and benefits, as well as of third-party impacts, required to develop policy alternatives; it has no access to expertise other than the inevitably tendentious testimony of expert witnesses; it has no capacity to implement and administer the policy recommended; and, above all, it lacks means to do any post-implementation measure of the effectiveness of the program and to make obviously necessary adjustments. In sum, the Supreme Court, in *Delgamuukw* has seemingly charged boldly into the "quintessentially political" area of government transfer payments without the capacity to develop policy, implement it through a program, or adjust it as problems develop other than through continual litigation.

Bearing those limitations in mind, what did the Court actually decide in *Delgamuukw*? To abridge the analysis of the case, I summarize below (with cross references to the numbered paragraphs of the case report) the key aspects of the decision from the perspective of a parliamentary draftsman instructed to translate it, to the extent possible, into a statute.

(1) Aboriginal title to land" derives from common law and therefore presumably includes resources on that land.

(1) Aboriginal title is subject to the conditions set out in para 7 below, but nevertheless is *sui generis*, that is, in a class by itself as determined by the aboriginals proving their use and occupation of it. (paras 109-15).

(1) The nature of aboriginal rights vary along a spectrum from mere use rights to aboriginal title:

(1) activities integral to the aboriginal culture but connected only tenuously to land that therefore confer aboriginal *rights* but not aboriginal title;

   (a) similar activities that are related to a particular piece of land that do not give rise to aboriginal title but confer an aboriginal *right* to use and occupy that land to perform those activities; and

(b) use and occupation of specific land from which aboriginals derive aboriginal *title*. (paras 138-139).

(2) Aboriginal title, which is *communal* and *inalienable*, is in effect a charge on the Crown's underlying title: it derives from use and occupation before the claim of British sovereignty, and aboriginal activities on it are not confined to activities integral to their distinctive culture but are subject to the conditions set out in para 7 (paras 11-15, 129, 140-59).

(3) To establish aboriginal title an aboriginal claimant must prove generally

(a) occupation before British sovereignty,

(b) if present occupation is relied on, continuity between present and pre-sovereignty occupation; and

(c) exclusive occupation. (paras 140-59, especially 143)

(4) Because aboriginal rights, including aboriginal title, are unique (*sui generis*), an aboriginal group claiming them is *not* bound by common law evidentiary standards, and, accordingly, oral history is admissible at least to prove current occupation has origins before the date of British sovereignty. (paras 82-84, 101).

(5) The existence and continuance of aboriginal title are subject to the three following conditions.

(a) Evidence that might strain the Canadian legal and constitutional structure is not admissible and, accordingly, may preclude proof of the existence of aboriginal title. (para 82).

(b) Lands held pursuant to aboriginal title cannot be used by aboriginals in a manner irreconcilable with the nature of the attachment (use, occupation activities) from which that title derives.
    "Irreconcilable" does not mean merely a non-conforming use but a use that would destroy its use for the "attachment" factor from which the title derives. (paras 125-32).

(c) Either the federal government or a provincial government may infringe on aboriginal title for any purpose it justifies as of *compelling and substantial* value to the community as a whole, if the infringement does not breach the government's fiduciary duty to the title-holders.
    In this context, *fiduciary duty* requires that the government consults the title-holders before infringing, act reasonably to minimize the infringement, and fairly compensate the title-holder for

its loss.[43] And *"compelling and substantial"* purpose includes any basic social or economic activity of the overall community. (paras 165-68).

(6) Aboriginal rights, including aboriginal title, cannot be extinguished directly by provincial law or even indirectly under the *Indian Act*, s. 88. (paras 179-83).

(7) Although aboriginal title is communal and generally inalienable, an aboriginal title-holder may transfer the land to the Crown for valuable consideration.

What did the Court actually decide in *Delgamuukw*? Not much. Although it purported to do a contextual analysis, in fact the court focused on aboriginal title or rights to land and resources and then declared those rights in abstract terms, which may give some comfort to aboriginal land claimants but no guidance to policy-makers at any level.

To draw that inference is not to criticize the court but rather, by indirection, to commend it for dealing diplomatically with the issue without seriously obtruding into the area of quintessential politics. Like the lower courts in *Delgamuukw* the Supreme Court attempts to turn up the thermostat to expedite promised settlements with aboriginal people that have already festered too long.

Root Problem

The root problem is not the judiciary. It is the breakdown of governance systems generally. Demonstrating great prescience, Theodore Lowi published a book in 1969 decrying the degeneration of governance from voter representation to, effectively, interest group representation ("identity politics"), from thoroughly analyzed, widely debated, principled policy decisions to negotiated deals. As he forcefully states:[44]

> The problem is that the new representation embodied in the notion of interest-group liberalism is a pathological adjustment to the problem. Interest-group liberal solutions to the problem of power provide the system with stability by spreading a sense of representation at the expense of democratic forms, and ultimately at the expense of legitimacy. Interest-group liberalism seeks pluralistic government, in which there is no formal specification of means or of ends. In pluralistic government there is, therefore, no substance. Neither is there procedure. There is only process.

This trend is serious in the United States, but it cannot completely overcome the constraints constitutionally enforced by the division of executive, legislative and administrative powers. Policy-making in the US is still dynamic, innovative and frequently bold, drawing substance from experience throughout North America.[45]

The problem is far more serious in Canada where, because of the lack of division of powers, actual power becomes increasingly centralized in the Prime Minister's Office. As a result, very major issues such as wealth transfers to aboriginal peoples can best be characterized as backroom deals. There is little useful, published policy analysis. There is virtually no legislative scrutiny. There is no effective parliamentary debate. There is only a deal to be pushed through a frequently protesting, sometimes recalcitrant, but largely ineffective legislative system.

Conclusion

This decline of governance has probably reached its nadir in relation to aboriginal settlements. The lack of effective, traditional governance is especially extraordinary when one considers that the estimated aggregate cost of settlements in B.C. alone will be $10-$12 billion in 1998 dollars.[46] And virtually all of that is in excess of the roughly $7-billion annual appropriation to the federal Department of Indian and Northern Affairs, some $4 billion a year of which is reallocated as block or earmarked grants to First Nations governments for local allocation.[47]

The costs of the present "policies" are enormous but undoubtedly would be acceded to if they resolved to resolve the "aboriginal problem" to achieve the objectives stated by President Johnson in 1964. To date, after examining the problems of some of the First Nations (Navajo, Samson Cree, Alaska Aboriginals), it is difficult to be optimistic about "deals" to force purportedly democratic governance systems on aboriginal communities. What is needed is greater exercise of what Trilling characterized as the liberal imagination. In Canada, however, that will be a monumental task, for it implies the need not just for improved policy-making but also for fundamental institutional change.

Notes

1 Okun, *Equality and Efficiency: the Big Tradeoff* (1975). But see W. Mitchell and R. Simmons, *Beyond Politics: Markets, Welfare and the Failure of Bureaucracy* 16-18 (1994), showing that to tilt the balance in favor of equality of result can have a corrosive effect on society. In 1964, at the outset of the US "War on Poverty," 367,000 Americans received food stamps at an annual cost of $800 million; by 1990 20 million people received food stamps and the annual cost had risen to some $13 billion. In 1994 the Republican congress enacted legislation that drastically reduced these transfers. To the extent they relied on them, transfers to US Indian recipients were reduced accordingly.

2 Economists in socialist countries, seeking means to induce individuals to be productive in state-owned industries or collective farms, become acutely aware of this problem. See E.H. Carr, *The New Society* 60 (1951), quoting Hawtrey who states "what differentiates economic systems from one another is the character of the motives they invoke to induce people to work"; see also J. Kornai, *Contradictions and Dilemmas in Studies on the Socialist Economy and Society* 124-30 (1986).

3 The Canadian examples are the various support programs ("pogey") to the Atlantic Provinces.

4 Lionel Trilling, Morals and the Novel, in *The Liberal Imagination: Essays on Literature and Society* 214-15, Doubleday Paperback ed. (1953). Examples are Dickens' *Bleak House*, Gogol's *Dead Souls* and Zola's *Germinal*.

5 See F. Cohen, *Handbook of Indian Law* 180-96 (1982 ed.).

6 See *American Indian Policy Review Commission, Final Report* (Task Force No.9) 44-46 (United States GPO, 1976). For a summary of current Congressional activities to implement the Great Society Program, see the website of the Department of Interior, Office of Self-Governance: http://doi.gov/oait/os-gwww.htm. Some 206 Tribes, supported by appropriations of $180 million are now involved in actual or experimental self-governance programs.

7 See Executive Order 13084, Consultations and Coordination with Indian Tribal Governments (14 may 1998), which stresses recognition of the quasi-autonomy of Indian tribes as "domestic dependent nations" and requires that bureaucrats cooperate accordingly. This is available on Internet: http://indian.senate.gov/13084.htm.

8 See T. Anderson, *Sovereign Nations on Reservations* 147 (1995).

9 This is crooked thinking by use of a dilemma that ignores a continuous series of possibilities between the two extremes presented: see R. Thouless and C. Thouless, *Straight and Crooked Thinking* 140, Item 5 (Headway Paperback, 2d ed. 1990).

10 A famous analysis of the Poor Laws and their successors is in K. Polanyi, *The Great Transformation: the Political and Economic Origins of Our Time* 68-102, Beacon Press, Boston (1944, paperback ed. 1957).

11 See id. at 82 6 id. at 101. At 84 Polanyi adds that in light of these traumatic events "...The Poor Law discussion formed the minds of Bentham and Burke, Godwin and Malthus, Ricardo and Marx, Owen and Mill, Darwin and Spencer.... ...A world was uncovered the very existence of which had

not been suspected, that of the laws governing a complex society. ...The form in which the nascent reality came to our consciousness was *political economy.*" [Italics added.] Alexis de Tocqueville, touring England in 1833 and, characteristically, carefully observed events there, noted the perverse incentives created by *Speenhamland* and the *Poor Law*, and forecast collapse: see A. de Tocqueville, memoir on Pauperism (1935); A. Jardin, Tocqueville 242-46, Farrar Straus, Giroux, NY (1988).

12 See F. Cohen, *Handbook of Indian Law* 50-52 (1982 ed.). There are few words more Protean than "nation" and "self-determination": see the excellent short essay on Nationalism in Vol.5, *The Encyclopedia of Philosophy*, Macmillan Inc. NY (1972). Nevertheless, these terms have been used since the Spanish conquest, through Chief Justice Marshall's landmark decisions on the early 1830s up to the present date (see n.7, *supra*) as if they had some definitive meaning.

13 See F. Cohen, *supra* n.18, at 62.

14 See F. Cohen, *supra* n.13, at 106-07.

15 See T. Anderson, *supra* n.8, at 142-45, who emphasizes the aboriginal communities were anything but homogeneous. See also D. Riesman, *The Lonely Crowd: A study of the Changing American Character* 225-35, Yale Univ. Press, New Haven (ab.ed.1961).

16 See F. Cohen, *supra* n.13, at 130-32; T. Anderson, *supra* n.16, at 105-06. Commenting on the Samson Cree scandal, the Globe and Mail editors recommend as one solution direct payment of all band revenues to individuals: Globe and Mail, p. A16 (27 April 1999).

17 See T. Anderson, *supra* n.16, at 94-95, 111-34.

18 See F. Cohen, *supra* n. 13, at 147-70; see also T. Anderson, *supra* n.16, at 139-45, 153-58.

19 See F. Cohen, *supra* n.13, at 157, 185-87; see also the *American Indian Policy Review Commission* 20-21 (1976).

20 See P. Tennant, *Aboriginal Peoples and Politics* 149-50 (1990).

21 This is not illusion. Although tribal leaders are largely involved, in most cases, with one source of revenue, transfer payments, the assumption is that they must acquire those skills before they can successfully build self-help communities. In effect, the new laws substitute ex post audits for ex ante bureaucratic control from Washington. See the Department of Interior, Bureau of Indian Affairs Website for details of the extensive audit program.

22 This Bill, sponsored by Rep. George Miller can be accessed on Internet through Thomas, the Library of Congress site.

23 These shares were non-transferable for 25 years, a period that was extended in 1996, presumably because most of the corporations were not sufficiently stable to issue securities to the public by way of primary or secondary trades.

24 See Black et al., *When Worlds Collide: Alaska Native Corporations and the Bankruptcy Code*, 6 Alaska L. Rev. 73, 74-77 and 87 (1995).

25 Several years ago—but not in an aboriginal context—the Fraser Institute collaborated in an in-depth study of GAI/NIT program experiments actually implemented in Canada and the USA. Unfortunately, the results relating to the effectiveness of the incentive design were inconclusive.

26 B. de Jouvenal, De la politique pure 248 (1963), quoted in Ellul, Politicization and Political Solutions, in K. Templeton (ed.), *The Politicization of Society* 211, 237 (1979).

27 J. Houghteling, *The Dynamics of Law* (1975).

28 See W. Friedmann, *Legal Theory* 422-29 (5th ed. 1967).

29 Kennedy. Form and substance in Private Law Adjudication, 89 Harvard L. Rev. 1685, 1688 (1976).

30 See W. Friedmann, n.28 supra, at pp. 275-91; and G. Himmelfarb, *On Looking into the Abyss, Untimely Thoughts on Culture and Society*, at 131-61. (Vintage Paperback 1995).

31 John Ralston Saul, *The Unconscious Civilization* 68 (Anansi Paperback, 1995).

32 See Kennedy, n.29 *supra*.

33 See W. Friedmann, n.28 *supra* at 292-311.

34 K. Llewellyn, Some Realism about Realism—Responding to Dean Pound, 44 Harvard L. Rev. 1222 (1931). See also Jones, An Invitation to Jurisprudence, 74 Col. L. Rev. 1023 (1974).

35 See R. Malloy, *Law and Economics: A Comparative Approach to Theory and Practice*, esp. pp. 2-12, 48-58 (1990).

36 G. Himmelfarb, *On Looking into the Abyss* 132-33 (Vintage Paperback 1995). *See also* R. Malloy, *supra* n.36, 76-85.

37 Turley, The Hitchhiker's Guide to CLS, Unger and Deep Thought, 81 Nw. U.L. Rev. 593-95 (1987), quoted in Malloy, supra n.36, at 77.

38 Malloy, Law and Economics, *supra* n.36, at 81-82.

39 J.M. Keynes, *The General Theory of Money, Interest and Employment* (383, Macmillan ed. 1973). The rhetoric of Keynes, directed at economic "madmen" is much diluted, but his idea seems most appropriate in the circumstances.

40 See Chayes, The Role of the Judge in Public Law Litigation, 89 Harv. L. Rev. 1281 (1976).

41 The Supreme Court acknowledged it did not have even the desirable aboriginal parties before it (para 185). It did not even consider the effects on third parties directly and adversely affected by hard transfer decisions.

42 This extends beyond common law in jurisdictions, such as Canada, where there is no constitutional protection against property expropriations where a legislature takes property and expressly denies any right to compensation.

43 T. Lowi, *The End of Liberalism* 62-63 (2d. ed. 1979).

44 Ironically, Senator Inouye, Vice Chairman of the Senate Committee on Indian Affairs, highlights as a model of First Nation governance the experience of the "Samson Cree Nation in Canada: see Speech to the Administration's Conference on Building Economic Self-Determination in Indian Communities (5Aug. 1998), web site http://indian.senate.gov.ecocon.htm. In Canada the Samson Cree Nation has been publicly excoriated as being politically corrupt (Globe and Mail, p.A16, 27 April 1999) and criticized by the Auditor General as financially out of control.

45 See the report Financial and Economic Analysis of Treaty Settlements in British Columbia (16 March 1999), prepared for the BC Government by Grant Thorton Management Consultants.

46 See 1999 Report of the Auditor General of Canada, c.10: Web Site http://www.oag-bvg.gc.ca/domino/reports.nsf/html.

References

T. Anderson, *Sovereign Nations or Reservations?: An Economic History of American Indians*, Pacific Research Institute for Public Policy. San Francisco (1995) This work contains an excellent appendix of References to US studies.

F. Cohen, *Handbook of Indian Law* (982 ed.).

J. Fallows, *Breaking the News: How the Media Undermine American Democracy*, Vintage Books, NY (paperback 1997).

G. Himmelfarb, *The De-Moralization of Society: From Victorian Virtues to Modern Values*, Vintage Books, NY (paperback 1995).

G. Himmelfarb, *On Looking into the Abyss: Untimely Thoughts on Culture and Society*, Vintage Books, NY (paperback 1995).

A. Jardin, *Tocqueville: A Biography*, Farrar Strauss Giroux, NY (Eng. transl. ed. 1988).

M. Kelman, *A Guide to Critical Legal Studies*, Harvard Univ. Press, Cambridge (paperback 1987).

J.M. Keynes, *The General Theory of Employment, Interest and Money* (1936), Macmillan, London (paperback 1973).

T. Lowi, *The End of Liberalism: The Second Republic of the United States*, W.W. Norton & Co., NY (1979).

R. Mallory, *Law and Economics: A Comparative Approach to Theory and Practice*, West, St. Paul (paperback 1990).

W. Mitchell and R. Simmons, *Beyond Politics: Markets, Welfare and the Failure of Bureaucracy*, Westview Press, Boulder (paperback 1994).

K. Polanyi, *The Great Transformation: The Political and Economic Origins of Our Time* (1994), Beacon Press, Boston (paperback 1957).

N. Postman, *Amusing Ourselves to Death: Public Discourse in the Age of Show Business*, Viking Penguin Books, NY (paperback 1985).

R. Thouless and C, Thouless, *Straight and Crooked Thinking* (1930), Headway Paperback (4th ed. 1990).

A. de Tocqueville, *Memoir on Pauperism*, Ivan R. Dee, Chicago (paperback ed. 1997).

Aboriginal Title as a Constitutionally Protected Property Right

Kent McNeil

Delgamuukw v. British Columbia[1] is undoubtedly one of the most important decisions the Supreme Court of Canada has ever handed down. It will have a continuing, long-term impact on the Aboriginal peoples' relationships with the federal and provincial governments, as well as on the constitutional division of powers in this country.[2] While there are many aspects of the decision that require analysis and discussion, this paper's focus is on the definition of Aboriginal title provided by the Court. In particular, I am going to discuss the status of Aboriginal title, not only as a *property right*, but also as a *constitutionally protected property right*. This will involve looking at the central position of property, especially *real* property, in the common law.[3] It will also involve examining the effect of constitutionalizing Aboriginal title, along with other Aboriginal rights, in 1982. Related to this is the question of how Aboriginal title can be infringed. Finally, I will return to property rights generally, and briefly consider the implications of *Delgamuukw* for the protection accorded to those rights by Anglo-Canadian law.

Notes will be found on pages 67–75.

1.   The Central Position of Real Property in the Common Law

Land was by far the most important form of wealth in England prior to the Industrial Revolution. Due to the feudal system, it also played a central role in the political, military and social structure of the country. So as the common law took form in the period following the Norman Conquest, disputes over land naturally predominated in the king's courts. Judicial decisions involving land accordingly played a major role in the development, not only of property law, but of other branches of English law as well.[4]

Because land was so important, protecting real property from arbitrary seizure by the king was at least as important as guarding it against other persons. The nobles who forced King John to sign *Magna Carta* in 1215 thought this protection to be of sufficient importance to warrant a key clause to curtail this abuse of royal power. Chapter 29 accordingly provided that "[n]o Freeman shall ... be disseised [i.e., dispossessed of his land] ... but by the lawful Judgment of his Peers, or by the law of the Land."[5] This restraint on the authority of the executive branch of government is still in force in Britain,[6] and would have been received in Canada as part of our constitutional law.[7] It is a basic aspect of the rule of law,[8] protecting real property against government taking except in accordance with law.[9]

However, the constitutional protection accorded to property rights by Anglo-Canadian law is only effective against the *executive*. Due to the doctrine of parliamentary sovereignty (or supremacy),[10] the *legislative* branch of government has no binding constitutional obligation to respect private property. But this does not mean that property is not a fundamental right in our legal system. On the contrary, it has been long been regarded as enjoying special status in English law, along with other fundamental rights and freedoms. William Blackstone, for example, the great compiler and categorizer of English law, said this in reference to the rights and liberties of British subjects:

> these may be reduced to three principal or primary articles; the right of personal security, the right of personal liberty, and *the right of private property*; because, as there is no other known method of compulsion, or of abridging man's natural free will, but by an infringement or diminution of one or other of these important rights, the preservation of these, inviolate, may justly be said to include the preservation of our civil immunities in their largest and most extensive sense.[11]

Modern enumeration of fundamental rights and freedoms also include the right of private property. Halsbury's *Laws of England*,[12] for example, lists the right to property under the constitutional law heading, "Duties and Rights of the Subject," along with liberty, the right to life, freedom of expression, freedom of conscience, and the right of association.

While lack of protection against legislative taking means that property rights do not enjoy the kind of constitutional status they have been accorded in the United States,[13] presumptions of statutory interpretation do provide limited protection against legislative infringement in Anglo-Canadian law.[14] There are two relevant presumptions. First, it is always presumed that the legislature does not intend to interfere with vested rights, particularly rights of property.[15] So if the legislature intends to take private property, it must express that intention clearly, as the courts will, if possible, construe the legislation as not interfering with property rights.[16] Secondly, the courts will presume that the legislature intends that compensation be paid for any private property that is taken, unless compensation is unequivocally denied.[17] Through this indirect means of interpretation of statutes, the courts have succeeded in providing property rights with limited protection against legislative taking.[18]

When Canada's Constitution was patriated in 1982, a conscious decision was made not to include property rights in the fundamental rights and freedoms guaranteed by the Charter.[19] However, Aboriginal rights were accorded constitutional protection outside the *Charter* by section 35 of the *Constitution Act, 1982*.[20] As Aboriginal title is an Aboriginal right, it is constitutionally protected.[21] Moreover, the *Delgamuukw* decision confirmed suggestions in earlier Supreme Court decisions that Aboriginal title is a form of property right.[22] We therefore need to examine the *Delgamuukw* decision in more detail to understand the proprietary nature of Aboriginal title.

2. Aboriginal Title as a Property Right

In *Delgamuukw*, Chief Justice Antonio Lamer[23] rejected the argument made by the Gitksan and Wet'suwet'en that Aboriginal title is tantamount to an inalienable fee simple estate.[24] But he also rejected the position of the Canadian and British Columbian governments that Aboriginal title has no independent content, being no more than a bundle of rights to engage in activities that are themselves Aboriginal rights, or, alternatively, that "aboriginal title, at most, encompasses the right to exclusive use and occupation of land in order to engage in those activities which are aboriginal rights themselves."[25] Instead, Lamer found that Aboriginal title lies in between these opposing positions. He described its content in this way:

> Aboriginal title is a right in land and, as such, is more than the right to engage in specific activities which may be themselves aboriginal rights. Rather, it confers the right to use land for a variety

of activities, not all of which need be aspects of practices, customs and traditions which are integral to the distinctive cultures of aboriginal societies. Those activities do not constitute the right *per se*; rather, they are parasitic on the underlying title. However, that range of uses is subject to the limitation that they must not be irreconcilable with the nature of the attachment to the land which forms the basis of the particular group's aboriginal title. This inherent limit, to be explained more fully below, flows from the definition of aboriginal title as a *sui generis* interest in land, and is one way in which aboriginal title is distinct from a fee simple.[26]

The Chief Justice went on to elaborate on this description of Aboriginal title. Commenting on *St. Catherine's Milling and Lumber Co. v. The Queen*,[27] he said subsequent cases have demonstrated that the Privy Council's description of it as "a personal and usufructuary right" "is not particularly helpful to explain the various dimensions of aboriginal title." [28] He continued:

> What the Privy Council sought to capture is that aboriginal title is a *sui generis* interest in land. Aboriginal title has been described as *sui generis* in order to distinguish it from "normal" proprietary interests, such as fee simple. However, as I will now develop, it is also *sui generis* in the sense that its characteristics cannot be completely explained by reference either to the common law rules of real property or to the rules of property found in aboriginal legal systems. As with other aboriginal rights, it must be understood by reference to both common law and aboriginal perspectives.[29]

So Aboriginal title, while unlike other common law real property interests, is nonetheless "an interest in land."[30] Moreover, it is "a *right to the land* itself,"[31] which "encompasses the *right to exclusive use and occupation of land* held pursuant to that title for a variety of purposes, which need not be aspects of those aboriginal practices, customs and traditions which are integral to distinctive aboriginal cultures."[32] These descriptions of Aboriginal title clearly indicate that it is a real property right, though *sui generis* in nature.[33] This is confirmed by an observation the Chief Justice made respecting the general inalienability of Aboriginal title, other than by surrender to the Crown:

> This Court has taken pains to clarify that aboriginal title is only "personal" in this sense [i.e., in the sense of being inalienable], and does not mean that aboriginal title is a non-proprietary interest which amounts to no more than a licence to use and occupy the

land and cannot compete on an equal footing with other proprietary interests: see *Canadian Pacific Ltd. v. Paul*, [1988] 2 S.C.R. 654,
at p. 677.[34]

Nor do the other *sui generis* aspects of Aboriginal title referred to by the
Chief Justice diminish its status as a proprietary interest. The first of these is its
source in occupation of land "*before* the assertion of British sovereignty,
whereas normal estates, like fee simple, arise afterward."[35] There is a similarity here with the land titles of the French settlers who came to Canada
during the French régime—their property interests, which continued
after France ceded New France to Britain in 1763,[36] are not "normal estates, like fee simple," because their source is not English law, but the
French law that was in force prior to Britain's acquisition of sovereignty. However, in contrast with the situation of the French settlers, the
relevance of Aboriginal law to Aboriginal title appears to be its value,
along with proof of physical presence and use, in establishing occupation of land at the time of assertion of Crown sovereignty.[37] Once that
occupation has been shown, apparently Aboriginal title then exists as
a generic right that does not vary from one Aboriginal nation to another
in accordance with their diverse systems of law.[38] However, Aboriginal
law would probably be applicable *within* each Aboriginal nation to govern the land rights of the members *inter se*.[39]

Another *sui generis* aspect of Aboriginal title that distinguishes it
from common law real property interests is that it is *communal*. Chief
Justice Lamer put it this way in *Delgamuukw*:

> Aboriginal title cannot be held by individual aboriginal persons; it
> is a collective right to land held by all members of an aboriginal na-
> tion. Decisions with respect to that land are also made by that
> community.[40]

This is an extremely important passage in his judgment, as it provides a foundation for a right of self-government.[41] For the purposes of
this paper, however, it also reveals how the law of Aboriginal title appears to diverge from the usual common law position on legal personality. As a general rule, in Anglo-Canadian law title to property must be
vested in an individual person or persons, who can be either natural persons (human beings) or artificial persons (corporations). If a group of
people owns property, title must be vested in all the members of the
group *as individuals*. The group cannot, as an entity in its own right, hold
title because it lacks legal personality. It is for this reason that the common law does not permit unincorporated associations as such to hold
title to property.[42] By holding that Aboriginal title is "a collective right

to land held by all members of an aboriginal nation," Chief Justice Lamer cannot have meant that the members hold as individuals, as there would then be no significant distinction between this aspect of Aboriginal title and landholding by members of unincorporated associations, and so Aboriginal title would not be *sui generis* in this respect. Instead, he must have intended to accord a form of legal personality to Aboriginal nations.[43] If so, they have unique status in Anglo-Canadian law which probably enhances their claim to a right of self-government,[44] but does not affect the proprietary nature of their Aboriginal title.

A final *sui generis* aspect of Aboriginal title is the "inherent limit" mentioned in one of the passages already quoted from *Delgamuukw*, where Lamer said that Aboriginal lands cannot be used in ways that are "irreconcilable with the nature of the attachment to the land which forms the basis of the particular group's aboriginal title."[45] He referred to this as a "limit on the content of aboriginal title," and said that it is "a manifestation of the principle that underlies the various dimensions of that special interest in land—it is a *sui generis* interest that is distinct from 'normal' proprietary interests, most notably fee simple." [46] He then linked this inherent limit to the need to maintain the continuity of an Aboriginal nation's special relationship with their land: "That relationship should not be prevented from continuing into the future. As a result, uses of the land that would threaten that future relationship are, by their very nature, excluded from the content of aboriginal title." [47]

This inherent limit raises important issues that cannot be dealt with here, such as the potential impact of the pre-sovereignty practices, customs and traditions of particular Aboriginal nations on the uses they can make of their lands, and the implications of the limit for self-government.[48] But for the purposes of this paper, what needs to be understood is that the inherent limit does not diminish the proprietary nature of Aboriginal title. By way of analogy, consider zoning laws in Canadian cities. Those laws often place quite severe restrictions on the uses that fee simple owners can make of their lands, without affecting the proprietary nature of their title. Similarly, the inherent limit does not affect the characterization of Aboriginal title as proprietary. While the limit may restrict the uses which Aboriginal nations can make of their lands, their right of use and occupation is nonetheless exclusive,[49] and it is this right to exclude others, rather than a right to put the land to any use, that makes Aboriginal title proprietary.[50] But one effect of the limit is probably that there are uses to which some Aboriginal lands cannot be put by anyone as long as they are subject to Aboriginal title,[51] in the same way as there are uses to which zoned lands cannot be put as long as the zoning restrictions remain in force.

It is therefore clear from the *Delgamuukw* decision that Aboriginal title is a proprietary interest in land, though differing from what the Chief Justice called "normal" common law property interests, like the fee simple. Moreover, it includes a right to exclusive use and occupation. The proprietary nature and exclusivity of Aboriginal title are not affected by its *sui generis* aspects, which include its source in occupation of land prior to Crown sovereignty, its inalienability other than by surrender to the Crown, its communal nature, and restrictions on use arising from its inherent limit. But as mentioned earlier, Aboriginal title is not just a property right. Since the entrenchment of Aboriginal and treaty rights in section 35 of the *Constitution Act, 1982*, it is also a *constitutionally protected* property right. We now need to consider what this means, and the extent to which Aboriginal title can be infringed, notwithstanding its constitutional status.

3. Constitutional Protection and Infringement of Aboriginal Title

Section 35(1) of the *Constitution Act, 1982*,[52] provides: "The existing aboriginal and treaty rights of the aboriginal peoples of Canada are hereby recognized and affirmed." In *Delgamuukw*, Chief Justice Lamer said this about this provision:

> s.35(1) did not create aboriginal rights; rather, it accorded constitutional status to those rights which were "existing" in 1982. The provision, at the very least, constitutionalized those rights which aboriginal peoples possessed at common law, since those rights existed at the time s.35(1) came into force. Since aboriginal title was a common law right whose existence was recognized well before 1982 (e.g., *Calder* [*v. Attorney-General of British Columbia*, [1973] S.C.R. 313]), s.35(1) has constitutionalized it in its full form.[53]

The reason Aboriginal rights were accorded constitutional protection in 1982 was to protect them against interference by the *legislative branch of governments*.[54] This protection was not required against private persons and the *executive branch* because, to the extent that these rights are recognized as such by the common law, that law protects them, along with other legal rights, against interference by anyone, unless the interference is authorized by legislation.[55] But as we have seen, constitutional entrenchment was required if these rights were to be protected against *legislative* interference because, due to the doctrine of parliamentary sovereignty, even fundamental rights and freedoms are subject to legislative infringement if the intention to infringe them is unequivocally expressed.[56]

Of course constitutional entrenchment does not provide absolute protection against legislative infringement. Where *Charter* rights are concerned, section 33 (the "notwithstanding" clause) provides for legislative override, and section 1 subjects those rights "to such reasonable limits prescribed by law as can be demonstrably justified in a free and democratic society." While pointing out that these provisions do not apply to section 35 because it is outside the *Charter*,[57] the Supreme Court in *R. v. Sparrow*[58] created a test for infringement of Aboriginal rights that is similar in some respects to the approach it uses in applying section 1. Briefly stated, the *Sparrow* test requires the Crown to prove that any legislative (or legislatively authorized) infringement of Aboriginal rights is for a valid legislative objective that is compelling and substantial, and that the Crown's fiduciary obligations towards the Aboriginal peoples have been respected. If the Crown fails to do this, the infringement will be constitutionally invalid.[59]

In *Delgamuukw*, Chief Justice Lamer made it clear that the *Sparrow* justification test applies to infringements of Aboriginal title.[60] On why the constitutional rights of the Aboriginal peoples can be infringed at all, he said it was "important to repeat" what he had said in *R. v. Gladstone*:

> Because ... distinctive aboriginal societies exist within, and are part of, a broader social, political and economic community, over which the Crown is sovereign, there are circumstances in which, in order to pursue objectives of compelling and substantial importance to that community as a whole (taking into account the fact that aboriginal societies are part of that community), some limitation of those rights will be justifiable. *Aboriginal rights are a necessary part of the reconciliation of aboriginal societies with the broader political community of which they are part; limits placed on those rights are, where the objectives furthered by those limits are of sufficient importance to the broader community as a whole, equally a necessary part of that reconciliation.*[61]

Elaborating on the kinds of objectives that might justify infringement of Aboriginal title, the Chief Justice said this:

> In my opinion, the development of agriculture, forestry, mining, and hydroelectric power, the general economic development of the interior of British Columbia, protection of the environment or endangered species, the building of infrastructure and the settlement of foreign populations to support those aims, are the kinds of objectives that are consistent with this purpose and, in principle, can justify the infringement of aboriginal title. Whether a particular

measure or government act can be explained by reference to one of those objectives, however, is ultimately a question of fact that will have to be examined on a case-by-case basis.[62]

As most of these objectives—agriculture, forestry, and mining, for example—relate to *provincial* areas of jurisdiction, the issue of provincial power to infringe Aboriginal title arises here. But while Lamer specifically said in *Delgamuukw* that Aboriginal title can be infringed by the provinces,[63] he also held that Aboriginal title is under *exclusive* federal authority because it is within the core of federal jurisdiction over "Indians, and Lands reserved for the Indians."[64] As explained in detail elsewhere, in my opinion these two aspects of Lamer's judgment are irreconcilable, and so the issue of provincial power to infringe Aboriginal title will have to be re-examined by the Court.[65]

For the purposes of this paper, then, we will focus our attention on *federal* power to infringe Aboriginal title, which apparently arises from Parliament's authority over "Lands reserved for the Indians."[66] The first thing to note is that the power of Parliament to *extinguish* Aboriginal title, which undoubtedly existed prior to 1982,[67] was taken away by section 35(1) of the *Constitution Act, 1982*. In *R. v. Van der Peet*, Chief Justice Lamer said this in reference to Aboriginal rights generally, of which Aboriginal title is one manifestation:

> At common law aboriginal rights did not, of course, have constitutional status, with the result that Parliament could, at any time, extinguish or regulate those rights...; it is this which distinguishes the aboriginal rights recognized and affirmed in s.35(1) from the aboriginal rights protected by the common law. Subsequent to s.35(1) aboriginal rights *cannot be extinguished* and can only be regulated or infringed consistent with the justificatory test laid out by this Court in *Sparrow, supra* [n.33].[68]

As we have seen, the range of objectives that will meet the first branch of the justificatory test for *infringement* of Aboriginal title was stated by Lamer in *Delgamuukw* to be "fairly broad," including "the development of agriculture, forestry, mining, and hydroelectric power ... [and] the building of infrastructure and the settlement of foreign populations to support those aims."[69] What Lamer had in mind here does not appear to be limited to the taking of Aboriginal lands for *public* purposes, such as the construction of highways or state-owned hydroelectric projects. Instead, he seems to have also envisaged that Parliament could temporarily take Aboriginal lands and make them available to *private* individuals and corporations (his "foreign populations"), who would then engage in farming, forestry, mining, etc.[70] And as long as this was "of sufficient importance to the broader community as a whole"[71] (i.e., the Canadian public), the taking would be justifiable under the *Sparrow* test.

This means that the real property rights of the Aboriginal peoples are not just subject to legislative *regulation* in the public interest,[72] as are all property rights, for purposes such as environmental protection. Aboriginal title is also subject to legislative *taking*,[73] not only for direct public purposes such as the construction of highways and other infrastructure, but also for private development that has only a tangential connection with the public interest.[74] For example, if Aboriginal lands are suitable for agriculture, but are not being used by their Aboriginal titleholders for that purpose, it seems that Parliament can take them and allow farmers to use them if that would be of sufficient importance to Canadians as a whole. As I have stated elsewhere, this sounds very much like a modern-day equivalent of "a familiar justification for dispossessing Aboriginal peoples in the heyday of European colonialism in eastern North America—agriculturalists are superior to hunters and gatherers, and so can take their lands"[75]

What is even more remarkable about this judicial disregard for the sanctity of Aboriginal title[76] is that, unlike other property rights, it is supposed to be protected against legislative infringement by the Canadian Constitution. Given the kinds of objectives that Lamer considered to be sufficiently compelling and substantial for Aboriginal title to be infringed, one has to seriously question the value of this constitutional entrenchment.

However, the *Sparrow* justification test does include a couple of features that may serve to provide practical protection to Aboriginal title. First, the requirement that the fiduciary obligations of the Crown be respected includes a duty to consult with Aboriginal peoples when infringements of their Aboriginal rights are contemplated. In *Delgamuukw*, Lamer put it this way:

> aboriginal title encompasses within it a right to choose to what ends a piece of land can be put ... This aspect of aboriginal title suggests that the fiduciary relationship between the Crown and aboriginal peoples may be satisfied by the involvement of aboriginal peoples in decisions taken with respect to their lands. *There is always a duty of consultation.*[77]

The extent of this duty will depend on the circumstances, including the severity of the infringement. It could range from a minimum standard to discuss the matter where the infringement is relatively minor, up to a requirement of full consent where serious infringement is involved.

Even where the minimum standard applies, however, "this consultation must be in good faith, and with the intention of substantially addressing the concerns of the aboriginal peoples whose lands are at issue."[78]

Secondly, the duty to respect the Crown's fiduciary obligations includes a duty to pay compensation for infringements of Aboriginal title. In *Delgamuukw*, Chief Justice Lamer found that this duty arose out of the title's economic aspect. He elaborated as follows:

> Indeed, compensation for breaches of fiduciary duty are [*sic*] a well-established part of the landscape of aboriginal rights: *Guerin*, [*supra* n.22]. In keeping with the duty of honour and good faith on the Crown, fair compensation will ordinarily be required when aboriginal title is infringed. The amount of compensation payable will vary with the nature of the particular aboriginal title affected and with the nature and severity of the infringement and the extent to which aboriginal interests were accommodated.[79]

Moreover, as this duty to pay compensation is part of the justificatory test for infringements of Aboriginal title, the duty itself appears to be constitutional. This probably means that Parliament cannot avoid it by passing legislation, as it can where other, non-constitutional property rights are concerned.[80] So as a practical matter, this duty to pay compensation might well cause Parliament to exercise caution before infringing Aboriginal title, especially if the benefit of the infringement would go mostly to a province or a third party.[81]

4.   Implications of *Delgamuukw* for the Protection of Other Property Rights in Canada

For Canadians who are concerned about the protection of their private property rights from government interference, the *Delgamuukw* decision is anything but reassuring. It is sobering to compare the degree of protection that the Supreme Court accorded to the *constitutional* property rights of the Aboriginal peoples with the protection the courts have traditionally accorded to *common law* property rights. To quote again from Blackstone, "[s]o great moreover is the regard of the law for private property, that it will not authorize the least violation of it; *no, not even for the general good of the whole community.*"[82] Acknowledging parliamentary sovereignty, however, Blackstone had to concede that, for a new road to be constructed, for example, the legislature could and often did expropriate land for the public good upon payment of full compensation. However, only the legislature can authorize this because the executive has no authority to expropriate property, even for public purposes, without statutory authority.[83] Moreover, while in theory there would be nothing to prevent a legislature from expropriating land for reasons other than public purposes such as roads and other infrastructure, or without paying compensation, in practice this rarely happens, as legislatures are reluctant to infringe a fundamental common law right without good reason.[84]

In Canada various federal and provincial statutes govern the taking of private property for public purposes.[85] The Canada *Expropriation Act*,[86] for example, provides in section 4(1) that "[a]ny interest in land ... that, in the opinion of the Minister [of Public Works and Government Services], is required by the Crown for a public work or other public purpose may be expropriated by the Crown in accordance with the provisions of this Part."[87] However, as Professor Eric Todd has pointed out, "[t]he exercise of the power of expropriation interferes drastically with private property rights and therefore the courts generally construe expropriation statutes strictly and in favour of the individual whose rights are affected."[88] Moreover, any exercise of a power of expropriation has to comply strictly with the procedural requirements in the enabling statute. Failure to respect those requirements will render the expropriation invalid, exposing the expropriating authority to damages and/or an injunction for trespass or nuisance.[89]

We have seen that, despite the constitutional entrenchment of Aboriginal title, the Supreme Court in *Delgamuukw* said that it can be infringed to meet objectives that appear to go far beyond the kind of public purposes envisaged by expropriation statutes.[90] As long as the infringement is of sufficient importance to the general public, and the Crown's fiduciary obligations are respected, the constitutional rights of the Aboriginal peoples can be legislatively overridden. Moreover, there is no mention in *Delgamuukw* of any requirement for the kinds of procedural safeguards that are generally contained in expropriation statutes.[91] So in practice, if not in constitutional theory, Aboriginal title might enjoy greater protection against federal infringement under current expropriation legislation than it does under the Canadian Constitution. If this is correct, we should be very skeptical of the value of constitutional entrenchment of *any* property rights.

Acknowledgments

The invaluable research assistance provided by Chantal Morton for this paper is very gratefully acknowledged.

Notes

1 [1997] 3 S.C.R. 1010.

2 See Kent McNeil, *Defining Aboriginal Title in the 90's: Has the Supreme Court Finally Got It Right?* (Toronto: Robarts Centre for Canadian Studies, York University, 1998) (hereinafter McNeil, *Defining Aboriginal Title*); Kent Mc-Neil, "Aboriginal Title and the Division of Powers: Rethinking Federal and Provincial Jurisdiction" (1998) 61 *Sask. L. Rev.* 431 (hereinafter McNeil, "Aboriginal Title and the Division of Powers"); Kerry Wilkins, "Of Provinces and Section 35 Rights" (1999) 22 *Dalhousie L.J.* 185.

3 One could also look at the central place that land generally holds in Aboriginal cultures and legal systems: e.g., see Fred Plain, "A Treatise on the Rights of the Aboriginal Peoples of the Continent of North America," in Menno Boldt and J. Anthony Long, eds., *The Quest for Justice: Aboriginal Peoples and Aboriginal Rights* (Toronto: University of Toronto Press, 1985), 31, esp. 34; Leroy Little Bear, "Aboriginal Rights and the Canadian 'Grundnorm'," in J. Rick Ponting, ed., *Arduous Journey: Canadian Indians and Decolonization* (Toronto: McClelland and Stewart, 1986), 243; John J. Borrows and Leonard I. Rotman, *Aboriginal Legal Issues: Cases, Materials and Commentary* (Toronto: Butterworths, 1998), 1-4.

4 See generally S.F.C. Milsom, *Historical Foundations of the Common Law*, 2nd ed. (London: Butterworths, 1981); A.W.B. Simpson, *A History of the Land Law*, 2nd ed. (Oxford: Clarendon Press, 1986).

5 *Magna Carta*, 17 John (1215).

6 *Halsbury's Laws of England*, 4th ed. (London: Butterworths, 1973-86), vol. 8, para. 908 n.2. See also *Attorney-General v. De Keyser's Royal Hotel*, [1920] A.C. 508 (H.L.), at 569, where Lord Parmoor stated: "Since Magna Carta the estate of a subject in lands or buildings has been protected against the prerogative of the Crown."

7 *Magna Carta* would have been received as part of the applicable statute law in all the common law provinces. As a fundamental part of the British constitution, no doubt it applies in Quebec as well, despite the reintroduction of French civil law by the *Quebec Act*, 14 Geo. III (1774), c.83 (U.K.) (the Preamble to the *Constitution Act, 1867*, 30 & 31 Vict., c.3 (U.K.), provides that Canada shall have "a Constitution similar in Principle to that of the United Kingdom").

8 See *Entick v. Carrington* (1765), 19 How. S.T. 1029 (C.P.).

9 See James W. Ely, Jr., *The Guardian of Every Other Right: A Constitutional History of Property Rights*, 2nd ed. (New York: Oxford University Press, 1998), 13-14, 54-55.

10 On this doctrine, see R.F.V. Heuston, *Essays in Constitutional Law*, 2nd ed. (London: Stevens and Sons, 1964), 58-81; Stanley de Smith and Rodney Brazier, *Constitutional and Administrative Law*, 6th ed. (London: Penguin Books, 1986), 70-73; E.C.S. Wade and A.W. Bradley, *Constitutional and Administrative Law*, 11th ed. by A.W. Bradley and K.D. Ewing (London: Longmans, 1993), 65-75.

11 William Blackstone, *Commentaries on the Laws of England* (Oxford: Clarendon Press, 1765-69), vol. 1, at 129 (emphasis added). See also Herbert Broom, *Constitutional Law Viewed in Relation to Common Law*, 2nd ed. by George L. Denman (London: W. Maxwell and Son, 1885), 225-45.

12 *Supra* n.6, vol. 8, para. 833.

13 The Fifth Amendment to the American Constitution provides in part that no one shall be "deprived of life, liberty, or property, without due process of law; nor shall private property be taken for public use, without just compensation." For detailed discussion, see Ely, *supra* n.9.

14 See T.R.S. Allan, "Legislative Supremacy and the Rule of Law: Democracy and Constitutionalism" (1985) 44 *Cambridge L.J.* 111, at 117-25.

15 In *Attorney-General for Canada v. Hallet and Carey Ltd.*, [1952] A.C. 427 (P.C.), at 450, Lord Radcliffe said that "there is a well-known general principle that statutes which encroach upon the rights of the subject, whether as regards person or property, are subject to a 'strict' construction." See also Ruth Sullivan, *Driedger on the Construction of Statutes*, 3rd ed. (Toronto: Butterworths, 1994), 370-76.

16 See *Colet v. R.*, [1981] 1 S.C.R. 2, at 10.

17 See *Western Counties Railway Co. v. Windsor and Annapolis Railway Co.* (1882), 7 App. Cas. 178 (P.C.), at 188; *Commissioner of Public Works (Cape Colony) v. Logan*, [1903] A.C. 355 (P.C.), at 363-64; *Central Control Board (Liquor Traffic) v. Cannon Brewery Co. Ltd.*, [1919] A.C. 744 (H.L.), per Lord Atkinson at 752; *Manitoba Fisheries Ltd. v. R.*, [1979] 1 S.C.R. 101.

18 See also *Attorney-General v. Horner* (1884), 14 Q.B.D. 245 (C.A.), esp. per Brett M.R. at 256-7; *London and North Western Railway Co. v. Evans*, [1893] 1 Ch. 16 (C.A.), per Bowen L.J. at 28; *The Commonwealth v. Hazeldell Ltd.* (1918), 25 C.L.R. 552 (H.C. Aust.), per Griffith C.J. and Rich J. at 563; *Attorney-General v. De Keyser's Royal Hotel*, *supra* n.6, per Lord Atkinson at 542, Lord Parmoor at 576, 579; *Colonial Sugar Refining Co. v. Melbourne Harbour Trust Commissioners* (1927), 38 C.L.R. 547 (P.C.), at 559.

19 See J. McBean, "The Implications of Entrenching Property Rights in Section 7 of the Charter" (1988) 26 *Alta. L. Rev.* 548. *The Canadian Charter of Rights and Freedoms* consists of the first 34 sections of the *Constitution Act, 1982*, being Schedule B to the *Canada Act 1982*, c.11 (U.K.).

20 *Supra* n.19. Section 35(1) is quoted in text accompanying n.52, *infra*.

21 *Delgamuukw*, *supra* n.1, per Lamer C.J.C. at 1091-95 (para. 133-39).

22 See *Guerin v. The Queen*, [1984] 2 S.C.R. 335, per Wilson J. at 349, Dickson J. at 376-82; *Canadian Pacific Ltd. v. Paul*, [1988] 2 S.C.R. 654, at 677-78; *Roberts v. Canada*, [1989] 1 S.C.R. 322, at 340.

23 Lamer C.J.C. delivered the principal judgment, for himself, Cory and Major JJ. La Forest J. delivered a separate judgment for himself and L'Heureux-Dubé J., concurring in result but differing to some extent in his reasons. McLachlin J. simply said: "I concur with the Chief Justice. I add that I am also in substantial agreement with the comments of Justice La Forest." *Delgamuukw*, *supra* n.1, at 1135 (para. 209).

24 A fee simple is the greatest private interest in land available at common law. For all practical purposes, it is equivalent to ownership.

25 *Delgamuukw, supra* n.1, at 1080 (para. 110).

26 *Ibid.*, at 1080-81 (para. 111).

27 (1888), 14 App. Cas. 46, at 54.

28 *Delgamuukw, supra* n.1, at 1081 (para. 112).

29 *Ibid.* See also *St. Mary's Indian Band v. Cranbrook (City)*, [1997] 2 S.C.R. 657, at 666-67 (para. 14). On the *sui generis* nature of Aboriginal rights generally, see John Borrows and Leonard I. Rotman, "The *Sui Generis* Nature of Aboriginal Rights: Does It Make a Difference?" (1997) 36 *Alta. L. Rev.* 9.

30 This was apparent from the *St. Catherine's* decision itself, in which Lord Watson decided that Aboriginal title to land "is an interest other than that of the Province in the same" within the meaning of section 109 of the *Constitution Act, 1867*, 30 & 31 Vict., c.3 (U.K.), and that the beneficial interest in Aboriginal title lands would only become available to the provinces "as a source of revenue whenever the estate of the Crown is disencumbered of the Indian title": *supra* n.27, at 58-59. For discussion, see Hamar Foster, "Aboriginal Title and the Provincial Obligation to Respect It: Is *Delgamuukw v. British Columbia* 'Invented Law'?" (1998) 56 *The Advocate* 221.

31 *Delgamuukw, supra* n.1, at 1096 (para. 140) (emphasis in original). See also 1095 (para. 138).

32 *Ibid.*, at 1083 (para. 117) (emphasis added).

33 Note that, when considering Aboriginal and treaty rights apart from title, such as an Aboriginal right to fish or a treaty right to hunt, the Supreme Court has been careful to avoid applying what Dickson C.J. and La Forest J. referred to in *R. v. Sparrow*, [1990] 1 S.C.R 1075, at 1112, as "traditional common law concepts of property": see *R. v. Sundown*, [1999] 1 S.C.R. 393, at 411-12 (at para. 34-36). But those kinds of rights, which are communal rights to participate in "activities," are different from Aboriginal title because it is "the right to the land itself": *Delgamuukw, supra* n.1, at 1093-95 (para. 137-39).

34 *Delgamuukw, supra* n.1., at 1081-82 (para. 113). To this it might be added that alienability is not an essential attribute of real property, even at common law. Apart from statute, a fee tail estate was not alienable as such, though it could be converted into an alienable fee simple by barring the entail: see Simpson, *supra* n.4, at 90-91. Also, at common law the Crown could create inalienable fee simple estates: see Joseph Chitty, *A Treatise of the Law on the Prerogatives of the Crown* (London: Joseph Butterworth and Son, 1820), 386 n.(h). In *Pierce Bell Ltd. v. Frazer* (1972-73), 130 C.L.R. 575 (H.C. Aust.), at 584, Barwick C.J. said that a statutory restraint on alienation of land granted by the Crown would not reduce, or make conditional, the fee simple estate obtained by the grantee. Moreover, the Crown's underlying title to all land in its common law dominions is an inalienable real property interest: see Kent McNeil, *Common Law Aboriginal Title* (Oxford: Clarendon Press, 1989), 80-93, esp. 92 n.58. See also A.W.B. Simpson, "Real Property," in H.W.R. Wade, *Annual Survey of Commonwealth Law 1972* (London: Butterworths, 1973), 320, at 324, where the author, a foremost authority on English real property law, criticized the decision in *Milirrpum v. Nabalco Pty. Ltd.* (1971), 17 F.L.R. 141 (F.C. Aust.) (since overruled by *Mabo v. Queensland (No. 2)* (1992), 175 C.L.R. 1 (H.C. Aust.)) because, *inter alia*, it

contains a discussion of the concept of ownership which perpetuates what seems to be *an error—the idea that alienability is an essential feature of this concept.* Ownership is a notion based upon the central idea of there being a special relationship between a person or group and a thing, and this relationship is thought of as having such importance as to justify conferring upon the owner *a right of excluding others* from whatever use the thing is capable of and seems to be appropriate. In extremely intense cases of ownership the exclusion is automatic. For example only Odysseus could bend his bow, and only King Arthur could draw the sword from the stone.... *Hence it is a weak form of ownership which permits alienation*; in more intense forms *it is personal*, and thus it is that some forms of property are buried with the dead from whom they cannot be separated. [emphasis added]

35 *Delgamuukw, supra* n.1, at 1082 (para. 114) (emphasis in original).

36 See *Drulard v. Welsh* (1906), 11 O.L.R. 647 (Ont. Div. Ct.).

37 *Delgamuukw, supra* n.1, per Lamer C.J.C. at 1099-1100 (para. 146-48).

38 See Brian Slattery, "Varieties of Aboriginal Rights" (1998) 6:4-6 *Canada Watch* 71.

39 See Brian Slattery, "Understanding Aboriginal Rights" (1987) 66 *Can. Bar Rev.* 727, at 745-46; Kent McNeil, "Aboriginal Rights in Canada: From Title to Land to Territorial Sovereignty" (1998) 5 *Tulsa J. Comp. & Int'l L.* 253, at 285-91.

40 *Delgamuukw, supra* n.1, at 1082-83 (para. 115).

41 While the Court declined to deal with the issue of self-government directly (see *ibid.*, per Lamer C.J.C. at 114-15 (para. 170-71), La Forest J. at 1134 (para. 205)), it has been pointed out that Lamer's comments on the communal nature of aboriginal title and the decision-making authority of Aboriginal communities have important implications for self-government, as "[m]aking decisions about the care and use of land is a fundamental activity of government": Peter H. Russell, "High Courts and the Rights of Aboriginal Peoples: The Limits of Judicial Independence" (1998) 61 *Sask. L. Rev.* 247, at 272. For more detailed discussion, see McNeil, *supra* n.39, at 278-91.

42 See generally Dennis Lloyd, *The Law Relating to Unincorporated Associations* (London: Sweet and Maxwell Ltd., 1938); Harold A.J. Ford, *Unincorporated Non-Profit Associations: Their Property and Their Liability* (Oxford: Clarendon Press, 1959); S.J. Stoljar, *Groups and Entities: An Enquiry into Corporate Theory* (Canberra: Australian National University Press, 1973).

43 Note that there is a considerable body of case law on the legal capacity of Indian bands and band councils: e.g., see *Johnson v. British Columbia Hydro and Power Authority*, [1981] 3 C.N.L.R. 63 (B.C.S.C.); *Beauvais v. The Queen*, [1982] 4 C.N.L.R. 43 (F.C.T.D.); *Joe v. Findlay*, [1987] 2 C.N.L.R. 75 (B.C.S.C.); *Bannon v. Pervais*, [1990] 2 C.N.L.R. 17 (Ont. Dist. Ct.); *Ochapowace First Nation v. Araya*, [1995] 1 C.N.L.R. 75 (Sask. C.A.); *Chadee v. Norway House First Nation*, [1997] 2 C.N.L.R. 48 (Man. C.A.). However, the legal capacity of bands and band councils appears to be dependent on the fact that they have been created and granted statutory powers by the *In-*

dian Act, R.S.C. 1985, c.I-5: see *Whitebear Band Council v. Carpenters Provincial Council of Saskatchewan*, [1982] 3 C.N.L.R. 181 (Sask. C.A.); *Paul Band v. R.*, [1984] 1 C.N.L.R. 87 (Alta. C.A.); *Heron Seismic Services Ltd. v. Muscowpetung Indian Band*, [1991] 2 C.N.L.R. 52 (Sask. Q.B.); *Telecom Leasing Canada v. Enoch Indian Band of Stony Plain Indian Reserve No. 135*, [1994] 1 C.N.L.R. 206 (Alta. Q.B.); compare *Tawich Development Corporation v. Deputy Minister of Revenue of Quebec*, [1997] 2 C.N.L.R. 187 (C.Q.). For an argument that band councils do not owe their existence and powers solely to the *Indian Act*, see Kent McNeil, "Aboriginal Governments and the *Canadian Charter of Rights and Freedoms*" (1996) 34 *Osgoode Hall L.J.* 61, at 79-88. See also Geoffrey S. Lester, "Do Treaty Indians Have a Corporate Personality? A Note on the Pawis, Blackfoot and Bear Island Cases," [1990] 1 C.N.L.R. 1.

44 In practice, governments own land in their own right, though in Anglo-Canadian law the requirement of legal personality is satisfied by the theory that the indivisible Crown has title as a corporation sole. The difficulty posed by federalism is avoided in this regard by dividing the Crown into the Crown in right of Canada and the Crown in right of each province, making it possible for the Crown in right of Canada to sue the Crown in right of a province over title to land, and vice versa. But the collective nature of the Crown's title should be apparent because Crown land is not held for the benefit of the Crown itself, but for the benefit of the Crown's subjects: see *The Queen v. Symonds* (1847), [1840-1932] N.Z.P.C.C. 387 (N.Z.S.C.), per Martin C.J. at 395; *Williams v. Attorney-General for New South Wales* (1913), 16 C.L.R. 404 (H.C. Aust.). Similarly, an Aboriginal nation can be regarded as a *political* entity that holds title to the nation's lands on behalf of all the members of the nation.

45 *Delgamuukw, supra* n.1, at 1080 (para. 111), quoted at greater length in text accompanying n.26, supra.

46 *Ibid.*, at 1088 (para. 125).

47 *Ibid.*, at 1089 (para. 127).

48 On the latter issue, see McNeil, *Defining Aboriginal Title, supra* n.2, at 11-14.

49 See *supra* n.32 and accompanying text.

50 See quotation from Simpson, *supra* n.34.

51 See *Delgamuukw, supra* n.1, per Lamer C.J.C. at 1091 (para. 131): "If aboriginal peoples wish to use their lands in a way that aboriginal title does not permit, then they must surrender those lands and convert them into non-title lands to do so." Obviously any such use of the lands by persons other than the Aboriginal titleholders would also violate their Aboriginal title, though if authorized by a non-Aboriginal government this would raise the issue of whether the violation was a justifiable infringement, a matter to be discussed in Part 3 below.

52 *Supra* n.19.

53 *Delgamuukw, supra* n.1, at 1091-92 (para. 133).

54 This protection is accorded by s.52(1) of the *Constitution Act*, 1982, which provides: "The Constitution of Canada is the supreme law of Canada, and any law that is inconsistent with the provisions of the Constitution is, to the extent of the inconsistency, of no force or effect."

55 Constitutional entrenchment apart, in our parliamentary system of government legislatures can authorize the executive to infringe common law rights, including fundamental rights and freedoms: e.g., see *Attorney-General for Canada v. Hallet and Carey Ltd.*, *supra* n.15; *R. v. Halliday*, [1917] A.C. 260 (H.L.). Where, however, the executive lacks clear and plain statutory authority, it is prevented from interfering with legal rights by the rule of law: see *Entick v. Carrington*, *supra* n.8; *Roncarelli v. Duplessis*, [1959] S.C.R. 121. This vital protection against government interference is also manifested in the rule that the Crown and its officials cannot infringe the rights of British subjects by acts of state: see *Walker v. Baird*, [1892] A.C. 491 (P.C.); *Johnstone v. Pedlar*, [1921] 2 A.C. 262 (H.L.); *Eshugbayi Eleko v. Government of Nigeria*, [1931] A.C. 662 (P.C.), at 671; *Attorney-General v. Nissan*, [1970] A.C. 179 (H.L.); *Buttes Gas v. Hammer*, [1975] Q.B. 557 (C.A.), at 573.

56 *Supra* nn. 10-18 and accompanying text.

57 See *supra* nn. 19-20 and accompanying text.

58 *Supra* n.33, at 1102, 1108-19.

59 See also *R. v. Gladstone*, [1996] 2 S.C.R. 723, per Lamer C.J.C. at 762-80 (para. 54-84); *R. v. Adams*, [1996] 3 S.C.R. 101, per Lamer C.J.C. at 133-35 (para. 56-59); *R. v. Côté*, [1996] 3 S.C.R. 139, per Lamer C.J.C. at 189-90 (para. 81-83).

60 *Delgamuukw*, *supra* n.1, at 1107-14 (para. 160-69).

61 *R. v. Gladstone*, supra n.59, at 774-75 (para. 73), quoted in *Delgamuukw*, *supra* n.1, at 1107-08 (para. 161) (emphasis added by Lamer in *Delgamuukw*; "equally" emphasized in original). For critical commentary on this aspect of the *Gladstone* decision, see Kent McNeil, "How Can Infringements of the Constitutional Rights of Aboriginal Peoples Be Justified?" (1997) 8:2 *Constitutional Forum* 33.

62 *Delgamuukw*, *supra* n.1, at 1111 (para. 165). See also per La Forest J. at 1132-33 (para. 202).

63 *Ibid.*, at 1107 (para. 160).

64 *Constitution Act, 1867*, 30 & 31 Vict., c.3 (U.K.), s.91(24). Because Aboriginal title is under exclusive federal jurisdiction, Lamer concluded that since Confederation the provinces have had no constitutional authority to extinguish it: *Delgamuukw*, *supra* n.1, at 1115-23 (para. 172-83).

65 See McNeil, "Aboriginal Title and the Division of Powers," *supra* n.2.

66 See *Delgamuukw*, *supra* n.1, per Lamer C.J.C. at 1116-18 (para. 174-76).

67 *Ibid.*, at 1118 (para. 175).

68 [1996] 2 S.C.R. 507, at 538 (para. 28) (emphasis added).

69 *Supra* n.62 and accompanying text.

70 The taking of the lands would have to be temporary because if permanent it would *extinguish* the Aboriginal title, and as we have seen Parliament lost the power to extinguish Aboriginal title in 1982: see *supra* n.68 and accompanying text.

71 *Supra* n.61 and accompanying text.

72 Note that in *Sparrow*, *supra* n.33, at 1113, Dickson C.J.C. and La Forest J., for a unanimous Court, specifically rejected the public interest justification for infringements of Aboriginal rights: "We find the 'public interest' justi-

fication to be so vague as to provide no meaningful guidance and so broad as to be unworkable as a test for the justification of a limitation on constitutional rights." However, in *Gladstone* and *Delgamuukw*, Lamer C.J.C. seems to have embraced the public interest justification. See McNeil, *Defining Aboriginal Title, supra* n.2, at 17-21.

73 Harvesting timber and extracting minerals from land clearly involves taking, as those resources are included in Aboriginal title (*Delgamuukw, supra* n.1, at 1083-88 (para. 116-24)), and are part of the land until severed from it. Moreover, the value of real property is generally diminished by their removal. Even preventing the owner of minerals from accessing them is a form of government taking: see *British Columbia v. Tener*, [1985] 1 S.C.R. 533. Arguably, taking of natural resources, especially non-renewable resources like minerals, would involve extinguishment of the Aboriginal title to those resources, and therefore be prohibited by section 35(1): see supra n.68 and accompanying text.

74 Lamer seemed to think that economic development could be of sufficient importance for the general public to justify infringement of Aboriginal rights. In *Delgamuukw, supra* n.1, at 1108 (para. 161), he said:

> But legitimate government objectives also include "the pursuit of *economic and regional fairness*" and "the recognition of the historical reliance upon, and participation in, the fishery by non-aboriginal groups" [*Gladstone, supra* n.59] (para. 75). By contrast, measures enacted for relatively unimportant reasons, such as sports fishing without *a significant economic component* (*Adams, supra* [n.59]) would fail this aspect of the test of justification. [emphasis added]

Where the economic development is being carried out by a large corporation (as it usually is in the context of forestry and mining, for example), this sounds remarkably like a Canadian echo of the old refrain of American free-enterprise that what is good for General Motors is good for America.

75 McNeil, *Defining Aboriginal Title, supra* n.2, at 20.

76 I use the word "sanctity" in this context, not so much because property rights are at issue (though some writers, like Blackstone, *supra* n.11, vol. 2, at 1-15, esp. 2-3, have grounded property rights in natural law), but because Aboriginal title does have spiritual value for most, if not all, Aboriginal peoples: e.g., see authorities cited in n.3, *supra*.

77 *Delgamuukw, supra* n.1, at 1113 (para. 168) (emphasis added).

78 *Ibid.* See also *Cheslatta Carrier Nation v. British Columbia (Environmental Assessment Act*, Project Assessment Director), [1998] 3 C.N.L.R. 1 (B.C.S.C.); *Nunavik Inuit v. Canada (Minister of Canadian Heritage)*, [1998] 4 C.N.L.R. 68 (F.C.T.D.); *Halfway River First Nation v. British Columbia (Ministry of Forests)*, [1999] 4 C.N.L.R. 1 (B.C.C.A.). For discussion, see Sonia Lawrence and Patrick Macklem, "From Consultation to Reconciliation: Aboriginal Rights and the Crown's Duty to Consult" (2000) 79 *Can. Bar Rev.* 252.

79 *Delgamuukw, supra* n.1 at 1113-14 (para. 169).

80 Of course the denial of compensation, where non-constitutional rights are concerned, would have to be unequivocal: see cases cited in nn. 17-18, *supra*.

81 As discussed above (see *supra* nn. 69-74 and accompanying text), if Aboriginal title can be infringed for the purpose of resource development undertaken by corporations, much of the benefit may in fact go to those corporations.

82 Blackstone, *supra* n.11, vol. 1, at 139 (emphasis added).

83 See Broom, *supra* n.11, at 231: "no man's property can legally be taken from him or invaded by the direct act or command of the sovereign, without the consent of the subject, given expressly or impliedly through parliament." See also Keith Davies, *Law of Compulsory Purchase and Compensation*, 3rd ed. (London: Butterworths, 1978), at 9-10; Graham L. Fricke, ed., *Compulsory Acquisition of Land in Australia*, 2nd ed. (Sydney: The Law Book Company Limited, 1982), 5-6, esp. 5 n.3; *Rugby Water Board v. Shaw Fox*, [1973] A.C. 202 (H.L.), per Lord Pearson at 214 ("compulsory acquisition and compensation for it are entirely creations of statute"). Note, however, that there is an exception to this where the Crown seizes or destroys property in time of war, in which case it must pay compensation, except where the destruction occurred as a direct result of battle: see *Attorney-General v. De Keyser's Royal Hotel*, *supra* n.18; *Commercial and Estates Co. of Egypt v. The Board of Trade*, [1925] 1 K.B. 271 (C.A.), esp. per Atkin L.J. at 294-7; *Burmah Oil Co. v. Lord Advocate*, [1965] A.C. 75 (H.L.); *Halsbury's Laws of England*, *supra* n.6, vol. 8, para. 920. See also Eric C.E. Todd, *The Law of Expropriation and Compensation in Canada*, 2nd ed. (Toronto: Carswell, 1992), at 20.

84 For an instance of this, see the controversy arising out of the British Parliament's response to *Burmah Oil Co.* case, *supra* n.83, discussed in A.L. Goodhart, "The Burmah Oil Case and the War Damage Act 1965" (1966) 82 L.Q.R. 97.

85 See Todd, *supra* n.83, at 7-16, 26-27; *Canadian Encyclopedic Digest*, Ontario 3rd ed. (Toronto: Carswell), Title 61 - Expropriation (March 1998), §25-50.

86 R.S.C. 1985, c. E-21.

87 Note that subsections (2) to (7) of section 4 include special provisions regarding expropriation of Cree-Naskapi lands, Sechelt lands, Yukon First Nations settlement land, and Tetlit Gwich'in Yukon land. Analysis of these provisions would involve constitutional questions and an examination of the specific land claims agreements to which the provisions relate, matters that are outside the scope of this paper. Also, there is probably a constitutional limitation on federal expropriation, as the taking would have to be related to a federal head of power: see Todd, supra n.83, at 32, and generally Andrée Lajoie, *Expropriation et fédéralisme au Canada* (Montréal: Les Presses de l'Université de Montréal, 1972).

88 Todd, *supra* n.83, at 26. E.g., see *Blue Haven Motel Ltd. v. Burnaby (District)* (1965), 52 D.L.R. (2d) 464 (B.C.C.A.); *Saratoga Holdings Ltd. v. Surrey (District)* (1971), 18 D.L.R 371 (B.C.C.A.); *Park Projects Ltd. v. Halifax (City)* (1981), 22 L.C.R. 244, at 252 (N.S.E.C.B.), affirmed (1982), 25 L.C.R. 193 (N.S.C.A.). Moreover, the courts will not imply a power of expropriation that is not clearly expressed: see *Simpson v. South Staffordshire Water Works Co.* (1865), 34 L.J. Ch. 380, esp. per Lord Westbury L.C. at 387; *Winnipeg (City) v. Cauchon* (1881), Man. R. (Armour) temp. Wood 350 (Man. Q.B.); *Thomson v. Halifax Power Co.* (1914), 16 D.L.R. 424 (N.S.S.C); compare *Har-*

ding v. *Cardiff (Township)* (1881), 29 Gr. 308 (Ont. H.C.), affirmed (1882), 2 O.R. 329 (Ont. Div. Ct.). For discussion and further references, see Todd, at 26-29. In this respect, the approach of the courts is in keeping with general principles of statutory interpretation: see supra nn. 14-18 and accompanying text. See also *Canadian Encyclopedic Digest, supra* n.85, §59-74.

89 See *Dominion Iron and Steel Co. v. Burt*, [1917] A.C. 179 (P.C.), esp. at 185; *R. v. Lee* (1917), 16 Ex. C.R. 424, esp. at 428, affirmed (1919), 59 S.C.R. 652; *Re Magnone* (1957), 23 W.W.R. 415 (B.C.S.C.), esp. at 417. For discussion and further references, see Todd, *supra* n.83, at 29-31; *Canadian Encyclopedic Digest, supra* n.85, §18-24.

90 On what constitutes a public work or purpose, see *R. v. O'Halloran*, [1934] Ex. C.R. 67; *Vaughan Construction Co. v. Nova Scotia (Attorney-General)* (1967), 60 D.L.R. (2d) 692 (N.S.S.C.); *Thompson v. R.*, [1978] 5 W.W.R. 635 (Man. Q.B.); *Pineridge Property Ltd. v. British Columbia District No. 57 Board of Education* (1982), 40 B.C.L.R. 221 (Co. Ct.); *Grauer Estate v. R.* (1986), 1 F.T.R. 51. Compare *Piccirillo v. British Columbia (Minister of Forests and Lands)* (1988), 47 D.L.R. (4th) 513 (B.C.S.C.). See also *Semiahmoo Indian Band v. Canada*, [1998] 1 C.N.L.R. 250 (Fed. C.A.), involving a surrender of reserve land, in lieu of expropriation, for expansion of a Canada Customs facility. As the Crown simply retained the land without using it "for customs facilities or *any other public purpose*" (p.253, emphasis added), Isaac C.J. for a unanimous Court held that the Crown had breached its fiduciary duty to the Band in obtaining the land. At pp. 264-65, he said: "While the Crown must be given some latitude in its land-use planning when it actively seeks the surrender of Indian land for a public purpose, the Crown must ensure that it impairs the rights of the affected Indian Band as little as possible, which includes ensuring that the surrender is for a timely public purpose."

91 See Todd, *supra* n.83, 39-81; *Canadian Encyclopedic Digest, supra* n.85, §125-373.

Solution or Problem?

GEOFF PLANT AND MELVIN H. SMITH

> *The following is an excerpt from a conference discussion on the ramifications of the Delgamuukw decision in British Columbia. The two main speakers are Geoff Plant, counsel for the B.C. government during the Delgamuukw trial who was elected to the B.C. Legislative Assembly and is currently opposition critic of the Attorney General's office; and Melvin H. Smith, Q.C., former constitutional advisor to four previous B.C. governments, columnist, university lecturer and author of the best-selling book,* Our Home or Native Land?

Geoff Plant

The starting point for my remarks is the now famous statement of Supreme Court Chief Justice Antonio Lamer in the last paragraph of his reasons for judgment in *Delgamuukw*. He said: "Ultimately it is through negotiated settlements with good faith and give and take on all sides, reinforced by the judgments of this Court, that we will achieve what I stated in *Van der Peet*, the basic purpose of Section 35(1), the reconciliation of the pre-existence of aboriginal societies with the sovereignty of the Crown. Let us face it, we are all here to stay."

This is not the first time that the courts have encouraged the resolution of aboriginal claims by negotiation. Justice Macfarlane of the B.C. Court of Appeal expressed a similar sentiment in the *Meares Island* case in 1985. If this statement by Chief Justice Lamer is not the first such statement, it is easily the most powerful. It is a strong hint from the highest court in Canada that the only path to reconciliation is negotiation.

So what lies behind this judicial exhortation? Let me make a suggestion. Perhaps the command to settle is in effect an admission that the framework of legal principles that the Court has around the ideas of aboriginal rights in title is simply unworkable. In other words, the Court has encouraged negotiation because it recognized that the aboriginal rights doctrine that it created has made the business of government, as a practical matter, virtually impossible.

In support of this idea, I want you to consider the following scenario as an example of the model of pre-treaty government created by the Court in *Delgamuukw*. A district forest manager in a small town in British Columbia receives an application for a cutting permit. Before the cutting permit can be issued, this manager, most likely a registered forester by training, must make a decision about the existence, location, and nature of potentially conflicting aboriginal rights or title. This, of course, is over and above all of the other things that district forest managers have to do as part of the planning of the harvesting of forest resources. To make a decision, this official must examine the oral history of whatever aboriginal groups may have had a connection to the proposed license area in 1846, a time when the non-aboriginal population of British Columbia consisted of a few dozen fur traders.

Since oral histories are often jealously guarded, the oral history in question may in fact be completely inaccessible, or accessible only at a price. Assuming, however, we get over that threshold and oral history can be obtained, it will then need to be understood. As someone who has engaged in that exercise at some length, I can assure you that this is not by any means a straightforward task. Once that is done, the official then will be required to weigh that history from the "aboriginal perspective." He must also ensure—and, as the Chief Justice of British Columbia discovered, woe betide him if he does not—that the oral history is placed "on an equal footing" with other historical evidence, if there is any. From the evidence of historic use and occupation, the official must then determine whether there are aboriginal rights or title on the affected land, and who has them. In this context it may be useful to you, but it probably won't be to the official, to observe that no court has yet made a judicial determination about the existence of aboriginal title over any specific parcel of land anywhere in British Columbia outside Indian reserves. We have tests for the proof of title, which time does not permit me to critique, but we as yet have no example of their application.

However, having decided—miraculously, I suggest—who if anyone has what aboriginal rights, if any, the official must next determine whether the proposed forest harvesting activity is, first, in pursuance of a judicially acknowledged legitimate public policy objective; and second, is consistent with the honour of the Crown. He will make these decisions knowing that he will probably have to defend them in court, and recognizing that the principles which govern the exercise of this discretion are in flux and will probably change significantly between the day he makes his decision and the day the case actually finally reaches the Supreme Court of Canada. You will recall that the Chief Justice reserved to *his* Court the role in respect of giving effect to reconciliation. It is "this Court" were the words that he used.

So our official will probably have to be prepared to defend his decision on the basis of principles and criteria which are in fact unknown to him at the time he makes it. Moreover, while he might hope that there would be a useful framework of principles to guide him, our unlucky civil servant also knows that the question of whether his decision can be justified is, to use the language of *Delgamuukw*, "ultimately a question of fact that will have to be examined on a case-by-case basis."

The complications don't end there. Even if the aboriginal interest can be identified with certainty, the official will, as the Court in *Delgamuukw* admits, face difficulties in determining the precise value of that aboriginal interest in the land, and any grants, leases, or licenses given for its exploitation. However, having helpfully admitted that there will be such difficulties, the Supreme Court of Canada has given him absolutely no guidance in how to resolve them, going so far as to cheerfully admit that, "these difficult economic considerations obviously cannot be solved here."

Of course, depending on circumstances, the official—whose life I'm sure you now truly envy—may have to do more than consult with the affected First Nation. He may need to obtain its consent. What he will know for certain before he makes that decision is that he won't know for certain whether he has to consult and obtain consent, or consult, or do something in between consulting and getting consent. He certainly won't know that until long after he has made the decision. All of this, I suggest respectfully and humbly, is—and this is the framework of principles that the Court gave us in *Delgamuukw*—a recipe for bureaucratic, if not economic, paralysis.

As a framework of legal principles that are intended to guide the actions of government, it is entirely impracticable. It is, I suggest, a nightmare. It is no wonder that the Court, which created this framework of principles, has urged the parties to negotiate settlements. But negotiate on what basis? It's worth pausing for a moment to consider the challenge of undertaking principled treaty negotiations when the fundamental principles underlying the rights at issue are in flux, or admittedly uncertain.

An example: in *Delgamuukw*, after 13 years of litigation, the Court refused to embark upon a consideration of the plaintiff's claims to rights of self-government. In the words of the Chief Justice: "The issue of self-government will fall to be determined at trial." A trial which, I remind you, the Court takes pains at several points during the judgment to strongly urge the parties never to participate in, because of course the preferred alternative is negotiation. Well, the fact is that the Gitksan and the Wet'suwet'en claim self-government rights. So what then is the basis upon which they will be negotiated? If there is no existing aboriginal right to self-government—and there *is* no recognized aboriginal right to self-government as yet—then there is nothing, I suggest, that can be recognized or affirmed as such under Section 35(1) of the *Constitution Act, 1982*.

What then is the principled basis upon which governments could negotiate Section 35 self-government rights in a treaty? During legislative debate on the Nishga treaty, which is the experience that I have most recently had as a legislator in British Columbia, the government of British Columbia maintained that anything can be negotiated and given Section 35 protection in a treaty. I say, with respect, that that approach ultimately undermines respect for the idea of aboriginal rights, rather than enhances it. But I do recognize the difficulty of attempting to approach the project of treaty-making from a principled perspective, when the principles are impractical, incomplete, and in flux.

Not surprisingly, therefore, there are a number of difficulties with the current B.C. treaty process. Time permits me to give only one example. The issue is the identification of the proper parties to treaty negotiations.The root of the problem is that when the B.C. treaty process began in 1991, aboriginal groups were able to identify themselves in preparation for negotiations. Anyone could participate by making a claim, and they could ask for anything. There were no preconditions. It was unnecessary, for example, for a claimant group to establish its identity as a First Nation, or that it held aboriginal title or rights. All that was required was a statement of intent to negotiate.

Now, I acknowledge the rationale of this approach. One of the flaws in earlier treaty processes is that the white man, if you will, predetermined the scope of negotiations, and the identity of the claimant group. In effect, this meant that the process and its objectives and results were essentially imposed upon First Nations. Not surprisingly, the arrangements forced upon the signatories to these treaties lacked informed acceptance from the start. Therefore, there is great force in the argument that First Nations need to have meaningful influence over the treaty-negotiation process if they are to have any confidence in its outcome.

At the same time, it makes no sense to conclude treaties if there is doubt whether the groups negotiating are those who possess the aboriginal rights and title, which are the fundamental justification for the whole exercise in the first place. The issue here is what the relationship should be between aboriginal rights and the treaty process. In the context of this specific problem, earlier governments chose not to resolve that issue in the interest of making some progress in the treaty process. The consequence, eight years and millions of dollars later, is that questions are being raised—questions rooted in an analysis of *Delgamuukw*—about the ability of the groups who are at the treaty table in British Columbia to conclude binding agreements that will resolve aboriginal rights and title claims with certainty.

Dateline: *The Interior News*, a newspaper published in Smithers, British Columbia, May 12, 1999. A story under the following headline: *Kitsegucla Chiefs Present Demands to Two Ministers*. As the article indicates, a group of Gitksan hereditary chiefs traveled to Victoria in April. There they met with two cabinet ministers to present a list of demands for local control of forest resources and a sawmill. Vernon Milton, chief Skogmlaha says: "In spite of *Delgamuukw*, a decision that is a year-and-a-half old, there has been no real change in the way the province conducts forestry operations in that region."

Well, taking what he says at face value, I'm tempted to suggest that it's not difficult to see why there has been no real change in forestry operations in British Columbia. No government ministry with responsibility for lands or resources could do the things that the Supreme Court of Canada in *Delgamuukw* has required of it with any kind of responsible efficiency.

So I return to my original question: What did the Court mean when it said that the pathway to reconciliation is negotiated settlements? The unanswered question is whether aboriginal rights and title—that is, the constitutionalized common-law rights, recognized and affirmed under Section 35(1) of the *Constitution Act*—can be practically reconciled with the day-to-day exercise of Crown sovereignty, which is the underpinning of our economy, at least of the economy of British Columbia. Is there not something odd about a judgment which, having expressly set out to clarify legal principles organized around the idea of reconciliation, then concludes by arguing that it is only through negotiated settlements that reconciliation can in fact be achieved? I suggest that this amounts to an admission that the principles at stake, which are purportedly fundamental, are unworkable. And I leave for consideration the question that if the principles at stake are truly unworkable, are they not also ultimately unsound?

Mel Smith

In an earlier paper, Professor Brian Slattery points out that the Supreme Court of Canada's decision in *Delgamuukw* can be looked upon as either a major departure from established legal precedent (what he called the judicial discretion view), or alternatively, as merely the latest manifestation of an ever-evolving view of the common law on the subject of aboriginal rights, a sort of a natural progression. I believe he holds to the latter view. I might be inclined to agree with him if there were case law in recent years to support the view that indeed the law has been evolving over time. But on the subject of aboriginal rights as it relates to land, I can find no case law on the subject. Oh yes, references made oftentimes to the *Guerin* case of 1984, but that was a case involving a breach of fiduciary duty relating to reserve lands. Reference was also made to the 1990 *Sparrow* case, but that is a case involving aboriginal priorities over fishing for food and ceremonial purposes. These are not cases involving aboriginal land rights.

In fact, before *Delgamuukw*, the most recent case on which the Supreme Court of Canada gave judgment involving aboriginal land rights was the *Bear Island* case in Ontario. I'd suggest that to some degree, the *Bear Island* case was to Ontario what the *Delgamuukw* case was to BC. True, there were treaty rights in issue in that case, but the question of aboriginal land rights was also squarely in issue. Both the Supreme Court of Ontario and the Court of Appeal of Ontario ruled against the claim to aboriginal land rights. The Supreme Court of Canada dismissed the appeal in August 1991 in a brief, two-page judgment that supported many of the findings of the trial judge, which in many respects were similar to those of Chief Justice McEachern's findings in *Delgamuukw*. So I fail to see that the case law leading up to *Delgamuukw* gives support for the view that the Supreme Court of Canada decision in that case is merely but a further evolution of the state of the law on aboriginal rights relating to land.

Rather, I see it as a major departure, an audacious departure, from all that has gone before, by a Court that has come under the influence of the report of the *Royal Commission on Aboriginal Peoples*, and of what the Chief Justice refers to in his judgment as the writings of certain academics that he refers to as "the critical literature." Lots of so-called critical literature, lots of reference to the *Royal Commission on Aboriginal Peoples* report—but very little case law or precedents to support the Court's decision.

What has the Court done in this case? I could summarize it in five or six points.

First, as far as British Columbia is concerned, it has drastically undermined the Crown ownership of as much as 94 percent of the province's land mass. In short, I believe the Court has seriously weakened the meaning and scope of the assertion of British sovereignty in 1846 over the territory of what is now British Columbia. Sovereignty was supposed to do two things: establish English law and its institutions in the territory; and place ownership of all the land in territory in the hand of the Crown in right of the colony, and subsequently the province. It seems to me that the Court's decision has potentially seriously weakened both objectives. Sovereignty would not have been threatened if the Court had found that aboriginal title meant what it has traditionally meant until now; i.e. that it is a user right. But the Court has gone much further than this and found aboriginal title to mean an exclusive right which can almost amount to full ownership, save the requirement to hold it collectively and sell it only to the Crown.

Second, the Court has put almost insurmountable hurdles in the way of the provincial government over present and future land resources decisions. Geoff Plant outlined in detail some of those hurdles which have to be faced in the administration of the land laws of the province in the face of the decision of the Supreme Court. And I agree with him 100 percent. The task is absolutely impossible. The Court says there must be a compelling and substantial legislative objective in order to override aboriginal title wherever it exists. The Court acknowledges that the general economic development of the province may in some cases meet that test, without indicating what those cases are. In some cases, the prior aboriginal interest would need to be preserved, perhaps by allowing natives to have rights of co-management over any tenure granted.

On the matter of compelling and substantial legislative objective, I couldn't help but be amused by a throwaway line in the Court's judgment that suggested that sport fishing wouldn't fall into a compelling and substantive legislative objective. Little did the Court know that the sport-fishing industry in British Columbia has about five times the economic impact of the commercial fishery. Talk about being out of touch with the B.C. realities. There is a perfect illustration.

Moreover, the Court in *Delgamuukw* states that the government can only grant a tenure if it consults. In some cases, that may have to amount to aboriginal consent. Which cases? We don't know. And so on it goes.

Third, the decision has supplanted the common law with a new system of law in which equal credence is to be given in aboriginal cases to the "aboriginal perspective."

Fourth, it has replaced the long established rules of evidence in civil cases with two sets of rules now, one for aboriginal cases only.

Fifth, the Court failed to confirm that in constitutional terms the right to make laws in this country is fully vested in either parliament or provincial legislatures.

Finally, almost as an afterthought, the Court gave the final coup-de-grace to British Columbia in holding that lands covered by aboriginal title, wherever they are, are lands reserved for the Indians under Section 91(24) of the *Constitution Act*, and therefore under federal jurisdiction. That seems to mean that the federal government, if it so chose, could legislate a full range of land-use management laws over those parts of British Columbia covered by aboriginal title, wherever those parts may be found to be.

Terry Morley, a respected political scientist at the University of Victoria and a man not noted for hyperbole, says this of the *Delgamuukw* case: "This distant and disdainful Court places the economic prosperity of British Columbia in grave peril. Today, a Court in faraway Ottawa with modes of reason foreign to B.C.'s sensibilities has revived our colonial state, and made itself and its subordinate judges our effective rulers." That this has brought about massive uncertainty in British Columbia is an understatement. This isn't just semantics, or some play on words. The uncertainty created by this case is a reality in British Columbia.

The mining industry has all but left the province of British Columbia. No doubt there are other factors that govern that decision as well, but certainly the *Delgamuukw* case is one prominent factor. The forest industry is in little better shape. *Globe and Mail* columnist Jeffrey Simpson wrote that the forest industry would be foolish to spend another nickel on capital plant in British Columbia. Someone asked yesterday, "Is the Torrens system affected?" Who knows whether we have a good safe holding and marketable title that the land registry office of the province assures to the holder of a fee simple interest in British Columbia? Who knows whether that is still the case in the light of the *Delgamuukw* case?

There are at least three solutions. First, more litigation will be necessary. *Delgamuukw* in a sense decided nothing, but undermined everything. Further litigation will be necessary to clarify concepts raised in that case but not fully and properly dealt with. And a future B.C. government, hopefully, will be more inclined to take more of a stand to protect provincial interests in court than has been the case in the recent past. That might well result in the Court pulling back on some of these issues.

We might also get some elucidation in future cases as to just what to base negotiations upon. It's all very well to talk about negotiation. But on what basis? The Court gave us very little help on that issue. At some stage in future litigation, somebody will point out that the British Columbia government has paid its price to the native people. When we entered Confederation in 1871, we agreed to establish reserves under Section 13 of our Terms of Union. We did that in spades over 50 years. Of the approximately 2,300 reserves in the whole of Canada by 1924, 1,600 were in British Columbia.

Now, I am not an advocate for the native people living on reserves. I think the system has been a miserable failure. The current treaty-making process is only building on what has been 130 years of failure. I am referring to B.C.'s obligations on entering into Canada. We developed differently in B.C. Treaties on the Prairies likewise resulted in the establishment of reserves. We achieved the same result in British Columbia prior to our entry into Confederation, and subsequently by the establishment of 1,600 reserves that set aside areas of settlement and fishing sites for the use and benefit of the native people. Unfortunately, the Supreme Court of Canada totally ignored the historical context of British Columbia in its judgment. An aspect that Chief Justice McEachern spent 84 pages of his judgment dealing with was totally cast aside. No, no, treaty-making. It has to be treaty-making.

I suggest that it will be adjudicated upon by the Supreme Court as to whether we as a province have met our obligation. I don't question for a moment that there is such a thing as aboriginal rights which have to be compensated for. But British Columbia may well have done its job. Yet this background has been totally disregarded thus far both in the courts and in the negotiating process. So more litigation will be necessary.

Land claim negotiations of sorts will no doubt hobble along and continue. That will be the second solution. Yet these two solutions will not be enough. In B.C. alone, 50 treaties are yet to be negotiated. Many other bands are not in the treaty-making process, and they either want to negotiate separately or not at all. Litigation is challenging the process in certain cases. All this would take many years. We cannot wait that long. The uncertainty, and what it is doing to the economy of British Columbia, cannot allow it to wait that long.

So a third element is necessary. That element is appropriate legislation, similar to the situation in Australia. In this respect, Australia is strikingly similar to British Columbia. Australia entered into no treaties with its aboriginal people. In 1992 the High Court ruled that native title existed in Australia, but it soon became apparent that the application of the ruling was not compatible with workable and certain land management, which is just what we are finding in British Columbia. After more than a year of deliberation in Australia, the *Comprehensive Native Title Act* was introduced by Prime Minister Keating and subsequently passed. It endeavours to strike a balance between the rights of the aboriginal people, as found in the *Mabo* decision on the one hand, and workable and certain land management on the other.

We need something similar in the Canadian context. We need a federal statute that decries that the granting of any land tenure by the provincial government shall have the effect of lawfully infringing any aboriginal title over the land area covered by the tenure. By any tenure, I include Crown lands, timber licenses, mineral leases, agricultural leases, grazing permits, and rights of way.

In addition, aboriginal title that could be proved in specific cases would continue to exist over untenured Crown land, but only so long as the land remains untenured. Next, federal legislation would establish a statutory regime to provide fair compensation to any aboriginal group that can establish the loss of aboriginal title over any land included in those tenures, based on a graduating scale of compensation set out in the statute, governed by the nature and extent of the aboriginal interest infringement upon it. Finally, a federal statute would establish a duly qualified special tribunal composed of judges, or people having special knowledge in relation to land management and land assessment, to settle the measure of compensation after a full hearing based on the statutory criteria.

I am well aware that in Canada the situation is different from than Australia in that we have constitutionalized rights under Section 35. The Supreme Court of Canada has made it plain in the *Van der Peet* case that aboriginal title can be the subject of regulation. What I am proposing is a regulatory scheme that does just that. This compensation would be primarily monetary compensation awarded on the basis of strict criteria. It would not be, as it is at the present time in land claim negotiations, whatever the traffic will bear, or go to whoever is the best negotiator, speaks the loudest, and makes the best case. We in Canada should embark upon this more rational approach to dealing with this difficult problem. We must deal fairly, but it must be done in a balanced way. Ultimately, this is a matter for governments to decide.

Questions

Brian Slattery   As I listened to Mel Smith, I was reminded of Burke's reflections on the French Revolution. Burke warns us against losing touch with our past—the customs, practices and accommodations built up over many years, and the fundamental principles that inform them. And he warns us against the spirit of what might be called rationalist constructivism, where we look at the world as if it were invented yesterday, and set out some fundamental principles and attempt to construct everything anew. I wondered in listening to Mel whether he wasn't operating more in the mode of rationalist constructivism, rather than in the spirit that seeks to grapple with our past and take full account of it.

In relation to the question whether *Delgamuukw* is a dangerous innovation or a natural progression in the jurisprudence, I notice that Mel didn't mention the major United States Supreme Court cases from the 1820s and 1830s. Those cases are interesting for Canada because they represent an attempt to grapple with British law and British policy before the American Revolution, which of course was carried over to Canada. I notice that he didn't mention the *St. Catherine's Milling* case, where a majority of judges on the Supreme Court did recognize the existence of aboriginal title. Nor did he mention the Privy Council decision, which recognized a form of aboriginal title under the Royal Proclamation. Nor, very surprisingly, did he mention the *Calder* case, which of course is a British Columbia case, where the majority of Supreme Court judges recognized the existence of aboriginal title. Nor did he mention that in the *Guerin* case, the Supreme Court specifically said that it was dealing with reserve lands, but it was dealing with them on the basis of principles that applied to aboriginal land because, in this respect, there was no difference between the two. Nor did he mention that in the *Bear Island* case, the Supreme Court of Canada specifically said that it was confining its ruling to the question of whether or not there was an adhesion to a treaty, and said it did not necessarily agree with the principles laid down in the lower courts.

If you take full account of that jurisprudence, it's reasonably clear that whether that you like that jurisprudence or not, it's there, and if you follow it through in a reasonable way, *Delgamuukw* can be seen as an evolution, certainly not an innovation. In any case, I think that whatever we may think of that jurisprudence, it is at least at attempt to come to grips with our past. And when I say our past, I don't mean simply the past of us, Canadians viewed at large, but the past that includes the past of aboriginal peoples who were the first people here, and who are a living part of our heritage and tradition.

Mel Smith   Well, I would have dealt with some of these in more detail if I'd had more time. But the Royal Proclamation has been found not to apply to the province of British Columbia, in any event, by innumerable courts including the Supreme Court of Canada in the *Calder* case, and certainly the courts in British Columbia. About the *Calder* case, I don't get as excited about the *Calder* case as those who claim that it's a great move in the direction of aboriginal rights and aboriginal title. That case went through three levels of courts. The Supreme Court of British Columbia threw the case out; the Court of Appeal of British Columbia unanimously, five judges to nothing, threw it out; and the Supreme Court of Canada threw it out. It didn't allow the appeal in the *Calder* case. The question in the *Calder* case was not so much whether aboriginal title was or was not a fact, but whether or not it was extinguished. Three judges said it wasn't extinguished; three judges said it was; and the seventh dismissed the appeal on other grounds.

As far as the US cases are concerned, the US cases have been around for a while. They've been adjudicated upon by the courts in Canada up to now, and for one reason or another largely distinguished from the present context of things.

Finally, the *St. Catherine's* case was very important, I like that case. I think Professor Slattery is right, and maybe I should have made reference to it. Let me just give you one small quote from the *St. Catherine's* case. Justice Taschereau said in that case: "The practice of the crown over the years in dealing with Indian claims did not imply that the Indians had legal title to the land." Taschereau said that to find otherwise would mean: " … that all progress of civilization and development in this country is, and always has been, at the mercy of the Indian race. Some of the writers cited by the appellants, influenced by sentimental and philanthropic considerations, do not hesitate to go as far. But legal and constitutional principles are in direct antagonism with their theories." I think that's an appropriate quote in today's context.

As far as grappling with our past, I'm all for grappling with our past. I think the particular past of British Columbia that I briefly touched upon is something that ought to be taken into careful consideration by the courts. In a sense the negotiating process, and also the Supreme Court of Canada in *Delgamuukw*, proceeded on the basis that there is no past. In that respect, it's faulty.

Kent McNeil   I have a question for Mr. Plant, but before I ask that, I just want to comment on Mr. Smith's response to Professor Slattery's comments. Regarding the *St. Catherine's* case and the judgment of Mr. Justice Taschereau I think one has to look not at that judgment, but the judgment of the Privy Council, the highest court in the British Empire at the time. The Privy Council said that aboriginal title, or Indian title as it called it, is an interest in land other than that of the province. And it said as well that the beneficial interest in aboriginal title lands only becomes available to the province after aboriginal title has been surrendered by a treaty. That was what the highest court said. What Justice Taschereau said really is not very relevant, given that decision.

Secondly, the reason why there is so little case law between *St. Catherine's* and the *Calder* decision is that in 1927 the Parliament of Canada enacted an amendment to the Indian Act, which made it virtually impossible for aboriginal peoples to bring claims before the courts. They could not hire legal counsel, they could not raise money to bring claims. This was done specifically to prevent the aboriginal nations of British Columbia from going to the courts to assert their claims. And I think that's one of the most oppressive pieces of legislation that Canada has ever produced, and I think we should be ashamed.

Then the *Calder* case comes along, and six judges say there is such a thing as aboriginal title in British Columbia. They split fifty-fifty over the issue of the application of the Royal Proclamation. And they also split over the question of extinguishment. Well, in the *Delgamuukw* decision, the issue of extinguishment prior to B.C. joining Confederation is no longer an issue.

So I think one has to take the history as it is, rather than picking out bits of it that just seem to support one's own case.

I also wanted to comment very briefly on the Australian situation and *the Native Title Act* there. That legislation has not produced a solution in Australia. If one thinks that that would be the solution to problems in Canada, I would be quite amazed at that kind of approach. Maybe I should give Mr. Smith a chance to respond to that.

Mel Smith   I referred to Mr. Justice Taschereau in the Supreme Court of Canada in the *St. Catherine's Milling* [case] because I think Professor Slattery made reference to the decision of the Supreme Court of Canada in *St. Catherine's*. I think the legislation that you referred to about outlawing claims is a dark chapter in our history. Fortunately that Act was repealed, I think in 1951. So it was around for about 25 years. I think the *Native Title Act* and the process that has been followed in Australia, from what I understand it, and I don't profess to be an expert on the Australian situation by any means, has been subject to amendment. I believe it's a work in progress.

I believe we have to step out of the box in Canada to deal with this issue, to deal with it fairly, and deal with it expeditiously. We must not think that we're limited in the dealing of it with either just litigation or negotiation. I think we need all the policy tools at our disposal to deal with what is indeed a most difficult and complex question. If they're having difficulties with aspects of the *Native Title Act* in Australia, so be it. But it seems to me, a lot of the secondary and collateral issues can be decided by legislation to make decision-making on the main issues much more easy, and much more expeditious. I don't think we should reject other possibilities of dealing with this issue.

Kent McNeil   My question concerns the example that Geoff Plant gave of the forestry official trying to make a decision about what to do when granting a forestry license, or lease, or whatever. I think one of the problems here is the authority of that official to grant the license in the first place if, in fact, he first comes to the decision that there is aboriginal title. Then he comes to that position and he has to decide with respect to infringement whether there is a valid legislative objective, and whether the fiduciary obligations of the crown are being respected. But I would put it to you that the official actually has no authority to make those kinds of decisions, never even gets to that point unless that official can point to some specific legislation that gives the official the power to make decisions that infringe aboriginal title. And without that specific legislative authority, the official can't do anything further. And the reason for that is that in our constitutional system, our parliamentary system, executive officers cannot make decisions that infringe on people's rights without fair and plain legislative authority to do that. And that's basic to the rule of law in this country. So I just wondered where you would see the authority for that official to make those kinds of decisions, and whether there is any such legislation in British Columbia. I'm not aware of any.

Geoff Plant   Well first of all, let's explore the implications of that helpful piece of insight. The presumption then is that there is probably no provincial official capable of granting a cutting permit in British Columbia, which means that if you thought my scenario was kind of grim one, get ready for the Kent McNeil version of what aboriginal title really means. The scenario I outlined contemplated that a regional manager or a district manager, which are defined terms in the *Forest Act* of British Columbia, would be making the kinds of decisions that they are currently authorized legislatively to make, which include granting cutting permits and related documents.

Now I cannot claim to be an expert on what is becoming a burgeoning jurisprudence around attacking, by way of judicial review, the issuance of tenures under the *Forest Act* of British Columbia, which is a developing body of law. But if the premise in your question is that the Forest Act would not be capable as a matter of law of operating in a way to authorize a delegated official, like a district manager, to have the power to grant a cutting permit which would take effect according to its terms subject to the resolution of the issues that I talked about, then I think you are launching what seems to me to be a more fundamental attack on the ability of the province to regulate and control the management of the public lands. That's an interesting question. Maybe it's just that I'm a bit Pollyanna-ish, but I assume that the courts in *Delgamuukw* and other decisions are not actually intending to completely conceptually destroy the basis of land and resource management by the provincial government. I think they are just trying to constrain it. But I may have misunderstood your question.

Kent McNeil   Well, calling them public lands, I think, begs a question. I think no provincial official would think of granting a forestry permit over lands that are held by fee simple, or over lands that are held by...

Geoff Plant   That's your Section-109 point. Which is to say that so long as what purports to be the Crown lands of British Columbia are in fact lands that are burdened by aboriginal title, then as Mel Smith has indicated, their 91(24) [*Constitution Act, 1867*] lands, at best, are subject to a different set of principles. If that's so, then I think the Supreme Court of Canada has actually rewritten the constitution in a way that's pretty significant. Whether conceptually it represents just a gradual evolution or not is one of those questions that I could tell you people who hold chainsaws and use them for a living in order to feed their families in British Columbia, and there are some thousands of people who do that, would have a hard time wrestling with.

One of the striking things about the Supreme Court of Canada judgment—when you read it divorced from the judgments below, and particularly when you read it divorced from the evidentiary context from which it arises—is that the judgment is remarkably ahistorical from a British Columbia perspective. There is almost nothing of the history of British Columbia in that judgment, and we could argue about what that history should mean. But let me give you in two sentences, one theory. It may be a bad theory, but let me give it to you.

If you had told the Fathers of Confederation—that is, those who negotiated the terms of union on behalf of what was to become the province of British Columbia in 1871—that because there was something called aboriginal title, the province was in fact acquiring no practical ownership of the Crown lands, they would have gone back to the bargaining table. As a reconstruction of what the pact of Confederation was from the province's perspective, that is pre-eminently a position that can only be argued by people who won't look at it through the lens of defending the basic premise upon which British Columbia entered Confederation, which was "give us the lands, because we don't have any money. We need the lands in order to develop an economy."

Kent McNeil: They should have read the Royal Proclamation then.

Converting the Communal Aboriginal Interest into Private Property

Sarnia, Osoyoos, the *Nisga'a* Treaty and Other Recent Developments

JACK WOODWARD

The Communal Aboriginal Interest in Aboriginal Title

Delgamuukw[1] makes it clear that aboriginal title—first described as a "personal and usufructuary right"[2] and more recently as a *sui generis* interest in land "best characterized by its general inalienability, coupled with the fact that the Crown is under an obligation to deal with the land on the Indian's behalf when the interest in surrendered"[3]—is a right to the land itself.[4] Aboriginal title arises from First Nations' possession of lands before the assertion of British sovereignty and crystallized into a burden on the underlying title of the Crown at the time of assertion of sovereignty.[5]

For the purposes of this paper, aboriginal title has the following important attributes:

Notes will be found on pages 101–102.

(1) Aboriginal title is a collective interest in land and not an individual right. It is a collective right to land held by all members of an aboriginal nation. Decisions with respect to that land must be made by that community.[6]

(2) Aboriginal title lands cannot be transferred, sold or surrendered except to the Crown.[7]

(3) Aboriginal title is a right to the land itself.[8]

(4) Aboriginal title is a right to exclusive use and occupation.[9]

(5) Aboriginal title lands have an inherent limit—they cannot be used for purposes that are irreconcilable with the First Nations attachment to the land without surrender.[10]

(6) Unextinguished aboriginal title is constitutionally entrenched.[11]

The first attribute is important in determining *who* can make the decision to modify aboriginal title. The other attributes are important in determining *how* the communal interest in aboriginal title can be modified or converted into private interests.

Who may make the decision to modify the communal interest? (*Sarnia*)

The recent decision in *Sarnia*[12] makes it clear that a fundamental aspect of aboriginal title is that because it is a communal interest, the decision to modify (in this case, surrender) must be made by the collective decision of the community as a whole, in accordance with aboriginal law. *Sarnia* was a claim for the recovery of four square miles in the City of Sarnia which were, by Treaty, formerly part of the Chippewas reserve and which the Band claimed had never been surrendered. The property owners traced their title to a Crown patent issued in 1853. The Band claimed against Canada, Ontario and 2,000 property owners for recovery of the land or alternatively for damages against the Crown. The Court held that the *Royal Proclamation, 1763*[13] continued in effect and that the common law of aboriginal title incorporates the surrender procedures evidenced by Crown practice.[14] A valid surrender, in this case, required that the aboriginal title land be purchased by the Crown at a public meeting of the Indians assembled for that purpose by the Governor or his equivalent.[15] The Court held that "the decision to surrender must be made by the collective decision of the community as a whole, not by some faction of the community or even by a group of chiefs." The "only way to make the surrender and to evidence it is by some public meeting or assembly of Indians held for that purpose."[16] On the particular facts of *Sarnia*, there was no evidence of any community meeting held to consider the surrender. Therefore, Justice Camp-bell found it unnecessary to decide whether the Chippewas of Sarnia had a general practice of collective consensus decision making or ma-jority decision making, either of which attained the status of an internal decision protocol or an aboriginal right in relation to the surrender of aboriginal title.[17] As there was no collective decision of the community to cede aboriginal title to the Crown, the purported surrender was held to be invalid. Thus the Crown patent was invalid and aboriginal title to the land continued to exist.

Sarnia deals with how aboriginal title lands reserved by treaty may be surrendered. The question of who may surrender aboriginal title in reserve lands is more complex. The Court in *Guerin*[18] held that the In-dian interest in reserve lands and unextinguished aboriginal title lands was the same.[19] The question arises whether a band can make the col-lective community decision to surrender aboriginal title in reserve lands. There is no problem with a band effecting a surrender of the ab-original title in reserve lands, where the band is the successor to the ab-original group holding aboriginal title at sovereignty (see note 24). However, where the band is not the successor to the aboriginal group, or is the joint successor with other bands, the situation becomes more complicated, especially in light of the *Osoyoos*[20] case discussed below.

How is Aboriginal title converted into Private Interests? (*Osoyoos*)

To convert aboriginal title lands into fee simple estates, the communal interest in the former must be modified in such a way as to ensure a good title in the latter. Since 1982, the two main ways by which this may be accomplished are by voluntary surrender under the *Indian Act*[21] (subject to the discussion of the *Osoyoos* case below) or by a land claims agreement.[22]

(i)   *Surrender under the Indian Act*

The present *Indian Act* reflects the land surrender procedure first set out in the *Royal Proclamation, 1763*. Reserve land must be surrendered absolutely before it can be sold to non-Indians.[23] Surrenders of reserve land must be made to the Crown, must be assented to by a majority of the electors of the band,[24] and must be accepted by the Governor in Council.[25] As such, it may contain all the essential elements for surren-der of aboriginal title. However, the recent case of *Osoyoos* suggests that a surrender of the reserve interest may not, in all cases, have the effect of modifying aboriginal title in the reserve lands. The majority of the Court in *Osoyoos* seems to suggest that the reserve interest, at least for the purpose of section 35 of the *Indian Act*, may be expropriated without necessarily affecting aboriginal title to these lands.[26] This case concerned whether the Osoyoos Band could tax an irrigation canal right of way expropriated under section 35 of the *Indian Act*. The Court found that an Order in Council, which granted rights of exclusive enjoyment and possession of the right of way, issued pursuant to section 35 of the *Indian Act* operated to extinguish the reserve interest in the lands.[27] The Court suggested that expropriation of the reserve interest did not amount to extinguishment of the aboriginal title.[28] Justice Lambert, dissenting, held that if the Band has aboriginal title to the lands within the geographic boundaries of the reserve (as is the case in most reserves in British Columbia) then section 35 of the *Indian Act* should not be read as extinguishing the reserve interest.[29] He found that the Indian interest in reserve land is an interest that is now described as aboriginal title.[30] It is not difficult to see the anomalies that might arise if *Osoyoos* is extended to the surrender provisions of the *Indian Act*. A band could surrender the reserve interest absolutely, thereby allowing the Crown to create third party interests which may nevertheless still be subject to an existing aboriginal title.

The modified defence of bona fide purchaser for value without notice

In *Sarnia*, the Court held that a Crown grant, to which 2,000 property owners in the City of Sarnia traced their title, was invalid because there had been no extinguishment of the aboriginal title in those lands. However, Justice Campbell held that the treaty rights and aboriginal title in the disputed lands were extinguished by the application of a defence of *bona fide* purchaser for value without notice combined with an equitable limitation period of 60 years. The Court applied the equitable limitation period, in part because the purchasers had occupied the lands for a very long time and had no way of discovering the defect in the original grant, even with due diligence; and because there was a potential adequate remedy against the Crown for damages for breach of fiduciary duty. The Court recognized that "the defence of good faith purchaser for value without notice is a fundamental aspect of our real property regime designed to protect the truly innocent purchaser who buys land without any notice of a potential claim by a previous owner." [31] Thus on the facts of this case, Justice Campbell held that the aboriginal and treaty rights were extinguished in the disputed land at the end of the equitable limitation period and crystallized into a damage claim against the Crown.[32]

Extinguishment by Limitations Acts

Justice Campbell in *Sarnia* held that various federal and provincial statutory limitation periods both pre- and post-Confederation were not applicable to extinguish aboriginal title in lands reserved by Treaty because Parliament had no power to unilaterally extinguish a treaty right, and even if such a power existed it could only extinguish treaty rights, or aboriginal title, if its intention to do so was clear and plain. The Province had no jurisdiction to extinguish title, and section 88 of the *Indian Act* did not incorporate such laws by reference (and because the lands in question were reserved by Treaty the paramountcy set out in section 88 would also operate to render provincial limitations statutes inapplicable).[33]

In *Stoney Creek Indian Band*,[34] Justice Lysyk reached a similar conclusion on the effect of provincial limitation periods. He held that the B.C. *Limitations Act*[35] was constitutionally inapplicable to bar a claim for damages arising out of trespass to reserve lands because the Province was constitutionally incompetent to legislate with respect to the occupancy or possession of reserve lands, and section 88 of the *Indian Act* did not apply to referentially incorporate provincial laws in respect of reserve lands.[36]

The situation with respect to the application of a provincial Limitation Act may be different where the action for recovery of land invalidly surrendered is brought in federal court. In *Apsassin*,[37] the Court held that s. 39 of the *Federal Court Act* (which incorporated applicable provincial limitation periods to claims brought in federal court) operated to bar a claim against the federal Crown for damages for breach of fiduciary duty in relation to the original surrender of *reserve* lands. However, it is important to note that no argument was advanced that s.39 was constitutionally inapplicable to extinguish aboriginal title since the claim was brought prior to the constitutional entrenchment of aboriginal title (and treaty and other rights) through s.35(1) of the *Constitution Act, 1982*.[38]

(ii) Conversion of Aboriginal Title into fee simple estate by land claims agreements (The Nisga'a Treaty)

In areas where aboriginal title has been addressed through land claims agreements, each agreement is unique as to how aboriginal title is treated. Modern treaties have sought to avoid extinguishment language and instead have sought to "modify" aboriginal title in such a way as to achieve the certainty of extinguishment without its political ramifications. The *Nisga'a Final Agreement* (NFA) constitutes the full and final settlement in respect of the aboriginal rights, including aboriginal title, of the Nisga'a Nation.[39] The NFA exhaustively sets out the Nisga'a's s. 35(1) rights. The NFA modifies Nisga'a aboriginal title to a fee simple estate in areas to be known as Nisga'a lands or Nisga'a fee simple lands.[40] The Nisga'a may dispose of the whole of its estate in fee simple to any person.[41] The governance or jurisdictional control of the Nisga'a Lands by the Nisga'a Government does not cease upon the sale of its interest in the land.[42] The Nisga'a Government has the authority to establish its own land title or land registry system.[43] The interests or estates created under the Nisga'a laws in respect of estates or interests that are recognized and permitted by federal or provincial laws of general application will be consistent in respect of those interests or estates with federal and provincial laws of general application, other than the provincial Torrens system and any federal land title or land registry laws.[44] The *NFA* also removes Nisga'a Lands from federal jurisdiction under s. 91(24) of the *Constitution Act, 1867*,[45] and the *Indian Act*. The *Sechelt Agreement-in-Principle*[46] (*Sechelt AIP*) effectively contains the same concepts with respect to aboriginal title lands as evidenced in the *NFA*.

Modification of the aboriginal title interest

The wording of the modification provisions in the *NFA* and the *Sechelt AIP* state that "for greater certainty, aboriginal title will be modified and *continues* as the estate in fee simple" [emphasis mine].[47] There is no express surrender of the aboriginal title; however, the agreement requires the First Nation's free, full, voluntary and fully informed collective intention to consent to the modification of their aboriginal title. Thus aboriginal title is converted into a fee simple estate with respect to the proprietary interest and becomes a treaty right. It would seem that the continuing fee simple aboriginal title can be used for purposes that are irreconcilable with the nature of the First Nation's attachment to the land. This is logically inconsistent as the root of aboriginal title is the First Nation's connection with the land. Thus it might be more appropriate to say that aboriginal title is surrendered and a new treaty right is created which is a fee simple estate.

Potential uncertainty of third party fee simple title

The fee simple estate that the First Nation may grant to a third party may be subject to another First Nation's interest. For example, the Gitanyow assert aboriginal title to lands covered by the *NFA* which may affect any fee simple estates granted by the Nisga'a to third parties. A question arises whether in such a case the Gitanyow could seek recovery of the land in question from the third party. *Delgamuukw* recognized that joint aboriginal title to land is possible and that joint aboriginal title may place inherent limitations on the way in which each First Nation uses their aboriginal title lands.[48] Both the *NFA* and *Sechelt AIP* have identical provisions to deal with this contingency.[49] If it is determined that an aboriginal group other than the Nisga'a Nation have rights under s. 35(1) of the *Constitution Act, 1982* that are adversely affected by a provision of the *NFA*, that provision will cease to operate to the extent that those rights are adversely affected. This may create uncertainty for third party rights.

Treaty Negotiation must be in Good Faith (Luuxhon)

This problem has already surfaced in an action initiated by the Gitanyow alleging that in signing the *NFA* the Crown was not negotiating in good faith with the Gitanyow. In *Delgamuukw*, Chief Justice Lamer stated that "the Crown is under a moral, if not legal, duty to enter into and conduct those negotiations in good faith." [50] Since *Delgamuukw*, the lower courts have recognized the requirement for good faith negotiations where British Columbia and Canada have entered into treaty negotiation with First Nations. In *Luuxhon*,[51] an action was commenced by the Gitanyow Hereditary Chiefs on behalf of the Gitanyow First Nation against Canada and British Columbia. Two questions were posed for the Court: first, whether Canada and British Columbia, having undertaken to negotiate a treaty with the Gitanyow, were fixed with an obligation to negotiate in good faith; and second, whether by signing the *NFA*, and thereby giving the Nisga'a rights to territory subject to a Gitanyow claim to aboriginal title, the Crown had violated their obligation to consult with the Gitanyow in good faith. The Gitanyow First Nation has significant overlap of traditional territory with the Nisga'a and asserts aboriginal rights and title to areas contained in the *NFA*. Justice Williamson proceeded to determine only the first question and did so as a question of law. He held that the Crown has a legal obligation to negotiate treaties in good faith with aboriginal peoples. Further that this obligation applies equally to Canada and the provinces and is rooted in the fiduciary relationship existing between the Crown and aboriginal peoples through s. 35(1) of the *Constitution Act, 1982*. Justice Williamson relied on the judgment of Melvin J. in the *Chemanius* case.[52]

Conclusion

Aboriginal title may be distinct in comparison with traditional common law interests in land, however it is hardly unique when compared with other non-common law interests in land. Non-common law interests in law are recognized in most of the lands formerly constituting the British Empire, particularly the former colonies in Africa and Asia. In the majority of these jurisdictions, the "native" land law (customary law) contains elements very similar to those ascribed to aboriginal title in *Delgamuukw*. Yet in these jurisdictions, customary land law has coexisted with the transplanted English common law and has, in some instances, resulted in the evolution of legal interests in land that contain incidents of both the customary law and the common law. For example, since customary interests in land have been at the centre of Ghanaian land law since colonial times, most transactions in land come into contact with customary law at some point, and the free market economy has adapted to function efficiently. In Canada, as Chief Justice Lamer stated in *Delgamuukw,* the jurisprudence on aboriginal title is somewhat underdeveloped.[53] This is an understatement. The implications of *Sarnia, Osoyoos* and *Luuxhon* for the conversion of the communal interest in aboriginal title lands into private interests are far reaching. As stated above, *Sarnia* held that a Crown grant was not effective to give title where the collective has not effected a valid surrender of aboriginal title. The Court fashioned a modified *bona fide* purchaser without notice defence to deal with the situation of innocent third party purchasers for value with an apparently valid Crown grant. This doctrine may not be readily applicable to modern grants. It would be difficult to argue that private parties do not now have notice of aboriginal title claims in British Columbia. Even private interests on reserve lands may be less certain than previously thought. *Osoyoos,* by suggesting that expropriation of the reserve interest does not necessarily affect the aboriginal title interest in reserve lands, leaves uncertain private interests in these lands. Similarly, title to lands granted by the Nisga'a under the *NFA* to third parties may be problematic. *Luuxhon* raises the problem of overlaps and begs the question of what happens to private rights granted by a collective who may only have joint title to the lands in question.

Notes

1 *Delgamuukw v. British Columbia*, [1997] 3 S.C.R. 1010 [hereinafter *Delgamuukw*].
2 *St. Catherine's Milling and Lumber Co. v. The Queen* (1888), 14 A.C. 46 (P.C.) at 45.
3 *Guerin v. The Queen*, [1984] 2 S.C.R. 335 at 382 [hereinafter *Guerin*].
4 *Delgamuukw, supra* note 1 at para. 140.
5 *Ibid.* at para. 145.
6 *Ibid.* at para. 115.
7 *Ibid.* at para. 113.
8 *Ibid.* at para. 140.
9 *Ibid.* at para. 117.
10 *Ibid.* at para. 128.
11 *Ibid.* at paras. 133, 134.
12 *Chippewas of Sarnia Band v. A.G. (Canada) et al.* (unreported, April 30, 1999) 95-CU-92484 Ont. S.C. [hereinafter *Sarnia*].
13 *Royal Proclamation, 1763*, R.S.C., 1985, App. II, No.1.
14 *Sarnia, supra* note 12 at pp. 84, 98, 101, 116, 122.
15 *Ibid.* at pp. 101,102.
16 *Ibid.* at 86.
17 *Ibid.* at pp. 62, 63.
18 *Guerin, supra* note 3 at 379.
19 *Delgamuukw, supra* note 1 at para. 120.
20 *Osoyoos Indian Band v. The Town of Oliver* (unreported, May 4, 1999) Victoria V03036 (B.C.C.A.) [hereinafter *Osoyoos*].
21 *Indian Act*, R.S.C. 1985, c. I-5 [hereinafter *Indian Act*].
22 It may be that voluntary abandonment of the First Nation's attachment to the land will extinguish aboriginal title but this is beyond the scope of this paper.
23 *Indian Act*, R.S.C. 1985, c. I-5, ss. 37-38.
24 Of note, is *Corbiere v. Canada (Minister of Indian and Northern Affairs)* (unreported, May 20, 1999) File No.: 25708 (S.C.C), which may change the definition of electors in the *Indian Act* to include both on and off-reserve members.
25 *Indian Act*, R.S.C. 1985, c. I-5, s. 39.
26 *Osoyoos, supra* note 20 at para. 85.
27 *Ibid.* at para. 105.
28 *Ibid.* at para 85.
29 *Ibid.* at paras. 33-36.
30 *Ibid.* at para. 34.
31 *Sarnia, supra* note 12 at 228.
32 *Ibid.* at 230.
33 *Ibid.* at 226-227.
34 *Thomas et al. v. Alcan Aluminum*, [1999] 1 C.N.L.R. 92 (B.C.S.C.).
35 *Limitations Act*, R.S.B.C. 1979, c.236.

36 While Justice Lysyk's order has been overturned by the Court of Appeal in *Stoney Creek Indian Band v. Alcan Aluminun Ltd.*, [1999] B.C.J. No. 2169 (QL) on procedural grounds, his reasoning on the ussues was untouched.

37 *Blueberry River Indian Band v. The Queen* [1995] 4 S.C.R. 344.

38 *Constitution Act, 1982*, being Schedule B to the *Canada Act 1982* (U.K.), 1982, c.11.

39 *Agreement between the Government of Canada, the Province of British Columbia and the Nisga'a Nation*, the Nisga'a Final Agreement, initialled August 4, 1998 at c. 2, art. 22 [hereinafter *NFA*].

40 *Ibid.* at c. 2, art. 25 and at c. 3, art. 3.

41 *Ibid.* at c. 3, art. 4.

42 *Ibid.* at c. 3, art. 5.

43 *Ibid.* at c. 11, arts. 46 and 50.

44 *Ibid.* at c. 11, art. 46.

45 *Constitution Act, 1867* (U.K.), 30 & 31 Vict. c. 3.

46 *Agreement-in-Principle between the Government of Canada, the Province of British Columbia and the Sechelt People*, the Sechelt Agreement-in-Principle, dated April 16,1999 [hereinafter Sechelt AIP].

47 *NFA, supra* note 39 at c. 1, art. 24 and Sechelt AIP, *ibid.* at c. 1, art. 1.9.2.

48 *Delgamuukw, supra* note 1 at paras. 158-159.

49 *NFA, supra* note 39 at c. 1, arts. 33-35 and Sechelt AIP, *supra* note 44 at c. 1, art. 1.13.

50 *Delgamuukw, supra* note 1 at para. 186.

51 *Luuxhon v. The Queen* (unreported, March 23, 1999) Vancouver C981165 (B.C.S.C.) [hereinafter *Luuxhon*].

52 *Chemanius First Nation et al. v. B.C. Assets and Lands Corp. et al.* (unreported, January 7, 1999) Victoria 983940 (B.C.S.C.).

53 *Delgamuukw, supra* note 1 at para. 119.

What My Elders Taught Me
Oral Traditions as Evidence in Aboriginal Litigation

ALEXANDER VON GERNET

Introduction

This paper is an effort to share with others some of the wisdom of my elders.[1] When I say "elders" I do not mean my parents, grandparents or other relatives. Nor am I referring to any of my First Nations friends such as the late Chief Jacob Thomas. Rather, I am talking about my academic mentors who used both oral communication and numerous learned treatises to instruct me in the skills of my profession. Among other things, they showed me how archaeological data, written documents, and oral traditions are used in methodological conjunction to illuminate the past. After summarizing what I was taught about oral traditions,[2] I will offer a few observations on the *Delgamuukw* case.

I would like to begin by reviewing some modern perspectives on reconstructing the past in the present. At the risk of obscuring the full range of opinions, I will simplify matters and focus on two rival epistemologies located at the extreme ends of a continuum.

Notes will be found on pages 118–121.

Historical Objectivism

At one end of the spectrum of approaches is an interpretative position known as historical objectivism or positivist history. This position has a commitment to the reality of the past, a belief that there is a single solution or one "true" history, and a tendency to eliminate other possibilities. Its sprawling set of assumptions includes the notion that historical facts are embedded in documents and need only be extracted; hence, there is a focus on the collection and critical analysis of documentary materials to ascertain their origins, date and trustworthiness. There is a sharp separation between fact and fiction. Facts are independent of interpretation. The historian should have an attitude of neutral objectivity and disinterest and should never be an advocate or propagandist. The result is an authoritative, chronologized text about what "actually happened" in the past.[3]

The Postmodernist Critique

Historical objectivism, in various incarnations, has been the dominant paradigm in Western historiography. But it in recent decades it has been challenged as problematic by an intellectual movement loosely organized under the rubric "postmodernism." This alternative position is, in many respects, a type of historical relativism in which interpretation changes in relation to changing circumstances. It is also a type of idealism in which humans are said to adjust not to a world as it really is, but to a world as they imagine it to be. Instead of a single, "true" history, there is pluralism, with multiple locations of historical knowledge. A value-free, empirical, objective history is an impossible ideal: historians can never free themselves from their own biases and all pasts are culturally mediated and socially constructed. Historical works written by "expert" historians; anthropologists and members of other academic guilds are socially constituted as authority and have no privileged claims on universal truth. They are closer to ethnocentric ideology than to scientific objectivity. There is no past to be *re*constructed—only many, equally "true" or equally fictitious pasts to be *con*structed. There are no objective means of distinguishing between truth and falsehood since reality is what each individual believes it to be. As such, postmodernism is primarily a critique of many basic tenets of objectivism and positivism rather than a viable alternative.[4]

The Role of Oral Traditions

Oral traditions have an important role in the contested terrain between historical objectivism and postmodernism. While they have often focused on written documents, historical objectivists have not totally ignored oral sources and have incorporated them into their reconstructions of the past after first subjecting them to varying degrees of scrutiny. In a recent study, I reviewed numerous examples of Aboriginal oral traditions which contained useful facts about remote periods in history, as well as many instances in which scholars employed this evidence in standard historical reconstructions.[5]

Critics of the objectivist approach believe that oral traditions should not be mined for facts to be used as evidence in positivist histories, but should stand on their own as valid alternatives to such histories and regarded as worthy of study in their own right. Postmodernists raise questions about who is empowered or authorized to tell the story about the past, who controls the authentication process, and whose voices are included and whose are excluded or marginalized. Indeed, the term "voice" is prominent in the fashionable language of postmodernist discourse. It is with the "return of voice" that marginalized or minority groups, including Aboriginal peoples, can reclaim the past from "expert" academics, construct their own pasts, assert social power and claim rights. It is argued that oral traditions, in particular, can challenge biased, hegemonic history based on written records; democratize elitist historical disciplines; and give balance to an historical record.[6]

Reputable scholars draw from both ends of the continuum and try to situate their work in a comfortable middle ground. Unfortunately, excessive fidelity to the postmodernist end of the spectrum as well as a number of peculiar misconceptions have fostered untenable generalizations in the academic community, in First Nations political rhetoric and in Aboriginal litigation. I will briefly explore only a few of those generalizations.

Bias

It is frequently suggested that history, as told by outsiders, is inherently biased, politically motivated, and amounts to an assertion of dominance and power over those whose past is being told. The voices of First Nations people are believed to be essential because only they can confront the distorting cultural biases that allegedly inform "expert" views of Aboriginal history. These biases are said to include, for example, the notion that Aboriginal societies were static and without history until after contact with "progressive" European cultures.[7] However, non-Aboriginal archaeologists first corrected this bias by demonstrating that the cultures of First Nations people underwent constant change prior to European contact, challenging the racist attitudes of nineteenth-century evolutionism and outdated ideas of progress.[8] Significantly, the bias was confronted internally, in the absence of trendy postcolonial theory and without recourse to oral traditions or an overt challenge from First Nations people.[9] Clearly, it is not necessary to be an Aboriginal person to identify and overcome distorting biases.

Many also assume that the written record produced by Europeans is inherently biased because it was not produced by Aboriginal people but by strangers who had little understanding of the people they were writing about. How, then, does one explain the fact that written accounts by missionaries, fur traders, soldiers, explorers and other newcomers are commonly used to support Aboriginal claims? Good examples are the records of Hudson's Bay Co. trader William Brown and Peter Ogden which were relied upon by the Gitksan and Wet'suwet'en plaintiffs in the *Delgamuukw* trial to challenge the idea that an Aboriginal land-tenure system developed in response to the European fur trade.[10]

The postmodernists are correct in their observation that Western historical disciplines can become tools for use in the subordination and domination of non-Western peoples. Yet it must be conceded that these same disciplines also become the tools of resistance. Many First Nations people have overcome their long-felt mistrust of Western approaches and have used modern science in research, exhibition and education[11] to challenge other versions of their history,[12] to support Aboriginal rights,[13] or to oppose development on their lands.[14] As one Blackfoot Elder said, archaeology "had done more for the betterment of native peoples than all of the missionary and government agents had ever done." [15] Archaeology is a source of information that is independent of written accounts and can help to ensure that history is not only written by the winners.[16] Critics who charge that Western anthropologists and archaeologists are inherently biased because of their non-Aboriginality, or who argue that their research and findings harm First Nations interests,[17] must also be prepared to explain why it is that archaeological data often provides compelling support *for* Aboriginal claims.[18]

Those First Nations activists who claim that unflattering academic views of their history are the result of Western prejudices are just as likely to accept positive contributions emerging from the research of non-Aboriginal scholars.[19] In many respects, historical objectivism, including the scholarly apparatus that goes with it, has become the dominant posture of modern Aboriginal intellectuals involved in the public representation of their history.[20] Others have been influenced by postmodernist literature and are employing this relatively new Western approach to dismantle colonial thought.[21] Curiously, Aboriginal intellectuals who see the use of oral traditions by Western historians as a form of cultural appropriation have themselves appropriated the discourse of Western postmodernism to make the argument.[22] Many First Nations writers have voluntarily incorporated Western scholarship into their own 'voice,' partly because modern anthropology, history and other disciplines frequently challenge rather than perpetuate the myths used to assert dominance and power over Aboriginal people.[23]

Aboriginal people are humans like everyone else and their voices can be just as self-serving and biased as the writings of non-Aboriginal people. This makes it particularly important that all assertions about the past, whether written or oral, are subjected to scrutiny and are not accepted at face value for any reason, including political expediency or cultural sensitivity. Unlike heritage, which often makes the past an exclusive possession created to protect group interests, history is an open inquiry into any and every past; it is comprehensive, collaborative and open to all.[24] Members of any given culture are not inherently better qualified to give an accurate representation of themselves and their history. No scientific or moral arguments can be advanced for restricting the study of the past to members of the group being investigated, or for giving any group exclusive proprietary rights to its history. On the contrary, the history of any people is greatly enriched because individuals from outside the group study it.[25] Charges of cultural appropriation[26] are often misguided and based on an outdated view of scholarly practice. In my view, James Henderson, a prominent Aboriginal legal scholar, is simply wrong when he alleges that efforts to understand Aboriginal pasts using a foreign world view "is the essence of cognitive imperialism and academic colonization." [27]

There are many reasons why the perspective of the people whose past is being explored must be given serious consideration, but the absence of bias and assurances of accuracy are certainly not among them. Postmodernists agree that voices coming from the inside are not necessarily free from bias. Indeed, most argue that since *all* voices are inherently biased, *all* stories about the past are equally valid alternatives. Despite many attractions, this position also has profound limitations. When taken to its obvious radical conclusion, postmodernism leads to a conundrum. It is a socially constructed Western ideology that cannot present itself as a better alternative to its older competitor without creating a privileged position for itself, thereby undermining its own ideals. It must also dilute its own relativism or be charged with tolerating morally repugnant or socially noxious historical theories. Furthermore, in its extreme form, it offers only a debilitating nihilism that denies the existence of a basis for knowledge and precludes any consensus on what happened in the past. The notion that there is no past to be reconstructed and that all stories are equally true is contrary to common human experience and is rejected by most Aboriginal as well as non-Aboriginal people. More importantly, it is an entirely impractical epistemology when dealing with situations in which decisions about what happened *must* be made.

The Orality-Literacy Continuum

A second problem that deserves attention is the common tendency to dichotomize orality and literacy. While the terms 'oral' and 'orality' have often been contrasted with 'written' and 'literacy,' [28] these seemingly obvious distinctions are rather slippery in practice. [29] Aboriginal cultures have often been characterized as 'oral.' [30] Since it is no longer possible to generalize validly about oral or literate individuals, it would be a mistake to divide entire cultures along these lines. There is now a widespread academic consensus that orality and literacy should not be regarded as a dichotomy. Even literacy may not represent a pole, now that the world has entered an era of 'post-literate' communication. Simply put, orality and literacy are no longer among the reasons for distinguishing between Aboriginal and non-Aboriginal peoples. [31]

It is often forgotten that alphabetic systems are not the only form of writing in Aboriginal North America. [32] Prior to European contact, there were systems of writing without words which constituted a non-alphabetic form of literacy. Since there is nothing inherent in orality that fosters accurate transmission of information, and since the memories of Aboriginal people are no different from those of other humans, it comes as no surprise that First Nations people had *aides-mémoire* such as notched or marked sticks, dendroglyphs, wampum and pictography. The fact that these exist is in and of itself evidence that the people who invented them understood the limitations of memory. They not only illustrate how oral traditions frequently depend on mnemonic cues, but serve to undermine generalizations about how "Canada's First Nations had no written history." [33]

For millennia, Aboriginal people had writing *without* words. Over the course of the last few centuries, many have also written *with* words. This makes for a situation that is far more complex than advocates of a simple orality-literacy dichotomy would have us believe. In some cases, missionaries adapted European languages to indigenous sound systems. In other instances, native speakers modified European writing for their own use. Still others devised and perfected entirely new systems, including syllabaries, ideographic script such as hieroglyphic writing and countless orthographies. [34]

Then there is English—a language that (either through a voluntary strategy of adaptation or, more often, involuntary participation in that catastrophic experiment known as the residential school) has become the lingua franca and the basis of literacy for the majority of First Nations people in Canada. [35] For some peoples, such as the Inuit of the Arctic, English literacy has been a recent development. [36] In other parts of Canada, however, Aboriginal peoples have been speaking and writing in English for more than three centuries. [37] The degree to which written sources have been incorporated into oral documents has often been underestimated. Scholars working in many different countries have noted this phenomenon, known as "feedback." The feedback effect is common in oral traditions related in all but the most remote areas of the world.[38] Throughout the twentieth century, First Nations people have increasingly consulted the corpus of written research in the public domain,[39] while at the same time drawing on their rich inventory of non-recorded oral traditions.

Aboriginal Traditions and Non-Aboriginal Traditions

A third popular but untenable generalization posits a stark distinction between Aboriginal and non-Aboriginal historical traditions. Anthropologists discovered long ago that temporal orientation is, to a certain extent, a cultural construction. The past is not always remembered lineally, sequentially, chronometrically or calendrically. For this reason, history may involve compression or telescoping of time, or may even be conceived of in cyclical terms.[40] Unfortunately, these insights have led to extreme forms of cultural relativism, in which differences are frequently accepted without question. Maurice Bloch recognized this as part of a "recurrent professional malpractice of anthropologists to exaggerate the exotic character of other cultures."[41] Extreme relativism is an exaggeration because if every culture conceived of things in entirely unique ways, no culture but our own would be comprehensible to us. In other words, if members of other cultures really did have entirely different concepts of time and history, we simply could not do what we obviously do, that is communicate with them.[42] Just as ethnocentrism assumes that everyone thinks alike, so too extreme relativism takes it for granted that all cultures are completely different. Frequently, neither position is founded on solid cross-cultural research.

Having examined numerous studies and researched this issue at some length, I have come to the conclusion that the contrast between the two "traditions" or "perspectives" is fraught with oversimplification, generalization, and reductionism. First Nations cultures are rich in their diversity. While it is appropriate to recognize and celebrate differences between these cultures and more recent immigrants, facile dichotomies between linear and cyclic, between an interest in the past and a timeless present, or between a caricatured non-Aboriginal historical tradition and a monolithic Aboriginal historical tradition are overstated and contrary to evidence.[43] In the case of Aboriginal claims, such dichotomies can lead to the type of divisive "us" and "them" mentality that limits intercultural communication and ultimately works against consensus-building.

The Delgamuukw Trial Judgement

Oral traditions figured prominently in the *Delgamuukw* trial.[44] Some judges in earlier years may have been guilty of a mechanical application of the rules of evidence which rendered entire classes of materials inadmissible even before they could be weighed against other evidence. This was not the case here, for many of the oral documents tendered by the Gitksan and Wet'suwet'en, either through *viva voce* testimony or in the form of written affidavits, were admitted as evidence. It was only after careful deliberation that Chief Justice McEachern ultimately gave them little weight. I recently had occasion to study the trial decision and am preparing a detailed analysis; for now, I will confine my remarks to a few observations on the published reaction to the decision.

There is a widespread consensus that in his Reasons for Judgement, Justice McEachern volunteered several unnecessary remarks in a language reminiscent of nineteenth-century evolutionism. His notion that the Aboriginal plaintiffs were a "primitive" people prior to contact with Europeans and his use of Western technologies as a yardstick to measure progress[45] was offensive, not only to the First Nations plaintiffs, but to the many non-Aboriginal academics who have struggled hard to overturn such ethnocentrism. For these reasons, his judgement has been justifiably criticized.[46] It has also been charged that Justice McEachern's treatment of ancient documents is not in accord with mainstream historical scholarship.[47] Since the Chief Justice appears to have adopted the long-abandoned view that such documents largely speak for themselves,[48] this criticism also has validity. Complaints about his treatment of oral traditions, on the other hand, have in my view generally been unfair and off the mark.

Justice McEachern has been chastised for ignoring context in his use of written documents and for failing to subject these sources to further corroboration before giving them probative value.[49] However, in a classic example of dammed if he does and dammed if he doesn't, some of his detractors have accused him of "ethnocentric biases," and an "ethnocentric vanity verging on racism"[50] for applying these same, commonly accepted principles of research to oral documents. There have been complaints that the Judge's narrative "is about the unchallengeable authority of the now familiar 'Western scientific tradition' "[51] and that his dismissal of Aboriginal oral traditions is based on a "naive positivism."[52] Julie Cruikshank criticizes Justice McEachern for being overly concerned about the "reliability" of oral traditions and for seeing the value of oral traditions exclusively in terms of their contribution to a positivistic reconstruction of "what really happened." She advances the thesis that "the court's decision to present and evaluate oral tradition as positivistic, literal evidence for 'history' is both ethnocentric and reductionist, undermining the complex nature of such testimony because it fails to address it on its own terms." She asserts that "there is in anthropology an extensive body of literature which guides scholarly analysis of oral tradition; in that literature, concerns about 'literal truth' of oral traditions were superseded almost a century ago." [53]

Critics like Cruikshank ignore two important facts. First, the Aboriginal plaintiffs *themselves* tendered oral traditions as truthful statements about what really happened and it was they who went to great lengths to establish the historicity and trustworthiness of these traditions by pointing to internal training, testing and validation procedures and by calling on independent, scientific corroboration. It seems clear that many Gitksan believe that their oral traditions come from the past, are about a remote past, and can be used as evidence to construct history in a positivistic sense.[54] More specifically, both lay and expert witnesses relied upon the traditions to prove the connection between precontact and present societies, ancient land use and territorial boundaries.[55] Whatever their usual role within the community, once oral traditions are offered as insights into a past that is contested or otherwise under investigation and are marshaled in support of an argument in a dispute with outsiders, they are either transformed into or specifically generated as *evidence* and can no longer be addressed solely on their own terms.

Secondly, Cruikshank's assertion that anthropologists no longer have an interest in the historicity of oral traditions and no longer seek to extract facts about what "actually" happened in the past represents a rather narrow slice of the range of approaches having currency in the second half of the twentieth century.[56] Cruikshank's antipositivism has by no means superseded other approaches. True, some historians and anthropologists, including myself, have gone beyond what "really happened" and developed an interest in what people believe might have happened. They acknowledge the legitimacy of self-representation and write accounts outlining how a group of people conceive of their histories on their own terms and construct their own historical consciousness within their own frameworks of analysis. Nevertheless, since some oral traditions are demonstrably containers of facts about the past, scholars continue to combine them with other evidence in standard positivist histories.[57]

A careful reading of his Reasons for Judgement suggests that Justice McEachern's critical approach to oral traditions was not stimulated entirely by his personal predilections or the ideology of his profession, but was also inspired by mainstream academic opinion. For instance, he cited a lengthy excerpt from Bruce Trigger's *Time and Traditions*, in which one of the most influential Canadian anthropologists of this century noted that oral traditions are as much about the present as the past, that they are reworked from generation to generation, that they require careful evaluation, and that when used uncritically they can be a source of much confusion.[58] Since this scholar was among the many 'learned authors' who reminded the judge to be cautious,[59] it is unfair to intimate that Justice McEachern's critical approach was not in accord with modern anthropological thinking. Or, as other critics claim, that his approach was generated "exclusively within the framework of western jurisprudence," arose from a "Canadian legal ideology," and conveyed an "orientation lag between current academic approaches and conservative judicial practice."[60] By admitting oral documents into evidence, recognizing that they are not *prima facie* proof of the truth of the facts stated in them, taking note of the context in which they were generated, evaluating them for internal consistency, comparing them with other available evidence, and carefully weighing them, the judge did precisely what his critics suggest he should have done with written documents.[61]

Delgamuukw in the Supreme Court of Canada

Chief Justice Antonio Lamer of the Supreme Court of Canada noted that the *Delgamuukw* appeal raised "an important practical problem relevant to the proof of aboriginal title which is endemic to aboriginal rights litigation generally—the treatment of the oral histories of Canada's aboriginal peoples by the courts."[62] The Court's response to Justice McEachern's decision will undoubtedly influence the way in which lower courts approach Aboriginal oral traditions for many years to come. Although I have studied the decision in considerable detail, I again offer only a few preliminary remarks.

Since the trier of fact is in direct contact with the mass of evidence, the Supreme Court has been reluctant to interfere with the findings of fact made by a trial judge.[63] Indeed, the Court refused to question Justice McEachern's decision to reject the testimony of two anthropologists who served as expert witnesses on behalf of the Aboriginal plaintiffs.[64] However, when it came to the same trial judge's decision to assign little weight to the oral traditions, the Court waived the principle of noninterference and offered a lengthy critique. The Chief Justice argued that such appellate intervention was warranted because the trial judge did not have the benefit of the principles laid down in the *R. v. Van der Peet* case, which instructed courts to appreciate the unique evidentiary difficulties inherent in adjudicating Aboriginal claims and to adopt a special approach that does not undervalue the evidence presented by First Nations people. Since Aboriginal rights are defined by reference to pre-contact practices (or, in the case of title, pre-sovereignty occupation), the Court reasoned that written documents are usually unavailable and oral documents are often "the only record of their past." Hence, the "Aboriginal perspective" must be accorded "due weight" by the courts. The oral evidence given by Aboriginal people must be accommodated and "placed on an equal footing with the types of historical evidence that the courts are familiar with, which largely consists of historical documents." [65]

The Supreme Court agreed with the trial judge that the *adaawk* and *kungax* oral traditions of the Gitksan and Wet'suwet'en people were admissible out of necessity as exceptions to the hearsay rule, but disagreed with his decision not to give them independent weight. The Chief Justice feared that since the deficiencies identified by the trial judge are inherent in all oral traditions (an assumption that is, incidentally, demonstrably false), such traditions would be consistently "undervalued" in Canadian courts. [66] Furthermore, the trial judge apparently erred when he discounted the "recollections of aboriginal life" on the grounds that they did not demonstrate land use beyond 100 years ago; here, Justice McEachern had "expected too much." [67] Finally, the trial judge erred in his treatment of oral documents adduced in the form of territorial affidavits. He should not have rejected them on the grounds that their contents were not known in the general community, that the subject matter was disputed, and that they had been generated in the context of land claims discussions. [68] Since conclusions on issues of fact might have been very different had the trial judge assessed the oral traditions "correctly," the Supreme Court suggested that his factual findings cannot stand and that a new trial was warranted. [69]

The *Delgamuukw* decision is in keeping with a recent trend that has effectively lowered the standard of proof in Aboriginal and treaty rights cases. [70] In my view, the decision is problematic because, while lowering the standard is well intentioned, the rationale for doing so is based on misconceptions that can be traced back to the earlier *Van der Peet* decision.

In *Van Der Peet*, Chief Justice Lamer held that since producing "conclusive" evidence about Aboriginal practices, customs and traditions prior to contact with Europeans is a "next-to impossible task," the evidence relied upon may relate to Aboriginal practices "post-contact," provided these have their "origins pre-contact" or "can be rooted in the pre-contact societies." [71] This is apparently intended to overcome "the evidentiary difficulties in proving a right which originates in times where there were no written records." [72] Such reasoning will appear puzzling to anyone familiar with modern approaches to reconstructing the past.

First, even if it were possible to obtain conclusive evidence about the past, the conclusiveness of such evidence would have nothing to do with whether it relates to pre- or post-contact times. Suggesting that pre-contact evidence is more difficult to obtain than post-contact evidence is indulging in a baseless generality, since there is nothing inherent in the latter evidence that lessens the difficulties. For reasons I need not detail here, the written records generated during the period after European contact and the oral traditions collected in recent times are not necessarily more conclusive than archaeological evidence that serves as the basis of much of our knowledge about pre-contact life. In fact, in many cases, a good argument can be made that the archaeological record (which, after all, was generated by Aboriginal people living at the time), must be preferred over later written and oral records, which can only be projected into the past through inferential argument.[73]

It is of course true that the pre-contact record does not contain all the perishable components of land use and practices, which might form the basis of title and rights. As Justice Mahoney said in *Hamlet of Baker Lake v. Minister of Indian Affairs and Northern Development*, "snow houses leave no ruins."[74] Yet reconstructing pre-contact Aboriginal land use and associated practices such as hunting and fishing is not at all a "next-to-impossible task," particularly with the emergence of archaeozoology, archaeobotany and other specialized fields which have provided valuable insights into subsistence activities. In some instances, extensive knowledge is now available about all the different animal and plant species hunted, fished or collected by a particular Aboriginal group, the time of year during which they inhabited a particular campsite, the amounts of edible meat they obtained, how they butchered and cooked their food and how they disposed of their garbage.[75] In many cases, we are also able to outline, with a reasonable degree of certainty, socio-political systems and even ideology, symbolism and religion.[76] If disputing parties invested as much money in state-of-the-art archaeological fieldwork as they now do on lawyers, they might be surprised at the result.

Secondly, if it is indeed "next-to-impossible" to produce evidence from pre-contact times, how is anyone to overcome the hurdle of demonstrating that the post-contact practices, customs and traditions have their "origins pre-contact" or "can be rooted in the pre-contact societies"? There is no practical way of untying this Gordian knot, although it can be cut by adopting the type of inferential argument known as analogical reasoning. This involves carefully projecting a post-contact known (the source-side of the analogy) back into a pre-contact unknown (the subject side of the analogy). When done properly, this sophisticated method has successful applications.[77] In the hands of the untrained, however, it is prone to misuse and can easily turn into circular reasoning.[78] A skilled ethnohistorian can project written records and oral traditions into the past, but to 'root' a practice in pre-contact times requires at least some independent evidence of the type only archaeology can provide.

The Supreme Court's rationale is at least partly based on a well-known necessity argument that, together with the circumstantial probability of reliability argument, constituted the original common law justification for admitting oral traditions as exceptions to the hearsay rule. The necessity justification seems straightforward enough since there is no dependable way of consulting a witness once he is dead. Resorting to other types of evidence is essential; otherwise a claimant would never be able to prove anything. That this *necessarily* means recourse to oral traditions is, however, an unwarranted assumption. In my experience as an expert witness in numerous Aboriginal litigations from Newfoundland to British Columbia, I have always incorporated oral traditions as part of my evidence whenever they were available. Yet, I have never encountered a case in which oral traditions were absolutely necessary because they were "the only record of their past." On the contrary, in most parts of the country the material date (either European contact or assertion of sovereignty) is beyond the temporal scope of many oral traditions and it usually becomes necessary to tender other evidence.

The Supreme Court's instruction that oral traditions be "placed on an equal footing" with historical documents[79] has already become a source of much confusion and speculation. Does the Court mean that oral traditions be placed on an equal footing because they may contain at least some features of historicity which are *not*, in the Court's words, "tangential to the ultimate purpose of the fact-finding process at trial— the determination of the historical truth"?[80] Does equal footing mean that oral traditions should be subjected to the same rigorous tests routinely conducted by historians on written materials? Or does the Court have in mind something closer to the postmodernist end of the spectrum—perhaps an approach that gives "due weight" to any Aboriginal voice merely because of its Aboriginality and irrespective of whether it is tangential to the task or fails standard tests? Of course, the latter approach risks an imbalance in which oral traditions will be consistently and systematically *over*valued in the courts below because who will dare question an elder? The rejection of McEachern's critical analysis will almost certainly be regarded by some not merely as an effort to level the field or lower the standard, but as an outright abandonment of the rigorous scrutiny that is essential to any fact-finding process. When taken to its logical conclusion this would seem unworkable in conflict resolution and, as others have noted,[81] it would open the way for a radical reinvention of the law itself.[82]

It is unfortunate that the Supreme Court in *Delgamuukw* has perpetuated the untenable orality/literacy and Aboriginal/non-Aboriginal dichotomies, since the net effect has been to isolate oral traditions as an exotic species of evidence. I hasten to add that I do not place the blame on the learned justices but, rather, on the absence at trial of expert witnesses qualified to assess the tendered oral documents, form opinions on their strengths and weaknesses, and demonstrate how these commonly-used sources are best used in methodological conjunction with other evidence.

Conclusions

My elders taught me that a respect for people's beliefs should not preclude scientific inquiry.[83] Furthermore, I learned that reducing all human ideas to a common level conflicts with the fact that our modern scientific understanding, despite all its shortcomings and possibilities for misuse, remains qualitatively different from other belief systems and more closely approximates what is external to the individual.[84] That this understanding emerged from the Western intellectual tradition should not disqualify it as a suitable framework for studying Aboriginal pasts. It has given rise to methods that remain the most comprehensive, inclusive and flexible available.[85] Although it is incapable of arriving at absolute truth, it is a way to knowledge that can be both dependable and reliable.[86] When used as a tool of oppression, a Western approach can do much harm to First Nations people, but when used responsibly and fairly it can serve members of all cultures well. This is particularly true when the rigour of positivism incorporates some of the more important and useful messages of the postmodernist critique.

The relativistic orientation of postmodernism (much like the anthropological cultural relativism from which it is partly derived) leads to a fuller appreciation of First Nations and the ethical and moral principles underlying the actions, beliefs and practices of their members.[87] That complete objectivity is unobtainable is also an important lesson, although it must never become an excuse for abandoning the positivist ideal.

Courts simply do not have the ivory-tower luxury of pronouncing that all stories about the past are socially constituted and equally true. Aboriginal litigations are invariably fact-finding exercises and usually involve making decisions about what actually happened in history. However, while judges may have brilliant legal minds, they often lack the specialized training that is required to reconstruct Aboriginal pasts. Fortunately, there are competent expert witnesses who do have the requisite skills, have spent their lives working with the same types of evidence, and are able to assist courts in their difficult tasks. Since judgements issued by courts impact the lives of many Canadians, it is absolutely essential that decisions be informed by the best research available today.

As a participant in numerous litigations across the country, I have adopted an approach that I believe is most useful in resolving the complex historical issues before the courts. In accord with mainstream scholarship,[88] this approach tries to achieve a rapprochement between various scholarly disciplines and to effect a balance between historical objectivist and postmodernist, or between positivist and relativist positions. It recognizes the legitimacy of self-representation and acknowledges that what people believe about their own past must be respected and receive serious historical consideration. At the same time, it assumes that there was a real past independent of what people presently believe it to be, and that valuable information about that past may be derived from various sources including oral histories and traditions. It accepts that both non-Aboriginal and Aboriginal scholars can be biased, that various pasts can be invented or used for political reasons, and that a completely value-free history is an impossible ideal. Nevertheless, it postulates that the past constrains the way in which modern interpreters can manipulate it for various purposes. While the actual past is beyond retrieval, this must remain the aim. The reconstruction that results may not have a privileged claim on universal 'truth,' but it will have the advantage of being rigorous. The approach rejects the fashionable notion that because Aboriginal oral histories and traditions are not Western, they cannot be assessed using Western methods and should be allowed to escape the type of scrutiny given to other forms of evidence.[89] Ultimately, the perspective is in accord with Bruce Trigger's belief that public wrongs cannot be atoned by abandoning scientific standards in the historical study of relations between Aboriginal and non-Aboriginal people.[90]

Notes

1 This paper is based in part on research conducted while preparing several studies commissioned by the Department of Indian and Northern Affairs (see von Gernet 1996, 1998), as well as on the author's forthcoming book on the use of oral histories and traditions in reconstructing Aboriginal pasts. All references contained in the footnotes are listed alphabetically in the references cited section.

2 I follow the common scholarly practice of distinguishing between oral history and oral tradition. Although the literature is not always consistent, oral histories are most often defined as recollections of individuals who were eyewitnesses or had personal experience with events occurring within their lifetime. Oral traditions, on the other hand, are oral narratives about past events transmitted by word of mouth over at least a generation.

3 Carr 1961: 5-7; Fogelson 1989: 135; Hedican 1995: 25-29; Kellner 1975: 291; Krech 1991: 351-352; Lowenthal 1996: 106-111; Miller 1992b: 56; Novick 1988: 1-2; Tough 1990: 6.

4 Cohen 1994: 4, 241; Cruikshank 1994a: 162-163; Culhane 1992: 70; Fienup-Riordan 1988; Fogelson 1989: 135, 138; Grace 1998; Hill 1988: 3; Krech 1991: 352; Novick 1988: 3, 16-17, 523; Tough 1990: 6-7; Trigger 1995: 319-321; 1998: 5-6, 15.

5 Von Gernet 1996.

6 Cohen 1994: 79; Cruikshank 1988: 198; 1992a: 33; 1992b: 8; 1994a: 147-148; 1994b: 403, 417; Culhane 1992: 68; Finnegan 1992: 48; Fisher 1992: 46-47; Fortune 1993; Kew 1994: 83, 92; McDonald et al. 1991: 75; Moss and Mazikana 1986: 19, 73; Perdue 1980: xix; Quintana 1992: 86; Reimer 1981: 30-31; 1984: 2; Seligman 1989: 176-177; Thompson 1988: 5-6; Treaty 7 Elders 1996: 327-329; Trigger 1998: 15; cf. O'Farrell 1979: 5.

7 Fortune 1993: 92; Gisday Wa and Delgamuukw 1988: 37; Henderson 1997: 21-23.

8 Pryce 1992: 38; Trigger 1980; 1989; 1995: 324; 1998: 22-23.

9 Trigger 1998: 22-23.

10 Gisday Wa and Delgamuukw 1988: 39-40; Ray 1990: 15-19; 1991.

11 Anawak 1989: 48-49; Bielawski 1989: 231-232; Cruikshank 1992b: 9.

12 McDonald et al. 1991: 77.

13 Sioui 1992: 82-89.

14 Wickwire 1991: 53-54, 69.

15 quoted in Fox 1989: 31.

16 Gathercole 1990: 1; Rubertone 1989: 32, 37-43.

17 e.g., Callison 1995: 168; Deloria 1995.

18 Devine 1991: 16.

19 Trigger 1982: 7.

20 Ciborski 1990: 244; von Gernet 1995: 123.

21 e.g., Henderson 1995: 207; 1997: 23.

22 e.g., Callison 1995.

23 At the same time, this Western scholarship is also engaged in debunking tenacious myths entertained by some Aboriginal people. These include the

idea that Indians did not practice scalping until after Europeans taught them how, as well as the notion that the United States Constitution was closely patterned on the League of the Iroquois (Axtell 1988: 252; Tooker 1988).

24 Lowenthal 1996: 119-120, 128-129; Washburn 1987: 95-96.

25 Trigger 1982: 8.

26 Callison 1995.

27 Henderson 1997: 23. This is not to say that the reconstructions of outsiders are always more accurate. In fact, some local histories told by First Nations people have been shown to be more accurate than those offered by their non-Aboriginal neighbours (Meighan 1960: 60).

28 e.g., Ong 1982.

29 Finnegan 1992: 5-6, 50.

30 See, for example, Gisday Wa and Delgamuukw (1988: 33). They are also commonly regarded as 'preliterate' (e.g., Gover and Macaulay 1996: 60), although this term is fraught with an implicit technological determinism and evolutionary connotation (Chamberlin 1997: 8; McRanor 1997: 81-82).

31 Battiste 1984: 37-39; Edwards and Sienkewicz 1990: 6, 215; Finnegan 1992: 141; Goody 1987: xii-xiv; Heath 1984: 54; Pomedli 1992: 335-336; Pylypchuk 1991: 55-56; Sherzer and Woodbury 1987: 9-10; Tannen 1982a: 3; 1982b; Urion 1991: 6-7.

32 Battiste 1984: 28-31; Daly 1993: 223; Vastokas 1996: 57; Walker 1981.

33 McLeod 1992: 1279.

34 Battiste 1984; Walker 1981.

35 Miller 1996.

36 Petrone 1988: xi-xiii; see also Moses and Goldie 1998.

37 Petrone 1983: vii, 169.

38 Cohen 1994: 230; Henige 1974: 96-103; 1982: 81-83; Sturtevant 1966: 31-32; Vansina 1985: 31, 156-157; von Gernet 1995: 120-123.

39 Spurling 1988: 74; Sturtevant 1966: 31-32; Trigger 1985: 167; von Gernet 1994b: 12-13.

40 Allen and Montell 1981: 25-26; Fontana 1969: 370; Fortune 1993: 90; Hallowell 1937: 652, 665-666; Henderson 1995: 223-224; Henige 1974: 2, 14; McClellan 1970: 116, 118; Mills 1994: 30; Morantz 1984: 174; Ratelle 1992: 4; Stone 1993: 3, 63-72; Sypher et al. 1994: 54; Vansina 1985: 173.

41 Bloch 1977: 285.

42 Bloch 1977: 283; Hedican 1995: 28.

43 Layton 1989: 4; Williams and Mununggurr 1989: 73.

44 The disputing parties and the judge subsumed under the rubric 'oral histories' a number of different oral documents which, according to the definitions given *supra*, are more properly characterized as oral traditions, since they depend on the intergenerational transmission of successive memories.

45 McEachern 1991: 208, 221, 222.

46 Asch 1992; Asch and Bell 1994; Burns 1992; Cassidy 1992; Cruikshank 1992a; 1994b: 411-413; Culhane 1992; Daly and Mills 1993; Fisher 1992; Fortune 1993; Foster 1992; Frideres 1998: 67; George 1992; Gover and Macaulay 1996; Jeffrey 1992; McLeod 1992: 1282-1283; Miller 1992a; 1992b; Mills 1994: 3-33, 177-187; 1995; Monet and Skanu'u 1992; Pylypchuk 1991:

72-73; Ray 1990; 1991; Ridington 1992a; 1992b; Schwartz 1992; Slattery 1992; Sterritt 1992; Stone 1993: 122-143; Storrow and Bryant 1992; Tennant 1992; Wetzel 1995: 85-86; Wilson 1992; Wilson-Kenni 1992.

47 Fisher 1992; Fortune 1993; Miller 1992a: 6; 1992b.

48 McEachern 1991: 251.

49 Asch and Bell 1994: 514-515, 537; Culhane 1992: 78; Fisher 1992: 44, 46-47; Fortune 1993: 101-102.

50 McLeod 1992: 1283-1284.

51 Fortune 1993: 114.

52 Miller 1992b: 55-56, 62.

53 Cruikshank 1992a: 26, 37, 38.

54 Anonymous 1992; Asch and Bell 1994: 542; Cassidy 1992: 6-7; Culhane 1992: 68; Fortune 1993: 95; Gisday Wa and Delgamuukw 1988: 26-27, 34-36; Jeffrey 1992: 58; Joseph 1994: ix; McEachern 1991: 243, 258-259, 263-270, 272; McLeod 1992: 1288; McRanor 1997: 69; Mills 1994: 17-18, 74; Monet and Skanu'u 1992: 3, 30, 32, 36, 38, 92, 110, 139; Ray 1990: 14; Stone 1993: 127-129; 137-138.

55 McEachern 1991: 243-245,252, 258.

56 Brown 1991; Harris 1968; Krech 1991; Layton 1989; Trigger 1989; Vansina 1985.

57 For a brief review see von Gernet 1996.

58 McEachern 1991: 246.

59 McEachern 1991: 259.

60 Asch and Bell 1994: 505; Cruikshank 1992a: 40; Stone 1993: 122.

61 Culhane 1992: 78; Fisher 1992: 44, 46; Fortune 1993: 102. Critics who, because of strong commitments to a postmodernist relativism, decry the tendency of Canadian courts to apply Western principles of rigorous scholarship to Aboriginal oral documents, offer little in the way of alternatives. Joel Fortune, for example, conveniently resorts to the well-worn excuse that this is "beyond the scope" of his commentary (Fortune 1993: 107).

62 Lamer et al.1997: 1027.

63 Lamer et al. 1997: 1064-1065, 1070.

64 Lamer et al. 1997: 1071.

65 Lamer et al. 1997: 1065-1077.

66 Lamer et al. 1997: 1072-1074.

67 Lamer et al. 1997: 1075-1076.

68 Lamer et al. 1997: 1076-1078.

69 Lamer et al. 1997: 1079.

70 Gover and Macaulay 1996: 56-59.

71 Lamer et al. 1996: 205.

72 Lamer et al. 1996: 207.

73 Unlike oral documents, which because they are generated in the present can raise suspicions about their pastness, the antiquity of the archaeological record is generally indisputable.

74 Gover and Macaulay 1996: 48, 58.

75 e.g., von Gernet 1992b.

76 von Gernet 1992a; 1993. Aboriginal religious beliefs can also be reconstructed with a tolerable degree of certainty from written records produced by Europeans shortly after first contact (e.g., von Gernet 1994a).

77 e.g., von Gernet 1993.

78 It is, for example, inappropriate to argue that a post-contact practice has an origin pre-contact and at the same time infer the pre-contact practice solely from post-contact evidence.

79 Lamer et al.1997: 1069.

80 Lamer et al.1997: 1068-1069.

81 Fortune 1993: 95-96.

82 It does not appear that the Supreme Court is ready for such a reinvention; as the Chief Justice says, the accommodation that accords due weight to the perspective of Aboriginal peoples, must be done in a manner which "does not strain" the Canadian legal structure (Lamer et al. 1997: 1066).

83 Fontana 1969: 366-370; Sturtevant 1966: 22-23; Trigger 1982: 6; Washburn 1987; Wiget 1982: 181-182.

84 Trigger 1995: 323.

85 Axtell 1997: 23.

86 Feder 1990: 12.

87 Hedican 1995: 26.

88 Krech 1991: 352.

89 Wilson 1997.

90 Trigger 1982: 8.

References

Allen, Barbara, and William L. Montell (1981). *From Memory to History: Using Oral Sources in Local Historical Research*. American Association for State and Local History, Nashville, Tennessee.

Anawak, Jack (1989). Inuit Perceptions of the Past. In *Who Needs the Past? Indigenous Values and Archaeology*, edited by R. Layton, pp. 45-50. Unwin Hyman, London.

Anonymous (1992). Science Supports Ancient Legends. *National Geographic* 181(3): Geographica.

Asch, Michael (1992). Errors in *Delgamuukw*: An Anthropological Perspective. In *Aboriginal Title in British Columbia: Delgamuukw v. The Queen*, edited by F. Cassidy, pp. 221-243. Oolichan and Institute for Research on Public Policy, Lantzville, B.C. and Montreal, P.Q.

Asch, Michael, and Catherine Bell (1994). Definition and Interpretation of Fact in Canadian Aboriginal Title Litigation: An Analysis of *Delgamuukw*. *Queen's Law Journal* 19: 503-550.

Axtell, James (1988). *After Columbus: Essays in the Ethnohistory of Colonial North America*. Oxford University Press, Oxford.

Axtell, James (1997). The Ethnohistory of Native America. In *Rethinking American Indian History*, edited by Donald L. Fixico, pp. 11-27. University of New Mexico Press, Albuquerque.

Battiste, Marie Ann (1984). *An Historical Investigation of the Social and Cultural Consequences of Micmac Literacy.* Unpublished Ed.D. Dissertation, School of Education, Stanford University.

Bielawski, Ellen (1989). Dual Perceptions of the Past: Archaeology and Inuit Culture. In *Conflict in the Archaeology of Living Traditions*, edited by Robert Layton, pp. 228-236. Unwin Hyman, London.

Bloch, Maurice (1977). The Past and the Present in the Present. *Man* 12(2): 278-292.

Brown, Donald E. (1991). *Human Universals.* McGraw-Hill, New York.

Burns, Peter T. (1992). Delgamuukw: A Summary of the Judgement. In *Aboriginal Title in British Columbia: Delgamuukw v. The Queen*, edited by Frank Cassidy, pp. 21-34. Oolichan Books and The Institute for Research on Public Policy, Lantzville, B.C. and Montreal, P.Q.

Callison, Cynthia (1995). Appropriation of Aboriginal Oral Traditions. *University of British Columbia Law Review* Special Issue: 165-181.

Carr, Edward H. (1961). *What is History?* Vintage, New York.

Cassidy, Frank (editor) (1992). Rethinking British Columbia: The Challenge of *Delgamuukw*. In *Aboriginal Title in British Columbia: Delgamuukw v. The Queen*, edited by Frank Cassidy, pp. 5-17. Oolichan Books and The Institute for Research on Public Policy, Lantzville, B.C. and Montreal, P.Q.

Chamberlin, J. Edward (1997). Culture and Anarchy in Indian Country. In *Aboriginal and Treaty Rights in Canada: Essays in Law, Equality, and Respect for Difference*, edited by Michael Asch, pp. 3-37. UBC Press, Vancouver.

Ciborski, Sara (1990). *Culture and Power: The Emergence and Politics of Akwesasne Mohawk Traditionalism.* Ph.D. Dissertation, Department of Anthropology, University at Albany, State University of New York, Albany, New York.

Cohen, David W. (1994). *The Combing of History.* Cambridge University Press, Cambridge.

Cruikshank, Julie (1988). Myth and Tradition as Narrative Framework: Oral Histories from Northern Canada. *International Journal of Oral History* 9(3): 198-214.

——— (1992a). Invention of Anthropology in British Columbia's Supreme Court: Oral Tradition as Evidence in *Delgamuukw v. B.C. BC Studies* 95: 25-42.

——— (1992b). Oral Tradition and Material Culture. *Anthropology Today* 8(3): 5-9.

——— (1994a). Claiming Legitimacy: Prophecy Narratives From Northern Aboriginal Women. *American Indian Quarterly* 18(2): 147-167.

——— (1994b). Oral Tradition and Oral History: Reviewing Some Issues. *The Canadian Historical Review* 75(3): 403-418.

Culhane, Dara (1992). Adding Insult to Injury: Her Majesty's Loyal Anthropologist. *BC Studies* 95: 66-92.

Daly, Richard (1993). Writing on the Landscape: Protoliteracy and Psychic Travel in Oral Cultures. In *They Write Their Dream on the Rock Forever: Rock Writings of the Stein River Valley of British Columbia*, by Annie York, Richard Daly and Chris Arnett, pp. 223-260. Talonbooks, Vancouver.

Daly, Richard, and Antonia Mills (1993). Ethics and Objectivity: AAA Principles of Responsibility Discredit Testimony. *Anthropology Newsletter* 34(8): 1,6.

Deloria, Vine, Jr. (1995). *Red Earth, White Lies: Native Americans and the Myth of Scientific Fact.* Scribner, New York.

Devine, Heather (1991). The Role of Archaeology in Teaching the Native Past: Ideology or Pedagogy? *Canadian Journal of Native Education* 18(1): 11-22.

Edwards, Viv, and Thomas J. Sienkewicz (1990). *Oral Cultures Past and Present.* Basil Blackwell, Cambridge, Massachusetts.

Feder, Kenneth L. (1990). *Frauds, Myths, and Mysteries: Science and Pseudoscience in Archaeology.* Mayfield, Mountainview, California.

Fienup-Riordan, Ann (1988). Robert Redford, Apanuugpak, and the Invention of Tradition. *American Ethnologist* 15: 442-455.

Finnegan, Ruth (1992). *Oral Traditions and the Verbal Arts: A Guide to Research Practices.* Routledge, London.

Fisher, Robin (1992). Judging History: Reflections on the Reasons for Judgment in *Delgamuukw v. B.C. BC Studies* 95: 43-54.

Fogelson, Raymond D. (1989). The Ethnohistory of Events and Nonevents. *Ethnohistory* 36: 133-147.

Fontana, Bernard L. (1969). American Indian Oral History: An Anthropologist's Note. *History and Theory* 8: 366-370.

Fortune, Joel L. (1993). Construing *Delgamuukw*: Legal Arguments, Historical Argumentation, and the Philosophy of History. *University of Toronto Faculty of Law Review* 51(1): 80-117.

Foster, Hamar (1992). It Goes Without Saying: The Doctrine of Extinguishment by Implication in Delgamuukw. In *Aboriginal Title in British Columbia: Delgamuukw v. The Queen*, edited by Frank Cassidy, pp. 133-160. Oolichan Books and The Institute for Research on Public Policy, Lantzville, B.C. and Montreal, P.Q.

Fox, W.A. (1989). Native Archaeology in Ontario: A Status Report. *Arch Notes* 89(6): 30-31.

Frideres, James S. (1998). *Aboriginal Peoples in Canada: Contemporary Conflicts.* 5th Edition. Prentice Hall Allyn and Bacon, Scarborough, Ontario.

Gathercole, Peter (1990). Introduction. In *The Politics of the Past*, edited by Peter Gathercole and David Lowenthal, pp. 1-4. Unwin Hyman, London.

George, Herb (Satsan) (1992). The Fire Within Us. In *Aboriginal Title in British Columbia: Delgamuukw v. The Queen*, edited by Frank Cassidy, pp. 53-57. Oolichan Books and The Institute for Research on Public Policy, Lantzville, B.C. and Montreal, P.Q.

Gisday Wa and Delgam uukw (1988). The Address of the Gitksan and Wet'suwet'en Hereditary Chiefs to Chief Justice McEachern of the Supreme Court of British Columbia. [1988] 1 *Canadian Native Law Reporter* at pp. 17-72.

Goody, Jack (1987). *The Interface Between the Written and the Oral.* Cambridge University Press, Cambridge.

Gover, Brian J., and Mary L. Macaulay (1996). "Snow Houses Leave No Ruins": Unique Evidence Issues in Aboriginal and Treaty Rights Cases. *Saskatchewan Law Review* 60: 48-89.

Grace, Damian (1998). A Strange Outbreak of Rocks in the Head. *The Sydney Morning Herald*, January 21, p. 13.

Hallowell, A. Irving (1937). Temporal Orientation in Western Civilization and in a Pre-Literate Society. *American Anthropologist* 39: 647-670.

Harris,Marvin (1968). *The Rise of Anthropological Theory*. Thomas Y. Crowell, New York.

Heath, Shirley B. (1984). Oral and Literate Traditions. *International Social Science Journal* 36(1): 41-57.

Hedican, Edward J. (1995). *Applied Anthropology in Canada: Understanding Aboriginal Issues*. University of Toronto Press, Toronto.

Henderson, James (Sákéj) Youngblood (1995). Míkmaw Tenure in Atlantic Canada. *Dalhousie Law Journal* 18: 196-294.

——— (1997). *The Míkmaw Concordat*. Fernwood, Halifax.

Henige, David (1974). *The Chronology of Oral Tradition: Quest for a Chimera*. Clarendon Press, Oxford.

——— (1982). *Oral Historiography*. Longman, London.

Hill, Jonathan D. (1988). Myth and History. In *Rethinking History and Myth: Indigenous South American Perspectives on the Past*, edited by Jonathan D. Hill, pp. 1-17. University of Illinois Press, Urbana.

Jeffrey, Alice (Miluulak) (1992). Remove Not the Landmark. In *Aboriginal Title in British Columbia: Delgamuukw v. The Queen*, edited by Frank Cassidy, pp. 58-61. Oolichan Books and The Institute for Research on Public Policy, Lantzville, B.C. and Montreal, P.Q.

Kellner, Hans D. (1975). Time Out: The Discontinuity of Historical Consciousness. *History and Theory* 14(3): 275-296.

Kew, Michael (1994). Anthropology and First Nations in British Columbia. *BC Studies* 100: 78-105.

Krech, Shepard III (1991). The State of Ethnohistory. *Annual Review of Anthropology* 20: 345-375.

Lamer, C.J. et al. (Supreme Court of Canada) (1996). Dorothy Marie Van der Peet (Appellant) v. Her Majesty the Queen (Respondent) and the Attorney General of Quebec et al. (Interveners). [1996] 4 *Canadian Native Law Reporter* at pp. 117-286.

——— (1997). Delgamuukw v. British Columbia. [1997] 3 *S.C.R.* at pp. 1010-1141.

Layton, Robert (1989). Introduction: Who Needs the Past? In *Who Needs the Past? Indigenous Values and Archaeology*, edited by R. Layton, pp. 1-20. Unwin Hyman, London.

Lowenthal, David (1996). *Possessed by the Past: The Heritage Crusade and the Spoils of History*. Free Press, New York.

McClellan, Catharine (1970). Indian Stories About the First Whites in Northwestern America. In *Ethnohistory in Southwestern Alaska and the Southern Yukon*, edited by Margaret Lantis, pp. 103-133. University Press of Kentucky, Lexington, Kentucky.

McDonald, J. Douglas, Larry J. Zimmerman, A.L. McDonald, William Tall Bull, and Ted Rising Sun (1991). The Northern Cheyenne Outbreak of 1879: Using Oral History and Archaeology as Tools of Resistance. In: *The Archae-*

ology of Inequality, edited by Randall H. McGuire and Robert Paynter, ed., pp. 64-78. Blackwell, Cambridge, Massachusetts.

McEachern, C.J.B.C. (British Columbia Supreme Court) (1991). Delgamuukw et al. v. The Queen in right of British Columbia et al. 79 *D.L.R. [Dominion Law Reports]* (4th): 185-640.

McLeod, Clay (1992). The Oral Histories of Canada's Northern People, Anglo-Canadian Evidence Law, and Canada's Fiduciary Duty to First Nations: Breaking Down the Barriers of the Past. *Alberta Law Review* 30(4): 1276-1290.

McRanor, Shauna (1997). Maintaining the Reliability of Aboriginal Oral Records and Their Material Manifestations: Implications for Archival Practice. *Archivaria* 43: 64-88.

Meighan, Clement W. (1960). More on Folk Traditions. *Journal of American Folklore* 73: 59-60.

Miller, Bruce G. (1992a). Introduction [to Theme Issue on Anthropology and History in the Courts]. *BC Studies* 95: 3-6.

――――― (1992b). Common Sense and Plain Language. *BC Studies* 95: 55-65.

Miller, J.R. (1996). *Shingwauk's Vision: A History of Native Residential Schools.* University of Toronto Press, Toronto.

Mills, Antonia (1994). *Eagle Down is our Law: Witsuwit'en Law, Feasts, and Land Claims.* University of British Columbia Press, Vancouver.

――――― (1995). Cultural Contrast: The British Columbia Court's Evaluation of the Gitksan-Wet'suwet'en and Their Own Sense of Self-Worth as Revealed in Cases of Reported Reincarnation. *BC Studies* 104: 149-172.

Monet, Don, and Skanu'u (Ardythe Wilson) (1992). *Colonialism on Trial: Indigenous Land Rights and the Gitksan and Wet'suwet'en Sovereignty Case.* New Society, Philadelphia, PA and Gabriola Island, B.C.

Morantz, Toby (1984). Oral and Recorded History in James Bay. In *Papers of the Fifteenth Algonquian Conference,* edited by William Cowan, pp. 171-191. Carleton University, Ottawa.

Moses, Daniel David, and Terry Goldie (editors) (1998). *An Anthology of Canadian Native Literature in English.* 2nd Edition. Oxford University Press, Toronto.

Moss, William W, and Peter C. Mazikana (1986). *Archives, Oral History and Oral Tradition: A RAMP Study.* United Nations Educational Scientific and Cultural Organization, Paris.

Novick, Peter (1988). *That Noble Dream: The "Objectivity Question" and the American Historical Profession.* Cambridge University Press, Cambridge.

O'Farrell, Patrick (1979). Oral History: Facts and Fiction. *Quadrant* 148: 4-8.

Ong, Walter J. (1982). *Orality and Literacy: The Technologizing of the Word.* Methuen, London.

Perdue, Theda (1980). *Nations Remembered: An Oral History of the Five Civilized Tribes, 1865-1907.* Greenwood Press, Westport, Connecticut.

Petrone, Penny (editor) (1983). *First People, First Voices.* University of Toronto Press, Toronto.

Petrone, Penny (editor) (1988). *Northern Voices: Inuit Writing in English.* University of Toronto Press, Toronto.

Pomedli, Michael M. (1992). Orality in Early Greek and Cree Traditions. In *Papers of the Twenty-Third Algonquian Conference*, edited by William Cowan, pp. 334-343.

Pryce, Paula (1992). The Manipulation of Culture and History: A Critique of Two Expert Witnesses. *Native Studies Review* 8(1): 35-46.

Pylypchuk, Mary Anne (1991). The Value of Aboriginal Records as Legal Evidence in Canada: An Examination of Sources. *Archivaria* 32: 51-77.

Quintana, Antonio G. (1992). The Archivist and Oral Sources. In *Documents that Move and Speak: Audiovisual Archives in the New Information Age*, pp. 84-89. K.G. Saur, München.

Ratelle, Maurice (1992). *Le "Two Row Wampum" ou Les voies parallèles*. Québec, Ministère de l'Énergie et des ressources, Direction des Affaires Autochtones. Québec City.

Ray, Arthur J. (1990). Creating the Image of the Savage in Defence of the Crown: The Ethnohistorian in Court. *Native Studies Review* 6(2): 13-29.

———— (1991). Fur Trade History and the Gitksan-Wet'suwet'en Comprehensive Claim: Men of Property and the Exercise of Title. In *Aboriginal Resource Use in Canada: Historical and Legal Aspects*, edited by Kerry Abel and Jean Friesen, pp. 301-315. University of Manitoba Press, Winnipeg.

Reimer, Derek (1981). Oral History and Archives: The Case in Favor. *Canadian Oral History Association Journal* 5: 30-33.

Reimer, Derek (editor) (1984). *Voices: A Guide to Oral History*. Provincial Archives of British Columbia, Victoria, B.C.

Ridington, Robin (1992a). Fieldwork in Courtroom 53: A Witness to *Delgamuukw* v. B.C. *BC Studies* 95: 12-24.

———— (1992b). Fieldwork in Courtroom 53: A Witness to *Delgamuukw*. In *Aboriginal Title in British Columbia: Delgamuukw v. The Queen*, edited by F. Cassidy, pp.206-220. Oolichan and Institute for Research on Public Policy, Lantzville, B.C. and Montreal, P.Q.

Rubertone, Patricia E. (1989). Archaeology, Colonialism and 17th-century Native America: Towards an Alternative Interpretation. In *Conflict in the Archaeology of Living Traditions*, edited by Robert Layton, pp. 32-44. Unwin Hyman, London.

Schwartz, Bryan (1992). "The General Sense of Things: " Delgamuuk[w] and the Courts. In *Aboriginal Title in British Columbia: Delgamuukw v. The Queen*, edited by Frank Cassidy, pp. 161-177. Oolichan Books and The Institute for Research on Public Policy, Lantzville, B.C. and Montreal, P.Q.

Seligman, Haim (1989). Is Oral History a Valid Research Instrument? *International Journal of Oral History* 10(3): 175-182.

Sherzer, Joel and Anthony C. Woodbury (1987). Introduction In: *Native American Discourse: Poetics and Rhetoric*, edited by Joel Sherzer and Anthony C. Woodbury, pp. 1-16. Cambridge University Press, Cambridge.

Sioui, Georges E. (1992). *For an Amerindian Autohistory*. McGill-Queen's University Press, Montreal and Kingston.

Slattery, Brian (1992). The Legal Basis of Aboriginal Title. In *Aboriginal Title in British Columbia: Delgamuukw v. The Queen*, edited by Frank Cassidy, pp.

113-132. Oolichan Books and The Institute for Research on Public Policy, Lantzville, B.C. and Montreal, P.Q.

Spurling, B. (1988). Archaeology and the Policy Sciences. *Canadian Journal of Archaeology* 12: 65-85.

Sterritt, Neil (Medig'm Gyamk) (1992). It Doesn't Matter What the Judge Said. In *Aboriginal Title in British Columbia: Delgamuukw v. The Queen*, edited by F. Cassidy, pp.303-307. Oolichan and Institute for Research on Public Policy, Lantzville, B.C. and Montreal, P.Q.

Stone, Helen (1993). *Living in Time Immemorial: Concepts of "Time" and "Time Immemorial."* Unpublished M.A. thesis, Canadian Studies, Carleton University, Ottawa.

Storrow, Marvin R.V. and Michael J. Bryant (1992). Litigating Aboriginal Rights Cases. In *Aboriginal Title in British Columbia: Delgamuukw v. The Queen*, edited by F. Cassidy, pp.178-192. Oolichan and Institute for Research on Public Policy, Lantzville, B.C. and Montreal, P.Q.

Sturtevant, William C. (1966). Anthropology, History, and Ethnohistory. *Ethnohistory* 13: 1-51.

Sypher, Howard E., Mary L. Hummert, and Sheryl L. Williams (1994). Social Psychological Aspects of the Oral History Interview. In *Interactive Oral History Interviewing*, edited by Eva M. McMahan and Kim L. Rogers, pp. 47-61. Lawrence Erblaum Associates, Hillsdale, New Jersey.

Tannen, Deborah (1982a). The Oral/Literate Continuum in Discourse. In *Spoken and Written Language: Exploring Orality and Literacy*, edited by Deborah Tannen, pp. 1-16. Ablex, Norwood, New Jersey.

——— (1982b). The Myth of Orality and Literacy. In *Linguistics and Literacy*, edited by William Frawley, pp. 37-50. Plenum Press, New York.

Tennant, Paul (1992). The Place of Delgamuukw In British Columbia History and Politics—and vice versa. In *Aboriginal Title in British Columbia: Delgamuukw v. The Queen*, edited by Frank Cassidy, pp. 73-91. Oolichan Books and The Institute for Research on Public Policy, Lantzville, B.C. and Montreal, P.Q.

Thompson, Paul (1988). *The Voice of the Past: Oral History*. 2nd edition. Oxford University Press, Oxford.

Tooker, Elisabeth (1988). The United States Constitution and the Iroquois League. *Ethnohistory* 35(4): 305-336.

Tough, Frank (1990). Introduction: Advocacy Research and Native Studies. *Native Studies Review* 6(2): 1-12.

Treaty 7 Elders and Tribal Council (1996). *The True Spirit and Original Intent of Treaty 7*. McGill-Queen's University Press, Montreal and Kingston.

Trigger, Bruce G. (1980). Archaeology and the Image of the American Indian. *American Antiquity* 45(4): 662-676.

——— (1982). Ethnohistory: Problems and Prospects. *Ethnohistory* 29(1): 1-19.

——— (1985). *Natives and Newcomers: Canada's "Heroic Age" Reconsidered*. McGill-Queen's University Press, Kingston and Montreal.

——— (1989). *A History of Archaeological Thought*. Cambridge University Press, Cambridge.

———— (1995). Archaeology and the Integrated Circus. *Critique of Anthropology* 15(4): 319-335.

———— (1998). Archaeology and Epistemology: Dialoguing across the Darwinian Chasm. *American Journal of Archaeology* 102(1): 1-34.

Urion, Carl (1991). Changing Academic Discourse About Native Education: Using Two Pairs of Eyes. *Canadian Journal of Native Education* 18(1): 1-22.

Vansina, Jan (1985). *Oral Tradition as History.* University of Wisconsin Press, Madison, Wisconsin.

Vastokas, Joan M. (1996). History Without Writing: Pictorial Narratives in Native North America. In *Gin Das Winan: Documenting Aboriginal History in Ontario*, edited by Dale Standen and David McNab, pp. 48-64. Champlain Society Occasional Papers 2. Champlain Society, Toronto.

von Gernet, Alexander (1992a). New Directions in the Construction of Prehistoric Amerindian Belief Systems. In *Ancient Images, Ancient Thought: The Archaeology of Ideology*, edited by S. Goldsmith, S. Garvie, D. Selin, & J. Smith, pp. 133-140. Archaeological Association, University of Calgary, Calgary, Alberta.

———— (1992b). Archaeological Investigations at Highland Lake: 1991 Field Season. In *Annual Archaeological Report, Ontario* 3 (1992): 74-79.

———— (1993). The Construction of Prehistoric Ideation: Exploring the Universality-Idiosyncrasy Continuum. *Cambridge Archaeological Journal* 3(1): 67-81.

———— (1994a). Saving the Souls: Reincarnation Beliefs of the Seventeenth-Century Huron. In *Amerindian Rebirth: Reincarnation Belief among the North American Indians and Inuit*, edited by Antonia Mills and Richard Slobodin, pp. 38-54. University of Toronto Press, Toronto.

———— (1994b). Archaeology as Discourse: An Editorial Essay. *Ontario Archaeology* 57: 3-22.

———— (1995). The Date of Time Immemorial: Politics and Iroquoian Origins. In *Origins of the People of the Longhouse*, edited by A. Beckerman and G. Warrick, pp. 119-128. Ontario Archaeological Society, North York, Ontario.

———— (1996). *Oral Narratives and Aboriginal Pasts: An Interdisciplinary Review of the Literature on Oral Traditions and Oral Histories.* 2 vols. Research and Analysis Directorate, Indian and Northern Affairs Canada, Ottawa.

———— (1998). *Handbook for Creating a Record of Aboriginal Oral Histories and Traditions.* Research and Analysis Directorate, Indian and Northern Affairs Canada, Ottawa.

Walker, Willard (1981). Native American Writing Systems. In *Language in the USA*, edited by Charles A. Ferguson and Shirley B. Heath, pp. 145-174. Cambridge University Press, Cambridge.

Washburn, Wilcomb E. (1987). Distinguishing History from Moral Philosophy and Public Advocacy. In *The American Indian and the Problem of History*, edited by Calvin Martin, pp. 91-97. Oxford University Press, New York.

Wetzel, Michael G. (1995). *Decolonizing Ktaqmkuk Mi'kmaw History.* Masters of Laws Thesis, Dalhousie University, Halifax, Nova Scotia.

Wickwire, Wendy C. (). Ethnography and Archaeology as Ideology: The Case of the Stein River Valley. BC Studies 91-92: 51-78.

Wiget, Andrew O. (1982). Truth and the Hopi: An Historiographic Study of Documented Oral Tradition Concerning the Coming of the Spanish. *Ethnohistory* 29(3): 181-199.

Williams, Nancy M., and Daymbalipu Mununggurr (1989). Understanding Yolngu Signs of the Past. In *Who Needs the Past? Indigenous Values and Archaeology*, edited by Robert Layton, pp. 70-83. Unwin Hyman, London.

Wilson, Angela C. (1997). Power of the Spoken Word: Native Oral Traditions in American Indian History. In *Rethinking American Indian History*, edited by Donald L. Fixico, pp. 101-116. University of New Mexico Press, Albuquerque.

Wilson, Dora (Yagalahl) (1992). It Will Always Be The Truth. In *Aboriginal Title in British Columbia: Delgamuukw v. The Queen*, edited by F. Cassidy, pp.199-205. Oolichan and Institute for Research on Public Policy, Lantzville, B.C. and Montreal, P.Q.

Wilson-Kenni, Dora Time of Trial: The Gitksan and Wet'suwet'en in Court. *BC Studies* 95: 7-11.

2 Impact in British Columbia

An Overview of Treaty Negotiations before and after *Delgamuukw*

Alec C. Robertson

In December 1993, the British Columbia Treaty Commission began receiving First Nations into the tripartite six-stage treaty negotiation process. Four years later, when the Supreme Court of Canada delivered its judgment in *Delgamuukw*, there were 51 First Nations in the process representing about 70 percent of the aboriginal population of B.C. They were organized into 43 negotiating tables of which 34 were in the fourth and principal stage of the process, negotiating the substantive terms of their treaty.

Although one or two agreements in principle were close, none had yet been reached. The Nisga'a remained the only First Nation that had completed an agreement in principle and they were outside the Treaty Commission process. However, it was well understood by 1997 that treaties would not come quickly. There were no precedents for modern treaties in British Columbia and it would take time to hammer out fundamental issues like "certainty" and "taxation," as the Nisga'a and Sechelt negotiations have demonstrated. It will take longer to hammer out the several 'treaty models' that are required to reflect the diversity of British Columbia and its aboriginal groups. The Nisga'a model may have some application in northwestern B.C. but its mix of lands and resources will not fit much of the rest of the province. There need to be models for First Nations that are urban, suburban, rural, interior, north-eastern, and trans-boundary. Each model requires government to work out the appropriate set of policies and mandates. Once the models are in place, it is expected that treaty making will move more quickly.

From the perspective of non-aboriginal British Columbia, it is worth reiterating the benefits of the decision by the provincial government to participate in treaty negotiations as a mechanism for dealing with aboriginal land claims. This approach has delivered stability and the economy has largely escaped a repetition of the protests that were so prevalent in 1990, before the treaty process began.

The Treaty Commission's role included identifying obstacles to progress, and a number of obstacles had emerged by December 1997.

The first was labeled "System Overload" by the Treaty Commission. The process was open to all who could qualify as a "First Nation," without regard to size or capacity to negotiate a comprehensive treaty. The Task Force that designed the process expected about 30 First Nations on the basis of historic and linguistic groupings. Fifty-one have entered the process, many of which are Indian Act band councils representing single communities of a larger linguistic group. The Task Force had underestimated the success of the Indian Act in fragmenting the traditional governance systems that had held the original nations together. Even tribal councils sometimes have difficulty retaining their members. A number of communities threatened to separate from tribal councils and enter the process on their own until the Treaty Commission adopted policies that effectively precluded the practice.

There is a very real need for the Principals (Canada, British Columbia, and the First Nations Summit) to agree on the criteria, including size and capacity, for determining an appropriate negotiating unit, or to mandate the Treaty Commission to do so. Alternatively, Canada and British Columbia need to disclose clearly what they will and will not negotiate with smaller aboriginal groups.

Canada and the province each have six negotiating teams. The latter stages of an AIP negotiation will require virtually an entire team. Realistically, the two governments can sustain active concurrent negotiations with 10 to 12 tables. The natural consequence of system overload is that the governments will focus their resources where they expect to make the most progress. By December 1997, the governments were focusing their resources on about 10 tables. The Treaty Commission referred to these as "fast-track" tables to distinguish them for funding purposes from the remainder, who were on a slower track.

While it suits some First Nations to proceed at a slower pace, others have the capacity to negotiate at a faster pace and wish to do so, as they are borrowing heavily to stay in the process. Further, the fast track tends to favour smaller First Nations. The larger tribal councils in the fourth stage require time to organize their mandates, but once mandated, expect to negotiate at a faster pace.

At the same time, capacity on the government side has been declining. The province, with no depth of experience in treaty making to build on, has lost personnel through budget cuts and attrition, not only in the Ministry of Aboriginal Affairs but also in key areas of the "dirt ministries" vital to treaty negotiations, such as Environment Land & Parks, Forests, and Energy & Mines. The province has the least capacity, which meant that it was setting the pace of negotiations.

System Overload remains a critical problem and has been underscored and accentuated by the findings and repercussions of the *Delgamuukw* judgment.

Overlapping land claims was another growing problem exacerbated by the number of smaller First Nations. There has been no incentive for First Nations to resolve their overlaps, and in many cases there is cultural resistance to provoking antagonism towards their neighbours. However, unresolved overlapping claims can undermine treaty negotiations. The litigation by the Gitanyow Hereditary Chiefs, arising out of the Nisga'a AIP, demonstrates the need for both governments to adopt new policies to address overlaps in treaty negotiations, and the Treaty Commission has urged them to do so.

Approaches to negotiations and mandates were also a source of friction.

The approach adopted by the two governments was to negotiate a complete treaty package, not a series of incremental agreements. There are obvious tactical reasons for this approach, but the approach does not suit protracted negotiations. It means that substantive negotiations began with the easiest subjects and the deal-breakers of lands, resources and cash are left until the end. It also means that interim measures are rarely negotiated, on the grounds that interim measures cannot be justified until the treaty lands are identified. This approach was frustrating to First Nations who were borrowing money to remain in the process, and needed to demonstrate to their people that treaty negotiations could produce tangible benefits to offset the mounting debt.

Mandates are influenced by each party's perception of the other party's legal rights. When negotiations fail, the alternative is litigation.

By December 1997, differing perspectives as to the nature and extent of aboriginal rights were affecting negotiations. The aboriginal perspective was an historical, lawful claim of aboriginal title within their traditional territories, a title tantamount to ownership. Indeed, the agreement of the public governments to enter into treaty negotiations was initially perceived by many First Nations as a symbolic act of mutual recognition: the Crown was recognizing aboriginal title and jurisdiction in traditional territories, and First Nations were recognizing the underlying title and jurisdiction of the Crown in those territories. That mutual recognition has never been acknowledged by the two governments or their negotiators. The perspective of the governments, as reflected in statements by government negotiators when pressed, was to acknowledge only the undefined, site-specific, activity-based aboriginal rights upheld by the B.C. Court of Appeal in *Delgamuukw. Aboriginal tile was never mentioned.*

By December 1997, there were some First Nations close to suspending negotiations because they believed their members would not accept a treaty based on the governments' perspective of their rights. At the same time, a well funded lobby group was publicly criticizing provincial mandates as being unduly generous and treating aboriginal rights as more consequential than the rights upheld by the B.C. Court of Appeal in *Delgamuukw.*

The Impact of *Delgamuukw*

On December 11, 1997, the Supreme Court of Canada handed down its reasons for judgment in *Delgamuukw.* The shock waves have not yet subsided.

Aboriginal title is said to exist in British Columbia as a substantive legal right, the aboriginal equivalent to fee simple ownership. Wherever aboriginal title is established or acknowledged, the Crown's jurisdiction is limited and the provincial share of that jurisdiction is minimal. While the Court has expressly stated that the province can infringe on aboriginal title, legal scholars have pointed to the Court's confirmation that land subject to aboriginal title is firmly entrenched in federal jurisdiction under the Constitution, and question the legal basis for provincial infringement. This is one of the most unsettling aspects of the judgment and will require further direction from the Court.

A provincial economy and administration predicated upon provincial ownership of and jurisdiction over all Crown land has been thrown into question.

There is also the huge question of compensation for past, present and future infringement and how that compensation is to be calculated. As of which date did compensable infringement begin: in colonial times; when B.C. joined Canada; or in 1982 when aboriginal rights became constitutionally protected? To what extent do the Crown grants that support private ownership create compensable claims?

The extent of aboriginal title is unknown. Clearly isolation and freedom from overlaps will favour aboriginal title. While some language in the judgment suggests that large areas may be subject to aboriginal title, the Court's description of a spectrum of aboriginal rights, varying in the degree of their connection to land, suggests that trial judges may have a broad discretion in deciding the extent of aboriginal title within any territory.

The Court's requirement that aboriginal title can only be claimed by the successors to the aboriginal nation that occupied the territory in 1846 may well require the reconfiguration of a number of First Nations now in the treaty process and help to address one aspect of System Overload. The Court's requirement that government must, in good faith, negotiate with all aboriginal groups claiming an interest in the area under negotiation, should provide the incentive to address overlaps.

It is also important to recognize that the Court, by making no specific finding of aboriginal title but providing a near unanimous dissertation on its consequences, was setting the stage for negotiations and concluded the judgment with a strong message to that effect.

The Status of Treaty Negotiations after *Delgamuukw*

Immediately following *Delgamuukw*, the Treaty Commission proposed to the Principals that they select appropriate representatives and work together to settle the modifications to mandates, approaches and to the treaty process itself that would be required to revitalize the treaty negotiations. The Principals agreed, and a list of issues was settled which included the issues identified by the Treaty Commission. Priority was to be given to accelerating land and resource negotiations at treaty tables. Preliminary meetings were held in March 1998 and substantive meetings in April 1998.

Canada tabled a proposal that would enable lands and resources to be negotiated in three phases. Firstly, as interim measures at the beginning of negotiations, with the tacit recognition that Canada would have to participate in the funding of interim measures. This is important as Canada is not required under the cost-sharing Memorandum of Understanding (MOU) to fund interim measures, and that has been a major obstacle to their negotiation. The second and intermediate phase is the negotiation of economic development agreements involving lands and resources to provide employment and capacity building. These would ultimately be incorporated into the third phase when treaty lands and resources are settled.

At the last set of substantive meetings in April 1999, the province tabled a proposal to accelerate the negotiation of land, resources and cash, with an overarching agreement to be negotiated among the Principals over the next six months that would address specific issues important to the province. The meetings concluded on the understanding that Canada and the First Nations Summit would respond to BC's proposal.

The Summit neither accepted nor rejected the proposal, but instructed its leaders to continue negotiations and report back to the Summit at the end of June. The province responded by withdrawing from further tripartite negotiations and by refusing to reappoint the Chief Commissioner of the B.C. Treaty Commission whose term had just expired.

The province sought to pursue bilateral negotiations with each of Canada and the Task Group of the Summit, but I understand that both wanted the tripartite negotiations to continue. I am told that tripartite meetings among the three Principals have resumed with the object of both improving the treaty negotiation process and accelerating the negotiation of lands and resources.

I understand that treaty negotiations continue at the various treaty tables, but the level of activity is generally low while the parties wait for new mandates to be developed.

The Options Facing British Columbia

It might be useful to look at the options facing British Columbia to test whether there are realistic alternatives to a tripartite negotiation process for resolving these critical issues. I offer the following brief commentary on some of the options facing non-aboriginal British Columbia. The list, I am sure, is incomplete.

(1) Persuade Canada to legislate limits to aboriginal title or to compensation payable for past infringements.

Delgamuukw confirmed that only the federal government can legislate in relation to aboriginal rights, and aboriginal title is a constitutionally protected aboriginal right. That means legislation must meet a strict test of justification, administered by the courts, that takes into account not only the legitimacy of the purpose, but also the fiduciary relationship between Canada and its aboriginal peoples. Furthermore, the "notwithstanding clause" in the Constitution used to override certain constitutional rights does not apply to aboriginal rights. Legislation diminishing aboriginal rights or compensation for past infringements is unlikely to survive the legal hurdles it would face, even if it survived the political firestorm it would ignite.

(2) Encourage litigation as a means of mapping the extent of aboriginal title and determining how compensation is to be fixed.

Litigation is always an option when parties won't negotiate or negotiations fail. It is not the first choice for many reasons. Critical court decisions will inevitably be appealed through to the Supreme Court of Canada taking 7 to 10 years altogether. The expense is enormous, and if there are counterclaims, the party that launched the lawsuit cannot unilaterally stop it. The parties have no control over the outcome and the results can be unpredictable or, as in Calder and Delgamuukw, inconclusive.

Litigation is best used strategically. When negotiations reach an impasse, it is appropriate to consider the costs and benefits of litigation, as well as its effect on each of the parties and on the negotiations. The *Sechelt* decision to litigate their claim of aboriginal title was strategic. They have made it clear that they can be persuaded to come back to the table. The province made a strategic decision in 1995 when it suspended negotiations with the Gitksan, thereby compelling the Delgamuukw appeal to be heard by the Supreme Court of Canada. Even when used strategically, litigation is risky.

(3) Demand that the federal government assume full responsibility for negotiating treaties.

The rationale here is that land subject to aboriginal title is, under *Delgamuukw*, within the exclusive jurisdiction of the federal government. Some aboriginal groups look upon Delgamuukw as confirming their view that only Canada can negotiate treaties with aboriginal nations. But land subject to aboriginal title has not been mapped, and land not subject to aboriginal rights or title belongs beneficially to the province. If deals are to be struck that reconcile provincial rights with aboriginal rights, the province must participate.

Delgamuukw, by clarifying the extent of federal jurisdiction and the concomitant fiduciary obligations, does imply that the federal government will have to assume a larger role in treaty negotiations and assume a larger burden of the associated costs.

(4) Continue tripartite treaty negotiations.

This appears to be the only viable alternative, and the post-*Delgamuukw* environment is now more supportive of those negotiations.

There is no longer debate as to whether aboriginal rights are substantial legal rights, or whether they can be settled for less cash and little, if any, land. The public, and particularly the resource sector, is expecting government to resolve the uncertainty they are experiencing and that resolution must come through negotiation. Even industries wishing to negotiate resource developments directly with aboriginal groups will need to avoid either antagonizing the government that claims jurisdiction or finding themselves embroiled in complex legal issues.

There is a very real need for the Principals to continue the negotiations among themselves to settle the new rules that will apply not only to treaty negotiations, but also to the consultation process with First Nations that *Delgamuukw* mandates. Even though the latter principally affects the province, Canada has a constitutional responsibility for developments affecting lands subject to aboriginal rights and must play a role in arriving at a consultation mechanism that is accessible, workable, and expeditious.

The Litigation Factor

Aboriginal litigation attracts media attention and the media are now speculating that First Nations will prefer litigation to negotiation.

I think the opposite is true. The Treaty Commission closely monitored First Nation reactions after *Delgamuukw* and the overwhelming response has been a desire to get on with negotiations. First Nations have a healthy distrust of litigation for the reasons already mentioned, plus two others.

I have been told many times that First Nations find it culturally degrading to expose their Elders, their rituals, their myths and oral histories to unsympathetic and adversarial court proceedings.

More concretely, litigation will not address their core issues of unemployment, rising birthrates, low socioeconomic expectations, dependency, and lack of capacity to effectively use the land rights that a court might ultimately award many years in the future. Treaty negotiations can't resolve all these issues, but their focus is on addressing core problems by providing an economic base, infrastructure and funding to stabilize the community and move it towards self-sufficiency. Treaty negotiations allow First Nations to shape the ways their needs will be addressed, litigation doesn't.

If the Principals do not make solid progress in revitalizing treaty negotiations, then litigation will increase. But I believe the prevailing view is the one cryptically expressed by Chief Joe Mathias at a recent business gathering: "Litigation is still a crap shoot. We're here to negotiate."

Treaty Costs and Compensation

My task was to set the stage by providing an overview of treaty negotiations before and after *Delgamuukw*. Another issue involves treaty costs and compensation. My thesis that tripartite negotiations offer the only realistic means of reconciling aboriginal and non-aboriginal objectives has a point relevant to both.

The perception that *Delgamuukw* will unduly increase the cost of treaties must not obscure the fact that most First Nations have compelling reasons to negotiate. The Nisga'a, who came within one judicial vote of aboriginal title to the Nass Valley and have strong leadership and depth of experience in negotiations, elected to continue to finalize their treaty after Delgamuukw. The current circumstances of their people, their culture, and their economy are compelling reasons to pursue the deal they have already made. If a final agreement is as imminent as claimed, there will soon be an opportunity to assess the incremental cost of Delgamuukw for treaty negotiations.

My second point relates to the role of compensation for past infringements in treaty negotiations. Since the beginning of treaty negotiations, First Nations have demanded that compensation for past wrongs be a separate head of negotiations. Both governments have refused, arguing that treaties were to address the future and not the past. It is understandable that governments would wish to avoid a recitation and evaluation of every wrong that has occurred since colonial times. However, the reality of treaties is that their benefits, including fiscal payments, have among other purposes, compensation for past infringements *because the treaty will require the First Nation to release all claims for past infringements.*

In short, the issue of compensation for past infringements is arguably most appropriately and efficiently settled in the context of treaty negotiations. Even as a separate topic of negotiation, that context will enable the give and take necessary to arrive at the package that each party can accept.

Author's Note

Some 18 months after this paper was presented, it can be said that the tripartite meetings among the Principals did resume and have produced initiatives from the federal and provincial governments to negotiate lands and resources at an earlier stage in the process in the expectation that this will accelerate negotiations generally. In addition, activity has increased at the treaty negotiation tables, particularly at those tables on the fast track. In April 1999, the first Agreement in Principle under the BCTC process was signed with the Sechelt Nation, and as of February 2000, the two governments have tabled offers to six other First Nations in the process.

Delgamuukw and Diplomacy
First Nations and Municipalities in British Columbia

Paul Tennant

Introduction

The *Delgamuukw* ruling is a major contribution to Canadian legal and political thought. It has relevance for every Canadian interested in what Canada was, is, and will be. However, it is we British Columbians, both aboriginal and newer-comers, who are the most immediately and directly affected. In my view, the public discussion of the ruling in our province has so far focused too much on the details and too little on the principles, with the result that particular interpretations have lacked context and have at times been highly misleading. Unfortunately, both aboriginal spokespersons and their critics may have produced the general impression that the ruling is a victory for aboriginal peoples that leaves little room for the rest of us, and may even make the treaty process pointless.

The ruling is certainly a victory for aboriginal peoples. It validates what British Columbia Indian leaders have believed and claimed ever since colonial settlement began. It recognizes that aboriginal title ex-

This paper is a much revised version of a talk delivered to the Greater Vancouver Chapter of the Institute of Public Administration of Canada, April 26, 1998.

ists, defines it as a right to land, and places it within the guarantee provided by section 35 of the *Constitution Act, 1982*. But there are a number of reasons why ruling is by no means a defeat for the province, or for the rest of us.

Two of these reasons are especially significant. First, the ruling does not make aboriginal title automatic or universal. Each First Nation has the responsibility of demonstrating that the ruling's criteria are met. A First Nation's present-day area of aboriginal title will rarely, if ever, include all of its traditional territory. The court states explicitly that some First Nations may not be able to demonstrate that they have any non-reserve lands under aboriginal title.

Second, and of the most fundamental importance, the ruling makes clear that the outcomes of the whole range of normal legislative actions of the province (from authorizing resource development to the creation of towns and cities) have been and remain legitimate even where such actions have infringed upon aboriginal title. This aspect of the ruling has escaped some of the critics, who seem to believe that the ruling has the effect of destroying the province's ability to govern. While nothing as dramatic has occurred, it remains the case that First Nations do emerge with enhanced legal and constitutional standing.

What has been missing in our public thinking and public policy is a concern for ensuring that the new constitutional reality is reflected in the practical relations between First Nations and the rest of us. Most of these relations will exist at the local level, between First Nations and their neighbouring communities. The province has been loath to acknowledge this bit of practical reality, let alone to allow it to be fully reflected in the treaty process.

The approach of starting with the principles of *Delgamuukw* opens the way to developing creative strategies that can be undertaken at the local level to meet the varying needs of differing localities. In a modest way, these strategies can open the way for real participation by ordinary people in the political setting that is most meaningful to them; that is, in their own local community. These strategies can thus lessen the dangers that arise when officials have to make decisions in advance of public understanding and support. These strategies can be undertaken not only outside the treaty process (but still with the long-term purpose of strengthening that process), but also outside the immediate control and interference of the province (with the long-term purpose of strengthening local communities and enhancing community self-government, both aboriginal and Municipal).

In this paper, I begin by identifying three principles arising from *Delgamuukw* that relate directly to local communities, and then say something about the views held by opponents of the three principles.

Next, I comment on the place of First Nations in British Columbia and discuss ways that they and Municipalities should relate to each other, giving detailed attention to the principles and practice of local diplomacy. I conclude with comments on the relevance of the principles to the BC Treaty Process and a discussion of the benefits of First Nation-Municipal diplomacy.

Three Fundamental Principles in *Delgamuukw*

Primary among the principles set out in the *Delgamuukw* ruling is that of *reconciliation* between aboriginal interests and those of the larger Canadian public or polity. This reconciliation is to be achieved not through the courts, not through legislated imposition, but through negotiation between aboriginal peoples and the Crown. This principle is driven home in the ruling's closing, when Chief Justice Antonio Lamer states:

> Ultimately, it is through negotiated settlements, with good faith and give and take on all sides, reinforced by the judgments of this Court, that we will achieve ... 'the reconciliation of the pre-existence of aboriginal societies with the sovereignty of the Crown'. Let us face it, we are all here to stay.

The second major principle, emphasized in *Delgamuukw* but already well developed in previous Canadian jurisprudence relating to aboriginal interests, is that of the *honour of the Crown*. In general, this principle requires that Parliament, legislatures, and governments act consistently and in good faith in honouring agreements and in respecting aboriginal rights and interests. The historic embodiments of this principle are the *Royal Proclamation, 1763* and the related Treaty of Niagara.

Maintaining the honour of the Crown is itself a moral obligation, one that requires not merely the legalistic following of the letter of legislation and agreements, but also having appropriate laws and policies in the first place. The ruling makes clear that the honour of the Crown is at stake in achieving reconciliation through negotiation. As the Chief Justice states, "the Crown is under a moral, if not a legal, duty to enter into and conduct these negotiations in good faith."

The third major principle is that local aboriginal communities (whether Indian, Métis, or Inuit) are *unique and distinct legal and constitutional entities within Canada*. Indian and Inuit communities are unique in having their origins prior to Canada's, distinct in having retained their pre-contact identities, and unique and distinct in possessing collective rights particular to their own history and place. In previous cases the Supreme Court has not hesitated to use the term "distinct society" as the measure of an aboriginal community (and, of course, to define an aboriginal right as a practice or circumstance integral to a particular society's distinct identity).

Within our own province, the simple but utterly important constitutional reality is that every recognized local native Indian community (that is, First Nation) has both its identity and its rights confirmed and guaranteed. This constitutional status of First Nations, which is a status Municipalities can for the moment only dream of, was evident prior to *Delgamuukw*, but it is amplified in by the ruling. First Nations and their rights are here to stay.

While other principles can be identified in the ruling, the three that I have enumerated are the most significant. Although the resulting consequences are many, in our context today in British Columbia, the *Delgamuukw* principles lead us directly to two further principles or ideals. The first of these is *co-equality of local communities*. The second, following from the first, is *diplomacy as the guiding principle* in relations between First Nations and their neighbouring communities.

Taking the practical steps to embody and implement these principles requires no change to any legislation and does not depend on any permission from, or action by, either the Department of Indian Affairs or the Ministry of Municipal Affairs (let alone the Ministry of Aboriginal Affairs). The main impediment is the hesitancy on each side to regard communities on the other side as co-equal. But the hesitancy is more entrenched on the non-aboriginal side. Part of the Municipal hesitancy is the result of taking the prominent critics too seriously. It is also the case that many Municipal leaders have not yet had the opportunity to familiarize themselves with the place and role of First Nations. For these reasons, I shall deal with the critics and the place of First Nations before dealing with the two further principles and with their implementation.

The Critics

The *Delgamuukw* ruling brings major elements of certainty to the legal and constitutional debates about aboriginal rights. Within British Columbia, the ruling provides the final legal and constitutional rebuttal to the major myths, assumptions, and doctrines that underlie and explain hostility to native claims in general, and to the principle of aboriginal title in particular.

Fortunately, of course, court pronouncements do not end political or public debate. However, the ruling does place the province's most prominent critics of aboriginal rights in the unenviable position of being out of step with the nation's highest court, and with established legal thought in the rest of the country. Also, as they have been consistently for the last 15 years, the critics remain out of step with public opinion in the province, which continues to support the principles of aboriginal rights and of treaty negotiations.

In their desire to have British Columbia exempt from *Delgamuukw* and from the policy beliefs that have been long-established in the rest of Canada, and in their belief that the provincial majority has the right to impose its views on ethnic minorities, the prominent B.C. critics are taking the same approach as Parti Quebecois leaders in Quebec. In effect, the critics want a special status for British Columbia, one in which we British Columbians can pick and choose among the rulings of Canada's highest court and can return to those idyllic days when the majority could dictate or deny aboriginal rights. The fact that the prominent critics are fervent opponents of special status for Quebec says much about the consistency and depth of their thinking.

As their hot-line shows, newspaper columns, and public statements have made clear, the prominent critics do not agree with the three principles that make up the core of the *Delgamuukw* ruling. The critics are reluctant to accept that First Nations are distinct societies with collective rights within Canada and British Columbia and they have little respect for the honour of the Crown. Many of the critics assume that we live in a populist republic in which there is no higher political God than current majority sentiment expressed on an issue-by-issue basis, locally or province-wide. Nor do the critics wish to promote reconciliation; instead, they wish to impose solutions rather than to negotiate in good faith with First Nations.

During the debates on whether Quebec should be recognized as a distinct society, both supporters and opponents at least agreed on one thing—both sides sported bumper stickers proclaiming "My Canada Includes Quebec." Federal Reform Party supporters, at least in my neighborhood and among my acquaintances, were enthusiastic about this slogan. I have been suggesting that the time is right for a new bumper sticker with a new slogan, this time proclaiming "My British Columbia Includes First Nations." Sadly, I have to report that none of my Reform Party acquaintances seems too keen on the idea.

The Place of First Nations

British Columbia English has still not evolved uniform terminology to refer to aboriginal groups, with the inevitable result that there is often misunderstanding and confusion as to the scope and applicability of both claims and rights. Our leading reporters and columnists still make fundamental errors. Among native Indians, the village-level community is the primary social and political entity (although the language group, consisting of several communities of common cultural heritage, can also be important politically).

Until recent decades, the word "nation" was commonly used in British Columbia and the rest of Canada to refer to village or tribal-level Indian communities. The *Royal Proclamation* uses "tribe" and "nation" as synonyms, while the *Oxford English Dictionary* continues to give "tribe of North American Indians" as one major definition of "nation." Although the word is a provocative irritant to the major critics who seem to assume that any Indian "nation" must be bent on joining the United Nations as a sovereign entity, the word remains perfectly ordinary and acceptable in the aboriginal context—and politically neutral to those knowledgeable about our history. The term "tribal nation" is at times used to refer to the comprehensive, but still very much locally-based, cultural group (for example, Nisga'a, Okanagan, Sto:lo).

"First nation" has emerged in the last decade as the most common term in this province for village-level community, although at times (as in the B.C. treaty process itself) it is used more loosely. With few, if any, exceptions, each First Nation continues to have a legal identity as a particular "Indian band" formed and operating under the *Indian Act*. For the purpose of this paper, the word "community" means a First Nation—or a Municipality.

What must be understood is that among native Indian populations in British Columbia it is only the local community (that is, First Nation) that can possess aboriginal title and other aboriginal rights. Individual Indians (and sub-groups such as houses or clans) can exercise aboriginal rights, but only as members of a particular First Nation. No province-wide or countrywide Indian grouping has or can have any constitutional status or ability to possess aboriginal rights.

For most practical purposes, Municipalities do not need to concern themselves with any aboriginal grouping other than First Nations, who will also be *Indian Act* bands for various legal purposes. The same will generally be true for school boards and regional districts, although here there is greater likelihood that the local tribal nation will be of importance. (The larger towns and cities, however, do have substantial numbers of aboriginal residents who may be represented by such interest groups as the United Native Nations or Métis associations.)

How, then, should First Nations and Municipalities go about thinking about each other and dealing with each other? As I have indicated, I believe that the *Delgamuukw* ruling leads us to two further principles or ideas: first, *co-equality of local communities*; second, *diplomacy as the guiding principle* in relations between First Nations and Municipalities.

Co-Equality of First Nations and Municipalities

The principle of equality of individual persons is one of the foundations of Canadian political and constitutional thought. At one time, this principle was highly controversial, with opponents pointing to the actual individual differences in such matters wealth, education, character, gender, personal abilities, ethics, and civic contributions. Yet today we take for granted that each person is of equal moral worth entitled to equal civil rights and equal political voice. I suggest that we apply this same sort of thinking to local communities—that we regard First Nations and Municipalities as fundamentally equal to each other.

For First Nations and Municipalities to regard each other as of equal moral worth requires some fresh thinking on both sides. From the First Nations' perspective, Municipalities can quite understandably be seen not only as mere creations of the province, but also as undignified creatures kept on a rather short leash. The Municipal model is made even less palatable when the prominent critics present it as one First Nations should follow. (The Sechelt First Nation is often said to have accepted such a model; however the Sechelt negotiated the terms of its own special legislation with Parliament, rather than with the provincial legislature.) In essence, the Municipal model rests on the same principles as does Indian band government under the *Indian Act* and is thus the polar opposite of the models of aboriginal self-government that First Nations are pursuing. It is in good part for these reasons that First Nations were generally opposed to allowing Municipalities a role of their own in the treaty process.

My impression is that there is no uniform Municipal perspective on First Nations. Any such perspective at the present time would likely focus on practical aspects, noting that First Nations typically have much smaller populations and much higher rates of social and economic problems. What is quite clear is that Municipal leaders do not at present look upon First Nations as sources of models or ideas or support that could be of benefit to Municipalities.

Nevertheless, from a perspective that embraces both First Nations and Municipalities, there is a substantial similarity. In the human dimension, both are collectivities of local residents who have similar daily and longer-term concerns. In the governance dimension, both are local governing authorities. The day-to-day activities, issues, and operations handled by their officials are amazingly similar. As a rough estimate, I would say that eighty percent of the time and effort of First Nations politicians and officials is spent on the same things that occupy Municipal politicians and officials.

Given these actual similarities, it seems to me a small step to accept First Nations and Municipalities as having equal moral worth. Perceiving the two as having equal human value does not mean that either will be forced to be identical to the other. For this reason, I suggest the term "co-equality," rather than simply "equality"—to indicate that First Nations and Municipalities are different and will remain so, but also to acknowledge that they are also fundamentally similar insofar as they are composed of local communities of British Columbians, led by community governments concerned with local needs.

Accepting the principle of co-equality of First Nations and Municipalities opens the door for leaders on each side to come to realize that the other can be an important source of support and ideas for improving local government and for strengthening the role of local communities in the B.C. Treaty Process. More immediately, however, accepting the principle of co-equality points to diplomacy as the foundation of relations between the two communities, and as the direct and pragmatic way to move leaders on each side step-by-step through the doorway to better understanding and practical benefits.

The Principle of Diplomacy between Communities

It is perhaps necessary, given the fearful misperceptions of some of the critics, that I stress that I am here merely adapting some elements of international diplomacy, and that I am doing so strictly as a means towards better community relations at the local level. I am not proposing local embassies, suggesting border checkpoints, or contemplating immunity from parking tickets.

Diplomacy has three working assumptions that are especially germane. First, participants are equal. Second, recognition of similarities and common goals provides a basis for dealing with differences. Third, having regularized channels of communication lessens the chance of conflict and simplifies resolving any that does occur. Put simply, diplomacy is the art and practice of neighbourliness.

The methods of diplomacy are many, but formal protocol is always one major attribute. Protocol allows each side to display the symbols of its history and values, and it allows each side to demonstrate its respect for the history and values of the other. Protocol also allows each side to display its leaders and to acknowledge the position of leaders on the other side. Protocol prevents surprises (including unintended omissions or insults), and so provides predictability. Mutual respect for protocol is a mark of mutual respect between the participants and is itself thus an important manifestation of neighbourliness.

Protocol is most visible and routinized in the planning and conducting of scheduled formal events, but it is a factor in all communications and interactions—as shown in the fact that knowing when and how to "dispense with protocol" is itself as aspect of protocol. Protocol can be looked upon as the aspect of diplomacy that creates and maintains a secure and stable framework for informal and speedy communication and co-operation.

The Practice of Diplomacy at the Local Level

Many neighbouring First Nations and Municipalities already have good relations. Typically, these rest on agreements or contracts relating to specific services or activities. However, in few, if any, cases has fully developed diplomacy been attained— that is, the existence of an active relationship having the following features:

(1) The councils and officials on both sides genuinely accept the principle of co-equality and regard good relations as a policy imperative.

(2) Each government invites representatives of the other to all major official community functions, where their presence is acknowledged and welcomed.

(3) There are regular events intended specifically and primarily to demonstrate the principle of co-equality and the desire for good relations. For example, perhaps each council hosts an annual feast/banquet for the councillors and senior officials of the other community.

(4) Individual councillors and senior staff are personally acquainted with their counterparts in the other community's government and are reasonably well informed about the issues and concerns facing them. There is no hesitancy about picking up the phone to talk with a counterpart, and visits to the other's office or work location occur informally as a matter of course.

(5) There is an ongoing issues audit. Current issues of common concern are identified, as are future issues that may cause friction. Explicit common action is taken to resolve issues before they become of wider concern.

(6) Official symbols, such as coats of arms, maces, crests, and talking sticks, may be designed or modified to take account of the presence and history of the other community and to symbolize co-equality. Less obvious symbols, such as street, subdivision, and building names, may also be relevant.

(7) Leaders on both sides are well aware of the fundamental differences between the two communities and thus of the asymmetry inherent in their relationship. For example, families or houses or clans are seen as components of community on the aboriginal side and so the Municipal mayor knows the worth of an invitation to a potlatch and values the respect he or she conveys (and gains) by attending a First Nations family funeral.

(8) In general, among leaders and public on both sides there is a sense of satisfaction with the relations between their communities, a recognition that in a certain sense they form a shared local community, and an automatic willingness to regard each other as local allies against provincial and federal impositions.

Attaining a state of fully developed inter-community diplomacy is not an over-night task. Given that First Nations generally have fewer resources and that their officials face debilitating demands upon their time and attention, the initiatives will in practice often have to come from the Municipal side. Given that minorities with grievances have long memories, and that many good words have been offered without follow-up in the past, those making the initiative will in some cases need extra-strength patience and credibility. In most cases, however, the beginnings have already been accomplished; in British Columbia, the Union of B.C. Municipalities and the First Nations Summit have played an important leadership roles in this endeavour.

In a few cases, relations are already on a promising and evolving foundation. The Tsleil-Waututh (Burrard First Nation) and North Vancouver District, and the Katzie First Nation and Pitt Meadows provide two examples. There are relevant models also in the corporate sector, with perhaps the most notable and progressive example of relations with First Nations having been developed and put into practice by B.C. Tel, through its Aboriginal Liaison Officer, Paul Peters.

Where beginnings have not been made, and in those few cases where relations are actively hostile, indirect or outside facilitation may be appropriate. An indirect beginning could take the form of hiring a researcher to organize local volunteers (jointly from both communities) to prepare a history of key historical developments in both communities, to collect documents and photographs for display in a place welcoming to members of both communities, and to provide a list of the major annual events and ceremonies in both communities. A more direct beginning could involve hiring a consultant in the emerging specialty of community-level diplomacy. Here, a first stage could be an assessment of the state of relations and factors bearing upon including, in the case of larger communities, the role of the media.

My eight-point check list merely illustrates the general themes of diplomatic relations at the community level. Every locality will have its own variations and innovations. The larger First Nations and Municipalities will need to consider having a senior official specializing in relations with the other community—or perhaps they could jointly appoint one person to work for both. The danger associated with such specialization is that regular senior officials may tend to view community diplomacy as outside their own responsibility. What is certain, however, is that in the initial stages every large Municipality will need to have one person or committee to whom councillors and staff can turn for prompt protocol guidance in contacting the First Nation and in developing the diplomatic relations.

The B.C. Treaty Process

The B.C. Treaty process is critical for all First Nations and important to most Municipalities. Yet too many burdens have been placed upon it. Even were it not overloaded with two many tables and too little funding, the process could not by itself develop the widespread prior trust, respect, and confidence that are essential if the final treaties are to be more than words on paper. Much has been said about the need for education of the non-aboriginal public to this end, but the reality is that those not directly affected have little motive to pay attention to it, and those whose interests are directly affected will dismiss it as propaganda.

The First Nations who have entered the treaty process have for the most part failed to appreciate fully that the treaty process is part of the provincial and federal political processes. The strategies that worked for First Nations during their isolation under the *Indian Act,* when the larger public was politically irrelevant, will not work today. The philosophy and the idealism that kept the land struggle alive cease to be helpful guides to action once the struggle has been won. New approaches are needed when the Promised Land has been attained, especially when parts of it have other inhabitants. Community level diplomacy offers one of these approaches.

The Benefits of Local Diplomacy

The immediate benefits of community-level diplomacy are just that: immediate benefits in the form of better decisions and better programs and, less tangibly, in the satisfaction that derives from good government and the minimizing of disagreement.

Two British Columbia examples illustrate my point. Both are cases in which a First Nation had its principal reserve within a Municipality and wanted to develop condominiums. In one case, the proposal, its first phase now complete, has been the centrepiece of continual friction and public hostility (including a road blockade by Whites), even though the development is picayune compared to giant transportation facilities already imposed on the reserve by the province. Almost unknown is the harmonious relation that has developed in the other case. Here, an escalating controversy over the First Nations' desire for Municipal street connections quickly subsided when a Municipal councillor sought advice on how to approach the First Nation. Neither side had any doubt about the wisdom of proceeding diplomatically. Before too long, the road was built and the condo development went ahead, with agreement that the Municipality's building standards would be met, and enforced by the Municipality's inspectors. Pragmatism prevailed—not least because the Chief and Council realized that Municipal inspection approval would bring a better price for the condos.

In the longer term, most Municipalities and almost all First Nations can build on local diplomacy to gain benefits from the treaty process. Municipalities have complained much about their lack of influence in the process, but in their Pavlovian turning to the province for a solution, they have missed seeing the opportunity waiting at home with their neighbours.

Direct bilateral local diplomacy outside the treaty process, but focusing specifically on treaty subject headings, provides a rich potential for both Municipalities and First Nations to further their common and individual interests—especially by giving them the opportunity to identify those interests in the first place. This potential is greatest in the major urban areas, but it exists almost everywhere. The relevant subject headings will differ somewhat from place to place, but most will be the everyday matters of local government. First Nation self-government provisions will, of course, be front and centre.

For First Nations, the benefits of this bilateral diplomacy outside the treaty process are substantial. Casting off the old inward-looking philosophy and accepting the new diplomacy opens ways to creative problem solving and positive community development within the First Nations themselves. Community empowerment comes through reaching out and coming to know one's neighbours. Hence, the seeming paradox that the First Nations most committed to strong self-government are those that will most welcome involvement with Municipalities.

Local diplomacy opens the way to meaningful public education. Treaty-oriented local diplomacy brings Municipal leaders, who form the established core of public opinion leaders throughout the province, into a focused learning situation that deals directly with the matters that are the subjects of the critics' misperception and misinformation. Indeed, giving local community leaders the opportunity and the incentive to link their communities' interests to the treaty process seems to be the only workable way of engendering local-level and province-wide appreciation of the treaty process.

(It might even be the case that the treaty process overload could be reduced, to the advantage of all parties, if First Nations were to propose that for the next several years the negotiating tables would not deal with the matters the First Nations wished in the meantime to pursue with their Municipal neighbours. The tables could thus focus on the more economically and politically sensitive subject headings, presumably those relating to natural resources allocation and development.)

Generally, however, the most tangible benefit to the First Nations would be the possibility of Municipal support for their positions at the treaty tables. Municipal leaders do have a representative role that is independent of the *Municipal Act* and in this role, acting on behalf of their communities, they can provide a powerful political resource for First Nations to call upon. Positions and proposals that had been co-operatively developed locally would be both technically and politically more difficult for the so-called "senior" governments to interfere with or to oppose.

Following a Yukon precedent, a First Nation could even include a Municipal representative on its negotiating team. Who knows, since the Agreement establishing the B.C. Treaty Process allows any party to bring any matter to the table, a First Nation could even propose that the local treaty grant self-government and constitutional status to its partner Municipality.

Community, Resource Rents and Tenure

BUD SMITH, QC

On December 11, 1997, when the Supreme Court of Canada decision in *Delgamuukw v. The Queen* (1997) 153 DLR (4) 193 was rendered, the constitutional arrangement between Canada and British Columbia effectively thereby was amended.

It no longer can be asserted that this Province exclusively may make laws in relation to "property" within its boundaries. That constitutional authority, derived from s. 92(13) of the *British North America Act*, at least in the matter of land, now must be shared.

Similarly, it is unclear what, if any, lands, including timber and wood thereon, the Province holds exclusive management and sales authority over as long has been assumed under the authority of s. 92(5) *BNA Act*.

In 1871, British Columbia agreed all sums due from lands, mines and minerals would belong to the Province subject to any Interest other than that of the Province. That constitutional arrangement found in s.109 *BNA Act*, post-*Delgamuukw*, and given any rational interpretation of the Supreme Court of Canada decision, must mean at minimum, resource rent now taken from Crown land will be subject to sharing beyond the exclusive benefit of the province's general revenue fund.

British Columbia earns a substantial part of its income by developing or harvesting land-based resources for exchange in a relatively open export economy. This province's historic sense of itself and definition of community long has been welded to the resource base of that land.

To the extent people have participated in or been excluded from that resource economy very often also has been a function of the way community has been defined. Whatever are the academic subtleties from generation to generation, community at its core, invariably reflects the Webster Dictionary description of "people linked by common interests living in a particular place." If the devil be in the detail, then in this instance, the detail is determining what we accept as being the common interest.

Since the explosion of European contact with people of the Americas in the late 1400s, rarely has there been an instance of balance between the interests of transoceanic migrants and those of indigenous populations.

The North America Free Trade Agreement (NAFTA) countries have pursued three distinct policies to accommodate cultural difference. The notion of a cultural mosaic in Canada, the melting pot concept in the United States, and the idea of convergence in Mexico characterize each NAFTA country's respective constitutional, political, and economic development.

In the NAFTA countries, there has been a consistency in the marginalization of many indigenous populations. Indigenous populations of each country have advanced a request for respect of traditional lands. After talking has failed in each country, claims to pre-contact rights and land title have been asserted successfully in Court by indigenous people.

The decision in *Delgamuukw* is not an aberration from settled law by an isolated, out-of-tune Supreme Court of Canada. In fact, the decision builds upon a series of cases adjudicating aboriginal issues, and at its core does not deviate greatly from rulings made by other Courts in common law jurisdictions.

Delgamuukw evokes many responses. Perhaps the most unproductive response is pursuit of some legal or political silver bullet that can negate its impact. The sooner will it be the better that we accept that *Delgamuukw* is neither good, nor bad; that *Delgamuukw* is neither praise worthy, nor blame worthy; *Delgamuukw* is simply the law. It is a piece of the constitutional framework upon which we now will continue the ever-unfinished tasks of building our community.

For merchants of the status quo, the need to contemplate such a profound constitutional rearrangement will be unsettling. Those who trade on uncertainty may see short term opportunity. For most of us, *Delgamuukw* requires redefining many elements of what we call community and of what we see as our common interest, our community interest.

For most of this province's history, community interest has assumed that aboriginal title did not exist in British Columbia. Indeed "community" frequently has not been inclusive of aboriginal people. In the main, as a Province, we have actually or implicitly subscribed through our actions to the notion expressed by Premier Sir Richard McBride, who in 1909 was reported by the *Montreal Gazette* as stating that because the Indians had "accepted the white man's machinery, for the policing and general direction of the country, they tacitly confessed themselves conquered. Surely we do not have to go to war and injure a helpless people to technically perfect a title to any part of Canada." In 1973, the British Columbia government, reflecting those same values, unilaterally included the Kamloops Indian Reserve within the boundaries of the then newly amalgamated City of Kamloops. That decision was reversed in January, 1976 following a change of government.

By mutual consent reflecting a better understood common interest, the City of Kamloops and Kamloops Indian Band since have grown a broad community relationship that includes joint Council meetings; development of a major City recreation facility on land leased from the Band; common fire protection service; a common liquid waste management system; and mutual planning for future water, recreation, road, and development services. Today's relationship has built progressively from a set of values much different than that which was manifested in 1973.

While the values now active at Kamloops were not constitutionally mandated, they more importantly reflect a voluntary attitude shift by the community's decision-makers. The area's land now holds greater economic, environmental, cultural, social, and recreation value because enlightened self interest about the idea of what makes community gradually is being redefined.

Moving forward from December 11, 1997, finding the way to creatively benefit communities post-*Delgamuukw*, in some manner, will mean reallocating the resource rent and other bounty taken from British Columbia lands. Reallocation cannot be yet another add-on to the present resource extraction cost regime. That reallocation will not be imposed. Reallocation can come about only upon the new constitutional reality of this province being accepted by its elite and its decision-makers.

Perhaps the place of greatest opportunity, need, and risk for such a reallocation to begin is in working forests across British Columbia. That is the case, in part, because those forests now are the focus for much change and considerable community division. Using the fact of the decision in *Delgamuukw* could be the catalyst required to initiate that focus from a foundation point more fundamental than now is being considered.

For several years there has been a need for change in our forests. Change that augments stewardship, recognizes aboriginal claims, fosters innovation, enhances the annual cut, is attractive to capital, and supports creation of jobs. Achieving all or even any of those goals requires change to our foundational system of ownership and tenure. While understanding the need, and occasionally testing the waters, decision-makers have declined to visit the system at its foundation. Instead decision-makers of all stripes have chosen to maintain the tenure status quo, whilst piling onto it a veritable mountain of centralized regulation. That choice has been made in substantial part, because to test the foundations so fundamentally would provoke significant negative response from the many who have a vested interest in that status quo.

All too often, fundamental change in our province is advanced only after roundly vilifying what is being replaced. That process necessitates much focus on problems of the past and insufficient focus on opportunities for the future. In the context of forests, the tenure system has served beneficially in a number of respects. Most importantly, it has been the cornerstone around which relative economic stability has been made available to communities, especially in the interior. As a consequence, current social, physical, educational, health and cultural infrastructure was made possible, in contrast to consequential results of the earlier itinerant nature of mechanical conversion in the forests.

As the current tenure system has matured, we have witnessed a tendency to capital-intensive, centralized conversion facilities producing a relatively uniform dimensional wood product. That phenomenon works against creative species utilization, marginalizes innovators, diminishes good stewardship, reduces the resource's job potential, and has led to over-administration. The greatest imbalance from those results appears to visit itself on communities closest to the resource. Coincidentally, those communities often are places with relatively large aboriginal populations.

The current forest tenure system once was an extraordinarily powerful tool which rewarded innovators and created conditions for building the single most important economic engine in the province. Today, that same tenure system works against innovators and has become a major impediment to challenging the status quo in our most significant natural resource. If *Delgamuukw* does nothing else, it will cause the status quo to be challenged in every aspect of land use across British Columbia.

Responding to that challenge will be a seminal test for the leadership of our province in every community, every resource industry, and every public policy institution.

Shortly after the decision in *Delgamuukw* was given, Chief Herb George addressed members of the Shuswap Tribal Council and others, including myself, at a meeting in Kamloops.

Chief Jules invited me from the floor to speak. As I approached the speaking area, a thought occurred to me, and I talked about the inherent symbolism in having a successful plaintiff and one of the named (by office) unsuccessful defendants standing together on the same platform.

Symbolic in two important ways. From all trials there is a winner, which usually means there is a loser. If you pass over the chance for dialogue and eschew the ever-present opportunity to avoid litigation, the risk taken is that you will be the loser. My standing next to Chief George enabled Shuswap people to see a symbolic picture of the fact that trials lead to winning, or to losing.

The second and more important symbol seen that evening is that once the trial is over, people who have represented opposing positions can stand together to begin the task of openly moving forward in search of common interests.

Recognizing litigation leads to a kind of tyranny imposed by the word "or" as in winners or losers, all potential parties to future litigation surrounding issues of aboriginal title should reflect carefully before proceeding. The Crown ignored 115 years of opportunity to seek alternatives to litigation and, as a result, has had its constitutional authority amended, in the case of the Province; and likely must carry a significant financial obligation, in the case of Canada. Aboriginal communities likely have little to gain through further litigation, and potentially a good deal to lose as the details of occupancy, infringement, and justification are defined within the very real constraints articulated in *Delgamuukw* (see postscript).

If we so choose, post-*Delgamuukw*, we can move forward on several vexing issues rooted in how this land is used. Forests may be amongst the most important places to begin. The very nature of that resource speaks to the utility of finding common interest about its stewardship and use. To begin that journey will require the discarding of preconceived notions about ownership and tenure.

Should they choose, public policy leaders can decide on those changes, confident vested interests can be answered by asserting change is required following the Supreme Court of Canada ruling in *Delgamuukw*. In that regard, *Delgamuukw* may prove to be a heaven-sent opportunity to address, without preconditions, the intertwined issues of title, tenure, ownership, stewardship, community benefit, harvesting technique, and resource rents.

When the Supreme Court of Canada said aboriginal title is a burden on the Crown's underlying title, it did not thereby also say aboriginal title is a burden on people. How we as people—aboriginal and non-aboriginal people alike—choose to address that Crown title burden will be a function of how we address our own responsibility to ourselves, to the law, and to our community.

Lands in this province were improperly taken, according to the very legal tradition brought here by those who did the taking. Common to all NAFTA countries are grievances from that taking, which must be settled honourably before any community can move forward. We can favourably settle grievances AND find a common community interest.

We do have choices. We can choose to argue about compensation or infringement or occupancy. We alternatively can focus on identifying a common community interest, from which a remodelled constitutional foundation for governance can be built.

Each of us bears some responsibility for the choice that will be made. May we be given the strength and grace to carry our own share of that responsibility.

Postscript

On January 20, 2000 Justice George Lamperson gave reasons for his Supreme Court of British Columbia judgement in *Chief Ron Ignace et al. (Appellants) and the Registrar of Land Titles, Kamloops Land Titles District (Respondent)* confirming the Registrar's refusal to register a certificate of pending litigation pertaining to an aboriginal title claim. This judgement relies upon and reaffirms the British Columbia Court of Appeal decision in *Ukw v. BC* (1987), 16 BCLR (2d) 145 (CA), which decision precludes an aboriginal title claimant from filing a *lis pendens* under the Land Title Act. Justice Lamperson ruled "there is nothing in the *Delgamuukw* decision which supports the Band's contention that *Ukw* no longer applies." The Lamperson ruling is being appealed. The appellants requested a five judge panel at the Court of Appeal to argue the *Ukw* decision should be reversed. That request was denied. The appeal was heard the last week of June, 2000.

The underlying issues involve the nature and extent of aboriginal title over lands registered in fee simple to owners of the property known as Six Mile Ranch, on which a significant equestrian, agritourism, golf, hotel, condominium, and marina development has been approved.

Using the Six Mile Ranch project as a test case to advance the value of *Delgamuukw* for aboriginal communities likely will prove to have been an unwise choice. Registering a *lis pendens* on development approved lands, usually has potential to induce a cash settlement from the developer. The Six Mile Ranch developer, however, has chosen to litigate and apparently has the resources and will to see the issue through on legal principle. The Province has not pursued a monetary settlement of the aboriginal title claim and cannot compromise the fee simple interests without attracting great liability.

The fee simple / aboriginal title issues in the *Ignace* appeal are not unique to the Six Mile Ranch and the Court of Appeal decision will have impact on every fee simple title in British Columbia.

The underlying claim to aboriginal title at the Six Mile Ranch is not self-evident and has not been pursued by Skeetchestn Indian Band or the Secwepemc Aboriginal Nation through their own currently active litigation process. Details about occupancy, beyond the mere assertion of occupancy, so far have not been made evident. Meeting the *Delgamuukw* tests and discussion about infringement and justification will be an extraordinary challenge for the aboriginal title claimants at Six Mile Ranch.

Almost assuredly the *Ignace* case will stand as an example of why reliance on *Delgamuukw* for litigation which is not grounded upon a solid underlying claim of aboriginal title, may result in a substantial diminution of *Delgamuukw*'s value for all aboriginal communities.

Land Claim Settlements
Who Should Pay, Ottawa or Victoria?

MELVIN H. SMITH, QC

The question that I am called upon to answer is, assuming there are to be land-claim settlements, which level of government is to pay for them—the federal government or the government of British Columbia, or both? I will endeavour to show that there is a clear answer to that question to be found in the constitutional documents that brought British Columbia into Confederation in 1871.

However, a preliminary observation is necessary. Very little has been said to date about the *measure* of compensation that ought to be paid to relinquish aboriginal title in specific cases in light of the decision of the Supreme Court of Canada in *Delgamuukw*. Obviously the measure of compensation should vary, depending on how heavy the burden of aboriginal title is in a site-specific situation. For example, the burden of aboriginal title will be the greatest in areas that are and have been occupied since 1846 on a daily basis by native communities for their settlements or other daily uses. On the other hand, those areas that are more remote and are less frequented by a native presence will have a much lighter burden of aboriginal title upon them and therefore the degree of compensation should be much less. It may well be that in British Columbia, much of the lands heavily burdened with aboriginal title are already included in Indian reserves set aside "for the use and benefit" of various native bands throughout the province.

These are difficult judgments to make. I do not believe that these decisions ought to be the subject of negotiation because I have little confidence in government negotiators holding the line or following any fixed criteria on these kind of issues. From what I see, the tendency is for government negotiators to make endless concessions and pay any price to reach an agreement regardless of the high cost to the public interest. Because of the difficulty in making determinations on what I call the *weight* of aboriginal title, I am of the view that these issues should be decided by a court comprised of judges with some expertise in determining land values and arriving at decisions on the measure of compensation in an expeditious way. Australia has followed this course.

Which level of government ought to pay the bill?

The natural tendency is to respond by suggesting that both Ottawa and Victoria ought to share the cost. Certainly this is the basis on which land claims negotiations have been proceeding thus far. But to suggest a joint sharing of costs is to totally ignore the historical and constitutional relationship on native matters that was established in 1871, when British Columbia entered Confederation. Specifically, I am speaking of section 13 of the Terms of Union entered into between Canada and British Columbia and approved 127 years ago on July 20. People's eyes tend to glaze over when I talk about the Terms of Union, but they ought not to, for the Terms of Union are as much a part of the Constitution of Canada as is the Charter of Rights and Freedoms or section 35, which recognizes aboriginal and treaty rights, or any other section of the Constitution.

It is important to realize that these Terms of Union are not some archaic, dead-letter document that are of use only to archivists and students of history. They set out rights and obligations that are very much alive and well. A clear illustration of this occurred a few years ago in respect of the Terms of Union of Prince Edward Island's entry into Canada in 1870. One of the terms of Prince Edward Island's entry into Confederation was that the federal government would at all times provide a ferry link from the mainland to Prince Edward Island. This had been done continuously since Confederation through the CNR, which operated a daily ferry service. In the mid-1970s, a lawful strike interrupted the ferry service between the mainland and Prince Edward Island. The government of Prince Edward Island sued the government of Canada for a breach of the Terms of Union by Ottawa for not maintaining the ferry link. Prince Edward Island was successful before the Supreme Court of Canada and was awarded a substantial claim in damages against Ottawa.

Let me dip back into British Columbia history. British Columbia does not owe its origins to its entry into Confederation in 1871 or even to the Canadian Confederation of 1867. The Crown Colony of Vancouver Island was established by Royal Grant in 1849 and a second colony comprising the mainland of British Columbia was established a few years later. Both colonies were united by Imperial legislation in 1866 to become the area that we now know as British Columbia.

James Douglas, the Chief Factor for the Hudson's Bay Company on Vancouver Island was appointed Governor of the island colony in 1851. By instructions from his Company's head office, Douglas was advised "to consider the natives as the rightful possessors of such lands *only as they occupy by cultivation or had houses built on* such lands at the time when the Island came under the undivided sovereignty of Great Britain in 1846." All other land was "to be regarded as waste, and applicable for the purposes of civilization" (Emphasis added).

To ensure friendly relations with the natives, who far outnumbered the handful of white settlers, Douglas went beyond his instructions and began to enter into agreements with certain native tribes around Victoria, Saanich, Fort Rupert and Nanaimo. Over a six-year period, Douglas entered into 14 such agreements. The agreements preserved to the Indians their village sites and farmlands and permitted them to continue hunting and fishing in unoccupied areas. Even though these agreements were expressly made by the Hudson's Bay Company and not the Crown, subsequent judicial interpretations have found them to be treaties between the Crown and the tribes involved. They are known as the "Douglas" Treaties. Douglas's efforts of this kind were not supported in London and so he discontinued the practice. Apart from a portion of the Peace River district that is included in Treaty 8 negotiated by the federal government in 1899, these are the only "treaties" that exist in British Columbia.

Although abandoning treaty-making as such, Douglas by no means forsook dealing with the native interest. As an alternative, he embarked upon a vigorous policy of establishing Indian reserves. This was a most significant development for it established a direction in white-native relations in this province that is distinct from early colony policy in the rest of Canada. (Supporters of modern-day treaty making are quick to commend Douglas for his early treaty-making efforts, but are inclined to ignore his even more significant efforts at establishing reserves.)

By 1858, the province's non-native population was swelling in the wake of a gold rush. Demand boomed for quality land in good locations for white settlers. Douglas, by now Governor of both the Island and Mainland colonies, responded by establishing Indian reserves. With input from the Indians, he allotted land for band villages, burial grounds, cultivation, and hunting. Indians were also entitled to the free use of all unoccupied lands until taken up by settlers by pre-emption or homesteading. By 1871, 120 Indian reserves had been established throughout the Colony. But this was only the beginning.

When B.C. entered Confederation in 1871, Ottawa assumed legislative responsibility for its "Indians and Lands reserved for Indians" under the terms of the *British North America Act, 1867*. Article 13 of B.C.'s Terms of Union with Canada placed other obligations on Ottawa. It reads:

> *The charge of the Indians* and the trusteeship and management of the lands reserved for their use and benefit, shall be assumed by the Dominion Government, and a policy as liberal as that hitherto pursued by the British Columbia Government, shall be continued by the Dominion Government after the Union. (Emphasis added)

Article 13 goes on to require the Province to provide tracts of land for the establishment of additional Indian reserves "of such extent as it has hitherto been the practice of the British Columbia Government." **In sum, the expressed constitutional obligation of the Province was to provide lands for more reserves. Nothing more. Any and all other constitutional obligations to the native people rested on Ottawa's shoulders.**

No mention was made in the Terms of Union of "Indian title." This was no mere oversight. Just a year earlier in 1870, the legislation that constituted Manitoba as a province specifically mentioned unextinguished Indian title and how it would impact on land conveyances. It is inconceivable that the question of Indian title, so fresh in the mind of federal authorities in 1870 in respect of Manitoba, would be overlooked only one year later when B.C.'s entry to Canada was under consideration. **The better view is that there was recognition by federal authorities in 1871 that B.C. was dealing with the Indian matter differently, i.e. by the establishment of reserves.**

The practice of establishing Indian reserves without entering into treaties sets B.C. apart from the rest of Canada in dealing with the Indian interest. This is born out by the fact that of 2,323 Indian reserves throughout Canada today, 1,634 of them are located in British Columbia. Critics have made much of the fact that, while many in number, the reserves established in B.C. are small in size in comparison to the fewer but larger reserves established on the Prairies. Smallness is due in part to the differences in the topography of the two regions and also due to varying habits, wants and pursuits of the Indians themselves.

On the coast at least, large blocks of agricultural land are in short supply. Moreover, the coastal Indian economy was mainly derived from the products of the sea. Hence coastal reserves tended to include pocket-sized settlements in valley bottoms and fishing sites along the coast or along riverbanks. In the B.C. interior, reserves were somewhat larger to provide for some measure of future farming and ranching. By contrast, the Prairies were blessed with semi-open plains of vast proportions. The federal government could afford to be generous in allocating reserves on the Prairies and still have adequate land for settlers.

That said, the per capita difference is not all that great. The total area of reserves in Canada is 2.68 million hectares. In B.C., the total area of reserves is 344 thousand hectares or 13 per cent of the total of Canada. B.C. has 17 percent of Canada's status Indians. Incidentally, the total land area contained in Indian reserves throughout Canada comprises 10,021 square miles, which the Canadian Almanac describes as "one of the largest land holdings in the free world."

By the passage of Order in Council PC.1265, dated July 19, 1924, the federal government formally acknowledged that B.C. had satisfied all its obligations of Article 13 of the Terms of Union respecting the furnishing of lands for Indian reserves and described the process as a "full and final settlement of all differences between the governments of the Dominion and the Province." Such an acknowledgment by the federal government is support for the position of every B.C. government up to 1991 that B.C. had fully discharged its obligations to its Indians even though it had done so differently from the rest of Canada.

What has been the practice elsewhere in Canada? Treaty-making has been the usual practice. But have provinces been involved in treaty-making? With the exception of Québec, all Indian treaties entered into since 1867 have seen the federal government as the sole signatory on behalf of government. In northern Québec the situation is different because the constitutional obligation of the government of Québec is different. When the vast northern territories were added to Québec by federal legislation in 1912, it was expressly conditional upon *Québec* obtaining surrenders of aboriginal rights. Consequently, when the government of Québec entered into modern treaties with the Cree and Inuit of northern Québec in 1975, and the Naskapi Indians in 1978, the government of Québec obtained similar surrenders.

No similar express constitutional obligation falls on the government of British Columbia. In fact, the very opposite is the case because section 13 of B.C.'s Terms of Union imposes on the federal government "the charge of the Indians."

Why then has the present government of B.C. involved itself in the treaty-making business? Did the B.C. government wrongfully conclude that because the government of Québec entered into treaties, B.C. is obliged to do likewise? Was there a serious analysis made of the constitutional differences between Québec and British Columbia on this issue before B.C. plunged headlong into the process? Apparently not.

This is not merely some kind of academic issue akin to how many angels can dance on the head of a pin. The answer to it determines whether the Canadian taxpayer at large or the B.C. taxpayer will pick up the tab for land claim settlements in this province. More than that, the Crown land is owned by the Province. If the responsibility for settling claims is the federal government's alone, as I suggest it is, then the federal government should be required to buy from the province, presumably at fair market-value, any land or resources it wished to include in a land claim agreement. This might have the desirable effect of lessening the tendency of government land claim negotiators to be as generous as they seem willing to be with the public's land and resources.

Over and over in *Delgamuukw*, the Supreme Court of Canada emphasizes that the Province of British Columbia cannot legislate in relation to Indians because that is a matter exclusively given to the federal Parliament under section 91(24) of the Constitution. The Court also said that the provincial government cannot extinguish aboriginal title. The opposite side of the same coin is in section 13 of the Terms of Union, which places the obligation for the "charge of the Indians" exclusively in the hands of the federal government. It seems to me that he who calls the tune constitutionally (in this case the federal government alone) should pay the piper. The government of British Columbia should not only leave land claim negotiations and entering into treaties to the federal government but it should seriously consider serving notice on the federal government that it expects to be indemnified for any failure of the federal government to discharge its obligation toward the Indians as required of it under section 13 of the Terms of Union.

3 Impact in Alberta, Saskatchewan and Manitoba

The Effect upon Alberta Land Claims

Tom Flanagan

At first glance, the *Delgamuukw* decision may seem to have little or no bearing upon native land claims in Alberta. In *Delgamuukw*, the Supreme Court of Canada held that aboriginal title may still exist in British Columbia because it has not been extinguished through negotiated agreement or appropriate legislation. All of Alberta, however, has been surrendered to the Crown through five of the Numbered Treaties:

Treaty 4 (extension)	1894
Treaty 6	1876
Treaty 7	1877
Trcaty 8	1899
Treaty 10	1906

Each of the Numbered Treaties states, in the words of Treaty 6, that the Indian signatories "do hereby cede, release, surrender and yield up to the Government of the Dominion of Canada, for her Majesty the Queen and Her successors forever, all their rights, titles and privileges, whatsoever, to the lands" described in the treaty.[1] If all bands signing treaties have given up their aboriginal rights and title to land, *Delgamuukw*

Notes will be found on pages 181–182.

at most might have relevance to a few Alberta bands, such as the Lubicon Cree or the "Aseniwuche Winewak Nation" (previously the Métis of Grande Cache), whose members claim to still possess aboriginal rights and title because they have not adhered to any treaty.[2] If this were all, *Delgamuukw* would only affect the rights of a small number of Alberta bands in remote locations and would hardly justify being discussed at a national conference. I believe, however, that the matter is more complicated than appears at first glance. While the direct impact of *Delgamuukw* upon Alberta and the other prairie provinces may be small, its indirect impact may turn out to be very great because of the way that the Supreme Court treated oral traditions in that case.

Prior to the 1990s, oral traditions played only a limited role in native-rights litigation. In the 1935 *Dreaver* case, the Exchequer Court heard testimony from Chief Dreaver, who had been present at the signing of Treaty 6 in 1876, and allowed him to state his understanding of the "medicine chest" clause in that treaty.[3] In 1971, Justice Morrow heard oral evidence from Indians who had witnessed the signing of Treaties 8 and 11. But neither of these cases had high legal (as compared to political) impact. Justice Morrow's decision was overturned on appeal, and *Dreaver* remained little known and was not even reported until the 1970s. Moreover, both cases exemplified not oral traditions in the true sense of stories passed down across generations, but non-literate witnesses recounting their own memories of events witnessed decades ago.

The Supreme Court of Canada said in the *Horse* case (1988) that treaties should be interpreted in accordance with the normal rule for contracts, "that extrinsic evidence is not to be used in the absence of ambiguity."[4] In other words, the *Horse* rule was that oral traditions could be used as an aid to interpretation where courts found the wording of a treaty unclear. More recently, the Supreme Court's *Badger* decision (1996) opened the door even more widely to the use of oral traditions. Justice Peter Cory wrote:

> The treaties, as written documents, recorded an agreement that had already been reached orally and they did not always record the full extent of the oral agreement .... The treaties were drafted in English by representatives of the Canadian government who, it should be assumed, were familiar with common law doctrines. Yet, the treaties were not translated in written form into the languages ... of the various Indian nations who were signatories. Even if they had been, it is unlikely that the Indians, who had a history of communicating only orally, would have understood them any differently. As a result, it is well settled that the words in the treaty must not be interpreted in their strict technical sense nor subjected to

rigid modern rules of construction. Rather, they must be interpreted in the sense that they would naturally have been understood by the Indians at the time of the signing.[5]

The Court's decision in *Badger* did not turn entirely, or even chiefly, on oral tradition; but it did make use of oral tradition, as recounted by a Cree Elder, to help interpret the words of Treaty 8 as well as the accompanying promises made by government representatives during the negotiations.

The judicial standing of oral traditions received a further boost in 1997, when the Supreme Court of Canada handed down its *Delgamuukw* decision. The technical reason why the Court ordered a new trial in that case was its finding that the trial judge, although he had admitted the oral histories of the Gitksan and Wet'suwet'en as evidence, "went on to give these oral histories no independent weight at all."[6] Chief Justice Antonio Lamer laid down the following principle:

Notwithstanding the challenges created by the use of oral histories as proof of historical facts, the laws of evidence must be adapted in order that this type of evidence can be accommodated and placed on an equal footing with the types of historical evidence that courts are familiar with, which largely consists of historical documents.[7]

The Chief Justice was rightly concerned that, in cases like *Delgamuukw*, involving facts from a time when no written records existed, it might be impossible for native plaintiffs to make out any case at all if oral traditions were not given independent weight.[8]

There are, however, some important differences between *Delgamuukw* and treaty litigation. In *Delgamuukw*, there was no text to interpret because there was no treaty; the Indian plaintiffs were offering their oral traditions as evidence about their occupancy of land prior to the time when white settlers were present to write down their observations. In contrast, treaty cases focus on the interpretation of a text, and Indian oral traditions recount events which are also recorded in conventional documents. Indeed, Indian peoples had already become at least partially literate when the later treaties were signed.

In 1836, the Methodist missionary James Evans developed a syllabic form of writing for the Cree language.[9] Syllabics were quickly adopted by missionaries of other faiths and adapted to other native languages of the north, such as Dene and Inuktitut. Henry Faraud, who founded the first Oblate mission at Fort Chipewyan, used syllabics from the outset as a tool of evangelization.[10] After Indian converts learned to read Christian texts and hymns in their own languages, they used syllabics for secular purposes, such as sending letters.[11] Father René Fumoleau's book, *As Long As This Land Shall Last,* contains a photographic reproduction of a letter written in syllabics in 1883 by two Chipewyan chiefs.[12]

To be sure, only a relatively small number of northern native people were literate in any language by 1899, but they would all have understood the importance of writing. Those who had converted to Christianity attended religious services involving the Bible, prayer books, and hymnals. All aboriginals, whether Christian or not, had been dealing with fur traders for over a century and so had come into contact with written contracts, bills of sale, and account books. According to the documentary evidence of the treaty negotiations, the Indians understood the importance of the written treaty and were anxious to obtain copies of it. The Cree chief Keenoshayo said at Lesser Slave Lake in 1899: "We want a written treaty, one copy to be given to us, so we shall know what we sign for."[13]

The courts will, no doubt, take such factors into account when they weigh the importance of oral traditions in treaty litigation. Nonetheless, I suspect that the *Delgamuukw* decision may tend to raise the status of oral traditions in treaty litigation. Is it likely that Canadian courts, having swung the door wide open to oral traditions in aboriginal rights litigation, will leave it barely cracked in treaty cases? There will be strong pressure to adopt the *Delgamuukw* approach, whatever that turns out to be in practice, across the board.

This would mean repudiation of the quite limited approach to oral traditions taken in *Horse.* Advocates of aboriginal rights detest the *Horse* decision and are continually inviting the Supreme Court to overrule it.[14] Their goal is to promulgate a transformed understanding of treaties in which the written words of the agreement are not determinative because, as Sharon Venne puts it, "the written text expresses only the government of Canada's view of the treaty relationship: it does not embody the negotiated agreement."[15]

Not surprisingly, the Royal Commission on Aboriginal Peoples (RCAP) adopted a similar point of view:

> The commission believes that the unique nature of the historical treaties requires special rules to give effect to the treaty nations' understanding of the treaties. Such an approach to the content of the treaties would require, as a first step, the rejection of the idea that the written text is the exclusive record of the treaty.[16]

The real target in all of this is extinguishment, that is, the surrender of aboriginal title.[17] "The treaty nations," wrote RCAP, "maintain with virtual unanimity that they did not agree to extinguish their rights to their traditional lands and territories but agreed instead to share them in some equitable fashion with the newcomers."[18] RCAP conceded that "the text of the post-1850 treaties clearly provides for the extinguishment of Aboriginal title" but argued that we cannot rely upon the text because "the people of the treaty nations reject that outcome."[19] Moreover, aboriginal people could not have surrendered their title because they did not understand the legal language of the treaties and their own cultures and languages did not contain concepts like rights, surrender, and extinguishment. "Thus, it is possible that Aboriginal title continues to coexist with the Crown's rights throughout the areas covered by treaties, despite the Crown's intention to include a cession of Aboriginal title."[20]

RCAP's conclusion was that Canada should henceforth act on the basis of this novel and untested legal theory and regard aboriginal peoples as co-owners of all land, even though they signed agreements extinguishing their land rights, have received substantial benefits for doing so, and continue to seek punctilious fulfilment of those treaty clauses from which they draw benefits. The Commission's call for the "implementation and renewal of treaties"[21] comes down in the end to a one-sided reading of the treaties. Implementation means that clauses conferring benefits must be fulfilled to the letter, while renewal means that clauses involving the surrender of rights must be ignored, reinterpreted, or replaced.

An early victory of this view of treaties occurred in the campaign against Treaty 11. In 1973, sixteen chiefs in the Northwest Territories and northern Alberta attempted to register a caveat on about 400,000 square miles of land ceded by Treaties 8 and 11. They succeeded in persuading Justice Morrow of the Supreme Court of the Northwest Territories that "notwithstanding the language of the two Treaties there is sufficient doubt on the facts that aboriginal title was extinguished that such claim for title should be permitted to be put forward by the caveators."[22] At trial, the would-be caveators produced a series of Elders who had been present (mostly as children) at the signing in 1921 and who testified, in the words of Chief François Paulette:

> No lands have ever been surrendered or ceded in the first treaty. It was sort of a peace treaty ....
>
> No land was mentioned. That peace treaty was with regard to whether the white people can come in without any conflict with the Indians and the Indians have no conflict with the white people.[23]

This view of the treaty was widely disseminated through Father Fumoleau's book. Morrow's decision in the *Paulette* case was overturned on appeal, but the political victory had been won. The federal government entered into negotiations with the Dene and Metis of the Northwest Territories (but not Alberta) for a new land-claim agreement.

The repudiation of treaties has not yet spread to other parts of Canada, perhaps because conditions in the Mackenzie Valley were unique. Land there was still under the jurisdiction of a federal territory, so a provincial government did not have to agree to give up control of its Crown lands. Also, reserves had never been taken up, relatively little land had been alienated to private owners, and native people were still a demographic majority outside of Yellowknife.

Delgamuukw's elevation of oral traditions will abet the guerrilla warfare in the courts, in which aboriginal advocates are attempting to undo extinguishment by gradually undermining the Crown's control of public lands and natural resources. A recent example is a case decided by the Provincial Court of Saskatchewan in 1998, which acquitted two Dene from Buffalo Narrows of the charge of hunting moose illegally on the Primrose Lake Air Weapons Range. Basing this part of his judgment largely on Dene oral tradition, the judge held that Treaty 10, even though it contains the usual clause about surrender of title to the land, actually meant that "the land would thereafter be *shared* along principled lines."[24] The decision was overturned on appeal;[25] but if it had stood, it would have deprived Saskatchewan of its control over resource development on Crown land, compelling the province to get permission from one or more Indian bands every time a project is contemplated. There might also have been implications about compensation for past developments in which the Crown acted as if it had a clear title.

Another example is the *RioAlto* case now wending its way through the Alberta courts. RioAlto Exploration sought and obtained permission in the normal way from the Ministry of Environmental Protection to run seismic lines in the Treaty 8 area. The Fort McKay First Nation, alleging that seismic exploration would interfere with its members' trap-lines, asked the Court of Queen's Bench for "an Order of Mandamus compelling the Minister of Environmental Protection to consult with the Applicants regarding the scope, nature and extent of the impact of all exploratory activities approved by that minister on the exercise of the Treaty and Aboriginal rights of the Applicants."[26] What the band is after is the right to approve, and receive compensation for, any economic development on Crown land in what it considers its traditional territory—in effect, a form of co-ownership with the province. Counsel for the band will base an argument on the Treaty's guarantee of the continued right to hunt and fish on Crown land. The language of the treaty is inconvenient, because it says that hunting and fishing can continue "saving and excepting such tracts as may be required or taken up from time to time for settlement, mining, lumbering, trading or other purposes." [27] In response, the McKay First Nation will quote the oral promise of the treaty commissioners:

> But over and above the provision, we had to solemnly assure them that only such laws as to hunting and fishing as were in the interest of the Indians and were found necessary in order to protect the fish and fur-bearing animals would be made, and that they would be as free to hunt and fish after the treaty as they would be if they never entered into it.[28]

They will also bring forward various oral traditions purporting to show that their people never intended to give up their land rights.

The dockets of courts in Alberta and other western provinces are already filled with cases in which aboriginal litigants intend to argue that the treaties do not mean what they appear to mean, and that the written texts can only be understood in the light of aboriginal oral traditions. Aboriginal researchers have been laying the foundations of this campaign for more than 25 years by systematically collecting interviews with tribal Elders. Much of this material has been published in books such as *The Spirit of the Alberta Indian Treaties* and *The True Spirit and Original Intent of Treaty 7*.[29] One only has to glance through these books to find numerous examples of oral traditions purporting to show that Indians never intended to surrender their land rights in the treaties. Consider this conversation of Jean-Marie Mustus with interviewer Richard Lightning in 1975:

> *Lightning:* Do you know how much land was given up or sold to the white man?
>
> *Mustus:* The amount of land they gave up was written down on paper. I am wondering whether it was one foot underground or more. It was written down, but I do not know where the paper could be found.
>
> *Lightning:* And you do not know how much was to be used?
>
> *Mustus:* No, I do not know, but whatever they selected for themselves they kept; the rest was taken. I do not recall my grandfather telling me about the depth underground.
>
> *Lightning:* Did he ever tell you anything about underground minerals or oil?
>
> *Mustus:* Yes, these things were mentioned, as was the timber within the reserve; the Indians had a right to anything underground.[30]

This sort of quotation will be marshalled in support of continuing Indian rights over mineral and timber resources.

This is not just a problem for Alberta or the prairie provinces. Treaties 3 and 5 cover parts of north-western Ontario as well as Manitoba; and Treaty 9, negotiated in 1905-06 and expanded by adhesions in 1929-30, covers more than two-thirds of the entire province of Ontario. These are Numbered Treaties and will have to be construed by the courts in the same way as the other Numbered Treaties that cover the prairie provinces. The southern part of Ontario was surrendered by a large number of earlier treaties that present additional issues, but there is no reason to doubt they will be equally open to reinterpretation based on oral traditions.

As an example of what to expect in Ontario, Patrick Macklem has recently argued that the extinguishment of aboriginal title in Treaty 9 is only "apparent." [31] According to Macklem's "expansive interpretation of the right to hunt, trap, and fish," [32] the province cannot undertake or authorize any development that would cause aboriginal hunting, fishing, and trapping to become less successful than they have been, "measured by reference to the fruits of past practice." [33]

If extinguishment is undermined in the courts by such an "expansive" interpretation of hunting rights, buttressed by the oral traditions that *Delgamuukw* has so powerfully endorsed, it will produce an awkward duplication of property rights. Indian bands will not receive ownership rights as such, but rather veto rights, or perhaps the right to be consulted, on economic development projects that might affect hunting, fishing, and trapping in "traditional territories" whose boundaries are at present not defined. Provinces will lose the ability they now have to undertake or authorize projects on their own authority. It is, moreover, inevitable that bands will have overlapping conceptions of their traditional territories, so that provincial authorities may have to deal with two or more bands, not just for major projects like dams, but for minor projects like seismic lines. Such an impossibly cumbersome system of dual or multiple property rights would stultify economic activity.

In any case, it seems likely that the *Delgamuukw* decision is destined to reverberate across Alberta, the other prairie provinces, and Ontario—wherever land-surrender treaties are in place. Native litigants will mobilize oral traditions to bolster their claims that, whatever the treaties appear to say, their aboriginal rights and title are unextinguished. They will appeal to the authority of *Delgamuukw* to persuade courts to place their oral traditions "on an equal footing" with the texts of the treaties. If provincial governments hope to retain the control of Crown land that they have enjoyed in the past, their litigators will have to learn to deal with oral traditions more effectively than they have done in the past.

Epilogue

In the highly publicized *Donald Marshall* decision, released September 17, 1999, the Supreme Court of Canada drove the final nail in the coffin of *Horse*, holding in effect that extrinsic evidence must always be used in interpreting treaties.[34] *Donald Marshall* did not deal with oral traditions as such, but rather with a presumed contemporary oral understanding of the treaty to be inferred from documentary evidence. Although not a definitive precedent for the mandatory use of oral traditions in interpreting the Numbered Treaties, it is further evidence that the Supreme Court is moving in that direction.

Notes

1 Treaty 6, in John Leonard Taylor, *Treaty Research Report: Treaty Six (1876)* (Treaties and Historical Research Centre, Indian and Northern Affairs Canada, 1985), p. 60.

2 On the Lubicon, see Thomas Flanagan, "Adhesion to Canadian Indian Treaties and the Lubicon Lake Dispute," *Canadian Journal of Law and Society* 7 (1992), pp. 185-205. The Aseniwuche Winewak Nation have a long history of making claims as Metis; see Trudy Nicks, "Grande Cache: The Historic Development of an Indigenous Alberta Métis Population," in Jacqueline Peterson and Jennifer S.H. Brown, eds., *The New Peoples: Being and Becoming Métis in North America* (Winnipeg: University of Manitoba Press, 1985), pp. 163-181. They recently presented themselves as an Indian nation in an appeal to the Tax Assessment Review Board of the Municipal District of Greenview, No. 16, 1998.

3 Delia Opekokew, "A Review of Ethnocentric Bias Facing Indian Witnesses," in Richard Gosse, James Youngblood Henderson, and Roger Carter, eds., *Continuing Poundmaker and Riel's Quest: Presentations Made at a Conference on Aboriginal Peoples and Justice* (Saskatoon: Purich, 1994), p. 197.

4 *R. v. Horse* [1988] 2 W.W.R., p. 300.

5 *R. v. Badger* [1996] 133 D.L.R. (4th), p. 344.

6 *Delgamuukw v. British Columbia* [1997] 153 D.L.R. (4th), p. 235.

7 Ibid., p. 232.

8 Ibid., p. 239.

9 Regna Darnell, "Cree Syllabics," *The Canadian Encyclopedia* (Edmonton: Hurtig, 1985), vol. 1, pp. 438-439.

10 Henry Faraud, *Dix-hit ans chez les sauvages* (Paris: Régis Ruffet, 1866), pp. 117-118, 155.

11 Telephone interview with Raymond Huel, Department of History, University of Lethbridge, June 22, 1998.

12 René Fumoleau, *As Long as This Land Shall Last* (Toronto: McClelland and Stewart, n.d.), pp. 32-33.

13 Charles Mair, *Through the Mackenzie Basin: A Narrative of the Athabasca and Peace River Treaty Expedition of 1899* (London: Simpkin, Marshall, Hamilton, Kent & Co., 1908), p. 62.

14 E.g., Monique M. Ross and Cheryl Y. Sharvit, "Forest Management in Alberta and Rights to Hunt, Trap and Fish under Treaty 8," *Alberta Law Review* 36 (1998), p. 648; Alan Pratt, "The Numbered Treaties and Extinguishment: A Legal Analysis," Discussion Paper for the Royal Commission on Aboriginal Peoples, May 1995, pp. 41-43; Royal Commission on Aboriginal Peoples, Report (Ottawa: Minister of Supply and Services, 1996), vol 2, p. 29.

15 Sharon Venne, "Understanding Treaty 6: An Indigenous Perspective," in Michael Asch, ed., *Aboriginal and Treaty Rights in Canada: Essays on Law, Equality, and Respect for Difference* (Vancouver: University of British Columbia Press, 1997) p. 173.

16 RCAP, *Report*, p. 35.

17 Michael Asch and Norman Zlotkin, "Affirming Aboriginal Title: A New Basis for Comprehensive Claims Negotiations," in Asch, *Aboriginal and Treaty Rights in Canada*, p. 209.

18 RCAP, Report., p. 45.

19 Ibid.

20 Ibid., p. 47.

21 Ibid., p. 50.

22 Fumoleau, *As Long as This Land Shall Last*, p. 13.

23 Trial transcript, p. 157. Glenbow Alberta Institute, William G. Morrow Papers, M 1865, box 1, file 1.

24 *R. v. Catarat and Sylvestre*, Provincial Court of Saskatchewan, August 26, 1998, typescript, p. 39.

25 *R. v. Catarat and Sylvestre*, Saskatchewan Court of Queen's Bench, August 25, 1999.

26 Originating Notice, *Ahyasou et al. v. RioAlto et al.*, February 13, 1998, s. 5.

27 Treaty 8, in Dennis F.K. Madill, *Treaty Research Report: Treaty Eight* (Treaties and Historical Research Centre, Indian and Northern Affairs Canada, 1986), p. 128.

28 Madill, *Treaty Eight*, pp. 122-123.

29 Richard Price, ed., *The Spirit of the Alberta Indian Treaties* (Ottawa: Institute for Research on Public Policy, 1979); Treaty 7 Elders et al., *The True Spirit and Original Intent of Treaty 7* (Montreal and Kingston: McGill-Queen's University Press, 1996).

30 Price, *Spirit of the Alberta Indian Treaties*, p. 146.

31 Macklem, "The Impact of Treaty 9," in Asch, *Aboriginal and Treaty Rights in Canada*, p. 97.

32 Ibid., p. 116.

33 Ibid., p. 133.

34 *Donald John Marshall v. the Queen*, September 17, 1999, paragraph 13, www.droit.umontreal.ca.

Interpretation
of the Prairie Treaties

NORMAN ZLOTKIN

> Respect for the unique position of Canada's First Peoples—and
> more generally for the diversity of peoples and cultures making up
> the country—should be a fundamental characteristic of Canada's
> civic ethos.
>
> *Report of the Royal Commission on Aboriginal Peoples*, v. 1, 685.

Introduction

Prairie First Nations and the federal and provincial governments disagree on whether the numbered treaties are land surrender documents.
In this paper, I suggest that the Supreme Court of Canada decision in
Delgamuukw v. British Columbia[1] will make it easier for treaty First Nations from the prairies to contend that the written versions of their
treaties are inaccurate statements of their solemn agreements with the
Crown. The decision will enable them to put forward their own understanding of their treaties, based on their own oral histories. *Delgamuukw* also indicates the kinds of limitations a court would place on
"treaty title" if it found a prairie treaty was not a land surrender document. More generally, *Delgamuukw* illustrates the inappropriateness of
litigation as a method of resolving the complex, ongoing issues be
tween First Nations and the Crown.

Notes will be found on pages 194–196.

The Prairie Treaties

Following the policy set out in the Royal Proclamation of 1763, the Crown negotiated 11 "numbered" treaties between 1871 and 1921 with the First Nations inhabiting the northern and western parts of the Dominion of Canada east of the Rocky Mountains.[2]

The written versions of the numbered treaties covering the Prairie Provinces (as well as parts of northeastern British Columbia, northwestern Ontario and the Northwest Territories) indicate they are land surrender documents. Governments read the treaties in this fashion, and rely on the land surrender provisions as one source of their ownership and authority over lands and resources.

In form, the 11 post-Confederation numbered treaties closely resemble one another. In the words of the Honourable Alexander Morris, who negotiated Treaties 3 through 6:

> The treaties are all based upon the models of that made at the Stone Fort in 1871 and the one made in 1873 at the north-west angle of the Lake of the Woods with the Chippewa tribes, and these again are based, in many material features, on those made by the Hon. W. B. Robinson with the Chippewas dwelling on the shores of Lakes Huron and Superior in 1860 [sic].[3]

Although differing in certain details, the written versions of the numbered treaties contain the same core provisions as the Robinson treaties of 1850. In exchange for surrendering "all their right and title" to their lands, the First Nations were to receive annuities in perpetuity and "reserves" for their own use. Treaties Nos. 1 to 7 (1871-1877),[4] which were designed to open the west to agricultural settlement, were also to provide tools, livestock and seed grain to those First Nations who took up farming.[5] The numbered treaties also included a guarantee of hunting and fishing rights.

There are major differences between the treaties as they are written in English and the First Nations' understanding of the agreements they signed. The First Nations view the treaties as representing a recognition by the Crown of their inherent sovereignty. First Nations believe that, by means of their treaties, they entered into ongoing political arrangements with the Crown by which they "retained sovereignty over their people, lands, and resources, both on and off the reserves, subject to some shared jurisdiction with the appropriate government bodies on the lands known as 'unoccupied Crown lands'." [6] They do not view either historic or modern treaties as fixed contracts, but rather as a means of establishing ongoing political and legal relationships between

Aboriginal collectivities and the Crown. In their view, relationships established through treaties should be based on a mutual recognition and affirmation of rights and interconnections between both parties.

Looking at these different perspectives in more detail, the written texts of the numbered treaties include land surrender provisions, by which First Nation parties surrender their rights over great expanses of territory. In exchange, the treaties include the following rights and benefits to be retained or given to First Nations.

(1) Reserves were to be established within the ceded territories for the exclusive use and benefit of the First Nations that signed the treaties.

(2) Small cash payments were to be given to members of the First Nation parties to the treaties. Thereafter, annuity payments would be given to them and their descendants.

(3) In the prairie treaties, farming implements and supplies were promised as an initial outlay. Thereafter, hunting and fishing materials such as nets and twine were to be furnished on an annual basis.

(4) Rights to hunt, fish and trap over the ceded territories were guaranteed.

(5) The government was to establish and maintain teachers and schools on reserves.

(6) Flags, medals and suits of clothing were to be given to the chiefs and headmen of each band.

(7) In the prairie treaties, a "medicine" chest for the use of the First Nations was promised.

According to the First Nation understanding, treaties confirmed principles and rights, which were to be enjoyed by First Nations in perpetuity. These principles and rights include the following:

(1) First Nations retained their sovereignty over their people, lands and resources both on and off reserve, subject to some shared jurisdiction over the lands known as "unoccupied Crown lands." This is understood as the recognition of the right of self-government.

(2) The Crown promised to provide for First Nation economic development in exchange for the right to use the lands covered by treaty.

(3) The treaties promised revenue sharing between the Crown and First Nations.[7]

Though the numbered treaties use the language of extinguishment, the First Nations who signed them do not see them as extinguishment documents but as agreements with the Crown to establish ongoing political and social relations and to allow European settlement. From a First Nation perspective, the "surrender" of Aboriginal rights and title was not on the table when the prairie treaties were negotiated.

The language often used by First Nations to express the goal of the treaty process is "sharing" with non-Aboriginal people, but it is sharing based on a clear recognition of the legitimacy of underlying Aboriginal title. As Professor Leroy Little Bear of Harvard University states:

> The Indian concept of land ownership is certainly not inconsistent with the idea of sharing with an alien people. Once the Indians recognized them as human beings, they gladly shared with them. They shared with Europeans in the same way they shared with the animals and other people. However, sharing here cannot be interpreted as meaning the Europeans got the same rights as any other native person, because the Europeans were not descendants of the original grantees, or they were not parties to the original social contract. Also, sharing certainly cannot be interpreted as meaning that one is giving up his rights for all eternity.[8]

Chief Harold Turner of the Swampy Cree Tribal Council indicates that the concept of sharing is broadly held within Aboriginal communities and was the basis of Aboriginal negotiations with Canada from the time of the historic treaties. As he stated during the hearings of the Royal Commission on Aboriginal Peoples:

> Our ancestors did not sign a real estate deal as you cannot give away something you do not own. No, the treaties were signed as our symbol of good faith to share the land. As well, the treaties were not signed to extinguish our sovereignty and our form of government.[9]

As for the question of the nature of ownership and underlying title, Professor Little Bear states:

> [Living Aboriginal peoples] are not the sole owners under the original grant from the Creator; the land belongs to past generations, to the yet-to-be-born, and to the plants and animals. Has the Crown ever received a surrender of title from these others?[10]

The *Sioui* Case

In order to understand the effect of *Delgamuukw* on treaty First Nations in the Prairies, one must first examine the 1990 Supreme Court decision in *R. v. Sioui*.[11] *Sioui* involved the exercise of treaty rights to hold a traditional religious ceremony within a provincial park in Quebec. Four Hurons were charged with cutting down trees, camping and making fires in a provincial park, contrary to the Quebec *Parks Act*.[12] The right to practice traditional customs and religious rites was the subject of a treaty made in 1760.[13]

The judgment deals with several issues. It repeats the rule from earlier cases that treaties and statutes relating to Indians should be liberally construed and uncertainties resolved in favor of the Indians.[14] It states that the question of capacity to enter a treaty must be seen from the point of view of the Indians at the time of the treaty.[15] As is the situation with Aboriginal rights, First Nations can have treaty rights on lands for which they did not have Aboriginal title.[16] *Sioui* holds that an agreement concerning something other than territory, such as political or social rights, can be a treaty[17] within the meaning of section 88 of the *Indian Act*,[18] (and, presumably, within the meaning of section 35 of the *Constitution Act, 1982*).

Sioui states that a treaty with a First Nation is an agreement *sui generis* that is neither created nor terminated according to the rules of international law.[19] A treaty is characterized by the intention to create obligations, the presence of mutually binding obligations, and a certain measure of solemnity.[20] The historical context is important in determining whether a document is a treaty.[21] Factors useful in determining the existence of a treaty include: continuous exercise of a right in the past and at present; the reasons why the Crown made a commitment; the situation prevailing at the time of signature; evidence of relations of mutual respect and esteem between the negotiators; and the subsequent conduct of the parties.[22] If there is ambiguity as to whether a document is a treaty, the court must look at extrinsic evidence to determine its legal nature.[23] Most importantly, the Court stated that a treaty cannot be extinguished without the consent of the Aboriginal parties.[24]

The treaty in *Sioui* did not define the territory over which the customs and religious rites could be exercised. Therefore, the Court held that the treaty must be interpreted by determining the intention of the parties at the time it was entered into.[25] The Court concluded that both parties contemplated that the rights guaranteed by the treaty could be exercised over the entire territory frequented by the Hurons at the time, so long as the carrying on of the customs and rites was not incompatible with the current use made by the Crown of the territory.[26]

Justice Lamer stated it has to be assumed that the parties intended to reconcile the Hurons' need to protect the exercise of their customs and the desire of the British to expand.[27]

In other words, as long as the exercise of the treaty right is not incompatible with the government's use of the Crown lands in question, the treaty right remains available for use by the treaty First Nation. But if the government selects or allows a use of the land that is incompatible with the exercise of the treaty right, then the treaty right becomes unexercisable at that location. *Sioui* does not recognize any requirement that the First Nation be consulted over the land use and its potential effect on treaty rights.

This approach was followed by the Supreme Court in *R. v. Badger*,[28] which articulates a "visible incompatible use" test when determining whether prairie treaty First Nations can exercise treaty rights to hunt as guaranteed by the *Natural Resources Transfer Agreement*. Once again, the treaty First Nation has no input into the decision whether land can be put to uses inconsistent with treaty hunting rights.

Delgamuukw and Treaty Interpretation

In *Delgamuukw*, the Supreme Court took the opportunity to confirm its approach to oral history in the treaty context, as set out in *Sioui* and the earlier cases, *R. v. Simon*[29] and *R. v. Taylor*.[30] In addressing the Aboriginal rights question in *Delgamuukw*, Chief Justice Lamer wrote:

> In cases involving the determination of Aboriginal rights, appellate intervention is also warranted by the failure of the trial court to appreciate the evidentiary difficulties inherent in adjudicating Aboriginal claims when, first, applying the rules of evidence and, second, interpreting the evidence before it. As I said in *Van der Peet*, at para. 68:
>
> > In determining whether an aboriginal claimant has produced evidence sufficient to demonstrate that her activity is an aspect of a practice, custom or tradition integral to a distinctive aboriginal culture, *a court should approach the rules of evidence, and interpret the evidence that exists*, with a consciousness of the special nature of aboriginal claims, and of the evidentiary difficulties in proving a right which originates in times where there were no written records of the practices, customs and traditions engaged in. *The courts must not undervalue the evidence presented by aboriginal claimants simply because that evidence does not conform precisely with the evidentiary standards that would be applied in, for example, a private law torts case.*[31] [Emphasis in original.]

The Court justifies this approach by reference to the legal nature of Aboriginal rights in Canadian law, rights which are "aimed at the reconciliation of the prior occupation of North America by distinctive Aboriginal societies with the assertion of Crown sovereignty over Canadian territory."[32] When dealing with evidence, courts are to give "due weight to the perspective of Aboriginal peoples."[33]

The Court goes on to state that:

> Notwithstanding the challenges created by the use of oral histories as proof of historical facts, the laws of evidence must be adapted in order that this type of evidence can be accommodated and placed on an equal footing with the types of historical evidence that courts are familiar with, which largely consists of historical documents. This is a long-standing practice in the interpretation of treaties between the Crown and Aboriginal peoples.[34]

The Court relies on *Sioui* and *Taylor* for the liberal rules of treaty interpretation, and goes on to quote Chief Justice Dickson in *Taylor*, who said that given that most Aboriginal societies "did not keep written records," the failure to take into account oral history would "impose an impossible burden of proof" on Aboriginal peoples, and "render nugatory" any rights that they have.[35]

It must be kept in mind that most treaty litigation has occurred in the context of hunting and fishing rights. Although hunting rights are of great importance to treaty First Nations, in cases such as *Taylor* and *Simon*, it has been unnecessary for the courts to address basic questions concerning the relationship between First Nations and the Crown. Litigation in Canada has not addressed fundamental questions such as the treaty relationship between the First Nation parties and the Crown. Crown sovereignty has been assumed without question. And, prior to 1982, treaty cases were decided in the context of Parliamentary sovereignty. Parliament was sovereign, and had no legal duty to recognize treaty rights. Parliament had the authority to limit or even abolish treaty rights without the consent of the First Nation parties to the treaties. Legislation inconsistent with the continued exercise of treaty rights took priority over treaty rights, even if Parliament had not considered the effects of proposed legislation or regulation on treaties.[36]

Since the coming into effect in 1982 of section 35(1) of the *Constitution Act, 1982*, Parliament has not been able to interfere with constitutionally protected treaty rights without meeting the justification test developed by the Supreme Court in *Sparrow*.[37]

Delgamuukw and "Treaty Title"

To summarize, *Delgamuukw* may make it easier for First Nations to put before the courts their own understandings, based on their oral histories, of the prairie treaties. However, oral histories will not provide clear answers to many of the difficult questions around treaty interpretation. Litigation occurs on a case-by-case basis, and requires a dispute between parties. Most treaty litigation has occurred in the context of a prosecution by the Crown for an alleged violation of federal or provincial legislation in which the defendant has raised a treaty rights defence. With few exceptions,[38] courts have not had to address the difficult question of whether the numbered treaties are land surrender treaties.

If land issues are litigated and oral histories are given serious consideration, courts may find that some or all of the prairie treaties are not land surrender treaties. Courts may conclude that prairie treaty First Nations have an existing "treaty title," which is similar to Aboriginal title in some ways but different in others because of the treaty relationship.

It must also be recalled from *Delgamuukw* that Aboriginal rights, including Aboriginal title, even though recognized and affirmed by section 35(1) of the Constitution Act, are not absolute.[39] Those rights may be infringed by federal and provincial governments[40] if the infringements satisfy the two-stage test for justification: first, the infringement must be in furtherance of a legislative objective that is compelling and substantial;[41] and second, the infringement must be consistent with the special fiduciary relationship between the Crown and Aboriginal peoples.[42] The range of legislative objectives that can justify the infringement of Aboriginal title is fairly broad. As stated in *Delgamuukw*, most of these objectives can be traced to the reconciliation of the prior occupation of North America by Aboriginal peoples with the assertion of Crown sovereignty. Such reconciliation entails the recognition that distinctive Aboriginal societies exist within, and are part of, a broader social, political and economic community.[43]

The list of governmental activities that can justify the infringement of Aboriginal title is wide-ranging. *Delgamuukw* lists agriculture, forestry, mining, hydroelectric development, general economic development, protection of the environment and endangered species, the building of infrastructure and the settlement of foreign populations to support these aims as the kinds of objectives that will allow infringement. Whether a particular measure or government act can be justified by reference to one of those objectives is ultimately a question of fact to be determined on a case-by-case basis.[44]

Given the conclusion in *Delgamuukw* that Aboriginal rights are not absolute, it is extremely unlikely that future courts would find treaty rights or treaty title to be absolute. In *Delgamuukw*, the Supreme Court held that three aspects of Aboriginal title are relevant to the manner in which the fiduciary duty operates with respect to the second stage of the justification test.[45] These aspects are likely to be found most relevant to treaty title.

First, Aboriginal title encompasses the right to exclusive use and occupation of land. The court states that this is relevant to the degree of scrutiny to be given to the infringing measure or action.[46] In contrast, treaty title may not involve the exclusive use and occupation of lands, but a shared responsibility between First Nations and the Crown. The example given by the Court, however—that governments may have to accommodate the participation of Aboriginal peoples in resource development[47]—seems to fit a model of shared responsibility.

Second, the Crown's fiduciary obligation may be satisfied by involving Aboriginal peoples in decisions concerning their lands.[48] Involving treaty First Nations in decisions concerning Crown lands would also fit a model of shared responsibility. With Aboriginal title, the Court suggests that in most cases the standard will be significantly higher than mere consultation.[49] Shared decision-making, rather than mere consultation, may fit the First Nation understanding of treaty rights. The Court states that some cases may even require the full consent of an Aboriginal nation, particularly when provinces enact hunting and fishing regulations in relation to Aboriginal lands.[50] This would be particularly true for treaty First Nations, because without the guarantees of continued hunting and fishing rights, they would not have signed the treaties.

Third, lands held pursuant to Aboriginal title have an economic component. This suggests compensation is relevant to the question of justification. Fair compensation will ordinarily be required when Aboriginal title is infringed.[51] Compensation would be just as relevant when considering the infringement of treaty rights.

Alternatives to Litigation

Although *Delgamuukw* provides a more positive environment for treaty First Nations when they engage in litigation, one would not expect treaty First Nations to rush to court. Just as the *Delgamuukw* case does not settle the many outstanding issues between the Gitksan and Wet'suwet'en nations and the Crown, litigation will not settle the most basic issues between treaty First Nations and the Crown. First Nations see the purpose of their treaties with the Crown as the creation of an ongoing relationship based on mutual respect and accommodation. Such a relationship cannot be achieved through litigation. Treaty First Nations, Canada and the provinces must work out together a means of living with one another in the new millennium. A satisfactory relationship must involve respect for the "spirit and intent" [52] of the treaties rather than a denial of the basic nature of the treaty relationship.

For some time there has been a consensus among organizations representing First Nations that their treaty relationship with the Crown must be re-examined and renewed. The Bilateral Constitutional Task Force on Treaties and Treaty Rights found that "Treaty First Nations were unanimous in the call for a process in which treaty issues could be negotiated and resolved." [53] At the 1987 First Ministers Conference on Aboriginal Matters, the Assembly of First Nations put forward a proposed constitutional amendment that would have committed the Government of Canada "to clarify, renovate or implement ... each treaty ... [at the request of] the aboriginal peoples concerned." [54] The results of such negotiations would be set out in either an amendment to a treaty, an adhesion to a treaty, or a new treaty. [55] In 1992 the Charlottetown Accord recognized the necessity for such a renewal process. [56]

In 1996, the Royal Commission on Aboriginal Peoples recommended that "the federal government establish a continuing bilateral process to implement and renew the Crown's relationship with and obligations to the treaty nations under the historical treaties, in accordance with the treaties' spirit and intent." [57] It went on to list principles of interpretation to be used in the treaty renewal process along with the following basic presumptions:

> There is a presumption in respect of the historical treaties that
>
> - treaty nations did not intend to consent to the blanket extinguishment of their Aboriginal rights and title by entering into the treaty relationship;
>
> - treaty nations intended to share the territory and jurisdiction and management over it, as opposed to ceding the territory, even where the text of an historical treaty makes reference to a blanket extinguishment of land rights; and
>
> - treaty nations did not intend to give up their inherent right of governance by entering into a treaty relationship, and the act of treaty making is regarded as an affirmation rather than a denial of that right. [58]

The Saskatchewan Treaty Table

In 1998, Judge David M. Arnot, the Treaty Commissioner for Saskatchewan, presented a report entitled *Treaties as a Bridge to the Future*[59] to the Minister of Indian Affairs and the Federation of Saskatchewan Indian Nations. The report was developed through an ongoing process of dialogue involving the Office of the Treaty Commissioner, the Federation of Saskatchewan Indian Nations, the Government of Canada and the Government of Saskatchewan.[60] The report outlines a vision for the future based on the treaty relationship between Saskatchewan First Nations and the Crown. The report deals with the process of an evolving treaty relationship, including the basic issues of governance and fiscal relations, issues that are unsuitable for resolution in the courts. It emphasizes the policy areas of education, child welfare and justice. The role of the government of Saskatchewan is addressed. The report recognizes the necessity of public support for the treaty process, and calls for public education and public acts of treaty renewal.

The Saskatchewan "Treaty Table" may be seen as a step towards implementing the Royal Commission recommendations on renewal of the historic treaties. It provides a model for the treaty renewal process in which to address First Nation issues in the context of their ongoing relationship with the Crown. This model also avoids the inevitable uncertainties of litigation.

Notes

1 [1998] 1 C.N.L.R. 14.
2 There are also historical treaties covering parts of British Columbia and Ontario. Prior to the Royal Proclamation, treaties of peace and friendship were signed with several First Nations of the Maritimes and Quebec.
3 A. Morris, *The Treaties of Canada with the Indians*, Facsimile Edition, (Toronto, Coles Publishing Co., 1971) at 285.
4 The complete text of Treaties Nos. 1 to 7 and adhesions thereto are found in Morris, *ibid.*, 313-375. The texts of all the numbered treaties have been published in booklets by the Queen's Printer, Ottawa.
5 *Ibid.*, 288.
6 D. Opekokew, *The First Nations: Indian Governments in the Community of Man* (Regina, Federation of Saskatchewan Indians, 1982) at 16.
7 *Ibid.*, 16-17.
8 L. Little Bear, "Aboriginal Rights and the Canadian 'Grundnorm'" in J.R. Ponting, ed., *Arduous Journey: Canadian Indians and Decolonization* (Toronto: McClelland and Stewart, 1986) at 246.
9 Transcripts of the Public Hearings of the Royal Commission on Aboriginal Peoples, the Pas, Manitoba, May 20, 1992, at 252.
10 *Supra*, note 8, at 247.
11 [1990] 1 S.C.R. 1025, 70 D.L.R. (4th) 427, [1990] 3 C.N.L.R.127, 56 C.C.C. (3d) 225, 109 N.R. 22 [hereinafter cited to C.N.L.R.]
12 R.S.Q. 1977, c. P-9.
13 For the story of the Treaty of 1760, see D. Schulze, "The Murray Treaty of 1760: The Original Document Discovered" [1998] 1 C.N.L.R. 1.
14 *Supra*, note 11, at 134.
15 *Ibid.*, 136.
16 *Ibid.*, 139. See *R. v. Adams*, [1996] 3 S.C.R. 101, [1996] 4 C.N.L.R. 1, 110 C.C.C. (3d) 97, 202 N.R. 89, and *R. v. Cote*, [1996] 3 S.C.R. 139, [1996] 4 C.N.L.R. 26, 110 C.C.C. (3d) 122, for a rejection of the proposition that claims to Aboriginal rights must be grounded in an underlying claim to Aboriginal title.
17 *Ibid.*
18 R.S.C. 1985, c. I-6.
19 *Supra*, note 11, at 135.
20 *Ibid.*, 139.
21 *Ibid.*, 140.
22 *Ibid.*, 140-141.
23 *Ibid.*, 143.
24 *Ibid.*, 152.
25 *Ibid.*, 155.
26 *Ibid.*, 157.
27 *Ibid.*
28 [1996] 2 C.N.L.R. 77, 195 N.R. 1 (S.C.C.)

29 [1985] 2 S.C.R. 387, [1986] 1 C.N.L.R. 153, 23 C.C.C. (3d) 238, 24 D.L.R. (4th) 390, 71 N.S.R. (2d) 15, 171 A.P.R. 15, 62 N.R. 366.

30 [1981] 3 C.N.L.R. 114, 62 C.C.C. (2d) 227, 34 O.R. (2d) 360 (S.C.C.)

31 *Supra*, note 1, at 47.

32 *Ibid.*

33 *Ibid.*, 48.

34 *Ibid.*, 49-50.

35 *Ibid.*, 50.

36 See, for example, *R. v. Sikyea*, [1964] S.C.R. 642, 49 W.W.R. 306, 44 C.R. 266, 50 D.L.R.(2d) 80, *R. v. George*, [1966] S.C.R. 267, 47 C.R. 382, 55 D.L.R. (2d) 386, 33 C.C.C. 137, *Hamlet of Baker Lake v. Minister of Indian Affairs*, [1979] 3 C.N.L.R. 17, [1980 1 F.C. 518 (F.C.T.D.)

37 *R. v. Sparrow*, [1990] 1 S.C.R. 1075, [1990] 3 C.N.L.R. 160, [1990] 4 W.W.R. 410, 46 B.C.L.R. (2d) 1, 70 D.L.R. (4th) 385, 56 C.C.C. (3d) 263, 111 N.R. 241.

38 e.g., *Re Paulette*, [1973] 6 W.W.R. 97 and 115, 39 D.L.R. (3d) 45,42 D.L.R. (3d) 8, reversed on other grounds [1976] 2 W.W.R. 193, 63 D.L.R. (3d) 1. affirmed on other grounds [1977] 2 S.C.R.628, [1977] 1 W.W.R. 321, 72 D.L.R. (3d) 161, 12 N.R. 420 (N.W.T.).

39 *Supra*, note 1, at 75.

40 *Ibid.*

41 *Ibid.*

42 *Ibid.*, 76.

43 *Ibid.*, 78.

44 *Ibid.*

45 *Ibid.*

46 *Ibid.*

47 *Ibid.*, 79.

48 *Ibid.*

49 *Ibid.*

50 *Ibid.*

51 *Ibid.*, 79-80.

52 For a discussion of what is meant by the "spirit and intent" of the treaties, see the Assembly of First Nations & Canada, *Report of The Bilateral Constitutional Task Force on Treaties and Treaty Rights* (Ottawa, 6 February 1987) at 6-9. The Report was prepared for consideration by the participants in the Aboriginal constitutional process prior to the 1987 First Ministers Conference on Aboriginal Affairs [FMC]. See also H. Cardinal, "Treaties Six and Seven: The Next Century" in I. A. Getty and D. B. Smith, ed., *One Century Later[:] Western Canadian Reserve Indians Since Treaty 7* (Vancouver: University of British Columbia Press, 1978) 132; Opekokew, *supra*, note 6, at 11-13.

53 *Ibid.*, 10.

54 Doc. 830-276/016, s. 35.02(1), (2). The proposed amendment was tabled at a Ministerial Meeting in Ottawa, 13 March 1987, prior to the 1987 FMC.

55 *Ibid.*, s. 35.02(3).

56 Meeting of the First Ministers and Aboriginal and Territorial Leaders, "Charlottetown Accord—Draft Legal Text, October 9, 1992," s.35.6(2)-(6). This text did not receive formal approval from governments before the referendum in October 1992.

57 *Report of the Royal Commission on Aboriginal Peoples*, v. 2, 57.

58 *Ibid.*, 58.

59 D. M. Arnot, *Statement of Treaty Issues: Treaties as a Bridge to the Future* (Saskatoon: Office of the Treaty Commissioner, 1998).

60 *Ibid.*, vii.

Will *Delgamuukw* Eclipse the Prairie Sun?
Implications for the Prairie Treaties

KENNETH J. TYLER

> What we speak of and do now will last as long as the sun shines and the river runs, we are looking forward to our children's children, for we are old and have but few days to live.
>   Mistahwahsis, Fort Carlton (22 August, 1876)[1]

Thus spoke Mistahwahsis, a leading chief of the Saskatchewan River Cree, on the eve before the signing of Treaty Number Six, employing an image that was already hackneyed.[2] The Treaties, those solemn compacts that are, or should be, fundamental to a fit and proper relationship between First Nations and the rest of Canadian society,[3] were supposed to last forever. They have survived, even though (according to a common assumption across virtually the entire spectrum of enlightened Canadian opinion) the whole history of Canada has been littered with broken covenants, unfulfilled promises, and legitimate expectations dashed.[4] Indeed the Treaties have now been re-invigorated, rescued from obscurity on occasion by a vigilant Supreme Court,[5] and enshrined in our Constitution by section 35 of the 1982 *Constitution Act*.

Notes will be found on pages 221–225.

The Treaties are especially important to the Prairie Provinces where practically the entire landmass is notionally covered by Treaties 1, 2, 3, 4, 5, 6, 7, 8 and 10.[6] Despite occasional rumours of potential claims by the Dakota Indians[7] and the Métis, federal and provincial governments have confidently operated on the assumption that the question of Aboriginal title has been settled on the Prairies. As the shocks from the *Delgamuukw* decision reverberated through British Columbia, Prairie governments believed they could adopt the stance of detached observers.

That detachment may yet prove to be justified, but the security of the Crown's title is not quite so clear as it once was. In the wake of the *Delgamuukw* decision, while the sun may still shine and the rivers yet flow, two lawsuits have recently been filed by Treaty groups in the Province of Alberta. Similar claims are anticipated by First Nations in other parts of the Prairie Provinces, which call into question what has long been regarded as the very essence of the Treaties.

Chief Florence Buffalo has filed one of the lawsuits in the Alberta Court of Queen's Bench on behalf of the Samson Cree Nation claiming, among other things, a declaration of unextinguished Aboriginal title and existing aboriginal and treaty rights in, under and to all the natural resources in central Alberta between the Oldman and North Saskatchewan Rivers and extending as far east as the 112th Meridian of Longitude,[8] together with an alleged Treaty right to shared use of the surface of that land. She also seeks special and general damages in the amount of $10 billion against each of the defendant federal and provincial Crowns, together with an accounting for the value of all natural resources, extracted from the land, and all royalties, revenues and other payments related to such extraction.[9]

The Statement of Claim in the other lawsuit was filed on the same date as that of the Samson Cree Nation (26 February 1999) on behalf of all of the Indian Bands in Treaty Seven. In that action, the Plaintiffs claim a declaration that they have not ceded, released, surrendered or yielded up their Aboriginal title and right to the Treaty Seven Territory[10] and that they continue to possess a legal interest in it. They do not quantify the amount of damages they seek against the defendant federal and provincial Crowns, but do indicate that the award should be based upon a breach of fiduciary duty and loss of Treaty rights and benefits and be augmented by exemplary, punitive, and aggravated damages.[11]

It is not the purpose of this paper to comment specifically on these particular pleadings (the writer has no involvement in either of the actions) but rather to consider the basic issue which they raise—the validity, interpretation and legal effectiveness of the Prairie Treaties.

It is abundantly clear that neither action can possibly succeed if the written text of the Treaties is accepted. Treaty Six, to which the Samson Cree Nation had adhered in 1877,[12] declared in its opening substantive clause:

> The Plain and Wood Cree Tribes of Indians, and all other the Indians inhabiting the district hereinafter described and defined, do hereby cede, release, surrender and yield up to the Government of the Dominion of Canada for Her Majesty the Queen and her successors forever, all their rights, titles and privileges, whatsoever, to the lands included within the following limits ...

And then after describing the territorial boundaries of the Treaty, which included the northerly portion of Chief Buffalo's claim, the Treaty text continued:

> And also all their rights, titles and privileges whatsoever, to all other lands, wherever situated, in the North-West Territories, or in any other Province or portion of Her Majesty's Dominions, situated and being within the Dominion of Canada;
> The tract comprised within the lines above described, embracing an area of one hundred and twenty-one thousand square miles, be the same more or less;
> To have and to hold the same to Her Majesty the Queen and her successors forever;

Similarly, Treaty Seven declares:

> And whereas the said Commissioners have proceeded to negotiate a treaty with the said Indians; and the same has been finally agreed upon and concluded as follows, that is to say: the Blackfeet, Blood, Piegan, Sarcee, Stony and other Indians inhabiting the district hereinafter more fully described and defined, do hereby cede, release, surrender, and yield up to the Government of Canada for Her Majesty the Queen and her successors forever, all their rights, titles and privileges whatsoever to the lands included within the following limits, ...
> ... and also all their rights, titles and privileges whatsoever, to all other lands wherever situated in the North-West Territories, or in any other portion of the Dominion of Canada:
> To have and to hold the same to Her Majesty the Queen and her successors for ever:

On their face, these Treaty provisions would seem to be a complete answer to the Plaintiffs' claims, in the absence of any other provision in the Treaties themselves that might purport to replace or preserve the aboriginal interests so exhaustively surrendered. Both Treaties Six and Seven do, of course, promise reserves, and preserve the right to hunt throughout the surrendered tract. Treaty Six also promises protection for existing fishing practices. None of these provisions, however, go any significant distance towards validating the Plaintiffs' sweeping claims.

Both the Samson Cree Nation and the Treaty Seven Plaintiffs acknowledge the existence of the Treaties in their Statements of Claim.

In the Queen's Bench action, the Samson Cree Nation declares:

11. According to the printed version of *Treaty No. 6*, the Plain and Wood Cree tribes of Indians and other Indians ceded, released, surrendered and yielded up to the Government of the Dominion of Canada for Her Majesty the Queen all their rights, titles and privileges whatsoever to lands contemplated by the Treaty in consideration of the recognition, retention and granting of various rights and benefits. However, under *Treaty No. 6*, the Indian tribes and Indian Nations party thereto or who adhered thereto as a minimum did not cede, release, surrender or yield up any rights, titles and privileges whatsoever to Natural Resources.

12. At the time of the adhesion in 1877 to *Treaty No. 6* by Plaintiffs' ancestors, Plaintiffs had aboriginal title and rights to the lands and Natural Resources of the Traditional Lands. In *Treaty No. 6*, the Indians party thereto and more particularly the ancestors of the Plaintiffs through their adhesion and in virtue of the negotiations, undertakings, commitments and representations of Her Majesty's representatives, agreed only to share the surface of the Traditional Lands with Her Majesty the Queen. This was the intention and understanding of the Indian signatories and adherents. Plaintiffs and their ancestors did not surrender by *Treaty No. 6* their aboriginal title and aboriginal rights in and to the Natural Resources.

13. Despite adhesion to *Treaty No. 6*, Plaintiffs and their ancestors have continued to have existing and unextinguished aboriginal title and rights in and to the Natural Resources.

In the Federal Court action the Treaty Seven Plaintiffs recite the provisions that appear to provide for the complete extinguishment of all land-related rights, but then proceed to say:

39. Contrary to the above provisions in Treaty 7 the Plaintiffs deny that they ceded, released, surrendered or yielded up their Aboriginal title or right over the Treaty 7 Territory.

40. The Plaintiffs understanding was that Treaty 7 was a treaty of peace and that they were agreeing to share the Treaty 7 Territory with the Crown in exchange for the promises made during Treaty 7 discussions by the representatives of the Crown.

41. The Plaintiffs further state that Treaty 7 does not mention the resources, either renewable and non-renewable, on the Treaty 7 Territory and it is not the understanding of the Plaintiffs that they ceded, released, surrendered or yielded up their Aboriginal title or right to such resources.

In addition to their principal claim that they had not agreed to the surrender of their lands and the natural resources, the Plaintiffs also advanced alternative claims. The Samson Cree Nation alleges that the surrender of their interest in their traditional lands and the natural resources was conditional on the fulfilment of the Treaty promises by the Crown, which they assert have not been fulfilled.[13] The Treaty Seven Plaintiffs allege that if their ancestors did, indeed, surrender their Aboriginal title and rights they did so only for the purpose of permitting the federal Crown to hold the lands and resources in trust for their benefit. They allege that by purporting to alienate some of the Treaty Seven lands and resources within the Treaty area to private parties, and by purporting to transfer the whole of its interest to the Province of Alberta, by the 1930 *Natural Resources Transfer Agreement*, the federal Crown breached its trust obligation to the Plaintiffs, and compensation is now due.

Not long ago, such a frontal attack on the written text of the Treaties would have seemed quixotic. Treaties for the cession of Indian land rights have been part of Canada's history since long before Confederation. In the *Calder* case,[14] Justice Emmett Hall, in a dissent now vindicated by the *Delgamuukw* decision, declared:

Surely the Canadian treaties, made with much solemnity on behalf of the Crown, were intended to extinguish the Indian title. What other purpose did they serve? If they were not intended to extinguish the Indian right, they were a gross fraud and that is not to be assumed.[15]

It is true that in *Simon v. The Queen,* the Supreme Court repudiated the notion that Treaties, by definition, must include a land cession.[16] Nevertheless, it has remained quite willing to enforce extinguishment provisions included in the text of a Treaty, even against a First Nation whose representatives may never have signed the agreement. In *Attorney General of Ontario v. Bear Island Foundation*[17] the Supreme Court unanimously affirmed the lower courts' rejection of a claim of Aboriginal rights and title to the Temagami region of northeastern Ontario. The Ontario government had relied upon the 1850 Robinson Huron Treaty under the terms of which the Indian parties had "fully freely and voluntarily surrender[ed], cede[d], grant[ed], and convey[ed] unto Her Majesty, her heirs and successors forever, all their right, title, and interest to, and in the whole of" a vast portion of northern Ontario, including the Temagami region. The Temagami people, however, alleged that they had never entered into the 1850 Robinson Huron Treaty, although it was established in evidence that they had received Treaty Annuities and a small reserve. The Supreme Court tersely noted:

> It is unnecessary, however, to examine the specific nature of the aboriginal right because, in our view, whatever may have been the situation upon the signing of the Robinson-Huron Treaty, that right was in any event surrendered by arrangements subsequent to that treaty by which the Indians adhered to the treaty in exchange for treaty annuities and a reserve.[18]

The *Bear Island* decision would appear to be clear authority for the proposition that the legal effectiveness of the extinguishment provisions of a Treaty is not dependent upon the explicit acquiescence of those terms by each Treaty First Nation. However, the primary proposition advanced by the Samson Cree Nation and the Treaty Seven Bands is not that they should not be bound by the terms of their respective Treaties—the point unsuccessfully advanced by the Temagami in *Bear Island.* What these new Plaintiffs are alleging is that the *real* Treaties are not the ones set out in the heretofore accepted written texts.

Scarcely more than a decade ago, such a suggestion would have been readily dismissed. In *R. v. Horse*[19] a group of Treaty Six Indians were charged with night hunting by means of lights, contrary to the Saskatchewan *Wildlife Act.* Under Paragraph 12 of the *Natural Resources Transfer Agreement* Indians were required to obey the laws of the Province unless they were hunting for food on unoccupied Crown lands or other lands to which they had a right of access. The land on which they were hunting was privately owned, and they were hunting without the permission of the owner. Among the defences which counsel advanced on behalf of the accused was the argument that the Indians of Treaty Six had a right of access to privately owned land because, under the terms of the Treaty, their ancestors had only agreed to share the land with incoming settlers, rather than to give it up. In the Supreme Court of Canada, Justice J.W. Estey, for a unanimous Court, noted that the text of Treaty Six provided that:

> Her Majesty further agrees with her said Indians that they, the said Indians, shall have right to pursue their avocations of hunting and fishing throughout the tract surrendered as hereinbefore described, subject to such regulations as may from time to time be made by her Government of her Dominion of Canada, and <u>saving and excepting such tracts as may from time to time be required or taken up for settlement</u>, mining, lumbering or other purposes by her said Government of the Dominion of Canada, or by any of the subjects thereof, duly authorized therefor, by the said Government.[20]

Since the lands on which Mr. Horse and his companions were hunting had been taken up for settlement by one of Her Majesty's subjects, the Court seemed to be clearly of a mind to dismiss this claim. However, counsel for the Accused insisted that the historical record would vindicate the claim that Treaty Six had guaranteed his clients access to privately owned land for hunting purposes. He requested that the Court examine the record of the negotiation of the Treaty as compiled by the pre-eminent Treaty Commissioner, Lieutenant Governor Alexander Morris. Justice Estey was clearly uncomfortable with this suggestion:

> I have some reservations about the use of this material as an aid to interpreting the terms of Treaty No. 6. In my view the terms are not ambiguous. The normal rule with respect to interpretation of contractual documents is that extrinsic evidence is not to be used in the absence of ambiguity; nor can it be invoked where the result would be to alter the terms of a document by adding to or subtracting from the written agreement. This rule is described in *Cross on Evidence* (6th ed. 1985), at pp. 615-16:
>
> > Extrinsic evidence is generally inadmissible when it would, if accepted, have the effect of adding to, varying or contradicting the terms of a judicial record, a transaction required by law to be in writing, or a document constituting a valid and effective contract or other transaction. Most judicial statements of the

rule are concerned with its application to contracts, and one of the best known is that of Lord Morris who regarded it as indisputable that:

> Parol testimony cannot be received to contradict, vary, add to or subtract from the terms of a written contract or the terms in which the parties have deliberately agreed to record any part of their contract. [*Bank of Australasia v. Palmer*, [1897] A.C. 540, at p. 545][21]

Justice Estey proceeded to note that the rule requiring the liberal interpretation of Indian treaties in favour of the Indians adequately protected their interests and was not incompatible with the parol evidence rule:

> The parol evidence rule has its analogy in the approaches to the construction of Indian treaties. This Court in *Simon v. The Queen*, [1985] 2 S.C.R. 387, was concerned with the proper interpretation of an Indian treaty by the courts. Dickson C.J. stated at p. 404: "An Indian treaty is unique; it is an agreement *sui generis* which is neither created nor terminated according to the rules of international law". An early judgment in *Nowegijick v. The Queen*, [1983] 1 S.C.R. 29, referred more broadly to the rules of interpretation properly applicable in a court of law to an Indian treaty. Dickson J. (as he then was) there stated, at p. 36: " ... treaties and statutes relating to Indians should be liberally construed and doubtful expressions resolved in favour of the Indians".[22]

After noting that parol evidence rule also applied to the interpretation of international treaties, Justice Estey went on to say: "In my opinion there is no ambiguity which would bring in extraneous interpretative material."[23] Nevertheless, he did ultimately agree to examine Morris' account "as a useful guide to the interpretation of Treaty No. 6" and a means of seeing the Treaty "in its overall historical context."[24] After reviewing the Treaty Commissioner's narrative, Justice Estey concluded that the historical record was entirely congruent with the plain meaning of the Treaty's written terms and affirmed the convictions.

While the *Horse* decision was somewhat ambiguous on the question of the application of the parol evidence rule,[25] it left little doubt about the Supreme Court's belief in the primacy of the written Treaty text.

Until three years ago, therefore, the prospects for any challenge to the extinguishment provisions of any of the Prairie Treaties would have seemed distinctly unfavourable. There was a widespread understanding, reflected in Justice Hall's judgment in *Calder* that the very purpose of the numbered Treaties was to obtain the surrender by the Indians of their land and resource claims. The *Horse* case suggested that while the courts were prepared to look at extrinsic historical evidence, it was only as a guide to interpretation and to provide context for the Treaty text. *Bear Island* indicated that the written terms of a Treaty would be enforced against a particular First Nation if it accepted Treaty benefits, even if it might not have given its conscious acquiescence to the written terms.

Those apparent certainties have been thrown into question, however, by more recent pronouncements of the Supreme Court. In *R. v. Badger*[26] the Court revisited the question of the right to hunt on private lands. It distinguished *Horse* by indicating that a distinction should be drawn between "occupied" private lands (which had been dealt with in the earlier decision) and "unoccupied" private lands which were arguably at issue in the more recent case.[27] Of possibly greater significance than the hunting rights issue,[28] however, was Justice Cory's comments, for the majority, on Treaty interpretation:

> [W]hen considering a treaty, a court must take into account the context in which the treaties were negotiated, concluded and committed to writing. The treaties, as written documents, recorded an agreement that had already been reached orally and they did not always record the full extent of the oral agreement: see Alexander Morris, *The Treaties of Canada with the Indians of Manitoba and the North-West Territories* (1880), at pp. 338-42; *Sioui, supra,* at p. 1068; *Report of the Aboriginal Justice Inquiry of Manitoba* (1991); Jean Friesen, *Grant me Wherewith to Make my Living* (1985). The treaties were drafted in English by representatives of the Canadian government who, it should be assumed, were familiar with common law doctrines. Yet, the treaties were not translated in written form into the languages (here Cree and Dene) of the various Indian nations who were signatories. Even if they had been, it is unlikely that the Indians, who had a history of communicating only orally, would have understood them any differently. As a result, it is well settled that the words in the treaty must not be interpreted in their strict technical sense nor subjected to rigid modern rules of construction. Rather, they must be interpreted in the sense that they would naturally have been understood by the Indians at the time of the signing.[29]

The suggestion that there might be a distinction between the agreement reached orally and the written text raises a potentially troublesome question. Which then are the actual treaties? The documents we have labelled and accepted as treaties for more than a hundred years? Or the verbal understandings reached with the different groups of Indian signatories? The recent case of *R. v. Sundown*[30] also emphasizes the importance of the particular understanding reached at the time the Treaty was made. Justice Cory, speaking for a unanimous Court, declared:

> Treaty rights, like aboriginal rights, are specific and may be exercised exclusively by the First Nation that signed the treaty. The interpretation of each treaty must take into account the First Nation signatory and the circumstances that surrounded the signing of the treaty. Lamer C.J. was careful to stress the specific nature of aboriginal rights in *R. v. Van der Peet*, [1996] 2 S.C.R. 507. At para. 69 he wrote:
>
> > The fact that one group of aboriginal people has an aboriginal right to do a particular thing will not be, without something more, sufficient to demonstrate that another aboriginal community has the same aboriginal right. The existence of the right will be specific to each aboriginal community. [Emphasis added.][31]

This principle is equally applicable to treaty rights. Dickson C.J. and La Forest J. also emphasized the specific nature of aboriginal and treaty rights in *R. v. Sparrow*, [1990] 1 S.C.R. 1075, when they discussed the correct test to apply under s. 35(1) of the *Constitution Act, 1982*. At p. 1111 this appears:

> We wish to emphasize the importance of context and a case-by-case approach to s. 35(1). Given the generality of the text of the constitutional provision, and especially in light of the complexities of aboriginal history, society and rights, the contours of a justificatory standard must be defined in the specific factual context of each case. [Emphasis added][32]

Thus, in addition to applying the guiding principles of treaty interpretation, it is necessary to take into account the circumstances surrounding the signing of the treaty and the First Nations who later adhered to it.[33]

As the Court had noted in *Badger*, Treaty negotiations were often not all conducted in one place or with the same parties:

> The Indian people made their agreements orally and recorded their history orally. Thus, the verbal promises made on behalf of the fed-

eral government at the times the treaties were concluded are of great significance in their interpretation. Treaty No. 8 was initially concluded with the Indians at Lesser Slave Lake. The Commissioners then travelled to many other bands in the region and sought their adhesion to the Treaty. Oral promises were made with the Lesser Slave Lake band and with the other Treaty signatories and these promises have been recorded in the Treaty Commissioners' Reports and in contemporary affidavits and diaries of interpreters and other government officials who participated in the negotiations.[34]

Does this suggest that each of the nine different Treaties applicable to land in the Prairie Provinces should really be seen as many times that number of binding agreements? That would seem to be a misreading of the Court's comments. Notwithstanding the increased emphasis on context and the Indian point of view, nothing in either the *Badger* or the *Sundown* case suggests that the actual Treaty is anything other than the written document. While the Court may be increasingly insistent on considering the Indian point of view before committing itself to any particular interpretation of a Treaty term, it has not yet endorsed the view that the oral understanding, rather than the written text, is the *real* Treaty, or that the written text should be disregarded if it is contradicted by historical evidence of a completely inconsistent Indian viewpoint. Nevertheless, the increasing sensitivity of the Court to the Indian understanding of Treaty terms may provide some encouragement to those who, like the Samson Cree Nation and the Treaty Seven Plaintiffs, may wish to mount a direct challenge to the written text of the Treaties themselves.

The suggestion that the numbered Treaties did not actually involve a cession of land and resource rights is not entirely new. Indeed it was advanced in the Supreme Court of the Northwest Territories in 1973 in connection with Treaties Eight and Eleven, when Justice Morrow found that a group of 16 Indian chiefs from the western portion of the Territories had presented a *prima facie* case that their bands had possessed Aboriginal rights to the territories north of the 60th parallel found within the boundaries of Treaties Eight and Eleven, and that there was sufficient doubt that the Aboriginal title of the Indians had been extinguished by the two Treaties to permit the chiefs to register a caveat on the lands of the Territories giving notice of their claim.[35]

The case, which was based on a Registrar of Land Title's reference to the Supreme Court on the question of the registrability of a caveat, proceeded in a rather unusual manner. The Crown immediately objected to the Court's jurisdiction to hear the matter and when it failed on that motion, it withdrew from the case. Although the Court appointed a local lawyer as *amicus,* it does not appear that he attempted to call any evidence to support the validity of the written text of the treaty.[36] The evidence of the historians, anthropologists and Elders called by the caveators thus went in virtually unchallenged and uncontradicted. The decision was overturned by a majority in the Northwest Territories Court of Appeal, without reference to the strength or weakness of the caveators' case.[37] The Supreme Court of Canada unanimously upheld the Court of Appeal's decision on the narrow ground that caveats could not be registered against unpatented Crown lands under the federal *Land Titles Act.*[38]

The evidence led in the Supreme Court of the Northwest Territories in the *Paulette* case emphasized that there were no reserves in the Northwest Territories. This lent some plausibility to the claims of several Elders that land issues had not been dealt with during the negotiation of Treaty Eleven and at the adhesions to Treaty Eight with respect to the Indians living north of the 60th parallel.[39] Whatever might have been the case in the Northwest Territories in the 1970s, where witnesses to Treaty Eleven were still available to testify, the documentary evidence provides an ample basis for demonstrating that the Indians of the Prairie Provinces were well aware that the subject matter of the Treaties was land. There is also some evidence that they understood that their rights to natural resources were also being surrendered.

In 1817, in the Red River Valley of what is now Manitoba, Lord Selkirk entered into a Treaty with certain Ojibwa and Cree chiefs for the cession of all of the land within two miles on either side of the Red River, from its mouth to the junction with the Red Lake River in what is now Minnesota, and for two miles on either side of the Assiniboine River from its mouth to the Rivière aux Champignons, located a little to the west of Portage La Prairie.[40] In return for this land, the Ojibwa and Cree were each promised one hundred pounds of good and merchantable tobacco annually to be delivered to the Forks of the Red and Assiniboine in the case of the Ojibwa, and to Portage La Prairie in the case of the Cree.[41]

As the years passed, the Selkirk Treaty became a source of controversy and confusion. Some Indians claimed that no Treaty was ever signed, others that the Chiefs who signed it did not know what they were subscribing to, still others that the Chiefs had not sold the land, but only leased it for a season, and yet others that the Chiefs had sold land, but not the land described in the deed. Many Métis questioned the validity of the Treaty on the grounds that the Indians who had executed it were relative newcomers to the country and possessed no Aboriginal title there.[42] It may be possible to doubt the understanding of the Chiefs who entered into the Selkirk Treaty as to the purport of their actions. But the very controversy that grew up around it ensured that the Indians in the area that was to be encompassed by Treaty One became well aware of the nature of land cession treaties. In 1869, before the Hudson's Bay Company had given up its rights to Rupertsland, a group of new settlers from Canada learned very quickly that the Indians were well aware of the boundaries of the Selkirk Treaty and were very anxious to negotiate new Treaty arrangements with the incoming Canadian authorities. It was also very clear that the Indians understood that land would be the central focus of the new Treaty relationship. The settlers attempted to establish themselves along Rat Creek, a stream to the north of the Assiniboine, which flowed into the Whitemud River. They were immediately accosted by members of the Portage Band under Chief Yellow Quill who pointed out that they were trespassing on land not covered by the Selkirk Treaty, and warned them off. The settlers appealed to Hudson's Bay Company Governor William McTavish who dispatched James McKay, a respected Métis member of the Council of Assiniboia, to intercede with the Band. After considerable discussion, the Councillor was able to persuade the Band to accept the following temporary arrangement:

> We, the undersigned Indians of Portage la Prairie, have, in accordance with Gov. McTavish's request, agreed among ourselves to allow any Canadians who may come with the intention of settling, to settle at Rat Creek on the lower, or the east side, and on the whole of the farming land down to the Portage and downwards to Manitobah Lake.

> We strongly object to any old settlers going up to Rat Creek to settle, we mean those who have settled below this for some time past ... We give a lease of the land above mentioned for the term of three years, fully expecting that some arrangements will be made with us before the expiration of the three years, about our lands. We further agree to allow the settlers that may settle at Rat Creek the privilege of going three miles landward, to the mountain, or into the woods for their building timber or for firewood.[43]

After the transfer of Rupertsland to Canada, the problem of settlers establishing themselves and cutting wood outside of the Selkirk Treaty area resurfaced, prompting another Chief of the Portage Band to post the following notice on the church door in the community of Portage la Prairie:

To all whom it may concern

Whereas the Indian title to all lands west of the Fifty mile boundary line at High Bluff has not been extinguished &

Whereas those lands are being taken up & the wood thereon cut
off by parties who have no right or title thereto,

I hereby warn all such parties that they are infringing on lands that
as yet virtually belong to the Indians & do hereby caution them to
desist, on pain of forfeiting their labour.[44]

Moosoos ^{His}
Mark

The Métis witness to the Notice,[45] who would seem to have forwarded
a copy of it to Lieutenant Governor Adams G. Archibald, explained the
reason for the Chief's action:

The Chief complains that people come and cut wood without leave
and permission and that it is not right.

That the woods belong to the Indians and it seems to them that the
people are stealing.

That in the smallest bargains, an agreement is come to between
parties but here there was none, and he would like to have some
understand [sic] about it.

The Chief says that the most of the tribe are out on the Hunting
grounds and that he was left in charge, and that it is not right to
cut their wood without even consulting them.[46]

The Portage Band was not alone in seeking an understanding concerning their lands. When the prospective Lieutenant Governor William McDougall made his abortive attempt to enter the Hudson's Bay
Company Territory from the United States in the late autumn of 1869,
he was met by the Ojibwa Chief Kewetaosh and his band from the vicinity of Roseau River. The Chief demanded to know if it were true
that Canada had purported to buy his land from the Hudson's Bay
Company.

He then proceeded to lay claim to the country from Pembina to the
Assinaboine, and from the high lands on the west to the Lake of

the Woods. He said his ancestors had never sold their title to any part of it—they had only <u>lent</u> as much as a man could see under a horse's belly on both sides of the River to the Company, and he now wanted to know what I was going to do with his land. ...

I replied to his speech through an interpreter ... I was glad to see him and his band, and hoped we would be able to make a satisfactory agreement about any land of his we might require. I explained the nature of the arrangement with the H. B. Company, which I assured him left his rights, whatever they might be just as they stood before.... I then produced a map of the Territory and asked him to point out the bounds of the land to which he and his band laid claim. This proposal was evidently something he did not expect, and a good deal of consultation took place between him and his companions. I told them that I merely wished to find out the extent of the country they <u>claimed</u>; that I was not prepared ei ' er to admit their claim or deny it, but before we could negotiate, must know what it was they pretended to own—that there were other Indian bands, especially towards the Lake of the Woods, who would probably claim some part of the territory he had described as belonging to his band. It then came out that three chiefs— "Peguis," [47] near Lake Winnipeg, "Fox," of Prairie Portage, and "Gros Oreille" of Oak Point, towards Lake of the Woods, and himself, agreed last winter upon a division of the country between them, and that his claim was to be limited to the country bounded by Scratching River and the Government Road on the north, Pembina Mountain on the West, White mouth River on the East and the American Boundary on the South. [48]

William McDougall subsequently reported from his Pembina exile [49] that he had received a friendly letter from "the Indian Chief 'Pegwis', who lives at Winnipeg, in which he strongly condemns the conduct of the French half-breeds ... He wishes to see me, to shake hands and bargain about his land." [50] At his first interview with the newly arrived Lieutenant Governor Archibald, Chief Henry Prince, son of Peguis, raised the question of payment for his lands. [51] So too did a delegation of six chiefs, including the son of "Les Grandes Oreilles," who met the Lieutenant Governor two days after the interview with Chief Prince. They indicated that they had been waiting all summer, having been informed that Archibald would make a Treaty with them "about their lands" as soon as he arrived. [52]

Lieutenant Governor Archibald diverted these requests by promising that he would meet the Indians the following spring and make a

Treaty with them at that time. By the end of May 1871, the Portage Band began to lose patience. It met in council and passed a number of resolutions, which they forwarded to the Lieutenant Governor. They objected to the manner in which they were being treated by the settlers and to the fact that their band members were being imprisoned for violations of Canadian law before a Treaty had been made. They demanded payment of £5 for every member of their band who might be arrested and £1 per day for every day that such a member was detained in prison. The Band explained these unusual resolutions as follows:

> Why we pass these resolutions at our council held today is because that we never have yet seen or received anything for the land and the woods that belong to us, and the settlers use to enrich themselves. We might not have felt so hard at the present time at the usage we have rec^d of late, had we ever rec^d any remuneration for the said lands & woods that ... [illegible] belong to us. ... We feel sorry to have to express these resolutions at our Council today, but ... [illegible] necessity compels us to do so. We always thought & wished to be friendly with you (the settlers) but can now see that you look upon us as children & we feel that you are treating us the same.

> What was said last fall by the Governor we still remember all. We were promised by Governor Archibald that we should be treated with etc. early this spring.[53]

It will be seen therefore, that before the first of the Numbered Treaties was entered into, the documentary record gives considerable evidence that the Indian parties were well aware that the subject matter of the Treaties would be land, and they were also concerned about at least one of the natural resources connected with land—namely timber. Their understanding of the issues was sophisticated and they resented being treated like children. Indeed it was the Indians, far more than the government, who were insistent upon a bargain involving lands.

During the negotiations themselves, land issues were paramount. Spokespersons for the Indians put forward a proposal that would have resulted in their retention of large tracts of land that they could use as a source of resource income. As Lieutenant Governor Archibald reported: "... the Indians seem to have false ideas about the meaning of a Reserve. They have been led to suppose that large tracts of ground were to be set aside for them as hunting grounds, including timber lands, of which they might sell the wood as if they were proprietors of the soil." [54]

The Treaty Commissioners rejected this proposal, arguing that since the Indians would be able to hunt over the unoccupied portion of the Treaty lands there was no need for reserves larger than would be necessary for them to use for farming purposes should they choose to take up that vocation. After long and hard bargaining, and the granting of a number of concessions in other areas, including the amount of the annuities, the Indians accepted a treaty which contained clauses respecting lands similar to those proposed by the Crown's representatives.[55]

The documentary record shows that the question of mineral rights was raised and expressly dealt with during the negotiations of another of the Numbered Treaties—Treaty Three, concluded in 1873. As Treaty Commissioner Lieutenant Governor Alexander Morris reported:

> They asked what reserves would be given them, and were informed by Mr. Provencher that reserves of farming and other lands would be given them as previously stated, and that any land actually in cultivation by them would be respected. They asked if the mines would be theirs; I said if they were found on their reserves it would be to their benefit, but not otherwise. They asked if an Indian found a mine would he be paid for it, I told them he could sell his information if he could find a purchaser like any other person.[56]

The historical record discloses that throughout the negotiation of the numbered treaties in the 1870s the Indian parties were remarkably well informed about the previous proceedings in connection with other Treaties. Thus the Indians who gathered to sign Treaty Two at Manitoba Post in late August of 1871 were reported to be fully familiar with the terms of Treaty One concluded at Lower Fort Garry just 18 days earlier.[57] A striking example of the rapid and effective communication occurred in 1876, when Treaty Commissioners were dispatched to what is now Northern Manitoba to take adhesions from various bands to Treaty Five, concluded in the previous year. Thomas Howard, one of these Commissioners arrived at The Pas on 5 September 1876, just 13 days after Treaty Six had been concluded more than 350 kilometres up the Saskatchewan River. He attempted to obtain the Band's agreement to the terms of Treaty Five but encountered a real problem because Treaty Six contained more generous provisions with respect to reserve size and initial cash payments:

> ... I proceeded to explain the terms of the treaty that I desired to receive their adhesion to. The Chiefs immediately stated that they wanted to make a treaty of their own, and it was only after great

difficulty that I could make them understand that in reality it was not a new treaty they were about to make.

They had heard of the terms granted the Indians at Carlton, and this acted most prejudicially at one time against the successful carrying out of my mission; but I at last made them understand the difference between their position and the Plain Indians, by pointing out that the land they would surrender would be useless to the Queen, while what the Plain Indians gave up would be of value to her for homes for her white children. They then agreed to accept the terms offered if I would agree to give them reserves where they desired; ...[58]

A common issue raised by several of the Indian parties throughout a number of the Treaty negotiations which further demonstrated the general awareness of the Indian negotiators of relevant events in the Euro-Canadian world was the question of the Hudson's Bay Company's sale of Rupertsland to Canada. As early as April 1871, Chief Sweetgrass, the leading Cree Chief who would sign Treaty No. 6 at Fort Pitt in 1876, sent a message from Edmonton to Lieutenant Governor Archibald: "We heard our lands were sold and we did not like it; we don't want to sell our lands; it is our property, and no one has a right to sell them." [59]

At the negotiation of Treaty Four in what is now Southern Saskatchewan the discussions were held hostage for a considerable period in a dispute concerning the Hudson's Bay Company. All speakers deferred to Chief "Gambler" until the matter was talked through. The Chief was fairly vague at first in describing the cause of the Indian's complaint. But he did accuse the Company of stealing the land, in terms that clearly suggested that he understood the land to include the natural resources. On the fourth day of the negotiations the following exchange occurred:

> THE GAMBLER: "When one Indian takes anything from another we call it stealing, and when we see the present we say pay us. It is the Company I mean."
>
> LIEUT-GOV. MORRIS: "What did the Company steal from you?"
>
> THE GAMBLER: "The earth, trees, grass, stones, all that which I see with my eyes."[60]

Finally, although Chief Gambler would not clearly articulate the issue, Chief Pis-qua[61] stepped forward at the end of the long day and put the troublesome question on the table:

Pis-Qua (the plain) pointing to Mr. McDonald, of the Hudson's Bay Company—"You told me you had sold your land for so much money, £300,000. We want that money.[62]

The Lieutenant Governor was able to fend off this request by indicating that the payment of money to the Company for the sale of its rights did not stand in the way of Her Majesty paying the Indians for their rights.

While many more examples could be given, the documentary records of the Treaty negotiations and the preceding events would seem to offer ample evidence that the Indian parties understood that a purchase of land was a central purpose of the Treaties. There is also evidence from at least some of the negotiations that they also understood that natural resources, including timber and minerals were included in the surrenders that they made.

Although it only surfaces sporadically, there is also considerable evidence from the years following the making of the Treaties that the Indian parties understood that they had surrendered their Aboriginal title in return for the Treaty rights of reserves, annuities, and other benefits. Often the evidence of this understanding occurred when Aboriginal spokespersons complained about the non-fulfilment of Treaty promises, as for example in the case of the meeting of Treaty Six and Four Chiefs near Fort Carlton in the summer of 1884 to air their grievances. After reciting a number of complaints, the Chiefs are reported to have declared:

That requests for redress of these grievances have been again & again made without effect. They are glad that the young men have not resorted to violent measures to gain it. That it is almost too hard for them to bear the treatment received at the hands of the government after its "sweet promises" made to get their country from them. They now fear they are going to be cheated.[63]

A similar point was made by spokesperson Louis O'Soup on the occasion of the 1911 Delegation of Saskatchewan and Manitoba Indians to Ottawa. O'Soup and others had collected grievances from a number of Bands in the southern portions of the Prairie Provinces and travelled down to Parliament Hill to confront Minister of Indian Affairs Frank Oliver with them. One of the grievances related to a requirement that Indians should pay duty on gifts of horses that were made to them by their U.S. friends and relatives. As O'Soup explained:

Long ago we never saw a boundary line. The people on either side just travelled across. Our friends are across the boundary line and when we go to see them they give us some small ponies and when we bring [them] to this side of the line they are taken away from us, no matter how small, if we have not $12.50 to pay for the horse. We find it hard because we are poor. We don't blame you. The people of the United States are rich and so are Canadians but you take our little ponies from us although we gave you the country and you are making money on the country we gave you and we have not money to pay for the ponies. The Indian thinks the Gov't is hard, because the pony is not worth much to a white man but the Indian can ride about on him and see his neighbour.[64]

Even into the late 1960s similar comments can be found. For example, in the well-known polemic by Harold Cardinal, *The Unjust Society*, [65] the following passage concerning the Treaties can be found:

Our people talked with the government representatives, not as beggars pleading for handouts, but as men with something to offer in return for rights they expected. To our people, this was the beginning of a contractual relationship whereby the representatives of the queen [*sic*] would have lasting responsibilities to the Indian people in return for the valuable lands that were ceded to them.

The treaties were the way in which the white people legitimized in the eyes of the world their presence in our country. It was an attempt to settle the terms of occupancy on a just basis, legally and morally to extinguish the legitimate claims of our people to title to the land in our country. There never has been any doubt in the minds of our people that the land in Canada belonged to them. Nor can there have been any doubt in the mind of the government or in the minds of the white people about who owned the land, for it was upon the basis of white recognition of Indian rights that the treaties were negotiated. Otherwise, there could have been nothing to negotiate, no need for treaties. In the language of the Cree Indians, the Indian reserves are known as *the land that we kept for ourselves* or *the land that we did not give to the government*. In our language, *skun-gun*.[66]

In the early 1970s federal government funding for Aboriginal organizations, and in particular, for land claims research, led to a number of programs in which Elders were interviewed to gain their perspective on the meaning of the Treaties. The writer participated in some of those efforts, on behalf of the Indian Association of Alberta and the Federation of Saskatchewan Indians. The material collected was undoubtedly of considerable value, but like all oral histories varied greatly in quality and reliability. Some informants were so concerned about the accuracy of what they would relate that they would not speak of any event that they had not personally witnessed. Others told fantastic tales of devious conspiracies—how the white men gathered together all of the smartest people from all of Europe to meet in Winnipeg for weeks so that they could calculate the most effective means to trick the Indian out of his lands. During these research projects, the story of the "top six inches" was uncovered. The assertion that at the Treaty negotiations the white man had told the Indians that he only wanted the top six inches of the soil to allow his people to farm and that the title to everything else would remain with the Aboriginal people.[67] The story was far from universal, however. It competed with other accounts claiming that the Indians had not sold any land at all, that they only agreed to share it with the newcomers, that they had sold the land, but not the animals, that they had sold the land but not the trees or the grass.

Given the considerable volume of evidence from historical documents relating to the Indian understanding of the Treaties and the pre-*Delgamuukw* jurisprudence on Treaty interpretation, it might have seemed pointless to attempt to challenge the Treaty provisions which purport to extinguish Indian interests in lands and resources outside of reserves. That, however, may no longer be the case. Two aspects of the *Delgamuukw* decision in particular have introduced a considerable element of uncertainty.

The first relates to oral tradition. Following up his admonition in the *Van der Peet* case to respect the Aboriginal perspective and to interpret the laws of evidence in a manner which respects the difficulties inherent in the attempts by Aboriginal people to prove their claims, Chief Justice Antonio Lamer declared in *Delgamuukw* that:

> This appeal requires us to ... adapt the laws of evidence so that the aboriginal perspective on their practices, customs and traditions and on their relationship with the land, are given due weight by the courts. In practical terms, this requires the courts to come to terms with the oral histories of aboriginal societies, which, for many aboriginal nations, are the only record of their past. Given that the aboriginal rights recognized and affirmed by s. 35(1) are defined by reference to pre-contact practices or, as I will develop below, in the case of title, pre-sovereignty occupation, those histories play a crucial role in the litigation of aboriginal rights.

A useful and informative description of aboriginal oral history is provided by the *Report of the Royal Commission on Aboriginal Peoples* (1996), vol. 1 (*Looking Forward, Looking Back*), at p. 33:

The Aboriginal tradition in the recording of history is neither linear nor steeped in the same notions of social progress and evolution [as in the non-Aboriginal tradition]. Nor is it usually human-centred in the same way as in the western scientific tradition, for it does not assume that human beings are anything more than one--and not necessarily the most important--element of the natural order of the universe. Moreover, the Aboriginal historical tradition is an oral one, involving legends, stories and accounts handed down through the generations in oral form. It is less focussed [*sic*] on establishing objective truth and assumes that the teller of the story is so much a part of the event being described that it would be arrogant to presume to classify or categorize the event exactly or for all time.

In the Aboriginal tradition the purposes of repeating oral accounts from the past is broader than the role of written history in western societies. It may be to educate the listener, to communicate aspects of culture, to socialize people into a cultural tradition, or to validate the claims of a particular family to authority and prestige. ...

Oral accounts of the past include a good deal of subjective experience. They are not simply a detached recounting of factual events but, rather, are "facts enmeshed in the stories of a lifetime". They are also likely to be rooted in particular locations, making reference to particular families and communities, This contributes to a sense that there are many histories, each characterized in part by how a people see themselves, how they define their identity in relation to their environment, and how they express their uniqueness as a people.

Many features of oral histories would count against both their admissibility and their weight as evidence of prior events in a court that took a traditional approach to the rules of evidence. The most fundamental of these is their broad social role not only "as a repository of historical knowledge for a culture" but also as an expression of "the values and mores of ... [that] culture": ... [References omitted] Dickson J. (as he was then) recognized as much when he stated in *Kruger v. The Queen*, [1978] 1 S.C.R. 104, at p. 109, that "[c]laims to aboriginal title are woven with history, legend, politics and moral obligations". The difficulty with these features of oral histories is that they are tangential to the ultimate purpose of the fact-finding process at trial--the determination of the historical truth. Another feature of oral histories which creates difficulty is that they largely consist of out-of-court statements, passed on through an unbroken chain across the generations of a particular aboriginal nation to the present-day. These out-of-court statements are admitted for their truth and therefore conflict with the general rule against the admissibility of hearsay.

Notwithstanding the challenges created by the use of oral histories as proof of historical facts, the laws of evidence must be adapted in order that this type of evidence can be accommodated and placed on an equal footing with the types of historical evidence that courts are familiar with, which largely consists of historical documents. This is a long-standing practice in the interpretation of treaties between the Crown and aboriginal peoples ... [references omitted]. To quote Dickson C.J., given that most aboriginal societies "did not keep written records", the failure to do so would "impose an impossible burden of proof" on aboriginal peoples, and "render nugatory" any rights that they have (*Simon v. The Queen*, [1985] 2 S.C.R. 387, at p. 408). This process must be undertaken on a case-by-case basis.[68]

The injunction to place oral histories on an equal footing with traditional documentary does not, of course, mean that the documentary evidence should be disregarded, or that the word of the Elders will always be accepted. Those challenging such testimony, however, will bear some special burdens. The events referred to will be beyond the personal knowledge of the witnesses. In some senses Elders will be testifying as quasi-experts in the oral tradition of their people, but there will be only very limited possibilities for the Crown to test or challenge their expertise. The Crown is also very unlikely to be able to find its own witnesses from within the Aboriginal communities to dispute the Plaintiffs' version of the tribal tradition. A good understanding of the history of the Plaintiff's community will undoubtedly be of great assistance, both in cross-examination of opposing witnesses and in placing a coherent account of the Treaties based on the documentary evidence before the Court. So too will a sympathetic understanding of the influences and social pressures which might lead people to a sincere belief in an unreliable version of past events. No one would not expect to obtain an accurate, complete, and disinterested understanding of the history of Canadian Banking at a convention of Prairie grain farmers, but if you appreciate the relationship between banking and farming, you can still obtain some information of value from the farmers on the subject.

The second manner in which the *Delgamuukw* decision has made an assault on the Treaties more likely and attractive relates to the definition of Aboriginal title itself. Prior to the decisions in *Van der Peet* and *Adams,* Aboriginal title was generally assumed to be merely the bundle of Aboriginal rights that related to the land.[69] The *Adams* case made it clear that Aboriginal title was more than this but did not tell us just what it was. However, in *Delgamuukw,* Chief Justice Lamer declared:

> As *Adams* makes clear, aboriginal title confers more than the right to engage in site-specific activities which are aspects of the practices, customs and traditions of distinctive aboriginal cultures. Site-specific rights can be made out even if title cannot. What aboriginal title confers is the right to the land itself.[70]

If the previous understanding of the meaning of Aboriginal title had been maintained, one might have questioned the utility of challenging the extinguishment provisions of the Treaty. After all, on ordinary contract principles if it is clear that the Crown's principal objective in entering into the Treaties was to obtain a surrender of Aboriginal title, and if it were shown that such a surrender was not given, one might conclude that the Agreements were a nullity, either on the basis of *non est factum* or a complete failure of consideration. Such a finding would call into question the existing Treaty rights of the Prairie Indians, and if they were then required to prove Aboriginal rights to the use of particular resources in particular areas based upon the date of European contact, they might have great difficulty in doing so, particularly when one appreciates the historical migrations of the different tribal groups. Certainly it would have been very difficult to claim ownership of the entire oil and gas and other mineral resources of the Prairies based on an integral to culture and date of contact model. However, by holding that Aboriginal title entitles the title holders to use lands for any purpose not incompatible with traditional use, the Supreme Court has made challenges to the essential validity of the Treaties much more attractive.

None of the above should be seen as suggesting that the Prairie Treaties are in mortal danger, or as minimizing the difficulties which an Aboriginal challenger to them will face. Furthermore, the symbolic importance of the Treaties to Prairie First Nations should not be discounted. Should it become clear that a particular lawsuit is more likely to tear down a Treaty than to give it an agreeable re-interpretation, many Aboriginal people may have second thoughts about pursuing it.

Nevertheless, while it would be foolish to suggest that the *Delgamuukw* decision has produced the same profound uncertainty on the Prairies that it has in British Columbia, the ground is not quite so firm under one's feet east of the Rockies today as it once was.

Notes

1 Alexander Morris, *The Treaties of Canada with the Indians of Manitoba and the North-West Territories, including the Negotiations on which they were based, and other Information relating thereto,* 1991, Fifth House Publishers, Saskatoon, (Originally published 1880) p. 213.

2 See. *Ibid* pp. 202, 208 and 235 for use of the sun and river images by Treaty Commissioner Morris, and pp. 219, 227 and 238 by spokesperson for the Cree. At the Treaty Six negotiation Chief Sweetgrass prayed that the Treaty should continue "as long as this earth stands and the river flows," *Ibid* p. 236.

3 See Royal Commission on Aboriginal Peoples, *Report* Vol. 1 *Looking Forward, Looking Back* pp. 178-179.

4 In this short paper it is not possible to deal with the question of whether or not Canada's Treaties with Aboriginal people have been faithfully fulfilled or not. The writer is of the view that although Treaty fulfilment was not a major concern of British and Canadian authorities in the development of their Indian policies, they did make conscientious attempts to fulfil Treaty undertakings in most cases. The majority of so-called "breaches" of the Treaties identified by modern critics of the Crown's record in this respect actually relate to questions of interpretation of what the Treaties meant. See, for example, the Royal Commission on Aboriginal Peoples comments on the "Non-Fulfilment of Treaty Promises" *ibid.* at pp. 176-178. Such clear breaches of the Treaties as did occur were more likely to be the result of in-efficiencies and incompetence than malevolence—as, for example, in the case of the many outstanding Treaty land entitlements on the Prairies (which are now being addressed under formulas which appear to take into account and compensate for the delay in implementing the promises). No doubt, one could justifiably criticize the Crown for its post-1885 detribalization policy, which was clearly contrary to the basic understanding on which the Treaties were made and perhaps for its failure to maintain laws prohibiting alcohol on reserves. However, in cataloguing Treaty breaches, one should not forget that they were not always one-sided. Many of the earliest Treaties were also breached by the Indian parties who broke their engagements to maintain peace and neutrality vis-à-vis either the French or the British.

5 See *R v. Sioui,* [1990] 1 S.C.R. 1025; (1990), 70 D.L.R.(4th) 427; 56 C.C.C.(3d) 225; 109 N.R. 22; 30 Q.A.C. 280; [1990] 3 C.N.L.R. 127. The Supreme Court found that an agreement entered into by General Murray with a group of Huron Indians was a Treaty. The agreement provided that if the Hurons abandoned their French Allies and returned to their homes, they would not be molested or interrupted in their journey and would be allowed the free exercise of their religion, their customs, and the liberty of trading with the English.

6 The extreme northeastern tip of Manitoba is, by an accident of history, not included within the defined boundaries of any Treaty. Treaty Five was extended to what is now northern Manitoba in 1909-10, before Manitoba's boundaries were extended to Hudson's Bay and the 60th parallel in 1912. The area added to Manitoba almost, but did not quite coincide, with the

new Treaty Five territory on the north and east. When Treaty Nine extended to Hudson's Bay in 1929-30, the Treaty terms did not define areas outside the Province of Ontario. The small area excluded (between Cape Tatnum and the Ontario boundary) is undoubtedly dealt with by one of the Treaties or the other, however, since both contain the recital that the Indian signatories gave up "all their rights, titles and privileges whatsoever to all other lands wherever situated."

7 The Dakota have been refused the right to enter into Treaties because the eight bands now in Saskatchewan and Manitoba entered British Territory from the U.S. in 1862 following the Minnesota Sioux War. A ninth Sioux Band near Wood Mountain, Saskatchewan is largely descended from the remnants of Sitting Bull's followers who had entered Canada in 1876 following the Battle of the Little Bighorn, and never returned to the U.S. with their Chief.

8 The meridian runs just east of Vegreville and just west of Hanna, Alberta.

9 Statement of Claim, *Chief Florence Buffalo acting on her own behalf and on behalf of all the other citizens and members of the Samson Cree Nation and the Samson Cree Nation v. Her Majesty the Queen in Right of Canada and Her Majesty the Queen in Right of Alberta,* Action No.9903 03870 (Edmonton) Court of Queen's Bench of Alberta, filed 26 February, 1999.

10 The approximate area covered by Treaty Seven extends from the U.S. Border on the south, the British Columbia Border on the west, the Red Deer River on the north and a line running from the junction of the Red Deer River and the South Saskatchewan just east of the present Saskatchewan boundary, to the western end of the Cypress Hills, and then south to the 49th parallel. The north-eastern boundary does not actually follow the Red Deer River, but rather a line produced from a point east of Buffalo Lake to the junction of the Red Deer and South Saskatchewan Rivers. It will be noticed that there is a significant overlap between the two claims.

11 Statement of Claim, *Kainaiwa Nation (Blood Tribe) and Chief Chris Shade, suing on his own behalf and on behalf of the Members of The Kainaiwa/Blood Tribe, Peigan Nation and Chief Peter Strikes with a Gun, suing on his own behalf and on behalf of the Members of the Peigan Nation, Siksika Nation and Chief Darlene Yellow Old Woman Munroe, suing on her own behalf and on behalf of the Members of The Siksika Nation, Tsuu Tina Nation and Chief Roy Whitney, suing on his own behalf and on behalf of the members of The Tsuu Tina Nation, Bearspaw Band and Chief Darcy Dixon, suing on his own behalf and on behalf of the members of The Bearspaw Band, Chiniki Band and Chief Paul Chiniquay, suing on his own behalf and on behalf of the members of The Chiniki Band, Wesley Band and Chief John Snow Sr., suing on his behalf and on behalf of the members of The Wesley Band v. Her Majesty the Queen in right of Canada and Her Majesty the Queen in Right of Alberta,* File No. T-340-99, Federal Court, Trial Division, filed 26 February 1999.

12 The group that became Samson's Band adhered to Treaty Six at Blackfoot Crossing on 25 September 1877 (3 days after the signing of Treaty Seven at the same location) as part of Bobtail (Kiskaquin)'s Band.

13 The Samson Cree Nation makes other alternative claims relating to self-government and tax exemptions that will not be canvassed in this paper.

14 *Calder v. Attorney General of British Columbia*, [1973] S.C.R. 313; (1973), 34 D.L.R. (3d) 145; [1973] 4 W.W.R. 1; 7 C.N.L.C. 91.
15 *Ibid.* at 394 (S.C.R.)
16 [1985] 2 S.C.R. 387; (1985), 24 D.L.R.(4th) 390; 23 C.C.C.(3d) 238; 62 N.R. 366; 71 N.S.R.(2d) 15; 171 A.P.R. 15; [1986] 1 C.N.L.R. 153.
17 [1991] 2 S.C.R. 570; (1991), 83 D.L.R.(4th) 381; [1991] 3 C.N.L.R. 79.
18 *Ibid.* at 575 (S.C.R.)
19 [1988] 1 S.C.R. 187; (1988), 47 D.L.R.(4th) 526; [1988] 2 W.W.R. 289; 39 C.C.C.(3d) 97; [1988] 2 C.N.L.R. 112.
20 *Ibid.* at 199. Emphasis in original quote by Justice Estey (not in the text of Treaty Six).
21 *Ibid.* at 201-202.
22 *Ibid.* at 202.
23 *Ibid.* at 203.
24 *Idem.*
25 It did appear somewhat incongruous for Justice Estey to both cite the rule which provides that extrinsic evidence cannot be received in the absence of ambiguity, to find no ambiguity, and then to consider the extrinsic evidence in any event.
26 [1996] 1 S.C.R. 771; (1996), 133 D.L.R.(4th) 324; 105 C.C.C.(3d) 289; 195 N.R. 1; 37 A.L.R.(3d) 153; 181 A.R. 321; [1996] 4 W.W.R. 457; [1996] 2 C.N.L.R. 77.
27 In fact, the Court concluded that the land on which Mr. Badger had been hunting was not "unoccupied." It reached the contrary conclusion with respect to the place where Mr. Ominiyak, one of two other individual Treaty Eight Indians whose appeals were heard jointly with Badger's, had been charged with hunting.
28 The Court concluded that Indians did have the right to hunt on unoccupied private land or land that had not been put to a use that was visibly incompatible with hunting, on the theory that Treaty Eight had guaranteed Indians the right to hunt on lands that were not taken up for settlement or other purposes. This guarantee was accepted as providing the "right of access" required by paragraph 12 of the *Natural Resources Transfer Agreement*. The actual findings in the three cases before the Court, however, indicated that the concept of "visible incompatible use" would be fairly broadly interpreted. As a result it is doubtful that Indian hunters received much of a practical victory in the case. It seems likely that in most cases where it could be said that private land was not put to such a use, the hunter would likely be able to maintain a successful due diligence defence.
29 *R. v. Badger, supra* n. 26 at 798-799.
30 *R. v. Sundown*, [1999] S.C.J. No. 13 (QL).
31 Emphasis added by Justice Cory.
32 Emphasis added by Justice Cory.
33 *R. v. Sundown, supra* n. 30 at paragraph 25.
34 *R. v. Badger, supra* n. 26 at 800-801.
35 *Re Paulette and the Registrar of Titles (No. 2)* (1973), 42 D.L.R.(3d) 8 (N.W.T.S.C.). The Court's conclusions are at pp. 39-40.

36 *Ibid.* at 11-12.

37 *Paulette v. The Queen; sub. nom. Re Paulette et al. and Registrar of Titles (No. 2)*, (1975), 63 D.L.R.(3d) 1 (N.W.T.C.A.). Four of the five judges held that the applicable Land Titles legislation did not permit the registration of caveats on unpatented Crown land. One of those four also found that Aboriginal rights and title were not caveatable interests. The fifth judge dissented and would have affirmed the lower court ruling.

38 *Paulette v. The Queen; sub. nom. Re Paulette et al. and Registrar of Titles (No. 2)*, [1977] 2 S.C.R. 628; (1976), 72 D.L.R.(3d) 161; 12 N.R. 420; [1977] 1 W.W.R. 321; [1977] C.N.L.B. (No.1) 5. Although the chiefs lost the case with respect to the caveat, they did achieve a political victory, because in the aftermath of the case the federal government agreed to enter into land claims negotiations with the NWT Dene, Gwitch'en and Inuvialuit notwithstanding the terms of the Treaties.

39 It should also be appreciated that the concept of Aboriginal title was much less certain than it is in the wake of *Delgamuukw*. In *Baker Lake (Hamlet of) v. Minister of Indian Affairs and Northern Development (No. 2)*, [1980] 5 W.W.R. 193; (1979), 107 D.L.R.(3d) 513; [1980] 1 F.C. 518; [1979] 3 C.N.L.R. 17 at 579 (F.C.) Justice Mahoney declared that the Baker Lake Inuit were "entitled to a declaration that the lands comprised in District E2 ... are subject to the aboriginal right and title of the Inuit to hunt and fish thereon." Such declaration seems confused in light of Chief Justice Lamer's pronouncements in *Van der Peet, Adams*, and *Delgamuukw*.

40 There were additional lands at Fort Douglas, Fort Daer and Grand Forks, stretching six miles in radius around those posts.

41 A copy of this Treaty may be found in Morris *Treaties* pp. 298-300.

42 The various alleged defects of the Selkirk Treaty were summarized in A.G. Archibald, letter to the Secretary of State for the Provinces, 20 December, 1870, Archibald Papers, Provincial Archives of Manitoba, MG 12 A 1, Doc. No. 155.

43 Joutupotang *et al.*, Indian Agreement witnessed by Jas. McKay et al., Portage la Prairie, 14 June, 1869, reproduced in "Indian Titles in the North-West," *Toronto Globe*, 4 September, 1869. There are a number of other accounts of this incident. See, for example, "Further Correspondence by J.J. Hargrave in the *Montreal Herald* on the Beginning of the Resistance, in W.L. Morton (ed.), *Alexander Begg's Red River Journal and Other Papers Relative to the Red River Resistance of 1869-1870* (Toronto: The Champlain Society, 1956) p. 431.

44 Moosoos, Notice, 17 December, 1870, Archibald Papers, Doc. No. 150.

45 Fred Bird. Bird likely drafted the notice for Moosoos.

46 *Idem.*

47 Presumably this was a reference to Peguis's son Henry Prince, as Peguis had died 5 years earlier.

48 William McDougall to the Secretary of State for the Provinces, 5 Nov., 1869, Secretary of State for the Provinces Records, National Archives of Canada, RG 6 C 1, Vol. 316, File 995/69.

49 McDougall's attempt to enter Rupertsland in order to establish himself before the scheduled transfer of the Territory from the H.B.C. to Canada was forcibly prevented by a group of French Métis. He remained for several weeks in Pembina, in what is now North Dakota, before returning to Ontario in December of 1869.

50 William McDougall to Joseph Howe, 29 November, 1869, Secretary of State for the Provinces Records, Vol. 316, File 995/69.

51 Notes of an Interview between the Lieutenant Governor of Manitobah and Henry Prince (Miskookenu) Chief of the Salteaux and Swampies at the St. Peter's Parish School on the morning of Tuesday, the 13th Sept. 1870, Archibald Papers, Document No. 22.

52 A.G. Archibald to Secretary of State for the Provinces, 21 September, 1870, reprinted in House of Commons, *Sessional Papers (No. 20), 1871* p. 18.

53 Yellow Quill *et al.* to His Excellency the Lieutenant Governor of Manitoba, 30 May, 1871, Archibald Papers, Document No. 332.

54 Adams G. Archibald to the Secretary of State for the Provinces, 29 July, 1871, in Indian Affairs Records, National Archives of Canada, R.G. 10 , Vol. 363, File M 634.

55 The Portage Band, under Chief Yellow Quill, however, managed to exact an extra 25 square miles of reserve land for his band in addition to the 32 acres per capita offered to the other Treaty One Bands. See Morris, *Treaties* pp. 25-43 and 313-316.

56 Morris, *Treaties*, p. 50. See also p. 70.

57 *Ibid.* at pp. 31 and 41.

58 *Ibid.* at p. 162.

59 Messages from the Cree Chiefs of the Plains, Saskatchewan to His Excellency Governor Archibald, 13 April 1871, Archibald Papers, Document No. 272.

60 Morris, *Treaties* at p. 102.

61 Usually referred to as "Pasqua."

62 Morris, *Treaties* at p. 106.

63 J. Ansdell Macrae to Indian Commissioner Dewdney, 25 August 1884, in Indian Affairs Records, R.G. 10, Vol. 3697, File 15423.

64 Notes of representations made by delegation of Indians from the West, A. Gadie interpreter, 24 Jan., 1911 in Indian Affairs Records, R.G. 10, Vol. 4053, File 379, 203-1.

65 (Edmonton: Hurtig, 1969).

66 *Ibid.* at p. 29. (Emphasis in original).

67 See for example, Interview with Lazarus Roan, 30 March 1974, in Richard Price (ed.), *The Spirit of the Alberta Indian Treaties*, (Montreal: Institute for Research on Public Policy, 1980), p. 115.

68 *Delgamuukw v. British Columbia*, [1997] 3 S.C.R. 1010 at paragraphs 84-87.

69 See, for example *Baker Lake, supra* n. 39.

70 *Delgamuukw* at paragraph 138.

4 Impact in Ontario

Take Your Time and Do It Right
Delgamuukw, Self-Government Rights and the Pragmatics of Advocacy

Delgamuukw and Inherent Self-Government Rights

The failure of the Charlottetown proposals[1] in 1992 brought to an end a decade of sustained political effort to make specific provision in our constitution for aboriginal rights of self-government,[2] and likely postponed indefinitely any prospect of protecting such rights through explicit constitutional amendment.[3] It did not, however, diminish aboriginal peoples' own conviction that they have, and always have had, inherent self-government rights.[4] In the years that followed, attention turned with new intensity to the task of determining whether, as a matter of law, Canada's constitution might *already* protect inherent self-government rights: to whether, that is, such rights might qualify as "existing aboriginal rights" recognized and affirmed by section 35(1) of the *Constitution Act, 1982*.[5]

The notion that the constitution does indeed already protect the exercise, as Canadian law, of at least some inherent aboriginal rights of self-government has, of course, both proponents and opponents. Its

---

Notes will be found on pages 245–263.

proponents include the Royal Commission on Aboriginal Peoples ("RCAP"),[6] a substantial majority of the legal scholars, aboriginal and non-aboriginal, who have written about the issue,[7] and, most recently, the government of Canada, for which the inherent right's existence as a feature of mainstream law is now official policy.[8] The journals and RCAP's reports and studies are replete with legal and moral arguments that promote and facilitate judicial accreditation of such rights. Opposition to the notion (again, both aboriginal and non-aboriginal) has, for its part, appeared most often in the popular media, in considered critiques from outside the legal academy[9] and in the decisions of Canadian and commonwealth courts, which, so far, have rarely, if ever, upheld aboriginal peoples' claims to have free-standing, enforceable self-government rights.[10]

Several things about these patterns are interesting and surprising. It is, for one thing, unusual to see so much agreement among interested legal academics about an issue that is, by any standard, so controversial. It is rare, as well, to see both the federal government and a royal commission two of whose members were current or former judges accepting or asserting as law a position that courts, when asked in actual cases, have continued to resist. It is striking that the judicial and the academic opinion about the inherent right have diverged so conspicuously, and that these streams of opinion have seemed, on this issue, to give one another so little weight. And it is remarkable how little communication and interaction there seems to have been between those who support aboriginal peoples' inherent self-government rights and those who are apprehensive about them.

Small wonder, then, that everyone concerned with self-government issues anticipated so eagerly the Supreme Court's decision in *Delgamuukw*.[11] *Delgamuukw* was not, of course, the first case in which the court had occasion to shape the law on self-government; at least three earlier decisions had given preliminary, if indirect and uncoordinated, indications about the issue.[12] It was, however, the first Supreme Court case in which a claim to a constitutional right of self-government, anchored in traditional practice and forms of social organization and based on a thorough factual record, was at the heart of the business before the court. The two strong dissents supporting self-government in the B.C. Court of Appeal had only increased the sense of anticipation.[13] Few believed the Supreme Court could decide the *Delgamuukw* appeal without indicating clearly whether our constitution leaves room for aboriginal rights of self-government.

We all know what happened. The Supreme Court, having decided already to send the case back to trial, declined not only to determine the claim of self-government on its merits but even to offer substantive guidance for future litigation.[14] In one important sense, it decided nothing. And because the court *decided* nothing about the law on self-government, it is tempting and natural to suppose that it *told* us nothing of interest about that law.

Part of my purpose here is to dispute that supposition. My personal view is that the Supreme Court's decision *not* to decide the fate of self-government rights in *Delgamuukw* was the best possible contribution to the self-government conversation that it could have made in the circumstances, and that it told us some very important things about the orientation of self-government law. By deferring the issue as it did, and in the manner it did, the court, in my judgment, defined and shifted the ground on which the destiny of the inherent right, considered as a feature of existing Canadian law, is to be determined.

To begin with, I think the court made it clear that it is not eager to close the discussion, or the door, on inherent self-government rights. It would have been as easy as pie for the court to expunge such rights altogether from the universe of Canadian legal and constitutional discourse. All it had to do was express its agreement with the courts below that any self-government rights that the Gitksan and Wet'suwet'en may ever have had were extinguished, at the latest, when British Columbia joined Confederation in 1871.[15] After more than 10 years of litigation, that conclusion, well supported by existing authority,[16] would have been the line of least resistance. Instead, the Supreme Court elected, for the time being, to keep the ball in play. To me, that decision is highly significant. It means that the court is open to persuasion, in a proper case, that such rights survive and that they qualify for constitutional protection as existing aboriginal rights; it is prepared, in principle, to accept that inherent right claims may well have a credible basis in mainstream law. From now on, it will be more difficult for the inherent right's opponents to rely exclusively on blanket extinguishment arguments to dispatch such claims.

For someone of my persuasion, this is extremely good news. I am, for the record, someone whose Canada leaves room for constitutionally protected rights of aboriginal self-government. I believe, as well, that a responsible mainstream court could conclude today, on the basis of credible and attractive legal arguments, that many, if not all, traditional aboriginal collectivities have self-government rights entitled to protection under Canada's current constitution, even without the benefit of a constitutional amendment.[17] I find it encouraging, therefore, that the Supreme Court of Canada has indicated publicly its willingness to continue entertaining such arguments. So too, no doubt, do the lawyers, legal scholars, researchers and bureaucrats who have devoted themselves to the development of such arguments.

It would, however, be a mistake, in my view, for proponents of inherent self-government rights to assume that credible legal or even moral arguments will be enough, on their own, to convince the courts to take responsibility for including such rights within the constitution's protection. Attractive as I find the best such arguments on their legal merits, they are not, by any measure, so compelling, legally, that no responsible court could decide the question otherwise. Most judicial authority, as I have said, still opposes acknowledgement of existing self-government rights.[18] And there is, as some have already noted, a certain rhetorical awkwardness about arguing now, after five unsuccessful efforts in fifteen years to amend the constitution to provide for self-government rights, that such rights, in fact, have been there all along.[19]

In these circumstances, a worthy legal argument equipping courts to embrace inherent self-government rights is little more than an instrument available for their use; it almost certainly will not itself give them reason enough to embrace such rights, unless, on other grounds, they already find mainstream accreditation of the inherent right attractive and appropriate.

The Supreme Court's decision in *Delgamuukw* to defer the self-government issue is a signal that it is open, for now, to persuasion on this ground, as well. It is, however, also a sign—to me, an unmistakable one—that the court is going to *need* such persuasion: that it is deeply troubled by the magnitude, and the consequences, of the decision it is being asked to make about self-government rights. Consider, in this context, the following passage from the majority judgment:

> The broad nature of the claim at trial also led to a failure by the parties to address many of the difficult conceptual issues which surround the recognition of aboriginal self-government. The degree of complexity involved can be gleaned from the *Report of the Royal Commission on Aboriginal Peoples*, which devotes 277 pages to that issue. That report describes different models of self-government, each differing with respect to their conception of territory, citizenship, jurisdiction, internal government organization, etc. We received little in the way of submissions that would help us to grapple with these difficult and central issues. Without assistance from the parties, it would be imprudent for the Court to step into the breach.[20]

This observation came, remember, at the culmination of legal proceedings whose trial record included 318 days of evidence, 56 days of legal argument, roughly 35,000 pages of transcript evidence and over 50,000 pages of exhibit evidence.[21] It is difficult to imagine a clearer indication of the court's own sense that something pretty crucial has been missing from the discussion, or of its sense of unreadiness for the huge—and, once undertaken, inescapable—task of integrating such rights somehow into the mainstream constitutional order.

I must say I find the court's reticence here to be well founded. The fact is that we don't yet have a shared and trustworthy understanding, even in outline, of how self-government rights would work within our mainstream legal arrangements, or of the impact they would have on them. This being so, it is hardly surprising that there has been some public apprehension. In these circumstances, and in the absence of clearer intuitions about these basic legal practicalities, it is hardly grounds for complaint that the courts are wary of being the ones to accord such rights full institutional credibility. It is reasonable for them first to insist on substantive assistance with these issues.

For those of us whose project it is to open the constitution to inherent self-government rights, therefore, the most compelling current task is, almost certainly, to address constructively and candidly that legitimate sense of judicial unreadiness. The mainstream courts' receptiveness to the merits of the legal and moral arguments that could anchor such rights seems sure to depend, in significant part, on our success or failure in this endeavour.

Any realistic effort to carry out this task, however, must begin from an appreciation of the nature and the weight of the public apprehension that, for better or worse, already exists about inherent self-government rights. In practical terms, that apprehension represents and expresses the case that advocates of self-government rights have to meet. What makes this enterprise still more challenging is that it must proceed throughout in a way that continues to honour the integrity of the collective aboriginal experience that inherent self-government rights exist, if they make any difference at all, to preserve and to promote.

I want in the rest of this article to explore what such an enterprise entails. The first step is to grasp more concretely why inherent rights of self-government matter, and why they give pause.

Why the Inherent Right Matters

For aboriginal communities, their members and supporters, acknowledgement that they have enforceable rights to govern themselves—to resume responsibility for their own collective destinies[22]—may well now be the minimum price that the mainstream legal system must pay to earn from them a modicum of respect.[23] For centuries now, such communities have done everything humanly possible to maintain the integrity and vitality of their own traditions, languages, ceremonies and other authoritative internal arrangements, and to continue fulfilling their ancestral obligations to one another and to the rest of creation,[24] despite catastrophic changes to their physical and economic circumstances, inexorable pressures from non-aboriginal settlement and often concerted efforts by settler peoples to undermine and marginalize their most sensitive and deeply grounded relationships.[25] To qualify as a meaningful departure from this history of interference and exploitation, mainstream acknowledgement of such rights must begin from a respect for both the fact and the legitimacy of aboriginal difference:[26] must dedicate sufficient "constitutional space for aboriginal peoples to be aboriginal," to borrow Donna Greschner's wonderful phrase.[27] This entails respecting and protecting communities' power, and indeed duty, to defend such individuals, lands and resources as may remain to them against mainstream "laws and policies which are demonstrably threatening to their culture," [28] and generally to address their own needs and imperatives in ways that they themselves consider effective and appropriate, even when those aims and ways differ substantially from what we in the mainstream culture might have done or preferred.[29] This, in turn, necessarily involves "the significant letting go of Canadian government power over the lives of Aboriginal citizens" [30] and accepting that self-governing aboriginal communities are bound sometimes to make mistakes (even by their own reckoning) that it cannot be our business, uninvited, to correct.

Respect for the integrity of aboriginal difference is, therefore, the first imperative that defines inherent right advocacy. It requires that we oppose all unnecessary restrictions on fundamental aboriginal values and on the governance arrangements integral to the enduring aboriginal legal traditions. Below this threshold, any mainstream arrangement to preserve or acknowledge self-government rights ceases to offer them meaningful legal protection, and forfeits its authenticity.

Public Apprehensions about Self-Government

What the Apprehensions Are

For those in the non-indigenous mainstream, on the other hand, the prospect of giving enforceable legal effect to inherent self-government rights may be troubling for any of several complex and layered reasons. For some, especially those in positions of real power or legal authority, judicial confirmation now of inherent self-government rights would most probably register, apart from everything else, as a strong rebuke: a rebuke to decades, perhaps centuries, of careful, considered practice informed by accepted conceptions of permissible conduct and of the public interest. For if aboriginal peoples today possess inherent self-government rights, it follows necessarily that they have always had such rights, at common law, in Anglo-Canadian jurisprudence,[31] and that a very great deal that has happened to aboriginal peoples and communities since the Crown asserted sovereignty in North America has been, by domestic Canadian standards, in breach of those rights. To be judged and found wanting, according to enforceable standards one has no choice but to accept, for having failed to respect legal rights that one's predecessors considered too insubstantial to bother extinguishing is, undoubtedly, not a welcome experience.

Other widely shared apprehensions, which reinforce but do not depend upon such discomfiture,[32] concern the practical consequences of constitutional protection for self-government rights. Most such apprehensions fit within at least one of three general kinds.

Concerns about Capacity and Readiness
Transitions from colonial to indigenous forms of governance require patience and particular care, some commentators suggest, especially given the impatience and the unrealistically high expectations that such transitions often prompt in community members themselves. Even at the best of times, there are real risks of failure and frustration: outcomes that can undermine communities' social vitality and the legitimacy, in the eyes of their members, of their self-government efforts.[33] These risks seem to some to be acute in many of Canada's aboriginal communities, for two reasons: because of the truly staggering scale of deprivation, despair, abuse and dysfunction that one too often finds in such communities, problems of a kind and scale beyond the contemplation of the collective coping mechanisms traditional to aboriginal societies;[34] and because of the fear (of some) that many such communities have too few members with sufficient leadership skills, technical expertise or practical experience to meet the collective's needs in these highly complex and difficult circumstances.[35] Indications that leaders in some aboriginal communities have not used effectively even the very limited powers now available to them makes many outsiders, especially, still more cautious about the prospect of their having more power.[36]

Concerns about Vulnerable Individuals
According to several commentators, individuals living in aboriginal communities[37] are especially vulnerable to the power of their aboriginal governments: not so much because those governments happen to be aboriginal, but because such communities share a number of features each of which they say contributes independently to the risk of excessive centralization of official power. In the first place, transitions from colonial to local rule are, on this view, themselves occasions and incentives for

those in power at the time to consolidate their authority by trading on their prestige.[38] Second, when communities have no tradition of selecting their leaders regularly and democratically,[39] and their governments obtain the vast majority of their wealth through fiscal transfers from sources outside the community,[40] those governments have much less incentive to account to community members for their conduct or to make a point of addressing community members' needs or concerns, because they are effectively insulated from the consequences of residents' disapproval. Finally, individual rights and freedoms, generally speaking, are, in the view of these commentators, more vulnerable in small, homogeneous communities, because such arrangements encourage highly personal styles of community management and discourage both the diversity of overlapping minorities that tend to foster respect for such rights, and the articulation of separate roles and powers within government that tend to be required to protect them.[41]

Published reports of favoritism,[42] personal harassment,[43] misuses of funds,[44] unaccountable leadership[45] and other alleged abuses of political authority by chiefs or other band officials in some communities[46] only lend credibility to these apprehensions.[47] The Royal Commission on Aboriginal Peoples, for example, received more than 200 submissions expressing concerns about ethics and conflicts of interest in aboriginal governments.[48] Such reports and experiences, it seems safe to suppose, contributed significantly to the reluctance of aboriginal voters to support the explicit constitutional entrenchment of their inherent self-government rights pursuant to the Charlottetown Accord.

No issue better illustrates this kind of apprehension, among both aboriginal and non-aboriginal people, than the concern about the fate of aboriginal women if today's band governments were constitutionally empowered. Although it seems widely accepted that neither sexual nor domestic abuse, nor any of the other usual incidents of patriarchy or sexism, was characteristic of North American native societies before they began to have regular contact with the Europeans,[49] it seems equally clear, at least to several commentators, that substantial numbers of aboriginal men today, including many in positions of community leadership, have engaged in such practices and acted upon such attitudes to the disadvantage of the women in their communities.[50] During negotiations that led to the Charlottetown Accord, for example, it became clear that many aboriginal women simply did not believe that male aboriginal leaders, armed with constitutionally protected rights of self-government, could be trusted, left to their own devices, to respond fairly and respectfully to the women's interests or to give sufficient priority to their need for protection from abuse.[51] The Native Women's Association of Canada ("NWAC") has insisted that mainstream human rights standards, and mainstream courts, remain available for the protection of aboriginal women in communities acting pursuant to rights of self-government.[52] It considered these protections so crucial to the safety and well-being of Canada's aboriginal women, and so different from the positions being taken by the four aboriginal organizations participating officially in the Charlottetown negotiations, that it brought legal proceedings seeking independent representation at those negotiations.[53]

Concerns about Mainstream Society and Its Institutions

To some commentators, apprehensions such as these matter not just for their own sake as signs of an altruistic regard for disadvantaged peoples, but also because the aboriginal peoples of Canada are entitled, as Canadian citizens, to the ongoing assurance that the law will protect their rights as individuals no less fully than it protects the rights of the other citizens of Canada.[54] To them, it would be awkward, at best, for Canada's federal and provincial governments, each of which is subject to enforceable obligations to respect and protect the constitutional rights of individuals, to have to provide ongoing financial support to aboriginal governments that recognized, and were subject to, no such constraints.[55]

These and other commentators, including the Royal Commission on the Economic Union,[56] have expressed public worry about what could happen to the institutions and arrangements on which Canadians and their governments now routinely depend if Canada were suddenly to accredit as many as 600 truly self-governing aboriginal communities,[57] especially given the breadth and strength of the powers and the immunities that such communities are sometimes said to expect.[58] For some critics, the mere existence of so many additional governments, each with its own internal structures, conventions and priorities, poses serious risks of fragmentation in a country whose national institutions already sometimes seem dangerously weak,[59] and whose need for economic integration can only continue to grow.[60] Others have emphasized the risks that such potentially different approaches and outlooks pose to the country's defining and fundamental values.[61] Still others doubt the possibility of creating workable intergovernmental arrangements that could possibly accommodate so many distinct aboriginal polities that are at once so small and so poorly resourced, and insist that self-government cannot work unless there is significant consolidation of aboriginal communities into larger governance units that have the power to bind all their members.[62]

Why the Apprehensions Matter

For these—and occasionally as well for other, less credible[63]—reasons, many non-native individuals and institutions, and some aboriginal people themselves, continue in some measure to fear, and even some-times to oppose, the notion of aboriginal governments having consti-tutional protection.[64] According to published reports, the Chretien government, having recognized the potential for public opposition to this notion, gave serious thought in 1995 to backing away from its ear-lier promise to treat the inherent right of self-government as an exist-ing aboriginal right.[65]

Considered as reasons to withhold the constitution's protection from inherent self-government rights,[66] these various apprehensions are open to criticism on several grounds. Members of surviving aborig-inal communities, whose cultures and institutional arrangements have already endured much worse, and whose ancestors were not given the option of weighing the merits and implications of settler peoples' self-government claims, will be forgiven for finding many of them ironic, if not precious, and for observing how little faith those who express them seem to have in the staying power of the mainstream system.[67] No less ironic, or unfair, from their standpoint is the inference that aboriginal peoples are now disqualified from governing themselves precisely be-cause of all the disruption and deprivation suffered in their communi-ties at the hands of the settler peoples.[68] Others are bound to find convenient, if not colourable, some non-native critics' sudden expres-sions of tender concern for the welfare of native women and other vul-nerable individuals engaged with aboriginal communities.[69] Still others, who have documented our courts' propensity, when adjudicat-ing the claims of aboriginal peoples, to rely on unacknowledged and unacceptable assumptions about the superiority of mainstream tradi-tions and arrangements, are apt to conclude, with some justification, that most of the apprehensions being expressed by self-government's critics are further examples of this pattern, and of such assumptions.[70] Still others, asked to imagine settler society's powerlessness to deal with rogue inherent right communities, may insist on recalling the "very large club" that mainstream governments will continue to hold over aboriginal peoples dependent on their fiscal transfers.[71]

Personally, I share these reservations about the critique of self-gov-ernment rights. For these and similar reasons, I do not believe it justi-fies rejection or abandonment of the project of earning such rights mainstream judicial acceptance. I do believe firmly, however, that one cannot pursue that project responsibly without acknowledging the cur-rency and appeal of that critique and without engaging it on its merits. This is so, in my view, for at least three reasons.

First, whatever else one may say about the critique or about its proponents, it does identify some real problems that need attention, like it or not, if effective self-government arrangements are to endure and flourish, even under the special protection of the constitution.[72] Practically speaking, it is going to take patience, care, and special effort to situate such arrangements, and such rights, in relation to the rest of the mainstream order. Underestimating the difficulty of these challenges will not make them easier to address.

Second, whatever the law may say, the success or failure, in Canada, of self-government initiatives is going to depend, indefinitely, on how much support and co-operation they receive from non-aboriginal Canadians.[73] Mainstream Canadians, generally speaking, are likely to be less supportive of the self-government rights and arrangements of aboriginal peoples if they are apprehensive about the impact such arrangements may have on the individuals living in self-governing communities,[74] on themselves, or on Canadian society generally. Hostility or resistance from the non-native public may very well make prohibitively time-consuming, expensive and difficult the already daunting tasks of restoring, realizing and protecting indigenous forms of government for contemporary use.[75]

Finally—and most important, for here we come full-circle—the very existence of this critique, and of the concerns it expresses, cannot help but affect the perceptions and the intuitions of the courts that, sooner or later, will have to determine the destiny, within our law, of inherent self-government rights. It seems to me all but inconceivable that Canadian courts will treat such rights as constitutional rights unless they are confident that the existing law equips them to address, in practical ways and case by case, the kinds of concerns that self-government's critics have identified. It is extremely important to appreciate why this is so.

As I suggested earlier, the task of integrating into our mainstream legal order inherent rights of self-government, and with them the substantially different cultural orientations that such rights presuppose and exist to protect, would be a major conceptual challenge for our courts in the best of circumstances, precisely because it would propel them against the current, and into uncharted waters.[76] I am among those who believe that it is just and appropriate—and, from a legal standpoint, more than defensible—for courts, despite these disincentives, to make this task their own. Even so, one is bound to acknowledge the effort, and the professional courage, it will require of them to do so, especially in the absence of explicit constitutional text that compels, or even encourages, them to embrace it. If self-government's proponents are going to expect Canadian judges to undertake so pervasive a project, they are going to have to establish, at a minimum, not only that it deserves their support and interest, but that they can recognize and engage in it, as judges, in full conscience.[77] In the current vernacular, that means demonstrating that rights of self-government can be "reconciled with the sovereignty of the Crown." [78]

It is this additional task that the public apprehensions about self-government complicate. Many of them, taken full strength, suggest that self-government rights and powers, unchecked, could pose significant risks to values, institutions and arrangements considered fundamental to, and constitutive of, the Canadian legal and constitutional order. The character of those apprehensions, the basis they often appear to have in observable fact and the hold they seem, from the coverage, to have on the public imagination make them especially difficult for mainstream courts to ignore.[79] Our courts would almost certainly consider it irresponsible to recognize and enforce such rights within Canadian law without first satisfying themselves that our legal system, as a whole, can absorb and manage such risks.

The paramount concern is that section 35(1) of the *Constitution Act, 1982*, if it protected inherent rights of self-government at all, would protect them so well as to deprive the mainstream orders and branches of Canadian government of the effective capacity to prevent or contain such potential risks to the mainstream constitutional order.

It was Ian Binnie who first articulated this concern (several years before his own appointment to the bench), almost immediately after the Supreme Court of Canada first prescribed, in *Sparrow*,[80] the kind and degree of protection that section 35(1) was to give aboriginal rights:

> ... the *Sparrow* doctrine makes it improbable that the judicial concept of Aboriginal rights will extend to such key objectives as Aboriginal self government. The application of the Supreme Court's interpretations of section 35 in *Sparrow* would afford too much immunity from other levels of government to Aboriginal communities, many of which lie cheek by jowl with non-Aboriginal communities in densely populated areas of southern Canada. "Constitutionalizing" a right to Aboriginal self-government would, in light of *Sparrow*, leave the courts with inadequate mechanisms to regulate the overlapping interests of communities occupying contiguous territory.[81]

If one accepts Binnie's premises, it seems almost impossible to quarrel with his conclusion. In the absence of clear constitutional text instructing them to do so, Canadian judges are most unlikely to take responsibility for extending *Sparrow*'s protection to rights of self-government if they are frightened, as judges, by the consequences of doing so, no matter how many scholars and royal commissions tell them—correctly, in my view—that it would be the right thing for them to do. And accrediting constitutional rights that pose uncontainable threats to basic mainstream institutions or fundamental mainstream values would certainly frighten them.[82]

How to Address Them

If all this is so, then the second imperative shaping inherent right advocacy must surely be to show that, and how, it is possible to integrate such rights harmoniously into the larger legal framework for which the mainstream courts are responsible. Success at this undertaking depends on perseverance in two related tasks: reducing to a minimum the *avoidable* tensions and apprehensions that now attend the notion of aboriginal self-government, and demonstrating, in response to the challenge Binnie posed years ago, that Canada's legal system already provides sufficient means to ensure that self-government rights could not be exercised, even with the constitution's protection, in ways or for purposes that would do violence to the principles and arrangements on which our legal order depends. I want to consider each of these tasks briefly, and in turn.

Minimizing Avoidable Apprehensions

Meeting the first of these expectations means increasing mainstream public confidence in the enterprise of aboriginal self-government by improving the public understanding of what self-government is, why it matters, and how it is intended that it will operate.[83] Efforts to do so might usefully call greater attention to the complementarity that already exists, especially at the higher levels of generality, between aboriginal peoples' various defining traditions and values and those of the mainstream culture,[84] and to the extent to which aboriginal practice and precedent has already informed and improved the development of mainstream political institutions in North America.[85] Success at this part of the larger task, however, will be difficult, it seems to me, unless there is real progress, soon, at two others.

The first is for aboriginal peoples themselves, especially, to begin addressing the reasons for the apparent loss, within significant numbers of aboriginal communities, of trust and confidence in those communities' leadership and governance arrangements.[86] It is, to begin with, essential that mainstream Canadians not be further tempted to regard aboriginal peoples' legal traditions and governance forms as anthropological ephemera: as talismans suitable only for the purposes of nostalgia. We (in the mainstream) need instead to be encouraged in every way to perceive and experience, even if only from a distance, the living presence of those laws and arrangements and their power, even today, to organize, shape and constrain the activity that takes place within aboriginal collectivities.[87] It is, from this standpoint, vital that the members of communities seeking mainstream affirmation of their self-government rights communicate, by practice and example, their own ongoing conviction in the resonance and the authority of those forms and traditions.[88] It is equally important to seek to dispel mainstream perceptions (and predisposition to believe) that power in aboriginal communities is being used arbitrarily and irresponsibly. As long as those who live in such communities are widely perceived to be suffering under unresponsive and sometimes untrustworthy leadership, and as long as aboriginal women are perceived to face aggravated risks of abuse and marginalization in their own communities, Canada's non-native governments are going to be reluctant to relax the supervisory powers they now exert over such communities, and mainstream courts, in all likelihood, reluctant to be the ones to set aside protected constitutional space for community laws and governance. This is so regardless of where responsibility ultimately lies for the deterioration of conditions in those communities.[89]

The other is for those who would find self-government rights in the constitution to start being much more specific about the parameters—legal, political and operational—of the rights being claimed. The greater the public uncertainty about what such rights might possibly mean, about the size and composition of the self-governing aboriginal collectivities and about the interface between such units and existing mainstream governments, the less eager the courts are going to be—as *Delgamuukw* itself illustrates—to assume the responsibility for locating such rights within the existing constitution.[90] Fortunately, the self-government options proposed for consideration in the RCAP Final Report,[91] the recent developments in the Canadian law of aboriginal rights,[92] and the federal government's recent willingness to proceed on the basis that the inherent right is already in the constitution[93] should make it much easier than it would have been even five years ago to begin thinking more concretely about self-government issues.

Protecting Fundamental Mainstream Values
Progress toward minimizing the avoidable apprehensions about the potential impact of aboriginal rights of self-government will encourage, and free, the courts to be more receptive to the legal arguments already available in support of such rights. Even complete success at that task, however, seems most unlikely to eliminate altogether the kinds of risks to which Binnie alluded: the risk that the exercise of such rights would threaten values and institutions fundamental to the Canadian constitutional order and that section 35(1) of the *Constitution Act, 1982* would protect such rights so well that mainstream courts and governments

could not contain such threats as they arose.[94] This second challenge, therefore, deserves and requires independent attention.

A full and proper answer to it is, of course, far beyond the scope of this article. It is my view, however, that our courts already have all the power they need to constrain, as necessary, the exercise of existing aboriginal rights of self-government in the interest of preserving truly fundamental Canadian values and institutions.[95] This is so, in brief, because our courts, in giving effect to *any* rights enforceable within mainstream law, have both the power and the duty to define the scope of such rights in a way that ensures their ongoing harmony with the arrangements and values essential to the legal system on which the protection of those rights depends.[96] Properly understood, the task of protecting our legal system's integrity—what the court in *Mabo* called its "skeleton of principle"[97]—from the harms that could result from misuse of self-government rights requires not a one-time-only assessment, winner take all, of the havoc such rights could conceivably cause but continuing alertness to the need for systemic harmony in the ongoing work of articulating, case by case, what such rights mean (and protect) and what they do not.

The more serious danger may be that the courts will find it too easy, and too tempting, to constrict the protected scope of self-government rights in the course of applying them. The purpose of the harmonization exercise is not to find ways of domesticating, to the point of impotence or uniformity, what are, after all, supposed to be *inherent* rights. The virtue of including self-government rights within the constitution's protection—at least for those of us who believe that doing so *has* some virtue—just is, again, to secure constitutional space within which aboriginal difference, its sources and foundations, are authoritative, not just inconveniences in need of ongoing management, and within which respect for aboriginal difference is enforceable. Constraining more than necessary authoritative expressions or examples of aboriginal difference would, I suggested earlier, compromise the integrity of any undertaking from the courts, and from our constitutional order, to protect self-government rights.[98] Where fundamental values or institutions are not at risk, therefore, it will be extremely important that courts approach such rights with restraint and respect, in order to maximize the protected space available to inherent right communities for self-direction and -realization.

Conclusion

The Supreme Court's recent predilection, in cases about aboriginal rights, has been to deliver broad, sometimes exploratory judgments that organize the law for application in lower courts, sometimes even when the case before them has not required that they do so. *Delgamu-ukw* itself is one recent example, as regards aboriginal title. Despite that predilection, however, the court took pains in *Delgamuukw*, as it had once before in *Pamajewon*, to avoid deciding the fate of claims to inherent self-government rights. By doing so, in the way it did so, it signalled both its openness to further legal argument designed to establish a place for such rights within mainstream legal doctrine and its profound discomfort with the uncertainty and the apprehension that could result from acceptance of such rights as constitutional rights.

Taken together, these indications amount to an invitation to proponents of self-government rights to demonstrate that, and how, such rights might integrate into the larger legal and constitutional framework for which the courts themselves are responsible. It will be a prudent invitation for us to accept, before the next self-government case appears before the courts. For if it is forced to decide the issue without being shown a cogent way of addressing the risks that self-government rights, at their worst, could pose to aboriginal peoples and to the rest of society, the Supreme Court will, I am almost certain, close the door on such rights. It will not expose the rest of the legal order to risks that it does not believe it can contain.

Successful mainstream advocacy for inherent self-government rights, therefore, is going to take more than defensible legal (or even moral) arguments supportive of the existence of such rights. It will also require concerted ongoing efforts to satisfy two other, sometimes contrary, imperatives: on the one hand, demonstration that our courts will continue to be able, even after giving constitutional effect to such rights, to protect the coherence and the integrity of the mainstream order and the arrangements and values that define it, and, on the other, vigilant and ongoing opposition to all unnecessary restrictions on the scope and exercise of such rights. Achieving that aim means finding and maintaining equipoise between these imperatives: a hard and delicate task, to be sure, but one that is, in my view, both essential and achievable.

Acknowledgments

This is a revised and expanded version of chapter one of my LL.M. thesis, *Unchartered Territory: Fundamental Canadian Values and the Inherent Right of Aboriginal Self-Government* (University of Toronto, 1998). Special thanks to Patrick Macklem, Kent McNeil, David Beatty, Eileen Hipfner, Greg Levine, Jonathan Rudin, Lorne Sossin and Deborah Wilkins for their encouragement and for comments that materially improved the text. Any missteps that remain are despite their best efforts, not because of them.

Notes

1 See Canada, *Consensus Report on the Constitution: Charlottetown* (Final Text, 28 August 1992) (Ottawa: Minister of Supply and Services, 1992) ("Charlottetown Accord") and *Draft Legal Text* (9 October 1992).

2 In 1983, a special committee of the House of Commons had recommended federal legislative recognition, and constitutional entrenchment, of a form of aboriginal self-government: see Canada, H.C., Special Committee on Indian Self-government, *Indian Self-Government in Canada* (Ottawa: Minister of Supply and Services, 20 October 1983) esp. at 43-46. Sections 37-37.1 of the *Constitution Act, 1982*, being Schedule B to the Canada Act 1982 (U.K.), 1982, c. 11 ("*Constitution Act, 1982*"), repealed in 1983 and 1987, respectively, by ss. 54 and 54.1, had made provision for four constitutional conferences to be devoted specifically to aboriginal issues. Self-government dominated agendas at those conferences. For commentary on them, see, e.g., Brian Schwartz, *First Principles, Second Thoughts: Aboriginal Peoples, Constitutional Reform and Canadian Statecraft* (Montreal: Institute for Research and Public Policy, 1986) ("Schwartz, Second Thoughts"); Douglas Sanders, "The Constitution, the Provinces, and Aboriginal Peoples" in J. Anthony Long & Menno Boldt, eds., *Governments in Conflict? Provinces and Indian Nations in Canada* (Toronto: University of Toronto Press, 1988) 151 at 165-169; Kathy L. Brock, "The Politics of Aboriginal Self-Government: A Canadian Paradox" (1991) 34 Can. Pub. Admin. 272.

3 See, e.g., Jeffrey Simpson, "The Grand Talk of Constitutional Reform for Aboriginals Is a Mirage" *[Toronto] Globe & Mail* (15 August 1995) A16.

4 See, e.g., Assembly of First Nations, First Nations Circle on the Constitution, *To the Source* (1992) ("*To the Source*") at 13-23; Canada, *Report of the Royal Commission on Aboriginal Peoples*, vol. 2 (Ottawa: Minister of Supply and Services, 1996) ("2 RCAP Final Report") esp. at 139.

5 See, e.g., Kent McNeil, "Envisaging Constitutional Space for Aboriginal Governments" (1994) 19 Queen's L.J. 95 ("McNeil, 'Constitutional Space'").

6 See 2 RCAP Final Report, note 4 above, at 166-169, 186-213. The Royal Commission had announced its support for the inherent right in at least two earlier reports: *Bridging the Cultural Divide: A Report on Aboriginal People and Criminal Justice in Canada* (Ottawa: Minister of Supply and Services, 1996) ("RCAP, *Bridging*") esp. at 219-224, and *Partners in Confederation: Aboriginal Peoples, Self-Government and the Constitution* (Ottawa, Minister of Supply and Services, 1993) ("RCAP, *Partners*") at 29-45.

7 See, e.g., Shaun Nakatsuru, "A Constitutional Right of Indian Self-Government" (1985) 43 U. T. Fac. L. Rev. 72; Darlene M. Johnston, "The Quest of the Six Nations Confederacy for Self-Determination" (1986) 44 U.T. Fac.L.Rev. 1; Bruce Clark, *Native Liberty, Crown Sovereignty: The Existing Aboriginal Right of Self-Government in Canada* (Montreal: McGill-Queen's University Press, 1990); Michael Asch & Patrick Macklem, "Aboriginal Rights and Canadian Sovereignty: An Essay on *R. v. Sparrow*" (1991) 29 Alta L. Rev. 498; Patrick Macklem, "First Nations Self-Government and the Borders of the Canadian Legal Imagination" (1991) 36 McGill L.J. 382 ("Macklem, 'Borders'"); Patrick Macklem, "Ethnonationalism, Aboriginal Identities, and the Law" in Michael D. Levin, ed., *Ethnicity and Aboriginality: Case Studies in Ethnonationalism* (Toronto: University of Toronto Press, 1993) 9 ("Macklem, 'Ethnonationalism'"); Patrick Macklem, "Distributing Sovereignty: Indian Nations and Equality of Peoples" (1993) 45 Stanford L. Rev. 1311 ("Macklem, 'Distributing Sovereignty'"); Patrick Macklem, "Normative Dimensions of an Aboriginal Right of Self-Government" (1995) 21 Queen's L.J. 173; Bruce Ryder, "The Demise and Rise of the Classical Paradigm in Canadian Federalism: Promoting Autonomy for the Provinces and First Nations" (1991) 36 McGill L.J. 308; Brian Slattery, "Aboriginal Sovereignty and Imperial Claims" (1991) 29 Osgoode Hall L.J. 101; Brian Slattery, "First Nations and the Constitution: A Question of Trust" (1992) 71 Can. Bar Rev. 261 ("Slattery, 'Question of Trust'"); Brian Slattery, "The Organic Constitution: Aboriginal Peoples and the Evolution of Canada" (1995) 34 Osgoode Hall L.J. 101; Hamar Foster, "Forgotten Arguments: Aboriginal Title and Sovereignty in *Canada Jurisdiction Act* Cases" (1992) 21 Man. L.J. 343; Donna Greschner, "Aboriginal Women, the Constitution and Criminal Justice" [1992] U.B.C. L. Rev. (Sp. Ed.) 338; Alan Pratt, "Aboriginal Self-Government and the Crown's Fiduciary Duty: Squaring the Circle or Completing the Circle?" (1992) 2 N.J.C.L. 163; Mark Walters, "British Imperial Constitutional Law and Aboriginal Rights: A Comment on *Delgamuukw v. British Columbia*" (1992) 17 Queen's L.J. 350 ("Walters, 'Comment on *Delgamuukw*'"); Mark D. Walters, "*Mohegan Indians v. Connecticut* (1705-1773) and the Legal Status of Aboriginal Customary Laws and Government in British North America" (1995) 33 Osgoode Hall L.J. 785 ("Walters, '*Mohegan Indians*'"); Mark D.Walters, "The 'Golden Thread' of Continuity: Aboriginal Customs at Common Law and Under the Constitution Act, 1982" (1999) 44 McGill L.J. 711; John Borrows, "Constitutional Law from a First Nations Perspective: Self-Government and the Royal Proclamation" (1994) 28 U.B.C. L. Rev. 1; McNeil, "Constitutional Space," note 5 above; Kent McNeil, "Aboriginal Rights in Canada: From Title to Land to Territorial Sover-

eigny" (1998) 5 Tulsa J. Comp. & Int'l. L. 253 ("McNeil, 'Aboriginal Rights' "); Delia Opekokew, "The Inherent Right of Self-Government As an Aboriginal and Treaty Right" in *The Inherent Right of Aboriginal Self-Government*, papers presented to Canadian Bar Association, Continuing Legal Education Program, Annual Meeting, 1994 ("CBA, *The Inherent Right*"), vol. 2; Mei Lin Ng, *Convenient Illusions: A Consideration of Sovereignty and the Aboriginal Right of Self-Government* (LL.M., Osgoode Hall Law School, York University, 1994) [unpublished]; Peter W. Hutchins, Carol Hilling & David Schulze, "The Aboriginal Right to Self-Government and the Canadian Constitution: The Ghost in the Machine" (1995) 29 U.B.C. L. Rev. 251 (" 'Ghost in the Machine' "); Peter W. Hogg, *Constitutional Law of Canada*, 4th ed., abridged (Toronto: Carswell, 1997) at 573, 589.

For commentaries that express doubt—some regretfully, some not—about the sufficiency of the legal basis in the existing constitution for meaningful rights of aboriginal self-government, see Schwartz, *Second Thoughts*, note 2 above, at 385-390; W.I.C. Binnie, "The Sparrow Doctrine: Beginning of the End or End of the Beginning?" (1990) 15 Queen's L.J. 217; Harry S. LaForme, "Indian Sovereignty: What Does It Mean?" (1991) 11 Can. J. Native Studies 253; Sylvain Lussier, "Réflexions sur 'Partenaires au Sein de la Confédération' et le Droit 'Inherent' à l'Autonomie Gouvernementale" in CBA, *The Inherent Right*, vol. 1; Kenneth J. Tyler, "Another Opinion: A Critique of the Paper Presented by the Royal Commission on Aboriginal Peoples Entitled: *Partners in Confederation*" in CBA, The Inherent Right, vol. 1; Bob Freedman, "The Space for Aboriginal Self-Government in British Columbia: The Effect of the Decision of the British Columbia Court of Appeal in *Delgamuukw v. British Columbia*" (1994) 28 U.B.C. L.Rev. 49; Bradford W. Morse, "Permafrost Rights: Aboriginal Self-Government and the Supreme Court in *R. v. Pamajewon*" (1997) 42 McGill L.J. 1011 ("Morse, 'Permafrost Rights' "). See also, in the popular press, William Johnson, "Modern Myths: Elements of Self-government Haven't Been Perpetuated" *The [Montreal] Gazette* (7 July 1992) B3.

8 See Canada, Department of Indian Affairs and Northern Development, *Federal Policy Guide: Aboriginal Self-government: The Government of Canada's Approach to Implementation of the Inherent Right and the Negotiation of Aboriginal Self-government* (Ottawa: Minister of Public Works and Government Services Canada, 1995) ("*Federal Policy Guide*") esp. at 3-4.

Between 1990 and 1995, Ontario government policy also recognized that First Nations have inherent rights of self-government "under the Constitution of Canada." See Bob Rae, "The Road to Self-determination," in Frank Cassidy, ed., *Aboriginal Self-Determination* (Lantzville, B.C.: Oolichan Books, 1991) ("*Aboriginal Self-Determination*") 150 at 152, and *Statement of Political Relationship* between Ontario and the First Nations in Ontario, 6 September 1991.

9 See notes 32-65 below and the text accompanying them. According to a 1995 Insight Canada research survey commissioned by the federal Department of Indian Affairs, 53% of Canadians believed that aboriginal peoples weren't ready to assume self-government powers, and only 46% believed

that aboriginal peoples should be given more autonomy. By comparison, about 70% of Canadians polled in 1993 had supported ratifying the Charlottetown proposals that would have entrenched the inherent self-government rights. See Jack Aubry, "Canadians Wary of Native Autonomy" *Calgary Herald* (1 June 1995) A7.

By no means all the newspaper coverage of self-government issues has been negative. For examples of generally supportive reports or analyses in the public media, see Ruth Teichroeb, "Democracy on the Reserve: Reserve Proves Model of Democracy" *Winnipeg Free Press* (10 April 1992) B21 ("Teichroeb, 'Model of Democracy'"); Peter Ferris, "Native Self-government: Change That Can Help Everyone" *Winnipeg Free Press* (31 May 1992) A7; Robert Sheppard, "Maybe It's Racist, But It's a Good Thing" *[Toronto] Globe & Mail* (2 June 1992) A17; Stephen Hume, "Time to Pop the Self-government Bogeyman Bubble" *Vancouver Sun* (7 October 1992) A15; "Self-government and the Charter" [editorial] *[Toronto] Globe & Mail* (15 October 1992) A30; Ruth Teichroeb, "Native Self-rule: Is It a Dead End? Victims Are Trying to Reclaim Control" *Winnipeg Free Press* (14 July 1996) B2 ("Teichroeb, 'Victims Are Trying'").

10 For Canadian and commonwealth cases rejecting assertions of free-standing rights or powers of aboriginal governance, see, e.g., *Doe d. Sheldon v. Ramsay* (1852), 9 U.C.Q.B. 105, Burns J.; *R. v. Beboning* (1908), 17 O.L.R. 23 (C.A.); *Sero v. Gault* (1921), 50 O.L.R. 27 (S.C.); *Logan v. Styres* (1959), 20 D.L.R. (2d) 416 (Ont. H.C.); *Isaac v. Davey* (1974), 5 O.R. (2d) 610 (C.A.), aff'd. on other grounds (*sub nom. Davey v. Isaac*), [1977] 2 S.C.R. 897; *Coe v. Commonwealth of Australia* (No. 1) (1979), 24 A.L.R. 118 (H.C.A.); *Re Stacey and Montour and The Queen* (1981), 63 C.C.C. (2d) 61 (Que. C.A.); *A.G. Ontario v. Bear Island Foundation* (1984), 15 D.L.R. (4th) 321 (Ont. H.C.J.) at 407, aff'd. on other grounds (1989), 58 D.L.R. (4th) 117 (Ont. C.A.), aff'd. without reference to the point [1991] 2 S.C.R. 570; *Delgamuukw v. The Queen in right of B.C.* (1991), 79 D.L.R. (4th) 185 (B.C.S.C.) ("*Delgamuukw (S.C.)*"), aff'd. on this point [1993] 5 W.W.R. 97 (B.C.C.A.) ("*Delgamuukw (C.A.)*"), rev'd. on other grounds [1997] 3 S.C.R. 1010 ("*Delgamuukw*"); *Coe v. Commonwealth of Australia (No. 2)* (1993), 118 A.L.R. 193 (H.C.A.); *Walker v. New South Wales* (1994), 182 C.L.R. 45 (H.C.A.); *R. v. Pamajewon*, [1993] 3 C.N.L.R. 209 (Ont. (Prov. D.)), aff'd. on other grounds (1994), 95 C.C.C. (3d) 97 (Ont. C.A.) ("*Pamajewon (C.A.)*"), aff'd. [1996] 2 S.C.R. 821 ("*Pamajewon*"); *R. v. Williams*, [1995] 2 C.N.L.R. 229 (B.C.C.A.). For Canadian and commonwealth judgments that suggest at least some basis for argument in support of existing aboriginal rights of self-government, see *Connolly v. Woolrich* (1867), 17 R.J.R.Q. 75 (S.C.) at 83-84, 138, 1 C.N.L.C. 70 at 78-79, 132, aff'd. *sub. nom. Johnstone v. Connolly* (1869), 17 R.J.R.Q. 266, 1 C.N.L.C. 151 (Q.B.); *Arani v. Public Trustee of New Zealand*, [1920] A.C. 198 (P.C.); *Delgamuukw (C.A.)*, Lambert J.A. (dissenting in part), Hutcheon J.A. (dissenting in part); *Casimel v. Insurance Corp. of British Columbia* (1993), 82 B.C.L.R. (2d) 387 (C.A.); *R. v. Bear Claw Casino Ltd.*, [1994] 4 C.N.L.R. 81 (Sask. Prov. Ct.), and *Mushkegowuk Council v. The Queen in right of Ontario* (1999), 178 D.L.R. (4th) 283 (Ont. S.C.J.), set aside

without reference to the point (2000), 184 D.L.R. (4th) 532 (Ont. C.A.). *Pamajewon* (C.A.), *ibid.*, gives both sides some comfort.

For Supreme Court of Canada consideration of aboriginal self-government, see note 12 below.

11 *Ibid.*

12 In *Sparrow v. The Queen*, [1990] 1 S.C.R. 1075 ("*Sparrow*"), the court made it clear (at 1103) that "there was from the outset never any doubt that sovereignty and legislative power, and indeed the underlying title, to [aboriginal] lands vested in the Crown." In *Matsqui Indian Band v. Canadian Pacific Ltd.*, [1995] 1 S.C.R. 3, it allowed its approach to a question of statutory procedure to be shaped in part by a federal policy supportive of aboriginal self-government. And in *Pamajewon*, note 10 above, a case whose facts, for this purpose, were about as unsympathetic as one could easily imagine, the court showed considerable restraint in dismissing the suggestion that self-government rights protected from mainstream regulation a large-scale commercial gaming operation that a band council had organized on its reserve. See also, most recently, *Corbière v. The Queen in right of Canada*, [1999] 2 S.C.R. 203 at 248-249 (¶¶52-53), where the minority judgment, with the concurrence of the majority (*ibid.* at 224 (¶20)), again gently deferred an argument based on self-government rights, this time in response to a claim that statutory residency requirements for *Indian Act* band council elections violate the equality rights guaranteed in s. 15(1) of the *Canadian Charter of Rights and Freedoms*, Part I of the *Constitution Act, 1982* ("*Charter*" or "*Charter of Rights*").

13 See *Delgamuukw* (C.A.), note 10 above, at 305 (¶¶783-785), 348-353 (¶¶963-984), 359-364 (¶¶1011-1030), Lambert J.A.; at 394-396 (¶¶1163-1173), Hutcheon J.A.

14 See *Delgamuukw*, note 10 above, at 1114-1115 (¶¶170-171), Lamer C.J.C.; at 1134 (¶205), La Forest J.

15 See *Delgamuukw* (S.C.), note 10 above, at 437-455, 473; *Delgamuukw* (C.A.), note 10 above, at 148-153 (¶¶151-175), Macfarlane J.A.; at 222-226 (¶¶470-485), Wallace J.A.

16 See note 10 above.

17 Tempting though it is, I cannot pause here to substantiate this conclusion in any detail. I am satisfied, though: (1) that social organization with some recognizable form of governance and laws is a precondition to the kinds of aboriginal rights that the Supreme Court of Canada has already recognized (see, e.g., *Delgamuukw*, note 10 above, 1099-1100 (¶¶147-148), quoting *Hamlet of Baker Lake v. Minister of Indian Affairs & Northern Development*, [1980] 1 F.C. 518 (T.D.) at 559; *Mabo v. Queensland (No. 2)* (1992), 175 C.L.R. 1 (H.C.A.) ("*Mabo*"), at 59-62); McNeil, "Aboriginal Rights," note 7 above, at 285-289; (2) that jurisdiction and governance arrangements were, as a matter of anthropological fact, characteristic generally of North American aboriginal societies identifiable as such (see Catherine Bell & Michael Asch, "Challenging Assumptions: The Impact of Precedent in Aboriginal Rights Litigation" in Michael Asch, ed., *Aboriginal and Treaty Rights in Canada: Essays on Law, Equality, and Respect for Difference* (Vancouver: UBC Press,

1997) (*"Aboriginal and Treaty Rights"*) 38 esp. at 64-71); (3) that colonial law provided for pre-existing indigenous legal arrangements to survive and continue to operate in British colonies, subject only to the power of duly authorized colonial legislatures to extinguish them (see, e.g., Walters, "Comment on *Delgamuukw*," note 7 above; Walters, *"Mohegan Indians,"* note 7 above), and (4) that nothing that any duly authorized Imperial, colonial or Canadian legislature is known to have done exhibited a sufficiently clear and plain intention to extinguish aboriginal communities' pre-existing rights and powers of self-government (see, e.g., 2 RCAP Final Report, note 4 above, at 206-213).

18 See note 10 above and the text accompanying it.

19 Ken Tyler, not one of the inherent right's most ardent supporters, has framed the situation with characteristic flair:

> Were the Aboriginal governments secretly inducted into the Confeder- ation partnership on the 17th of April, 1982? There is no evidence that any of the participants in the patriation of the Canadian constitution thought they were doing any such thing. Neither the Queen, nor the Prime Minister, nor any of the Provincial Premiers, nor any member of the Canadian or United Kingdom Parliaments made any mention of such a momentous event. Representatives of the First Nations them- selves, far from greeting their long-awaited acceptance into the Canadi- an family, rushed to the English Courts in a desperate and unsuccessful attempt to block an initiative which there were convinced placed their Aboriginal and Treaty rights in mortal danger. Since 1982 we have had four First Minister's [sic] Conferences devoted exclusively to Aborigi- nal Constitutional Reform plus the Charlottetown process, in each of which the major priority for the Aboriginal participants was to have the 'right of self-government' entrenched in the Constitution. Surely it would require some very startling new evidence, and some very con- vincing arguments, to persuade Canadians that all of these efforts were unnecessary, and all of the earnest concerns of the Aboriginal people were unwarranted, because the framers of the *Constitution Act, 1982* had unwittingly accomplished all that they desired:

Tyler, note 7 above, at 25. See also Brian Schwartz, "The General Sense of Things: *Delgamuukw* and the Courts" in Frank Cassidy, ed., *Aboriginal Title in British Columbia: Delgamuukw v. The Queen* (Lantzville, B.C.: Oolichan Books, 1992) 161 (Schwartz, "General Sense") at 174 ("The 1982 Consti- tution recognizes the 'existing' rights of aboriginal peoples. Can the courts, in good intellectual conscience, suddenly 'discover' that these rights all along contained rights for self-government that would require a massive set of negotiations, leading to a certain kind of outcome?")

20 *Delgamuukw*, note 10 above, at 1115 (¶171).

21 See *Delgamuukw, ibid.* at 1070 (¶89); *Delgamuukw* (S.C.), note 10 above, at 199.

22 See 2 RCAP Final Report, note 4 above, at 139-141.

23 As a non-aboriginal person, mindful of the differences of view among ab- original peoples and communities themselves, I say this with some trepida-

tion; please discount and cross-check this observation accordingly. But see first Mary Ellen Turpel, "Aboriginal Peoples and the Canadian *Charter*: Interpretive Monopolies, Cultural Differences" (1989-90) 6 Can. Hum. Rts. Y.B. 3 ("Turpel, 'Interpretive Monopolies' ") esp. at 25-26, 33-34, 45; P.A. Monture-OKanee & M.E. Turpel, "Aboriginal Peoples and Canadian Criminal Law: Rethinking Justice" [1992] U.B.C. L. Rev. (Sp. Ed.) 239 ("Rethinking Justice") at 262-263; Asch & Macklem, note 7 above, esp. at 517, and the other sources cited in this paragraph in the text. Compare Audrey D. Doerr, "Building New Orders of Government: The Future of Aboriginal Self-Government" (1997) 40 Can. Pub. Admin. 274 at 275.

24 For accounts of such efforts in two unrelated aboriginal communities, see Johnston, note 7 above (Iroquois) and John J. Borrows, "A Genealogy of Law: Inherent Sovereignty and First Nations Self-Government" (1992) 30 Osgoode Hall L.J. 291 (Anishnabek). Compare James (Sakej) Youngblood Henderson, "First Nation Legal Inheritances in Canada: The M'ikmaq Model" (1996) 23 Man. L.J. 1 ("Henderson, 'Legal Inheritances' "); J. Edward Chamberlin, "Culture and Anarchy in Indian Country" in *Aboriginal and Treaty Rights*, note 17 above, 3.

25 There are, of course, too many useful accounts of colonial oppression of aboriginal peoples in Canada to list in a single footnote. For a representative sampling of good brief accounts, however, see James R. Miller, "The Historical Context of the Drive for Self-Government" in Richard Gosse, James Youngblood Henderson & Roger Carter, eds., *Continuing Poundmaker and Riel's Quest* (Saskatoon: Purich Publishing, 1994) ("*Poundmaker*") 41 esp. at 42; Mary Ellen Turpel, "Patriarchy and Paternalism: The Legacy of the Canadian State for First Nations Women" (1993) 6 C.J.W.L. 174 ("Turpel, 'Patriarchy' ") at 181-182; Mary Ellen Turpel-Lafond, "Enhancing Integrity in Aboriginal Government: Ethics and Accountability for Good Governance," research study prepared for the Royal Commission on Aboriginal Peoples, 1995 ("Turpel-Lafond, 'Enhancing Integrity' ") at 9-15; James Youngblood Henderson, "All Is Never Said" in *Poundmaker, ibid*. 423 esp. at 428, and the sources cited in these publications. See also Sidney L. Harring, *White Men's Law: Native People in Nineteenth Century Canadian Jurisprudence* (Toronto: Osgoode Society, University of Toronto Press, 1998).

26   To me, to be a First Nations person in Canada means to be free to exist politically and culturally (these are not separate concepts): to be free to understand our roles according to our own cultural and political systems and not according to a value system imposed upon us by the Indian Act for over 100 years, nor by role definition accepted in the Anglo-European culture:

Turpel, "Patriarchy" *ibid*. at 185. See also Turpel, "Interpretive Monopolies," note 23 above, at 33.

27 See Greschner, note 7 above, at 342.

28 LaForme, note 7 above, at 263. See also "Rethinking Justice," note 23 above, at 263.

29 See LaForme, *ibid*. at 263-264 ("It is this capacity to deal with threats to cultural survival, in a manner that may be drastically different from that re-

quired by other elements of Canadian society, which is needed to ensure the survival of Aboriginal cultures"); Macklem, "Distributing Sovereignty," note 7 above, at 1354 ("Indian government involves more than the conferral of special rights to engage in particular activities: It also involves rights to determine how, when, where and by whom such activity can occur, and the possibility that such decisions will be made in ways that conflict with nonindigenous political values ..."); RCAP, *Bridging*, note 6 above, at 277.

30 Patricia Monture-OKanee, "Thinking About Aboriginal Justice: Myths and Revolution" in *Poundmaker*, note 25 above, 222 at 230. See also Tyler, note 7 above, at 7-8.

31 This is so, of course, whether or not such rights, as a matter, of history, had ever received "the legal recognition and approval of European colonizers": see *Delgamuukw*, note 10 above, at 1092-1093 (¶¶134-136), quoting (at ¶136) *Côté v. The Queen*, [1996] 3 S.C.R. 139 ("Côté") at 174 (¶52).

32 See, e.g., Richard Gosse, "Charting the Course for Aboriginal Justice Reform Through Aboriginal Self-Government" in *Poundmaker*, note 25 above, 1 at 16.

33 Roger Gibbins & J. Rick Ponting, "An Assessment of the Probable Impact of Aboriginal Self-Government in Canada" in Alan Cairns & Cynthia Williams, eds., *The Politics of Gender, Ethnicity and Language in Canada* (Toronto: University of Toronto Press, 1986) 171 at 189, 192, 220-221. See also Miles Morrisseau, "Will Self-government Set Natives Against Each Other?" *The [Montreal] Gazette* (18 August 1992) B3 ("And what will be left of the fragile unity that now exists [among aboriginal peoples] when we have only ourselves to blame?").

34 See Mary Ellen Turpel, "Reflections on Thinking Concretely About Criminal Justice Reform" in *Poundmaker*, note 25 above, 206 at 209 ("Problems of alcohol and solvent abuse, family violence and sexual abuse, and youth crime—these are indications of a fundamental breakdown in the social order in Aboriginal communities of a magnitude never known before"); Monture-OKanee, note 30 above, at 227 ("We cannot look to the past to find the mechanisms to address concerns such as abuse, because many of the mechanisms did not exist. The mechanisms did not exist because they were not needed").

35 Gibbins & Ponting, note 33 above, at 191; David C. Hawkes & Allen M. Maslove, "Fiscal Arrangements for Aboriginal Self-Government" in David C. Hawkes, ed., *Aboriginal Peoples and Government Responsibility: Exploring Federal and Provincial Roles* (Ottawa: Carleton University Press, 1989) 93 at 123; Jeffrey Simpson, "Just What Is a 'Nation' and How Can It Work Like A Province?" *[Toronto] Globe & Mail* (27 February 1997) A18; Barry Cooper & David Bercuson, "An Abdication of Responsibility: Ottawa Must See Through the Job of Transferring Lands to Natives" *The [London] Free Press* (23 January 1999) F6. See also *To the Source*, note 4 above, at vi ("While all the people spoke of the need for change, many also said, almost in the same breath, that they are not ready for it. They are afraid, and their fears need to be addressed").

36 See, e.g., Gerald Flood, "Native Woman, Elder Fear Self-government" *Winnipeg Free Press* (8 October 1992) B5 (quoting a native elder in Manitoba as

saying "aboriginal leaders have failed in their efforts to improve conditions, and now expect to be trusted with more power"); Tom Oleson, "Native Self-rule: Is It a Dead End? Know Sovereignty Before Building It" *Winnipeg Free Press* (14 July 1996) B2 ("[Self-government] might receive more public sympathy . . . if there could be a clearer perception that the bands could run well the business they already have authority over"); Gordon Gibson, "It's a Matter of Principles" *National Post* (30 October 1999) B7 ("Gibson, 'Principles'").

37 Even, perhaps especially, the non-aboriginal people, according to some accounts. See, e.g., Cooper & Bercuson, note 35 above.

38 See Gibbins & Ponting, note 33 above, at 190; Schwartz, *Second Thoughts*, note 2 above, at 396.

39 See William Johnson, "Not All Are Leaping on Native Self-government Bandwagon" *The [Montreal] Gazette* (5 May 1992) B3 ("Johnson, 'Bandwagon'"); William Johnson, "Native Self-government: Let's Pay Attention" *The [Montreal] Gazette* (12 May 1992) B3 ("Johnson, 'Let's Pay Attention'"); "Band Councils Must Be Accountable" [editorial] *The [Brantford] Expositor* (24 March 1999) A6 ("Must Be Accountable").

40 "If a high proportion of total revenues are provided by an external authority, can the accountability link between the aboriginal government and its citizens be as strong and effective as in situations in which the community itself is the major source of government revenues?": Hawkes & Maslove, note 35 above, at 113. See also *ibid.* at 123; 2 RCAP Final Report, note 4 above, at 345-346; Richard Simeon, "Sharing Power: How Can First Nations Government Work?" in *Aboriginal Self-Determination*, note 8 above, 99 at 105; Schwartz, *Second Thoughts*, note 2 above, at 396; William Johnson, "What Would Indian Self-government Look Like? Big, Very Big" *The [Montreal] Gazette* (20 May 1992) B3 ("Johnson, 'Big, Very Big'"); William Johnson, "Why Native Leaders Don't Want Charter of Rights in Their Government" *The [Montreal] Gazette* (10 October 1992) B5 ("Johnson, 'Don't Want Charter'"); Tom Flanagan, "An Unworkable Vision of Self-Government" (March 1997) 18 Policy Options 19 at 20.

41 See generally Schwartz, *Second Thoughts, ibid.* at 394-396; Bryan Schwartz, "Bryan Schwartz Takes a Close Look at Aboriginal Self-government" *[Toronto] Globe & Mail* (4 August 1992) A12 ("Schwartz, 'Close Look'"); Gibbins & Ponting, note 33 above, at 216-219; Roger Gibbins, "Citizenship, Political, and Intergovernmental Problems with Indian Self-Government" in J. Rick Ponting, ed., *Arduous Journey: Canadian Indians and Decolonization* (Toronto: McClelland & Stewart, 1986) 369 ("Gibbins, 'Problems'") at 374-376; Johnson, "Bandwagon," note 39 above; Johnson, "Big, Very Big," *ibid.*; Flanagan, *ibid.* at 20-21; Jodi Cockerill & Roger Gibbins, "Reluctant Citizens? First Nations in the Canadian Federal State" in J. Rick Ponting, ed., *First Nations in Canada: Perspectives on Opportunity, Empowerment, and Self-Determination* (Toronto: McGraw-Hill Ryerson, 1997) 383 at 393-394; Gibson, "Principles," note 36 above.

42 See, e.g., Iris Yudal, "Chiefs Abuse Power, Funds, Group Charges" *Winnipeg Free Press* (21 February 1992) B23; Ruth Teichroeb, "Democracy on the Reserve: Limits Sought on Powers of Chiefs" *Winnipeg Free Press* (6 April 1992)

B13 ("Teichroeb, 'Limits' "); Wendy Dudley, "MP Sees Pitfalls in Self-rule" *Calgary Herald* (12 September 1994) B1; Rudy Platiel, "Native Councils Facing Challenges from Within" *[Toronto] Globe & Mail* (15 May 1996) A8; "Must Be Accountable," note 39 above; Nahlah Ayed, "Self-government a Mess, Native Coalition Testifies" *Toronto Star* (3 March 1999) A6; Andrew Duffy, "First Nation Women Want Ombudsman to Fight Corruption" *Sault Star* (3 March 1999) B9.

43 See, e.g., Heidi Graham, "Natives 'Rebels' Meet in Bid to 'Get Self-government Stalled' " *Winnipeg Free Press* (29 March 1992) B14; Patrick Nagle, "Male Domination Heightens Fear of Self-rule" *Calgary Herald* (1 April 1992) B8; Teichroeb, "Limits," *ibid.*; Ruth Teichroeb, "Democracy on the Reserve: Mother Who Reported Abuse Ostracized" *Winnipeg Free Press* (8 April 1992) B18 ("Teichroeb, "Mother Ostracized' "); Ruth Teichroeb, "Democracy on the Reserve: Family Pays Heavy Price for Reporting Sex Abuse" *Winnipeg Free Press* (8 April 1992) B18 ("Teichroeb, 'Heavy Price' "); Flood, note 36 above; Platiel, *ibid.*; Cockerill & Gibbins, note 41 above, at 393-394; Ayed, *ibid.*

44 See, e.g., "Native Group Fears Dictatorial Ways" *Calgary Herald* (21 February 1992) A9; Yudal, note 42 above; Teichroeb, "Limits," note 42 above; Platiel, note 42 above; "Must Be Accountable," note 39 above; Ayed, *ibid.*; Duffy, note 42 above; Rick Mofina, "Allegations of Native Fraud Soaring" *Vancouver Sun* (10 November 1999) A6.

45 See generally Turpel-Lafond, "Enhancing Integrity," note 25 above, at 1-23.

46 Some communities, of course, have no such problems: see, e.g., Teichroeb, "Model of Democracy," note 9 above. For a somewhat more favorable account of the internal accountability practices and attitudes among leaders of aboriginal communities generally, see Simon McInnes & Perry Billingsley, "Canada's Indians: Norms of Responsible Government Under Federalism" (1992) 35 Can. Pub. Admin. 215.

47 See 2 RCAP Final Report, note 4 above, at 345 ("There is a widespread perception in some communities that their leaders rule rather than lead their people, and that corruption and nepotism are prevalent"); Turpel-Lafond, "Enhancing Integrity," note 25 above, at 19 ("Without the existence of [internal conflict of interest guidelines], the trust and confidence in the integrity of a band council to act in the interest of all members is significantly lessened due to the inability to require individuals to account for their conduct"). See also "Inherent But Unclear" [editorial] *Winnipeg Free Press* (11 April 1992) A6; Johnson, "Big, Very Big," note 40 above; Peter O'Neil, "Self-rule for Natives Arouses Hopes, Doubts" *Vancouver Sun* (7 October 1992) A4 ("O'Neil, 'Hopes, Doubts' "); Johnson, "Don't Want Charter," note 40 above; "Must Be Accountable," note 39 above.

48 Turpel-Lafond, "Enhancing Integrity," *ibid.* at 1. See also *To the Source*, note 4 above, at 21 ("many of our witnesses ... worried that additional power could be abused by some of the leaders").

49 See, e.g., *To the Source*, *ibid.* at 59; Thomas Isaac & Mary Sue Maloughney, "Dually Disadvantaged and Historically Forgotten?: Aboriginal Women and the Inherent Right of Aboriginal Self-Government" (1992) 21 Man. L.J. 453 at 454-457; Greschner, note 7 above, at 339-340; Joyce Green, "Constitu-

tionalizing the Patriarchy: Aboriginal Women and Aboriginal Government" (1993) 4 Const. Forum 110 at 112; Turpel, "Patriarchy," note 25 above, at 180; Monture-OKanee, "Myths and Revolution," note 30 above, at 227. But see also Emma LaRocque, "Re-examining Culturally Appropriate Models in Criminal Justice Applications" in *Aboriginal and Treaty Rights*, note 17 above, 75 at 83-84.

50 See, e.g., *To the Source, ibid.* at 59-61; Isaac & Maloughney, *ibid.*; Nagle, note 43 above; Teichroeb, "Limits," note 42 above; Teichroeb, "Mother Ostracized," note 43 above; Teichroeb, "Heavy Price," note 43 above; Ruth Teichroeb, "Democracy on the Reserve: Professor Says Indian Women Have Reason to Fear Autonomy" *Winnipeg Free Press* (8 April 1992) B18 ("Teichroeb, 'Professor Says' "); Turpel, "Patriarchy," note 25 above, at 181-182; Green, *ibid.* esp. at 112; John Borrows, "Contemporary Traditional Equality: The Effect of the *Charter* on First Nation Politics" (1994) 43 U.N.B.L.J. 19 ("Borrows, 'Equality' ") esp. at 46; Karina Byrne, "Indian Women Want Protection" *Winnipeg Free Press* (27 March 1994) A3; Patricia Robertson, "Native Women Demand Role" *Winnipeg Free Press* (18 May 1996) A11; LaRocque, *ibid.*

51 In the words of Sharon McIvor, at the time a spokesperson for the Native Women's Association of Canada ("NWAC"), "It's really scary to know that these guys are going to be in complete control, they are going to be able to do whatever they want. ... We are lost; if you non-Indian Canadians don't put pressure on your people to help look after our rights, then we are dead in the water": "Native Women Fear Autonomy Will Hide Sex Abuse" *Calgary Herald* (29 July 1992) A9. See also, e.g., *To the Source, ibid.* at 61 ("Women who have been raped, beaten, sexually harassed, overlooked, excluded, ignored, or otherwise oppressed by Aboriginal men are hardly eager to trust the men to look after their interests"); Susan Delacourt, "Natives Divided Over Charter" *[Toronto] Globe & Mail* (14 March 1992) A4 ("Delacourt, 'Natives Divided' "); Peter O'Neil, "Native Women Push for Human Rights" *Vancouver Sun* (14 March 1992) A3 ("O'Neil, 'Native Women Push' "); Sarah Scott, "The Native Rights Stuff: Many Women Fear Self-government Without Charter Guarantees" *The [Montreal] Gazette* (28 March 1992) B5 ("Scott, 'Native Rights Stuff' "); Nagle, note 43 above; Teichroeb, "Limits," *ibid.*; Teichroeb, "Professor Says," *ibid.*; "Native Fights for Charter" *Calgary Herald* (23 April 1992) A12 ("Native Fights for Charter"); Flood, note 36 above; Green, *ibid.*; Byrne, *ibid.*; Borrows, "Equality," *ibid.* at 41-46; LaRocque, *ibid.* esp. at 93-95. Compare Ayed, note 42 above.

52   Aboriginal women have sexual equality rights. We want those rights respected. Governments simply cannot choose to recognize the patriarchal forms of government which now exist in our communities. The band councils and Chiefs who preside over our lives are not our traditional forms of government ... Recognizing the inherent right to self-government does not mean recognizing the patriarchy created by a foreign government:

NWAC, "Statement on the Canada Package" (Ottawa: NWAC, 1992) at 7, quoted in Borrows, "Equality," *ibid.*, at 41. See also Michele Rouleau, "Proposal for Native Self-government Could Deny Fundamental Human Rights to Women" *The [Montreal] Gazette* (23 October 1992) B3; Green, *ibid.*; LaRocque, *ibid.* esp. at 93-95.

There is, of course, controversy, especially among aboriginal peoples, about the extent to which these views of the current male aboriginal leadership are fair and, assuming that they are fair, about whether recourse to external tribunals and standards is, as NWAC maintains, the most appropriate way of addressing that reality in self-governing aboriginal communities. These issues, unfortunately, lie beyond the scope of the present work. The academic sources cited here and in notes 49-51 above provide a useful range of views about them. For additional contributions and viewpoints, see, e.g., Turpel, "Interpretive Monopolies," note 23 above; Mary Ellen Turpel, "Aboriginal Peoples and the Canadian Charter of Rights and Freedoms: Contradictions and Challenges" (1989) 10 Can. Woman Studies (Nos. 2 & 3) 149; Wendy Moss, "Indigenous Self-Government in Canada and Sexual Equality Under the *Indian Act*: Resolving Conflicts Between Collective and Individual Rights" (1990) 15 Queen's L.J. 279; Ruth Teichroeb, "Democracy on the Reserve: Solidarity Vital, Province's Native Leaders Say" *Winnipeg Free Press* (10 April 1992) B1; "Native Women Urged to Ignore 'White Feminists'" *Calgary Herald* (31 July 1992) A10; Margaret A. Jackson, "Aboriginal Women and Self-Government" in John H. Hylton, ed., *Aboriginal Self-Government in Canada* (Saskatoon, Purich Publishing, 1994) 180.

53 *The Queen v. Native Women's Association of Canada*, [1994] 3 S.C.R. 627. For commentary on this litigation and the context from which it arose, see Green, *ibid.* and Borrows, "Equality," *ibid.* at 42-44.

54 See. e.g., Canada, *Report of the Royal Commission on the Economic Union and Development Prospects for Canada*, vol. 3 (Ottawa: Minister of Supply and Services, 1985) ("3 Macdonald Report") at 371; Gibbins & Ponting, note 33 above, at 205, 218-219; Schwartz, "General Sense," note 19 above, at 172; "Inherent But Unclear," note 47 above; Cockerill & Gibbins, note 41 above, at 383-384, 388, 390-391, 398-399.

55 Schwartz, *Second Thoughts*, note 2 above, at 394; Gibbins, "Problems," note 41 above, at 376.

56 3 Macdonald Report, note 54 above, at 368-371.

57 "At this point we cannot assume that self-government can be implemented without inflicting serious damage to democratic principles, to the intergovernmental structures of the Canadian federal state, and to the citizenship rights of Canadian Indians": Gibbins, "Problems," note 41 above, at 376. See also Binnie, note 7 above, esp. at 218, 225; William Johnson, "Mercredi Has No Mandate, But That Doesn't Stop Him" *The [Montreal] Gazette* (26 June 1992) B3; Philip Authier, "Quebec Lawyers Slam Native Self-government: It Poses 'Unprecedented Threat to Province's Powers,' Legal Paper Says" *The [Montreal] Gazette* (22 July 1992) B1; Schwartz, "Close Look," note 41 above; Bob Cox, "Self-rule Scenario Packs Potential for Future Conflict, Author Says" *Vancouver Sun* (29 September 1992) A8; "Reformer Inflaming Issues, Says Minister" *Calgary Herald* (8 February 1994) A9; Cockerill & Gibbins, note 41 above, esp. at 385-387.

58 See, e.g., Johnson, "Big, Very Big," note 40 above; Ted Byfield, "Native Self-government Goes Beyond What Canadians Think" *Financial Post* (21-23 March 1992) S3; Tyler, note 7 above, at 7-10.

59 See, e.g., Johnson, "Bandwagon," note 39 above; Authier, note 57 above; Schwartz, "Close Look," note 41 above; Milo Cernetig, "Reform Attacks Native Self-rule" *[Toronto] Globe & Mail* (5 October 1992) A1 at A1, A4.

60 See Jeffrey Simpson, "The Words Are Magnificent, But Can They Be Realistically Implemented" *[Toronto] Globe & Mail* (28 February 1997) A18 (review of RCAP Final Report).

61 See "Aboriginal Gamble" [editorial] *Winnipeg Free Press* (2 June 1992) A6; Authier, note 57 above; Gordon Gibson, "Where the Aboriginal Report Takes a Wrong Turn" *[Toronto] Globe & Mail* (26 November 1996) A19 ("Gibson, 'Wrong Turn' "); Cockerill & Gibbins, note 41 above, at 383-384, 387-388.

62 See 3 Macdonald Report, note 54 above, at 370-371; Gibbins & Ponting, note 33 above, at 209-213; Cockerill & Gibbins, *ibid.* at 385-387.

63 See, e.g., Gordon Gibson, "Let's Not Use Racism to Tackle Native Needs: Isolating Aboriginal People from the Mainstream Is a Mistake" *[Toronto] Globe & Mail* (1 June 1992) A15.

64 See, e.g., Byfield, note 58 above; Susan Delacourt, "Native Self-government Difficult Sell, Clark Says" *[Toronto] Globe & Mail* (2 June 1992) A1, at A1-A2; Peter O'Neil, "B.C. Tories Voice Fears Over Native Government" *Vancouver Sun* (4 June 1992) A4; Sandro Contenta, "Native Deal Stirs Deep Fears in Quebec" *Toronto Star* (19 July 1992) A10; "Go Slowly on Self-government: Canadians Deserve More Than Vague Concepts" [editorial] *The [Montreal] Gazette* (24 January 1994) B2; Oleson, note 36 above; Gibson, "Wrong Turn," note 61 above; "Must Be Accountable," note 39 above.

From this standpoint, it hasn't helped, either, that aboriginal communities have gone to court in recent years asserting constitutionally protected rights: to abduct community members and subject them, without consent, to tribal rituals involving physical punishment (*Thomas v. Norris*, [1992] 2 C.N.L.R. 139 (B.C.S.C.)); to hear on reserve, exclusively before a jury composed of community members, sexual assault charges brought against a community elder, despite objections from the complainant (also a community member) that she could not be safe, or be fairly heard, in such circumstances (*R. v. A.F.* (1994), 30 C.R. (4th) 333 (Ont. (G.D.)), aff'd. (1997), 101 O.A.C. 146 (C.A.)); to withhold band membership and related entitlements from women born and raised in the community merely because they had "married out" (*Sawridge Band v. The Queen*, [1996] 1 F.C. 3 (T.D.), rev'd. [1997] 3 F.C. 580 (C.A.)), and to promote and engage in high-stakes gaming completely free of any provincial or federal supervision (*Pamajewon*, note 10 above).

65 Jim Bronskill, "Liberals Wavered on Promise: Native Self-government Memorandum" *Calgary Herald* (6 May 1996) A8. In the end, the federal government confirmed its original intention to proceed on the basis that the constitution already protects the inherent right: *ibid.*; *Federal Policy Guide*, note 8 above.

66 There are, of course, other reasons for identifying such concerns and taking them seriously. Several of those cited above with concerns about self-government made it clear that their intention was not to discourage its eventual constitutional entrenchment or accreditation, but only to identify pitfalls that would have to be addressed in the course of design or implementation. See, e.g., Gibbins & Ponting, note 33 above, at 174, 193, 235; Schwartz, *Second Thoughts*, note 2 above, at 396; Green, note 49 above, at 119; Cockerill & Gibbins, note 41 above, at 384. The final report of the Royal Commission on Aboriginal Peoples itself acknowledges that there are grounds for many of these concerns and suggests concrete proposals for dealing with them in the course of giving effect to inherent self-government rights: see 2 RCAP Final Report, note 4 above, at 326-353. See also notes 72-82 below and the text accompanying them.

67 "[H]ave faith that your own system of laws is flexible enough and will not crumble if you accept that First Nations have a right to administer their own justice": Blaine Favel, "First Nations Perspective of the Split in Jurisdiction" in *Poundmaker*, note 25 above, 136 at 139. See also Monture-OKanee, note 30 above, at 224-225. Compare Asch & Macklem, note 7 above, at 517.

68 See, e.g., Macklem, "Distributing Sovereignty," note 7 above, at 1360; Teichroeb, "Victims Are Trying," note 9 above. Compare J. Anthony Long & Katherine Beaty Chiste, "Indian Governments and the Canadian Charter of Rights and Freedoms" (1994) 18 Am. Ind. Culture & Rsch. J. 91 at 103-111.

69   Concern for aboriginal women is piously invoked by closet opponents of aboriginal self-determination who reject the idea and practice of aboriginal sovereignty and use a new-found solidarity with women as an expedient and politically correct justification for their resistance. This belief in an inherent or irremediable chauvinism of aboriginal men, worse than the chauvinism of non-aboriginal men, must be shown for what it is: false, pernicious and racist:

Greschner, note 7 above, at 339. See also, Borrows, "Equality," note 50 above, at 46-47. Compare Turpel-Lafond, "Enhancing Integrity," note 25 above, at 2, 5.

70 Patrick Macklem has explored these issues most thoroughly and consistently. See, e.g., Asch & Macklem, note 7 above; Macklem, "Borders," note 7 above; Macklem, "Ethnonationalism," note 7 above; Patrick Macklem, "What's Law Got to Do With It? The Protection of Aboriginal Title in Canada" (1997) 35 Osgoode Hall L.J. 125. See also Colin H. Scott, "Custom, Tradition, and the Politics of Culture: Aboriginal Self-Government in Canada" in N. Dyck & J.B. Waldram, eds., *Anthropology, Public Policy, and Native Peoples in Canada* (Montreal: McGill-Queen's University Press, 1993) 311 esp. at 327, and Turpel, "Interpretive Monopolies," note 23 above, at 33-35.

71 "The point to stress here is that any continued dependency on fiscal transfers from the broader Canadian community gives the federal and provincial governments a very large club that can be used to force Indian compliance with conventional norms of taxation": Gibbins, "Problems," note 41 above,

at 370. See also Gibbins & Ponting, note 33 above, at 233; Hawkes & Maslove, note 35 above, at 123; O'Neil, "Hopes, Doubts," note 47 above ("One government official pointed out that few if any aboriginal governments will be self-sufficient. Any that abuse individual rights will have trouble getting government co-operation.")

72 See, e.g., 2 RCAP Final Report, note 4 above at 326-353.

73 "In reconstructing our world we cannot just do what we want. We require a measure of our oppressors' co-operation to disentangle ourselves from the web of enslavement they created": Borrows, "Equality," note 50 above, at 23. Compare Bradford W. Morse, "Indigenous Laws and State Legal Systems: Conflict and Compatibility" in Bradford W. Morse & Gordon R. Woodman, eds., *Indigenous Law and the State* (Dordrecht: Foris Publications, 1988) (*"Indigenous Law"*) 101 at 114 ("The challenge today is to find a mix of solutions which can respond to the different needs and circumstances of indigenous peoples. To do so will require the support of the general community, which means that some minimum standards must be adhered to in order to gain that approval and tolerance").

74 See Turpel-Lafond, "Enhancing Integrity," note 25 above, at 2, 5, quoted below at note 89. See also *ibid.* at 39-40.

75 For tangible evidence that this is so, one need only recall the unprecedented hostility directed toward aboriginal fishers in Atlantic Canada, especially by the non-aboriginal fishers there, in the days and weeks following the Supreme Court's confirmation, in *Marshall v. The Queen*, [1999] 3 S.C.R. 456 (*"Marshall"*), that Mi'kmaq peoples have treaty rights to earn a moderate livelihood from trade in fish and game. See, e.g., Jeffrey Simpson, "The Cost of Expectations" *[Toronto] Globe & Mail* (29 October 1999) A19; Rick Mofina, "Police Were Braced for Violence After Native Fishing Ruling, Report Says" *National Post* (21 February 2000) A10. See also note 79 below and the text accompanying it.

76 See notes 19-22 above and the text accompanying them.

77 Compare *Mabo*, note 17 above, per Brennan J. (for the plurality) at 29-30:

> In discharging its duty to declare the common law of Australia, this Court is not free to adopt rules that accord with contemporary notions of justice and human rights if their adoption would fracture the skeleton of principle which gives the body of our law its shape and internal consistency ... Whenever such a question [here, about overturning some well-established pre-existing common law rule] arises, it is necessary to assess whether the particular rule is an essential doctrine of our legal system and whether, if the rule were to be overturned, the disturbance to be apprehended would be disproportionate to the benefit flowing from the overturning.

> See also Jeremy Webber, "The Jurisprudence of Regret: The Search for Standards of Justice in *Mabo*" (1995) 17 Sydney L. Rev. 5 at 27-28.

78 *Van der Peet v. The Queen*, [1996] 2 S.C.R. 507 (*"Van der Peet"*) at 539 (¶31); *Delgamuukw*, note 10 above, at 1096 (¶141).

79 The large number of intervenors and the significant economic dimensions of the 1996 [Supreme Court] decisions [on Aboriginal rights] are

a clear indication to the court that they [sic] must be constantly aware of the practical and political consequences of their decisions in this area. Decisions which are detrimental to existing non-Aboriginal government and economic interests are bound to result in increased public criticism as Canadian citizens feel the impact of Supreme Court decisions in their daily lives:

Catherine Bell, "New Directions in the Law of Aboriginal Rights" (1998) 77 Can. Bar Rev. 36 at 65-66. Compare Jonathan Rudin, "One Step Forward, Two Steps Back: The Political and Institutional Dynamics Behind the Supreme Court of Canada's Decisions in *R. v. Sparrow, R. v. Van der Peet* and *Delgamuukw v. British Columbia*" (1998) 13 J. L. & Social Pol'y. 67 at 68 ("In the area of Aboriginal rights, the Court cannot provide much support in the face of significant political opposition to the expansion of such rights"). As Rudin observes, the courts cannot afford to ignore the political climate in which they proceed, because they must depend on other branches of government, and on public co-operation, to give effect to their decisions: *ibid.* at 79-89.

Events in the fall of 1999 provided a clear real life example. In November of that year, the Supreme Court of Canada, having endured two months of unremitting public concern and controversy over its treaty rights decision in *Marshall*, note 75 above, took the unprecedented step of issuing written reasons clarifying, and emphasizing the narrow dimensions of, that decision in response to an intervener's [!] motion requesting rehearing of the matter. See *Marshall v. The Queen*, [1999] 3 S.C.R. 533. It is worth recalling, too, that both the United States government and the Georgia state courts refused to enforce the U.S. Supreme Court's landmark decision on aboriginal sovereignty in *Worcester v. Georgia*, 31 U.S. (6 Peters) 515 (1832): see, e.g., Philip Bobbitt, *Constitutional Fate: Theory of the Constitution* (New York: Oxford University Press, 1982) at 111-114 and the sources cited there.

80 *Sparrow*, note 12 above.

81 Binnie, note 7 above, at 218. See also *ibid.* at 225, 234.

82 Consider, for instance, the court's evident anxiety in *Gladstone v. The Queen*, [1996] 2 S.C.R. 723 ("*Gladstone*") at 774-775 (¶¶73-75) about how to accommodate within mainstream commercial arrangements the constitutionally protected right of the Heiltsuk to harvest herring spawn on kelp for commercial purposes and in commercial quantities.

83 The results of a 1992 study, based on the constitutional reform proposals for self-government as of September, 1991, support the hypotheses that public attitudes toward aboriginal self-government correlate affirmatively with cultural and economic security and "that providing factual information about Aboriginal self-government would result in an attitude change towards favouring Aboriginal self-government": see Marlene Wells & J. W. Berry, "Attitudes Toward Aboriginal Self-Government: The Influences of Knowledge, and Cultural and Economic Security" (1992) 12 Can. J. Native Studies 75 esp. at 85. "Many people," Wells & Berry add, "have heard of Aboriginal self-government but are unfamiliar with the meaning. As a result, many people may hold inaccurate beliefs about it. The results of this study

suggest that if people knew more about the meaning of Aboriginal self-government they would hold more positive attitudes towards it" (*ibid.*).

84 See, e.g., James W. Zion, "Searching for Indian Common Law" in *Indigenous Law*, note 73 above, 121 at 123-125. But see Turpel, "Interpretive Monopolies," note 23 above, at 30 for a pointed warning about the risks, built into such efforts, of overlooking important differences among distinct aboriginal cultural systems.

85 See, e.g., Henderson, "Legal Inheritances," note 24 above, esp. at 9; Bruce Johansen, *Forgotten Founders: Benjamin Franklin, the Iroquois and the Rationale for the American Revolution* (Ipswich, Mass.: Gambit Inc., 1982); RCAP, *Partners*, note 6 above, at 40; Menno Boldt & J. Anthony Long, "Tribal Philosophies and the Canadian Charter of Rights and Freedoms" in Menno Boldt & J. Anthony Long, eds., *The Quest for Justice: Aboriginal Peoples and Aboriginal Rights* (Toronto: University of Toronto Press, 1985) 165 at 170; Greschner, note 7 above, at 345-347, and the sources cited in these works.

86   We must also establish trust and communication between our leaders and the people. The Elders said: listen to your grassroots. The youth said: walk your talk. Leaders must assure the people that the grassroots will be involved in rebuilding and reimplementing self-government. The grassroots feel that their leaders have left them behind. The leaders must also be consistent: if they talk about self-government, they should act according to their own traditions and values, not the Indian Act. Again, education and communication are essential:
To the Source, note 4 above, at vi.

87 For one very helpful such account, see Henderson, "Legal Inheritances," note 24 above.

88 "In fact, the chance of Canadian law accepting First Nations legal principles would be substantially weakened if the First Nations did not continue to practice their own laws within their own systems": John Borrows, "With or Without You: First Nations Law (in Canada)" (1996) 41 McGill L.J. 629 at 663. See generally *ibid.* at 657-664. The project that Borrows, Trish Monture, Sakej Henderson and others have undertaken to make indigenous laws and legal traditions accessible, to their own people and to others, as objects of reflection and study (see *ibid.* at 661 n. 166) seems to me to have some real potential to add substance to mainstream perceptions of those traditions.

89 As Mary Ellen Turpel-Lafond observed in her report about these issues to RCAP:
    [The adversarial character of some disputes between Aboriginal citizens and their governments] is the consequences [sic] of an absence of alternative internal political structures to address grievances regarding ethics and accountability in Aboriginal governments. Meanwhile, increased media attention is being paid to these allegations and internal debates. Without appropriate responses or initiatives, public confidence in self-government initiatives on these matters, already tentative in many regions, faces further erosion. What is required by Aboriginal leaders is to squarely address these concerns and the underlying problems from which they stem.

...

> Any widely-held perception that First Nations' governments act arbitrarily, unilaterally and capriciously and are not accountable to their people, whether legitimate or otherwise, will have adverse effects upon the opportunities for First Nations to implement self-government and assume greater recognition for First Nations' governments. Indeed, increased negative attention to the activities of the former are particularly susceptible to being seized upon to discredit self-government.

Turpel-Lafond, "Enhancing Integrity," note 25 above, at 2, 5. See also *ibid.* at 39-40; RCAP, *Bridging*, note 6 above, at 275-277. For some confirmation of Turpel's observations about the impact of such concerns on public attitudes, see notes 42-53 above and the text accompanying them.

90 See, e.g., note 20 above and the text accompanying it; compare *Pamajewon*, note 10 above, esp. at 834 (¶27), where the court expressed its displeasure at the "excessively general terms" in which communities were framing their claims to have constitutional rights of self-government. And even before these two cases, the court had emphasized, as a general matter, the importance of "identify[ing] precisely the nature of the claim being made" in aboriginal rights litigation: see, e.g., *Van der Peet*, note 78 above, at 551-553 (¶¶51-54).

91 See 2 RCAP Final Report, note 4 above.

92 See especially *Nikal v. The Queen*, [1996] 1 S.C.R. 1013; *Van der Peet*, note 78 above; *Gladstone*, note 82 above; *Adams v. The Queen*, [1996] 3 S.C.R. 101; *Côté*, note 31 above; *Delgamuukw*, note 10 above.

93 See note 8 above and the text accompanying it.

94 See notes 79-82 above and the text accompanying them.

95 I say this, just to be clear, without assuming that inherent right communities and governments would, as such, be subject to the *Charter of Rights*. My own view is that the *Charter* most probably would not, and should not, apply, as such, to communities exercising aboriginal rights of self-government. For that discussion, see Kerry Wilkins, "... But We Need the Eggs: The Royal Commission, the Charter of Rights, and the Inherent Right of Aboriginal Self-Government" (1999) 49 U.T.L.J. 53.

96 For earlier adumbrations of this general approach, see Bruce H. Wildsmith, *Aboriginal Peoples and Section 25 of the Canadian Charter of Rights and Freedoms* (Saskatoon: Native Law Centre, University of Saskatchewan, 1988) at 2, 24-29, 50-52 and "Ghost in the Machine," note 7 above, at 293-298. See also Dan Russell & Jonathan Rudin, *Native Alternative Dispute Resolution Systems: The Canadian Future in Light of the American Past* (Toronto: Ontario Native Council on Justice, 1992?) at 154-155. For my own elaboration and defence of this conclusion, see my LL.M. thesis *Unchartered Territory: Fundamental Canadian Values and the Inherent Right of Aboriginal Self-Government* (University of Toronto, 1999), esp. chapters 2 and 4.

97 See *Mabo*, note 17 above, at 29-30, Brennan J. (for the plurality), quoted above at note 77.

98 See notes 22-31 above and the text accompanying them. Concern about this kind of risk has given rise to doubts about the "cultural authority" of main-

stream courts to interpret, apply and enforce aboriginal peoples' self-government rights. See, e.g., Gibbins & Ponting, note 33 above, at 229-230; Turpel, "Interpretive Monopolies," note 23 above, esp. at 4-6, 23-26, 45; RCAP, *Bridging*, note 6 above, at 277-279; Kelly Gallagher-Mackay, "Interpreting Self-Government: Approaches to Building Cultural Authority," [1997] 4 C.N.L.R. 1.

References

Cases

Adams v. The Queen, [1996] 3 S.C.R. 101.

Arani v. Public Trustee of New Zealand, [1920] A.C. 198 (P.C.).

A.G. Ontario v. Bear Island Foundation (1984), 15 D.L.R. (4th) 321 (Ont. H.C.J.), aff'd. (1989), 58 D.L.R. (4th) 117 (Ont. C.A.), aff'd. [1991] 2 S.C.R. 570.

Casimel v. Insurance Corp. of British Columbia (1993), 82 B.C.L.R. (2d) 387 (C.A.).

Coe v. Commonwealth of Australia (No. 1) (1979), 24 A.L.R. 118 (H.C.A.).

Coe v. Commonwealth of Australia (No. 2) (1993), 118 A.L.R. 193 (H.C.A.).

Connolly v. Woolrich (1867), 17 R.J.R.Q. 75 (S.C.), 1 C.N.L.C. 70, aff'd. *sub. nom. Johnstone v. Connolly* (1869), 17 R.J.R.Q. 266, 1 C.N.L.C. 151 (Q.B.).

Corbière v. The Queen in right of Canada, [1999] 2 S.C.R. 203.

Côté v. The Queen, [1996] 3 S.C.R. 139.

Delgamuukw v. The Queen in right of B.C., [1997] 3 S.C.R. 1010, rev'g. in part [1993] 5 W.W.R. 97 (B.C.C.A.), rev'g. in part (1991), 79 D.L.R. (4th) 185 (B.C.S.C.).

Doe d. Sheldon v. Ramsay (1852), 9 U.C.Q.B. 105.

Gladstone v. The Queen, [1996] 2 S.C.R. 723.

Hamlet of Baker Lake v. Minister of Indian Affairs & Northern Development, [1980] 1 F.C. 518 (T.D.).

Isaac v. Davey (1974), 5 O.R. (2d) 610 (C.A.), aff'd. *(sub nom. Davey v. Isaac)*, [1977] 2 S.C.R. 897.

Logan v. Styres (1959), 20 D.L.R. (2d) 416 (Ont. H.C.).

Mabo v. Queensland (No. 2) (1992), 175 C.L.R. 1 (H.C.A.).

Marshall v. The Queen [1999] 3 S.C.R. 456, rehearing denied [1999] 3 S.C.R. 533.

Matsqui Indian Band v. Canadian Pacific Ltd., [1995] 1 S.C.R. 3.

Mushkegowuk Council v. The Queen in right of Ontario (1999), 178 D.L.R. (4th) 283 (Ont. S.C.J.), set aside (2000), 184 D.L.R. (4th) 532 Ont.C.A.

Nikal v. The Queen, [1996] 1 S.C.R. 1013.

Pamajewon v. The Queen, [1996] 2 S.C.R. 821, aff'g. (1994), 95 C.C.C. (3d) 97 (Ont. C.A.), aff'g. [1993] 3 C.N.L.R. 209 (Ont. (Prov. D.)).

R. v. A.F. (1994), 30 C.R. (4th) 333 (Ont. (G.D.)), aff'd. (1997), 101 O.A.C. 146 (C.A.).

R. v. Bear Claw Casino Ltd., [1994] 4 C.N.L.R. 81 (Sask. Prov. Ct.).

R. v. Beboning (1908), 17 O.L.R. 23 (C.A.).

The Queen v. Native Women's Association of Canada, [1994] 3 S.C.R. 627.

Sawridge Band v. The Queen, [1996] 1 F.C. 3 (T.D.), rev'd. [1997] 3 F.C. 580 (C.A.).

Thomas v. Norris, [1992] 2 C.N.L.R. 139 (B.C.S.C.).

R. v. Williams, [1995] 2 C.N.L.R. 229 (B.C.C.A.).

Sero v. Gault (1921), 50 O.L.R. 27 (S.C.).

Sparrow v. The Queen, [1990] 1 S.C.R. 1075.

Re Stacey and Montour and The Queen (1981), 63 C.C.C. (2d) 61 (Que. C.A.).

Van der Peet v. The Queen, [1996] 2 S.C.R. 507.

Walker v. New South Wales (1994), 182 C.L.R. 45 (H.C.A.).

Worcester v. Georgia, 31 U.S. (6 Peters) 515 (1832).

Books, Monographs and Collections of Essays

Michael Asch, ed., *Aboriginal and Treaty Rights in Canada: Essays on Law, Equality, and Respect for Difference* (Vancouver: UBC Press, 1997) ("*Aboriginal and Treaty Rights*").

Assembly of First Nations, First Nations Circle on the Constitution, *To the Source* (1992).

Philip Bobbitt, *Constitutional Fate: Theory of the Constitution* (New York: Oxford University Press, 1982).

Frank Cassidy, ed., *Aboriginal Self-Determination* (Lantzville, B.C.: Oolichan Books, 1991) ("*Aboriginal Self-Determination*").

Bruce Clark, *Native Liberty, Crown Sovereignty: The Existing Aboriginal Right of Self-Government in Canada* (Montreal: McGill-Queen's University Press, 1990).

Richard Gosse, James Youngblood Henderson & Roger Carter, eds., *Continuing Poundmaker and Riel's Quest* (Saskatoon: Purich Pub., 1994) ("*Poundmaker*").

Sidney L. Harring, *White Men's Law: Native People in Nineteenth Century Canadian Jurisprudence* (Toronto: Osgoode Society, University of Toronto Press, 1998).

Peter W. Hogg, *Constitutional Law of Canada*, 4th ed., abridged (Toronto: Carswell, 1997).

The Inherent Right of Aboriginal Self-Government, papers presented to Canadian Bar Association, Continuing Legal Education Program, Annual Meeting, 1994 ("CBA, *The Inherent Right*").

Bruce Johansen, *Forgotten Founders: Benjamin Franklin, the Iroquois and the Rationale for the American Revolution* (Ipswich, Mass.: Gambit Inc., 1982).

Bradford W. Morse & Gordon R. Woodman, eds., *Indigenous Law and the State* (Dordrecht: Foris Publications, 1988) ("*Indigenous Law*").

Native Women's Association of Canada, "Statement on the Canada Package" (Ottawa: NWAC, 1992).

Dan Russell & Jonathan Rudin, *Native Alternative Dispute Resolution Systems: The Canadian Future in Light of the American Past* (Toronto: Ontario Native Council on Justice, n.d.).

Brian Schwartz, *First Principles, Second Thoughts: Aboriginal Peoples, Constitutional Reform and Canadian Statecraft* (Montreal: Institute for Research and Public Policy, 1986).

Bruce H. Wildsmith, *Aboriginal Peoples and Section 25 of the Canadian Charter of Rights and Freedoms* (Saskatoon: Native Law Centre, University of Saskatchewan, 1988).

Articles and Essays

Michael Asch & Patrick Macklem, "Aboriginal Rights and Canadian Sovereignty: An Essay on *R. v. Sparrow*" (1991) 29 Alta L. Rev. 498.

Catherine Bell, "New Directions in the Law of Aboriginal Rights" (1998) 77 Can. Bar Rev. 36.

Catherine Bell & Michael Asch, "Challenging Assumptions: The Impact of Precedent in Aboriginal Rights Litigation" in *Aboriginal and Treaty Rights* 38.

W.I.C. Binnie, "The Sparrow Doctrine: Beginning of the End or End of the Beginning?" (1990) 15 Queen's L.J. 217.

Menno Boldt & J. Anthony Long, "Tribal Philosophies and the Canadian Charter of Rights and Freedoms" in Menno Boldt & J. Anthony Long, eds., *The Quest for Justice: Aboriginal Peoples and Aboriginal Rights* (Toronto: University of Toronto Press, 1985) 165.

John Borrows, "Constitutional Law from a First Nations Perspective: Self-Government and the Royal Proclamation" (1994) 28 U.B.C. L. Rev. 1.

John Borrows, "Contemporary Traditional Equality: The Effect of the *Charter* on First Nation Politics" (1994) 43 U.N.B.L.J. 19.

John Borrows, "With or Without You: First Nations Law (in Canada)" (1996) 41 McGill L.J. 629.

John J. Borrows, "A Genealogy of Law: Inherent Sovereignty and First Nations Self-Government" (1992) 30 Osgoode Hall L.J. 291.

Kathy L. Brock, "The Politics of Aboriginal Self-Government: A Canadian Paradox" (1991) 34 Can. Pub. Admin. 272.

J. Edward Chamberlin, "Culture and Anarchy in Indian Country" in *Aboriginal and Treaty Rights* 3.

Jodi Cockerill & Roger Gibbins, "Reluctant Citizens? First Nations in the Canadian Federal State" in J. Rick Ponting, ed., *First Nations in Canada: Perspectives on Opportunity, Empowerment, and Self-Determination* (Toronto: McGraw-Hill Ryerson, 1997) 383.

Audrey D. Doerr, "Building New Orders of Government: The Future of Aboriginal Self-Government" (1997) 40 Can. Pub. Admin. 274.

Blaine Favel, "First Nations Perspective of the Split in Jurisdiction" in *Poundmaker* 136.

Tom Flanagan, "An Unworkable Vision of Self-Government" (March 1997) 18 Policy Options 19.

Hamar Foster, "Forgotten Arguments: Aboriginal Title and Sovereignty in *Canada Jurisdiction Act* Cases" (1992) 21 Man. L.J. 343

Bob Freedman, "The Space for Aboriginal Self-Government in British Columbia: The Effect of the Decision of the British Columbia Court of Appeal in *Delgamuukw v. British Columbia*" (1994) 28 U.B.C. L.Rev. 49.

Kelly Gallagher-Mackay, "Interpreting Self-Government: Approaches to Building Cultural Authority," [1997] 4 C.N.L.R. 1.

Roger Gibbins, "Citizenship, Political, and Intergovernmental Problems with Indian Self-Government" in J. Rick Ponting, ed., *Arduous Journey: Canadian Indians and Decolonization* (Toronto: McClelland & Stewart, 1986) 369.

Roger Gibbins & J. Rick Ponting, "An Assessment of the Probable Impact of Aboriginal Self-Government in Canada" in Alan Cairns & Cynthia Williams, eds., *The Politics of Gender, Ethnicity and Language in Canada* (Toronto: University of Toronto Press, 1986) 171.

Richard Gosse, "Charting the Course for Aboriginal Justice Reform Through Aboriginal Self-Government" in *Poundmaker* 1.

Joyce Green, "Constitutionalizing the Patriarchy: Aboriginal Women and Aboriginal Government" (1993) 4 Const. Forum 110.

Donna Greschner, "Aboriginal Women, the Constitution and Criminal Justice" [1992] U.B.C. L. Rev. (Sp. Ed.) 338.

David C. Hawkes & Allen M. Maslove, "Fiscal Arrangements for Aboriginal Self-Government" in David C. Hawkes, ed., *Aboriginal Peoples and Government Responsibility: Exploring Federal and Provincial Roles* (Ottawa: Carleton University Press, 1989) 93.

James Youngblood Henderson, "All Is Never Said" in *Poundmaker* 423.

James (Sakej) Youngblood Henderson, "First Nation Legal Inheritances in Canada: The M'ikmaq Model" (1996) 23 Man. L.J. 1.

Peter W. Hutchins, Carol Hilling & David Schulze, "The Aboriginal Right to Self-Government and the Canadian Constitution: The Ghost in the Machine" (1995) 29 U.B.C. L. Rev. 251.

Thomas Isaac & Mary Sue Maloughney, "Dually Disadvantaged and Historically Forgotten?: Aboriginal Women and the Inherent Right of Aboriginal Self-Government" (1992) 21 Man. L.J. 453.

Margaret A. Jackson, "Aboriginal Women and Self-Government" in John H. Hylton, ed., *Aboriginal Self-Government in Canada* (Saskatoon, Purich Publishing, 1994) 180.

Darlene M. Johnston, "The Quest of the Six Nations Confederacy for Self-Determination" (1986) 44 U.T. Fac.L.Rev. 1.

Harry S. LaForme, "Indian Sovereignty: What Does It Mean?" (1991) 11 Can. J. Native Studies 253.

Emma LaRocque, "Re-examining Culturally Appropriate Models in Criminal Justice Applications" in *Aboriginal and Treaty Rights* 75.

J. Anthony Long & Katherine Beaty Chiste, "Indian Governments and the Canadian Charter of Rights and Freedoms" (1994) 18 Am. Ind. Culture & Rsch. J. 91.

Sylvain Lussier, "Réflexions sur 'Partenaires au Sein de la Confédération' et le Droit 'Inhérent' à l'Autonomie Gouvernementale" in CBA, *The Inherent Right*, vol. 1.

Patrick Macklem, "Distributing Sovereignty: Indian Nations and Equality of Peoples" (1993) 45 Stanford L. Rev. 1311.

Patrick Macklem, "Ethnonationalism, Aboriginal Identities, and the Law" in Michael D. Levin, ed., *Ethnicity and Aboriginality: Case Studies in Ethnonationalism* (Toronto: University of Toronto Press, 1993) 9.

Patrick Macklem, "First Nations Self-Government and the Borders of the Canadian Legal Imagination" (1991) 36 McGill L.J. 382.

Patrick Macklem, "Normative Dimensions of an Aboriginal Right of Self-Government" (1995) 21 Queen's L.J. 173.

Patrick Macklem, "What's Law Got to Do With It? The Protection of Aboriginal Title in Canada" (1997) 35 Osgoode Hall L.J. 125.

Simon McInnes & Perry Billingsley, "Canada's Indians: Norms of Responsible Government Under Federalism" (1992) 35 Can. Pub. Admin. 215.

Kent McNeil, "Aboriginal Rights in Canada: From Title to Land to Territorial Sovereignty" (1998) 5 Tulsa J. Comp. & Int'l. L. 253.

Kent McNeil, "Envisaging Constitutional Space for Aboriginal Governments" (1994) 19 Queen's L.J. 95.

James R. Miller, "The Historical Context of the Drive for Self-Government" in *Poundmaker* 41.

Patricia Monture-OKanee, "Thinking About Aboriginal Justice: Myths and Revolution" in *Poundmaker* 222.

P.A. Monture-OKanee & M.E. Turpel, "Aboriginal Peoples and Canadian Criminal Law: Rethinking Justice" [1992] U.B.C. L. Rev. (Sp. Ed.) 239.

Bradford W. Morse, "Indigenous Laws and State Legal Systems: Conflict and Compatibility" in *Indigenous Law* 101.

Bradford W. Morse, "Permafrost Rights: Aboriginal Self-Government and the Supreme Court in *R. v. Pamajewon*" (1997) 42 McGill L.J. 1011.

Wendy Moss, "Indigenous Self-Government in Canada and Sexual Equality Under the *Indian Act*: Resolving Conflicts Between Collective and Individual Rights" (1990) 15 Queen's L.J. 279.

Shaun Nakatsuru, "A Constitutional Right of Indian Self-Government" (1985) 43 U. T. Fac. L. Rev. 72.

Delia Opekokew, "The Inherent Right of Self-Government As an Aboriginal and Treaty Right" in CBA, *The Inherent Right*, vol. 2.

Alan Pratt, "Aboriginal Self-Government and the Crown's Fiduciary Duty: Squaring the Circle or Completing the Circle?" (1992) 2 N.J.C.L. 163.

Bob Rae, "The Road to Self-Determination," in *Aboriginal Self-Determination* 150.

Jonathan Rudin, "One Step Forward, Two Steps Back: The Political and Institutional Dynamics Behind the Supreme Court of Canada's Decisions in *R. v. Sparrow, R. v. Van der Peet* and *Delgamuukw v. British Columbia*" (1998) 13 J. L. & Social Pol'y. 67.

Bruce Ryder, "The Demise and Rise of the Classical Paradigm in Canadian Federalism: Promoting Autonomy for the Provinces and First Nations" (1991) 36 McGill L.J. 308.

Douglas Sanders, "The Constitution, the Provinces, and Aboriginal Peoples" in J. Anthony Long & Menno Boldt, eds., *Governments in Conflict? Provinces and Indian Nations in Canada* (Toronto: University of Toronto Press, 1988) 151.

Brian Schwartz, "The General Sense of Things: *Delgamuukw* and the Courts" in Frank Cassidy, ed., *Aboriginal Title in British Columbia: Delgamuukw v. The Queen* (Lantzville, B.C.: Oolichan Books, 1992) 161.

Colin H. Scott, "Custom, Tradition, and the Politics of Culture: Aboriginal Self-Government in Canada" in N. Dyck & J.B. Waldram, eds., *Anthropology, Public Policy, and Native Peoples in Canada* (Montreal: McGill-Queen's University Press, 1993) 311.

Richard Simeon, "Sharing Power: How Can First Nations Government Work?" in *Aboriginal Self-Determination* 99.

Brian Slattery, "Aboriginal Sovereignty and Imperial Claims" (1991) 29 Osgoode Hall L.J. 101.

Brian Slattery, "First Nations and the Constitution: A Question of Trust" (1992) 71 Can. Bar Rev. 261.

Brian Slattery, "The Organic Constitution: Aboriginal Peoples and the Evolution of Canada" (1995) 34 Osgoode Hall L.J. 101.

Mary Ellen Turpel, "Aboriginal Peoples and the Canadian Charter of Rights and Freedoms: Contradictions and Challenges" (1989) 10 Can. Woman Studies (Nos. 2 & 3) 149.

Mary Ellen Turpel, "Aboriginal Peoples and the Canadian *Charter*: Interpretive Monopolies, Cultural Differences" (1989-90) 6 Can. Hum. Rts. Y.B. 3.

Mary Ellen Turpel, "Patriarchy and Paternalism: The Legacy of the Canadian State for First Nations Women" (1993) 6 C.J.W.L. 174.

Mary Ellen Turpel, "Reflections on Thinking Concretely About Criminal Justice Reform" in *Poundmaker* 206.

Mary Ellen Turpel-Lafond, "Enhancing Integrity in Aboriginal Government: Ethics and Accountability for Good Governance," research study prepared for the Royal Commission on Aboriginal Peoples, 1995.

Kenneth J. Tyler, "Another Opinion: A Critique of the Paper Presented by the Royal Commission on Aboriginal Peoples Entitled: *Partners in Confederation*" in CBA, *The Inherent Right*, vol. 1.

Mark Walters, "British Imperial Constitutional Law and Aboriginal Rights: A Comment on *Delgamuukw v. British Columbia*" (1992) 17 Queen's L.J. 350.

Mark D. Walters, "*Mohegan Indians v. Connecticut* (1705-1773) and the Legal Status of Aboriginal Customary Laws and Government in British North America" (1995) 33 Osgoode Hall L.J. 785.

Mark D. Walters, "The 'Golden Thread' of Continuity: Aboriginal Customs at Common Law and Under the Constitution Act, 1982" (1999) 44 McGill L.J. 711.

Jeremy Webber, "The Jurisprudence of Regret: The Search for Standards of Justice in *Mabo*" (1995) 17 Sydney L. Rev. 5.

Marlene Wells & J. W. Berry, "Attitudes Toward Aboriginal Self-Government: The Influences of Knowledge, and Cultural and Economic Security" (1992) 12 Can. J. Native Studies 75.

Kerry Wilkins, "... But We Need the Eggs: The Royal Commission, the Charter of Rights, and the Inherent Right of Aboriginal Self-Government" (1999), 49 U.T.L.J. 53.

James W. Zion, "Searching for Indian Common Law" in *Indigenous Law* 121.

Statutes

Constitution Act, 1982, being Schedule B to the *Canada Act 1982* (U.K.), 1982, c. 11.

Canadian Charter of Rights and Freedoms, Part I of the *Constitution Act, 1982*.

Government Documents and Reports

Canada, Consensus Report on the Constitution: Charlottetown (Final Text, 28 August 1992) (Ottawa: Minister of Supply and Services, 1992).

Canada, *Consensus Report on the Constitution: Draft Legal Text* (9 October 1992).

Canada, H.C. Special Committee on Indian Self-government, *Indian Self Government in Canada* (Ottawa: Minister of Supply and Services, 20 October 1983).

Canada, Department of Indian Affairs and Northern Development, *Federal Policy Guide: Aboriginal Self-Government: The Government of Canada's Approach to Implementation of the Inherent Right and the Negotiation of Aboriginal Self-Government* (Ottawa: Minister of Public Works and Government Services Canada, 1995).

Canada, *Report of the Royal Commission on Aboriginal Peoples*, vol. 2 (Ottawa: Minister of Supply and Services, 1996).

Canada, *Report of the Royal Commission on the Economic Union and Development Prospects for Canada*, vol. 3 (Ottawa: Minister of Supply and Services, 1985).

Canada, Royal Commission on Aboriginal Peoples, *Bridging the Cultural Divide: A Report on Aboriginal People and Criminal Justice in Canada* (Ottawa: Minister of Supply and Services, 1996).

Canada, Royal Commission on Aboriginal Peoples, *Partners in Confederation: Aboriginal Peoples, Self-Government and the Constitution* (Ottawa, Ministry of Supply and Services, 1993).

Statement of Political Relationship between Ontario and the First Nations in Ontario, 6 September 1991.

Unpublished Theses

Mei Lin Ng, *Convenient Illusions: A Consideration of Sovereignty and the Aboriginal Right of Self-Government* (LL.M., Osgoode Hall Law School, York University, 1994) [unpublished].

Robert Kerry Wilkins, *Unchartered Territory: Fundamental Canadian Values and the Inherent Right of Aboriginal Self-Government* (LL.M., University of Toronto, 1998).

Newspaper and Magazine Articles

"Aboriginal Gamble" [editorial] *Winnipeg Free Press* (2 June 1992) A6.

Jack Aubry, "Canadians Wary of Native Autonomy" *Calgary Herald* (1 June 1995) A7.

Philip Authier, "Quebec Lawyers Slam Native Self-government: It Poses 'Unprecedented Threat to Province's Powers,' Legal Paper Says" *The [Montreal] Gazette* (22 July 1992) B1.

Nahlah Ayed, "Self-government a Mess, Native Coalition Testifies" *Toronto Star* (3 March 1999) A6.

"Band Councils Must Be Accountable" [editorial] *The [Brantford] Expositor* (24 March 1999) A6.

Jim Bronskill, "Liberals Wavered on Promise: Native Self-government Memorandum" *Calgary Herald* (6 May 1996) A8.

Ted Byfield, "Native Self-government Goes Beyond What Canadians Think" *Financial Post* (21-23 March 1992) S3.

Karina Byrne, "Indian Women Want Protection" *Winnipeg Free Press* (27 March 1994) A3.

Milo Cernetig, "Reform Attacks Native Self-rule" *[Toronto] Globe & Mail* (5 October 1992) A1.

Sandro Contenta, "Native Deal Stirs Deep Fears in Quebec" *Toronto Star* (19 July 1992) A10.

Barry Cooper & David Bercuson, "An Abdication of Responsibility: Ottawa Must See Through the Job of Transferring Lands to Natives" *The [London] Free Press* (23 January 1999) F6.

Bob Cox, "Self-rule Scenario Packs Potential for Future Conflict, Author Says" *Vancouver Sun* (29 September 1992) A8.

Susan Delacourt, "Natives Divided Over Charter" *[Toronto] Globe & Mail* (14 March 1992) A4.

Susan Delacourt, "Native Self-government Difficult Sell, Clark Says" *[Toronto] Globe & Mail* (2 June 1992) A1.

Wendy Dudley, "MP Sees Pitfalls in Self-rule" *Calgary Herald* (12 September 1994) B1.

Andrew Duffy, "First Nation Women Want Ombudsman to Fight Corruption" *Sault Star* (3 March 1999) B9.

Peter Ferris, "Native Self-government: Change That Can Help Everyone" *Winnipeg Free Press* (31 May 1992) A7.

Gerald Flood, "Native Woman, Elder Fear Self-government" *Winnipeg Free Press* (8 October 1992) B5.

Gordon Gibson, "It's a Matter of Principles" *National Post* (30 October 1999) B7.

Gordon Gibson, "Let's Not Use Racism to Tackle Native Needs: Isolating Aboriginal People from the Mainstream Is a Mistake" *[Toronto] Globe & Mail* (1 June 1992) A15.

Gordon Gibson, "Where the Aboriginal Report Takes a Wrong Turn" *[Toronto] Globe & Mail* (26 November 1996) A19.

"Go Slowly on Self-government: Canadians Deserve More Than Vague Concepts" [editorial] *The [Montreal] Gazette* (24 January 1994) B2.

Heidi Graham, "Natives 'Rebels' Meet in Bid to 'Get Self-government Stalled' " *Winnipeg Free Press* (29 March 1992) B14.

Stephen Hume, "Time to Pop the Self-government Bogeyman Bubble" *Vancouver Sun* (7 October 1992) A15.

"Inherent But Unclear" [editorial] *Winnipeg Free Press* (11 April 1992) A6.

William Johnson, "Mercredi Has No Mandate, But That Doesn't Stop Him" *The [Montreal] Gazette* (26 June 1992) B3.

William Johnson, "Modern Myths: Elements of Self-government Haven't Been Perpetuated" *The [Montreal] Gazette* (7 July 1992) B3.

William Johnson, "Native Self-government: Let's Pay Attention" *The [Montreal] Gazette* (12 May 1992) B3.

William Johnson, "Not All Are Leaping on Native Self-government Bandwagon" *The [Montreal] Gazette* (5 May 1992) B3.

William Johnson, "What Would Indian Self-government Look Like? Big, Very Big" *The [Montreal] Gazette* (20 May 1992) B3.

William Johnson, "Why Native Leaders Don't Want Charter of Rights in Their Government" *The [Montreal] Gazette* (10 October 1992) B5.

Rick Mofina, "Allegations of Native Fraud Soaring" *Vancouver Sun* (19 November 1999) A6.

Rick Mofina, "Police Were Braced for Violence After Native Fishing Ruling, Report Says" *National Post* (21 February 2000) A10.

Miles Morrisseau, "Will Self-government Set Natives Against Each Other?" *The [Montreal] Gazette* (18 August 1992) B3.

Patrick Nagle, "Male Domination Heightens Fear of Self-rule" *Calgary Herald* (1 April 1992) B8.

"Native Fights for Charter" *Calgary Herald* (23 April 1992) A12.

"Native Group Fears Dictatorial Ways" *Calgary Herald* (21 February 1992) A9.

"Native Women Fear Autonomy Will Hide Sex Abuse" *Calgary Herald* (29 July 1992) A9.

"Native Women Urged to Ignore 'White Feminists'" *Calgary Herald* (31 July 1992) A10.

Tom Oleson, "Native Self-rule: Is It a Dead End? Know Sovereignty Before Building It" *Winnipeg Free Press* (14 July 1996) B2.

Peter O'Neil, "B.C. Tories Voice Fears Over Native Government" *Vancouver Sun* (4 June 1992) A4.

Peter O'Neil, "Native Women Push for Human Rights" *Vancouver Sun* (14 March 1992) A3.

Peter O'Neil, "Self-rule for Natives Arouses Hopes, Doubts" *Vancouver Sun* (7 October 1992) A4.

Rudy Platiel, "Native Councils Facing Challenges from Within" *[Toronto] Globe & Mail* (15 May 1996) A8.

"Reformer Inflaming Issues, Says Minister" *Calgary Herald* (8 February 1994) A9.

Patricia Robertson, "Native Women Demand Role" *Winnipeg Free Press* (18 May 1996) A11.

Michele Rouleau, "Proposal for Native Self-government Could Deny Fundamental Human Rights to Women" *The [Montreal] Gazette* (23 October 1992) B3.

Bryan Schwartz, "Bryan Schwartz Takes a Close Look at Aboriginal Self-government" *[Toronto] Globe & Mail* (4 August 1992) A12.

Sarah Scott, "The Native Rights Stuff: Many Women Fear Self-government Without Charter Guarantees" *The [Montreal] Gazette* (28 March 1992) B5.

"Self-government and the Charter" [editorial] *[Toronto] Globe & Mail* (15 October 1992) A30.

Robert Sheppard, "Maybe It's Racist, But It's a Good Thing" *[Toronto] Globe & Mail* (2 June 1992) A17.

Jeffrey Simpson, "The Cost of Expectations" *[Toronto] Globe & Mail* (29 October 1999) A19.

Jeffrey Simpson, "The Grand Talk of Constitutional Reform for Aboriginals Is a Mirage" *[Toronto] Globe & Mail* (15 August 1995) A16.

Jeffrey Simpson, "Just What Is a 'Nation' and How Can It Work Like a Province?" *[Toronto] Globe & Mail* (27 February 1997) A18.

Jeffrey Simpson, "The Words Are Magnificent, But Can They Be Realistically Implemented" *[Toronto] Globe & Mail* (28 February 1997) A18 (review of RCAP Final Report).

Ruth Teichroeb, "Democracy on the Reserve: Family Pays Heavy Price for Reporting Sex Abuse" *Winnipeg Free Press* (8 April 1992) B18.

Ruth Teichroeb, "Democracy on the Reserve: Limits Sought on Powers of Chiefs" *Winnipeg Free Press* (6 April 1992) B13.

Ruth Teichroeb, "Democracy on the Reserve: Mother Who Reported Abuse Ostracized" *Winnipeg Free Press* (8 April 1992) B18.

Ruth Teichroeb, "Democracy on the Reserve: Professor Says Indian Women Have Reason to Fear Autonomy" *Winnipeg Free Press* (8 April 1992) B18.

Ruth Teichroeb, "Democracy on the Reserve: Reserve Proves Model of Democracy" *Winnipeg Free Press* (10 April 1992) B21.

Ruth Teichroeb, "Democracy on the Reserve: Solidarity Vital, Province's Native Leaders Say" *Winnipeg Free Press* (10 April 1992) B1.

Ruth Teichroeb, "Native Self-rule: Is It a Dead End? Victims Are Trying to Reclaim Control" *Winnipeg Free Press* (14 July 1996) B2.

Iris Yudal, "Chiefs Abuse Power, Funds, Group Charges" *Winnipeg Free Press* (21 February 1992) B23.

The Spirit of *Delgamuukw* and Aboriginal Oral Traditions in Ontario

DAVID T. MCNAB

The Elders have said that things are now not at all what they appear to be; it is also said that things always happen for a reason. More than anything else these notions best characterize the spirit of *Delgamuukw* in Ontario.[1] This paper is a pre-colonial approach to understanding the spirit of *Delgamuukw* in Ontario.

Land Claims are political creatures. *Delgamuukw* has had an impact on my life. Late in 1987, the head of the Ontario Native Affairs Directorate, a lawyer and a former high-ranking public servant in British Columbia, tried to get me to act as an expert witness for the British Columbia provincial government in the *Delgamuukw* case.[2] He even offered me release time from the Directorate to do the job. When that failed, he got the Deputy British Columbia Attorney General to call me. He called; I said no thank-you. I refused. He was upset, having apparently already been told that I would say yes to his request.

But, if nothing else, the head of the Directorate was persistent. When that did not succeed, early in 1988 he asked one of the lawyers who was acting for the province to call me privately and confidentially.

Notes will be found on pages 278–283.

He told me that I would be useful in this case because of what I had written in my doctoral dissertation about the Fort Victoria treaties, negotiated by Governor James Douglas in the early 1850s, as well as my description of British Imperial Aboriginal policy. I was perplexed by his reasoning but figured simply that he had not read my dissertation. Either he was getting bad advice or he was simply desperate. Be that as it may, I resisted and said no. Our head was infuriated. I was not following orders like a good bureaucrat. And he had lost all credibility with me.[3] From then on, we were on a collision course on many land and treaty rights issues—which led to my leaving the provincial government late in 1991, after the Temagami blockades of 1988-1989 and the events of the summer of 1990 at Oka and elsewhere.

The concept of circles of time is a representation of Aboriginal history that is not bounded by time or by place. This notion of history has been an "obsession" of the Mayans. Miguel Leon-Portilla, in his *Time and Reality in the Thought of the Maya*, has provided a thoughtful analysis of the significance and meaning of circles of time. Time is represented symbolically and ontologically by the concept of kinh, which means the Sun. Its "travel creates the day." In this sense, the concept of day "is simply a presence or cycle of the sun."[4] Known among the Maya, it also applies to all Aboriginal people, including the First Nations of Ontario.[5] It is most often seen in their drawings and in their images from their oral traditions, rather than being stated explicitly in their written works.[6]

This idea of circles of time is common to all indigenous peoples including the Anishnabe.[7] In the mid-nineteenth century, in his writings, *Kahgegagahbowh*, George Copway described the concept succinctly: "The Ojibwas, as well as many others, acknowledged that there was but one Great Spirit, who made the world; they gave him the name of good or benevolent; *kesha* is benevolent, *monedoo* is spirit; Ke-sha-mon-e-doo. They supposed he lived in the heavens; but the most of the time he was in the *Sun*. They said it was from him they received all that was good through life and that he seldom needs the offering of his Red children, for he was seldom angry."[8] The Sun, the sustainer of life, is also a metaphor of time.[9]

Too often in the past, the continuing power and presence of Aboriginal oral traditions, like Aboriginal spirituality, have been either overlooked, ignored or dismissed as inconsequential. As a result, this history has been written and viewed only through the lens of written history based on documents left by Euro-Canadian visitors about what they believed they saw for a fleeting moment in time within the context of European imperial history. This approach frequently has left a highly distorted portrayal of Aboriginal people. It is epitomized by pen and ink, as the Elders of the Walpole Island First Nation have reminded us: "When we were created we were made without those advantages; we have no pen or ink to write, we have nothing but a little piece of flesh called a heart, to remember by ..." [10] This metaphor of the heart binds together Aboriginal people and their languages and their cultures. It is altogether different than just history with the written documents left out. Aboriginal cultures are knowledge-based in terms of both land and water.[11] First Nations' oral traditions are a powerful cultural force and part of their toolbox of survival. Aboriginal people have a holistic view of history within which they see circles of time, which are ever expanding and infinite. This is their way of knowing and comprehending their spiritual place in the world of the Creator.[12] In the oral traditions, the landscape, or Mother Earth, is seen as inseparable from their memory of that landscape. It is important to see the inside of events, through the eyes of the sacredness of Mother Earth. Put another way, Aboriginal oral traditions see the history of mankind as one with and inseparable from nature.[13]

Without "pen or ink," First Nations remember and understand, through their stories, their internal and external landscapes of being and becoming. There are no boundaries and no beginning or end points. In short, there is no periodization of history. Their history is both separate and parallel to the history of Canada, as understood by non-Aboriginal people—the history of the newcomers. In this way, Aboriginal oral traditions also evoke and speak to the European past and have much to offer. They provide a necessary corrective, a balance, as well as a deeper understanding of what we know today as Canada.

For Aboriginal people, circles of time are part of the natural world and nature, of life and living. Every living thing has a relationship to every other, and the events that occur in one's lifetime have an immediate impact on one's children and grandchildren. The seventh generation is immediate and close. We are then within circles of time.[14] Aboriginal people have protected and conserved their Homelands—their Territories—since time immemorial. This is understood, and told, from the perspective of the First Nations, by their Elders. They tell who they are and, in spiritual terms, what their lands and waters mean to them. They have used the land and have shared in the harvesting of the uses of the land for thousands of years.[15]

The primary objective of Aboriginal people is spiritual—to protect the land, Mother Earth, and the waters of Turtle Island. This is a sacred trust, a trust to protect the land. The continuity and integrity of their lands are important to their survival as an indigenous people. Generations of First Nation members have used the land and have shared in its bounty and its uses. Moreover, they will continue to use this land

and teach their children about the Creator and the Land.[16] So this relationship is all-important. They owe their very survival to it. It is both simple and profound.

The events of the summer of 1990 at Oka and elsewhere across Canada, and since then, occurred in our time at the initiative of Aboriginal people to protect their lands and waters. To do this, they had no choice but to resist those who wished to destroy the land and themselves. Not to do this meant their own destruction, as well as the destruction of their children and grandchildren. It would have meant the end of their cultures and survival as Aboriginal people. They will continue to protect their lands and waters.

The twentieth century has drawn to a close. We are witnessing profound structural changes in the history of the world. The world of nineteenth-century European imperialism is over. Decolonization is continuing apace. This process has been characterized both by forces of construction and destruction. In Canada, to provide but one example, Aboriginal peoples are again reaffirming their inherent right to governance through diverse approaches and a variety of means. Their lands are ever so slowly being recovered, if not always respected. Aboriginal title is beginning to be understood and recognized. Treaties must be honoured and respected. For example, the *St. Anne Island* treaty of 1796, which involves free trade, sovereignty and border-crossing rights, must be honoured, rather than denied as it has been by the federal government to this day.[17]

One watershed in the twentieth century was the *Calder* case of 1973. This was a Supreme Court of Canada decision that found that Aboriginal title and rights did exist in the white justice system of Canada. It opened the legal doors for the prosecution of Aboriginal title and rights cases in Canada. *Calder* was followed by many constructive Supreme Court of Canada decisions that reaffirmed Aboriginal title and land rights and Treaties, including *Guerin*, *Simon*, *Sioui* and *Sparrow*, and most recently, *Delgamuukw*, to name but a few. The latter is also a spiritual watershed.[18]

On December 11, 1997, thirteen years to the day that Justice Donald Steele brought down his decision on Temagami, the Supreme Court of Canada dramatically rendered its judgment in the *Delgamuukw v. British Columbia* case, also identified as the Gitksan and Wet'suwet'en comprehensive claim.[19] It ordered a new trial based on the palpable errors of the trial judge. Prominent among these errors was the latter's discounting in its entirety the oral history and traditions of the Gitksan and Wet'suwet'en peoples.[20] Not to recognize this history is to deny Aboriginal people and their land rights, and to make a palpable error of legal judgment. This error was made both in the original trial of *Delgamuukw* and also by Justice Steele, the trial judge in the *Temagami* ruling in 1984.

Delgamuukw, like Temagami, is a case that rests largely on Aboriginal oral history and traditions. Relying in part on the findings in the Report of the Royal Commission on Aboriginal Peoples (1996),[21] the Supreme Court of Canada in *Delgamuukw* ruling stated that oral traditions are "not simply a detached recounting of factual events but, rather, are 'facts enmeshed in the stories of a lifetime.'" Moreover, they are "rooted in particular locations, making reference to particular families and communities." As a result, Aboriginal oral history is in fact "many histories, each characterized in part by how a people see themselves, how they define their identity in relation to their environment, and how they express their uniqueness as a people."

The Supreme Court stated that the "laws of evidence" in the Canadian justice system must accommodate Aboriginal oral history and traditions such that it "be placed on an equal footing with the types of historical evidence that courts are familiar with, which largely consists of historical documents. This is a long-standing practice in the interpretation of treaties between the Crown and Aboriginal peoples."[22] Not to recognize this history is to deny Aboriginal people and their land rights, and to make a palpable error of legal judgment. It is also dishonest and blatant racism. This error was made both in the original trial of *Delgamuukw* and also by Justice Steele in the *Temagami* ruling in 1984.[23]

If one accepts the oral history and traditions of the Temagami First Nation that it never participated in any Treaty at any time (and the historical evidence now points strongly in this direction), then it is likely that the Supreme Court would have found in favour of the Temagami First Nation, had the case been heard in 1997 rather than in 1991. Coupled with the fiduciary obligations of the Crown, the issue of whether the Teme-Augama Anishnabai (TAA) ever entered into a "passive adhesion" to the *Robinson Huron* treaty of 1850 would have been rendered a moot point.

In retrospect, the Temagami First Nation was too far ahead of the Canadian justice system. Steele discounted the Temagami oral history and traditions, as did the trial judge in *Delgamuukw*. Where is the fairness and justice in all of this? Who is indeed on trial? If one accepts the Supreme Court's premise that "we are all here to stay,"[24] then it is absolutely necessary for the courts to order a new trial for the Temagami First Nation on their Aboriginal title and land rights. Echoing the Covenant Chain of Silver, we are joined together. Circles of time ...

Notes

1 An earlier version of this paper has been published as part of the "Introduction" to McNab, *Circles of Time: Aboriginal Land Rights and Resistance*, Wilfrid Laurier University Press, 1999. See also my " 'What Liars those People Are': The St. Anne Island Speech of the Walpole Island First Nation given at the Chenail Ecarte River on August 3, 1815," *Social Sciences and Humanities Aboriginal Research Exchange*, 1, 1, Fall-Winter, 1993,10,12-13,15; "A Few Thoughts on Understanding Propaganda after Oka," Social Sciences and Humanities Aboriginal Research Exchange, 1, 1, Fall-Winter, 1993,18-21; "Treaties and an Official Use of History," *The Canadian Journal of Native Studies*, XIII, 1, 1993,139-43; Edited and an "Introduction," (with S. Dale Standen), *Gin Das Winan Documenting Aboriginal History in Ontario*, Occasional Papers of The Champlain Society, 2, Toronto: The Champlain Society, 1996, 66 pps; " 'The Promise That He Gave To My Grand Father was Very Sweet': The Gun Shot Treaty of 1792 at the Bay of Quinte," Research Note, *The Canadian Journal of Native Studies*, 16, 2, 1996,293-314; "Who is on trial? Teme-Augama Anishnabai Land Rights and George Ironside, Junior: Reconsidering Oral Tradition," Research Note, *The Canadian Journal of Native Studies*, 18,1,1998,117-34.

2 The trial judge's ruling in this case can be found in the *Canadian Native Law Reporter*, Special Edition, 1991, 5 C.N.L.R.,v-381. The trial began in Smithers, British Columbia on May 11, 1987 and after 318 days of evidence, ended on June 30, 1990.

3 For a description of the trial in this case see Arthur J. Ray, "Creating the Image of the Savage in Defence of the Crown: The Ethnohistorian in Court," *Native Studies Review*, Special Issue on "Advocacy and Claims Research: Edited by Frank Tough and Arthur J. Ray, Volume 6, Number 2, 1990,13-29.

4 Miguel Leon-Portilla, *Time and Reality in the Thought of the Maya*, Second Edition, Enlarged, Norman: Oklahoma University Press, 1988, (1968), pps. xvii-xxii; 18-19.

5 See, for example, Olive Patricia Dickason, *Canada's First Nations, A History of Founding Peoples from Earliest Times*, Second Edition, Toronto: Oxford University Press, 1997, pps. 2-3. More often than not, the concept is not explained by Aboriginal people since it is an assumption of their Weltanschauung and the bases of it are oral and not written. See also *Report of the Royal Commission on Aboriginal Peoples*, Ottawa: The Commission, 1996, "People to People, Nation to Nation," Highlights from the *Royal Commission on Aboriginal Peoples*; Volume 1, "Looking Forward, Looking Back."

6 See, for example, N. Scott Momaday, *In the Presence of the Sun, Stories and Poems, 1961-1991*, New York: St. Martin's Press, 1992, pps. xvii-xx, 73-107.

The sun is both metaphor and myth, embodying the supernatural as well as the natural worlds. Leon-Portilla has explained that the "sun does not rest, however. When it is apparently "devoured" in chi-kin, its setting, it goes into the lower world, crosses it, and triumphantly is reborn." Time has no beginning and no end; it is not linear. The sun's "cycles only seem to terminate." But in reality they do not. Leon-Portilla has written that the "Maya priests computed 'scores of suns' dating back hundreds of millions of years and, at the same time, forecast future cycles. If in their thought the day was a solar presence, time was the limitless succession of all solar cycles." By definition then *"kinh* spontaneously acquired its most ample meaning: duration that cannot be expressed because it has no limits, time, the sum of all possible solar cycles." To put it even more succinctly, *"kinh* gives life, destroys and recreates without end the reality in which men [meaning mankind] move and think."

Without "kinh," there is no history. With "kinh" the concept of history can be viewed as "circles of time." Moreover, as Leon-Portilla has argued through the "action of *kinh* all becomes present in time. Its burdens colour the four segments of the world. The countenances of the god-periods are successively oriented toward the great quadrants, determining the destiny and life of humanity and all existing things. Space, and that contained therein, acquire their true meaning due to the cycles of *kinh*. Furthermore from this perspective, "space and time are inseparable." This concept was all encompassing; it produced the Mayan "chronovision, the conception of a universe in which space, living things and mankind derive their reality from the ever-changing atmosphere of **kinh**." It also has informed their history as an active entity.

This idea of circles of time is common to all indigenous peoples including the Aboriginal Nations that are the focus of this work, the Ottawa or Odawa, the Ojibwa or Chippewa and the Potawatomi. In the mid-nineteenth century, in his writings, Kahgegagahbowh, George Copway described the concept succinctly: "The Ojibwas, as well as many others, acknowledged that there was but one Great Spirit, who made the world; they gave him the name of good or benevolent; *kesha* is benevolent, *monedoo* is spirit; Ke-sha-mon-e-doo. They supposed he lived in the heavens; but the most of the time he was in the *Sun*. They said it was from him they received all that was good through life. And that he seldom needs the offering of his Red children, for he was seldom angry." The Sun, the sustainer of life, is also a metaphor of time.

Historical events, as R.G. Collingwood observed, have an "inside" and an "outside." The outside of an event appears to be bounded by both time and place. However, the inside of an event is circular and is not a prisoner of time. At the same time the sense and character of place becomes extremely significant. Place is nature and the natural world. This world is animate, not dead. It has a life of its own and within nature is time and all living things including mankind. This concept of history is alien to European-trained historians and is not very well understood.

7 This idea of history as a circle of time can be seen in the star maps of the Cree and the legends or myths of the Algonquian peoples. What connects them is that they are all dreams of "Kinh" within a circle of time. See, for an Ojibwa perspective, Basil Johnston, *The Manitous, The Spiritual World of the Ojibway*, Toronto: Key Porter Books, 1995 and the reference below.

8 A. LaVonne Brown Ruoff and Donald B. Smith (editors), *Life, Letters & Speeches, George Copway (Kahgegagahbowh)*, Lincoln: University of Nebraska Press, 1997 (1850), page 81.

9 Too often in the past the continuing power and presence of the Aboriginal oral traditions, like Aboriginal spirituality, have been either overlooked, ignored or dismissed as inconsequential. As a result this history has been written and viewed only through the lens of written history based on documents left by European visitors about what they believed they saw for a fleeting moment in time within the context of European imperial history. This approach frequently has left a highly distorted portrayal of Aboriginal people. It is epitomized by "pen or ink."

For Aboriginal people circles of time are part of the natural world and nature, of life and living. Every living thing has a relationship to every other and the events that occur in one's lifetime have an immediate impact on one's children and grandchildren. The seventh generation is immediate and close. We are then within circles of time.

For a recent Cree view see Andrew Bainbridge, "The Rise of the Loving Son [Sun]," in *Co-existence? Studies in Ontario-First Nation Relations*, Frost Centre for Canadian Heritage and Development Studies, Trent University, 1992, pps. 6-10. Historical events, as R.G. Collingwood observed, have an "inside" and an "outside." The outside of an event appears to be bounded by both time and place. However, the inside of an event is circular and is not a prisoner of time. At the same time the sense and character of place becomes extremely significant. Place is nature and the natural world. This world is animate, not dead. It has a life of its own and within nature is time and all living things including mankind. This concept of history is alien to European-trained historians and is not very well understood.

10 Dean Jacobs, " 'We have but our hearts and the traditions of our old men': Understanding the Traditions and History of Bkejwanong," in David McNab and S. Dale Standen, Editors, with an "Introduction," *Gin Das Winan Documenting Aboriginal History in Ontario*, Occasional Papers of The Champlain Society, Number 2, Toronto: The Champlain Society, 1996, pps. 1-13.

11 For a different view from the perspective of the law see Paul Williams, "Oral Traditions on Trial" in David McNab and S. Dale Standen, Editors, with an "Introduction," *Gin Das Winan Documenting Aboriginal History in Ontario*, Occasional Papers of The Champlain Society, Number 2, Toronto: The Champlain Society, 1996, pps. 29-34.

12 Johnston, *The Manitous*.

13 These concepts are gradually having an influence on the way in which Europeans and non-Aboriginal people are now viewing their environment. The historian, Simon Schama, in his environmental approach to the history of landscape and memory in Europe and North America, has remarked on this relationship and its meaning for European-trained historians. He has argued that "the richness, antiquity, and the complexity of our [European and North American] landscape tradition" is a significant one. The environment is important to all of us "to show just how much we stand to lose" if we are not vigilant. Schama has pointed out that "instead of assuming the

mutually exclusive character of Western culture and nature, I want to suggest the strength of the links that have bound them together." This inseparability of culture and nature is one of the beginning points for understanding Aboriginal oral traditions.

14 Alexander Morris, *The Treaties of Canada with the Indians of Manitoba and the North-West Territories*, Toronto: Belfords, Clarke & Co. (Reprinted by Coles as a Coles Canadiana Reprint Series, 1971), 1880.

Mawedopenais, a Mide Chief of the Ojibwa, spoke to the Crown's commissioner and chief negotiator, Alexander Morris (1826-1889), at the Treaty #3 negotiations. As a spokesperson for the Rainy Lake and Rainy River people in this Treaty-making process, he was clear on the position of Aboriginal Nations and the title to their lands. He drew on the metaphor of the sun-of circles of time: "I lay before you our opinions. Our hands are poor but our heads are rich, and it is riches that we ask so that we may be able to support our families as long as the sun rises and the water runs."

Morris replied, disingenuously, indicating that he did not understand what Aboriginal title and the Treaty-making process meant for the Aboriginal Nations: "I am very sorry; you know it takes two to make a bargain; you are agreed on the one side, and I for the Queen's Government on the other. I have to go away and report that I have to go without making terms with you. I doubt if the Commissioners will be sent again to assemble this nation." This threat, implying the government approach of "divide and conquer" was not, as may be expected, well received by the Ojibwa Nation.

Treaty #3 was eventually negotiated and signed, but not on the basis of the Treaty document or as understood by Alexander Morris. He did not believe, as many people do to this day, that the Aboriginal Nations have been ready to share in the Treaty-making process with the riches in their heads. There was no balance in the "bargain" before or after the Treaty was signed. Morris and the federal government took too much away from the life of the Ojibwa. It has continued to do so here and elsewhere in Canada. From this unequal perspective, the negotiations were not successful. It was not the only Treaty that could be characterized in this fashion. Yet the Treaty issues do not die. They live within a circle of time for later generations. Aboriginal people never forget.

One hundred years later there is still a wide cultural gulf in the Treaty-making process which has intensified and has led to the abrogation of Aboriginal title and treaty rights and to the events of the summer of 1990. But the events at Oka were broader than the events at Kanesatake and Kahnawake. Similar situations also occurred in Ontario and in British Columbia.

The European, so-called scientific western tradition of history has seen, sometimes in its crudest forms, the relationship between people and the land and its uses as a separate category and process. From Aboriginal traditions these categories are wholly artificial and do not really exist. These have a holistic view and see land and man and nature and the uses that one makes of the lands and waters as one within a circle of time. They come from a single source-from the Creator who made all living things and nature. It is not enough to analyze each separately. The sum of the parts does not in this instance comprise the whole. This approach is simple, yet profound, for the way in which one sees the world.

European-university trained historians also tell stories. But they most often use written records produced by European and North American observers. Sometimes they pretend to speak of "scientific objectivity." These historians create and re-create the past, thereby trying to render what is seemingly incomprehensible, into a form of understanding about the context of their perspectives on time and place. Aboriginal traditions include knowledge about the relationship between people and the natural and the supernatural worlds. It is curiosity and the desire to know about oneself and the world in which one lives. It can through imagination become a vision of the present, embedded in the past and ever-becoming the future.

15 For an example see Dean Jacobs, " 'We have but our hearts and the traditions of our old men': Understanding the Traditions and History of Bkejwanong," in David McNab and S. Dale Standen, Editors, with an "Introduction," *Gin Das Winan Documenting Aboriginal History in Ontario*, Occasional Papers of The Champlain Society, Number 2, Toronto: The Champlain Society, 1996, pps. 1-13.

16 See Mary Laronde, "Co-management of Lands and Resources in N'Daki Menan," in *Rebirth, Political, Economic and Social Development in First Nations*, edited by Anne-Marie Mawhiney, Toronto: Dundurn Press, 1992, pps. 93-106.

17 McNab, *Circles of Time: Aboriginal Land Rights and Resistance*, Wilfrid Laurier University Press, 1999;"A Few Thoughts on Understanding Propaganda after Oka," *Social Sciences and Humanities Aboriginal Research Exchange*, 1, 1, Fall-Winter, 1993,18-21; "Treaties and an Official Use of History," *The Canadian Journal of Native Studies*, XIII, 1, 1993,139-43; " 'Water is Her Lifeblood': The Waters of Bkejwanong and the Treaty-Making Process," in *Earth, Water, Air and Fire: Studies in Canadian Ethnohistory*, Wilfrid Laurier University Press, 1998, pps. 35-63.

18 McNab, "A Few Thoughts on Understanding Propaganda after Oka," in *Social Sciences and Humanities Aboriginal Research Exchange*, Volume 1, No. 1, Fall-Winter, 1993, pps. 18-21.

At the same time fifteen years of Constitution-making have collapsed into disunity, separatism and regional antagonisms for the white visitors to Canada. The former Meech Lake Accord, the epitome of the old British Imperial centralist model of Confederation, stylishly referred to as "executive federalism," was defeated in the failure of the Meech Lake Accord in 1990. This was a clear Constitutional victory by Aboriginal people. They are in the Canadian Constitution. Although the Charlottetown Accord of 1992 was also a failure, the inherent right of Aboriginal people to Aboriginal governance, as well as their Aboriginal title and land rights, has since been reaffirmed.

Gradually, Canada is becoming similar in structure to what it was in pre-Confederation days. At that time British North America was a series of communities located along the Great Lakes and adjacent waterway systems. It comprised Euro-American and Aboriginal communities in an alliance of Nations within both Aboriginal and British Imperial confederacies.

It was a true meeting ground of diverse languages, cultures and communities. This is an illustration of how the past is an integral part of the present. Aboriginal title, time and resistance movements may well be common themes in Canada's disparate histories of its founding nations.

The foundation exists now for a constructive approach to the making of Canada on a Treaty basis. The Constitution of Canada recognizes Aboriginal people as "Indian, Inuit and Metis." It also shows some grudging respect for "existing Aboriginal and treaty rights." Why then did we have Aboriginal people opposed to the Meech Lake Accord, contributing dramatically to its failure in June 1990? Why did we have, some few weeks later, the violence and the blockades at Kanesatake, Oka and at Kahnawake in Quebec; the blockades of roads and railway lines in Ontario and British Columbia?

The answer lies in our disparate histories and our diverse cultures and understandings of them. To put it simply, Aboriginal people and the rest of Canada speak to one another from differing historical and cultural assumptions and experiences. These include languages, customs, governance, lands and waters as well as time and progress. This also helps to explain the repeated failures of Canada's Aboriginal policy or policies.

19 *Delgamuukw v. British Columbia*, File No. 23799, Heard June 16, 17, 1997 and the Judgment was rendered on December 11, 1997, pps. 31-32.

20 *Ibid., Delgamuukw v. British Columbia*, pps. 31-32.

21 See *Report of the Royal Commission on Aboriginal Peoples*, Ottawa: The Commission, 1996, Volume 1, "Looking Forward, Looking Back," page 33.

22 *Ibid., Delgamuukw v. British Columbia*, pps. 31-32.

23 Denial of the very existence of Aboriginal people is a form of racism. The relationship between the Teme-Augama Anishnabai (TAA), and the province has been characterized by a stubborn rejection of the TAA and their ancestral motherland, N'Daki Menan. After one hundred and fifty years, Ontario has refused to acknowledge their Aboriginal title and rights to their Territory. Negotiations had brought them the Bear Island Reserve, less than one square mile which they had to purchase using their own monies or face eviction by Ontario as squatters on their own lands. Land Cautions (1973) were placed on 4,000 square miles of N'Daki Menan. Such a legal Caution prevents first registration of titles by the Crown and thereby effectively puts a cloud on the title of the lands preventing or inhibiting economic development such as mining and land sales. This was followed by more than a decade of litigation from 1978 to 1990.

The legal case finally ended in seeming defeat in the white man's court of justice. Development was stopped by the "frozen cautions." The status quo ante bellum was maintained until the Cautions were lifted by a court action initiated by the NDP government of Bob Rae in 1993 and then finished off by the Harris government early in 1996. In spite of this recent litigation, the TAA's Aboriginal title and land rights to N'Daki Menan has never been resolved and the situation is much where it was in 1973 when the Cautions were placed on the land. Litigation in the white man's court does not always work.

24 *Ibid., Delgamuukw v. British Columbia*, at 273.

5   Impact in Québec

An Invaluable Lever for Québec's Aboriginal Communities

Claude Bachand

Introduction

My presentation is divided into two parts. The first is a brief statement about the principles of the *Delgamuukw* judgment. In the second part, I will offer some general comments on the practical implications of the December 1997 judgment for Québec's Aboriginal communities. I will also discuss three specific cases in which the logic set out in *Delgamuukw* has been applied, still applies, or should apply.

The *Delgamuukw* Decision

The *Delgamuukw* decision fundamentally offers a description of Aboriginal title in Canada and explains how that title may be established. It also sets out the specific criteria whereby it may be determined whether Aboriginal title has been infringed, as well as the rules that should be followed in such cases. *Delgamuukw* constitutes a precedent in this regard.

Although it mentions the existence of Aboriginal title, the case law never previously stated the exact content and complete scope of that title.[1] In 1973, *Calder v. Attorney General of British Columbia* recognized the

---

Notes will be found on page 292.

existence of Aboriginal title, but specifically stated that it was a right rooted in Aboriginal peoples' historic occupation, possession and use of traditional territories. In short, this right does not derive from the Royal Proclamation of 1763, treaties, or from the law, but from the historical occupation of the lands themselves. In 1984, the *Guérin* decision confirmed that Aboriginal title was inalienable. Four years later, *Canadian Pacific Ltd. v. Paul* stipulated that Aboriginal title was *sui generis* and different from other common Aboriginal rights: hunting, fishing, trapping and other rights.[2] In the meantime, s. 35 of the *Constitution Act, 1982* also constitutionalized and protected the treaty and other traditional rights of Aboriginal peoples.[3]

In 1997, *Delgamuukw* restated this case law, then vastly increased our knowledge of Aboriginal title. The judgment essentially states that an Aboriginal band holding such title may exclusively occupy and use, for varied purposes, the land for which it was recognized as having Aboriginal title.[4] Unless the lands affected by the title are surrendered to the Crown, Aboriginal title is inalienable.[5] In addition, title is collective in that it benefits the entire Aboriginal community affected. To put it plainly, this isn't merely a matter of hunting or fishing rights; we're talking about the right of the First Nations to occupy their lands and their ability to decide and to regulate the activities, including economic activities, that are carried out on those same lands.

The First Nations that hold Aboriginal title are not required to limit themselves to traditional activities on their lands, although they must ensure that the utilization of resources on those lands does not jeopardize the intimate relationship that links them to the lands or the nature of their historical occupation.[6] For example, if a band has fished on land since time immemorial, it would not be appropriate for that community to start up activities that might endanger marine wildlife.

To hold Aboriginal title, an Aboriginal group must prove three things: that it occupied the land in question before the assertion of British sovereignty; that this occupation was physical and continuous until the present; and that it .was, in general, the only group to have prerogatives and control over the land in question.[7]

However, Aboriginal title does not offer absolute protection for the First Nations that hold it or might hold it.[8] Governments may infringe title if they pursue pressing, serious and real objectives that are useful to society as a whole. Hydroelectric, logging or mining operations are examples of these kinds of important objectives. The *Delgamuukw* decision provides that each situation or planned operation must be justified or reviewed separately.

We now come to one of the most significant and new points in the judgment for Aboriginals in Canada, and particularly in Québec. *Delga-*

muukw stipulates that, prior to the implementation of projects that may infringe Aboriginal title, governments must consult Aboriginal bands affected by the projects in question. In certain major cases, these projects may not be carried out without the consent of the First Nations who have Aboriginal title. In a general way, *Delgamuukw* provides that governments will have to pay Aboriginals compensation in regard with the economic aspect of the title, but does not state the specific criteria for determining the value of such compensation. It states that the extent of the compensation will be based in particular on the severity of the title infringement.[9]

Following this brief review of the principles involved in *Delgamuukw*, let us now look at some of the practical implications of this judgment in and around Québec.

Delgamuukw: Its Practical Implications in and around Québec

Shortly after the decision was published in December 1997, a number of observers expressed considerable fears as to its consequences. In British Columbia, where 51 Aboriginal bands are negotiating with governments, the situation seemed particularly explosive.

In Québec, unlike British Columbia, 90 percent of lands occupied by Aboriginals are governed by modern treaties: the James Bay Agreement (1975) and the Northeastern Québec Agreement (1978). These regions are precisely where the Cree, Naskapis and Inuit live. The remaining 5 per cent of lands are occupied by 30,000 inhabitants. I mention this because *Delgamuukw* essentially applies to non-treaty lands that have not been surrendered.

Instead of resulting in a slew of land claims, it appears that in Québec, *Delgamuukw* first of all conferred new power on various Aboriginal communities in their relations with the federal and provincial governments in the numerous negotiations under way. It seems relatively clear that the prescriptions of *Delgamuukw* in regard to the obligation to consult Aboriginal nations and pay them appropriate compensation where their title has been infringed has been particularly helpful to them in strengthening their position in this relationship of power. As the constitutional law expert from the University of Toronto, Brian Slattery, said in December 1997, under this judgment, Aboriginals have become equals with their opposites at the various bargaining tables.[10]

In fact, even more than other important documents such as the report of the Royal Commission on Aboriginal Peoples and the United Nations recommendations, the *Delgamuukw* judgment has added serious legal weight to the traditional positions of Québec's Aboriginal communities on these specific points. While they can disregard a Royal

Commission's proposals, governments cannot afford to ignore the prescriptions of Supreme Court judgments without exposing themselves to legal action. *Delgamuukw* is thus an invaluable tool and lever in asserting Aboriginal political rights and Aboriginal title where circumstances require.

Nor should the public impact of a decision be neglected. Everyone in Aboriginal circles is familiar with the judgment and refers to it constantly. Once again, governments cannot shelve a judgment of this kind and hope it will be forgotten. They must comply with it and, moreover, are gradually altering their approaches to the Aboriginal communities on this subject, particularly in regard to their natural resource policies. If a planned project affects an Aboriginal title, governments must consult on and negotiate the activity and grant appropriate compensation.

I will now turn to three cases that concern Québec and neighbouring areas, cases in which *Delgamuukw* serves or may serve as a reference point in finding solutions to certain infringements of Aboriginal title, or to resolve land claims.

The first case is the mining project at Voisey's Bay in Labrador. A company wants to open a nickel, copper and cobalt mine at a location near Davis Inlet. These mining operations would undoubtedly have major consequences for the ecosystem of this region where Innu and Inuit live. In the report[11] published last spring on this mining project, the Canadian Environmental Assessment Agency, a federal government body, expressly analyzed the situation in relation to the guidelines set down in *Delgamuukw*. What were its conclusions? The Agency states in its report that, prior to authorizing any mining project, governments must first consult Aboriginals living in the region, involve them in the process of introducing this economic activity and compensate them in an appropriate manner. According to the Agency, governments cannot authorize the project, as they have previously done, and promise to negotiate with the First Nations at a later date. This is an actual case in which both the native communities and the government itself use Delgamuukw as a reference point.

Another example of the tangible influence of *Delgamuukw* is the hydroelectric project at Churchill Falls in Labrador, which would affect the Innu of both Labrador and Québec. The governments of Newfoundland and Québec are negotiating with the Innu to implement this new hydroelectric development project. Throughout the process, the Innu have publicly hammered home the principles of *Delgamuukw*: no hydroelectric development without consultation and the consent of the Innu community. The Innu further state that no new phase of operations can begin at Churchill Falls unless an agreement is reached on their territorial rights in the region. As may be seen from this brief overview, *Del-*

gamuukw has now strongly influenced the Aboriginal nations' argument in territorial negotiations and strengthened their positions relative to provincial governments.

A third interesting case in which the logic of *Delgamuukw* could apply is the situation of the islands claimed by the Cree and Inuit nations of Québec. These islands are located near the Québec coastline in the James Bay and Hudson Bay region. The islands and surrounding waters and seabed were until recently part of the Northwest Territories. With the creation of the territory of Nunavut on April 1, 1999, this region is now under the jurisdiction of the government of Iqaluit. The Cree and Inuit have historically occupied this area and these First Nations have a long tradition of hunting and trapping on the islands. The federal government has publicly acknowledged the problem since 1974. As a result of numerous disputes, progress on the issue has stopped and talks between the federal government and the Cree are at a standstill. In accordance with the explanations and criteria set out in *Delgamuukw*, it is highly likely that the Cree and Inuit hold Aboriginal title to the islands, waters and seabed. If this were the case, they could occupy and fully and freely use the land in question for their own purposes. The federal government would do well to reflect on this delicate situation which has already dragged on far too long.

To sum up, the *Delgamuukw* judgment is a legal decision of the highest importance. It explains, for the first time, the content of Aboriginal title, the criteria for establishing such title and the rules that must be followed when such title is threatened by third party activities. As we have seen in Québec, the judgment has conferred greater power on the Aboriginal communities in their dealings with the federal and provincial governments. They now carry invaluable legal weight to support their claims and demands and can press governments to consult and compensate them adequately where their Aboriginal title is infringed. In my opinion, the three cases I have cited show that the logic of *Delgamuukw* is now firmly rooted in the First Nations' arguments, that their constituent governments make express reference to it and that there is still considerable room for its practical application.

The legal consequences of this decision are numerous. It is fundamentally important that legislators understand these implications and attempt to address them adequately in their work in the House of Commons.

Notes

1 Mary C. Hurley, *Aboriginal Title: The Supreme Court of Canada Decision in Delgamuukw v. British Columbia*, Ottawa: Library of Parliament, 1998, p.1.
2 *Ibid.*, pp. 2-3.
3 Julien Bauer, *Le système politique canadien*. Paris: Presses universitaires de France, 1998, p. 80.
4 Hurley, *op. cit.*, pp. 9-10; Hugues Melançon, "Le titre aborigène en Cour suprême : la création d'un régime juridique dissuasif," *Recherches amérindiennes au Québec*, Vol. 28, No. 1, 1998, p. 123; André Émond, "L'affaire Delgamuukw ou la réactualisation du droit américain au regard des conditions d'existence et d'extinction du titre aborigène au Canada," *Les cahiers de Droit*, Vol. 39, No. 4, December 1998, p. 854; Andrew Purvis, "Our Home and Native Land," *Time*, December 22, 1997, pp. 18-19.
5 Cf. the statement by Phil Fontaine on this subject. Phil Fontaine, "Colonialist Approach to Aboriginal Issues," *Globe and Mail*, December 31, 1997, p. A23.
6 Hurley, *op. cit.*, p. 11.
7 Émond, *loc. cit.*, p. 855.
8 For a more thorough analysis, see Hugues Melançon, *loc. cit.*, pp. 123-24.
9 Hurley, *op. cit.*, pp. 17; Melançon, *loc. cit.*, p. 124.
10 Andrew Purvis. "Our Home and Native Land," *Time*, December 22, 1997, p. 19.
11 Government of Canada, Canadian Environmental Assessment Agency, *Report of the Environmental Assessment Panel—Voisey's Bay Project*, Ottawa, CEAA, 1999.

References

Case Law

Delgamuukw v. British Columbia, [1997] S.C.R.

Monographs and Articles

Bauer, Julien. *Le système politique canadien*. Paris: Presses universitaires de France, 1998, pp. 81-89.
Émond, André. "L'affaire Delgamuukw ou la réactualisation du droit américain au regard des conditions d'existence et d'extinction du titre aborigène au Canada," *Les cahiers de Droit*, Vol. 39, No. 4, December 1998, pp. 849-80.
Hurley, Mary C. *Aboriginal Title: The Decision by the Supreme Court of Canada in Delgamuukw v. British Columbia*, Ottawa: Library of Parliament, 1998, 19 pages.
Melançon, Hugues. "Le titre aborigène en Cour suprême : la création d'un régime juridique dissuasif," *Recherches amérindiennes au Québec*, Vol. XXVIII, No. 1, 1998, pp. 122-26.
Purvis, Andrew. "Our Home and Native Land." *Time*, December 22, 1997, pp. 18-19.

Smith, Melvin H. "The Delgamuukw Case: What Does it Mean and What Do We Do Now?" *Public Policy Sources*, No. 10, Fraser Institute, 1998, pp. 3-11.

Government Publications

Government of Canada, Canadian Environmental Assessment Agency. *Report of the Environmental Assessment Panel—Voisey's Bay Project*. Ottawa: CEAA, 1999.

Government of Québec, Secrétariat aux Affaires autochtones. *Partenariat, développement, actions*. Québec: Secrétariat aux Affaires autochtones, 1998, 41 pages.

Newspaper Articles

Delisle, Norman. "Les autochtones du Québec savourent le jugement de la Cour suprême," *Le Devoir*, December 13, 1997, p. A4.

Fontaine, Phil. "Colonialist Approach to Aboriginal Issues," *Globe and Mail*, December 31, 1997, p. A23.

Matas, Robert *et al.*, "Native Win on Land Rights," *Globe and Mail*, December 12, 1997.

National Implications and Potential Effects in Québec

PAUL JOFFE[1]

Introduction

The Supreme Court of Canada judgment in *Delgamuukw* v. *British Columbia*[2] continues to evoke a wide range of responses from Aboriginal peoples, non-Aboriginal governments, academics and interested observers. Its interpretation, meaning and impact are likely to vary in the different regions of Canada, based on varying circumstances, conditions and perspectives of all those concerned.

In reflecting upon the significance and implications of the *Delgamuukw* decision, it is prudent to view the decision as a "work in progress." First, like courts in other countries, Canadian courts are still in the process of coming to terms with the fundamental rights of Aboriginal peoples. Therefore, the evolution of judicial analysis of their land-related rights is likely to continue. Second, certain key aspects, such as the status of Aboriginal peoples and their rights to self-determination and self-government, have yet to be adequately considered. These additional elements could eventually have a profound effect on the approach and analysis by courts in Canada. Third, new constitutional decisions can bring key insights that cannot be ignored. In particular, the judgment of the Supreme Court of Canada in the *Québec*

Notes will be found on pages 319–344.

Secession Reference [3] *could prove to have a far-reaching influence on various aspects of the Delgamuukw* decision. In particular, the interpretation in the *Delgamuukw* judgment of s. 35(1) of the *Constitution Act, 1982* should not be assessed in isolation. Other constitutional provisions may be critical in arriving at a more complete understanding of the meaning and implications of what the Court has ruled. As the Supreme Court of Canada has confirmed in other cases, the "Constitution is to be read as a unified whole." [4] Fourth, one can anticipate the growing influence of international human rights norms on the interpretation of Aboriginal peoples' rights. Canadian courts have yet to adequately consider these existing and emerging international standards.

In order to assess some of the potential impacts in Québec (or any other region), it is important to not only examine the Supreme Court's decision but also reflect on other developments that may influence constitutional interpretations in the future.

This article will focus on the following:

(1) summarize some key aspects of the judgment, as well as the limitations that the Court devised;

(2) highlight certain aspects of the recent decision of the Supreme Court in the *Secession Reference*, which are likely to affect constitutional interpretation in the future;

(3) examine the bases for Aboriginal peoples' right to self-government, including a human rights analysis;

(4) describe past and present government actions in Québec, so as to determine if they are consistent with the Court's requirements in *Delgamuukw*; and

(5) conclude with some observations and recommendations.

Important aspects of the *Delgamuukw* decision

The Supreme Court of Canada's judgment in *Delgamuukw* includes a number of significant rulings. While certain interpretations break new ground, others confirm and reinforce prior judicial findings. Some of the key pronouncements may be summarized as follows:

(1) s. 35(1) of the *Constitution Act, 1982* provides a solid constitutional base for negotiations and the Crown "is under a moral, if not a legal, duty to enter into and conduct those negotiations in good faith." [5] Since the Court refers generally to s. 35(1), this duty of good faith negotiations can be said to apply to all rights under s. 35(1) and not only those concerning land. Regardless of what differences might exist in the var-

ious regions of Canada, this duty should become increasingly significant in assessing the fairness of any negotiations concerning Aboriginal and treaty rights.

(2) in regard to the use of Aboriginal peoples' oral histories as proof of historical facts, the Court ruled that "this type of evidence can be accommodated and placed on an equal footing with the types of historical evidence that courts are familiar with, which largely consists of historical documents."[6] The use of such oral evidence goes beyond cases dealing with the land rights of Aboriginal peoples, and applies generally to the interpretation of their treaties.[7]

(3) Aboriginal title "arises from the prior occupation of Canada by aboriginal peoples."[8] As the Court has previously indicated, Aboriginal rights are not dependent on any legislative or executive instrument for their existence.[9]

(4) Aboriginal title "is a collective right to land held by all members of an aboriginal nation."[10] This suggests that Aboriginal peoples, as distinct and organized societies, must have decision-making processes that are integral to the exercise of self-government.[11]

(5) Aboriginal title is a proprietary interest and can compete with other proprietary interests.[12]

(6) Aboriginal title encompasses the right to exclusive use and occupation of the land concerned,[13] including such uses as mineral rights.[14]

(7) Lands subject to Aboriginal title may be used by the Aboriginal titleholders for a variety of purposes that "need not be aspects of those aboriginal practices, customs and traditions which are integral to distinctive aboriginal cultures."[15]

At the same time, the Supreme Court imposes two limitations on the uses of lands subject to Aboriginal title:

(1) a restriction on Aboriginal title is that "the lands pursuant to title cannot be used in a manner that is irreconcilable with the nature of the claimants' attachment to those lands";[16] and

(2) "if aboriginal peoples wish to use their lands in a way that aboriginal title does not permit, then they must surrender those lands and convert them into non-title lands to do so."[17]

As Chief Justice Antonio Lamer explains it, these limitations derive from "a recognition of the importance of the continuity of the relationship of an aboriginal community to its land over time."[18] The rationale is further elaborated in the following terms:

> *Occupancy is determined by reference to the activities that have taken place*
> *on the land and the uses to which the land has been put by the particular*
> *group.* If lands are so occupied, there will exist a special bond be-
> tween the group and the land in question such that the land will
> be part of the definition of the group's distinctive culture ...
> [T]hese elements of aboriginal title create an inherent limitation
> on the uses to which the land, over which such title exists, may be
> put. For example, if occupation is established with reference to the
> use of the land as a hunting ground, then the group that success-
> fully claims aboriginal title to that land may not use it in such a
> fashion as to destroy its value for such a use (e.g. by strip mining
> it).[19] [Emphasis added.]

These limitations to Aboriginal title appear to be unnecessarily paternalistic and inflexible.[20] They may inadvertently contribute to undermining Aboriginal societies and legal systems by restricting future
options. It would be unfair to demand that Aboriginal peoples, the
original occupiers and possessors of the land, choose between retaining their Aboriginal title or else foregoing certain activities or ventures
on their traditional lands. The Supreme Court's objective appears constructive—that is, to ensure adequate protections for Aboriginal peoples against land uses that may be destructive of their relationship
with the land. Yet the Court's approach may be seriously questioned.
According to the Court's own prescription, the harmful activity could
still proceed, as long as the land is surrendered and Aboriginal title is
extinguished.[21]

Government practices of extinguishing Aboriginal rights have recently been characterized by the United Nations Human Rights Committee as incompatible with Aboriginal peoples' right to self-determination.
According to its April 1999 report, the Committee recommends to Canada that "the practice of extinguishing inherent aboriginal rights be
abandoned as incompatible with article 1[22] of the Covenant."[23] This human rights consideration clearly invites governments and courts in Canada to seek a more constructive approach.

Undoubtedly, safeguards against possible destructive uses on Aboriginal peoples' lands should be assured. However, they should be incorporated, through effective checks and balances, in the decision-
making of the peoples concerned—not through harmful practices of
extinguishment.

In addition, the profound relationship of Aboriginal peoples with
their lands and territories is a dynamic one. It includes vital economic,
social, cultural, political and spiritual dimensions. It may vary with
changing circumstances and conditions, often as a result of actions and

events that Aboriginal peoples may not fully control. The relationship reflects the priorities and values of the Aboriginal people concerned. Therefore, it should not be rigidly defined in terms of any single activity that fulfils a vital purpose at any period of time. Further, to limit future uses to those compatible with such activity is taking away an element of decision-making that belongs within the people affected. This limitation would only serve to penalize[24] Aboriginal peoples and would be inconsistent with their right to self-determination.

As indicated in the Introduction, the principles articulated in *Delgamuukw* may be affected by other judicial decisions in Canada. In this context, it is useful to examine briefly other relevant principles that are elaborated by the Supreme Court of Canada in the *Québec Secession Reference*.

Additional relevant principles in the *Québec Secession Reference*

The *Québec Secession Reference* was decided by the Supreme Court of Canada in 1996, subsequent to its ruling in *Delgamuukw*. It is common knowledge that the *Secession Reference* bears tremendous significance for any proposed secession from Canada. What may be less well known is that the judgment has potentially far-reaching implications for the Constitution of Canada as a whole. In the future, numerous constitutional cases in Canada are likely to be influenced or shaped in some way by the principles highlighted by the Court in this *Reference*.[25]

In the *Secession Reference*, the Court indicated that the constitutional texts enumerated in s. 52.(2) of the *Constitution Act, 1982* "are not exhaustive" and that "[t]he Constitution also 'embraces unwritten, as well as written rules.'"[26, 27] In particular, there are underlying constitutional principles that "animate the whole of our Constitution."[28] These include federalism, democracy, constitutionalism and the rule of law, and respect for minorities.[29]

The judgment generally includes Aboriginal peoples under the constitutional principle of "protection of minorities."[30] This characterization is likely adopted because Aboriginal peoples are lesser in number[31] than the majority population in Canada or any of its provinces. While Aboriginal peoples generally can avail themselves of minority rights protections,[32] they constitute distinct "peoples" with the right to self-determination and other fundamental collective rights.[33] Evidence that the Court did not intend to imply that Aboriginal peoples are simply "minorities" is found in another recent decision. In *R. v. Van der Peet*,[34] Chief Justice Lamer underlined the original occupation of North America by Aboriginal peoples and then stated: "It is this fact, and this fact above all others, which separates Aboriginal peoples from all other minority groups in Canadian society and which mandates their special legal, and now constitutional, status." [35]

Further, in regard to the protection of the Aboriginal and treaty rights of Aboriginal peoples, the Court highlighted in the *Secession Reference* that "the protection of these rights ... *whether looked at in their own right or as part of the larger concern with minorities*, reflects an important underlying constitutional value." [36] In other words, the safeguarding of Aboriginal and treaty rights may be also be viewed "in their own right" as an additional underlying constitutional principle.[37] As P. Russell has commented:

> The Court also discusses Canada's commitment to the rights of Aboriginal peoples as part of a concern for minority rights. But it also says that Aboriginal and treaty rights might also "be looked at in their own right" (§82) as an important underlying constitutional value. *This latter perspective is more appropriate given that Aboriginal peoples, unlike other minorities with constitutional rights, have an inherent and inalienable right to self-government which gives them a share of sovereign authority in Canada.*[38] [Emphasis added.]

In conclusion, the principle of safeguarding of Aboriginal and treaty rights may be invoked as part of the constitutional principle of "protection of minorities" or, more appropriately, as a separate constitutional principle and value. Either way, it is clear that the principle has equal weight with other underlying constitutional principles. As the Court explained in the *Secession Reference*, "[t]hese defining principles function in symbiosis. No single principle can be defined in isolation from the others, nor does any one principle trump or exclude the operation of any other." [39]

All of the underlying constitutional principles elaborated by the Court have the potential to bring new and important interpretations that benefit Aboriginal peoples. To what degree this occurs, may well depend on the imagination and skills of future Aboriginal negotiators and litigants. As will be illustrated in the discussion on self-government,[40] the principles of democracy and self-determination are especially relevant to Aboriginal peoples.

Aboriginal peoples' right to self-government— a key issue to resolve

In regard to the right to self-government, the Supreme Court concluded in *Delgamuukw* that there was insufficient evidence before it to make any judicial determination.[41] Consequently, the Court ruled that this issue should be determined when the case is sent back for a new trial.[42]

Chief Justice Lamer cautioned in passing that "rights to self-government, if they existed, cannot be framed in excessively general terms." [43] However, it makes little sense to attempt to determine contemporary rights of self-government based on the powers that were exercised by a particular people at an earlier period of history.[44] Such an approach would be inappropriate and unfair.[45] It would run counter to the notion of self-determination. As with any self-governing people, the nature and scope of powers exercised by an Aboriginal people in past situations would vary considerably, according to the needs, circumstances and available resources at any given point in time. As different needs and priorities arise, Aboriginal peoples must be free to exercise self-government powers that would effectively address new and impending challenges.

It would be difficult to conceive how an Aboriginal people that is considered to be an "organized society" [46] for the purposes of s. 35(1) of the *Constitution Act, 1982* and possessing collective[47] Aboriginal and treaty rights could be determined to have few or no rights of self-government.[48] How else could Aboriginal peoples make collective decisions concerning their land tenure systems or any other matters affecting them and their traditional territory? How would such peoples determine collectively their economic, social, cultural and political development? How would they maintain societal order, in accordance with their own perspectives and values?

To date, there is no "clear and plain" intent[49] that Aboriginal peoples in Canada gave up their pre-existing rights to self-government. Such an outright alienation or destruction of fundamental rights may not even be possible.[50] Further, it is now recognized that it was the brutal realities of an ongoing process of colonization that served to unjustly deny Aboriginal peoples their rights to both land and jurisdiction. As the Royal Commission on Aboriginal Peoples has emphasized:

> Regardless of the approach to colonialism practised ... the impact on indigenous populations was profound. Perhaps the most appropriate term to describe that impact is "displacement." Aboriginal peoples were displaced physically—they were denied access to their traditional territories and in many cases actually forced to move to new locations selected for them by colonial authorities. They were also displaced socially and culturally ... which undermined their ability to pass on traditional values to their children ... In North America, they were also displaced politically, forced by colonial laws to abandon or at least disguise traditional governing institutions and processes in favour of colonial-style municipal institutions.

... Aboriginal peoples lost control and management of their own lands and resources, and their traditional customs and forms of organization were interfered with in the interest of remaking Aboriginal people in the image of newcomers. This did not occur all at once across the country, but gradually ...[51]

A similar view has been acknowledged by the government of Canada:

Attitudes of racial and cultural superiority led to a suppression of Aboriginal culture and values. As a country, we are burdened by past actions that resulted in weakening the identity of Aboriginal peoples, suppressing their languages and cultures, and outlawing spiritual practices ... We must acknowledge that *the result of these actions was the erosion of the political, economic and social systems of Aboriginal people and nations.*[52] [Emphasis added.]

The right to self-determination, including self-government, is a crucial element to the ongoing survival[53] and development of Aboriginal peoples as distinct peoples. Adequate realization of this right is essential to the healing[54] and strengthening of Aboriginal societies, as well as their reconciliation in Canada. Arrangements for both exclusive and shared jurisdiction will likely prove to be a necessity in many situations in the Canadian federation.[55] However, it would be radical in the extreme for any government or court to determine that an Aboriginal people, as a "people," gave up their right to govern themselves and determine freely their economic, social and cultural development.[56]

In *Van der Peet*, Justice Claire L'Heureux-Dubé referred to reserve lands, Aboriginal title lands, and Aboriginal rights lands in raising the issue of Canadian sovereignty:

The common feature of these lands is that the Canadian Parliament and, to a certain extent, provincial legislatures have a general legislative authority over the activities of Aboriginal people, which is the result of the British assertion of sovereignty over Canadian territory. There are, however, important distinctions to draw between these types of lands with regard to the legislation applicable and claims of Aboriginal rights.[57]

However, what still has not been adequately addressed is the sovereignty of Aboriginal peoples within the Canadian constitutional context.[58] The Supreme Court of Canada has consistently concluded that Aboriginal peoples in Canada were recognized and treated as sovereign nations in early periods of history.[59] This sovereignty has never been expressly relinquished.[60] Yet, despite growing support for incorporation of Aboriginal sovereignty in the present constitutional framework,[61] this aspect has not been the subject of adequate examination and acknowledgment by the courts. As long as this serious omission continues, an imbalanced and unjust view of sovereignty in favour of federal and provincial governments may well be the result.[62]

Clearly, principles of sovereignty must be adequately enunciated, if we are to effectively address the self-government rights of Aboriginal peoples in the Constitution of Canada.[63] In developing a principled legal framework for the consideration of Aboriginal self-government, it is critical to also examine the underlying constitutional principle of democracy, as well as the right to self-determination. These basic aspects are of central importance to Aboriginal peoples and are therefore addressed below.

Democracy and self-determination in the Canadian constitutional context

In recent times, both the Royal Commission on Aboriginal Peoples and the government of Canada have concluded that section 35(1) of the *Constitution Act, 1982* includes the inherent right of Aboriginal peoples to self-government. As the Royal Commission underlines:

> At the heart of our recommendations is recognition that Aboriginal peoples *are* peoples, that they form collectivities of unique character, and that they have a right of government autonomy. Aboriginal peoples have preserved their identities under adverse conditions. They have safeguarded their traditions during many decades when non-Aboriginal officials attempted to regulate every aspect of their lives. *They are entitled to control matters important to their nations without intrusive interference. This authority is not something bestowed by other governments. It is inherent in their identity as peoples.* But to be fully effective, their authority must be recognized by other governments.[64] [Emphasis added.]

If principles of democracy and self-determination were also considered, it would be difficult to reach any other conclusion. In the *Secession Reference*,[65] the Supreme Court of Canada underlined throughout the judgment that "democracy" is one of the underlying constitutional principles governing interpretation of the Constitution. The Court indicated that values inherent in the notion of democracy include a "commitment to social justice and equality," as well as "respect for cultural and group identity."[66] These specific factors are directly relevant to the Aboriginal self-government debate.[67] The Court also added in general terms that "democracy is fundamentally connected to substantive goals, most importantly, the promotion of self-government." [68] This link between democracy and self-determination is recognized not only under Canadian constitutional law, but also at international law. As T. Franck explains:

> ... *self-determination is the oldest aspect of the democratic entitlement* ... Self-determination postulates the right of a people in an established territory to determine its collective political destiny in a democratic fashion and is therefore at the core of the democratic entitlement.[69]

Since self-determination is intimately tied to the democratic principle, one might query as to whether the right to self-determination is a part of the internal law of Canada. In the *Secession Reference*, the judgment states that "the existence of the right of a people to self-determination is now so widely recognized in international conventions that the principle has acquired a status beyond 'convention' and is considered a general principle of international law." [70]

The term "general principle of international law" is highly significant. According to international jurists, this term refers at least to rules of customary international law.[71] The term may also overlap with other principles.[72] However, the sentence and overall context in which the Supreme Court used the term, as well as the references cited on this point in the judgment,[73] lead to the conclusion that the Court was describing the right to self-determination as nothing less than customary international law.[74]

Canadian case law suggests that norms of customary international law are "adopted" directly into Canadian domestic law, without any need for the incorporation of these standards by statute.[75] This is true, as long as there is no conflict with statutory law or well-established rules of the common law.[76] In this way, the right to self-determination can be said to be a part of the internal law of Canada.[77] This has far-reaching positive implications that go beyond the Québec secession context, for any Aboriginal people who demonstrates it is a "people" [78] under international law.

Historically, non-Aboriginal governments in Canada have failed to recognize and respect the right of Aboriginal peoples to self-determination. However, in October 1996, the government of Canada formally declared in United Nations fora in Geneva that Canada is "legally and morally committed to the observance and protection of this right [of self-determination]" under international law in relation to indigenous and non-indigenous peoples.[79] This public declaration by Canada may be binding under international law, in accordance with the principle of good faith.[80]

Further, in regard to the right to self-determination, the Attorney General of Canada expressed the following position in the *Secession Reference*:

> ... the principles of customary law relating to the right of self-determination are applicable in the present case, because they do not conflict with the applicable Canadian domestic law. *Since these principles of customary law can be 'incorporated' into domestic law by Canadian courts, it is respectfully submitted that Canadian courts unquestionably have jurisdiction to apply them.*[81] [Emphasis added.]

Just as the *Canadian Charter of Rights and Freedoms* can provide avenues for the enforcement of customary international law within Canada,[82] so can the recognition and affirmation of Aboriginal and treaty rights in s. 35 of the *Constitution Act, 1982* do the same. This is especially true in relation to the exercise within Canada of the right of Aboriginal peoples to self-determination, as a customary law principle. As K. Roach provides: "In devising remedies, courts should be sensitive to the purposes of aboriginal rights, including the role of treaty-making and self-determination, while recognizing that they have a duty to enforce aboriginal rights."[83]

In the *Secession Reference*, the Supreme Court of Canada stated that "the recognized sources of international law establish that the right to self-determination of a people is normally fulfilled through internal self-determination—a people's pursuit of its political, economic, social and cultural development within the framework of an existing state."[84] Aboriginal peoples address to a vast degree their political, economic, social and cultural development through the exercise of their Aboriginal and treaty rights. Therefore, it is logical that s. 35 would provide one of the key avenues for recognition and enforcement of their right to self-determination.[85] As R. R. McCorquodale explains, self-government is an important political component of internal self-determination: "The 'internal' aspect of the right concerns the right of peoples within a State to choose their political status, the extent of their political participation and the form of their government ..."[86]

In responding to the specific questions[87] posed in the *Secession Reference*, the Supreme Court did not deem it necessary to elaborate on whether Aboriginal peoples in Québec constitute distinct "peoples" with the right to self-determination. At the same time, the Court gave a glimpse of its views. First, it indicated that the characteristics of a "people" include a common language and culture.[88] Second, in responding directly to the question concerning the international law right to self-determination, the Court stressed "the importance of the submissions made ... respecting the rights and concerns of Aboriginal peoples in the event of a unilateral secession, as well the appropriate means of defining the boundaries of a seceding Québec with particular regard to the northern lands occupied largely by aboriginal peoples." [89] This suggests that Aboriginal peoples' status and rights have a direct and substantial bearing on the question of self-determination under Canadian and international law.

Similarly, the Supreme Court in *Delgamuukw* did not engage in any in-depth analysis of the status of the Gitksan and Wet'suwet'en peoples involved. Yet, Chief Justice Lamer effectively recognized how their members share a common language and culture. In particular, the Chief Justice linked the oral histories of Aboriginal peoples to their distinct identity and uniqueness as peoples: "... there are many histories, each characterized in part by how a people see themselves, how they define their identity in relation to their environment, and how they express their uniqueness as a people." [90]

The importance to Aboriginal peoples of the right to self-determination, including the right to self-government, is hardly surprising. As H. Gros Espiell explains: "... human rights can only exist truly and fully when self-determination also exists. Such is the fundamental importance of self-determination as a *human right* and as a *prerequisite for the enjoyment of all the other rights and freedoms.*" [91] [Emphasis added.]

Moreover, countries such as Canada have a positive duty to recognize and respect the right to self-determination. In this regard, both international human rights covenants specifically provide that "State Parties to the present Covenant ... shall promote the realization of a right of self-determination, and shall respect that right, in conformity with the provisions of the Charter of the United Nations." [92]

In order for Aboriginal peoples to safeguard their collective rights and interests, including those relating to their lands and territories, it is insufficient to possess title alone. [93] Historically, Aboriginal peoples governed themselves as an integral part of their inherent rights. As confirmed by the Supreme Court of Canada, aboriginal rights are pre-existing rights not dependent for their existence on any executive order or legislative enactment. [94]

Currently, it is essential that the constitutional right of Aboriginal peoples to self-government be recognized. [95] This conclusion becomes all the more compelling when the human right to self-determination and the democratic principle are applied without discrimination [96] to Aboriginal peoples. In *Delgamuukw*, the Supreme Court has characterized the stewardship responsibility of Aboriginal peoples over their lands in terms of both present and future generations.[97] The fulfilment of this responsibility would hardly be feasible, in the absence of adequate self-government powers.

Aboriginal rights as inalienable human rights

It should be acknowledged that there are still governments who favour, in one form or another, the surrender and extinguishment of Aboriginal rights. As the debate in Canada now shifts to self-government, they claim that any such pre-existing Aboriginal right has been extinguished. These positions are exceedingly difficult to sustain, particularly if they are considered in a human rights context.

As an examination of contemporary international instruments would suggest,[98] basic indigenous rights are human rights.[99] Those international instruments that explicitly address the fundamental rights of indigenous peoples, such as the draft *U.N. Declaration on the Rights of Indigenous Peoples*, complement existing human rights standards in the *International Bill of Rights*.[100] They do so, by providing the social, economic, cultural, political and historical context relating to indigenous peoples.[101] In particular, the right to self-government constitutes a vital political aspect of the right to self-determination, which itself is a human right.[102] The Supreme Court of Canada has confirmed in the *Secession Reference* that the right to self-determination "has developed largely as a human right." [103] In the future, it would be important to analyze Aboriginal rights in a manner that fully includes a human rights perspective. If a human rights analysis were fully and consistently applied to Aboriginal rights, it is likely that their denial or infringement would be treated more seriously by governments and the judiciary.[104]

It is important to note that human rights have been declared repeatedly by the international community to be inalienable.[105] Clearly, they are not intended to be extinguished or otherwise destroyed.[106] Human rights instruments generally include provisions for some limitation or derogation,[107] but not the destruction of fundamental rights.[108]

Both of the International Covenants make clear that nothing in the Covenants can be construed as permitting the "destruction" of human rights.[109] Further, any "limitations" to the rights in the *International Covenant on Economic, Social and Cultural Rights* must be "compatible with the nature of the rights concerned." [110] In the *International Covenant on Civil and Political Rights*, State parties are permitted certain derogations from their human rights obligations under the Covenant "[i]n time of public emergency which threatens the life of the nation and the existence of which is publicly proclaimed." [111] However, any such derogations must be exercised without discrimination and are contemplated to be temporary. As A. Kiss explains, "limitations, like derogations, are exceptional, to be construed and applied strictly, and not so as to swallow or vitiate the right itself." [112]

Extinguishment of indigenous title, to the extent that it dispossesses indigenous peoples of their lands and resources and entails a loss of control over their own development, also denies them exercise of their right of self-determination. This point has recently been underlined by the U.N. Human Rights Committee in its concluding recommendations to Canada.[113] Further, the Committee adds:

> With reference to the conclusion by [the Royal Commission on Aboriginal Peoples] that without a greater share of lands and resources institutions of aboriginal self-government will fail, the Committee emphasizes that the right to self-government requires, *inter alia*, that all peoples must be able to dispose of their natural wealth and resources and that they may not be deprived of their own means of subsistence (art. 1, para.2).[114]

Not only has the Human Rights Committee applied the right to self-determination to Aboriginal peoples in Canada, but also it has highlighted the inextricable link between Aboriginal self-government and the adequacy of Aboriginal lands and resources. Moreover, in regard to the right to self-determination, the Committee "urges [Canada] to report adequately on implementation of article 1 of the [*International Covenant on Civil and Political Rights*] in its next periodic report." [115] In this way, the Committee has emphasized that the Aboriginal rights of Aboriginal peoples in Canada are human rights, which require government support and not neglect or extinguishment.

As outlined above, there is no specific authority to extinguish or otherwise destroy human rights. Rather, in regard to Aboriginal and treaty rights, the Canadian Constitution expressly requires the recognition and affirmation of these fundamental rights.[116] Also, the Crown's fiduciary responsibility in relation to Aboriginal peoples serves to reinforce Canada's national and international obligations and commitments concerning human rights. As D. McRae explained, in his 1993 commissioned report to the Canadian Human Rights Commission: "At the very least, such a [fiduciary] standard requires observance by the government of Canada of minimal standards for the protection of human rights ... In this regard there is an undoubted commitment in Canadian public policy to a high standard in the recognition and protection of human rights in respect of all peoples in Canada." [117]

Recently, the U.N. Committee on Economic, Social and Cultural Rights has highlighted the human rights of Aboriginal peoples, criticized Canada's extinguishment policies, and endorsed the recommendations of the Royal Commission on Aboriginal Peoples (RCAP). In its December 1998 Report, the Committee highlights the urgency of the situation in concluding as follows:

> The Committee views with concern the direct connection between Aboriginal economic marginalization and the ongoing dispossession of Aboriginal people from their lands, as recognized by the RCAP, and endorses the recommendations of the RCAP that policies which violate Aboriginal treaty obligations and extinguishment, conversion or giving up of Aboriginal rights and title should on no account be pursued by the State Party. Certainty of treaty relations alone cannot justify such policies. The Committee is greatly concerned that the recommendations of the RCAP have not yet been implemented in spite of the urgency of the situation.[118]

Based on all of the above, it can be concluded that Canada's obligations to respect human rights require that Aboriginal rights be explicit recognized and respected in government policy and practice. It is unjustifiable for federal and provincial governments to insist upon surrender of these rights through "agreements" with Aboriginal peoples, especially since s. 35(1) of the *Constitution Act, 1982* calls for their recognition and affirmation. Nor is it compatible with human rights considerations to suggest that Aboriginal self-government has been extinguished or is extinguishable.

In addition, increased respect and protection for Aboriginal rights, as human rights, is consistent with existing principles of constitutional interpretation. In particular, the doctrine of progressive interpretation,[119] includes the "living tree" doctrine. As originally stated by the Privy Council in *Edwards* v. *A.-G. Canada*: "The [*Constitution Act, 1867*] planted in Canada a living tree capable of growth and expansion within its natural limits." [120] This doctrine has been consistently reiterated by the Supreme Court of Canada. It is clearly applicable to the principles underlying Canada's Constitution, including democracy and the protection of Aboriginal and treaty rights.

As the Supreme Court stipulated in the *Secession Reference*, " ... observance of and respect for these [underlying constitutional] principles is essential to the ongoing process of constitutional development and evolution of our Constitution as a 'living tree', to invoke the famous description in *Edwards* v. *Attorney General for Canada* ..." [121] Moreover, in *A.-G. Canada* v. *Mossop*, the Court has indicated that this doctrine "is particularly well-suited to human rights legislation" [122] and that human rights considerations "must be examined in the context of contemporary values." [123] Further, the Court in *Hunter* v. *Southam Inc.* has explained how Canada's Constitution must be forward-looking— always capable of growth and development even in ways that may originally have been unforeseen:

> A constitution ... is drafted with an eye to the future ... Once enacted, its provisions cannot easily be repealed or amended. It must, therefore, be capable of growth and development over time to meet new social, political and historical realities often unimagined by its framers. The judiciary is the guardian of the constitution and must, in interpreting its provisions, bear these considerations in mind. [124]

Consequently, what is presently needed is a substantially revised approach to existing judicial analysis of Aboriginal peoples' fundamental rights. It is evident that Canadian courts should not rely excessively on the past activities of Aboriginal peoples, in order to determine their contemporary rights and powers. [125] While it remains important to adopt a contextual approach, [126] it is imperative to give increased weight to human rights and the underlying constitutional principles highlighted recently by the Supreme Court of Canada. In this way, the "new social, political and historical realities" faced by Aboriginal peoples could be effectively addressed through their own powers and initiatives.

Considering *Delgamuukw* in the Québec context

In considering the principles and rulings in *Delgamuukw* in the Québec context, a few observations can be made. First, many policies and actions of the Québec government in relation to Aboriginal peoples were implemented a number of years before the Supreme Court's decision. Therefore, Québec may be reluctant to revisit past actions, regardless of their degree of unfairness. Second, as will be demonstrated below, there is a common theme of unilateralism in government policies and actions both prior and subsequent to *Delgamuukw*. This unilateralism, s a means of government control, continues to breed distrust among Aboriginal peoples.

Third, government policies and strategies in Québec are determined to a large degree by its political agenda towards independence. Regardless of human rights considerations, Aboriginal peoples' status and rights are recognized solely in a manner that may not affect Québec's secessionist aspirations.

As in other regions of Canada, positive government initiatives do occur from time to time in Québec in relation to Aboriginal peoples. Yet, when one considers the wide range of urgent measures recommended by the Royal Commission on Aboriginal Peoples,[127] government efforts in Québec (like other regions of Canada) must be considered as lacking in many important respects.[128]

Any "advances" still tend to take place in a legal and political framework that reinforces ultimate domination and control by the Québec government and National Assembly. This continuing government trend to unilaterally impose an overall framework and conditions for negotiations is self-serving and colonial in nature. It violates the duty of governments to conduct negotiations in good faith.[129] Rather than encourage recognition of and respect for Aboriginal and treaty rights, contemporary government policies in Québec seek their eventual demise or disappearance. Examples of such acts are evidenced by the following.

(1) Denial of Cree and Inuit Aboriginal rights during land claims negotiations.

Under the *Québec Boundaries Extension Acts* of 1912, the Québec government had a constitutional obligation to recognize the territorial rights of Aboriginal peoples in northern Québec, while negotiating an agreement with the peoples concerned.[130] Yet, during the whole period of land claims negotiations, the Québec government refused to recognize that the Crees and Inuit had any Aboriginal title or rights in their vast traditional territories. As a result, the Aboriginal parties were compelled to negotiate an agreement, while being told that they had no Aboriginal rights. This failure of governments and Crown corporations has been recognized by the Supreme Court of Canada.[131] It was only after the James Bay and Northern Québec Agreement (JBNQA)[132] was signed by the parties in 1975 that the Québec government admitted that the Crees and Inuit had fundamental rights[133] and that it had constitutional obligations[134] under the *Québec Boundaries Extension Acts* of 1912.

(2) Unfair land selection criteria imposed.

The Cree and Inuit parties in the JBNQA negotiations were denied by Québec the right to select their own traditional lands for harvesting purposes,[135] if the lands selected had any known mineral potential.[136] As recounted by the Grand Council of the Crees:

> During the negotiation of the *JBNQA*, the Quebec government unjustly imposed specific criteria for land selection that excluded all Cree and Inuit traditional lands with mineral potential. This denied the Crees "the inherent right ... to enjoy and utilize fully and freely their natural wealth and resources."[137] It constituted a major violation of the aboriginal right to economic self-determination. It still serves to perpetuate our dependency. No land claims

agreement in Canada has prohibited aboriginal peoples from selecting lands with resource potential.[138]

(3)   *Purported extinguishment of Aboriginal rights.*[139]

Although a number of Aboriginal peoples were not party to the James Bay and Northern Québec Agreement,[140] their rights in and to the territory in northern Québec were purportedly extinguished by federal legislation approving and declaring valid the Agreement.[141] This third party "extinguishment" was insisted upon by the Québec government.[142] It is of doubtful constitutionality[143] and has been repeatedly denounced by the Commission des droits de la personne du Québec.[144] The effect of such actions by the government were described by the Opposition Party (Parti Québécois) at that time, as "extremely draconian." [145] Nevertheless, the government voted to defeat a motion to hear the views of Aboriginal third parties on the issue of extinguishment.[146] In this way, the Québec government acted in a manner that gravely violated principles of fundamental justice as well as the human rights of the Aboriginal peoples concerned.

It is also worth noting that the Commission des droits de la personne du Québec has indicated to the Royal Commission on Aboriginal Peoples that extinguishment, as a necessary pre-condition to any negotiation of territorial rights, is "unacceptable." [147] Extinguishment of indigenous peoples' rights has also been described as "another relic of colonialism." [148] While the *Programme du Parti Québécois* has for many years indicated that agreements will be concluded without extinguishment of the rights of Aboriginal peoples,[149] the Parti Québécois government has never acted on this commitment and still insists on extinguishment.

(4)   *Imposition of the 1985 National Assembly Resolution on Aboriginal Rights.*[150]

In March 1985, the National Assembly adopted a Resolution on Aboriginal peoples' fundamental status and rights despite the express objections of the peoples concerned.[151] The government unilaterally terminated negotiations on the wording of the Resolution, when Aboriginal leaders would not agree to Québec's proposed wording.[152] It would appear that a principal reason for imposing this Resolution on Aboriginal peoples was to purportedly demonstrate to the international community and Canadians how well the Québec government treats the first peoples in Québec.[153]

Notwithstanding the unilateral nature of the 1985 National Assembly Resolution, it has now been made the basis for Québec's 1998 policy on Aboriginal affairs.[154] Also, despite the rulings of the Supreme

Court of Canada,[155] the 1985 Resolution does not recognize that Aboriginal peoples have inherent or pre-existing rights. Their rights would be recognized only after an agreement has been reached on them with Québec. These government strategies show little respect for Aboriginal peoples and their fundamental rights.

(5) Terra nullius and indigenous peoples' rights

In June 1996, in *R. v. Côté*,[156] the Québec government argued before the Supreme Court of Canada that no Aboriginal peoples have possessed any Aboriginal rights in any part of the province for the past 450 years.[157] Consequently, the government alleged that s. 35 of the *Constitution Act, 1982* had no application in Québec in relation to the protection of Aboriginal rights.

To support its argument, the government urged the Supreme Court of Canada to apply the doctrine of *terra nullius*[158] *and attempted unsuccessfully to distinguish the Mabo* case[159] in Australia. This latter case had condemned the use of this doctrine against indigenous peoples as being racially discriminatory and colonial.[160] In response to this dispossession strategy, the Chiefs of the Assembly of First Nations of Québec and Labrador have unanimously condemned the discriminatory[161] positions taken in *Côté* by the Bouchard government.[162]

(6) Denial of Aboriginal peoples' status as distinct "peoples" [163]

Unlike its previous policy programmes, the 1997 *Programme* of the Parti Québécois (PQ) now classifies Aboriginal nations, along with the anglophone community, under the sub-heading "Historical Minorities." [164] Moreover, for purposes of self-determination and Québec sovereignty, the "Québec people" is simply declared to include all of its citizens.[165] This suggests that there exists only a single people in Québec. This PQ position is erroneous and undemocratic. In particular, it invalidly strips Aboriginal peoples of their right to self-identification[166] in the self-determination context.

In regard to Aboriginal peoples in Québec, their cultures and spirituality are not those of Quebecers. Aboriginal peoples each have their own way of life. They each clearly choose to identify as a distinct people themselves. While French-Canadians in Québec are likely to constitute "a people" for purposes of self-determination,[167] there is no Canadian or international law principle that would compel Aboriginal peoples against their will to identify as one people with Quebecers.[168]

(7) Denial of Aboriginal peoples' right to self-determination.

As long as Aboriginal peoples in Québec choose to self-identify as distinct peoples, it cannot be said that there is a single "Québec people" in the province with the right to self-determination.[169] The Bouchard government apparently believes that, if it refers to Aboriginal peoples as "nations" and not "peoples," it can continue to deny the first peoples their right to self-determination.[170] This position is as unjust[171] as it is futile. For purposes of self-determination, the term "peoples" includes "nations." This view is supported not only by international jurists,[172] but also by others in the context of Canadian domestic law.[173] In addition, it is racially discriminatory to deny Aboriginal peoples their status as "peoples" in order to deny them their human right to self-determination.[174]

(8) Forcible inclusion of Aboriginal peoples in a sovereign Québec.

The Québec government is of the view that it can include Aboriginal peoples and their traditional territories in any future Québec "state," without the consent[175] of the peoples concerned.[176] Despite its lack of legitimacy or validity,[177] this extreme and destabilizing strategy has never been repudiated by the government.

In relation to existing treaties, such as the James Bay and Northern Québec Agreement (JBNQA), the Québec government takes the position that it can unilaterally assume the obligations of the federal government and subject these treaties to a new Constitution in a secessionist Québec. However, the rights of Aboriginal peoples under existing treaties would take on different and uncertain interpretations that were never negotiated or agreed upon by the parties.[178] In regard to JBNQA, such unilateral alteration would constitute a fundamental breach,[179] contrary to its express terms and conditions as well as its spirit and intent.[180]

(9) Undermining future treaty making by Aboriginal peoples in Québec.

Québec's 1998 policy on Aboriginal affairs proposes the "recognition of responsibilities according to a so-called contractual jurisdiction concept." [181] Under this concept, agreements signed in the future "would not be covered by constitutional protection" and solely the "provisions relating to land aspects of a comprehensive land claim agreement will receive constitutional protection." [182] Thus, the "contractual jurisdiction" approach would serve to severely limit the treaty-making capacity of Aboriginal peoples in Québec, both now and in the future.

The "contractual jurisdiction" approach may also seek to seriously restrict the application of s. 35 of the *Constitution Act, 1982*, which confers constitutional protection on treaty rights of First Nations. Presently, section 35 does not limit such protection to treaty rights relating to land aspects. Also, Québec's new approach appears to contradict the 1985 National Assembly Resolution on Aboriginal Rights.[183] The strategy to move away from signing treaties with Aboriginal peoples appears to be a part of the official program of the Parti Québécois.[184]

(10) Self-serving principles in Québec's new Aboriginal policy.

In its 1998 policy on Aboriginal affairs, the Québec government imposes certain " fundamental reference points"[185] that entail significant constraints for First Nations. The reference points specified are: "territorial integrity," "sovereignty of the National Assembly," and "legislative and regulatory effectivity." Although the Crown is prohibited from "sharp dealing," [186] no explanation is offered in Québec's policy as to what each of these terms would mean.

The policy paper repeatedly emphasizes the notion of "territorial integrity." [187] despite its inappropriateness in a domestic context.[188] "Territorial integrity," as used by the Québec government, could have extensive implications in international law. To date, the Québec government has invoked this principle to suggest that Aboriginal peoples and their territories would be forcibly included in an independent Québec.[189] Such matters go far beyond the stated objectives of Québec's 1998 policy.[190]

Similarly, for the Québec government to impose such "reference points" as the "sovereignty of the National Assembly" and "legislative and regulatory effectivity" is blatantly self-serving. These terms strongly imply that Aboriginal peoples and governments would be subjugated or subordinated to the jurisdiction of the National Assembly. In international law, "effectivity" usually means "effective control," which suggests that ultimate control must rest with the National Assembly.[191] Also, in the context of Québec unilateral secession, "effective control" is what Québec authorities would need to demonstrate in seeking international recognition as an independent state.[192]

In summary, the Québec government has shown little respect to date for the fundamental rights of Aboriginal peoples. One sided principles have been imposed by the government to govern future negotiations. Any "progress" in Aboriginal peoples' issues still takes place within an overall unilateral framework that seriously undermines Aboriginal peoples' status and rights. In this context, the duty of Québec to enter into and conduct negotiations in good faith is not being respected. Although Québec's 1998 policy has been unanimously rejected by First Nations in the province,[193] the government has shown no signs of revising its document in conjunction with the peoples directly affected.

It is difficult to predict whether a more positive course will be adopted by the Québec government in the short term. Although some agreements will likely continue to be signed with Aboriginal peoples,

Québec's present strategies of unilateralism fail to meet any reasonable standard expected of a government. The Parti Québécois government may continue to tailor its policies concerning Aboriginal peoples so as to fit its sovereignist ambitions. However, the government cannot avoid or prevent the growing recognition in Canada and internationally of Aboriginal peoples' status as "peoples" with the right to self-determination. This increased recognition should have a most positive and profound effect on the dynamic of Aboriginal-Crown relations. Therefore, perhaps before the next referendum on Québec secession, the government may have little choice but to devise a more constructive approach.[194]

Conclusions

The judgment of the Supreme Court of Canada in *Delgamuukw* may be viewed in diverse ways as a positive and significant contribution to our understanding of Aboriginal title.[195] In some aspects, the Court's decision provides a new benchmark. However, it should not be seen as a complete or final pronouncement on this essential matter. Substantial shifts in judicial perspectives will likely be required.

In particular, greater attention is needed in relation to the status and rights of Aboriginal peoples under Canadian constitutional and international law. Principles underlying Canada's Constitution, such as "democracy" and the "protection of Aboriginal and treaty rights," should be accorded their full constitutional meaning and value in contemporary terms. The rights of present and future generations of Aboriginal peoples should not be unfairly limited by excessive focus on Aboriginal activities in early periods of history.

Further, notions of surrender or extinguishment of Aboriginal title should be replaced by new alternatives. As recommended by the U.N. Human Rights Committee, approaches are needed that are compatible with Aboriginal peoples' right to self-determination. In addition, judicial interpretation of Aboriginal land title and rights should not be artificially separated from Aboriginal jurisdiction. To date, Canadian courts have not yet addressed in any comprehensive way the right of Aboriginal peoples to self-government.

Aboriginal peoples possess an inherent right to self-government, as an essential political component of their right to self-determination. This right should be appropriately recognized under s. 35(1) of the *Constitution Act, 1982*. These conclusions are even more compelling, if the status of Aboriginal peoples and their collective human rights are accorded full and sensitive[196] consideration.

Clearly, the preferable route for resolving land, resource and self-government issues is, in most situations, through negotiations conducted in good faith.[197] However, carefully formulated litigation and effective judicial recourses are at times a necessary part of the overall process.[198] As stated in the *Report of the Royal Commission on Aboriginal Peoples*: "The courts can be only one part of a larger political process of negotiation and reconciliation ..."[199] And the Report adds:

> Because negotiation is preferable to litigation as a means of resolving disputes between the Crown and Aboriginal nations, "courts should design their remedies to facilitate negotiations between First Nations, governments and other affected interests."[200] Aboriginal peoples will secure substantive gains in negotiations only if courts order remedies that give Aboriginal parties more bargaining power than they have under Canadian law at present.[201]

The need for judicial remedies that enhance the negotiating positions of Aboriginal peoples has been illustrated repeatedly throughout Canada's history. Through constructive judicial guidance, unilateral or self-serving actions by non-Aboriginal governments against Aboriginal peoples would more likely be discarded. Instead, compliance with contemporary and emerging standards may well be the result.

There is little doubt that the process of recognizing and reconciling Aboriginal peoples' status and rights will continue into the long term. This does not mean that agreements between Aboriginal peoples and non-Aboriginal governments (or third party developers) cannot or should not proceed. Mutually beneficial agreements can be arrived at, if genuine respect for the first peoples, and their priorities and traditions of sharing, are an integral part of the discussions.[202]

Without these essential qualities of recognition, sharing and respect, no treaty or agreement will contribute to or ensure a climate of cooperation and reconciliation. The James Bay and Northern Québec Agreement[203] is an example of the long-range problems that can occur when such basic elements are lacking. Since this treaty was signed in 1975, the James Bay Crees have been in court virtually every year for the past twenty-odd years,[204] in order to defend their rights and ensure their just entitlements.[205] Clearly, purported extinguishments or surrenders of Aboriginal rights provide no assurance whatsoever that the result will contribute to a cooperative environment or to certainty in the future. The only certainty of an "extinguishment" strategy is that it generates mistrust.

What would seem crucial for any future negotiations concerning fundamental rights is the prior establishment of a principled framework.[206] This framework must be consistent with Aboriginal peoples' values, genuine democracy and relevant international norms.[207] This should be accomplished collaboratively by the parties or, as a last resort, by the courts.[208]

Aboriginal territories, lands, resources and self-determination are all issues that must be addressed on an urgent basis. Yet, there are still those who put budgetary considerations ahead of human rights and long-standing concerns for equality and justice. In this regard, serious reflection should be given to the words of Justice Rosalie Silberman Abella of the Ontario Court of Appeal: "We have no business figuring out the cost of justice until we can figure out the cost of injustice." [209]

Only then will we have the collective will to realize a critical precept underlined by Chief Justice Lamer in *Van der Peet* and reiterated in *Delgamuukw.* That is, that "the only fair and just reconciliation is ... one which takes into account the Aboriginal perspective while at the same time taking into account the perspective of the common law. True reconciliation will, equally,[210] place weight on each." [211] It is imperative that this perspective of intersocietal law include full respect for the collective and individual human rights of Aboriginal peoples. The inclusion of such a human rights dynamic may well prove to be a most positive catalyst—an essential component towards completing the "work in progress" that we find in *Delgamuukw.*

Notes

1 Member of the Québec and Ontario bars.
2 *Delgamuukw v. British Columbia*, [1997] 3 S.C.R. 1010, 153 D.L.R. (4th) 193, [1998] 1 C.N.L.R. 14 (S.C.C.), (1998) 37 I.L.M. 268.
3 *Reference re Secession of Québec*, [1998] 2 S.C.R. 217, (1998) 161 D.L.R. (4th) 385, 228 N.R. 203, (1998) 37 I.L.M 1342.
4 *Reference re Remuneration of Judges*, [1997] 3 S.C.R. 3 at 83, para. 107, per Lamer C.J.C.; *Reference re Secession of Québec, supra*, note 3, para. 50: "The individual elements of the Constitution are linked to the others, and must be interpreted by reference to the structure of the Constitution as a whole."
5 *Delgamuukw v. British Columbia*, note 2, *supra*, para. 186. Similarly, see *Nunavik Inuit v. Canada (Minister of Canadian Heritage)*, [1998] 4 C.N.L.R. 68 (F.C.T.D.), at 99, and at 101-102: "Where a national park is established, the impact will occur on title, the rights and the use of the land. There is, therefore, a duty to consult and negotiate in good faith [with Aboriginal peoples who claim rights] in such circumstances." The Nunavik Inuit decision was applied in Gitanyow First Nation v. Canada, [1999] 3 C.N.L.R. 89 (B.C.S.C.), where it was decided that, if the Crown enters into negotiations with a First Nation pursuant to B.C.'s treaty process, it has a duty to negotiate in good faith. Similarly, see *Chemainus First Nation v. British Columbia Assets and Lands Corporation*, [1999] 3 C.N.L.R., 8 at para. 26.
6 *Delgamuukw v. British Columbia, supra*, note 2, para. 87.
7 *Id.*
8 *Id.*, paras. 114 & 126.
9 *Guerin v. The Queen*, [1984] 6 W.W.R. 481 at 497, 13 D.L.R. (4th) 321 at 335, per Dickson J.; *Calder v. A.G. British Columbia*, [1973] S.C.R. 313 at 390, per Hall J.; *R. v. Van der Peet*, [1996] 2 S.C.R. 507, para. 30 (Lamer C.J.C.); *Delgamuukw v. British Columbia, supra*, note 2, para. 134.
10 Delgamuukw v. British Columbia, supra, note 2, para. 115.
11 K. McNeil, *Aboriginal Rights in Canada: From Title to Land to Territorial Sovereignty*, (1998) 5 Tulsa J. Comp. & Int'l L. 253 at 285ff. (relationship between communal nature of Aboriginal title and self-government). See also B. Slattery, "The Definition and Proof of Aboriginal Title" in Pacific Business & Law Institute, ed., *The Supreme Court of Canada decision in Delgamuukw*, conference materials (Vancouver, B.C.: 1998), 3.1 at 3.6: "... since decisions about the manner in which lands are to be used must be made communally, there must be some internal mechanism of communal decision-making. This internal mechanism arguably provides the core for the right of aboriginal self-government..."; and L. Mandell, "The Delgamuukw Decision" in Pacific Business & Law Institute, ed., *The Supreme Court of Canada decision in Delgamuukw, supra*, 10.1 at 10.7-10.8.
12 *Delgamuukw v. British Columbia, supra*, note 2, para. 113.
13 *Id.*, para. 117.
14 *Id.*, para. 122.
15 *Id.*, paras. 117 & 124. At para. 123 of the judgment, Lamer C.J.C. lists some of the critical literature supporting this point.

16 *Id.*, para. 125.
17 *Id.*, para. 131.
18 *Id.*, para. 126.
19 *Id.*, para. 128.
20 See, for example, R. Bartlett, *The Content of Aboriginal Title and Equality Before the Law*, (1998) 61 Sask. L. Rev. 377, at 388 ("inherent limit" is paternalistic and inconsistent with principle of equality).
21 This aspect of the judgment warrants reconsideration in the future. It makes little sense that certain uses, collectively determined by the Aboriginal people concerned, should require mandatory destruction of their existing Aboriginal title or rights contrary to their own wishes and systems of law. In no case should use and development of natural resources on Aboriginal peoples' traditional lands automatically involve "surrender" of Aboriginal title and rights. Rather, consistent with Aboriginal perspectives and values, arrangements of sharing should be explored.
22 *International Covenant on Civil and Political Rights* (1966), G.A. Res 2200 (XXI), 21 U.N. GAOR, Supp. (No. 16) at 49, U.N. Doc. A/6316, Can. T.S. 1976 No. 47 (1966). Adopted by the U.N. General Assembly on December 16, 1966 and entered into force March 23, 1976, art. 1, para 1: "All peoples have the right to self-determination. By virtue of that right they freely determine their political status and freely pursue their economic, social and cultural development."
23 See "Concluding observations of the Human Rights Committee" in United Nations Human Rights Committee, *Consideration of reports submitted by States parties under article 40 of the Covenant*, 7 April 1999, CCPR/C/79/ Add. 105, para. 8.
24 In *Delgamuukw v. British Columbia, supra*, note 2, at para. 132, Lamer C.J.C. emphasizes that the Court's limitation on Aboriginal title "is not ... a limitation that restricts the use of the land to those activities that have been traditionally carried out on it. That would amount to a legal straightjacket ..." Nevertheless, the limitation still carries what seems to be a severe and unfair "penalty" of surrender for derogating from judicially-prescribed conditions.
25 Since the decision in the *Québec Secession Reference* was rendered by the Supreme Court in August 1998, the underlying constitutional principles highlighted by the Court have been argued in other cases in a non-secession contex't. See, for example, *Samson et al. v. Attorney General of Canada et al.*, (1998) 155 F.T.R. 137, 165 D.L.R. (4th) 342 at para. 7 (principle of democracy unsuccessfully invoked in seeking to restrain Senate appointment by Governor General of Canada); and *Hogan et al. v. Attorney General of Newfoundland et al.*, Supreme Court, Newfoundland, 1997 St. J. No. 2526, decision of Riche J. filed January 14, 1999, QuickLaw version [1999] N.J. No. 5 (principles of protection of minority rights and rule of law unsuccessfully invoked in claiming invalidity of constitutional amendment concerning denominational rights).
26 *Reference re Remuneration of Judges of the Provincial Court of P.E.I., supra*, note 4, para. 92.

27 *Reference re Secession of Québec, supra,* note 3, para. 32.
28 *Id.,* para. 148. See also *Reference re Resolution to Amend the Constitution,* [1981] 1 S.C.R. 753, at 874, where it is said that the Constitution of Canada includes "the global system of rules and principles which govern the exercise of constitutional authority in the whole and in every part of the Canadian state."
29 *Reference re Secession of Québec, supra,* note 3, para. 32. See also R. Howse and A. Malkin, *Canadians are a Sovereign People: How the Supreme Court Should Approach the Reference on Québec Secession,* (1997) 76 Can. Bar Rev. 186, at 210: "These foundational norms ... do not merely form the justification for political conventions but are *binding legal principles which, now that the Constitution has been patriated, structure and govern the exercise of all constitutional change in Canada.*" [Emphasis added.]
30 *Reference re Secession of Québec, supra,* note 3, para. 82.
31 See also I. Schulte-Tenckhoff, *Reassessing the Paradigm of Domestication: The Problematic of Indigenous Treaties,* (1998) 4 Rev. of Const'l Studies 239, at 284: "... one trait is generally viewed as distinctive of Indigenous peoples, namely their historical relationship with the land, especially in former European settler colonies such as Canada—a relationship that is a fundamental component of their peoplehood. *Consequently, while many Indigenous peoples actually happen to be numerical minorities, minorities are not necessarily Indigenous peoples.*" [Emphasis added.]
32 The U.N. Human Rights Committee considers complaints of indigenous peoples, among others, in relation to art. 27 of the *International Covenant on Civil and Political Rights* (minority rights provision). See, for example, *Ominayak v. Canada,* U.N. Doc. CCPR/C/38/D/167/1984 (Human Rights Committee decision, March 28, 1990) ("historical inequities ... and more recent developments threaten the way of life and culture of the Lubicon Lake Band, and constitute a violation of article 27 so long as they continue"). See also *Lovelace v. Canada,* (No. 24/1977) *Report of the Human Rights Committee,* U.N. GAOR, 36th Sess., Supp. No. 40, at 166, U.N. Doc. A/36/40 (1981); and in (1981) 68 I.L.R. 17 (denying Indian woman who married a non-Indian the right to live on a reserve is a violation of art. 27 of the *International Covenant on Civil and Political Rights*).
33 S. J. Anaya, *Indigenous Peoples in International Law* (Oxford/New York: Oxford University Press, 1996), at 100: "International practice ... has tended to treat indigenous peoples and minorities as comprising *distinct but overlapping categories subject to common normative considerations.* The specific focus on indigenous peoples through international organizations indicates that groups within this rubric are acknowledged to have distinguishing concerns and characteristics that warrant treating them apart from, say, minority populations of Western Europe. At the same time, indigenous and minority rights intersect substantially in related concerns of nondiscrimination and cultural integrity." [Emphasis added.]

   See also J. Duursma, *Fragmentation and the International Relations of Micro-States [:] Self-Determination and Statehood* (Cambridge: Cambridge University Press, 1996), at 38: "One of the main differences between a

minority and a people is the fact that in the definition of minorities no relationship with a territory is demanded. A minority may well be long established in the territory of a State, but it need not have a particular
attachment to a specific area ... The longer a minority is established in a
given territory, the more chance there is that it will develop a particular
attachment to the territory. If a relationship exists, a minority could well
constitute a people." For a similar view, see A. Cristescu, Special Rapporteur, *The Right to Self-Determination: Historical and Current Development on the
Basis of United Nations Instruments*, U.N. Doc. E/CN.4/Sub.2/404/Rev.1
(1981) at 41, para. 279.

34 *R. v. Van der Peet, supra*, note 9.

35 *Id.*, at para. 30.

36 *Reference re Secession of Québec, supra*, note 3, para. 82 [emphasis added].

37 This point is made in C.-A. Sheppard, "The Cree Intervention in the Canadian Supreme Court Reference on Québec Secession: A Subjective Assessment," (1999) 23 vermont L. Rev. 845 at 856: "It may not be too
optimistic to consider that there has now emerged *an additional constitutional principle, distinct from the traditional principle of protection of minorities*,
i.e. protection of Aboriginal and treaty rights. [new para.] ... *Aboriginal
rights should not be viewed merely as a subspecies of minority rights.*" [Emphasis
added.]

38 P. Russell, "The Supreme Court Ruling, A Lesson in Democracy," *Cité Li-
bre*, English ed., vol. 26, no. 4, October-November, 1998, 29, at 30.

39 *Reference re Secession of Québec, supra*, note 3, para. 49. See also para. 91.

40 See sub-head "Democracy and self-determination in the Canadian constitutional context," *infra*.

41 *Delgamuukw v. British Columbia, supra*, note 2, paras. 170 per Lamer C.J.C.
and 205 per La Forest J.

42 *Id.*, at para. 171.

43 *Id.*, at para. 170. See, generally, *R. v. Pamajewon*, [1996] 2 S.C.R. 821
(S.C.C.); B. Morse, *Permafrost Rights: Aboriginal Self-Government and the Supreme Court in R. v. Pamajewon*, (1997) 42 McGill L.J. 1011. See also L.I.
Rotman, *Creating a Still-Life Out of Dynamic Objects: Rights Reductionism at the
Supreme Court of Canada*, (1997) 36 Alta. L. Rev. 1, at 2 (Supreme Court's
decision in Pamajewon focussed on gambling as a discrete issue, rather
than as part of the larger right of Aboriginal self-government).

44 *Cf. R. v. Pamajewon, supra*, note 43, para. 24: "In so far as they can be made
under s. 35(1), claims to self-government are no different from other
claims to the enjoyment of Aboriginal rights and must, as such, be measured against the same standard." In *R. v. Van der Peet, supra*, note 9, para.
46, the test for identifying Aboriginal rights was said to be as follows: "in
order to be an aboriginal right an activity must be an element of a practice,
custom or tradition integral to the distinctive culture of the Aboriginal
group claiming the right."

It is worth noting that, in *Delgamuukw v. British Columbia, supra*, note
2, the Supreme Court of Canada subsequently decided that lands subject
to Aboriginal title may be used by the Aboriginal titleholders for a variety

of purposes that "need not be aspects of those aboriginal practices, customs and traditions which are integral to distinctive aboriginal cultures" (para. 117). Therefore, it is possible that the right to self-government on Aboriginal title lands would also be interpreted by the Court as including a wide range of powers that are not necessarily linked to Aboriginal practices, customs and traditions integral to Aboriginal culture. In other words, the tests in *Van der Peet* and *Pamajewon* may not automatically be applied by the Court, in the case of Aboriginal title lands, for the purposes of determining Aboriginal peoples' right to self-government pursuant to s. 35(1) of the *Constitution Act, 1982*.

45 Fundamental rights can take on new meanings over time. In the human rights context, see *A.-G. Canada v. Mossop*, [1993] 1 S.C.R. 554, at 621, per L'Heureux-Dubé J: "… concepts of equality and liberty which appear in human rights documents are not bounded by the precise understanding of those who drafted them. Human rights codes are documents that embody fundamental principles, but which permit the understanding and application of these principles to change over time."

46 *Calder v. A.G. British Columbia*, [1973] S.C.R. 313, at 328: "… the fact that when the settlers came, the Indians were there, organized in societies and occupying the land as their forefathers had done for centuries." This passage is cited with approval in *Delgamuukw v. British Columbia*, note 2, *supra*, para. 189.

47 *Delgamuukw v. British Columbia*, note 2, *supra*, para. 115 per Lamer C.J.C.: "[Aboriginal title] is a collective right to land held by all members of an aboriginal nation. Decisions with respect to that land are also made by that community. This is another feature of aboriginal title which is *sui generis* and distinguishes it from normal property interests."

48 Legal literature in favour of recognition of Aboriginal rights to self-government includes: K. McNeil, *Aboriginal Rights in Canada: From Title to Land to Territorial Sovereignty, supra,* note 11; P. Hogg & M.E. Turpel, *Implementing Aboriginal Self-Government: Constitutional and Jurisdictional Issues,* (1995) 74 Can. Bar Rev. 187; P. Macklem, *Normative Dimensions of an Aboriginal Right of Self-Government,* (1995) 21 Queen's L.J. 173; A. Lafontaine, *La coexistence de l'obligation fiduciaire de la Couronne et du droit à l'autonomie gouvernementale des peuples autochtones,* (1995) 36 C. de D. 669; K. McNeil, *Envisaging Constitutional Space for Aboriginal Governments,* (1993) 19 Queen's L.J. 95; B. Slattery, *Aboriginal Sovereignty and Imperial Claims,* (1991) 29 Osgoode Hall L.J. 681; P. Macklem, *First Nations Self-Government and the Borders of the Canadian Legal Imagination,* (1991), 36 McGill L. R. 382; B. Ryder, *The Demise and Rise of the Classical Paradigm in Canadian Federalism: Promoting Autonomy for the Provinces and First Nations,* (1991) 36 McGill L.J. 308.

49 "Clear and plain" intent on the part of the Crown is said to be required when Aboriginal rights are allegedly extinguished by the Parliament of Canada. See, for example, *Delgamuukw v. British Columbia*, note 2, *supra*, para. 180, per Lamer C.J.

50 See text accompanying note 105, infra. See also W. Moss, "Inuit Perspectives on Treaty Rights and Governance" in Royal Commission on Aborig-

inal Peoples, *Aboriginal Self-Government [:] Legal and Constitutional Issues* (Ottawa: Minister of Supply and Services Canada, 1995) 55, at 92, where the inherent right of self-government from an Inuit viewpoint is described as "a pre-existing and fundamental human right and therefore not subject to extinguishment."

51 Royal Commission on Aboriginal Peoples, *Report of the Royal Commission on Aboriginal Peoples* (Ottawa: Canada Communication Group, 1996), vol. 1, at 139-140.

52 "Statement of Reconciliation" in Indian Affairs and Northern Development, *Gathering Strength—Canada's Aboriginal Action Plan* (Ottawa: Minister of Public Works and Government Services, 1997), at 4.

53 C. Brölmann & M. Zieck, "Indigenous Peoples" in C. Brölmann, R. Lefeber, M. Zieck, (eds.), *Peoples and Minorities in International Law* (Boston: Kluwer Academic Publishers, 1993) 187, at 219: "The survival of indigenous peoples requires more than merely the protection of their territorial basis. Their institutions, customs and laws, in short, their distinct cultures, need protection as well ... It is rather difficult to envisage how a culture in its broadest sense can be protected without granting some form of autonomy."

54 Royal Commission on Aboriginal Peoples, *Report of the Royal Commission on Aboriginal Peoples, supra,* note 51, vol. 3, at 5: "Current social problems are in large part a legacy of historical policies of displacement and assimilation, and their resolution lies in recognizing the authority of Aboriginal people to chart their own future within the Canadian federation." See also pp. 109, 201.

    See also Canadian Medical Association, *Bridging the Gap [:] Promoting Health and Healing for Aboriginal Peoples in Canada* (Ottawa: Canadian Medical Association, 1994) at 14: "It is recognized that self-determination in social, political and economic life improves the health of Aboriginal peoples and their communities. Therefore, the CMA encourages and supports the Aboriginal peoples in their quest for resolution of self-determination and land use." And at 13: "The health status of Aboriginal peoples in Canada is a measurable outcome of social, biological, economical, political, educational and environmental factors."

55 P. Hogg & M.E. Turpel, *Implementing Aboriginal Self-Government: Constitutional and Jurisdictional Issues, supra,* note 48, at 211 (agreements on self-government do not create the right, but settle mutually acceptable rules to govern the relationship between three orders of government).

56 Royal Commission on Aboriginal Peoples, *Report of the Royal Commission on Aboriginal Peoples, supra,* note 51, vol. 1, at 679: "There is no more basic principle in Aboriginal traditions than a people's right to govern itself according to its own laws and ways. This same principle is considered fundamental in the larger Canadian society and underpins the federal arrangements that characterize the Canadian Constitution." See also C. Bell, *New Directions in the Law of Aboriginal Rights,* (1998) 77 Can. Bar Rev. 36, at 71-72.

57 *R. v. Van der Peet, supra,* note 9, para. 117.

58 See, for example, P. Macklem, *Distributing Sovereignty: Indian Nations and Equality of Peoples*, (1993) 45 Stanford L. Rev. 1311, at 1367: "*From the perspective of both formal and substantive equality of peoples, indigenous peoples of North America can advance powerful claims* for a degree of sovereignty over their individual and collective identities." See also Royal Commission on Aboriginal Peoples, *Report of the Royal Commission on Aboriginal Peoples, supra*, note 51, vol. 5, at 162: "[Aboriginal, provincial and federal governments] share the sovereign powers of Canada as a whole, powers that represent a pooling of existing sovereignties."

See, generally, B. Slattery, *Aboriginal Sovereignty and Imperial Claims*, (1991) 29 Osgoode Hall L.J. 681; P. Joffe & M.E. Turpel, *Extinguishment of the Rights of Aboriginal Peoples: Problems and Alternatives*, A study prepared for the Royal Commission on Aboriginal Peoples, vol. 1, 1995, c. 4 ("Contending Sovereignties"); A. Bissonnette, *Le droit à l'autonomie gouvernementale des peuples autochtones: un phénix qui renaîtra de ses cendres*, (1993) 24 Revue générale de droit 5 at 22.

59 *R. v. Van der Peet, supra*, note 9, para. 37 (Lamer C.J.C.), para. 106 (L'Heureux-Dubé J.); *R. v. Côté*, [1996] 4 C.N.L.R. 26, para. 48 (Lamer C.J.C.); *R. v. Sioui*, [1990], 1 S.C.R. 1025, at 1052-1053.

See also A. Lajoie, et al., *Le statut juridique des peuples autochtones au Québec et le pluralisme* (Cowansville, Québec: Les Éditions Yvon Blais, 1996), at 95, 127 and 140, where it is indicated that, on occasion, the French had explicitly recognized the sovereignty of Aboriginal peoples (e.g. when negotiating the Great Treaty of Peace of 1701).

60 See, for example, M. Morin, *L'Usurpation de la souveraineté autochtone [:] Le cas des peuples de la Nouvelle-France et des colonies anglaises de l'Amérique du Nord* (Montréal: Les Éditions du Boréal, 1997), at 266; R. Dupuis & K. McNeil, *Canada's Fiduciary Obligation to Aboriginal Peoples in the Context of Accession to Sovereignty by Quebec* (Ottawa: Minister of Supply and Services Canada, 1995), vol. 2, Domestic Dimensions, at 50.

61 See also P. Hogg & M.E. Turpel, *Implementing Aboriginal Self-Government: Constitutional and Jurisdictional Issues, supra*, note 48; K. Yukich, *Aboriginal Rights in the Constitution and International Law*, (1996) 30 U.B.C. L. Rev. 235; P. Macklem, *Aboriginal Rights and State Obligations*, (1997) 36 Alta. L. Rev. 97, at 109 (respect for Aboriginal sovereignty underlies many arguments in favour of the inherent right of self-government).

62 B. Slattery, *Aboriginal Sovereignty and Imperial Claims*, (1991) 29 Osgoode Hall L.J. 681, at 690: "... native American peoples held sovereign status and title to the territories they occupied at the time of European contact and ... this fundamental fact transforms our understanding of everything that followed." See also P. Russell, *High Courts and the Rights of Aboriginal Peoples: The Limits of Judicial Independence*, (1998) 61 Sask. L. Rev. 247, at 275-276 (sovereignty in Canada should be shared); and M.D. Becker, *'We Are an Independent Nation': A History of Iroquois Sovereignty*, (1998) 46 Buffalo L. Rev. 981.

63 P. Russell, *Aboriginal Nationalism and Québec Nationalism: Reconciliation Through Fourth World Decolonization*, (1997) 8:4 Constitutional Forum 110

at 116: "It is only by sharing sovereignty that the relationship of Aboriginal peoples to the nation-states in which they live can move to one that is
fundamentally federal rather than imperial"; R. Whitaker, "Aboriginal
Self-Determination and Self-Government: Sovereignty by Inclusion," *Canada Watch* 5 (June/July 1997, no. 5) 69, at 73: "Sovereignty, Aboriginal
voices are telling us, is not an absolute, not a zero-sum of authority; it is
something that can, and should, be shared."

See also Royal Commission on Aboriginal Peoples, *Report of the Royal
Commission on Aboriginal Peoples, supra,* note 51, vol. 2(1), at 172: "The right
of self-determination is held by all the Aboriginal peoples of Canada ... It
gives Aboriginal peoples the right to opt for a large variety of governmental arrangements within Canada, including some that involve a high degree of sovereignty." In addition, see G. Erasmus, "Towards a National
Agenda" in F. Cassidy, (ed.), *Aboriginal Self-Determination* (B.C./Montreal:
Oolichan Books/Institute for Research on Public Policy, 1991) 171 at 173:
"... we have already a divided sovereignty in Canada. If we can put in place
a process that would allow for peaceful negotiations, we could finally recognize that First Nations can continue to enjoy their original responsibility and sovereignty. If so, we could end up in a situation where Canada
would have a number of sources of sovereignty and it could be practical—
it could work."

64 Royal Commission on Aboriginal Peoples, *Report of the Royal Commission on
Aboriginal Peoples, supra,* note 51, vol. 5, at 1-2.

See also Minister of Indian Affairs and Northern Development, *Ab-
original Self-Government: The Government of Canada's Approach to Implementa-
tion of the Inherent Right and the Negotiation of Aboriginal Self-Government*
(Ottawa: Public Works and Government Services, 1995); P. Hogg & M.E.
Turpel, *Implementing Aboriginal Self-Government: Constitutional and Jurisdic-
tional Issues, supra,* note 48, at 211; P. Hogg, *Constitutional Law of Canada,*
Loose-leaf Edition (Toronto: Carswell, 1997), vol. 1, at 27-46, n. 166; P.
Monahan, *Constitutional Law* (Concord, Ontario: Irwin Law, 1997), at 36.
Cf. P. Thibault, *Le rapport Dussault-Erasmus et le droit à l'autonomie gouverne-
mentale des peuples autochtones,* (1998) 9 N.J.C.L. 159, at 221-222.

65 *Reference re Secession of Québec, supra,* note 3.

66 *Id.* para. 64. The Court cited *R. v. Oakes,* [1986] 1 S.C.R. 103, at 136 in this
regard.

67 For a brief summary of other aspects of the judgment in the *Québec Secession Reference* that are relevant to Aboriginal peoples, see P. Joffe, "Québec's
sovereignty project and aboriginal rights" in *Canada Watch,* January-Febru-
ary 1999, nos. 1-2, 6.

68 *Id.,* para. 64.

69 T. Franck, *The Emerging Right to Democratic Governance,* (1992) 86 Am. J.
Int'l L. 46 at 52.

70 *Reference re Secession of Québec, supra,* note 3, para. 114.

71 See J.-M. Arbour, *Droit international public,* 3rd ed. (Cowansville, Québec:
Éditions Yvon Blais, 1997), at 116, where it is said that the expressions
customary international law and principles of international law are exactly

equivalent and should not be distinguished. See also Nguyen Quoc Dinh, P. Dallier & A. Pellet, *Droit international public*, 5th ed. (Paris: L.G.D.J., 1994), at 341.

See also A. Bayefsky, *International Human Rights Law [:] Use in Canadian Charter of Rights Litigation* (Toronto: Butterworths, 1992), at 10: "International jurisprudence sets two conditions for the existence of a customary rule of international law: (1) evidence of a sufficient degree of state practice, and (2) a determination that states conceive themselves as acting under a legal obligation."

72 I. Brownlie, *Principles of Public International Law*, 5th ed. (Oxford: Clarendon Press, 1998), at 19.

73 In support of its position, the Supreme Court cites two authors: A. Cassese, *Self-Determination of peoples: A legal reappraisal* (Cambridge: Cambridge University Press, 1995), at 171-172; K. Doehring, "Self-Determination" in B. Simma, ed., *The Charter of the United Nations: A Commentary* (New York: Oxford University Press, 1994), at 70. In both instances, the authors make no specific reference to "general principles of international law." Instead, both authors go further and describe the right to self-determination as now acquiring the status of a peremptory norm, i.e. *jus cogens*. Peremptory norms are described as "rules of customary law which cannot be set aside by treaty or acquiescence but only by the formation of a subsequent customary rule of contrary effect": see I. Brownlie, *Principles of Public International Law*, 5th ed. (Oxford: Clarendon Press, 1998) at 515.

It is not clear whether the Supreme Court of Canada necessarily views the right to self-determination as a peremptory norm, since it did not expressly use this term. However, the references cited by the Court clearly support the view that the term "general principle of international law," as used by the Court, refers at the very least to a rule of customary international law.

74 J. Duursma, *Fragmentation and the International Relations of Micro-States [:] Self-Determination and Statehood, supra*, note 33, at 77: "There is little doubt that the phrase [in the international human rights covenants] 'all peoples have the right of self-determination' is an accepted customary rule of international law."

See also S.J. Anaya, *Indigenous Rights Norms in Contemporary International Law*, (1991) 8 Arizona J. of Int'l & Comp. Law 1 at 29-30: "Beyond its textual affirmation, self-determination is widely held to be a norm of general or customary international law, and arguably *jus cogens* (a peremptory norm)."

75 A. Bayefsky, *International Human Rights Law [:] Use in Canadian Charter of Rights Litigation, supra*, note 71, at 5-10.

76 *Id.*, at 5.

77 These positions were argued by the Intervener Grand Council of the Crees in the *Secession Reference*. See *Factum of the Intervener Grand Council of the Crees (Eeyou Estchee)*, para. 76; *Factum of the Intervener Grand Council of the Crees (Eeyou Estchee)—Reply to Factum of the Amicus Curiae*, para. 83. (Factums submitted in this *Reference* are available on QuickLaw, database SCQR.)

78 While there is no legal definition of what constitutes a "people," the practice of the United Nations is to retain a very broad meaning of the term "peoples" for questions pertaining to self-determination. Both objective elements (e.g. common language, history, culture, race or ethnicity, way of life, and territory) and subjective elements (the will of a particular group to identify and assert its existence as a people) have been identified. See generally Secretariat of the Int'l Commission of Jurists, *East Pakistan Staff Study*, (1972) 8 Int'l Comm. of J. 23.

79 *Statements of the Canadian Delegation*, Commission on Human Rights, 53rd Sess., Working Group established in accordance with Commission on Human Rights resolution 1995/32 of 3 March 1995, 2nd Sess., Geneva, 21 October—1 November 1996, cited in *Consultations Between Canadian Aboriginal Organizations and DFAIT in Preparation for the 53rd Session of the U.N. Commission on Human Rights, February 4, 1997* (statement on art. 3, right to self-determination, on October 31, 1996).

80 *Nuclear Tests (Australia v. France)*, [1974] I.C.J. Rep. 253 at 268, para. 46: "Just as the very rule of *pacta sunt servanda* in the law of treaties is based on good faith, so also is the binding character of an international obligation assumed by unilateral declaration." And at 267, para. 43: "An undertaking of this kind, if given publicly, and with an intent to be bound, even though not made within the context of international negotiations, is binding."

This issue is discussed in P. Joffe, *International Practice, Québec Secession and Indigenous Peoples: The Imperative for Fairness, Non-discrimination and Respect for Human Rights*, (1997) 8.1 N.J.C.L. 97, at 99-101.

81 *Reply By the Attorney General of Canada to Questions Posed By the Supreme Court of Canada*, para. 8, available on QuickLaw, database SCQR.

82 G. La Forest, *The Expanding Role of the Supreme Court of Canada in International Law Issues*, (1996) 34 Can. Yearbook Int'l L. 89 at 97.

83 K. Roach, *Constitutional Remedies in Canada* (Aurora, Ontario: Canada Law Book, 1996), at 15-1. Roach adds at 15-3: "A purposive approach to remedies for aboriginal rights will recognize that both the history and future of aboriginal rights involve elements of self-determination."

84 *Reference re Secession of Québec, supra*, note 3, para. 126.

85 See also R. Dussault, "Redéfinir la relation avec les peuples autochtones du Canada: La vision d'avenir de la Commission royale" in G.A. Beaudoin et al., *Le fédéralisme de demain: Réformes essentielles/ Federalism for the Future: Essential Reforms* (Montreal: Wilson & Lafleur ltée, 1998) 345, at 349.

86 R. McCorquodale, *Self-Determination: A Human Rights Approach*, (1994) 43 Int'l & Comp. L.Q. 857, at 864. See also draft *U.N. Declaration on the Rights of Indigenous Peoples*, in U.N. Doc. E/CN.4/1995/2; E/CN.4/Sub.2/1994/56, 28 October 1994, at 105-115, reprinted in (1995) 34 I.L.M. 541, art. 31: "Indigenous peoples, as a specific form of exercising their right to self-determination, have the right to autonomy or self-government"; S. J. Anaya, *Indigenous Peoples in International Law, supra*, note 33, at 109 ("Self-government is the overarching political dimension of ongoing self-determination"); Royal Commission on Aboriginal Peoples, *Report of the Royal Commission on Aboriginal Peoples, supra*, note 51, vol. 2(1), at 175; A. Bucha-

nan, Federalism, Secession, and the Morality of Inclusion, (1995) 37 Arizona L. Rev. 53, at 54.

87 The three questions referred by the federal government to the Supreme Court of Canada were:

(1) Under the Constitution of Canada, can the National Assembly, legislature or Government of Quebec effect the secession of Quebec from Canada unilaterally?

(2) Does international law give the National Assembly, legislature or Government of Quebec the right to effect the secession of Quebec from Canada unilaterally? In this regard, is there a right to self-determination under international law that would give the National Assembly, legislature or Government of Quebec the right to effect the secession of Quebec from Canada unilaterally?

(3) In the event of a conflict between domestic and international law on the right of the National Assembly, legislature or Government of Quebec to effect the secession of Quebec from Canada unilaterally, which would take precedence in Canada?

88 *Reference re Secession of Québec, supra,* note 3, para. 125.

89 *Id.,* para. 139.

90 *Delgamuukw v. British Columbia, supra,* note 2, para. 85.

91 H. Gros Espiell, Special Rapporteur, *The Right to Self-Determination: Implementation of United Nations Resolutions,* Study for the Sub-Commission on Prevention of Discrimination and Protection of Minorities, (New York: United Nations, 1980), U.N. Doc. E/CN.4/Sub.2/405/Rev.1 at 10, para. 59. In this U.N. study, Gros Espiell also took the view that the right to self-determination did not extend to peoples already organized in an independent state. However, today this limited perspective enjoys little acceptance among international jurists. A much broader view has been expressed by the Supreme Court of Canada in *Reference re Secession of Québec, supra,* note 3, para. 138, and recently by the government of Canada.

92 Article 1, para. 3 of both the *International Covenant on Civil and Political Rights, supra,* note 22, and the *International Covenant on Economic, Social and Cultural Rights,* (1966), G.A. Res. 2200, 21 U.N. GAOR, Supp. (No. 16), 49, U.N. Doc. A/6319 (1966); Can. T.S. 1976 No. 46.

93 In *Delgamuukw v. British Columbia, supra,* note 2, para. 176, Lamer C.J.C. recognized (as did the courts below) that "separating federal jurisdiction over Indians from jurisdiction over their lands would have a most unfortunate result ... the government vested with primary constitutional responsibility for securing the welfare of the Canada's aboriginal peoples would find itself unable to safeguard one of the most central of native interests—their interest in their lands." Analogously, it would make little sense to recognize Aboriginal peoples' jurisdiction in respect to themselves but not their territories, lands and resources.

94 See cases cited in note 9, *supra.*

95 Report of the Special Committee, *Indian Self-Government in Canada* (Ottawa: Queen's Printer, 1983) ("Penner Report"), at 44: "The Committee recommends that the right of Indian peoples to self-government be explicitly

stated and entrenched in the Constitution of Canada." See also draft *United Nations Declaration on the Rights of Indigenous Peoples*, article 3: "Indigenous peoples have the right to self-determination. By virtue of that right they freely determine their political status and freely pursue their economic, social and cultural development."

In addition, see Canadian Human Rights Commission, *Annual Report 1993* (Ottawa: Minister of Supply and Services Canada, 1994) at 23: "... the inherent right of self-government must be agreed to exist; but more formal constitutional recognition of the fact would nevertheless contribute to the creation of a successful partnership."

96 E.-I. Daes, *Equality of Peoples Under the Auspices of the United Nations Declaration on the Rights of Indigenous Peoples*, (1995) 7 St. Thomas L. Rev. 493.

97 *Delgamuukw v. British Columbia*, *supra*, note 2, para. 154.

98 See, generally, the draft *United Nations Declaration on the Rights of Indigenous Peoples*; and the *Indigenous and Tribal Peoples Convention*, 1989, I.L.O. Convention No. 169, I.L.O., 76th Sess., reprinted in (1989) 28 I.L.M. 1382 (not yet in force in Canada).

99 See I. Cotler, "Human Rights Advocacy and the NGO Agenda" in I. Cotler & F.P. Eliadis, (eds.), *International Human Rights Law [:] Theory and Practice* (Montreal: Canadian Human Rights Foundation, 1992) 63, at 66: "... a ninth category [of human rights], one distinguishably set forth in the Canadian *Charter*—and increasingly recognized in international human rights law—is the category of *aboriginal rights*."

100 The *International Bill of Rights* is said to include the *Universal Declaration of Human Rights*, the *International Covenant on Civil and Political Rights*, and the *International Covenant on Economic, Social and Cultural Rights*.

101 Similar arguments are made in regard to the role of regional human rights instruments in reinforcing universal human rights norms: see, for example, C. Anyangwe, *Obligations of State Parties to the African Charter on Human and Peoples' Rights*, (1998) 10 African J. Int'l & Comp. L. 625, at 625.

102 All of the major international human rights instruments include references to the right to self-determination. See, for example, *Charter of the United Nations*, Can. T.S. 1945 No. 76; [1976] Yrbk. U.N. 1043; 59 Stat. 1031, T.S. 993, arts. 1, 55; *International Covenant on Civil and Political Rights*, art. 1; *International Covenant on Economic, Social and Cultural Rights*, art. 1; United Nations World Conference on Human Rights, *Vienna Declaration and Programme of Action*, adopted June 25, 1993, reprinted in (1993) 32 I.L.M. 1661, para. 2. See also S. J. Anaya, *Indigenous Peoples in International Law*, *supra*, note 33, at 90, n. 19 (references re self-determination is a human right); and U. Umozurike, *Self-Determination in International Law* (Hamden, Connecticut: Archon Books, 1972), at 46 et seq.

103 *Reference re Secession of Québec*, *supra*, note 3, para. 124.

104 See, for example, K. McNeil, *Aboriginal Title and the Division of Powers: Rethinking Federal and Provincial Jurisdiction*, (1998) 61 Sask. L. Rev. 431, where the author aptly questions the coherency of current judicial analyses that allow Aboriginal peoples' rights to be intruded upon by governments.

105 See, for example, the *Universal Declaration of Human Rights*, G.A. Res. 217 (III 1948), first preambular paragraph: "*Whereas* recognition of the inherent dignity and of the equal and inalienable rights of all members of the human family is the foundation of freedom, justice and peace in the world." Similar wording is found in the preamble of the two international human rights Covenants. See also *Charter of Paris for a New Europe, A New Era of Democracy, Peace and Unity*, November 21, 1990, reprinted in (1991) 30 I.L.M. 190: "*Human rights and fundamental freedoms are the birthright of all human beings, are inalienable and are guaranteed by law.* Their protection and promotion is the first responsibility of government. Respect for them is an essential safeguard against an over-mighty State. Their observance and full exercise are the foundation of freedom, justice and peace." [Emphasis added.]

106 "Extinguishment" is defined as "the destruction or cancellation of a right": *Black's Law Dictionary*, 6th ed. (St. Paul: West Publishing Co., 1990), at 584.

107 See, for example, the *Canadian Charter of Rights and Freedoms*, art. 1 ("reasonable limits prescribed by law as can be demonstrably justified in a free and democratic society"); and art 33 (derogation permitted solely in certain cases).

108 See also draft *U.N. Declaration on the Rights of Indigenous Peoples*, art. 44: "Nothing in this Declaration may be construed as diminishing or extinguishing existing or future rights indigenous peoples may have or acquire."

109 Art. 5, para. 1 of the Covenants: "*Nothing in the present Covenant may be interpreted as implying* for any State, group or person any right to engage in any activity or to perform any act aimed at the *destruction of any of the rights or freedoms recognized herein*, or at their limitation to a greater extent than is provided for in the present Covenant." [Emphasis added.]

110 Art. 4: "... the State may subject such rights only to such limitations as are determined by law *only in so far as this may be compatible with the nature of these rights* and solely for the purpose of promoting the general welfare in a democratic society." [Emphasis added.]

111 Art. 4.

112 A. Kiss, "Permissible Limitations on Rights" in L. Henkin, (ed.), *The International Bill of Rights [:] The Covenant on Civil and Political Rights* (New York: Columbia University Press, 1981) 290, at 290.

113 See text accompanying note 23, *supra*.

114 See "Concluding observations of the Human Rights Committee" in United Nations Human Rights Committee, *Consideration of reports submitted by States parties under article 40 of the Covenant*, 7 April 1999, CCPR/C/79/Add. 105, para. 8.

115 *Id.*, para. 7.

116 *Constitution Act*, 1982, s. 35(1).

117 D. McRae, *Report on the Complaints of the Innu of Labrador to the Canadian Human Rights Commission*, Ottawa, August 18, 1993, at 5.

118 United Nations Committee on Economic, Social and Cultural Rights, *Consideration of Reports Submitted by States Parties Under Articles 16 and 17 of the Covenant*, U.N. Doc. E/C.12/1/Add.31, 4 December 1998, para. 18.

119 P. Hogg, *Constitutional Law of Canada, supra,* note 64, vol. 2, at 33-17: "It is never seriously doubted that progressive interpretation is necessary and desirable in order to adapt the Constitution to facts that did not exist and could not have been foreseen at the time when it was written."

120 *Edwards v. A.-G. Canada,* [1930] A.C. 124 (P.C.) at 136.

121 *Reference re Secession of Québec, supra,* note 3, para. 52.

122 *A.-G. Canada v. Mossop,* [1993] 1 S.C.R. 554, at 621.

123 In *Mossop,* the Court was examining enumerated grounds of discrimination.

124 *Hunter v. Southam Inc.,* [1984] 2 S.C.R. 145 at 155.

125 See also J. Borrows & L.I. Rotman, *The Sui Generis Nature of Aboriginal Rights: Does it Make a Difference?,* (1997) 36 Alta. L. Rev. 9, at 39.

126 See also *Delgamuukw v. British Columbia, supra,* note 2, para. 201, per La Forest J. (approach adopted under s. 35(1) is a highly contextual one); and *Edmonton Journal v. A.-G. Alberta,* [1989] 2 S.C.R. 1326 (S.C.C.) at 1355-1356, per Wilson J. ("contextual approach" emanates from the interpretation clause in s. 1 of the *Canadian Charter of Rights and Freedoms*).

In regard to the inherent Aboriginal right to self-government, a contextual clause was included in a substantive provision of the now defunct Charlottetown Accord. See Draft Legal Text, October 9, 1992, s. 35.1 (3) (contextual statement) in K. McRoberts & P. Monahan, (eds.), *The Charlottetown Accord, the Referendum and the Future of Canada* (Toronto: Univ. of Toronto Press, 1993) at 348. In s. 35.1 (3) of the Draft Legal Text, it was provided that:

> The exercise of the [inherent] right [of self-government within Canada] includes the authority of duly constituted legislative bodies of the Aboriginal peoples, each within its own jurisdiction,
>
> a) to safeguard and develop their languages, cultures, economies, identities, institutions and traditions, and
>
> b) to develop, maintain and strengthen their relationship with their lands, waters and environment, so as to determine and control their development as peoples according to their own values and priorities and to ensure the integrity of their societies.

On the usefulness of a contextual approach concerning Aboriginal self-government, see P. Hogg & M.E. Turpel, *Implementing Aboriginal Self-Government: Constitutional and Jurisdictional Issues, supra,* note 48, at 192 *et seq.*; A. Bissonnette, *Le droit à l'autonomie gouvernementale des peuples autochtones: un phénix qui renaîtra de ses cendres, supra,* note 58, at 7-9.

127 Royal Commission on Aboriginal Peoples, *Report of the Royal Commission on Aboriginal Peoples, supra,* note 51, vol. 5, at 141 et seq. (summary of recommendations).

128 For example, a major shortcoming is the lack of an adequate land and resource base among Aboriginal peoples in Québec.

129 See note 5, *supra.*

130 Identical duties are provided in s. 2(c) of *An Act to extend the Boundaries of the Province of Quebec,* S.C. 1912, c.45 and in s.2(c) of the Schedule in *An Act respecting the extension of the Province of Quebec by the annexation of Ungava,*

S.Q. 1912, c. 7: "That the province of Québec will recognize the rights of the Indian inhabitants of the territory above described to the same extent, and will obtain surrenders of such rights in the same manner, as the Government of Canada has heretofore recognized such rights and obtained surrender thereof, and the said province shall bear and satisfy all charges and expenditures in connection with or arising out of such surrenders."

See also the terms and conditions pertaining to the *Rupert's Land and North-Western Territory Order*, 1870 in *Address to Her Majesty the Queen from the Senate and House of Commons of the Dominion of Canada*, Schedule (A), R.S.C. 1985, App. II, No. 9, 8 at 8-9: "... *upon the transference of the territories in question* to the Canadian government, the claims of the Indian tribes to compensation for lands required for purposes of settlement will be considered and settled *in conformity with the equitable principles which have uniformly governed the British Crown in its dealings with the aborigines* ..." [December 1867 Address].

131 *R. v. Sparrow*, [1990] 1 S.C.R. 1075 at 1103-1104: "... the James Bay development by Québec Hydro was originally initiated without regard to the rights of the Indians who lived there, even though these were expressly protected by a constitutional instrument; see the *Québec Boundaries Extension Act*, 1912, S.C. 1912, c. 45."

132 *James Bay and Northern Quebec Agreement and Complementary Agreements*, 1997 Edition (Québec: Les Publications du Québec, 1996).

133 Assemblée nationale, *Journal des Débats*, 4th Sess., 30th Legisl., vol. 17, No. 29, June 21, 1976, at 1597 (Québec Minister of Natural Resources, Jean Cournoyer). Apparently, these types of misrepresentations have characterized the treaty process since the early 1800s. See B. Clark, *Native Liberty, Crown Sovereignty [:] The Existing Aboriginal Right to Self-Government in Canada* (Montreal: McGill-Queen's University Press, 1990) at 202. "The treaties since the early 1800s were made by colonials. *To drive hard bargains the colonials led the natives to believe that they did not already have any strictly legal rights. The natives were induced to enter these treaties in order to acquire some legal rights, at least to small portions of the Indian territory, which small portions would be called their reserves.*" [Emphasis added.]

134 See the *ex post facto* statement of J. Ciaccia in the "Philosophy of the Agreement" in the James Bay and Northern Quebec Agreement, *supra*, note 132, at xx: "The Québec government has taken the position in these negotiations that it wanted to do all that was necessary to protect the traditional culture and economy of the native peoples, *while at the same time fulfilling its obligations under the Act of 1912.*" [Emphasis added.]

135 Reference is being made here to Category II lands, which are lands selected under JBNQA by the Aboriginal peoples concerned, where they are recognized to have exclusive hunting, fishing and trapping rights.

136 See N. Rouland, *Les Inuit du Nouveau-Québec et la Convention de la Baie James* (Québec: Association Inuksiutiit & Centre d'études nordiques de l'Université Laval, 1978) at 122, where this policy of Québec is described and criticized.

137 *International Covenant on Civil and Political Rights*, article 47.

138 Grand Council of the Crees (of Quebec), *Submission: Status and Rights of the James Bay Crees in the Context of Quebec's Secession from Canada* (Submission to the U.N. Commission on Human Rights, February 1992), at 100.

139 Royal Commission on Aboriginal Peoples, *Treaty Making in the Spirit of Coexistence: An Alternative to Extinguishment* (Ottawa: Supply and Services, 1995), at 17: "In light of divergent understandings of extinguishment clauses and the jurisprudence on treaty interpretation ... it cannot always be said with certainty that the written terms of an extinguishment clause will determine the clause's legal effect."

    In regard to the JBNQA, see generally S. Vincent & G. Bowers, (eds), *Baie James et Nord quebécois: dix ans après/James Bay and Northern Québec: Ten Years After* (Montréal: Recherches amérindiennes au Québec, 1985), where it is demonstrated that there is no common understanding whatsoever among representatives of the federal government, Québec government and various Aboriginal peoples as to what any purported "extinguishment" of rights under JBNQA might mean.

140 James Bay and Northern Quebec Agreement, *supra*, note 132.

141 Third party indigenous peoples affected by such purported "extinguishment" include: Innu (Montagnais), Algonquins, Atikamekw, Crees of Mocreebec (now in Ontario), Labrador Inuit, Labrador Innu, and Inuit in the Belcher Islands, N.W.T. The JBNQA, s. 2.14 includes an undertaking by the Québec government to negotiate with third party indigenous peoples, in respect to any "claims" which they may have in and to the northern territory. However, to date, no treaties have been signed with Aboriginal third parties, pursuant to this undertaking.

142 Commission des droits de la personne du Québec, *The Rights of Aboriginal Peoples [:] We must respect the rights of Native Peoples and deal with them accordingly* (Québec: January 1978) (Document 1), at 9-10: "*[T]he Québec government played a major role in inserting and maintaining the third party rights extinguishment clause in the federal bill* [i.e. s. 3(3) of the federal enabling legislation]. This issue was debated thoroughly while Bill C-9 was being studied, precisely because of the many protests it raised. These protests prompted the federal government to say it was prepared to review the provision. *It informed the Québec authorities of its intention, but the latter refused to review this condition of the agreement, which they deemed essential.* [new para.] *In summary, Québec played a decisive and dominant part in the overall affair,* and took action with direct and far-reaching implications for the territorial rights of the aboriginal peoples, the signatories and non-signatories of the agreement." [Emphasis added.]

143 P. Joffe & M.E. Turpel, *Extinguishment of the Rights of Aboriginal Peoples: Problems and Alternatives*, *supra*, note 58, vol. 1, 1995, at 315ff.

144 See, for example, Commission des droits de la personne du Québec, *The Rights of Aboriginal Peoples [:] We must respect the rights of Native Peoples and deal with them accordingly* (Québec: January 1978), at 21-23; Commission des droits de la personne du Québec, *Mémoire de la Commission des droits de la personne présenté à la Commission royale sur les peuples autochtones* (Montreal: novembre 1993) at 15, 26.

145 Assemblée nationale, *Journal des Débats, Commissions parlementaires*, Commission permanente des richesses naturelles et des terres et forêts, Entente concernant les Cris et les Inuit de la Baie James, 3rd Sess., 30th Legisl., November 6, 1975, No. 176, at B-6069 (J.-Y. Morin).

146 Assemblée nationale, *Journal des Débats, Commissions parlementaires*, Commission permanente des richesses naturelles et des terres et forêts, Entente concernant les Cris et les Inuit de la Baie James, 3rd Sess., 30th Legisl., November 7, 1975, No. 177, at B-6075.

147 Commission des droits de la personne du Québec, *Mémoire de la Commission des droits de la personne présenté à la Commission royale sur les peuples autochtones* (Montréal: November 1993) at 14; see also, at 43, the Commission's recommendation to permanently cast aside any pre-conditions requiring the extinguishment of rights.

148 D. Sambo, *Indigenous Peoples and International Standard-Setting Processes: Are State Governments Listening?*, (1993) 3 Transnat'l L. & Cont. Probs. 13 at 31. On the same page, the author adds: "No other people are pressured to 'extinguish' their rights to lands. This is racial discrimination. The practice of extinguishment must be eliminated." See also M. Seymour, *La Nation en question* (Montreal: Éditions de l'Hexagone, 1999), at 158 (old method of extinguishment of Aboriginal rights must be abandoned by Québec).

Studies that recommend alternatives to extinguishment include: Royal Commission on Aboriginal Peoples, *Treaty Making in the Spirit of Coexistence: An Alternative to Extinguishment* (Ottawa: Supply and Services, 1995); M. Jackson, *A New Covenant Chain: An Alternative Model to Extinguishment for Land Claims Agreements*, Report submitted to the Royal Commission on Aboriginal Peoples, February 1994; P. Joffe & M.E. Turpel, *Extinguishment of the Rights of Aboriginal Peoples: Problems and Alternatives, supra*, note 58, 3 vols.

149 *Programme du Parti Québécois [:] Des idées pour mon pays* (Montréal: Parti Québécois, 1994), at 21. Similarly, see also Parti Québécois, *La volonté de réussir: Programme et statuts du Parti Québécois* (Montreal: Parti Québécois, 1997), at 22.

150 See *Motion for the recognition of aboriginal rights in Québec*, adopted by the Québec National Assembly, March 20, 1985; *Motion portant reconnaissance des droits des autochtones*, adopted by Assemblée nationale du Québec, March 20, 1985.

151 See Assemblée nationale, *Journal des débats*, March 19, 1985, vol. 28,1 No. 38, at 2504, 2527-2528, where the objections of the Crees, Inuit, Mi'kmaq, Mohawks and Naskapis are brought to the attention of the Members of the National Assembly. All Liberal MNAs voted against the adoption of the Resolution, since it was said that the instrument had little or no content. See also Grand Council of the Crees, *Sovereign Injustice [:] Forcible Inclusion of the James Bay Crees and Cree Territory into a Sovereign Québec* (Nemaska, Québec, 1995), at 96-97.

152 The Québec government removed all draft provisions negotiated with Aboriginal peoples that it did not favour, e.g. existence of the federal fiduciary responsibility in relation to Aboriginal peoples. Moreover, the Resolution

provides that all future negotiations are to be based on the responses of the government to the positions of Aboriginal peoples (and not also on Aboriginal peoples' positions).

153 See, for example, J. Parizeau, *Pour un Québec souverain* (Montréal: VLB Éditeur, 1997), at 319, where the 1985 Resolution is referred to as an example of how "sensitive" the Québec government is to "minorities living on Québec territory."

154 Secrétariat aux affaires autochtones, *Partnership, Development, Achievement* (Québec: Gouvernement du Québec, 1998), at 17, where it is said that the National Assembly's resolution on the recognition of Aboriginal rights provides in part the "underpinning of Québec's action and identif[ies] the basic guidelines and principles for the strategic choices and proposed framework for intervention."

155 See cases cited, *supra*, in note 9.

156 *R. v. Côté, supra*, note 59.

157 The defendants in this important aboriginal and treaty fishing rights case were Algonquins, members of the Kitigan Zibi Anishinabeg (Desert River Band). As it has done in other cases, the Québec government was seeking far-reaching judicial conclusions denying the fundamental rights of other indigenous peoples, who were not parties to the case. Such practice is a violation of the rules of natural justice (*audi alteram partem*).

158 "*Terra nullius*" means "lands belonging to no one." The government also urged the Supreme Court of Canada to interpret the *Royal Proclamation of 1763* (often referred to as the "Indian Bill of Rights"), so as to preclude the recognition of indigenous land rights rather than to confirm them.

159 *Mabo et al. v. State of Queensland*, (1992) 175 C.L.R. 1 (High Court of Australia).

160 As Brennan J. of the High Court of Australia provides in *Mabo*, at 42: "Whatever the justification advanced in earlier days for refusing to recognize the rights and interests in land of the indigenous inhabitants of settled colonies, *an unjust and discriminatory doctrine of that kind can no longer be accepted.*" [Emphasis added.]

In rejecting Québec's argument in *Côté, supra*, note 59, para. 53, Chief Justice Lamer of the Supreme Court of Canada quoted the above words of Brennan J. and ruled as follows: "... the [Québec government's] proposed interpretation risks undermining the very purpose of s. 35(1) [of the Constitution Act, 1982] by *perpetuating the historical injustices suffered by aboriginal peoples at the hands of colonizers* who failed to respect the distinctive cultures of pre-existing aboriginal societies." [Emphasis added.]

161 Royal Commission on Aboriginal Peoples, *Report of the Royal Commission on Aboriginal Peoples, supra*, note 51, vol. 1, at 695: "To state that the Americas at the point of first contact with Europeans were empty uninhabited lands is, of course, factually incorrect. To the extent that concepts such as *terra nullius* and discovery also carry with them the baggage of racism and ethnocentrism, they are morally wrong as well."

See also S. Ratner, *Drawing a Better Line: Uti Possidetis and the Borders of New States*, (1996) 90 American J. Int'l L. 590, at 615: "*Terra nullius*, however, has no place in contemporary law. In the most literal sense, it is anachronistic ... But more important, the broader idea that the long-term inhabitants have no legally cognizable claim or title to is profoundly at odds with international human rights law and thus legally obsolete."

162 *Discriminatory and Colonial Positions Taken by the Government of Québec Before Supreme Court of Canada: Denial of the Existence of Aboriginal Rights in Québec,* Resolution No. 11/96, Secretariat of the Assembly of First Nations of Québec and Labrador, October 17, 1996.

163 E.-I. Daes, *Explanatory note concerning the draft declaration on the rights of indigenous peoples,* U.N. Doc. E/CN.4/Sub.2/1993/26/Add.1, at 2, para. 7.: "Indigenous groups are unquestionably 'peoples' in every political, social, cultural and ethnological meaning of this term. They have their own specific languages, laws, values and traditions; their own long histories as distinct societies and nations; and a unique economic, religious and spiritual relationship with the territories in which they have lived. It is neither logical nor scientific to treat them as the same 'peoples' as their neighbours, who obviously have different languages, histories and cultures."

164 Parti Québécois, *La volonté de réussir: Programme et statuts du Parti Québécois, supra,* note 149, at 18. The sub-heading "Historical Minorities" is placed under the heading "Citizenship." Cf. B. Melkevik, Le droit à l'identité et normes internationales: Minorités et peuples autochtones" in *Le Défi identitaire,* Cahiers d'études constitutionnelles et politiques de Montpellier I, Montpellier, 1996, 44, at 75 (Aboriginal peoples are "peoples" with economic, cultural and political heritages).

165 Parti Québécois, *La volonté de réussir: Programme et statuts du Parti Québécois, supra,* note 149, at 1: "The Québec people, composed of all of its citizens, is free to decide itself its status and its future." [Unofficial translation.] *Cf.* Parti Québécois, *Programme du Parti Québécois [:] Des idées pour mon pays* (Montréal: Parti Québécois, 1994), at 1, where it merely states that the "Québec people" exists, without indicating who is included and whether there are other peoples in the province.

166 *Indigenous and Tribal Peoples Convention, 1989* (No. 169), art. 1, para. 2, where "Self-identification" of indigenous and tribal peoples is regarded as "a fundamental criterion." See also R. McCorquodale, *Self-Determination: A Human Rights Approach, supra,* note 86, at 867. In F. Dumont, *Raisons communes* (Montréal: Boréal, 1995) at 63-64, the author seriously questions how Aboriginal peoples, against their will, can be included in the term "Québec nation" through the "magic of vocabulary."

167 See, for example, J. Brossard, *L'accession à la souveraineté et le cas du Québec,* 2nd ed. (Montréal: Les presses de l'Université de Montréal, 1995) (Supplément de D. Turp), at 182, where it is suggested that the best position to take is that the French-Canadian nation as a whole should exercise the right to self-determination; L. Dion, *Le Duel constitutionnel Québec-Canada* (Montréal: Les Éditions du Boréal, 1995), at 350 (French Canadians form a nation); L. Gagnon, "Débat: les mots taboos," *La Presse,* September 13, 1994, at B3 (true base of the Québec independence movement is the French-Canadian nation centred in Québec); M. Venne, "Le facteur culturel," *Le Devoir,* editorial,

April 23, 1999, at A8 (Quebecers' French-Canadian origins and the concept of founding peoples are the foundation of the sovereignist movement); P. Lemieux, "Être québécois, c'est être étatiste avant tout," *Le Devoir*, May 3, 1999, at A7 (author prefers to be referred to as "Canadien français," fears that definition of "québécois" reflects above all the values that a majority seeks to impose on others). Of course, nothing precludes French Canadians or others from self-identifying freely as Quebecers.

168 See also D. Lessard, "Les souverainistes cherchent un divorce à l'amiable," *La Presse*, March 27, 1999, at B1, where a CROP poll taken in Montreal between March 11-21, 1999 indicates more Quebecers are of the view that the Crees and Inuit constitute a people (80 per cent) and that Canadians constitute a people (86 per cent) than they are that Quebecers constitute a people (77 per cent).

169 See also M. Seymour, *La Nation en question, supra*, note 148, at 155 (there are eleven Aboriginal peoples and the Québec people living in whole or in part within the province of Québec).

170 See, for example, Secrétariat aux affaires autochtones, *Partnership, Development, Achievement, supra*, note 154, where Québec's latest policy fails to refer to Aboriginal peoples as "peoples" with the right to self-determination. See also T. Ha, "Quebec's borders are safe within Canada: Chrétien," *The Gazette*, Montreal, May 25, 1994, A1 at A2, where Lucien Bouchard, then leader of the Bloc Québécois, is quoted as follows: "The natives of Québec don't have a right of self-determination. It doesn't belong to them."

171 R. Guglielmo, *"Three Nations Warring in the Bosom of a Single State" [:] An Exploration of Identity and Self-Determination in Québec*, (1997) 21 Fletcher Forum of World Affairs 197, at 198: "Denial of well-articulated Cree arguments for self-determination has forced the Québécois secessionist movement to adopt a blatant double-standard and a line of reasoning fraught with contradictions, which greatly undermines the legitimacy of their own claims and reveals the racist strain which often underlies the *realpolitik* application of self-determination theory."

See also Assemblée nationale, *Journal des débats*, Commission d'étude des questions afférentes à l'accession du Québec à la souveraineté, 9 Oct. 1991, No. 5, at CEAS-137 (testimony of D. Turp), where in regard to self-determination and legitimacy, Turp indicates that "the aboriginal nations on their territory, are quite ahead of the francophones of Quebec, the anglophones of Quebec, all the Europeans and other nationalities on this territory." [Unofficial English translation.]

172 W. Ofuatey-Kodjoe, "Self-Determination" in O. Schacter & C. Joyner, eds., *United Nations Legal Order* (Cambridge: Cambridge Univ. Press, 1995) vol. 1, 349 at 354; H. Johnson, *Self-Determination Within the Community of Nations* (Leydon: A.W. Sijthoff, 1967), at 55: "In the discussions in the United Nations concerning the definition of the terms 'people' and 'nation' there was a tendency to equate the two. When a distinction was made, it was to indicate that 'people' was broader in scope. The significance of the use of this term centred on the desire to be certain that a narrow application of the term 'nation' would not prevent the extension of self-determi-

nation to dependent peoples who might not qualify as nations." See also discussion of "nations" and "peoples" in J. Duursma, *Fragmentation and the International Relations of Micro-States [:] Self-Determination and Statehood, supra*, note 33, at 14.

173 Royal Commission on Aboriginal Peoples, *Report of the Royal Commission on Aboriginal Peoples, supra*, note 51, vol. 2(1), at 178: "... the three Aboriginal peoples identified in section 35(2) encompass nations that also hold the right of self-determination." And at 182: "Aboriginal peoples are entitled to identify their own national units for purposes of exercising the right to self-determination. Given the variety of ways in which Aboriginal nations may be configured and the strong subjective element, any self-identification initiative must necessarily come from the people actually concerned." See also M. Seymour, *La Nation en question, supra*, note 148, at 16 ("peoples" and "nations" used almost synonymously).

Also, in *Worcester v. Georgia*, 31 U.S. (6 Pet.) 515 (1832), Marshall C.J. provides at 559: "The Indian nations had always been considered as distinct, independent political communities, retaining their original rights, as the undisputed possessors of the soil, from time immemorial ... *The very term 'nation', so generally applied to them, means 'a people distinct from the others.'* "

174 See *International Convention on the Elimination of All Forms of Racial Discrimination*, 660 U.N.T.S. 195, (1966) 5 I.L.M. 352. Adopted by U.N. General Assembly on December 21, 1965, opened for signature on March 7, 1966, and entered into force on January 4, 1969, art. 1, para. 1: "In this Convention, the term 'racial discrimination' shall mean any distinction, *exclusion, restriction* or preference based on race, colour, descent, or national or ethnic origin which has the *purpose or effect of nullifying or impairing the recognition, enjoyment or exercise, on an equal footing,* of human rights and fundamental freedoms in the political, economic, social, cultural or any other field of public life." [Emphasis added.]

175 This position of the Québec government is not shared by other commentators: see R. Janda, *La double indépendance [:] La naissance d'un Québec nouveau et la renaissance du Bas-Canada* (Montreal: Les Éditions Varia, 1998), at 93 (in regard to transferring Aboriginal peoples in the 1898 and 1912 territories to a new Québec state, their consent would be required); P. Hogg, *Principles Governing the Secession of Quebec*, (1997) 8.1 N.J.C.L. 19, at 44 (in view of their treaty rights, consent of the Crees and Inuit would be required regarding their northern territories). See generally M. Seymour, *La Nation en question, supra*, note 148, at 180-181 (Québec people cannot, in principle, have Québec accede to sovereignty without the consent of Aboriginal peoples); and at 184 (at moment when Québec declares its sovereignty, Aboriginal peoples would seem justified to exercise a right of association with Canada, but a response to their claims can avoid this). Should Aboriginal peoples not agree to join a sovereign Québec, secession might still be achieved for a portion of what is now the province of Québec. This could be the result of constitutional negotiations, in accordance with the legal framework and principles set out by the Supreme Court of Canada in *Reference re Secession of Québec, supra*, note 3.

176 On the possible use of force by the Québec government, see Grand Council of the Crees, *Sovereign Injustice*, note 151, *supra*, at 156-164; R. Séguin, "Iron hand possible, Quebec minister says," *Globe and Mail*, January 30, 1997, at A4. See also Statement of the Minister of Intergovernmental Affairs, Jacques Brassard, in Assemblée nationale, *Journal des débats*, 2nd sess., 35th legisl., November 12, 1997. For a strong criticism of Brassard's approach and argument, see A. Dubuc, "Babar et la partition," *La Presse*, editorial, November 15, 1997, at B2.

177 See, for example, M. Seymour, *La Nation en question, supra*, note 148, at 186, where the author states that Québec must not try to impose by force a sovereign state on Aboriginal peoples without trying simultaneously to satisfy their claims.

178 Grand Council of the Crees, *Sovereign Injustice [:] Forcible Inclusion of the James Bay Crees and Cree Territory into a Sovereign Québec, supra*, note 151, at 277-280.

179 In regard to JBNQA, see P. Hogg, *Principles Governing the Secession of Quebec, supra*, note 175, at 44: "[The Agreement] was negotiated in a federal context, and it provides for continuing Government obligations, some of which are owed by the Government of Canada ... and others by the Government of Québec ... Since Canada's obligations could no longer be fulfilled in an independent Québec, and would have to be assumed by the new state of Québec, a secession would constitute a breach of the Agreement. *The Agreement could be amended, of course, but only with the consent of the Aboriginal nations who are parties to it.*" [Emphasis added.] See also R. Howse and A. Malkin, *Canadians are a Sovereign People: How the Supreme Court Should Approach the Reference on Québec Secession*, (1997) 76 Can. Bar Rev. 186, at 210, n. 87: "Unilateral secession of Québec would mean that one level of government ... would no longer be able to carry out its obligations under the [JBNQA], and thus would constitute a fundamental breach of its terms."

180 In accordance with s. 35 of the *Constitution Act, 1982*, it is a constitutional requirement that Cree and Inuit treaty rights under JBNQA not be amended respectively without Cree or Inuit consent. Every chapter of JBNQA expressly requires the consent of the interested Aboriginal party, in the event of a proposed amendment.

181 Secrétariat aux affaires autochtones, *Partnership, Development, Achievement, supra*, note 154, at 22.

182 *Id.*

183 The 1985 National Assembly Resolution stipulates: "That this Assembly: ... Consider these [land claims] agreements and all future agreements of the same nature to have the same value as treaties." In addition, the 1985 Resolution urges the government to enter into agreements "guaranteeing" Aboriginal peoples the exercise of self-government and other fundamental rights. The text of this Resolution is reproduced in Secrétariat aux affaires autochtones, *Partnership, Development, Achievement, supra*, note 154, at 17-18.

184 See Parti Québécois, *La volonté de réussir: Programme et statuts du Parti Québécois, supra*, note 149, at 22 (in making the transition to a sovereign Québec,

existing "treaties" with Aboriginal peoples will be respected until they are replaced by new "agreements").

185 Secrétariat aux affaires autochtones, *Partnership, Development, Achievement, supra,* note 154, at 12.

186 *Sparrow v. The Queen, supra,* note 131, at 1107, per Dickson C.J.: "... no appearance of 'sharp dealing' should be sanctioned," quoting *R. v. Taylor and Williams,* (1981) 34 O.R. (2d) 360, at 367. See also *R. v. George,* [1966] S.C.R. 267, at 279 (Cartwright J. dissenting); and *Gitanyow First Nation v. Canada, supra,* note 5, at para. 74, where it is said that this duty to negotiate in good faith "must include at least the absence of any appearance of 'sharp dealing' ... disclosure of relevant factors ... and negotiation 'without oblique motive' ... " Similarly, in regard to judicial interpretation of treaties, see *R. v. Badger,* [1996] 2 C.N.L.R. 77, at 92, para. 41 ("[n]o appearance of 'sharp dealing' will be sanctioned").

See also J.S. Henderson, *Interpreting Sui Generis Treaties,* (1997) 36 Alta. L. Rev. 46, at 80: "It makes no difference whether the sharp dealings are in the negotiations or drafting of the treaties, or in the implementation of them. The courts have firmly stated that they do not tolerate or condone such conduct by the Crown."

187 Secrétariat aux affaires autochtones, *Partnership, Development, Achievement, supra,* note 154, at 11, 12, 19 and 21.

188 There is no articulated concept of "territorial integrity" of a province in Canadian law. As long as Québec remains a province, its boundaries are protected under Canada's Constitution: see *Constitution Act, 1871,* s. 3 and *Constitution Act, 1982,* s. 43. How the Québec government chooses to use the notion of "territorial integrity" in its 1998 policy on Aboriginal affairs is not explained.

At international law, the principle of "territorial integrity" applies to independent states and not provinces. In addition, this principle is not absolute and can only be successfully invoked if certain conditions are met: see *Reference re Secession of Québec, supra,* note 3, paras. 130, 154. See also T. Musgrave, *Self-Determination and National Minorities* (Oxford: Clarendon Press, 1997), at 235: "The maintenance or alteration of internal boundaries of an independent state is a matter which falls within the domestic jurisdiction of that state; it does not fall within the jurisdiction of international law."

189 Even if Québec could invoke the principle of territorial integrity, it likely would not be able to do so against the interests of the Aboriginal peoples concerned. See U. Umozurike, *Self-Determination in International Law, supra,* note 102, at 234, where it is said that "*the ultimate purpose of territorial integrity is to safeguard the interests of the peoples of a territory. The concept of territorial integrity is therefore meaningful so long as it continues to fulfill that purpose to all the sections of the people.*" [Emphasis added.]

190 While the policy document of Québec highlights the difficult socioeconomic and other conditions facing First Nations, it exploits this urgent situation by seeking to slip in the government's highly controversial political agenda. Future agreements with First Nations on such basic aspects as

essential services and community development should not be subject to such "reference points" as "territorial integrity." This is not only inappropriate but also unconscionable.

191 Evidence of such ultimate control by Québec has been incorporated into its 1998 policy. See, for example, Secrétariat aux affaires autochtones, *Partnership, Development, Achievement, supra,* note 154, at 22: "Should no agreement [with an Aboriginal nation] be negotiated or reached, of if one of the parties withdraws from an agreement already reached, Québec exercises its full jurisdiction."

192 The international law principle of "effectivity" is discussed in *Reference re Secession of Québec, supra,* note 3, paras. 140-146.

193 E. Thompson, "First Nations reject new policy," *The Gazette,* Montreal, May 20, 1998, at A5; M. Cloutier, "Les Premières Nations rejettent les propositions de Chevrette," *Le Devoir,* May 20, 1998, at A1. This does not mean that no agreements of any nature are being signed by First Nations and Québec. In relation to the Mohawks of Kahnawake, see K. Deer, "Québec Cabinet Signs Agreements," *The Eastern Door,* Kahnawake, March 26, 1999, at 1; A. Jelowicki, "Mohawks' tax picture changes," *The Gazette,* Montreal, March 31, 1999, at A4; M. Thibodeau, "Québec consent une exemption fiscale élargie aux Mohawks," *La Presse,* March 31, 1999, at A10.

194 See, for example, M. Seymour, *La Nation en question, supra,* note 148, where the author proposes a more constructive approach in Québec government policy, consistent with the right to self-determination of Aboriginal peoples.

195 See, for example, L. Mandell, "The Delgamuukw Decision," *supra,* note 11.

196 See *Sparrow v. The Queen, supra,* note 131, at 1112, per Dickson C.J.: "it is possible, and, indeed, crucial, to be sensitive to the aboriginal perspective itself on the meaning of the rights at stake."

197 *Montana Band of Indians v. Canada,* [1991] 2 F.C. 30, at 39, [1991] 2 C.N.L.R. 88, at 92: "Negotiated settlements of aboriginal claims are a distinct possibility in today's reality."

198 *MacMillan Bloedel v. Mullin,* [1985] 2 C.N.L.R. 58 (B.C.C.A.), at 77: "I think it fair to say that, in the end, the public anticipates that the claims will be resolved by negotiation and by settlement. This judicial proceeding is but a small part of the whole of a process that will ultimately find its solution in a reasonable exchange between governments and the Indian nations. Viewed in this context, I do not think that the granting of an interlocutory injunction confined to Meares Island can be reasonably said to lead to confusion and uncertainty in the minds of the public."

In regard to the right to an effective legal remedy, see also *Universal Declaration of Human Rights,* art. 8; *International Covenant on Civil and Political Rights,* art. 2, para. 6.

199 Royal Commission on Aboriginal Peoples, *Report of the Royal Commission on Aboriginal Peoples, supra,* note 51, vol. 2(2), at 562.

200 K. Roach, *Constitutional Remedies in Canada, supra,* note 83, at 15-3.

201 Royal Commission on Aboriginal Peoples, *Report of the Royal Commission on Aboriginal Peoples, supra,* note 51, vol. 2(2), at 564.

202 For a recent example of ensuring respect for the rights and priorities of Aboriginal peoples, see J. Green, "Panel: INCO may mine Voisey's Bay only after land claims," *Nunatsiaq News*, Iqaluit, April 16, 1999, at 13, where it is reported that a federal environmental assessment panel has determined that permission to develop a giant nickel mine in Labrador should proceed, but only after an agreement-in-principle on land claims is reached with the Inuit and Innu concerned. Should land claims discussions stall for unrelated reasons, then the panel recommended that at least an environmental co-management agreement should be negotiated as an interim measure.

203 James Bay and Northern Quebec Agreement, supra, note 132.

204 Inuit in northern Québec have been involved in considerably less litigation concerning JBNQA than the James Bay Crees.

205 For example, a recent Cree court action involves Ottawa, Québec, and 27 forestry companies: see M.-C. Ducas, "Les Cris en appellent aux tribunaux," *Le Devoir*, July 16, 1998, at A1; for strong criticisms of forestry practices in Québec, see also J.-R. Sansfaçon, "Le massacre forestier," *Le Devoir*, editorial, March 31, 1999, at A8; A. Gruda, "Le massacre à la scie," *La Presse*, editorial, April 13, 1999, at B2; L. Bélanger, "Nos forêts du Nord pourraient bien n'être plus un jour qu'un vague souvenir," *La Presse*, April 1, 1999, at B3. For a forestry industry viewpoint, see J. Gauvin, "La foresterie québécoise a fait des pas de géant," *La Presse*, April 15, 1999, at B3.

206 In addressing other complex issues of a legal and political nature, the Supreme Court of Canada has already largely adopted the notion of a principled framework. See *Reference re Secession of Québec, supra*, note 3, where the Court outlines a legal framework for secession negotiations that i) "emphasizes constitutional responsibilities as much as it does constitutional rights" (paras. 104, 151); ii) requires that such negotiations be "principled" (paras. 104, 149); iii) highlights the importance of underlying constitutional principles that govern the negotiations (paras. 49 *et seq.*, 88, 90, 93-95); iv) includes a "constitutional duty to negotiate" (paras. 69, 88 et seq.); and v) underlines that participants in such negotiations must "reconcile the rights, obligations and legitimate aspirations" of all those concerned (para. 104).

207 See P. Macklem, *Aboriginal Rights and State Obligations, supra*, note 61, at 113 et seq., where international norms are invoked in interpreting s. 35(1) of the *Constitution Act, 1982*.

208 In the event that self-government litigation proves to be a necessity, it would be especially beneficial for Aboriginal litigants to consider establishing certain fundamental principles as a first step. If carefully crafted, these principles could greatly assist all concerned parties to resolve their respective jurisdictions and interests through the negotiation process. In the absence of a principled framework, judicial consideration of self-government jurisdiction could prove to be a most imprudent risk.

For example, relevant principles might include recognition that: i) the right to self-government is a democratic entitlement of Aboriginal peoples; ii) Aboriginal peoples are "peoples" with the right to self-determination; iii) the right to self-determination is a part of the internal law of Canada; iv) the right to self-government is an important component of Aboriginal self-determination within Canada; and v) the right to self-determination, including self-government, is incorporated in s. 35 of the *Constitution Act, 1982.*

209 Cited in J. Keene, *Claiming the Protection of the Court: Charter Litigation Arising from Government "Restraint,"* (1998) 9 N.J.C.L. 97, at 114-115. These words of Madame Justice Abella have been endorsed by Supreme Court of Canada Judge Claire L'Heureux-Dubé: see *Making Equality Work,* Notes for an Address to the Department of Justice, December 10, 1996.

210 In regard to Aboriginal peoples, it is important to highlight here the concepts of "equality" that recently have been affirmed by the Supreme Court of Canada: i) True reconciliation, in accordance with s. 35(1) of the *Constitution Act, 1982,* requires that equal weight be accorded to Aboriginal and common law perspectives (see text accompanying this note); and ii) the principle of "protection of Aboriginal and treaty rights," either in its own right or as part of the principle of "protection of minorities," has equal weight with other underlying constitutional principles (see text accompanying note 39, *supra*).

These constitutional precepts of "equality" have yet to be adequately incorporated in judicial analyses pertaining to Aboriginal peoples and their basic status and rights. For example, Aboriginal peoples are firmly opposed to the surrender or extinguishment of their Aboriginal title and rights. Yet courts continue to ignore this central Aboriginal perspective. Also, aside from considerations relating to fiduciary duties and human rights, such surrender or extinguishment is wholly inconsistent with the constitutional principle of "protection of Aboriginal and treaty rights." No other people in Canada has its fundamental rights purportedly destroyed, in order to safeguard the people or rights concerned.

211 *R. v. Van der Peet, supra,* note 9, para. 50. This view is reiterated by Lamer C.J.C. in *Delgamuukw v. British Columbia, supra,* note 2, para. 81.

References

Doctrine

J. Borrows & L.I. Rotman, *The Sui Generis Nature of Aboriginal Rights: Does it Make a Difference?,* (1997) 36 Alta. L. Rev. 9.

P. Hogg & M.E. Turpel, *Implementing Aboriginal Self-Government: Constitutional and Jurisdictional Issues,* (1995) 74 Can. Bar Rev. 187.

A. Lafontaine, *La coexistence de l'obligation fiduciaire de la Couronne et du droit à l'autonomie gouvernementale des peuples autochtones,* (1995) 36 C. de D. 669.

P. Macklem, *Aboriginal Rights and State Obligations,* (1997) 36 Alta. L. Rev. 97.

P. Macklem, *Distributing Sovereignty: Indian Nations and Equality of Peoples,* (1993) 45 Stanford L. Rev. 1311.

R. McCorquodale, *Self-Determination: A Human Rights Approach,* (1994) 43 Int'l & Comp. L.Q. 857.

K. McNeil, *Aboriginal Rights in Canada: From Title to Land to Territorial Sovereignty*, (1998) 5 Tulsa J. Comp. & Int'l L. 253.

K. McNeil, *Aboriginal Title and the Division of Powers: Rethinking Federal and Provincial Jurisdiction*, (1998) 61 Sask. L. Rev. 431.

M. Seymour, *La Nation en question* (Montreal: Éditions de l'Hexagone, 1999).

B. Slattery, *Aboriginal Sovereignty and Imperial Claims*, (1991) 29 Osgoode Hall L.J. 681.

B. Slattery, "The Definition and Proof of Aboriginal Title" in Pacific Business & Law Institute, ed., *The Supreme Court of Canada decision in Delgamuukw*, conference materials (Vancouver, B.C.: 1998), 3.1.

Government documents, studies, etc.

Royal Commission on Aboriginal Peoples, *Report of the Royal Commission on Aboriginal Peoples* (Ottawa: Canada Communication Group, 1996), 5 vols.

Royal Commission on Aboriginal Peoples, *Treaty Making in the Spirit of Co-Existence [:] An Alternative to Extinguishment* (Ottawa: Minister of Supply and Services, 1995).

Secrétariat aux affaires autochtones, *Partenariat, développement, actions* (Québec: Gouvernement du Québec, 1998).

Secrétariat aux affaires autochtones, *Partnership, Development, Achievement* (Québec: Gouvernement du Québec, 1998).

Jurisprudence

Delgamuukw v. British Columbia, [1997] 3 S.C.R. 1010, 153 D.L.R. (4th) 193, (1998) 37 I.L.M. 268.

Reference re Secession of Québec, [1998] 2 S.C.R. 217, (1998) 161 D.L.R. (4th) 385, 228 N.R. 203, (1998) 37 I.L.M 1342.

R. v. Van der Peet, [1996] 2 S.C.R. 507.

International Instruments, Documents, etc.

Indigenous and Tribal Peoples Convention, 1989, I.L.O. Convention No. 169, I.L.O., 76th Sess., reprinted in (1989) 28 I.L.M. 1382 (not yet in force in Canada).

United Nations Committee on Economic, Social and Cultural Rights, *Consideration of Reports Submitted by States Parties Under Articles 16 and 17 of the Covenant*, U.N. Doc. E/C.12/1/Add.31, 4 December 1998.

United Nations Declaration on the Rights of Indigenous Peoples (Draft), in U.N. Doc. E/CN.4/1995/2; E/CN.4/Sub.2/1994/56, 28 October 1994, at 105-115, reprinted in (1995) 34 I.L.M. 541.

United Nations Human Rights Committee, *Consideration of reports submitted by States parties under article 40 of the Covenant*, 7 April 1999, CCPR/C/79/Add. 105.

6   Impact in the Maritimes

The Impact of *Delgamuukw* Guidelines in Atlantic Canada

*JAMES (SÁKÉJ) YOUNGBLOOD HENDERSON**

In *Delgamuukw v. British Columbia*,[1] the Supreme Court of Canada affirmed the inherent meaning of Aboriginal tenure (or title) and acknowledged its role in constitutional analysis. The message from the modern framers of the Constitution of Canada and the Supreme Court is that Aboriginal law, tenure and rights as well as treaty rights constitute a distinct constitutional order in s. 35(1) of the *Constitution Act*, 1982,[2] with its own implicate architecture, sources, traditions, and texts, that require constitutional equality with the other parts. The Supreme Court has found Aboriginal tenure is inherent in s. 35(1); its existence is constitutionally entrenched. All legislatures, Crown officials, and courts have the duty to protect Aboriginal tenure as part of the "supreme law of Canada" under s. 52(1); to relieve them of their duty would deny constitutional supremacy and its commitment to the rule of law.[3]

In *Delgamuukw*, the Supreme Court established "guidelines" for governments and courts to evaluate and protect Aboriginal tenure because it found the trial court's factual findings unreliable and ordered a new trial. The Court recognized these parallel land tenures have al-

---

*English translation. Guidance provided by *ababinilli*, *máheóo*, and *niskam*, although I assume full responsibility for interpretation. Notes will be found on pages 368–376.

ways existed in North America, that both sovereigns sought to reconcile the two land tenure systems by consensual treaties in the law of nations and British prerogative law, and that unpurchased Aboriginal tenure has not been extinguished or superseded by Canadian law.

The *Delgamuukw* guidelines affirm and recognize that Aboriginal tenure is *sui generis* tenure: an Aboriginal law generated system of land tenure protected by s. 35(1) of the *Constitution Act, 1982*. The sources, content, and meaning of a *sui generis* tenure exist not only in their physical possession on the land but also in Aboriginal worldviews, languages, laws, perspectives, and practices. A *sui generis* tenure does not take its source or meanings from European, British, Canadian law or practice, and exists independently of any recognition of the tenure. The Court has stressed it would be a mistake to seek answers to this *sui generis* legal system by drawing analogies to British property law or confusing it with doctrine of Crown tenure. The Dickson and Lamer Courts have rejected the inappropriate terminology and misleading categorization of content and proof of Aboriginal tenure of the older judicial precedent.

The *Delgamuukw* guidelines declare that Aboriginal tenure is a real property right in Canadian law: "the right to the land itself" that is distinguishable from Aboriginal rights.[4] Aboriginal tenure is the equivalent of the Crown's original title or tenure in British law. It is created by the overarching Aboriginal legal system that organizes all Aboriginal occupation and uses of land. Chief Justice Antonio Lamer declared the exclusive right to the use and occupation of land in an Aboriginal people means "the exclusion of both non-aboriginals and members of other aboriginal nations."[5] According to Aboriginal law, Aboriginal tenure is an "exclusive" right that is capable of being shared with other Aboriginal nations; but it is not controlled by the common law principles of exclusivity.[6]

The Court identified three "component rights" of Aboriginal tenure:

First, aboriginal title encompasses the right to exclusive use and occupation of land; second, aboriginal title encompasses the right to choose to what uses land can be put, subject to the ultimate limitation that those uses cannot destroy the ability of the land to sustain future generations of aboriginal peoples; and third, the lands held pursuant to aboriginal title have an inescapable economic component.[7]

As no other property right in Canada has been accorded constitutional protection, Aboriginal tenure and its component rights can prevent others from intruding on their lands.[8] These component rights carry a constitutional fiduciary duty to Canadian governments, which are entitled to equal protection of the law. If these component rights conflict with other constitutional authorities or rights, they may be subject to judicial reconciliation without the necessity of extinguishing Aboriginal rights.

The application of these guidelines to Atlantic Canada reveals that Aboriginal tenure was vested and reserved for the Aboriginal nations, tribes and peoples by compacts and treaties with the sovereign. Moreover, the sovereign by prerogative legislation prohibited any colonial or individual interference with these reserved tenures. Crown estates or settlements are derived from the treaty reconciliations, and remain part of the unpurchased Aboriginal tenure.[9]

The Wabanaki and Míkmaw compacts and treaties in Atlantic Canada specifically reserved their Aboriginal tenure. The sovereign expressly reserved their exclusive tenure in imperial law. In the British written version of the 1693 treaty, the sagamores and chief captains of the Confederacy agreed to allow British settlements under their Aboriginal law and tenure:

> That their Majesties' subjects the British shall and may peaceably and quietly enter upon, improve, and for ever enjoy all and singular their rights of lands, and former settlements and possessions with the eastern part of the said province of Massachusets [sic] Bay, without any pretension or claims by us, or any other Indians, and be in no wise molested, interrupted or disturbed by them.[10]

Additionally, this treaty provision affirmed colonial government within the Aboriginal territory. Article 3 of the 1713-14 treaties affirmed these settlements in Massachusetts Bay,[11] and the sovereign clarified and reserved the Aboriginal territory and free liberties back to 1693 treaty standard:

> Saving unto the said Indians their own Grounds, & free liberty for Hunting, Fishing, Fowling and all other their Lawful Liberties & Privileges, as on the eleventh day of August in the year of our Lord God One thousand six hundred & ninety three.[12]

The Wabanaki Compact (1725), concluded at Boston,[13] acknowledged the Wabanaki tribes were friends and subjects of the king, the British treaty commissioners candidly admitted they were not successful in getting the tribes to recognize King George as the sole owner and proprietor of New England and Nova Scotia.[14] The compact affirmed the existing treaties, but clarified article 3 of the 1713-14 treaties by dividing it into two separate articles, 3 and 4.[15] Article 3 of the Wabanaki Compact continued the treaty promises to British subjects:

> Shall and may peaceably and quietly enter upon Improve and forever enjoy all the singular Rights of God and former settlements[,] properties and possessions within the Eastern parts of the said province of the Massachusetts Bay Together with all Islands, inletts[,] Shoars [sic,] Beaches and Fishery within the same without any molestation or claim by us or any other Indians and be in no way molested[,] interrupted or disturbed therein.[16]

Article 4 emphasized the reservation of Aboriginal "lands, Liberties and properties" to the tribes:

> Saving unto the Penobscot, Naridgwalk and other Tribes within His Majesty's province aforesaid and their natural Descendants respectively all their lands, Liberties and properties not by them convey'd or sold to or possessed by any of the British subjects as aforesaid. As also the privilege of fishing, hunting, and fowling as formerly.[17]

Lieutenant Governor Dummer summarized his understanding of the land reservation clause in the following words:

> That the said Indians shall Peaceably Enjoy all their Lands & Property which have not been by them Conveyed and Sold unto, or possessed by the British & be no ways Molested or Disturbed in their planting or Improvement And further that there be allowed them the free Liberty and Privilege of Hunting Fishing & Fowling, as formerly.

> And whereas it is the full Resolution of this Government that the Indians shall have no Injustice done them respecting their Lands.[18]

By these treaty terms, the sovereign, the colonialists and the Confederacy agreed that in any dispute over land titles, the British subjects would carry the burden of proving their title by lawful purchase. "[I]f there should be any Dispute or Controversy hereafter between the British and you respecting the Titles or Claims of Land," the treaty commission told the Wabanaki leaders, "after a fair and lawful tryal, if the British cannot make out & prove their Title to the Lands Controverted they shall disclaim them; But if the British can make out their Titles then the Indian shall Disclaim the Lands so Controverted." [19]

Lieutenant Governor Dummer summarized his understanding of the reconciliation clause in the following words:

> I do therefore assure them that the several Claims or Titles (or so many of them as can be then had and Obtained) of the British to the Lands in that part of this Province shall be produced at the Ratification of the present Treaty by a Committee to be appointed by this Court in their present Session, and Care be taken as far as possible to make out the same to the satisfaction of the Indians and to distinguish & Ascertain what Lands belong to the British in Order to effectual prevention of any Contention or Misunderstanding on that Head for the future.[20]

Loron, one of the treaty negotiators in a 1751 treaty conference stated his understanding of the treaty: "Govr Dummer's treaty says we shan't loose a Foot of Ground." [21] Any British settler claim to contested land would have to be proved a title deriving from lawful purchase from the Wabanaki tribes, not the imperial sovereign.

Additionally, the British commissioners proposed to the Confederacy that an executed instrument in the name of the Government be delivered to the Confederacy "distinguishing and securing all your Rights." [22] The treaty commissioners suggested to the Massachusetts House of Representatives the establishment of a "Committee of able Faithful and Disinterested Persons" by the Government to "receive and adjust the claims of Lands in the parts Eastward of Sagadahock & Amoroscoggin Rivers & above Merry Meeting Bay," the only valid British settlement area under the compact.[23] The House read and accepted the proposal and returned them as Instructions to the treaty Commissioners.[24] The Commissioners stated that within twelve months of the conclusion of this "Treaty of Pacification," the commissioners would "ascertain the bounds of such claims & Challenges," "with a number of Indian chiefs appointed for that purpose." [25] "Before their Just right & Title hath been duly Enquired into & made Manifest, & the Indians have had the full knowledge & understanding of such rights & Title," the commissioners stated that no British settlements were to be made beyond those lands.[26] The Confederacy was ambivalent about the proposed claims commission concept, desiring the clarification document, but doubting the process, which was too much like a treaty conference. The Speaker informed the Commissioners that they could not accept the claims commission because such action would go "beyond our Instructions" from the Confederacy.[27]

The initial imperial Charter of 1621 and the 1717 and 1719 Commission to the Governors of Nova Scotia ordered the Governor to "send for the several heads of the said Indian Nations or clans, and promise them friendship and protection of His Majesty part."[28] Having made no existing treaties with Great Britain and wishing to remain nonaligned,[29] the Míkmaw delegates rejected the treaty no. 239 terms offered by the Nova Scotia delegates.[30] After hearing the new terms, the Míkmaq stated their own understanding of the words: they were supposed to "pay all the respect & Duty to the King of Great Britain as we did to ye King of France, but we reckon our selves a free People and are not bound."[31] On 15 December 1725, the Nova Scotia treaty commission, Major Paul Mascarene, in the Council Chamber in Boston, often new terms, which promised that the "Indian shall not be molested in their persons, Hunting[,] Fishing and Planting Grounds nor in any other their lawfull Occassions by His Majesty's subject or their Dependents."[32] The Míkmaq Delegates agreed to ratify the Wabanaki Compact at Annapolis Royal.

On 4 June 1726, the "Chiefs and Representatives [...] with full power and authority, by an unanimous consent and Desire of the said Indian Tribes, are come in Compliance with the Articles Stipulated by our Delegates as aforesaid" and do "Solemnly confirm & Ratify" the "1725 Compact."[33] Many copies of the ensuing 1726 ratification treaties exist, the multiple iterations and fragmentation of the treaties create many interpretative problems.[34] For unexplained reasons, the British scribes divided the Míkmaw ratification treaties into two separate documents: the first labeled "British to Indians,"[35] the second labeled "Indians to British."[36] Over one hundred Aboriginal peoples signed the agreement, some identifying themselves as chiefs of the Mikmaw Nation. Among those signing were the Chief and Delegates from "Cape Sable," the Chief of Annapolis Royal, Chignecto, Minas, Cape Breton and Newfoundland.[37] Thus, it was said that "all the Nova Scotia Tribes" entered into the compact.[38]

In the "British to Indians" written version of the treaty,[39] "His Most Sacred Majesty, George of great Brittain" promised the Míkmaq district chiefs "all Marks of Favour, Protection & Friendship." The written text of the treaty mistranscribed Nova Scotia's treaty commissioner Mascarene promises: "And I do further promise in the name of His honour the Lt Gov. R of the Province in Behalf of this Said Government, That the Said Indians shall not be Molested in their persons, Hunting, Fishing, [and Shooting &] Planting on their planting Grounds nor in any other Lawfull Occasions, by his Majesty's Subjects or their Dependants."[40] The sovereign promised legal enforcement of the treaty:

> [...] if any Indian are Injured by any of his Majesty's Subjects or their Dependants they shall have Satisfaction and Reparation made to them According to his Majesty's Law: Where of the Indians shall have the Benefit Equally with his Majesty's other subjects.[41]

By ratifying the Wabanki compact, the prerogative treaties, the "great King's Talk," recognized and affirmed Aboriginal tenure as a reserved for the chiefs, and granted peaceful occupation to those British settlers who had acquired an interest in Míkmaw tenure by a fair, honest, and consensual purchase.

Distinct from the private enterprises such as Massachusetts Bay colony and New England, the sovereign affirmed the unceded and unpurchased Aboriginal tenure in the prerogative commission creating the royal colony of the Nova Scotia.[42] The *1749 Commission* to Cornwallis, establishing the royal colony of Nova Scotia, renewed the 1719 order requiring treaty of friendship and protection with the Indian nations and provided no grants of land in fee simple for land already disposed of by the sovereign, i.e. the reserved Aboriginal "lands, Liberties and properties" of the Wabanaki Confederacy and Míkmaq Nation. The first condition of the commission stated the governor was "directed to make grants of such land in fee simple as are not already disposed of by his Majesty to any person that shall apply to you for the same."[43] Secondly, as a condition antecedent, the sovereign required that before the governor could grant any such land to British subjects, he had "by & with the advice and consent of our said Council to settle and agree with the Inhabitants of our Province for such Lands, Tenements, & hereditaments as now are or hereafter shall be in our power to dispose of."[44]

Reading these provisions together, the original constitution of Nova Scotia confirms that the reserved Aboriginal tenure could not be granted in fee simple by the governor, since they were already reserved for the Wabanaki Confederacy and Mikmaq nation. The Nova Scotia council had to settle and agree with the Mikmaw nation before any fee simple grants could be issued to colonists of their protected treaty lands.

This "settle and agree" provision, an affirmation of the treaty order established in the Wabanaki Compact, witnessed an elaboration of the requirement of fair and honest purchase of Aboriginal tenure by the Governor for the British sovereign. It also prevented any private purchase of Aboriginal tenure. Only if the Míkmaw Nation sold their ancient tenure and the Governor bought it for the Crown through prerogative treaties[45] could the Governor grant lands to the British settlers in fee simple.

The mandatory Governor-in-Council property agreement and settlement with the Aboriginal nations or tribes under the 1749 Commission, presumably by treaties, were reinforced by other prerogative limitations on the exercise of colonial authority by the Crown. First, His Majesty made all potential legislative power subject to the "further powers" of Royal Instructions and Commands under "our signet & sign manual or by order in our privy Council." Thus, the continuing supervision of Nova Scotia was to be carried out by the King-in-Council alone, acting through the issuance of prerogative Instructions. Second, the *Commission* also included a repugnancy clause; it required all law, statutes, and ordinances to be made "agreeable to the Laws and Statutes of this our Kingdom of Great Britain."

Thus, the relevant rules and principles of the United Kingdom's public law were also limitations of the colonial authorities and legislatures.[46] A crucial part of the Statutes of Great Britain was the *Statute of Frauds*,[47] which made written documents necessary in all transfer of legal estates, and applied to purchases of Aboriginal allodial tenure to the sovereign. In the subsequent treaties, however, the Míkmaw Nation did not yield up or sell their land to the Crown; they only agreed to small British settlements within their Aboriginal tenure.[48] Between August 13-15, 1749, at a Council meeting held on board the ship, the *Beaufort Transport*, Cornwallis entered into a renewal "upon the same footing" as the 1726 treaty with the Chignecto Míkmaq.[49] The existence of Aboriginal tenure in Atlantic Canada is a question of law rather than a question of fact as in British Columbia, since it was recognized and established by these imperial compact and treaties.

In Atlantic Canada, colonial law has viewed Aboriginal tenure as a part of the Crown tenure, not as a distinct or *sui generis* land tenure system recognized and vested in the Aboriginal nations and tribes in prerogative treaties. The Supreme Court's insight that Aboriginal tenure is a separate tenure from the common law tenure affirms the treaty reconciliation and resolves the third party interests under Crown grants as an issue of revenue sharing between the federal and provincial governments and Aboriginal peoples.

Most provinces of Atlantic Canada were created different than British Columbia. The constitution of Nova Scotia, New Brunswick, and Prince Edward Island were created by prerogative instruments and consist of treaty, royal commission and instruction to governors, and proclamation.[50] Prince Edward Island in 1873 and Newfoundland in 1949 admission to Canada was effected by an imperial statute and is similar to British Columbia.[51]

In the 1751 treaty negotiation with the Wabanaki Confederacy, Nova Scotia's treaty commissioner Mascarene invited the Wabanaki and "Micquemaques" to come to Chibucto to make peace, Mongaret of the Wabanaki Confederation said he would carry the message to them.[52] In the 1752 negotiations, Grand Chief Cope told the Nova Scotia council that the Míkmaq "should be paid for the land which the British had settled upon in this Country."[53] He agreed to "bring the other tribes of the Mickmack nation" to the treaty conference.[54] The Nova Scotia Council prepared an answer to the other tribes, in French and English, and promised that the Council "will not suffer that you be hinder from Hunting or Fishing in this Country as you have been use to do" and no person shall "hinder their settlements," especially on the "River Shibenaccadie," nor shall meddle with the land where you are." [55] On 22 November 1752, the Míkmaw chiefs affirmed the existing Wabanaki Compact (1725), and their 1726 and 1749 ratification treaties thus creating the Míkmaw Compact (1752).[56]

The Míkmaw Compact explicitly incorporated and continued the terns if Wabanaki Compact that reserved all Míkmaw lands, liberties, and properties to the Míkmaq that had not been conveyed or sold to the British in 1693, when no British subject possessed any land in Acadia or had purchased any of the Aboriginal tenure.[57] The Míkmaw Compact made the reserved Aboriginal tenure was a vested right by the treaty and an integral part of the constitutional law of the provinces. The Compact did not convey any Míkmaw tenure to the Crown or subjects; it merely accommodated the existing lawful settlements and provided compensation for their use of settlement lands.[58]

The Compact provided that British civil law, rather than political action, expressly protected the reservation of Míkmaw tenure. In an innovative treaty article, Article 8 provided that the Míkmaq were to be treated as equals to the British subjects and that in any controversy the Míkmaq would be protected in their treaty rights in "His Majesty's Courts of Civil Judicature." [59] This is a unique provision in Georgian treaties; the Míkmaw rejected political solutions and criminal law of the Wabanaki Compact in favour of civil remedies.[60] This legal implementation provision made the protection of the reserved Aboriginal tenure a vested legal right.

Six years after the compact, on 2 October 1758, and pursuant to the authority delegated to the sovereign by the Míkmaq, a legislative Assembly was convened in Nova Scotia. British constitutional conventions establish 1758 as the date of the reception of the British law in old Nova Scotia as a settled colony[61] that included New Brunswick.[62] British law was imported, except to the extent that the law was unsuitable to the circumstances of the colony, as for example, when inconsistent with the existing compact and treaties with the Aboriginal nations.[63] Since the Míkmaw Compact and its ratification treaties were an existing prerogative act made before the date of reception of the British common law,[64] no colonial legislation was required to implement the provisions of the compact and treaties. The compacts and treaties were imperial obligations and part of the existing prerogative constitution of Nova Scotia.[65]

After the end of the Seven Years War between the British and French,[66] in 1760, a Míkmaw delegation from French jurisdictions met with Governor-Chief Justice Belcher and the Legislative Assembly to renew and extend the compact to all parts of the Atlantic Canada previous held by the French.[67] The 1760 treaty affirmed the previous compact and treaties, specifically the legal protection of Aboriginal tenure by British law. Chief Justice Belcher described of the legal nature of protection and allegiance under the compact and treaties:

> Protection and allegiance are fastened together by links. If a link is broken the chain will be loose. You must preserve this chain entire on your part by fidelity and obedience to the Great King George the Third, and then you will have the security of his Royal Arm to defend you. I meet you now as His Majesty's graciously honored Servant in Government and in His Royal Name to receive at this Pillar, your public vows of obedience to build a covenant of Peace with you, as upon the immovable rock of Sincerity and Truth, to free you from the chains of Bondage, and to place you in the wide and fruitful Field of British Liberty.[68]

The "Field of British liberties," Belcher promised the assembled chiefs, would be "free from the baneful weeds of Fraud and Subtlety." [69] To ensure this, "[t]he Laws will be like a great Hedge about your Rights and properties—if any break this Hedge to hurt or injure you, the heavy weight of the Law will fall upon them and furnish their disobedience." [70]

The Míkmaw Compact, the inherited British *Statutes of Frauds*,[71] the 1761 Instructions,[72] and the 1763 Proclamation[73] protected the Aboriginal "lands, Liberties and properties" from any new settlements, interference or encroachment by colonial legislative assemblies, executive council, and the colonialists. Because of complaints to the British sovereign that "settlements had been made and possession taken of Land, the property of which they [the several Nations or Tribes of Indians] had by Treaties reserved to themselves by persons claiming the said lands under pretence of deeds of Sale and Conveyances illegally[,] fraudulently and surreptitiously obtained form the Indians," [74] These prerogative laws protected the tenure of Aboriginal nations and peoples in old Nova Scotia, Prince Edward Island, Newfoundland and Labrador, who had not signed any treaties nor sold or ceded their lands to the British sovereign. These laws were part of the constitution of the provinces, and they prohibited royal governors from surveying or passing patent to the reserved Aboriginal lands, requiring all persons to be removed from unceded or unpurchased Aboriginal lands. They ended and prohibited any private purchases of Aboriginal tenure, and conferred exclusively upon the sovereign a *sui generis* fiduciary duty, both contractually and equitably, to protect their Hunting Grounds until the sovereign purchased the lands.[75]

Prerogative treaties and law vested the Aboriginal tenure for the Aboriginal nations, as reserved allodial lands.[76] The provinces and colonies had protective and administrative obligations and services to the sovereign to protected the prerogative interests in the land, the provinces did not have any ownership, legal estate or beneficial interests in the unpurchased Aboriginal lands. At Confederation, the sovereign and the provinces agreed to assign these protective and administrative obligations or services to the federal dominion.[77] This change of administrative agents did not change the reserved *sui generis* tenure; these constitutional acts could not transfer to the federal government or the provinces "any legal estate in the Crown lands" beyond that acquired by the sovereign in the compact and treaties.[78] In Atlantic Canada, the "land reserved for the Indians" in s. 91(24) of the *Constitution [British North America] Act, 1867*[79] continued to be vested in Aboriginal nations by the explicit intent and wording of the British sovereign in the treaties and prerogative laws.[80]

The entire justification for establishing Crown land titles in Atlantic Canada was embedded in a presumption that because of prerogative acts and colonial statutes protected the reserved Aboriginal "lands, Liberties and properties," the Aboriginal lands was part of the sovereign land tenure. It was seen as a use right under the common law doctrine of Crown tenure in Britain. The *Delgamuukw* guidelines rejected this presumption, and affirmed that the unifying principle of Aboriginal tenure is *sui generis*, it exist by Aboriginal law distinct from the common law fiction of Crown's tenure.[81] The Supreme Court of Canada has taken pains to clarify that Aboriginal tenure is a proprietary interest and can compete on an equal footing with other proprietary interests,[82] but cannot be interpreted by the common law traditions:

> The inescapable conclusion from the Court's analysis of Indian title up to this point is that the Indian interest in land is truly *sui generis*. It is more than the right to enjoyment and occupancy, although, as Dickson J. pointed out in *Guerin*, it is difficult to describe what more in traditional [English] property terminology.[83]

In *Mitchell* v. *Peguis Indian Band*, Chief Justice Brian Dickson stated the controlling interpretative principle of treaty wording is the Aboriginal peoples understanding of the treaties:

> [...] that aboriginal understanding of words and corresponding legal concepts in Indian treaties are to be preferred over more

legalistic and technical constructions. This concern with aboriginal perspective albeit in a different context, led a majority of this Court in *Guerin*, to speak of the Indian interest in land as a *sui generis* interest, the nature of which cannot be totally captured by a lexicon derived from European legal systems.[84]

In 1985, the Supreme Court interpreted the 1752 treaty in the *Simon* case,[85] and overruled another colonial presumption in *Syliboy* that held "[t]he savages' right of sovereignty even of ownership were never recognized" by the Crown or international law.[86] This precedent had ended any discussion of Aboriginal ownership by the Canadian courts. Chief Justice Dickson characterized the *Syliboy* decision and its rejection of Aboriginal right to sovereignty and ownership as both substantively unconvincing and a biased product of another era in Canadian law that is inconsistent with a growing sensitivity to native rights in Canada.[87]

With the rebuttal of these legal presumptions in Atlantic Canada, the existing treaty reconciliations where the sovereign reserved and vested the Aboriginal tenure continues and has not been lawfully extinguished. The reserved Aboriginal tenure in the compact and treaties exists as distinct constitutional order of the Aboriginal peoples in the constitution of Canada. This is a different situation from Aboriginal tenure in British Columbia. The vesting of Aboriginal tenure in public law before the creation of legislative assemblies made the *sui generis* tenure beyond the scope of the provincial laws. Neither Nova Scotia nor New Brunswick could amend or violate the reserved Aboriginal tenure by prerogative treaties or the royal instructions or proclamation. In the legal context of pre-confederation, provincial acts could not be inconsistent with the prerogative treaties and laws, thus the provinces did not have jurisdiction to unilaterally extinguishing a vested Aboriginal tenure by creating small Indian reserves.

The constitutionally protected Aboriginal tenure in Atlantic Canada is the vested Aboriginal tenure in prerogative treaties and laws. Even if no treaty had reserved and vested the Aboriginal tenure, it would still a constitutionally protected tenure in the constitutional order. These existing prerogative laws were the source of federal delegated authority over lands reserved for the Indians in s. 91(24). In *St. Catherine's Milling* decision, where the judicial committee of the Privy Council explained at confederation the "natural" meaning of the phrase "Land reserved for the Indians" in s. 91(24) of the *Constitution [British North America] Act, 1867* was:

> sufficient to include all lands reserved, upon any terms or condition, for Indian occupation. It appears to be the plain policy of the

Act, in order to ensure uniformity of administration, all such lands, and Indian affairs generally, shall be under the legislative control of one central authority.[88]

In *Delgamuukw*, the Lamer Court held "Lands reserved for the Indians" by s. 91(24) itself was under federal jurisdiction, rather than provincial jurisdictions. Chief Justice Lamer found that federal jurisdiction over "Lands reserved for the Indians" included all unpurchased and unceded Aboriginal tenure and land rights in the province of British Columbia, as well as provincially-created Indian reserves.[89] Chief Justice Lamer confirmed these principles in a contemporary context:

> In *St. Catherine's Milling*, the Privy Council held that Aboriginal title was such an interest, and rejected the argument that provincial ownership operated as a limit on federal jurisdiction. The net effect of that decision, therefore, was to separate the ownership of lands held pursuant to Aboriginal title from jurisdiction over those lands. Thus, although on surrender of Aboriginal title the province would take absolute title, jurisdiction to accept surrenders lies with the federal government. The same can be said of extinguishment—although on extinguishment of Aboriginal title, the province would take complete title to the land, the jurisdiction to extinguish lies with the federal government.[90]

Additionally, Chief Justice Lamer noted, "even if the point were not settled, I would have come to the same conclusion." [91] No imperial acts have changed the vested Aboriginal tenure in the prerogative constitutional of Nova Scotia and New Brunswick between confederation and constitutional amendment in 1982, such as the western provinces in the *Constitution Act, 1930* [92] and the *Natural Resource Transfer Agreements, 1930.*[93]

The Lamer Court held that when British Columbia was admitted to confederation in 1871 "that jurisdiction over aboriginal title must vest with the federal government," [94] implying "the jurisdiction to legislate in relation to Aboriginal title," and "the jurisdiction to extinguish that title." [95] This vested jurisdiction operates to preclude provincial jurisdiction to make laws[96] or extinguish Aboriginal tenure or rights, "because the intention to do so would take the law outside provincial jurisdiction":[97]

> s. 91(24) protects a core of federal jurisdiction even from provincial laws of general application, through the operation of the doctrine of interjurisdictional immunity. That core has been described

as matters touching on "Indianness" or the "core of Indianness."
[...] It follows that aboriginal rights are part of the core of Indianness at the heart of s. 91(24).[98]

The division of powers precludes provincial regulation over land reserved for the Indians. As Lamer stated, "[t]he vesting of exclusive jurisdiction with the federal government over Indians and Indian lands
under s. 91(24), operates to preclude provincial laws in relation to
those matters."[99] This is a federal responsibility shared with the Aboriginal peoples of Canada in accordance with s. 35(1). These principles should apply to the admission of Prince Edward Island in 1873 and
Newfoundland in 1949 to confederation.

In Atlantic Canada, the Delgamuukw guidelines and principles
affirm the constitutional validity of Aboriginal tenure reserved in the
prerogative treaties and vested in imperial laws.[100] Reserved and unpurchased Aboriginal tenure in Atlantic Canada has not been extinguished by the sovereign or superseded by federal or provincial law or
settlement.[101] A unified Supreme Court of Canada in *Sparrow*, held
that s. 35(1) is not a codification of the existing or accumulated case
law on Aboriginal or treaty rights.[102] The Court affirmed that provincial or federal acts or regulations could not extinguish constitutional
rights of Aboriginal peoples. It held that s. 35(1) cannot be read so as
to incorporate the specific manner in which constitutional rights were
regulated before 1982,[103] and stated that federal-provincial statutory
or regulatory control of a constitutional right does not mean that the
right is extinguished, even if the control is exercised in "great
detail."[104] Finally, the Court stated that the sovereign's intention is
controlling and extinguishment of a constitutional right could only be
proven if the sovereign's written command is clear and plain.[105] The
Court declared that s. 35(1) not only creates a constitutional fiduciary
duty on the federal government for Aboriginal peoples but also operates as a "strong" limitation on the legislative powers of the federal
Parliament,[106] as well as provincial Legislatures.[107] No reason exists
why these constitutional principles do not apply in Atlantic Canada to
nullify any inconsistent provincial legislation prior to Confederation
or federal legislation after Confederation.

Together the British Columbia Court of Appeals and the Supreme
Court rejected federal and provincial Crown arguments that prior to
1982 unrecognized Aboriginal tenure was extinguished. It denied each
of their five extinguishment theories: that the assertion of Crown sovereignty had extinguished Aboriginal tenure; that colonial land legislation before Confederation extinguished the Aboriginal peoples'
relations to the land; that the creation of land grants by British Colum-

bia to settlers extinguished Aboriginal tenure because the Aboriginal people were precluded from sustaining their relationship to the land; that the establishment of federal Indian reserves in British Columbia extinguished Aboriginal tenure because the Aboriginal peoples "abandoned" their territory; and that s. 88 of the Indian Act allowed provincial laws of general application to extinguish Aboriginal rights. As Justice Hall had said to similar arguments in *Calder*, the Court said these arguments are "self-destructive." [108] Chief Justice Lamer declared that the Crown failed to establish any legal basis to justify the legal dispossession of Aboriginal peoples by provincial authority. [109]

In reviewing the trial judges' decision in *Delgamuukw*, the British Columbia Court of Appeal reversed the trial judge's conclusion that before Confederation there had been blanket extinguishment of Aboriginal tenure or rights. [110] The Court of Appeal held that a trial judge would have to make detailed determinations about the location and scope of existing Aboriginal tenure and the sovereign's clear and plain intent and wording to extinguish it. [111] This issue was not appealed to the Supreme Court, but should be applied to vested Aboriginal tenure in pre-confederation Atlantic Canada.

In *Delgamuukw*, the Lamer Court was faced with three specific extinguishment issues: whether the province of British Columbia, from the time it joined Confederation in 1871, until the entrenchment of s. 35(1) in 1982, had the jurisdiction to extinguish the tenure or rights of Aboriginal peoples in that province; if the province was without such jurisdiction, whether provincial laws of general application that were not "in pith and substance" aimed at the extinguishment of Aboriginal rights, could be implied to extinguish; and whether a provincial law, which could otherwise not extinguish Aboriginal tenure or rights, could be given that effect through referential incorporation by s. 88 of the federal *Indian Act*. [112]

The Court declared that the province never had constitutional authority to extinguish *sui generis* Aboriginal tenure, that it had never been extinguished in the past, and that Aboriginal tenure continues as a constitutionally protected tenure in British Columbia that must be respected by courts. [113] These principles and a similar conclusion should be applied to vested Aboriginal tenure in confederated Atlantic Canada.

The absence of any purchase or cession of the vested Aboriginal tenure by the sovereign prior to 1982 creates a Aboriginal peoples jurisdiction over all their "lands reserved for the Indians" in Atlantic Canada. In *Delgamuukw*, Chief Justice Lamer restated *Sparrow*'s principle that to be recognized and affirmed by s. 35(1) Aboriginal tenure or rights must have existed in April 17, 1982; rights that were extinguished by the sovereign before that time are not revived by the provision.[114] The Supreme Court in *Van der Peet* held that under s. 35(1), Aboriginal tenures and rights cannot be extinguished:

> At common law Aboriginal rights did not, of course, have constitutional status, with the result that Parliament could, at any time, extinguish or regulate those rights [...] it is this which distinguishes the Aboriginal rights recognized and affirmed in s.35(1) from the Aboriginal rights protected by the common law. Subsequent to s.35(1) Aboriginal rights cannot be extinguished and can only be regulated or infringed consistent with the justificatory test.[115]

Aboriginal tenure at federal common law is protected in its full form by its constitutionalization in s. 35(1)[116] by the federal government and Aboriginal peoples. No provincial authority exists over these lands, since the constitution and the federal common law are paramount to provincial laws.[117]

No Canadian court has ever found where the Aboriginal peoples in Atlantic Canada sold their vested treaty lands to the sovereign.[118] The last judicial review of the Nova Scotia Court of Appeal to review the legal record, Chief Justice MacKeigan in *Isaac* stated:

> No Nova Scotia treaty has been found whereby Indians ceded land to the Crown, whereby their rights on any land were specifically extinguished, or whereby they agreed to accept and retire to specific reserves, although thorough archival research might well disclose records of informal agreements, especially in the early 1800's when reserves were established by executive order. [...] I have been unable to find any record of any treaty, agreement or arrangement after 1780 extinguishing, modifying or confirming the Indian right to hunt and fish, or any other records of any cession or release of rights or lands by the Indians. [...] The review has confirmed that Indians have a special relationship with the lands they occupy, not merely a quaint tradition, but rather a right recognized in law.[119]

No archival evidence exists that they Aboriginal peoples sold or ceded their Aboriginal tenure to the British sovereign or that the sovereign authorized the executive orders or any extinguishment, modification, cession or purchase of the reserved lands. No sovereign acts provide for grants in fee simple contrary to prerogative treaties or laws. As Justice Lamer stated in *Sioui* about contemporary treaties in Quebec:

> The British Crown recognized that the Indians had certain ownership rights over their land ...[and] allowed them autonomy in their internal affairs, intervening in this area as little as possible.[120]

The lands reserved for the Indians in Atlantic Canada under prerogative acts have not been sold or transferred from Aboriginal tenure to Crown tenure.

In *Delgamuukw* the Court noted that Aboriginal title and rights recognized and affirmed by s. 35(1) are not absolute. According to the division of powers doctrine, Aboriginal rights may be infringed, both by the federal (e.g., *Sparrow*) and provincial (e.g., *Côté*) governments.[121] However, the Lamer Court declare that such justified infringements of s. 35(1) requires fair compensation to Aboriginal peoples:

> In keeping with the duty of honour and good faith on the Crown, fair compensation will ordinarily be required when Aboriginal title is infringed. The amount of compensation payable will vary with the nature of the particular Aboriginal title affected and with the nature and severity of the infringement and the extent to which Aboriginal interests were accommodated.[122]

This guideline affirms the existing principle of both common law and statute that the Crown may not expropriate a property interest without compensation, and applies the principle to external regulation of Aboriginal tenure. This is especially relevant when prerogative treaties and law vest the Aboriginal tenure in the Aboriginal nations, tribes, or peoples.

Any provincial or federal infringement of the reserved Aboriginal tenure under prerogative laws requires fair compensation. Both the Court of Appeal and the Supreme Court in *Delgamuukw* have suggested that compensation is appropriate for past federal and provincial regulation of Aboriginal tenure.[123] Justice Macfarlane for the majority of British Columbia Court of Appeal held that compensatory damages from the province might be the appropriate remedy for pre-1982 regulatory infringements of Aboriginal tenure.[124] Justice Gerard La Forest in the Supreme Court declared that Aboriginal tenure is a compensable right that can be traced back to *the Royal Proclamation, 1763*.[125] These principles are applicable to the actions of the provinces of Atlantic Canada toward Aboriginal law and tenures.

Fair compensation is a revenue-sharing issue between the Crown and the Aboriginal peoples, rather than an issue between the Aboriginal peoples and the purchasers from the Crown. The Supreme Court and the Privy Council held in *St. Catherine's* that the provinces under s. 109 could acquire a beneficial interest in Aboriginal territories as a source of revenue only when the estate of the Crown is disencumbered of the Indian tenure.[126] In *Delgamuukw*, the Court rejected the provincial Crown argument that the imperial Parliament in s. 109 of the *Constitution Act, 1867* "vested" the province with the underlying title to

Aboriginal tenure.[127] Moreover, the Lamer Court held that Aboriginal tenure in British Columbia was not extinguished by provincial or federal legislation and the province had not acquired beneficial interest under s. 109.

Since Aboriginal tenure in Atlantic Canada has not been disencumbered, neither the provincial nor federal Crown has any "ultimate" interest, since s. 35(1) has vested such unextinguished tenures in the Aboriginal peoples. Their Lordships of the Privy Council admitted in *St. Catherine's* that if the Ojibwa had been "the owners of fee simple of the territory" at Confederation, the province might not have derived any benefit from the cession, since the land was not vested in the sovereign at Confederation.[128] This is exactly the situation of the Wabanaki and Míkmaw tenure at Confederation: it was an explicit, vested sui-generis tenure recognized and affirmed by the British sovereign in the compact, treaties and prerogative law that would prevent the province or the federal government from deriving any beneficial interest over the reserved territory. Without a consensual sale and purchase of reserved Aboriginal tenure before 1982, the intangible future interest in the contemplation of the sovereign was never perfected, and under s. 35(1) of the *Constitution Act, 1982*, the reserved Aboriginal tenure is vested in the Aboriginal peoples according to their laws.

In sum, the vested Aboriginal tenure by prerogative treaties and law has been affirmed by s. 35(1) of the *Constitution Act, 1982* as a constitutional right to the land itself. The Aboriginal peoples had every right to rely on the Crown's promises that it intended to respect their tenure protected under their compact and treaties. They were entitled by their compact and treaties to assert their Aboriginal law over their reserved ancestral lands as a legal right, a civil right. They were entitled to have their settled expectations transformed into positive constitutional laws creating reliance-based rights. A fundamental principle of British law is that courts will assume that the British sovereign intends that the right of property of the inhabitants of any newly ceded territory will be fully respected.[129]

As the *Delgamuukw* constitutional principles and guidelines illustrate, the passage of time cannot validate an unconstitutional statutes or unlawful settlements and uses.[130] Colonial administration or regulation of these protected tenures or rights, either provincially or federally, could not legally extinguish this distinct legal realm or the reserved tenure, since such action would be a violation of the fundamental constitutional regime of Great Britain and Canada and *ultra vires*.[131] An act that is inconsistent with the constitution of Canada has never been and cannot become valid law, since its radical invalidity remains with the act until it is either repealed or struck down.[132]

Aboriginal and treaty tenures and rights do not cease to exist because the Crown's servants fail to secure them. To make the suggestion of implied extinguishment by colonial settlements of constitutional rights, especially those vested or protected Aboriginal tenure by prerogative laws, is to attempt to enshrine the perverse notion that rights are not to be legally protected in precisely those situations when protection is essential. In the response to *Delgamuukw* guidelines, it is now essential for the federal government to turn its resources to the issue of negotiation, compensation, and remedies for those who have been victimized by centuries of illegal and colonialist conduct. The highest court in Canada has again rejected Atlantic Canada's old colonial legal mentality and its defenses against Aboriginal tenure.

References

1 *Delgamuukw* v. *British Columbia.* [1997] 3 S.C.R. 1010.

2 *Constitution Act, 1982*, being Schedule B to the *Canada Act, 1982* (U.K.), 1982, c.11.

3 *Ibid. Re Reference by the Governor General in Council Concerning Certain Questions Relating to the Secession of Quebec from Canada* (1998), 161 D.L.R. (4th) 385 at paras. 71-2

4 *Delgamuukw, supra* note 1 at para. 138. *The Report of the Royal Commission on Aboriginal Peoples* (Ottawa: Minister of Supply & Services, 1996) [hereinafter *RCAP Report*] stated Aboriginal tenure as being "recognized and affirmed by s. 35(1) and described it as a "real interest in land that contemplates a right of right with respect to land and resources vol. 2 at 573.

5 *Ibid.* at para. 184.

6 *Ibid.* at para. 156. The court stated: "exclusivity is a common law principle derived from the notion of fee simple ownership and should be imported into the concept of Aboriginal title with caution."

7 *Ibid.* at para. 166. Compare to Justice L'Heureux-Dube's characterization in *R.* v. *Van der Peet*, [1996] 2 S.C.R. 507 at para. 115: "The traditional and main component of the doctrine of Aboriginal rights relates to Aboriginal title, i.e. the *sui generis* proprietary interest which gives Native people the right to occupy and use the land at their own discretion, subject to the Crown's ultimate title and exclusive right to purchase the land"; citing *St. Catherine's Milling and Lumber Co.* v. *The Queen* (1888), 14 A.C. 46 at 54 (P.C.) [hereinafter *St. Catherine's*]; *Calder* v. *Attorney-General of British Columbia*, [1973] S.C.R. 313, at 328, Judson J., and at 383, Hall J; and, *Guerin* v. *The Queen*, [1984] 2 S.C.R. 335, at. 378 and 382, Dickson J. (as he then was) "Aboriginal title lands are lands which the Natives possess for occupation and use at their own discretion, subject to the Crown's ultimate title" see *Guerin, ibid.* at 382.

8 *Delgamuukw, supra* note 1 at para. 155.

9 J.Y. Henderson, "Míkmaw Tenure in Atlantic in Atlantic Canada" (1995) 18(2) Dal. L. J. 216.

10 Cumming & Mickenberg, eds., *Native Rights in Canada* (Toronto: Indian-Inuit Assoc. of Canada, 1972), Art. 4 at 295.

11 *Ibid.* at 297 in Art. 3: "That her Majesty's Subjects, the British, shall & may peaceably & quietly enter upon, imprive [sic], & forever enjoy, all and singular their Rights of Land & former Settlements, Properties, & possessions with the Eastern Parts of the said Province of Massachusetts Bay and New Hampshire, together with all the Islands, Isletts, Shoars, Beaches, & Fisheries within the same, without any molestation or claim by us or any other Indians. And be in no ways molested, interrupted, or disturbed therein. Saving unto the said Indians their own Grounds, & free liberty for Hunting, Fishing, Fowling and all other their Lawful Liberties & Privileges, as on the eleventh day of August in the year of our Lord God One thousand six hundred & ninety three."

12 While this article is more specific than the *Wapapi Akonutomakononol,* see generally R.M. Leavitt and D.A. Francis, eds., *Wapapi Akonutomakonol. The Wampum Records. Wabanaki Traditional Law as recounted by Lewis Michell* (Fredericton, N.B.: Micmac-Maliseet Institute, 1990). The Wampum Records creates an "implemented fence" or boundary between the British and the Wabanaki legal jurisdictions, so that there would be no bothering one another anymore. The concept of "forever" is *askomiw.*

13 *E.g.,* Public Archives of Canada [PAC]; Colonial Office [CO] 5 898 at 173-174v.

14 Public Archives of Nova Scotia [PANS] Record Group [RG] 1, vol. 12 doc. 3 at 15, Dec. 1725; PAC, Manuscript Group [MG] 11; CO 217, Nova Scotia "A" [NSA] vol. 16 at 203, 207; *Native Rights, supra* note 10 at 300-02

15 *Ibid.* at art. 10. The Treaty Commissioners often used the distinguishing terms of "our and your Lands."

16 *Ibid.* art. 3.

17 *Ibid.* art. 4 .

18 J.P. Baxter, ed., *Documentary History of the State of Maine* (Portland, Me.: Fred L. Tower Co. & Maine Historical Society, 1916) [hereinafter DHM] vol. XXIII at 196 (22 Nov. 1725 in the House of Representatives).

19 *Ibid.* NSA American and West Indies, 1724-1725, 4 August 1726.

20 Letter with Enclosures, of Lieutenant Governor Dummer to Duke of Newcastle, 8 Jan. 1726. CO, 5/898.

21 DHM, supra note 18 vol. XXIII at 416 (Report of Conference at the Fort of St. George's Mass. Involving Nova Scotia's treaty commission Mascarene, 24 August, 1751)

22 DHM, *supra* note 18, at 196 (22 Nov. 1725.)

23 *Ibid.* at 196, Art. 1, 23 Nov. 1725.

24 *Ibid.* at 197.

25 *Ibid.* at Art. 2.

26 *Ibid.* at Art. 3.

27 *Ibid.* at 200 , 26 Nov. 1725.

28 Instruction to Governor Philips of Nova Scotia, June 19th, 1719, in L.W. Labaree, ed., *Royal Instructions to British Colonial Governors, 1670-1776,* vol. II (New York: D. Appleton, Century Co., 1935), No. 673 at 469 [hereinafter Labaree, Royal Instructions]. See "Statement prepared by the Council of Trade and Plantations for the King, September 8th, 1721": "It would likewise be for your Majesty's service that the sev. Governts of your Majesties Plantations should endeavor to make treaties and alliances of friendship with as many Indian nations as they can [...] ." Cited Levi, et al., "We Should Walk in the Tract Mr. Dummer Made" (Oct. 1st and 2nd 1992) at 35 [unpublished document distributed at New Brunswick Chiefs' Forum on Treaty Issues, St. John, New Brunswick].

29 "Family Treaty with the British Officials at Annapolis Royal , 7 January 1723" *The New England Courant* (7 January 1723). It was signed by the members of the Grand Claude family following the imprisonment of their relatives. See also Letter of John Doucett to the Board of Trade, 29 June 1722. PAC, MG11 CO 217/4 at 118. See also A.M. MacMechan, ed., *Original*

Minutes of His Majesty's Council at Annapolis Royal, 1720-1739 (Halifax: Public Archives of Nova Scotia, 1908) at 37-41 [hereinafter *Council Minutes*].

30 PAC, MG 11, CO 217, NSA, vol. 16 at 207; PANS CO 217, vol. 4 at 321, 348, 350.

31 *Ibid.* vol. 17 at 2, December 1725.

32 Enclosed in letter from Lt. Governor Armstrong to Council of Trade and Plantations [Newcastle] dated July 27, 1726, C. Headlam, ed., *Calendar of State Papers, Colonial Series*, America and West Indies, vol 29 fol. 77; PANS CO 217, vol. 4 at 321, 348, 350 (often labeled Number 239). In a 1751 treaty conference Mascarene that that he was at the ratification treaties at Casco Bay, Annapolis Royal, Chibucto, see *supra* note 21.

33 *Ibid.* Promises/Ratification of John Ducett, Lt. Gov. of Annapolis Royal to the Tribes in Nova Scotia, signed at Annapolis Royal 4 June 1725. PAC , MG11 CO 217, NSA ,vol. 5 at 3-4; *Ibid.* vol. 17 at 36-41; *Ibid.* vol. 38 at 108-108v, and 116-116v.; PANS CO 217, vol. 4 at 321; PANS CO 217, vol. 38 at 109 (the original parchment copy has not been found).

34 *Ibid.* See PAC, MG 11, CO 217, NSA, vol. 17 at 40; Promises/Ratification of Cape Sables, Annapolis River, Pontiquet, Minis and Passamaquady Indians to Gov. of N.S.PANS, Signed at Annapolis Royal 4 June 1726. CO 217, vol. 4 at 350; an identical text with different signatures is found in Promises/Ratification of St. John's, Passamaquady, Cape Sable, Chuabouacady, LaHave, Minas and Annapolis River Indians to Gov. of N.S. signed at Annapolis Royal 4 June 1726. PANS, CO 217, vol. 38, 108; PANS CO 217, vol. 4 at 320; Promises/Ratification of St. Jones, Cape Sables, Chubenakady, Rechibutou, Jediack, Minas, Chickanecto, Annapolis River, Eastern Coast Micmacs to Gov. of N.S., signed at Annapolis Royal 4 June 1726. PANS CO 217, vol. 38 at 116, also an identical text with different signatures.

35 *Ibid. British to Indians Treaty*, 1726 (U.K.), 12 Geo I. PAC , MG11 CO 217, NSA ,vol. 5 at 3-4; Promises/Ratification of John Ducett [also spelled as Doucette in the documents], Lt. Gov. of Annapolis Royal to the Tribes in Nova Scotia, signed at Annapolis Royal 4 June 1725. *Ibid.* vol. 17 at 36-41 (original parchment copy has not been found); *Ibid.* vol. 38: at 108-108v, and 116-116v. ; PANS CO 217, vol. 4 at 321; PANS CO 217, vol. 38 at 109.

36 *Ibid.* Promises/Ratification of Cape Sables, Annapolis River, Pontiquet, Minis and Passamaquady Indians to Gov. of N.S., signed at Annapolis Royal 4 June 1726. PAC, MG 11, CO 217, NSA, vol. 17 at 40; PANS, CO 217, vol. 4 at 350; CO 217, vol. 4 at 82-83.

37 PAC, NSA , MG11 CO 217, vol. 17 at 43.

38 *Ibid.* at 40-43.

39 CO 217, vol. 4 at 82.

40 *Ibid.* Compare, *supra* note 32. In some copies of the treaty the words "and Shooting &" appear.

41 *Ibid.*

42 Labaree, *Royal Instructions*, *supra* note 28, at 581-82.

43 *Ibid.* See generally L.W. Labaree, *Royal Government in America: A Study of the British Colonial System Before 1783* (New Haven, Conn.: Yale University Press, 1930).

44 *Ibid.* This section applies the British principle of continuity of laws to the new royal colony. This principle is called the doctrine of Continuity in British law, and reserved rights in the United States. The principle of continuity of property rights provides that property rights, once established, continue unaffected by a change of sovereignty unless positively modified or abrogated by the new sovereign (*Campbell* v. *Hall* (1774), 1 Cowp. 204. at 895-96). This principle has been held to apply to Aboriginal tenure by the highest courts in the United States, Great Britain, and Canada. See *Worcester* v. *Georgia,* 31 U.S.(6 Pet.) 515, 8 L. Ed. 483 (U.S. 1832) at 544 and 559; *Mitchel* v. *United States,* 34 U.S. (9 Pet.) 711 (1835) at 734 [hereinafter *Mitchel*]; *R.* v. *Symonds* (1847), [1840-1932] N.Z.P.C. Cases 387; *Nireaha Tamaki* v. *Baker* (1901), [1901] A.C. 561 at 579 (P.C.); *Re Southern Rhodesia* (1918), [1919] A.C. 211 at 234 (P.C.); *Amodu Tijani* v. *Southern Nigeria (Secretary),* [1921] 2 A.C. 399 at 404; *R.* v. *Calder, supra* note 7; *Guerin* v. *The Queen,* [1984] 2 S.C.R. 335 at 377-78, [1985] 1 C.N.L.R. 120. The Crown provided the correct procedure for settling and agreeing with the Inhabitants by public cession provisions of the *Royal Proclamation of 1763,* R.S.C. 1970, App. II, no.1 [hereinafter *Royal Proclamation*]; J. Borrows, "Constitutional Law from a First Nation Perspective: Self-Government and the Royal Proclamation" (1994) 28 U.B.C. L. Rev. 1 at 15-19; and B. Slattery, *The Land Rights of Aboriginal Canadian Peoples, as Affected by the Crown's Acquisition of Their Territories* (Saskatoon, Sk.: College of Law, University of Saskatchewan, 1979).

45 Labaree, *Royal Instructions, supra* note 42.

46 *Ibid.*

47 1677 (U.K.), 29 Car. II, c. 3

48 *Instructions, supra* note 42.

49 PANS RG 1, vol. 209; see letter Gov. Cornwallis to Duke of Bedford, PANS CO 217. The chiefs brought a copy of the treaty with them. One of the recorded treaties in the PANS was not Mascarene promises or the 1726 treaty, but rather the rejected proposed treaty of 1 Dec. 1725 (treaty no 239), *supra* note 30.

50 J. E. Read, "The Early Provincial Constitutions" (1948) 26 Can. Bar. Rev. 621,

51 *Prince Edward Island Term of Union, 1873* (U.K.) and *Newfoundland {British North America], Act, 1949* (U.K.), R.S.C. 1985, Appendix II, Nos. 12 and 32.

52 *Supra* note 21 at 417, 419

53 T. Akins, ed., *Selections from the Public Documents of the Province of Nova Scotia* (Halifax: Annand, 1869) at 671. (14 September 1752) This is the colonizers' version and text of the meeting. Míkmaq tradition says that the Grand Chief required payment for the British settlements.

54 *Ibid.*

55 *Ibid.* at 673 (16 September 1752).

56 *Native Rights, supra* note 10 at 307-09; Enclosure in letter of Gov. Hopson to Earl of Holdernesse, PANS, CO 217, vol. 40, at 371

57 *Ibid.,* Art. 1. The date of possession had to be before 1693 according to the Wabanaki Compact. See *Native Rights, supra* note 10 at 295. For actual

possession in 1693 to 1760, see A.H. Clark, *Acadia: The Geography of Early Nova Scotia to 1760* (Madison: University of Wisconsin Press, 1968).

58 Míkmaw Compact, 1752, in *Native Rights, supra* note 10 at Art. 5. This is the start of the Crown's notion of equalization payments and a redistributive economy.

59 *Ibid*. Art. 8 clarifies Article 6 of 1725 compact and Article 4 of 1726 and 1749 Míkmaw treaties. Article 6 the Wabanaki Compact, 1725 provided that "no private Revenge shall be taken" by either the Wabanaki or the British. Instead, both sovereigns agreed to submit any controversies, wrongs or injury between their people to His Majesty's Government for "Remedy or induse there of in a due course of Justice." Article 6 was affirmed by Míkmaq in 1726 and 1749, Article 7. Compared with the decline of feudal tenures, and corresponding development of central national legal systems, the European treaty order began to specify the effect of boundary changes on access to courts, jurisdictional clauses, and choices of law. Article VIII of the *Treaty of Utrecht* . The *Treaty of Paris* continued this article, but also began a reference to applying "the Law of Nations" to the disputes which might arise in the future. See A. Shortt and A.G. Doughty, eds., *Documents Relating to the Constitutional History of Canada 1759-1791*, vol. 1, 2nd ed. (Ottawa: J. de L. Taché, King's Printer, 1918).

60 *Simon* v. *R*, [1985] 2 S.C.R. 398, 62 N.R. 366 [hereinafter *Simon* cited to S.C.R.].

61 *Uniacke* v. *Dickson* (1848), 2 N.S.R. 287 (S.C. N.S.). P.W. Hogg, *Constitutional Law of Canada*, 3rd ed. (Toronto: Carswell, 1992) at 30, finds this dubious and argues that dates of reception thus derived are quite artificial and are really cut-off dates.

62 This is different from the idea that the first colonist carried as a birth right the British law and filled any legal void in the new territory. This idea was also limited by the courts' determination if they were suitable to the circumstance of the territory, such as prerogative treaties. Hogg *supra* 61 at Chapter 2, at 27-38. The 1763 Proclamation "annexed" Cape Breton and Prince Edward Island to old Nova Scotia's government, while reserving the Míkmaw Hunting Grounds in all places, thus creating a different date for the reception of British law. No other documents "annexed" the reserved Hunting Grounds to any colony or to the federal government.

63 Hogg, *supra* note 61 at 30, 32.

64 *Ibid.* at 28.

65 Sir W. Blackstone, *Commentaries on the Laws of England* (Oxford: Clarendon Press, 1765-69) vol. IV at 67-68. See especially, Justice Strong in *St. Catherines Milling and Lumber* v .R. (1887), 11 S.C. R. 577: "[A]t the date of confederation the Indian, by constant usage and practice of the crown, were considered to possess a certain proprietary interest in the unsurrendered lands which they occupied as hunting grounds; that this usage had either ripened into a rule of the common law as applicable to the American Colonies, or that such a rule had been derived from the law of nations and had in this way been imported into the Colonial law as applied to Indian Nations [...]" at 615-16

66 In Article 40 of the French Capitulation to the British in 1760, the King promised to maintain the tribes in their Aboriginal lands. See A. Shortt and A.G. Doughty, *supra* note 59 pt. 2, Sessional Papers No. 18. Article 40 continues the terms of the *Treaty of Utrecht*, and Art. II the *Treaty of Paris*, 1763 also reaffirmed it. Additionally, Article XXIII of the *Treaty of Paris* confirmed Article 40 of the Capitulation. Both the *Articles of Capitulation* and the *Treaty* ends any arguments about abrogation by hostilities or conquest. See especially, *Campbell v. Hall*, *supra* note 44 at 895-96 (articles of capitulation upon which the country is surrendered and the articles of peace by which it is ceded are sacred and inviolable according to their true intent and meaning).

67 PANSRG 1, vol. 37, doc. 14 (Treaties of Peace and Friendship with Mirimechi, Jediack, Pogmouch, and Cape Breton Micmacs at Halifax, 25 June 1761). For a list of the chiefs who had to ratify the compact See "Col. Fry Letter to Governor Belcher, 7 March 1760" [1760] London Magazine at 377 and *Collections of the Massachusetts Historical Society*, (Boston: The Society, from 1792) , vol. 10 at 115. The Wabanaki reaffirmed peace on the basis of their 1725 compact on 13 February 1760; B. Murdoch, *Epitome of the Laws of Nova Scotia*, vol. II (Halifax: J. Howe Publishers, 1832) at 384-5.

68 Míkmaw Compact, *supra* note 58; PAC NSA: American and West Indies, vol. 1 at 699-700. *Ibid.*

69 *Ibid.*

70 *Ibid.* The metaphor of "the Hedge" is directly related to the Wabanaki concept of "fence (implement)" (*lahkalusonihikon*) or territorial boundaries in the *Wapapi Akonutomakonol*, and its laws (*tapaskuwakonol*). Leavitt & Francis, *supra* note 12 at 56-57.

71 *Supra* note 47.

72 3 Geo. III; CO 217/19: 27-28; PANS Micro reel B-1028 4 May 1762. Implemented by Gov. Belcher Proclamation of 4 May 1762 and Act for the Regulation of Indian Trade, 1762 PANS, CO 217, vol. 19 at 33. See J. Singer, "Well Settled?: The Increasing Weight of History in American Indian Land Claims" (1994) 28 Georgia L. Rev. 481 at 503-508.

73 7 October 1763; Privy Council Register, Geo. III, vol. 3 at 102; PRO, c. 6613683; R.S.C. 1970, App. at 123-29. Original text is entered on the Patent Rolls for the regnal year 4 Geo. III, is found in the United Kingdom PRO: c. 66/3693 (back of roll); C.S. Brigham, ed., *British Royal Proclamations Relating to America*, vol. 12 (Worcester, Mass.: American Antiquarian Society, 1911) at 212-18; *Native Rights*, supra note 10 at 285-292.

74 1761 Instruction *supra* note 72 and 1763 Proclamation, *supra* note 73.

75 *Native Rights*, *supra* note 10 at 285-286.

76 See, Míkmaw Tenure in Atlantic Canada, *supra* note 9 at 267-296

77 *Ibid.* at 55.

78 *Ibid.* at 55.

79 U.K., 30 & 31 Victoria, c. 3.

80 *St. Catherine's*, *supra* note 7 at 55.

81 See Sir W. Blackstone, *Commentaries on the Laws of England*, vol. III (Oxford: Clarendon Press, 1765-69) at 43. A.V. Dicey, "The Paradox of the Land

Law" (1905) 21 L.Q. Rev. 221 at 222. A.W.B. Simpson, *A History of the Land Law*, 2nd ed. (Oxford: Oxford University Press, 1986) at 1.

82 *Delgamuukw, supra* note 1 at para. 113 (per Lamer C.J.C.)

83 *Ibid.* at para. 189 (per La Forest J), relying on *Guerin v. The Queen*, [1984] 2 S.C.R. 335, at 382 and *Canadian Pacific Ltd. v. Paul*, [1988] 2 S.C.R. 654 at 677.

84 [1990] 2 S.C.R. 85, [1990] 3 C.N.L.R. 46 at 82. J.Y. Henderson, "Interpreting *Sui generis* Treaties" (1997) 36(1) Alberta L. Rev. 46.

85 *R. v. Simon, supra* note 60 *reversing R. v. Syliboy*, [1929] 1 D.L.R. 307 and the Nova Scotia Court of Appeals on treaties in *Isaac v. The Queen infra* note 119; *R. v. Cope* 49 N.S.R. 555 at 564 (N.S.S.C.A.D.); *R. v. Simon* 49 N.S.R. (2d) 566, at 572-77 (N.S.S.C.A.D.).

86 *R. v. Syliboy, ibid.* at 313.

87 *Simon, supra*, note 60 at 399.

88 *Ibid.* at 59.

89 *Delgamuukw, supra* note 1 at para. 269.

90 *Ibid.* at para. 175.

91 *Ibid.* at para. 176.

92 (U.K.), 20 & 21 Geo. V, c. 26.

93 *Ibid.* at Schedules R.S.C. 1970, App. No. 25 at Para. 1 of Schedules.

94 *Ibid.* at para. 181.

95 *Ibid.* at para. 173ff. Similar reasoning was advanced for Aboriginal rights relating to land .The Court asserted that the federal government had: "the power to legislate in relation to other aboriginal rights in relation to land," which "encompasses within it the exclusive power to extinguish Aboriginal rights, including Aboriginal title."

96 *Ibid.* at para. 179.

97 *Ibid.* at para. 180.

98 *Ibid.* at para. 181. See generally, or intergovernmental or interjurisdictional immunity, J. Vaissi-Nagy, "Intergovernmental Immunity in Canada" in P. Lordon, *Crown Law* (Toronto & Vancouver: Butterworths, 1991) at ch. 5 at 129-169.

99 *Ibid.* at para. 179. Under the doctrine of paramountcy, where the federal government has a constitutional interest in property, provincial legislation over such interest, even if it that normally falls with its jurisdiction, is not binding, and federal legislation may override it and render it inoperative, *A.G. B.C. v. A.G. Canada (Johnny Walker case)*, [1924] A.C. 222, at 236-261 *Reference Re Waters and Water Powers*, [1929] S.C.R. 200 at 212-13, 223-26; *Alberta Government Telephones v. I.B.E.W.*, [1989] 2 S.C.R. 3181 *R. v Red Line Ltd.* (1930), 54 C.C.C. 271 (Ont. CA); *Re Young*, [1955] 5 D.L.R. 225 (Ont. CA.); *R. v. Glibbery* (1963) 36 D.L.R. (2d) 548 (Ont. CA); C.H.H. McNairn, "Crown Immunity from Statute—Provincial Governments and Federal Legislation: (1978), 56 Can. Bar. Rev. 145-150; K. Swinton, "Federalism and Provincial Government Immunity" (1979) 29 U.T.L.J. 1-50.

100 *Ibid.* at 1091-93. The Court refused to equate "existing" with the concept of being actual or exercisable. See *R. v. Eninew* (1984), 10 D.L.R. (4th) 137, 32 Sask. R. 237 (C.A.) [hereinafter *Eninew* cited to D.L.R.]. This ap-

proach answers the problem of how law can persist as order in a world of pervasive change and progression.

101 See generally Canada and the provinces position on Aboriginal land claims in the Atlantic Canada, J.Y. Henderson and A. Tanner, "Aboriginal Land Rights in the Atlantic Provinces" in K. Coates, ed. *Aboriginal land claims in Canada : a regional perspective* (Toronto: Copp Clark Pitman, 1992) at 131-167.

102 *R.* v *Sparrow*, [1990] 1 S.C.R. 1075 at 1105-06.

103 *Ibid.* at 1091 and 1109.

104 *Ibid.* at 1095-1101, 1111-1119. In *Denny* v. *The Queen*, [1990] 2 C.N.L.R. 115 at 263 (N.S.C.A.), the court affirmed the Aboriginal right to fish for food strictly on a constitutional interpretation of the *Constitution Act, 1982, supra* note 2 s.35(1) and independent of the force and effect of the terms of the Míkmaq treaties; court stated: "based upon the decision in *Isaac, infra* note 119 this [aboriginal] right has not been extinguished through treaty, other agreements or competent legislation. Given the conclusion that the appellants possess an aboriginal right to fish for food in the relevant waters, it is not necessary to determine whether the appellants have a right to fish protected by treaty."

105 *Ibid.* at 1098-99; *R.* v. *Alphonse*, [1993] 5 W.W.R. 401, 4 C.N.L.R. 19 (B.C.C.A.).

106 *Ibid.* at 1110.

107 *Ibid.* at 1115, 1110; *R.* v. *Howard*, [1994] 2 S.C.R. 299 , 3 C.N.L.R. 146 (S.C.C.), Gonthier J.

108 *Calder, supra* note 7 at 414.

109 *Delgamuukw, supra* note 1 at paras. 179-81, 183.

110 *Delgamuukw,* (1993) 104 D.L.R. (4th) 470, at 490 (B.C.C.A.). Hutcheon, J.A. for the minority opinion in the Court of Appeal agreed that there had not been blanket extinguishment of Aboriginal tenure, *ibid.* at 764.

111 *Ibid.*

112 *Ibid.* at paras. 173-183.

113 *Ibid.* at paras. 114, 126.

114 *Ibid.* at para. 172.

115 *Van der Peet, supra* note 7 at para. 28. Justice Heureux-Dubé agreed with the dissenting opinion in *R.* v. *Horseman*, [1990] 3 C.N.L.R. 95 at 117, 1 S.C.R. 901. In *Roberts* v. *Canada* [1989] 1 S.C.R. 322, Justice Wilson stated there is a law of Aboriginal title in the federal common law, at 340.

116 *Delgamuukw, supra* note 1 at para. 133-34.

117 *Bisallon* v. *Keable* [1983] 2 S.C.R.60 at 108.

118 See, Míkmaw Tenure in Atlantic Canada, *supra* note 9 at 259-267.

119 *Isaac v. The Queen* (1975) 13 N.S.R, (2d) 460 (N.S.C.A.D.) at 478-79, 483, 485. Chief Justice MacKeigan concluded that "The history of the next eighty-seven years discloses little concern for the Indians. The incoming settlers pushed them back to poorer land in the interior of the province. The government gradually herded them into reserves and made sporadic and unsuccessful attempts to convert them into agricultural people" (483-84). Before the Supreme Court of Canada in *Simon, supra*, note 60 the

Province of Nova Scotia argued that the Treaty of 1752 was not a valid treaty because it did not cede land to the Crown or delineate boundaries, and that occupancy by the white man under Crown grant or lease had extinguished the treaty reservation and gave absolute title in the land covered by the 1752 Treaty to the Crown (part VIII, 408-10). The Court found in unnecessary to come to a final decision on extinguishment by occupation of Crown grant or lease (at 405-406)

120 *R. v. Sioui*, [1990] 1 S.C.R. 1025 at 1055.

121 *Delgamuukw, supra* note 1 at para. 160. See, K. McNeil, " Aboriginal Title and the Division of Powers: Rethinking Federal and Provincial Jurisdiction" 1998 61(2) Sask. L. Rev. 431; and *Defining Aboriginal Title in the 90's. Has the Supreme Court finally got it Right?* (Toronto: Robarts Centre for Canadian Studies, 1998)

122 *Ibid.* at para. 169; also see *Sparrow, supra* note 102 at 1115, 110.

123 *Delgamuukw, supra* note 1 at para. 145.

124 *Ibid.*, B.C.C.A. at 537. The minority would have remitted the issues of damages to the trial judge.

125 *Ibid.* at para. 203.

126 *St. Catherine's, supra* note 7 at 46.

127 Section 109 provides: All lands, Mines, Minerals, and Royalties belonging to the several Provinces of Canada, Nova Scotia, and New Brunswick at the Union, and all Sums then due or payable for such Lands, Mines, Minerals or Royalties, shall belong to the several Provinces of Ontario, Quebec, Nova Scotia, and New Brunswick in which the same are situate or arise, subject to any Trusts existing in respect thereof, and to any Interest other than that of the Provinces in the same. *Constitution Act, 1867, supra* note 79.

128 *Ibid.* at 58.

129 *Oyekan v. Adele* [1957] 2 All E.R. 785 at 788 (P.C.).

130 *Delgamuukw, supra* note 1 at paras. 172-183.

131 *See also , Ref. Re Manitoba Language Rights* [1985] 1 S.C.R. 721, 744-45 (discussing section 52(1) of *Constitution Act, 1982* relationship to section 2 of the *Colonial Law Validity Act*)

132 *Manitoba (A.G.) v. Metro Stores (MTS) Ltd.*, [1987] 1 S.C.R. 110.132; *P.A.T.A. v. A.G. Canada* [1931] A.C. 310,313.

The Impact in Newfoundland and Labrador

ADRIAN TANNER

Introduction

For too long, the issue of aboriginal rights in Canada, and especially of land rights, has tended to be the preserve of specialists including lawyers, historians, civil servants, anthropologists and aboriginal political leaders. Discussion of these issues must be extended more broadly. Aboriginal rights will only gain the kind of respect that all laws must have in a democratic society when they become more widely understood.

It is important to examine the distinct repercussions this judicial decision is having in each region of Canada. I will consider the relevance of *Delgamuukw* to the rather special situation of aboriginal people in Newfoundland and Labrador. In that province there are four groups seeking settlement of their aboriginal land claims. Two of these claims, those of the Labrador Inuit Association and the Innu Nation, have been accepted by the federal Department of Indian Affairs and Northern Development. Negotiations have been under way for several years, and the Inuit negotiations are close to completion. The claims of the Mi'kmaq of the island of Newfoundland and the Labrador Métis Association have been rejected, but neither group accepts this as conclusive and are continuing their efforts to have their claims reconsidered.

Delgamuukw and Anthropology

On the face of things, my discipline of cultural anthropology has not fared too well so far in the hands of the Delgamuukw judiciary. The original judge refused to accept the testimony of two anthropologist expert witnesses, and the Supreme Court, while overturning most of the trial judge's findings, left this particular one alone. The anthropologists were accused of behaving too much like advocates, a function apparently reserved by the court exclusively for lawyers. However, there are other roles besides advocacy for anthropology in the elucidation of aboriginal title.

Aboriginal title arises in the way that the aboriginal group has occupied the land and cannot be equated with the Western concept of fee simple ownership or other familiar property law concepts. As noted in the *Delgamuukw* judgment, aboriginal title "must be understood by reference to both common law and aboriginal perspectives" and, as noted in the earlier Supreme Court *Van der Peet* judgement, involves "the reconciliation of the pre-existence of aboriginal societies with the sovereignty of the Crown." Aboriginal title is thus a compromise between the two perspectives, involving a two-way process. Not only must Western law expand to include unfamiliar principles, but aboriginal ideas must also adapt to Western concepts of property. In many other colonial and former colonial jurisdictions, such bridges between European common law and aboriginal understandings and practices have been commonplace for many years. In this respect, we in Canada have some catching up to do. This undertaking will require the kind of comparative approach that is already familiar to anthropology.

Anthropology does not just provide descriptions of the groups in question, their diverse ways of life, forms of social organization and ways of thinking. It also deals in the general principles and patterns that underlie culturally diversity of ideas and practices. One of these underlying principles is a general comparative understanding of property rights. All known societies, whether they have hunting and gathering, agricultural or industrial forms of production, recognize rights to territory and territorial resources. Property in land is commonly represented as a relationship, often deeply emotional and mystical, between a people and their land. However, in terms of rights, territorial property is more accurately seen as a relationship between *people* in the sense that some enjoy particular privileges with respect to the territory or resources in question, in relation to those who do not. For those groups who hold rights to their territory collectively, the "others" are those who are not members of the group.

Even if the societies involved may have had relatively simple hunting and gathering economies, their system of land tenure is often highly complex, with overlapping rights coming into play for different local sub-groups at different times of the year and covering different resources. Some rights to territory-based resources may be assigned to individuals, others to sub-groups, and still others to the whole society. While some rights may deal with the harvesting of territory-based resources, other rules may govern how particular parts of the resulting harvest is distributed. Consequently, land rights may be seen as more significant in the marking of social relations than as forms of wealth. While land under Western fee simple title can usually be freely bought and sold, this is not a common feature of land rights in non-industrial societies. The model of aboriginal title laid out in *Delgamuukw*—which refers to it as exclusively involving a collective right, one that can be sold, although only to the Crown—thus already represents a major transformation and simplification of not only prehistoric aboriginal land tenure practice, but also of some practices of aboriginal people that have continued to the present.

As stated above, cultural groups tend to express their territorial rights in emotional or even mystical terms, based on principles that they consider to be ultimate. In the *Delgamuukw* case, the connection to the land was traced by the aboriginal group through a series of individual lineages, each of which had its own oral accounts of their connections to their territories. In other parts of Canada, aboriginal people justify their connection to the land in terms of their relationship with spiritual entities connected to it. Among the Innu of Labrador, for example, human society is not seen as distinct from but part of that of animals and nature. Animals are thought of as "persons," as are the forces of Nature, and they all are seen as linked together in a single "society." Land-based geographic features are also thought of as spiritual "persons." The land thus forms a matrix of social relations between Innu local groupings, one that ties together this social model of Nature. Much of this kind of understanding has continued to the present despite the adoption by the Innu of Christianity in the nineteenth century.

While non-aboriginal Canadian representations of the basis of land title may seem very different from these aboriginal perspectives, both of them depend upon a connection between the land and a culturally based principle whose key characteristic is that it is ultimate. In the case of settler's title, its legitimacy is that it can be shown to derive from a Crown grant. As noted in the *Delgamuukw* decision, "[…] the inalienability of aboriginal lands is, at least in part, a function of the common law principle that settlers in colonies must derive their title from Crown grant and, therefore, cannot acquire title through purchase from aboriginal inhabitants." In colonial theory, when British sovereignty was declared in colonial territories, the Crown, as both connected to the deity and as the ultimate authority of the state, instantaneously acquired the underlying title to the territory. Unlike the test for aboriginal title, this did not require occupancy in order to be effective. This Euro-Canadian rationalization of land title can be seen, in its own way, to be as mystical and as legendary as those of the aboriginal people.

The Aboriginal Background
of Newfoundland and Labrador

Before 1949, Newfoundland had been a partly self-governing British colony. Its government had never recognized aboriginal people as having a distinct legal status, nor did it have any agency devoted to them. Most aboriginal people lived in the Labrador portion, which was effectively a colony within a colony in the sense that nobody, white or aboriginal, had the franchise, and government social services and facilities for the administration of justice were minimal. On the island portion, the Beothuk were driven to extinction by 1829. The Mi'kmaq were incorrectly seen by European settlers as interlopers from Nova Scotia, brought by the French to kill off the Beothuk. They were generally discriminated against, and as a consequence some of them tried to hide their aboriginal identity, while others remained in separate communities from the non-aboriginal Newfoundlanders.

At the time of Confederation in 1949, an under-the-table arrangement was made not to extend direct federal administration to the aboriginal people of the new province, unlike the situation in rest of Canada. Starting in 1964, the provincial government, with some federal funds, began to administer programs for aboriginal people, although at a more meager level than was the case in the rest of Canada. Moreover, instead of making the programs available specifically to aboriginal people, as in the rest of Canada, they were directed at anyone who happen to be living in any of a list of designated communities, whether these individuals were of non-aboriginal, aboriginal or mixed descent. In the case of the Labrador Inuit designated communities, a funding formula of 60 percent federal and 40 percent provincial was used, indicating the approximate proportions of aboriginal and non-aboriginal people assumed to be in the communities benefiting from the programs. The only Mi'kmaq community to have access to these programs was Conne River, and then only up to 1986. In that year, with the threat of court action and against the objections of both the federal government and the province, they became a band under the Indian Act and began to be funded under federal programs for status Indians. However, the dozen or so other Newfoundland Mi'kmaq communities, organized under the Federation of Newfoundland Indians, have not had access to such aboriginal programs, whether provincially or federal administered.

Canadians sometimes wonder if the interests of aboriginal people would have been better served had they been given the same citizen's rights and social programs at Confederation as all other Canadians, rather than assigning them a special legal status and reserves. Newfoundland offers in interesting empirical test case for this idea. Both before and since Confederation, Newfoundland has tried, as much as possible, to follow such a policy of non-discrimination and administrative integration. Despite this, however, the social conditions in Newfoundland's aboriginal communities are every bit as bad, and in many cases much worse, than are those to be found in the rest of Canada. The well-known case of Davis Inlet Innu is only the most notorious example of this unfortunate situation. By contrast, since the extension of the *Indian Act* to Conne River the community has been rejuvenated and social conditions have improved.

As the result of the distinctive history of contact, the situation of aboriginal land title in Newfoundland and Labrador has some unique features. In the case of the Labrador Inuit, the members of the group making the claim who will be the beneficiaries of any settlement are not narrowly defined in terms of their aboriginal status. They have to show connections to the northern coastal communities, even though a large number of them now no longer live there. This situation follows from the history of the Moravian communities, in which inter-marriage with European Newfoundlanders began in the 1800s. There are some parallels to the situation in the Mackenzie Valley of the Northwest Territories, where Métis have been included within the Dene claim.

The Innu are a single First Nation divided by their second language and with two claims, one from the Innu Nation of Labrador, the other from the Quebec Innu. This situation reflects the federal practice of authorizing land claims by provincially based organizations. However, the Labrador boundary with Quebec in no way reflects territorial divisions between Quebec-based and Labrador-based Innu bands—large parts of Labrador are actually the traditional lands of Quebec Innu. In fact it would have made more sense to deal with Quebec and Labrador Innu aboriginal title as involving a single block of land.

In the original Delgamuukw trial, the legendary history of the aboriginal group was called into question. In Newfoundland, it is the European settlers who have their own legends that the Mi'kmaq first became established on the island by the French to kill off the Beothuk. Even though these stories have been shown to be historically false, they have helped to shape government's negative attitudes towards the Mi'kmaq land claim. This claim raises fundamental issues of what constitutes proof of aboriginal occupancy at the time that British sovereignty was established.

Finally, the Labrador Métis claim is by descendents of marriages between Inuit and Europeans. Some of this group migrated into Innu territory in the upper Lake Melville region in the mid-nineteenth century, where they became specialized as trappers for the Hudson's Bay Company and developed a unique land tenure system along the major river valleys, based on individual trap lines. Because their occupation of this territory occurred after sovereignty was established, it faces the greatest difficulties to meet one of the tests laid out in *Delgamuukw*.

Delgamuukw and Land Claims in Newfoundland and Labrador

One significant finding of the *Delgamuukw* judgement deals with justifications for infringement on aboriginal title, as in the case of development projects. In the 1990 *Sparrow* decision, justification based on the conservation of a resource was addressed. In *Delgamuukw*, such projects are broadly outlined to include "the development of agriculture, forestry, mining, and hydroelectric power, the general economic development of [the region], protection of the environment or endangered species, the building of infrastructure and the settlement of foreign populations to support those aims." This infringement must take place in a way that acknowledges the priority interest of the aboriginal group which has an aboriginal right to the region. The group has the right to be involved in the decision over the use to which the land is put. They must be dealt with in good faith with the intention of substantially addressing their concerns. Depending on the degree to which the development infringes on aboriginal title, the consent of the group may be required. The court also noted that compensation would normally be required when aboriginal title is infringed upon.

At a minimum, the requirement for good-faith consultation before development can proceed only begins to addresses what has otherwise become a highly problematic situation for many aboriginal groups. Without the recognition of the principle that aboriginal title is a substantial interest that can be protected in the face of other competing interests, an absurd situation has existed. The federal government would recognized the validity of an aboriginal land claim, but before a settlement of the claim was reached major development projects could be undertaken, projects which could render these negotiations substantially meaningless. In fact, given that land claims negotiations generally take many years or decades to conclude, it was in the self-interest of a province or territory to promote as much development as possible in the area before reaching a settlement of the land claim. This is because it is more difficult to include in the settlement lands for which rights have already been assigned to a third party than it is for unencumbered land. While a fiduciary obligation rests on the federal government to settle outstanding aboriginal land title, provinces have no such legal obligation and it is in their interest to hold back, because of the benefits to be acquired from accelerating the resource development on the land in question.

Examples of this kind of situation existed in all parts of the country. A case in point in Atlantic Canada was the development of large areas of Labrador and adjacent parts of Quebec for low-level flight training by NATO air forces, beginning in 1980. The land claim of both the Innu Nation and the Labrador Inuit Association had been accepted as valid by the late 1970s. Before any meaningful negotiations of these claims had got under way, however, low-level flying had begun, and soon two major low-flying zones covering a large portion of the Innu and Inuit claim areas had been established. When the development was belatedly submitted to the Federal Environmental Impact Assessment Process, after the development was already in full gear, the Department of Defense insisted that the terms of reference of the assessment included the provision that any implications of the development for aboriginal land claims could not be addressed. Neither during or since have the concerns that have been raised by the Innu been adequately addressed

There are a number of development projects planned in Labrador in areas of outstanding aboriginal title, including the Voisey's Bay Nickel Mine/Mill; the proposed expanded Upper Churchill and the new Lower Churchill hydroelectric projects; and the Goose Bay to Red Bay section of the Trans-Labrador Highway. While the Labrador Inuit claim area includes Voisey's Bay, an agreement-in-principle has recently been signed. Thus this provision will be of more relevance to the Innu claim.

One of the significant parts of the *Delgamuukw* judgement was that the trial judge had erred in not taking account of the evidence of oral history. In Newfoundland the Mi'kmaq claim includes the assertion that they had been travelling back and forth between Nova Scotia and Newfoundland, where they had established themselves before European contact. Early European documentary evidence for this claim is sketchy. However, oral accounts of these crossings have been collected by anthropologists. Moreover, these oral accounts were documented as far back as 1912, long before there was any idea of a land claim. But, given that the *Delgamuukw* decision also establishes that prior occupation only need be established back to the time of British sovereignty, this may not be an essential point in any future Mi'kmaq legal case for aboriginal title.

A further issue related to the Newfoundland Mi'kmaq claims arises out of the Supreme Court Marshall decision, issued in 1999 after the Delgamuukw decision. The decision was based on a treaty with several groups that included the Mi'kmaq, and gives them rights to exploit and trade certain natural resources, including fish. If it can be shown that Mi'kmaq were occupying Newfoundland at the time of the treaty, then it could be that this group may be among the beneficiaries of the judgement. However, when in late 1999 a group of Mi'kmaq from outside the province came to Newfoundland with the intention of exercising fishing rights in the area, they did not have the support of local Mi'kmaq, and subsequently withdrew. The Mi'kmaq leadership announced they did not intend to exercise such rights before seeking an agreement on the matter with the province.

Conclusion

The modern aboriginal land claims process has been under way in Canada since 1973. Claims are internally adjudicated by the Indian Affairs Branch, which is not subject to public judicial review when it rejects claims. These and many other aboriginal rights cases end up in courts and are appealed to the highest levels. In the negotiations, provinces have what amounts to veto power over all matters, some of which are in the constitutional domain of the federal government. For some years the federal government has been told by the Supreme Court that it has been negligent in exercising its fiduciary responsibilities to Indians. So far, these admonitions have had little noticeable affect on federal actions. While the *Delgamuukw* decision has clarified a number of issues, it is not clear that this will lead to the rapid resolution of claims issues. Meanwhile, ordinary aboriginal people are in dire need of a resolution to these disputes.

Canada was initially forced into land claims by the Supreme Court, and has ever since chanted the mantra the settlement must come from political negotiations and not the courts. And yet it has become apparent the politically negotiated settlements themselves tend to lead to court action.

In my view, the task of deciding upon the validity of land claims is too important to be left to internal decisions of the Indian Affairs Branch. Moreover, neither Canada nor the aboriginal people can afford the time and expense of continual litigation all the way to the Supreme Court over aboriginal rights. I suggest we need a specialized judicial body with the training, expertise and facilities at its disposal to bring resolution to outstanding land claims, and to disputes arising out of aboriginal title. In the U.S. there was such a Claims Commission many years ago with these kinds of judicial powers. Unfortunately, the term "Indian Claims Commission" has already been used in Canada for different bodies with no judicial power or authority. We need a body with the specialized expertise and the authority required to deal with aboriginal issues, with the power to subpoena witnesses and take evidence under oath, and with the power to make binding decisions. We have wasted too much time already. In the meantime, the social conditions of aboriginal people, for whom land claims are intended to assist in their adjustment to having been overwhelmed by settlers, have steadily diminished.

Very recently, the announcement has been made of the intention to form an Independent Claims Body, with some of the kinds of judicial independence and powers I have suggested are needed. However, the proposed body will only deal with unresolved issues involved in "specific claims," that is, those that arise from failure to implement all the terms of treaties. Moreover, it will be limited to awards in cash, and then only up to a maximum of five million dollars. This may be a move in the right direction, but in my view the principle of an independent judicial claims body needs to be extend to the kinds of unresolved issues embedded in certain "comprehensive claims," where cash compensation is seldom the appropriate resolution.

Rights and Wrongs
Finding a Just Middle Ground in Land Claim Disputes

DON CAYO

Introduction

It is hard to recall a single case where native people in Canada have won much of lasting value unless, or until, they got in someone's way. Given the adversarial nature of court proceedings where someone wins and someone else loses, it is also hard to envisage any court ever finding an all-round satisfactory solution to a native rights or land claim case. So the best possible result in the Maritimes of the *Delgamuukw* ruling may well be that it helps put Mi'kmaq and Malecite people squarely in someone's way. The ruling has added one more arrow to natives' quiver of legal tools by giving their oral history the same weight as the written accounts of Europeans and their descendents. It may, at long last, give focus to negotiations for a just and rational redress of inequities.

Critics of the *Delgamuukw* ruling argue that oral history is fraught with opportunities to stray from the facts, perhaps particularly so in the North American native tradition where facts and myths are sometimes strung into seamless stories. These stories often put little emphasis on chronology, the single most important element of histories recorded in the European tradition. In such circumstances, it's easy to fear that the result will be inaccurate.

But it's naïve to believe that written history is necessarily any more correct. At best, accounts recorded at the time that events were unfolding can be expected to reflect the big picture no more accurately than newspaper accounts of today. At worst, they may be seriously skewed by deliberate manipulation, ignorance or prejudice. And the fact that historic accounts are interpreted in different ways by today's scholars, all of them claiming great objectivity, speaks for itself. Do not expect to find revealed truth on the lips or in the books of any group of self-interested people.

Patricia Olive Dickason, a Canadian historian who made her mark in recent decades by being one of the first academics to seriously consider native views of past events, has written about and discussed with the author of this paper the distortions that arise when only the victors get to record history. The victorious invariably cast themselves as the heroes of the piece.

Even today, in an era where the vanquished at last finding their voice, the real story may remain elusive. While a new breed of native historians may be quite properly at odds with Euro-centric views, Dr. Dickason believes they may come no closer to objective truth.

The first volume of the *Royal Commission on Aboriginal Peoples* deals extensively with the unreliability of the written record. For example, in relation to some of the earlier treaties, which it found fraught with ambiguities and unresolved paradoxes, it says:

> There is clear evidence that, at least at times, more got written down than was ever discussed with the aboriginals. And in some cases France talked about sovereignty only in discourse intended for the ears of competing European nations, never with natives who would have thrown them out.

So the prospect of the courts giving equal weight to competing versions of history need not be disturbing, providing they have the wisdom not to give total weight to any one account.

Indisputable marginalization

There are, however, some historical and modern-day facts that are beyond dispute—the well-documented marginalization of many natives and their communities. And these inequalities have a longer history in the Maritimes, one of the first parts of Canada to be settled by Europeans and their descendents, than in many other regions. Natives have been confined to ever-shrinking reserves on generally unproductive land from the time of the first extensive European settlement following the American Revolution. Their specific woes may have changed, but their general plight has not been alleviated by the superficially generous federal policies of recent decades.

In general, native people who leave the reserve seem to integrate a little better into the Maritimes' mixed communities, which have none of the native ghettos that characterize many Western Canadian cities. But those who remain on reserves may be a little worse off, particularly when it comes to welfare and unemployment. The *Royal Commission on Aboriginal Peoples* found welfare rates on Maritime reserves to be the highest in the land—77 percent of reserve residents are on assistance at some point in any given year. Other indicators of Canada-wide dysfunction that are scattered throughout the five-volume report, or recorded elsewhere, are more or less indicative of the situation in the Maritimes:

- Indians live, on average, eight years less than other Canadians do, and it's twice as common for their babies to die.

- Indians get sick more often than other people do; they're three times more apt to be injured in a car crash; one-and-a-half times more likely to be injured in a fall.

- They are eight times more susceptible to dying in a fire; six or seven times more likely to drown. They are three times more likely to kill themselves; six times more likely to be killed by someone else. They're seven times more likely to be poisoned.

- 10 percent of Canadian natives live in homes without piped water—90 times the national rate. Their houses may often be inadequate, but each is home to 30 percent more people than average.

- The total amount of land set aside for Indians in Canada is less than the Navaho own in Arizona.

- 73 percent of native people say alcohol abuse is hurting their people; 59 percent say drug abuse; 44 percent say family violence; 34 percent say suicide; 29 percent say sexual abuse; 16 percent say rape.

- Cases of abuse against women and against elders—people barging in and demanding money, for example—were not seen as problems in the past but have increased sharply, perhaps because of more frequent reporting. In the words of the Royal Commission report: "Indian men, unemployed and idle, are constantly humiliated by having their families supported by the welfare system. The little work that does exist on many native reserves ... is often awarded to women. A power struggle ensues when the native woman is the breadwinner, and the exercise of violence and intimidation may be the last resort of the down-trodden warrior."

- Only 31 percent of working-age Indians are employed. (The official unemployment rate makes the picture look a little better, but only because so many don't try to find work.)

- 65 percent of all working residents on reserves earn less than $10,000 a year. And less than two percent of all Indians, one-ninth of the national average, have incomes of more than $40,000. Overall, paycheques for Indians average about half as much as their non-native neighbours.

- Only 0. 6 percent of all natives have university degrees, compared with 4.4 percent for all Canadians.

- Native women are better educated than the men are, but no more likely to find work. And less than 16 percent of them earn $20,000 a year or more, compared with almost 35 percent of their non-Aboriginal sisters.

- Only 1,015 Indians in Atlantic Canada, or eight percent, own businesses—the second-lowest percentage in Canada. And virtually all native businesses in the region are tiny: 34 percent have no employees and another 54 percent have fewer than five.

Reasons for these dysfunctions can be, and have been, debated endlessly. Theories include the view that many individuals, often tempted by perverse policies into unwise choices, are authors of their own fate because they fail to pursue the opportunities that could be open to them as Canadians. That may or may not be so. While we ought to examine the pathologies of dependence when considering policy approaches, the reasons do not matter when we are assessing the high cost of this dependence and dysfunction, not only to the natives on Maritime reserves but also to the broader communities that pay for their myriad social programs.

Likewise, the reasons—failure to pursue job opportunities, racism, indifference and ignorance, or lack of opportunity—do not much matter when we examine the indisputable fact that native people, especially those who live on reserves, have long been excluded from the broader economy throughout the Maritimes.

This reality was underlined in conversation two years ago with Pat Francis, a new, young and progressive chief of the 350-member Woodstock reserve in the St. John River Valley. As is the case on almost all Maritime reserves, the Chief could count on his fingers the number of band members who had jobs off the reserve. One of his responses to the resulting problem of massive unemployment was to first write to, then have an employee visit, more than 60 non-native businesses. Each business was offered a free native employee—the band would pay the full cost of the informal apprenticeship—for a period of several months. The idea was that if the employee developed the skills needed and proved valuable, a job offer would follow. The exercise resulted in just one employer agreeing to try the experiment. Subsequently, one native woman was hired as a part-time waitress.

To those of us who believe that prosperity is not a zero-sum game—that wealthy and productive neighbours can enhance each other's earning power—this situation is counter-productive. Not to mention the human cost of miring thousands of people in dependence, and the ever-growing price tag for largely ineffective social services.

Little recent progress

Various native groups and leaders in the Maritimes have gone through the motions of making land claims in recent years. Aside from a few specific claims intended to recover compensation for fairly small patches of reserve land that can be proven to have been improperly appropriated by others, none have gone very far. None have had the backing of all Maritime natives and native groups, or even all in any one province. The provincial governments have, with only some very recent exceptions, shown little or no interest whatever in native issues and claims. And the federal government has not deigned that any of the claims to date were appropriate to be brought "to the table" for serious negotiation.

In scores of formal interviews and informal conversations with natives across New Brunswick, some of them senior leaders of groups that purport to have the authority to speak for all, I have heard a wide variety of land claim proposals. Frankly, some of them sound like pie-in-the-sky. Compared to cases that have been settled in other parts of the country, they seem to have little chance of succeeding in court, and no chance at all in negotiations. Claims include demands that the province's 8,000 or so native people be granted title to all of the land in New Brunswick; entitlement to 25 percent of all revenue from resource harvesting in the province; and the right to extract rent from non-native inhabitants.

Though no court precedent exists in the region, Maritime natives do have reason to hope they can establish a legal basis that their case is somewhat analogous to the situation in British Columbia—that they have never signed a treaty giving up their right to the land. A lower court in New Brunswick actually ruled in 1997 that this was the case. This judgment was thrown out on appeal, but only on the basis that the judge had weighed factors from his own knowledge and research rather than on the facts that were put before him. But the ruling, overturned or not, has dramatically changed the dynamics of the relationship between natives and non-natives in the province, and indeed through-out the Maritimes and parts of Quebec.

The case involved the right of natives to harvest wood from Crown land. During the several months between the ruling and the appeal, hundreds of native people took to the woods with their chainsaws. Despite the appeal court ruling, they continued to cut down trees.

Significantly, the provincial government and the huge New Brunswick forest industry began to take native issues and native claims more seriously. Several interim agreements have been reached with almost every band in the province, each allowing native people to harvest and sell specified amounts of wood. And the province appointed two respected jurists to study the situation and report back with recommendations for longer-term action.

The interim logging agreements are unsatisfactory to most natives, who believe they should have greater access to wood, as well as to the forest industry, which is worried about any cutting that does not fit within carefully drafted long-range plans. New Brunswick's forests are already logged to the limit, right to the edge of unsustainability. There is simply no room for additional cutters who aren't integrated into existing forest management plans.

The presence of native people in the woods and the very real threat that the court might grant them the right to stay—a threat that may be intensified by the *Delgamuukw* decision—places natives in someone's way, perhaps for the first time since the Malecite people sided with George Washington. They are in the way of the provincial government and logging interests like the influential Irving family of Saint John. And both the industry and the government are showing unprecedented willingness to talk with them.

Natives across provincial borders in parts of Quebec and Nova Scotia are also taking to Crown land with their chainsaws, although the activity is at this point on a smaller scale. But the Nova Scotia government, in particular, seems to be taking notice.

The talks taking place are neither comprehensive nor particularly well advanced. But they ought to be welcomed as the first attempts in modern memory to bring Maritime native people into the broader economy.

It seems clear from even a casual survey of the geography and settlement patterns of the Maritimes that it is politically impossible to turn over huge swaths of territory to a group of people out-numbered more than 100-to-1 by their non-native neighbours. The region is simply too densely populated. And even the more militant among Maritime natives concede that their neighbours are here to stay.

There are relatively large blocks of unsettled forestland in both New Brunswick and Nova Scotia. All of them are privately owned, designated as protected land, or leased by the Crown to forestry companies. The fishery is equally crowded with fewer geographic set-asides, but with quotas pushing the boundaries of sustainability and fully exploited by individual fishermen and fishing companies that have a legal right to do so.

If some form of involvement in the region's resource industries is the favoured way to give native people some access to an economy beyond their small and sparsely endowed reserves, then some form of co-management strategy seems to be the most practical answer. Co-management has proved effective in other parts of Canada, nowhere more so than in northwestern Saskatchewan, where the Meadow Lake Tribal Council is involved in the hugely successful management of 2.2 million hectares of Crown forest land.

Some reserves are making strides by adapting what is seen as a traditional approach of communal management to modern industries. The Conne River band of southern Newfoundland, for example, has virtually eradicated unemployment in an area traditionally starved for jobs. Band-owned enterprises include traditional trapping and crafts; out-fitting and eco-tourism; retailing; logging and milling; aquaculture and farming; and providing Internet and cable television service well beyond the boundaries of the reserve.

While this experiment is successful, it is also quite new. Given the widespread failure of communitarian economic management in many parts of the world, however, the jury is out as to how long it can continue to prosper.

The Meadow Lake model is an illustration of a graceful transition from community ownership to entrepreneurial individualism. It was designed from the outset to be what organizers call "a self-destructing co-operative." In communities with no tradition of entrepreneurship and where virtually no one had money to invest, the tribal council kick-started what has grown into a huge and environmentally friendly logging industry by buying all of the equipment needed and training people to operate it. But, as fast as skills were sufficiently developed and financing could be arranged, individual components of the operation were sold off to scores of different owners.

The centrepiece of the project was a deal between the tribal council and about 100 non-native employees to buy a money-losing, Crown-owned sawmill. The province was eager to sell, and the band exploited that eagerness by leveraging a co-management agreement for the 2.2 million hectares of land. Since that time, they have brought in a new partner—a company that built and operates Saskatchewan's first hardwood pulp mill. They have dramatically improved cutting practices, implemented widespread reforestation, and fostered the development of dozens of small mobile sawmills. When I visited the area two years ago, they had increased native employment on the land 25-fold and non-native employment three-fold, in less than a decade.

The area of northwestern Saskatchewan is less densely populated than any part of the Maritimes. But there are many parallels between the two regions. The Saskatchewan area is home to about the same number of native people from two different First Nations—Cree and Dene—echoing the Mi'kmaq-Malicite mixes in the East. Nearly a dozen native communities in both regions are widely scattered. The resource that is the basis of newfound prosperity in each area is widespread, but not particularly rich.

The biggest difference I observed was leadership. The Saskatchewan group, though divided at times by racial and political differences, has been able to come together to accomplish mutual goals. That has yet to happen on a large and sustained scale in the Maritimes.

But recent developments in the courts and on the land have created a climate in which Maritime governments and big industry are ready, perhaps even eager, to talk, given the high cost of depending on an uncertain wood supply. Although Maritime resources, especially wood and fish, are already fully exploited from a conventional harvesting perspective, the industries potentially have a long way to go in creating more wealth through adding value to the products they ship. I am confident that, if native people can find the right leadership and rally behind it and if both sides can avoid intractable confrontation, some mutually beneficial and satisfactory deals can be struck.

But that is not an outcome I expect if the big questions—rights to the land and access to economic activity—are settled in court.

7 Overall Economic Impacts

Costs and Coase
A Way Forward

OWEN LIPPERT

> The solution is essentially the transformation of the conflict from a political problem to an economic transaction. An economic transaction is a solved political problem.
>
> Abba Lerner, "The Economics and Politics of Consumer Sovereignty," *American Economic Review*, 62, May 1972, page 259.

> The delineation of rights is an essential prelude to market transactions.
>
> Ronald Coase, "The Federal Communications Commission," *Journal of Law and Economics*, 2, October 1959, pages 1-40.

> ... I believe that all of the parties have characterized the content of Aboriginal title incorrectly. The appellants argue that Aboriginal title is tantamount to an inalienable fee simple, which confers on Aboriginal people the rights to use those lands as they chose and which have been constitutionalized by s. 35(1). The respondents offer two alternative formulations ...The content of Aboriginal title, in fact, lies somewhere between these positions.
>
> ... its characteristics cannot be completely explained by reference either to the common law rules of real property or the rules of property found in Aboriginal legal systems.
>
> Chief Justice Antonio Lamer, *Delgamuukw v. British Columbia*, paragraphs 110-112.

Notes will be found on page 417.

Ludwig Wittgenstein, a famous philosopher from Vienna, it is reputed to have said, "If a question can be asked then it can be answered." The question raised by *Delgamuukw* is a simple one: can the question of who owns what land and why be resolved without bankrupting the country? The answer I try to provide here goes beyond the well-traversed legal and political approaches to one based on the economic insights provided by Ronald Coase, a University of Chicago economist and Nobel Laureate. The examples discussed in this paper come from British Columbia, but as others have argued, the questions raised may be valid in other provinces.

I examine the costs of doing nothing and the cost of doing something. Specifically, I examine the direct and indirect costs of negotiation and litigation. I conclude that for negotiation to cost less and to produce more economic growth than litigation, a workable set of property rights must be defined formally or informally. Coase provides considerable theoretical guidance in how to define and use property rights successfully. Ultimately, I conclude that the process of sorting out Aboriginal land claims may be better handled without the direct participation of governments. Aboriginal bands and resource users could arrive at their own agreements on the uses of, and rents paid on, Crown lands under Aboriginal title claim. It does not matter to resource users who they pay, but how much they pay. What governments would lose in resource rents, they would make back in more general taxes on economic activity which would surely rise.

What is the cost of doing nothing?

The first question decision-makers might ask themselves is, "What is the cost of doing nothing?"

The cost of doing nothing may be actually quite high. Well before *Delgamuukw*, the issue of Aboriginal title and lands claims had led to perceived higher risks for investments in B.C. Until quite recently, the B.C. forest industry enjoyed four years of strong markets and prices. During that time, capital investment remained low by historical standards. Today, profits go toward boosting internal rates of return to cover future risk or to acquisitions in other provinces and countries. Many reasons may explain why this is so, including high taxes, high labour costs and a heavy regulatory burden. Among them surely lurks the possibility of uncompensated or inadequately compensated expropriation through a possible land claims settlement.

In a recent Fraser Institute survey of mining company executives, my colleague Laura Jones reported that, "Uncertainty concerning the settlement of native land claims is identified as a deterrent to exploration investment in every province. However, it is considered the greatest liability in British Columbia, where 92 percent of survey respondents consider land claims uncertainty a serious deterrent to exploration investment. Of that 92 percent, 34 percent indicate that they would not invest in British Columbia due to the uncertainty surrounding claims."

Let me make very clear two important points about the costs of settling or not settling Aboriginal land claims. First, it is not a zero-sum game between Aboriginal and non-Aboriginal British Columbians. Economic uncertainty among non-Aboriginal citizens does not equal economic certainty for Aboriginal people. One side's loss is not the other's gain. *Delgamuukw* will lead to either more wealth-creating economic exchanges for all of us or for none of us, Aboriginal and non-Aboriginal alike. The price will be the same.

Second, when I talk of costs, I'm not referring to the land, itself. The land of British Columbia has no intrinsic economic value. Its only economic worth lies in its use as a source from which to extract natural resources or as a site for activities such as tourism and recreation. This statement is no less true for Aboriginal people. Ownership of land, no matter how defined, is not an end in itself: Aboriginal title agreements are just words on paper unless the land can be used for whatever purposes, including doing nothing with it.

If the land has no intrinsic value, what's important then to Aboriginal and non-Aboriginal people alike is how much, and in what ways, we can make use of the resources held within Crown lands. All of us want to enjoy immediate and long-term use of the land, whatever use that may be. All of us want to ensure the land can support varied uses, whether forestry, mining, recreation or preservation. In short, the more ways to achieve exchanges between landowners and land users, the more exchanges there will be and thus the greater the potential for wealth creation.

The ability of all British Columbians, Aboriginal and non-Aboriginal, to enjoy a higher material standard of living depends on increasing the quantum of exchanges through as many kinds of land uses as profitable within the market economy and permissible within the environmental and other land use regulations set by the legislature.

What is the cost of uncertainty?

Often one hears that the cost of unresolved land claims is uncertainty. The questions that need to be asked and answered are: "Uncertainty for whom? About what? And how will this uncertainty inhibit economic growth?"

Uncertainty in the context of Aboriginal title must mean something more than just not knowing what will happen in the future. Every enterprise dependent upon some form of access to Crown land, indeed every enterprise, faces the unknown. Is the uncertainty over the scope of Aboriginal title fundamentally different than the possibility of whopping new provincial taxes, fluctuations in the Canadian dollar, new American tariffs, slumping Asian markets, new competitors from South America, or the scientific discovery of new and cheaper substitutes for B.C.'s resource products? If a dollar off the bottom line is a dollar off the bottom line no matter what the cause, then Aboriginal title is just one more factor companies must take into account when risking their capital to produce wealth-creating exchanges.

The uncertainty that matters is how we might collectively and individually respond to such a state. The uncertainty surrounding Aboriginal title in B.C. is not whether it exists, but whether the federal government, the provincial government and the Aboriginal bands are capable of implementing it in an economically rational manner. Furthermore, are these three groups capable of understanding that the private sector, the wealth creators, will act rationally even if these groups do not. The private sector will swiftly alter its economic exchanges in response to the behavior of governments and Aboriginal bands.

The Cost of Doing Something

There are five relevant cost areas in which the behavior of governments and Aboriginal bands will be watched and judged:

(1)   costs to taxpayer of treaties and compensation;

(2)   treatment of existing leases and compensation for their abrogation;

(3)   direct government and Aboriginal rents applied to continuing leases;

(4)   transaction costs of defining the scope of Aboriginal title and negotiating its exercise; and

(5)   the costs of Aboriginal self-government to the extent they result from land transfers.

Whether these costs are borne directly or indirectly through taxation, the effect is the same fewer potential exchanges.

Costs to taxpayers of treaty settlements and compensation

The Delgamuukw decision opens the possibility that the definition and application of Aboriginal title will take place through the courts rather than through the existing treaty processes such as those that exist in British Columbia.[1]

There are three main public sector costs to be incurred in settling Aboriginal land claims, whether through the courts or through negotiations:

- land transferred;

- cash paid for land claimed but not transferred; and

- cash paid to compensate Crown licence holders on land transferred to Aboriginal bands.

Delgamuukw has introduced a whole new cost—the compensation to Aboriginal bands for past usage of lands for which they can prove Aboriginal title. Lamer wrote that the price of compensation starts at market value and could include all earnings since 1846. Though Aboriginal title does not apply to private property, the Crown must still compensate Aboriginal owners. What is the cost of compensating the Musqueam, Squamish, Capilano and Tsawwassen bands for the occupation and development of Vancouver?

The question on the surface raises the fears and expectations of billions of dollars to be paid out. But these fears and expectations may melt under scrutiny. Logically, a claim for compensation cannot be based on deriving a percentage of the current and accumulated market value of the land when that land only has the bulk of its value because of more than a century of development, however improperly the land was acquired. Chief Justice Lamer has done no one a favor with his scattered musings on the economic calculation of how to determine compensation. It makes more sense to take the value of the land at the time of the abrogation of Aboriginal title and to apply interest to that value. That said, the virtue of compound interest would make that sum astronomical. One bright bulb calculated that if the Manhattan tribe had converted the $24 dollars worth of trinkets into cash and placed it in an interest-bearing account, the sum today would nearly equal the value of New York City.

At some point the compensation figure, even if calculated on value at the time of alienation, becomes so large that the injury to the economy of creating that much more public debt hurts everyone including Aboriginal people, whether or not they pay taxes. After all, the compensation paid out will be in Canadian dollars, a currency whose value has steadily eroded over the last two decades in part because the massive accumulation of public debt.

A policy of compensation, however, may still provide some savings. One may well be the long-overdue redefinition of the Crown's financial role vis-à-vis Aboriginal bands. The general fiduciary responsibility of the Crown to Aboriginal people is "to protect them in the enjoyment of their Aboriginal rights and in particular in the possession and use of their lands." [2] Building from a now-discredited notion of wardship, the federal government slowly but steadily expanded the range of social welfare payments. As the 1985 *Nielsen Task Force* reported:

> The large portion [of Indian spending] devoted to status Indians and Inuit is commonly attributed to federal obligations under the treaties of the Indian Act. In fact, only 25 per cent of these expenditures can be directly attributed to these obligations. The remainder goes largely to services of a provincial and municipal nature and stem from decades of policy decisions designed to fill this void which have, by convention, come to be considered as though they were rights.[3]

If the federal and provincial governments through payments of compensation are fully meeting their constitutional "fiduciary responsibility," all other payments not strictly required by treaties must be considered as discretionary. They must be viewed by the same standard of equity and equality as applied to all other public payments to individuals and groups. Aboriginal people who are poor deserve the same public assistance as any other Canadian would expect to receive. At the same time, as income and means-testing applies to a range of benefits, there should be no exemptions on any basis and certainly not one based on some quasi-racial qualifications.

Moreover, as Aboriginal bands achieve self-government—in whatever form—one would expect them to assume the appropriate level of responsibility for social welfare spending. This is particularly true as bands assume ever-greater abilities to levy taxes.

Treatment of existing leases and compensation

Despite the size and mountainous nature of B.C.'s Crown land, very little of it is not covered by some lease, license or tenure, including timber rights and tree farm licenses, oil, gas and mineral exploration and extraction permits, grazing permits and road and pipeline right-of-ways. According to a 1992 Price Waterhouse study of the cost of land claims, resource industries dependent on access to Crown land, accounted for 200,000 jobs and $17.5 billion in annual revenues, one quarter of B.C.'s Gross Domestic Product.

Chief Justice Lamer does not address compensation for leaseholders directly in his decision. In his inattention to this critical issue, he is matched by the two governments and Aboriginal negotiators in the B.C. Treaty process who have been less than forthcoming as to how existing lease and license holders would be treated in the event of expropriation of their rights. All sides concede that some license holders may be expropriated. All sides concede that there should be fair compensation. The 1993 Cost-Sharing Memorandum of Agreement between the provincial and federal governments calls for the two levels of government to split the cost of compensating expropriated Crown land leaseholders. Yet suspicions persist as to the intentions of the governments, the closer the moment of actual expropriation nears. Why?

The reason is simple: the past behaviour of both governments. The federal government in canceling the Pearson Airport contract and the provincial government in canceling the ALCAN Kemano completion project, both resisted paying fair compensation except under extreme legal pressure. Both ultimately asserted that the legislature holds the prerogative to expropriate without fair or any compensation.

That position, however, has increasingly little legal justification. Osgoode Hall law professor Patrick Monahan has cogently argued that the Rule of Law has come to be interpreted in Canada as covering the contracts that governments enter into with private parties.[4] As licenses and leases are contracts, the federal and provincial governments are bound by the Rule of Law to pay compensation when these agreements are abrogated. Monahan states in his conclusion:

> This paper has argued that governments should be bound to the same moral standards as private citizens when its comes to the making and breaking of promises. Yet, at first blush, such a requirement might be thought to unduly limit the ability of the government of the day to achieve its preferred public policy objectives. In fact, however, the suggested limitations will operate to the long-term benefit of the state, rather than to its detriment. If governments are permitted to repudiate contracts at will, the state is effectively barred from undertaking permanently binding commitments. Anyone who is contemplating contracting with the government will be aware of the fact that, no matter how solemn the promise, the government can turn around the next day and "skip out" on the contract. This risk may lead the other party to decide that it would be better off investing its resources elsewhere, in jurisdictions which do offer protection for contractual expectations; alternatively, the private party may demand that the government pay a premium in order to discount the risk of future opportunistic behaviour by the state.

Rule of Law constitutional protection of contracts with governments, if substantiated in the courts, is one bit of good news for Canadians who are rightfully concerned over the lack of constitutional protection of property rights.[5] Aboriginal people, at least, can look forward to some constitutional protection of lands held by Aboriginal title.

Government and Aboriginal rents
and other opportunism costs

Government rents are taxes defined broadly. The bulk of government rents fall upon economic activity rather than the direct rent charged for access to Crown lands. The September 1997 *Quarterly Report* from B.C.'s Ministry of Finance and Corporate Relations predicts that provincial taxation on economic activity (personal and corporate income tax; sales taxes; and capital taxes) should bring in $6.624 billion and natural resource rents (petroleum and natural gas royalties; timber sales; and water rentals) will bring in only $945 million. Looking over the history of recent provincial revenues, natural resource rents are consistently about 15 percent of economic activity taxes and about 10 percent of total provincial revenues.

Let's then ask the question, "Would the full application of Aboriginal title give bands the ability to levy government rents and, if so, which ones?"

Delgamuukw specifies that the provincial government and certainly any private enterprise must consult and presumably receive the permission of the title-bearing band in order to use the resources on Crown land subject to Aboriginal title. In practice, this would lead to a classic exchange-of-hostages scenario. (In that scenario, both sides want their hostages back but fear that if they move first, the other side will renege.) The band, seeking to maximize its income, would seek the highest amount the market will bear in exchange for its permission. The provincial government, seeking to protect its income, would seek to surrender as little "rent" as possible by shifting or adding costs on the license-seeker or taxpayers in general.

This could lead to three possible outcomes:

- higher rents on access to Crown lands with the provincial government and the title-bearing Aboriginal band each levying rent;

- the same level of rents with the provincial government and title-bearing band either sharing the rent or one crowding out the other; and

- lower rents with the provincial government and title-bearing band lowering or vacating their respective rents in order to induce economic activity.

In the absence of an explicit market mechanism to determine rents on access to Crown land, e.g. an auction system, trial-and-error will determine which scenario will occur. Likely both the provincial government and the title-bearing band would at first seek to protect their revenues and each charge a rent. This could raise the cost of the resources to unprofitable levels and thereby reduce use, decreasing economic exchanges.

It is important to remember that any rent on land is a monopoly rent—with the monopoly position held by the lease-seeker. As Adam Smith writes in *The Wealth of Nations*

> The rent of land, therefore, considered as the price paid for the use of the land, is naturally a monopoly price. It is not at all apportioned to what the landlord may have laid out upon improvement of the land, or to what he can afford to take; but to what the farmer can afford to give.

Assuming then that the existing rents on Crown land have already reached the level at which lease-seeker will pay no more, the provincial government and title-bearing band must negotiate between themselves the splitting of rents with the overall level of rents either remaining constant or even lower.

The title-bearing band has a strong direct lever vis-a-vis the provincial government. Presumably without its permission, any economic development using Crown land resources could not proceed. However the Aboriginal band may be most in need of rent revenues. As a result, the band may seek a faster and less lucrative rent-sharing agreement.

The provincial government has weaker levers, but it does possess them. Victoria could either threaten not to approve a project or, in the extreme, seek Ottawa to alienate the land from Aboriginal title. This latter course would probably involve a lengthy legislative and legal battle with uncertain prospects for success. On the other hand, the provincial government may be in less immediate need of the rent revenue and, therefore, inclined to bargain longer to better its position in the final rent-sharing agreement.

Remember the full extent of the provincial government's exposure to lost resource rents is only 10 percent of its total revenue. Of course if some companies cannot access resources then their taxable income will also decrease, as will that of its employees. In time, however, the province would lose significant revenues, as much business and personal income tax revenues come from natural resource activity. The situation could become one of playing revenue "chicken."

In that game of chicken, Aboriginal bands have the disadvantage of not having the power to tax income except that of their own members. (Presumably, all federal transfers are being used to support essential activities.) It is an unanswered question of considerable importance whether Aboriginal bands can now freely set sales taxes, such as tobacco and real estate taxes on reserves and "conditionally surrendered" land.[6] If so, that might alter the balance.

Both sides, nonetheless, have the opportunity to block the other's rent seeking through a veto on a proposed resource development. As with any hostage negotiation, the ultimate fate of the hostages lies in *how* and *for how long* the two parties negotiate.

Indeed, it is a major thesis of this paper that exclusive focus on the direct government/Aboriginal rent misses the major portion of uncertainty and cost being created by the *Delgamuukw* decision—the cost of negotiations.

Transaction costs

A clearer evaluation of the economic impact of the *Delgamuukw* decision requires close attention to what economists call transaction costs.

Nobel laureate Ronald Coase advanced forcefully the economic importance of transaction costs in his two seminal articles (1937; 1961). Coase's work focused on the contract, the individual building block of economic exchange. Specifically he examined the costs of reaching and enforcing contracts. In the Coasean sense, transaction costs are defined as "the costs of measuring the valuable attributes of what is being exchanged and the costs of protecting rights and policing and enforcing agreements."[7] In terms of economic relationships—contracts, firms and markets—any actions, information or perceptions (or their lack of) that "impedes the definition, monitoring and enforcement of an economic transaction is a transaction cost."[8]

The cause of transaction costs lies in two major factors:

(1) ill-defined property rights; and

(2) incomplete and unequal information.

Following on Coase's approach, Yale economist Oliver Williamson points to two causes of pervasive transaction costs that are steeped in human nature:[9] "bounded rationality" (we think we act rationally, but often don't); and chronic opportunism (we promise, but don't always deliver).

Property rights

The economic purpose of property rights is to make the revenue-generating contracts and sales more economical to arrange. Such laws serve to reduce incidences such as the following:

• misunderstanding and conflict as to who can do what, with what;

• an inability to exchange one resource for another;

- stranding assets within the public domain, thus tempting individuals to seek to capture them through political means; and

- enticing political and bureaucratic interests to auction off access to public property at an accelerated rate, thus risking the economic and environmental losses associated with the "tragedy of the commons."

For Coase, the key to reducing transaction costs and achieving economic efficiency lies in defining defensible property rights. Property rights make possible allocative efficiency (complete benefits over complete losses) and technical efficiency (maximum possible output for given resources.) Coase asserts that it matters little who owns how much property, as long as somebody owns it and he or she has the ability to transact at a low cost.

For the reason of property rights alone, Coase holds that institutions matter. In particular, the law and the courts serve to clarify property rights when ownership is unclear or disputed. If the laws are clear and the courts well administered, then the transaction costs of assigning and defending property rights will be relatively low. If not, these costs will escalate.

Application to Delgamuukw

Delgamuukw has complicated the property right regime in B.C. and complexity is expensive. Lamer has re-defined both the substance of Aboriginal title and the rules of evidence to determine its presence.

Delgamuukw has in essence unbundled and reassigned the provincial government's rights to Crown land. Most particularly, the decision has made conditional on the approval of Aboriginal titleholders the government's ability to grant licenses to other users. At the same time, the decision does not assign to Aboriginal titleholders a full bundle of rights such as described by fee simple ownership. One can predict that this mixture of provincial and Aboriginal property rights over Crown land will prove to be unstable. To begin with, it will take at least a generation to map fully the extent of Aboriginal title in B.C., whether or not it is done by negotiation or litigation.

How does Lamer's *sui generis* property regime rate according to economic theory?

From an economic perspective, this *sui generis* property regime has severe problems. Ideally, Lamer should have chosen to grant Aboriginal title in fee simple ownership. From Adam Smith onwards, economists have shown that land will be better cared for and used more productively if owned in fee simple. Fee simple ownership creates incentives and reduces the transaction cost of exchanges.

The history of land tenure in British Columbia for the last 100 years has been of a struggle to create approximations of fee simple ownership in the form of tenures and licenses to overcome the inherent limitations of government ownership.

Even if initially inequitable to grant ownership of 95 percent of the B.C. land mass to 4.9 percent of the population, the sale and exploitation of that land would in time come to benefit all British Columbians. Remember that it is the use of the land and not its ownership that creates the economic exchanges leading to wealth. It would, in the long run, have made more economic sense for Aboriginal people to own all provincial Crown land, as long as they did so in traditional fee simple ownership.

Unfortunately, Lamer has placed a number of restrictions on how Aboriginal people may exercise their Aboriginal title, despite granting exclusivity of use. First and foremost, Aboriginal people cannot sell their interest in the land except to the Crown. This perpetuates the regime of section 89 of the *Indian Act* detailing how the real and personal property of Aboriginal people living on reserves cannot be alienated, pledged, or mortgaged except to the band or the Crown. Ostensibly, this protects Aboriginal people from losing their property. The effect, however, is to isolate Aboriginal people from the broader economy. Without the ability to pledge assets, they cannot receive financing—except through the government—for such everyday items as a car or a refrigerator. As a result, Aboriginal people on reserves were, and are, effectively denied access to consumer capital markets.

Mortgaged property, of course, is land at risk: failure to pay off the loan would lead to the asset being seized. Risk, nonetheless, is at the heart of economic growth. If Aboriginal people are prevented from risking their assets, they are prevented from achieving their full economic potential.

(Aboriginal individuals might argue that once they have regained effective Aboriginal title, the Court's restrictions could be ignored. If no one protests, then no court challenge to a mortgage would go forward.)

In addition, the *Act* imposes high administrative costs on many Aboriginal economic activities through a myriad of supervisory and approval processes. One look at the listings under INAC in the federal government phone book disabuses all claims of administrative efficiency. Some of these regulatory functions are now being delegated to band governments, but the effect is still the same. Government is government with all its justifications for the "inevitability of planning," in the words of Frederich Hayek. It will continue to seek to subjugate individual economic decisions to political control through manipulation of collective levers. Political restraint is rare.

The impairment of risk and the imposition of controls lead to a secondary effect, the loss of commercial reputation. Uncertainty over the ability to recover assets erodes confidence in Aboriginal enterprises. As a result, banks, suppliers, and retail merchants are reluctant to enter into commercial arrangements except when the federal government offers explicit guarantees. The laborious, and often politicized, process of securing such guarantees just adds more costs to doing business.

Aboriginal businesses do exist and do succeed. The reason for success more often lies in the ability of individual Aboriginal business leaders to thwart federal regulations than to secure federal largesse. Indeed, the attendant "moral hazard" risks to such government "risk-free" capital, one suspects, explains in part why too many Aboriginal economic development projects fail.

Second, Lamer's ruling restricts how Aboriginal bands may use the title-bearing land. They cannot use the land except in ways that are compatible with pre-contact practices. They cannot use the land in ways that would reduce the values making it subject to Aboriginal title in the first place. No strip mining, parking lots or possibly logging may be allowed on certain parcels. Such restrictions sound environmentally and culturally friendly, but are predicated on a very paternalistic notion of Aboriginal society. In essence, Aboriginal society, at least in its economic activity, is to be held within the bounds of its traditional practices. I read this restriction as a warning that the economic activity of Aboriginal bands is not supposed to evolve beyond a certain limit to be determined by the courts. The practical consequence is to give a veto to those whose interest lies in no commercial development of land. Again though, Aboriginal bands may choose to not recognize these strictures.

Third, the communal nature of Aboriginal title, though seemingly embraced by the Aboriginal band leadership, potentially skews the benefits toward the favored few in the Aboriginal political hierarchy. It also creates incentives for the "tragedy of the commons" effect, the neglect and over-exploitation of communal land, and the added negotiation costs to deal with the nominally consensual nature of band politics. The latter is particularly troublesome because of the possibility of projects being held hostage to the individual and family jealousies that afflict all communities.

There is a great deal said and written about cooperation and consensus as the means through which to advance economic growth. That is not how the world works. Economic growth is fundamentally dependent on risk—with its consequences of winners and losers. A market economy invariably changes people's lives. Some like it; some don't. Complete agreement simply is not possible. If consensus in a community is a requirement for economic exchanges, the result is probably no economic exchanges.

Incomplete and unequal information

Imbalances in information either *ex ante* or *ex post* an economic exchange can create opportunities for one party to take advantage of the other. In this way, information directly influences the efficiency of economic exchanges. If costs and/or benefits are hidden from one party or the other, they may enter unknowingly into inefficient exchanges. What may have started out as an efficient exchange degenerates during the course of the contract into an inefficient one, due to the behavior of the parties. Most commonly, parties may not know until well after the fact whether an exchange was efficient or not and therefore fail to adjust prices or some other factor in subsequent contracts.

As with property rights, institutions matter in the alignment of information to prevent abuses. Numerous laws, such as consumer protection laws, have been written to protect parties from information abuses. However imperfectly, the civil courts allow for parties to seek damages when an information abuse has occurred. The government itself is constrained from abusing its informational advantage by the Rule of Law, which restricts its ability to act arbitrarily.

Application to Delgamuukw

Applying all this to the discussion of *Delgamuukw* is fairly straightforward. If the cost of negotiating, monitoring and upholding economic exchanges using resources subject to Aboriginal title exceeds the benefits of those exchanges, then the exchanges will not take place—no matter how reasonable the direct rent may appear.

The question, then, is: "Has the Delgamuukw decision made the nature of the Aboriginal title on the Crown lands of British Columbia so complex, and the process of delineating it so potentially expensive, that the transactional costs of market exchanges based on the resources of these lands will exceed the market benefits?" That is, despite the interest of all parties to do business, will the costs of conducting business become too expensive?

For Coase, the cause of most so-called market failures does not lie in the inability either to provide certain goods (e.g., lighthouses) or to include externalities in the price of a good (e.g., pollution). The reason lies in high transaction costs that prevent private actors from negotiating a mutually acceptable contract.[10] Coase assumes economic actors can and will exchange anything if the cost of reaching a contract does not exceed the potential gain from the transaction.

Signaling costs

One of the ways that participants in an economic exchange overcome informational disparities is to signal their true position through a variety of means. Companies that wish to signal that they would not take advantage of their customers will advertise their commitment to service. Automobile repair shops will offer a money-back guarantee if you're not satisfied in 30 days.

Has the *Delgamuukw* decision removed the incentive from either the government or Aboriginal negotiators to signal their willingness to negotiate workable treaties? Or alternatively, "Has *Delgamuukw* so changed the potential outcome of land claims that neither side has sufficient understanding and support in their respective constituencies to risk sending a "good faith" signal?"

If the First Nations Summit's January 31 "Statement to Minister Stewart and Minister Cashore," was any indication, genuine "good faith" signals appear to be some way off in the future. The statement is confrontational in its tone and in its recommendations. As a result, the possibility of stalled negotiations certainly exists.

For example, the Summit document interprets Lamer as describing Aboriginal title as "similar to the concept of jurisdiction." Lamer certainly gives weight to Aboriginal title on Crown lands, but does not accord it jurisdiction outside of the framework of the Crown's sovereignty. Lawyers can debate the fine points of the law here, but from an economic perspective, precisely such confusion over who holds jurisdiction is a cause of future conflict and aborted economic exchanges.

The Summit called for an immediate interim freeze on any further alienation of land and resources. It is uncertain whether this means no new licenses and permits should issued or that all new licenses and all existing licenses should be frozen. In either case, such a freeze would quickly bring paralyze parts of the resource economy. Who would risk assets in expectation that the freeze would be lifted shortly? Stranded assets would be liquidated or abandoned.

The next step proposed by the Summit is to negotiate province-wide interim agreements and to determine how the treaty process "will be brought into line with the requirements of *Delgamuukw* and the report of the Royal Commission on Aboriginal People." This includes the complete funding of Aboriginal negotiators and the cancellation of all loans to date for that purpose.[11] "Excessive delay or failure" by the governments of Canada and B.C., the Summit stated, will be "interpreted as a breach of good faith and will contribute to the break down of the treaty process." While the Summit added, "The governments should not put us in a position to prove Aboriginal title," they note the number of cases continuing to come forward. The point is clear: litigation is an option and the governments can expect to "lose" more cases.

Certainly, the position of the Summit is a bargaining posture. The question is whether the very option of litigating all Aboriginal title now precludes "good faith" bargaining. That is, does the signaling of litigation overshadow the signaling of cooperation?

The risk is that the signaling of litigation in support of an aggressive interpretation of *Delgamuukw* will be interpreted by the non-Aboriginal public as cause for an equally aggressive reaction of non-cooperation.

Negotiation costs

The effect of all these factors is to contribute to the prospect of even higher negotiation costs. Just what are the current costs? Who really knows? The cost of negotiation, split between the federal and provincial governments across a bewildering variety of departments and ministries, cries out for review by the respective Auditors General. The formal costs of treaty process are estimated at about $20 million a year, but the associated costs to business and individuals might reach as high as $100 million a year, given there nearly 50 claims at various stages of negotiation.

Few would dispute that the negotiation costs of the B.C. Treaty process are high and the results mixed, as measured against even the expectations of the participants. As Erling Christensen, Executive Director of Native Issues Monthly, wrote:[12]

> the B.C. First Nations Summit, a treaty working group, has passed a resolution asking the Treaty Commission to go back to the federal and provincial government and inform them that funding is not adequate and the four year level be paid out over two years. This would adequately fund the process. At present, the process is under-funded by at least 50%.

It is difficult not to believe the negotiations have become a "rent-seeking" exercise on the part of politicians, bureaucrats, and consultants.

At the heart of the escalation of transaction costs associated with the B.C. treaty process are several fundamental flaws which *Delgamuukw* fails to address. These include:

- uncertainty of desired results;
- a large number of bargaining agents with ill-defined mandates;
- large, undefined assets under negotiation;
- weak incentives for timely completion; and
- numerous and unspecified opportunities for re-negotiation.

Where to from here?

A clear indication that *Delgamuukw* has significantly raised the potential level of transaction costs on economic exchanges dependent on Crown land resources is the question now being asked, "Will it be less expensive in the long-run to litigate or negotiate the scope and application of Aboriginal title?" This is remarkable since, as a rule, negotiation is always considered less expensive than litigation.

Given all the costs of the B.C. treaty process—in particular the transaction costs—it is a legitimate question to ask. Indeed, should we consider another means to resolve Aboriginal land claims.

There are two scenarios to resolve the situation:

- a litigation strategy; and

- a revised negotiation strategy.

(I assume a legislated solution such as Australia has done recently would be struck down in the Supreme Court because of the constitutional protection afforded Aboriginal title.)

Litigation strategy

Despite the natural aversion most of us have towards litigation, there are serious and compelling reasons for the provincial and federal governments to consider using the courts to define the scope of Aboriginal title in British Columbia. Indeed, given their interests, it is their optimal strategy. (Short, of course, of legislating a one-size-fits-all treaty.)

The first is certainty, itself. A court process will give the final word on the extent of a band's Aboriginal title. A final judgment will not be subject to judicial review, as might any negotiated treaty whether the plaintiffs are Aboriginal or non-Aboriginal. A court judgment would also enjoy a political finality that no treaty process can.

This is in part due to the ability of judges to better assess the legal arguments and evidence, oral or otherwise, put before him or her. Judges are the scientists of property rights and if ever there was a need for analytical rigor it is in the area of Aboriginal title. There are serious questions about the ability and propriety of government contract employees in negotiating deals on Aboriginal title of such scope and magnitude. Besides the obvious question of conflict-of-interest, government negotiators may be in violation of the Rule of Law.

Despite the economic criticisms leveled against the courts, they do help to reduce the pure transaction costs of incomplete and unequal information and the human tendency not to do what we promise. They are a means to achieve in the real world the preconditions of full communication, defined property rights, complete agreements and certain fulfillment of contracts. For instance, the enforcement of property rights and contracts requires a third party when compliance is no longer possible through negotiation.

Two factors adversely characterize court solutions: cost and delay. Though it is difficult to assess, given the current dysfunctional nature of the B.C. Treaty process, it would be less expensive and faster to litigate Aboriginal title. This is particularly true if the resulting treaties were to be subject to judicial review, as would likely happen.

One recognizes that, according to informal estimates by the federal Department of Justice, there are currently 500 Aboriginal cases before the Courts across Canada, each potentially costing up to $1 million to litigate. One-third of all British Columbia's Appeal Court judges have been assigned to Aboriginal cases and 15 percent of the Supreme Court's time over the next two years is budgeted for Aboriginal issues.

Still the quality of the process and the finality of the result recommend the litigation of Aboriginal title, particularly when the alternative is the questionable B.C. Treaty process. The litigation of Aboriginal title still leaves open the necessity of negotiations to apply the judgments of the courts.

A revised negotiation process

From an economic perspective of promoting economic exchanges, negotiations remain preferable to litigation. I argue that the Coase theorem provides a means to resolving the application of Aboriginal title to provide the greatest range and depth of economic exchanges.

Negotiation is the optimum strategy both for Aboriginal and non-Aboriginal citizens as economically rational actors.

The Coase theorem states that an economy will achieve full efficiency, *whatever the initial distribution of property,* if the costs of transacting a contract are zero. Princeton economist Avinash Dixit describes it this way:

> If all participants in the economy could be brought together, if initial ownership rights were assigned among these participants, and if they could costlessly make fully specified and fully binding agreements, then the outcome should be an efficient economic plan leaving only the division of spoils to be determined by the bargaining strengths of the participants.[13]

In practical terms, the Coase theorem requires a major revision of the B.C. Treaty process. In essence, it calls for the privatization of the process in so far as it deals with economic growth. Bluntly, Aboriginal bands should bypass the federal and provincial governments and negotiate directly with the individuals and companies seeking to use resources on Crown land they claim under Aboriginal title. Once an Aboriginal band and, let's say, a forest company, reach their own agreement on the extent and terms of logging a particular area, they can present that agreement to the federal and provincial government. In other words, the company and the band reach a private agreement on the details of an economic exchange.

For a forest company, what matters is the amount it pays in rents and transaction costs, *not to whom that money flows*. It matters not to the success of an economic exchange whether the provincial government or an Aboriginal band is the recipient of access rents.

Private agreements also have the advantage of flexibility. For instance, the participants can bind themselves to treating resources and other assets as private property. Self-imposed sanctions allow the parties to negotiate around ill-defined property rights and other uncertainties. (This raises the question of whether Aboriginal bands can be held liable in courts for their contracts based on lands bearing Aboriginal title. Civil liability is not an absolute necessity if other means are employed to reduce the risk of opportunism, e.g. performance bonds, staggered payments and the like.)

With the agreement between the Aboriginal band and the company in hand, the Aboriginal negotiators can present then present their own revenue-sharing proposal to the provincial government. Victoria or Saskatoon can then work out the numbers for itself in terms of lost resource rents versus the gain of not having to pay compensation, continued business and individual income tax; or the savings from turning over to the private sector and the Aboriginal band costs such as road construction, reforestation and environmental monitoring. It should be noted that all of these forestry-related costs to the province have for some time equaled or exceeded the province's direct resource rents from Crown lands. A provincial government would also take into account that the federal government has offered to pay half of foregone resource revenues in British Columbia, an offer it would surely extend to other provinces.

These private agreements would also help to clarify the economic circumstances of Aboriginal bands, thus providing critical information to the necessary self-government government negotiations, perforce held government-to-government.

The point is a simple one. As long as Aboriginal bands are locked into negotiations with governments, they are held hostage to government interests, which are largely to protect their own revenues and jurisdictional authority. That is a recipe for high and potentially destructive transaction costs. If Aboriginal bands are negotiating with private users of Crown resources, the critical issue is a wealth-creating economic exchange. Because they have a bottom line, business negotiations proceed with an efficiency unknown to political negotiations.

If the goal of Aboriginal people is economic growth rather than a fruitless pursuit of government recognition of some kind of Aboriginal sovereignty, then they should focus their attention on society's wealth creators rather than its status providers.

The risk exists, somewhat faint to my thinking, that the diversion of formerly provincial government rents to Aboriginal bands will severely hamper the fiscal ability of the provincial government to carry out its responsibilities. The reply is twofold. First, the provincial government is already doing too much and some retrenchment would make considerable economic sense. Second, as the Aboriginal community begins to derive more and more of its income from private wealth creation rather than public transfer payment, they will come to appreciate more fully that beyond a certain level government debt and expenditures represents a drag on the overall economy. As their attention focuses increasingly on economic growth as opposed public redistribution, they will not jeopardize new-found wealth to cling to the fraying safety of "wardship."

At the end of the day, Aboriginal people may find their best interest lies in moving beyond the stilted economics of *Delgamuukw* to more accepted economic principles for creating wealth.

Notes

1 For a background to the treaty process, see Owen Lippert, "Out of our Past: A New Perspective on Aboriginal Land Claims in B.C.," The Fraser Institute, 1995.

2 Brian Slattery, "Understanding Aboriginal Rights" (1987), 66 Canadian Bar Review, page 753.

3 Task Force on Program Review cited in Melvin H. Smith, Q.C., *Our Home or Native Land*, (Crown Western: Victoria, 1995), page 240.

4 Patrick Monahan, original manuscript, "Is the Pearson Airport legislation unconstitutional?: the rule of law as a limit on contract repudiation by government," 1996.

5 Critical market efficiencies rest upon the Rule of Law prevailing over the Rule of Man in the exercise of government: the greater the discretion of politicians and bureaucrats, the greater the opportunity for the misallocation of collectively-held resources. For reasons good and bad, politicians and bureaucrats, when faced with decisions beyond the application of existing law, will concentrate benefits on swing voters and well-organized interest groups and will disperse the costs among all taxpayers in the hope that a small marginal tax or debt liability increase will provoke little response. This is the "Public Choice" dilemma. The more the Rule of Law binds politicians and bureaucrats, then the less opportunity exists for either special favours or, conversely, special discriminations and punishments. The strengthening of the Rule of Law, therefore, lowers the chance of an arbitrary allocation of public resources for typically non-optimal purposes.

6 See Chief Manny Jules, "First Nations and Taxation," in eds. Stephen B. Smart and Michael Coyle, *Aboriginal Issues Today: A Legal and Business Guide*, (Self-Counsel Press: Toronto, 1997), pp. 154-167.

7 North 1990a, p. 27.

8 Avinash Dixit (1996) *The Making of Economic Policy: A Transaction-Cost Politics Perspective*. Munich Lectures in Economics 37 (Cambridge, MA: MIT Press, 1996), p. 37.

9 Williamson, 1985, pp. xii-xiii.

10 Coase's view that transaction costs are the primary cause of market failure should not be interpreted as denying other factors could not be present such as collective action problems.

11 Under the B.C. Treaty process, bands were given loans to support negotiations under the requirement that they would be paid back out of the proceeds of the ultimate settlement.

12 "Secrecy, Communications and Politics: The B.C. Treaty Process in Review," *Native Issues Monthly*, September 1994, page 5.

13 Dixit, 1996, p. 37.

Questions of Compensation
An Overview of Economic Impacts

J. KEITH LOWES

Introduction

In order to analyze the economic impact of the Supreme Court of Canada decision in *Delgamuukw*, it is necessary to make at least two distinctions. First, it is important to distinguish between the case as a legal decision and the case as a political event. Second, it is important to distinguish the matters actually decided from those left to further litigation. It is my thesis that, at least in the short term, the economic impact of the case as a political event will be more important than that as a legal decision, and that the impact of the undecided issues and will be more severe than that of those actually decided.

Legal Decision/Political Event

(a) Legal Decision

The case decided by the Supreme Court of Canada was changed substantially from that put before the Trial Judge and from that decided by the British Columbia Court of Appeal. The important issues of substance became issues of process. The practical question of who controls the lands and resources was diffused into that of the constitutional mechanism for reconciling Crown sovereignty with the fact of pre-existing indigenous occupation.

Notes will be found on page 424.

At trial, the Court was presented with a claim by a number of individual Chiefs to the "ownership" of and "jurisdiction" over a number of individual territories. The claims of ownership failed because the plaintiffs could not prove with sufficient certainty that their ancestors controlled the specific territories to the extent necessary to establish common law possessory title. The claims to jurisdiction also failed on the evidence. In addition, the Trial Judge concluded that aboriginal "jurisdiction" was contrary to the basic constitutional principles of the sovereignty of the Crown and the distribution of that sovereign power within the Canadian federation. The Trial Judge concluded that, in any event, any such ownership and jurisdiction was extinguished by Colonial enactments, which also extinguished any aboriginal rights short of ownership and jurisdiction.

The majority in the Court of Appeal supported the Trial Judge's conclusions about ownership and jurisdiction. It reversed him, however, on his conclusion about extinguishment: it declared that there were unextinguished and undefined aboriginal rights within the territory. It rejected the plaintiffs' attempt to recast their claims for ownership and jurisdiction of individual parcels to claims to communal aboriginal title over larger areas comprising those individual parcels.

Each of the plaintiffs appealed. They asked the Supreme Court of Canada for declarations that the Gitksan and Wet'suwet'en peoples had existing aboriginal title to territory comprising the individual parcels originally claimed by the individual plaintiffs. Since both the federal and provincial governments had conceded that the Trial Judge was wrong on the issue of extinguishment by the Colonial enactments, the issue of such extinguishment was not appealed by anyone. The provincial government, however, did appeal the Court of Appeal's decision that since joining Canada in 1871, British Columbia had no constitutional authority to extinguish aboriginal rights.

The Supreme Court of Canada ordered a new trial on the issue whether the plaintiffs, (representing the Gitksan and Wet'suwet'en peoples) had aboriginal title in the territory. Essentially, it decided that the tests applied by the Trial Judge more than six years earlier were too strict according to the standards which had been developed in other cases as *Delgamuukw* was proceeding through the Courts.

There are two judgements: one, by Chief Justice Antonio Lamer, concurred in by Justices Peter Cory and John C. Major; the other by Justice Gerard La Forest, concurred in by Justice Claire L'Heureux-Dubé. Justice Beverley McLachlin agreed with both.

The judgement of Justice La Forest is unremarkable. Although he agreed that there should be a new trial, he took the cautionary approach of not expounding on issues beyond the degree necessary to reach his decision. He confined his definition of "aboriginal title" to the traditional language used by Justice Judson in *Calder v. Attorney General of British Columbia*,[1] who stated: "... the fact is that when the settlers came, the Indians were there, organized in societies and occupying the land as their forefathers had done for centuries. This is what Indian title means ..."

Chief Justice Lamer took another approach. Noting that the Supreme Court of Canada had avoided defining aboriginal title, he set out general principles about the content of aboriginal title, the way in which it is protected by section 35(1) of the *Constitution Act, 1982* and the requirements necessary to prove it.

Chief Justice Lamer stated that aboriginal title encompasses the right to exclusive use and occupation of the land held pursuant to that title for a variety of purposes, which need not be aspects of those aboriginal practices, customs and traditions which are integral to distinctive aboriginal cultures. The protected uses, however, must not be irreconcilable with the nature of the group's attachment to that land. Aboriginal title is a right to the land itself.

In order to establish a claim to aboriginal title, the Chief Justice stated, the aboriginal group asserting the claim must establish that it occupied the lands in question at the time at which the Crown asserted sovereignty over the land subject to the title. The occupation must have been exclusive: however, joint title can arise from shared exclusivity. In determining whether sufficient occupation has been shown to establish aboriginal title, the "aboriginal perspective" on occupation must be taken into account together with the common law.

Chief Justice Lamer stated that constitutionally recognized aboriginal rights fall along a spectrum with respect to their degree of connection with the land. At one end, are aboriginal rights which are practices, customs and traditions integral to the distinctive aboriginal culture of the group claiming the right, but where the use and occupation of the land where the activity is taking place is not sufficient to support a claim of title to the land. In the middle are activities which might be intimately related to a particular piece of land, thus founding a site-specific right to engage in a particular activity. At the other end of the spectrum is aboriginal title itself.

Chief Justice Lamer affirmed that like other aboriginal rights, aboriginal title can be infringed by government, but that such infringement must be justified through the two-stage test set out in *Sparrow*.[2] On the first branch of the test, he stated that generally speaking, the economic development of the Province was a valid legislative objective for the purposes of justification. In determining whether the infringement met the second branch of the justification test (i.e. whether it was compatible with the fiduciary relationship between the Crown and the aboriginal peoples), The Chief Justice emphasized the requirement for consultation about the use of land subject to aboriginal title and compensation for the infringement.

(b) Political Event

The general statements of Chief Justice Lamer about aboriginal title and the consequent obligation of government to consult with the holders of aboriginal title about the use of lands subject to it have caused a good deal of confusion, controversy and concern in the province. It is not unusual to see the case described in the media as one "establishing" or "granting" aboriginal title in British Columbia. Many have argued that aboriginal title over large areas of the province can be easily established and, consequently, ought to be presumed between the provincial government and aboriginal claimants for the purposes of treaty negotiations and consultation protocols about land and resource use.

These arguments are having considerable effect. They are among a number of reasons driving a re-design of the treaty negotiation process. They inform demands by aboriginal groups for increased participation, if not a veto in land and resource use planning. They are probably influencing the current push to conclude negotiations with the Nishga. The effect is to increase the speed and turn up the volume in a process that is already confused and confusing.

Matters Decided/Matters Undecided

Theoretically, political pressures resulting from a major court decision might be helpful in resolving negotiations bogged down because of disputes about the parties' existing rights. This logjam-breaking role, however, requires a degree of certainty about the law that the *Delgamuukw* decision for good reason cannot, and does not, deliver. The decision leaves more issues undecided than it decides. Further, in those areas it does deal with, it lays down general principles that require refinement and the establishment of benchmarks—in other words, further litigation.

(a) Matters Decided

The primary reason for the ordering of a new trial was that the case as shaped at the trial was not amenable to the application of the principles which the Supreme Court of Canada had developed in other cases, as *Delgamuukw* was working its way through the courts. The pleading was directed at individual claims to specific parcels rather than to a communal claim to the entire territory. More importantly, the Supreme Court of Canada now required an appreciation of the "aboriginal perspective" and had developed a more flexible approach to the evidence, particularly of oral history, to provide this perspective. In essence, the general approach to aboriginal rights had shifted. A new trial was ordered so that the claims could be subjected to that new approach. Consequently, it is difficult to isolate issues that can be said to be conclusively determined.

The one hard conclusion arising from the case is that lands subject to aboriginal title (and aboriginal rights generally) are matters which fall within the scope of federal jurisdiction under section 91(24) of the *Constitution Act, 1867*. As a result, British Columbia has had no constitutional authority to extinguish aboriginal title since it joined Canada in 1871.

Other hard conclusions are difficult to find. Chief Justice Lamer's principles about aboriginal title are clearly articulated, but they are general and abstract. They need substance and the establishment of benchmarks. This can come only as a result of their application to specific, factual situations. The same can be said about the call by the Chief Justice for the development of a new appreciation of the "aboriginal perspective" and for the development of new rules of evidence directed at discovering that "aboriginal perspective."

(b) Matters Undecided

It is much easier to list the issues that the Court left undecided, either in the sense that they resulted in general principles needing further litigation to refine and flesh them out, or in the sense that they are issues which were simply left for another day.

A list of the former includes:

(1) The scope of section 91(24) of the *Constitution Act 1867* with respect to aboriginal rights, aboriginal title and the extinguishment thereof;

(2) The scope of changes to the rules of evidence to accommodate claims to aboriginal rights;

(3) The definition of "occupancy" as a test for aboriginal title;

(4) The scope and consequences of the "inherent limit" of aboriginal title;

(5) The application to specific fact situations of the various "spectra" identified by the Court: namely, the spectra of: aboriginal rights; degrees of judicial scrutiny of infringing legislation; requirements for consultation; priorities to aboriginal rights; and other methods of justifying infringements of aboriginal rights; and

(6) The concept of continuity of the "special relationship" of the aboriginal group and the land which justifies and founds aboriginal title.

Further, there are important legal issues that the Supreme Court did not deal with at all. Among these are:

(1) Self government;

(2) Colonial extinguishment;

(3) The mechanism for ultimately resolving the inconsistency of aboriginal rights with Crown Sovereignty or other, non-aboriginal, rights; and

(4) Remedies for the infringement of aboriginal rights past, present and future.

The latter two issues are, from a practical point of view, the most important. The central practical question is whether and to what extent aboriginal title and aboriginal rights limit the rights of others and the powers of government, particularly the power to make valid grants of lands and resources.

Conclusion

The decision of the Supreme Court of Canada in *Delgamuukw* has added even more uncertainty to an uncertain economic climate. Interpreted strictly, in terms of legal precedent, the decision lays down general principles at a high level of abstraction, reaffirms a case-by-case, fact specific approach, and does not deal at all with most of the issues of practical importance. This uncertainty is aggravated by a public focus that is more on what the case may *imply* than on what it actually says.

Notes

1 *Calder v. Attorney General of British Columbia* [1973] 1SCR313 (SCC) at page 328.
2 *R. v. Sparrow* [1990] 1 SCR 1075 (SCC).

Compensation after *Delgamuukw*
Aboriginal Title's
Inescapable Economic Component

Michael J. McDonald and Thomas Lutes

Introduction

As any observer of recent Canadian news can attest, aboriginal issues in Canada are once again atop the public and media agenda. The range of issues in the public eye is remarkable: from the applicability of sales tax to New Brunswick's aboriginal peoples; to the return of traditional lands to the First Nation at Ipperwash, Ontario; to the unprecedented fusion of aboriginal healing circles and the Canadian justice system in British Columbia's Bishop O'Connor case.

While such stories ride the crest of the latest wave of national media attention, the land claims process in British Columbia remains somewhat adrift following the December 1997 *Delgamuukw* decision. The implications of the Supreme Court of Canada's ruling in *Delgamuukw* that aboriginal title exists and contains an "economic component" poses a tremendous challenge to government, private industry and First Nations. In particular, the Crown faces judgment for its action—or inaction—in

---

Notes will be found on page 450.

resolving land and resource claims, not only in our courts of law but also in the forum of public opinion, with its jury of voting citizens.

The scenarios of economic doom voiced by a few politicians and public commentators since *Delgamuukw* was handed down have not allayed British Columbians' understandable concerns about the practical effects on their lives and on the effect of compensation to First Nations on the provincial economy. The entire land base of British Columbia is *not* about to be transferred to British Columbia's First Nations, and the entire provincial budget for the next quarter-century will *not* be directed to compensating the Province's aboriginal peoples. However, the continued unresolved infringement of aboriginal rights and title in British Columbia and the finalization of land claims and treaty negotiations *will* result in compensation from the Crown to First Nations. When compensation may be owed to First Nations and how compensation might be determined are the subjects of this paper, which is intended to present some practical options for decision-makers as they set out on the rather uncertain path blazed by *Delgamuukw*.

"Compensation" is used generically in this paper to refer both to damages awarded to aboriginal groups by our courts for unjustifiable infringement of their title, and to a portion of the payment made as part of a government settlement with First Nations. In our view, applying the term "compensation" to settlement or treaty payments is appropriate, since First Nations may, in many cases, be relinquishing, putting into abeyance, or agreeing to an exhaustive definition of their rights or title as part of these packages. Moreover, many land claim settlements will include compensation amounts for past unjustified infringements. The practical distinction between the two kinds of compensation is explained below.

The bulk of this paper is devoted to compensation issues, particularly for infringement of title, with a brief review of some of the important issues in the land claims settlement realm given at the end of the paper. We have chosen to focus on a detailed review of major compensation issues in this paper, although the complications arising from the taxation aspect of land claim settlements and self-government certainly merit their own discussion. Since our courts have so far said very little about exactly how compensation for infringement of aboriginal rights will be valued, much of the analysis in this paper is based on speculation.

The "Inescapable Economic Component" of Aboriginal Title

[A]boriginal title encompasses the right to *exclusive* use and occupation of land; second, aboriginal title encompasses the *right to choose* to what uses land can be put, ... and third, ... lands held pursuant to aboriginal title have an inescapable *economic component*. (Emphasis in judgment; Chief Justice Antonio Lamer in *Delgamuukw* v. *British Columbia* at 264)

In its short lifespan, the *Delgamuukw* decision has already been dissected, analyzed, celebrated, condemned and misrepresented like few Supreme Court of Canada decisions before it. It is certainly an historic decision, in which the Court's findings on the evidentiary use of aboriginal oral histories would alone have left the decision characterized as a landmark. It is the question of aboriginal title, however, which has drawn the most attention, including the fire of those who have characterized it as invented or "made-up" law.

One of the reasons for this criticism is surely that the portion of Chief Justice Antonio Lamer's judgment regarding the Canadian history and jurisprudence of aboriginal title is a model of brevity—exactly the type of concise judicial style for which he has become an ardent proponent. Unfortunately, this brevity results in a rather cursory treatment of the gradual but coherent jurisprudence relating to aboriginal title which has evolved in Canada over the last century and beyond. Admittedly, the Chief Justice's "fast-forwarded" treatment of aboriginal title jurisprudence does leave certain remarks in the judgment, such as the following statement, appearing to stand without solid foundation:

> Aboriginal title ... is a *right to the land* itself. Subject to the limits I have laid down above, that land may be used for a variety of activities, none of which need be individually protected as aboriginal rights under [the *Constitution*]. Those activities are parasitic on the underlying title. (Emphasis in judgment; *Delgamuukw* at 252)

Such wording, while perhaps bold in relation to the language in earlier aboriginal title decisions, is very much in keeping with aboriginal title's considerable legal pedigree. As University of Victoria Law Professor Hamar Foster argues in his March 1998 article in The Advocate, "the bare bones of the Delgamuukw judgment have deep roots in the common law, and in the history of what has, since the 1870s, been called the BC Indian Land Question." [1] The article is one of several excellent sources that supplement the somewhat skimmed analysis in *Delgamuukw* regarding the history of aboriginal title. [2]

Whatever the perceived weaknesses in *Delgamuukw*, the Supreme Court of Canada did speak clearly about the content of aboriginal title in the ruling. Chief Justice Lamer wrote concisely about the consequences of aboriginal title's economic component as follows:

> [A]boriginal title, unlike the aboriginal right to fish for food, has an inescapably economic aspect, particularly when one takes into account the modern uses to which lands held pursuant to aboriginal title can be put ... In keeping with the duty of honour and good faith on the Crown, fair compensation will ordinarily be required when aboriginal title is infringed. (*Delgamuukw* at 265).

The Chief Justice went on to note that since the issue of damages was not argued at the highest court level, it was unnecessary to determine how an appropriate level of compensation would be determined. He concluded, "it is best that we leave those difficult questions to another day." [3] While the day for these "difficult questions" may not arrive at the Supreme Court of Canada level for some time, the Federal and Provincial Governments can hardly afford to delay the reckoning of compensation issues. The occasions when compensation may be owed to aboriginal nations from the Crown are canvassed below, along with a brief discussion of some of the mechanisms and alternatives for compensation.

When Is Compensation Owed to First Nations?

Below, we examine the related but distinct circumstances in which the Crown will owe compensation to British Columbia's First Nations. The first situation involves government compensation when aboriginal peoples' rights, including title, have been infringed. An analysis of infringement compensation requires a fairly detailed review of the Supreme Court of Canada's rulings in *Delgamuukw* on justifying infringement, the Crown's fiduciary duty to First Nations, and the varying levels of compensation. We have included a discussion of two real-life scenarios as a means of mapping the possible compensation implications for First Nations, government and industry.

The second trigger for compensation is, of course, a result of the land claims settlement process currently under way in British Columbia. While land claims agreements will normally include a compensation element for infringement of aboriginal rights, the ultimate settlement will obviously be driven by policy, economics, and the reality of long-term negotiations, and not necessarily by judicially dictated principles of compensation.

Compensation for Infringement of Title

(a) Justifying Infringement: Satisfying the Valid Legislative Objective and the Fiduciary Duty Tests

Throughout their evolution in Canadian law, aboriginal rights have never been held to be absolute. The Supreme Court of Canada's 1990 ruling in *Sparrow* made this eminently clear:

Section 35(1) [of the *Constitution*] does not promise immunity from government regulation in twentieth century society, but it does hold the Crown to a substantive promise. The government is required to bear the burden of justifying any legislation that has some negative effect of any aboriginal right protected under [the *Constitution*]. (*R. v. Sparrow*, [1990] 3 C.N.L.R. 160 at 162)

A test for "justifying any legislation" that infringes aboriginal rights has been developed by our courts over the years. The "infringement test" involves a two-stage analysis, which is briefly summarized in the paragraphs below.

Assuming that the aboriginal right exists, the infringement must arise by reason of a compelling and substantial legislative objective, such as the reconciliation of First Nations' prior occupation in Canada with Crown sovereignty, the conservation of natural resources, or economic development priorities. In *Delgamuukw*, Chief Justice Lamer expanded upon the kinds of legislative objectives that might, depending upon the context, justify infringement of aboriginal title, and tailored his discussion to the British Columbia setting:

> In my opinion, the development of agriculture, forestry, mining, and hydroelectric power, the general economic development of the interior of British Columbia, protection of the environment or endangered species, the building of infrastructure in the settlement of foreign population to support those aims, are the kinds of objectives that are consistent with this purpose and, in principle, can justify the infringement of aboriginal title. Whether a particular measure or government act can be explained by reference to one of those objectives, however, is ultimately a question of fact that will have to be examined on a case-by-case basis. (*Delgamuukw* at page 263-264.)

The second requirement of the justification test is that the infringement must be consistent with the special fiduciary relationship between the Crown and aboriginal peoples. In applying this stage of the justification test to the infringement of aboriginal title, the Supreme Court in *Delgamuukw* held that the operation of the fiduciary duty, both in terms of the standard of scrutiny and the form of that duty, will depend on the nature of aboriginal title. In this regard, the Chief Justice noted the relevance of three particular aspects of aboriginal title:

- aboriginal title encompasses the right to exclusive use and occupation of the land;

- aboriginal title encompasses the right to choose to what uses the land can be put; and

- lands held pursuant to aboriginal title have an inescapable economic component.

The first aspect of aboriginal title, that it is a right to exclusive use and occupation of the land, means that in order to satisfy its fiduciary duty, the Crown will be required to demonstrate that both the process by which it allocated the land's resources, and the actual allocation of those resources, reflect the prior interest of the aboriginal titleholder. As Chief Justice Lamer explained:

> [T]his might entail, for example, that governments accommodate the participation of aboriginal peoples in the development of the resources of British Columbia, that the conferral of fee simples for agriculture, and of leases and licenses for forestry and mining reflect the prior occupation of aboriginal title in lands, that economic barriers to aboriginal uses of their lands (e.g., licensing fees) be somewhat reduced. The list is illustrative and not exhaustive ... . No doubt, there will be difficulties in determining the precise value of the aboriginal interest in the land and any grants, leases or licences given for its exploitation. These difficult economic considerations obviously cannot be solved here. (*Delgamuukw* at page 264)

This statement suggests that where the Province 'shares the wealth' of the land by ensuring some of the economic benefits and actual allocation of land and resources go to First Nations, it may *justifiably* infringe aboriginal title. In British Columbia, this resource sharing may be done at little or no cost to the Government where Crown tenures and licences are issued without charge.

Second, the fact that aboriginal title encompasses the right to choose to what uses the land can be put implies involvement of First Nations in decision-making with respect to their title lands. Further, this aspect of aboriginal title imposes a duty upon the Crown to consult the aboriginal group holding title, prior to the Crown dealing with the land. The Supreme Court described the range of consultation required as follows:

> The nature and scope of the duty of consultation will vary with the circumstances. In occasional cases, when the breach is less serious or relatively minor, it will be no more than a duty to discuss important decisions that will be taken with respect to lands held pursuant to aboriginal title. Of course, even in these rare cases when the min-

imum acceptable standard is consultation, this consultation must be in good faith, and with the intention of substantially addressing the concerns of the aboriginal people's whose lands are at issue. In most cases, it will be significantly deeper than mere consultation. Some cases may even require the full consent of an aboriginal nation, particularly when provinces enact hunting and fishing regulations in relation to aboriginal lands. (*Delgamuukw* at 265)

The definition of meaningful consultation in this context is perhaps the hottest topic in aboriginal law at the moment. The chasm between First Nations' and governments' understanding of the content of consultation will only create greater numbers of judicial review applications of government decisions where aboriginal rights are at stake.

Third, since aboriginal title has an inescapable economic component due to the modern uses to which aboriginal title lands can be put, the Court in *Delgamuukw* held that fair compensation will ordinarily be required whenever aboriginal title is unjustifiably infringed. In the Chief Justice's words, "the amount of compensation payable will vary with the nature of the particular aboriginal title affected and with the nature and severity of the infringement, and with the extent to which aboriginal interests were accommodated." [4] Clearly, the measurement of the economic component of aboriginal title and the compensation required will lead, in many cases, to difficult questions of law and economics.

(b) Why Damages Flow From a Breach of a Fiduciary Duty
Before analyzing the factors that will lead to varied levels of compensation for justifiable infringement, a brief summary of the law of damages for breach of fiduciary duty is in order, since compensation will normally arise if the Crown's fiduciary duty to First Nations is not fulfilled. Essentially, a 'fiduciary' is an individual or entity that has the ability to unilaterally exercise some discretion or power that affects a 'beneficiary's' interests. In addition, the beneficiary is somehow vulnerable to the fiduciary's exercise of power or discretion. [5]

In the aboriginal law context, compensation for breaches of the fiduciary duty is, in the words of Chief Justice Lamer in *Delgamuukw*, "a well-established part of the landscape of aboriginal rights." [6] One of the leading cases on fiduciary duties owed by the Crown to First Nations is *Guerin v. The Queen*, a 1984 decision of the Supreme Court of Canada. [7] In *Guerin*, the Federal Government was held to have breached its fiduciary obligation to protect the Musqueam Indian Band's interests when it negotiated a lease with the Shaughnessy Golf and Country Club on terms that were not revealed accurately to the Band. The

Band had surrendered the land under conditions that were not followed by the Crown in the subsequent lease, and the Crown did not
consult with the Band in accordance with its fiduciary duty. In its decision, the Supreme Court of Canada emphasized the following basic
principles of damages for breach of fiduciary duty:

- a "fiduciary" or trustee who defaults or breaches its duty must
  make restitution to the beneficiary;

- the fiduciary in breach is liable to place the beneficiary in the same
  position as he or she would have been if no breach had been committed; and

- unlike damages awarded by a court in tort law (such as negligence
  for personal injury) and contract law, a court considering damages
  for breaches of fiduciary duty need not always rigorously apply
  what are known as "limiting factors." These factors include *foresee-
  ability*, which limits an award if the wrongdoer should not reasonably have been able to predict the damage it caused; *remoteness*,
  which limits damages which are simply too far removed from the
  original act of the wrongdoer to be considered compensable; and
  causation, which is an insistence upon proving a direct link between
  an act and the resulting damage.[8]

In applying this general breach of fiduciary duty principles to the
specific facts in *Guerin*, the Court made the following findings:

- the Crown's breach of fiduciary duty was not in failing to lease the
  land, but was in leasing it when it could not lease it on the terms
  approved by the Band. The Band was therefore deprived of its land
  and the use to which it might have wanted to put the land - *i.e.*, to
  put it to the most advantageous use possible during the period
  covered by the unauthorized lease;

- the Band should be compensated for the lost opportunities for developing the land for the leasing period of up to 75 years, and the
  Band, as beneficiary, should get the benefit of any increase in market value of its land; and

- the Band should not have to prove that it would have developed
  the land even if the breach of duty had not occurred, since in fiduciary or trust situations, a court should make a presumption in favour of the beneficiary.

Essentially, the Supreme Court of Canada awarded damages to the
Band for what it had lost as a result of the Crown's breach: the lost opportunity to lease its land at a more favourable rate, which lost oppor-

tunity was assessed in light of what actually happened to land values after the breach had occurred. It should be noted that since breach of fiduciary duty damages are founded on trust-law principles, which import equity or the "conscience" of the court, judges are given much wider latitude in fashioning remedies for breaches of fiduciary duty than in typical contract or negligence situations. This equitable approach, with its wider range of compensation options, is a recognition of the fact that a beneficiary is particularly vulnerable to the acts of a fiduciary, who at all times should be acting in the best interests of the beneficiary.

One of the greatest challenges for governments in this area will be to avoid repetition of the result in the *Guerin* case for past and ongoing unjustifiable infringements. A wholesale application of compensation principles for breach of fiduciary duty in the aboriginal title context would force our courts, however reluctantly, to place a hard dollar value on aboriginal rights and title. This would have significant economic implications for government, particularly if many First Nations choose to leave the treaty negotiation table and litigate the overall title question regarding their traditional lands. Fortunately, at this point, only one such group (the Sechelt Indian Band) has filed such a suit, and it remains at the negotiation table.

(c) How the Amount of Compensation Will Vary
As noted above, the Supreme Court of Canada in *Delgamuukw* did not consider precisely how compensation would be valued on a dollar basis. The Court's clearest guidance, however, comes from Chief Justice Lamer's finding that compensation will vary with:

- the nature of the particular title at issue;

- the nature of the infringement;

- the severity of the infringement; and

- the extent to which aboriginal interests were accommodated.[9]

One of the implications of the Court's ruling on the variability of compensation is that government *can* minimize, and perhaps even eliminate, the amount of compensation it might otherwise owe to First Nations for ongoing and perhaps even past rights infringement. Throughout the analysis on compensation for unjustifiable infringement of title, it is important to keep in mind that it will certainly be necessary for First Nations to prove aboriginal rights and title where compensation damages are sought for breach of fiduciary duty by unjustified infringement of rights. In some cases, such as infringement on some reserve lands, proof of title will be a much easier exercise for a First Nation.

(d) The Nature of the Title at Issue

In determining compensation amounts, the general and particular aspects of aboriginal title will be vitally important. The *sui generis* (unique) nature of aboriginal title should prevent the blanket application of usual land valuation principles. The unique nature of aboriginal title was made clear in *Delgamuukw*:

> Aboriginal title has been described as *sui generis* in order to distinguish it from 'normal' proprietary interests, such as fee simple. However, as I will now develop, it is also *sui generis* in the sense that its characteristics cannot be completely explained by reference either to the common law rules of real property or to the rules of property found in aboriginal legal systems. As with other aboriginal rights, it must be understood by reference to both common law and aboriginal perspectives. (*Delgamuukw* at 241)

The Supreme Court of Canada did, however, put flesh to the conceptual framework in noting that the nature of aboriginal title includes the following four key factors, all of which are reviewed below:

- it is inalienable except to the Crown;
- its use by First Nations must not be irreconcilable with the aboriginal group's attachment to the land;
- it is communally held as a collective right by all members of a First Nation; and
- it is a right to exclusive use and occupation of the land.

The Inalienability of Aboriginal Title   The first aspect of title, that it is inalienable except to the Crown, suggests that to some extent, aboriginal title land should be devalued due to its lack of marketability. However, one can expect strong counter-arguments from First Nations that the inalienability of their land actually represents a distinctive element that cannot be defined by customary land valuations. Support for this view is found in *Delgamuukw*, where the Chief Justice ruled:

> Alienation [of native title land] would bring to an end the entitlement of the aboriginal people to occupy the land and would terminate their relationship with it ... . What the inalienability of lands held pursuant to aboriginal title suggests is that those lands are more than just a fungible commodity. The relationship between an aboriginal community and the lands over which it has aboriginal

title has an important non-economic component. The land has an inherent and unique value in itself, which is enjoyed by the community with aboriginal title to it. (*Delgamuukw* at 247-248)

It is not clear whether the concept of "inherent and unique value in itself" can be translated into a compensation amount. Perhaps the concept is more applicable to a consideration of whether infringement could be justified at all with compensation where the unique value of certain lands to an aboriginal nation is extremely high.

Besides this *Delgamuukw*-driven argument, the fact that our courts have traditionally defined marketable title as title which "at all times under all circumstances may be forced on an unwilling purchaser"[10]— i.e., in the case of aboriginal title, the Crown—indicates that a 'market' does exist for title land. In fact, the inalienability of title land, except to the Crown, may point toward fair market value as a minimum starting point for valuing aboriginal title. This argument is premised on the surrender of aboriginal lands to the Crown being compensated by way of expropriation law principles. Historically, numerous incidents of expropriation of both reserve lands and traditional lands (which many First Nations are now claiming fall within their aboriginal title land boundaries) have taken place. Railway rights-of-way, weapons ranges, fur trading posts and other expropriations have diminished aboriginal peoples' land base.

Compensation in such cases has normally been paid to First Nations at the time of expropriation. Such expropriation has been valued in accordance with general expropriation law principles, which include the premise that the owner should receive fair market value for the expropriated property, normally based on the use of the land on the date of the expropriation. Various methods can be used to determine value, including the direct sales approach (which compares comparable property values), the income approach (which considers income derived from the land) or the cost approach (which supplements the direct sales approach by considering land improvements that cannot otherwise be compensated for in the direct sales approach). In expropriation law, compensation greater than fair market value may be awarded if the owner is able to show that a special economic advantage is gained from the use of his land.

The use of the fair market value measurement in the expropriation context was adopted by the Royal Commission on Aboriginal Peoples in its 1996 Report to the Federal Government. The Royal Commission recommended that any expropriated lands now abandoned by the military or railroad companies be returned to First

Nations, or that the appropriate First Nations be provided with a right of first refusal on such lands. The Commission referred to fair market value in its conclusion:

> (f) If an Aboriginal community does not wish the return of expropriated lands because of environmental damage or other reasons, they receive other lands in compensation or financial compensation equivalent to fair market value; and

> (g) The content of such compensation package be determined by negotiation or, failing that, by the Aboriginal Lands and Treaties Tribunal.[11]

The Limitation on the Use of Title Lands   The Supreme Court of Canada was unequivocal in stating that aboriginals may not use their title lands in a manner "irreconcilable" with their attachment to the land. This was held in *Delgamuukw* to be roughly analogous to the restrictions in traditional property law against life estate holders ruining or destroying their property.[12] Again, one can expect arguments from the Crown that this limitation on aboriginal title should lead to some diminution in the value of title land. Indeed, in some cases, a particular aboriginal group's attachment to its land may be akin to a zoning restriction that renders otherwise more valuable land less desirable. For example, park land in large urban areas or Agricultural Land Reserve property in Richmond, which otherwise would have tremendous value for residential or commercial development, suffers from diminished market value by virtue of its zoning characteristics. Similarly, land held by a First Nation whose relationship to the land is such that little or no economic development is possible could be accorded a lower than market value.

Aboriginal Land is Communally Held   The fact that aboriginal title land cannot be held by individual aboriginal community members also means that decisions regarding the land are made by the community. It is difficult to assess how a court will evaluate this aspect of title. In our view, a court may agree to a slight diminution in the value of aboriginal title due to its communal nature, since decision-making as to that land will be made more cumbersome and time-consuming.

Exclusivity of Use   That aboriginal title allows for the exclusive use and occupation of the land by First Nations imports a wide variety of considerations. These include the fact that the very origins of aboriginal title are distinct from its fee simple counterpart. Aboriginal title is founded upon the undisputed occupation of present-day Canadian territory by aboriginal peoples prior to the assertion of Crown sovereignty. In Chief Justice Lamer's words:

> What makes aboriginal title *sui generis* is that it arises from possession *before* the assertion of British sovereignty, whereas normal estates, like fee simple, arise afterward ... (Emphasis in judgment; *Delgamuukw* at 242)

In other words, aboriginal title is not, like fee simple, dependent upon Crown grants for its existence. It predates European discovery and colonization of Canada, and survives British sovereignty.

The exclusivity of use is, in our view, an indicator that aboriginal title may be given additional value by a court up to or beyond the fair market value benchmark for fee simple lands. In a sense, aboriginal title land is similar to real property that is free from all zoning restrictions, and is therefore available for its highest and best use. This analogy must be tempered, of course, by the condition that an aboriginal group's use of the land must not be irreconcilable with its attachment to the land. Still, even with this limitation, exclusivity is perhaps the most important characteristic that will affect how a court might assess compensation for infringement of aboriginal title. This, in a sense, creates 'jurisdiction free' land insofar as there would otherwise be statutory limits on government-approved uses.

A few additional factors that will be consistent across all First Nations' lands bear mentioning. The first is that aboriginal rights, which include aboriginal title, are protected in the Canadian Constitution. This is a fundamental aspect of aboriginal title status; no other property rights are given such recognition in Canada. Secondly, Justice Gerard La Forest's concurring reasons in *Delgamuukw* included the following suggestion that the "honour of the Crown" and the degree of occupancy of title land will affect compensation amounts:

> It must be emphasized ... that fair compensation in the present context is not equated with the price of a fee simple. Rather, compensation must be viewed in terms of the right and in keeping with the honour of the Crown. Thus, generally speaking, compensation may be greater where the expropriation relates to a village area as opposed to a remotely visited area. I add that account must be taken of the interdependence of traditional uses to which the land was put. (*Delgamuukw* at 283)

In this passage, Justice La Forest seemed to be referring to one of the characteristics of aboriginal title, namely the relative exclusivity of use.

According to Justice La Forest, it seems that there is a range of aboriginal title lands which vary in their degree of exclusive occupancy and interdependence of uses, both of which will affect their value when it comes to compensation.

An important further distinction is that aboriginal title clearly includes subsurface mineral rights, whereas these rights are normally reserved in fee simple grants. The Supreme Court of Canada confirmed the mineral rights content of aboriginal title land in its 1995 decision, *Blueberry River Indian Band* v. *Canada*, in which the Band challenged the Federal Government's transfer of mineral rights as part of 1945 surrender by the Band of reserve lands to the Government.[13] In *Delgamuukw*, the Court cited the *Blueberry River* case and the *Indian Oil & Gas Act*[14] in its review of aboriginal title, noting that the legislation "presumes that the aboriginal interest in reserve land includes mineral rights."[15] This would have the effect of increasing compensation, particularly where extraction of minerals is not significantly irreconcilable with an aboriginal nation's attachment to its lands.

Of course, the determination of compensation does not end with a valuation of a First Nation's particular title to its land. The nature and severity of the infringement, as well as the Crown's efforts to accommodate aboriginal interests, will augment or diminish the amount of compensation the Crown will have to pay. While a valuation of the nature of title will depend entirely on aboriginal title's unique characteristics and on the distinctiveness of each First Nation's land holding, the remaining three compensation factors all contain some element of discretion on the part of the Crown. It is incumbent on the Crown to decide whether it will exercise such discretion in a manner that fulfills its fiduciary and other duties and reduces potential liability for compensation in the aboriginal law context.

(e) The Nature of the Infringement

That compensation should vary depending upon the nature of the infringement seems obvious. An intentional governmental act, or an act condoned by government, would normally be viewed by a court in a harsher light than an unintentional or passive infringement. One can envisage, for example, a court taking a softer approach as far as compensation level where infringement has occurred on land to which a First Nation did not previously claim title. Conversely, compensation would be enhanced where the infringement, such as the granting of forest tenures, takes place on land which the Crown has full knowledge is claimed as title land by a First Nation. It should be noted, however, that an unintentional or passive act of infringement by the Crown should not negate compensation; the honour of the Crown and the Crown's fiduciary duty to see to aboriginal peoples' interests place a considerable burden of knowledge and care on government. To some extent, this process has begun in that government has assisted First Nations in developing "Traditional Use Studies" to document important areas that may attract a greater fiduciary duty and greater compensation if infringement has occurred. This step may ultimately assist the Crown in its potential "due diligence" defences to breach of fiduciary duty claims.

(f) The Severity of the Infringement
The severity of infringement of aboriginal title is another strong determinant of the degree of compensation. Infringement that destroys or seriously diminishes a First Nation's connection to the land, or adversely affects its culture and identity, should result in much higher compensation than incidental infringement. The wholesale destruction of an area to which a First Nation holds title by strip mining or clear-cutting will clearly fall into a different compensation realm than the improper surveying, with its minimal impacts, of aboriginal title land. The duration of each infringement will be another aspect of its severity. For example, compensation for a one-time infringement should not match compensation for infringement of title caused by decades of the granting of forestry and mining licences on aboriginal lands which include village sites, burial grounds and sacred sites, as well as crucial hunting and gathering areas.

(g) Extent of Accommodation of Aboriginal Interests
This variable in the compensation calculation, perhaps more than any other, provides government with options for minimizing its exposure to compensation. The accommodation of First Nation interests comprises two major tasks for government. The first is to involve the First Nation in the development of the particular resources found on their land. This involvement may include joint decision-making; resource-sharing; the conferral of licences or lands to First Nations' communities and businesses; and the reduction of economic barriers to First Nations' involvement in resource development.[16] The conferral of licences to First Nations' communities and businesses would be an important aspect of accommodation.

The second governmental task, and perhaps the most important means of accommodating First Nations, will be to engage in a consultation process with First Nations prior to infringement of title. In *Delgamuukw*, the Chief Justice stressed the importance of consultation in the following passage:

> [T]he fiduciary relationship between the Crown and aboriginal peoples may be satisfied by the involvement of aboriginal peoples in decisions taken with respect to their lands. There is always a duty of consultation. Whether the aboriginal group has been consulted is relevant to determining whether the infringement of aboriginal title is justified, in the same way that the Crown's failure to consult an aboriginal group with respect to the terms by which reserve land is leased may breach its fiduciary duty at common law: *Guerin*. (*Delgamuukw* at 265)

The Chief Justice went on to note that the type and extent of consultation will vary from a duty to discuss important decisions when the infringement is trivial, to the full consent of a First Nation in some cases. The Chief Justice indicated that even when the minimal standard is consultation, that consultation must be in good faith and must be carried out with the intention of substantially addressing the First Nation's concerns. He noted that in the majority of infringement situations, the amount of input, involvement and discussion with the First Nation "will be significantly deeper than mere consultation."[17]

Infringement Scenarios: Reducing Crown Exposure to Compensation

Clearly, many resource and land use decisions taken in this Province will continue to raise the possibility of infringing on British Columbia First Nations' rights and title until broad land claims settlements or other resource agreements are reached. In many cases, it will be impossible for government to avoid paying compensation to First Nations for past infringements, whether such compensation is paid by way of a legal award or an out-of-court settlement. However, on a go-forward basis, it will be possible for government to assess the consequences of infringement decisions such as resource extraction and minimize or even eliminate compensation that may otherwise be owed to First Nations. As the following scenarios illustrate, the 'size of the cheque' that the Crown may have to write will depend, in many cases, upon involving the particular First Nation in a consultation process and in creating partnerships in developing the particular resource.

Scenario No. 1: Sale of Crown Land to Private Sector for Real Estate Development

Population pressure and urban growth in British Columbia may lead to the need to encroach on First Nations' traditional lands. Should government proceed to sell such land for residential development that is on or near traditional lands, it runs the real risk of unjustifiably infringing aboriginal title and incurring the concomitant liability to pay compensation. As noted above, the amount of this compensation would depend very much on the First Nation's particular title to the land, the severity and nature of the infringement, and the extent to which First Nations were consulted with and accommodated. Under this scenario, the unilateral sale of land that was later proven to be aboriginal title land, with no prior consultation with or no participation from the First Nation involved, could attract a considerable amount of compensation. Moreover, one could expect the First Nation to resist the development of the land by way of judicial review, injunction or filing a caveat with the Land Title Office claiming aboriginal title.

On the other hand, the Crown could minimize its compensation exposure, and help fulfil its fiduciary duty, by carrying out one or more of the following:

- at a minimum, engaging in meaningful consultation with the First Nation involved;

- engaging in full consultation to the extent of obtaining consent of the First Nation for the transfer;

- conferring some of the land to be developed to the First Nation, or offering other Crown land in the area to increase the size of the First Nation's Reserve;

- placing restrictions on the use of the Crown land involved in the transfer so as to minimize the impact of the change on the First Nation;

- considering the creation of a community facility, park, roads, utility improvements, etc., on the land so that the First Nation would also share in benefits and services;

- involving the First Nation in a joint decision-making process about the sale of the land; and/or

- directing a portion of the sale proceeds to the First Nation for infrastructure and community development.

As the range of processes above suggests, the Crown and First Nation involved are afforded the option of crafting an innovative, First Nation-specific arrangement. Of course, the parties may not be able to reach a mutually satisfactory agreement. Should government proceed with the land transfer in the absence of an agreement with the First Nation, the Crown could still reduce the compensation it must pay if it has engaged in meaningful, deep consultation with the First Nation. In all likelihood, in-depth consultation and a joint decision-making process will lead to agreements in many cases that would otherwise proceed to litigation.

Scenario No. 2: The Issuance of a Forest Licence under the Forest Act

One of the most common claims by First Nations that their title has been infringed will arise from the granting by the Provincial Government of *Forest Act* licences and tenures. With each judicial review by First Nations that quashes forestry approvals or licences granted on or near lands claimed as title lands, the Crown attracts the risk of an injunction restraining logging and/or, after logging has occurred, a lawsuit seeking compensation for infringement. Again, government's exposure may be limited by considering one or more of the following options:

- engaging in meaningful consultation with the First Nation prior to forest management decisions;

- obtaining the consent of the First Nation to the logging on its land;

- entering into joint decision-making / co-management agreements with the First Nation for development of the resource;

- requiring that the forest licence on aboriginal title land be a joint-tenure licence with the First Nation community;

- preferring aboriginal joint venture applications in the open bidding process;

- making forest licences conditional on the successful applicant entering into business arrangements with the First Nation;

- involving the First Nation significantly in higher level planning under the *Forest Practices Code*; and/or

- reducing stumpage for First Nation tenure-holders.

In both scenarios above, government will have to ensure that a proper legislative mandate is in place that allows government decision-makers to validly carry out such activities as consultation, joint decision-making and resource sharing. Without such legislative authority, decision-makers may run afoul of administrative law principles of natural justice and even of having certain legislation found to be unconstitutional. For example, in a 1996 Supreme Court of Canada decision, *R. v. Adams*, the Court considered Quebec fishing regulations that allowed only for aboriginal food fishing at the discretion of the Minister. The Court found that since the regulatory fishing scheme amounted to "a pure act of

Ministerial discretion" that gave no direction as to how the discretion should be exercised, it infringed the existing aboriginal right to fish for food.[18] The Supreme Court of Canada noted that while in normal situations, "unstructured administrative discretion"[19] would only be reviewed by courts after it was exercised to determine whether it complied with the *Canadian Charter of Rights and Freedoms*, infringement of aboriginal rights called for a different approach:

> In light of the Crown's unique fiduciary obligations towards aboriginal peoples, Parliament may not simply adopt an unstructured discretionary administrative regime which risks infringing aboriginal rights in a substantial number of applications in the absence of some explicit guidance. If a statute confers an administrative discretion which may carry significant consequences for the exercise of an aboriginal right, the statute or its delegate regulations must outline specific criteria for the granting or refusal of that discretion which seeks to accommodate the existence of aboriginal rights. In the absence of such specific guidance, the statute will fail to provide representatives of the Crown with sufficient directives to fulfill their fiduciary duties, and the statute will be found to represent an infringement of aboriginal rights ... .[20]

Certain legislation in British Columbia already contains important provisions for consultation with First Nations and considerations of their interests. The B.C. *Environmental Assessment Act*[21] includes several sections that mandate consultation which First Nations:

- section 7 requires that applications for Project Approval Certificates include information on consultation activities undertaken with First Nations and a summary of the First Nations' response;

- section 9, which calls for creation of a Project Committee to review the project, allows for First Nation representation on the Committee;

- section 14 provides for the Project Committee to make a written assessment of the adequacy of the project proponent's information distribution efforts, which may include specific measures providing for more detailed consultation with First Nations;

- section 17 provides for further input from First Nations as the project approval process attains various stages;

- section 22 calls for specific project report specifications, including particulars of potential impacts on aboriginal rights; and

- section 23 calls for the project report to include satisfactory plans on how the project proponent intends to carry out consultation with First Nations whose territory includes or is in the vicinity of the project.

The *Environmental Assessment Act* provisions on consultation were considered in a recent B.C. Supreme Court decision, *Cheslatta Nation v. British Columbia*,[22] in which a First Nation sought judicial review of various government decisions relating to a mine project. While Chief Justice Williams ruled that the common law duty of consultation with aboriginal peoples is "always present and always important," he noted that an additional statutory obligation to consult, which did not lessen the common law to consult, existed because of the *Act*.[23] This statutory obligation does not necessarily create a second tier of consultation; the case suggests that the content of the statutory obligation in the *Act*—good faith meaningful consultation—was essentially similar to the duty to consult at common law.

Two other statutes bear mentioning. Section 13 of the B.C. *Forest Act* requires that before entering into a forest licence, a regional manager must evaluate licence applications according to various criteria, including meeting Crown objectives of environmental quality, water management, fisheries, wildlife and cultural heritage resources.[24] This section could be viewed as providing authority for consultation and joint decision-making with British Columbia's First Nations. More specific authority is found in Ontario's *Crown Forest Sustainability Act*,[25] which includes the following section:

> (23) The Minister may enter into agreements with First Nations for the joint exercise of any authority of the Minister under this Part.

Such provisions are increasingly common in new and revised Canadian legislation relating to environment and resource use, and should prove important in ensuring that the Crown's obligation to consult and share resource decisions with First Nations is met.

The Effect of the *Limitation Act* on Infringement of Rights Decisions

The restrictions imposed in the B.C. *Limitation Act*[26] may affect the ability of some First Nations to bring to court certain claims for compensation for infringement of title that occurred many years ago. The *Limitation Act* does include provisions for postponing the running of time for limitations in, among others, breach of trust cases and in situations where material facts relating to an action have been willfully concealed. There is an ultimate 30-year limitation period even if the postponement of the running of time is found to exist. However, certain kinds of actions are not affected by limitation periods and may be brought at any time. These include actions for possession of land, where the person entitled to possession has lost possession in circumstances similar to trespass, and actions for declarations for title to property by any person in possession of the property. First Nations may, therefore, be able to avail themselves of these property exemptions.

In other cases, the *Limitation Act* provisions may be strictly applied to deny the ability of First Nations to proceed with lawsuits. For example, in *Roberts* v. *Canada*, a 1995 decision of the Federal Court Trial Division, the Court barred and extinguished an action by two British Columbia bands for damages against the Crown relating to a dispute about Reserve Lands.[27] This area of law may become fertile ground for creative legal arguments from both the Crown and First Nations in lawsuits whose subject is historical infringement of title. While it is beyond the scope of this paper to review the considerable jurisprudence on limitation issues relating to aboriginal rights, one might expect First Nations to argue strenuously that the Crown's trust-like or fiduciary duty toward them, and the very recent development of the concept and content of aboriginal title, should result in a postponement or elimination of limitation periods in some cases.

The Crown's Fiduciary Duty and the Involvement of Industry

In many cases of resource development, the consultation and decision-making process between the Crown and the First Nation will also involve the private company developing the resource. That company is likely to have more of the specific technical and environmental knowledge than the Government or the First Nation, and will normally assist the First Nation by providing information on the impact of the development on its lands. Industry will also be involved in many cases in joint-venture business relationships with First Nations. In practical terms, the involvement of industry at this stage may allow the Crown to off-load a portion of its fiduciary duty on to the private sector.

In addition, the requirement of the Crown to provide economic benefits to First Nations may fulfil a portion of the Crown's fiduciary duty, limit its own liability for compensation, and do so without drawing from the government's coffers. Moreover, the Province may well reap the economic benefits inherent in private-sector-First Nations' dealings, such as maximizing taxation revenues and reducing the size of the compensation package under later land claims settlements. These economic benefits may be possible, for example, where industry has reached an agreement with the First Nation to provide the Band with an annual payment from a project on aboriginal title land. Such a payment might not only be taxable by the government in the hands of the First Nation but, depending upon the circumstances, would not be tax-deductible by the business. Further, one could foresee government arguing that the payments made to the First Nation by industry should minimize the Crown's financial obligations to the First Nation in any land claims settlements or infringement lawsuits by the First Nation. First Nations may insist upon written assurances that any benefits conferred to them from agreements with the private sector relating to resource development on their lands not be used by the Crown to diminish later claims for compensation. This area is further complicated by the conflict between the need for confidentiality between the First Nation and private sector in any business negotiations, and the Crown's fiduciary duty to each First Nation to ensure that its best interests are maintained.

Clearly, the Government-Industry-First Nation triangle presents a myriad of uncertainties. It also offers numerous options for creative business planning, consultation and joint decision-making that could alleviate the Crown's burden while fostering economic growth. The *Delgamuukw* decision has not magically removed British Columbia's resources from the negotiation table—it has, however, placed another seat at that table.

Compensation in Land Claims Settlements

(a) Negotiation: The Preferred Approach

Chief Justice Lamer's urging in *Delgamuukw* to government and First Nations to resolve title and rights issues by way of negotiation is only the latest judicial admonition that the negotiated approach is the best solution to outstanding title issues. The Chief Justice's closing comments in the case are unusually blunt:

> [T]his litigation has been both long and expensive, not only in economic but in human terms as well. By ordering a new trial, I do not necessarily encourage the parties to proceed to litigation and to settle their dispute through the courts ... Moreover, the Crown is under a moral, if not a legal, duty to enter into and conduct those negotiations in good faith. Ultimately, it is through negotiated settlements, with good faith and give and take on all sides, reinforced by the judgments of this Court, that will achieve ... "the reconciliation of the pre-existence of aboriginal societies with the sovereignty of the Crown." Let us face it, we all are here to stay. (*Delgamuukw* at 273)

Delgamuukw has already spawned or revitalized litigation on behalf of First Nations for past and present infringement of title and rights. Such lawsuits will multiply if outstanding issues are left unresolved and if the Crown proceeds with resource development in the Province without a sound consultation policy. As suggested in the section on compensation in the infringement context, a "brush-fire" approach to resolving infringement of title will leave the Crown open to the political and financial risks of ongoing and uncertain litigation. The honour of the Crown, the fiduciary duty owed by government to First Nations, and the growing public sentiment opposing continued disputes with First Nations should lead to an accelerated land claims settlement process. Fortunately, compensation in a land claim settlement context allows the parties tremendous latitude for crafting agreements and nearly unlimited scope for a meeting of the minds; lawsuits leave compensation decisions to the judiciary, which is constrained by a fairly narrow range of remedies.

(b) The Content of Land Claims Settlements

Land claims settlements are essentially modern-day equivalent of treaties. Such agreements can include an element for compensation for past and ongoing infringement of aboriginal rights, plus compensation of some kind for an extinguishment of rights, for the holding of certain or all rights in abeyance, or for an exhaustive definition of the rights of a particular First Nation. This definition will include delineation of geographical boundaries for aboriginal title land and land on which aboriginal rights may be exercised.

Other aspects in land claims settlements may include some recognition of any existing fee simple lands and private rights on lands in and around the settlement area; water, forestry, sub-surface and fisheries resource management provisions; archeological and cultural agreements, including protection for artifacts and burial sites; self-government and policing provisions; environmental assessment and protection provisions; and taxation considerations, including, in some cases, wider scope for governmental taxation of aboriginal peoples.

(c) The Financial Component

Of all these items up for negotiation under a land claims settlement, perhaps the most contentious and high profile will be the amount of financial compensation paid to the aboriginal group. A lump-sum amount may include amounts for land given up, past infringements, ongoing use of traditional aboriginal territory by third parties, compensation for past grievances such as lost cultural artifacts and, in some cases, an amount acknowledging the harm caused by the residential school system. Of course, an amount representing any extinguishment or exhaustive definition of aboriginal rights would be included. Of this amount, a considerable portion may be allocated toward aboriginal title land previously removed from the First Nation or given up as part of the settlement. Valuation methods will obviously be left to the parties. However, one can assume that some formula, perhaps fair market value plus or minus a premium that varies depending upon the nature of the land and rights at issue, will be adopted. The utility of any such formula across the Province's many land settlement negotiations is uncertain since the nature of each First Nation's attachment to its land will vary tremendously. As lawyer Jack Woodward has pointed out, even the existing Canadian treaties may hold little value as precedents for land claim settlements:

> There are a great many ... treaties in Canada, even in B.C., but they are all virtually useless as a guide to the quantum of compensation which will be paid for such a cession of title. Most such treaties were products of the peculiar political circumstances of their times. To state the obvious, the aboriginal parties almost never had adequate legal advice when entering these compacts. Currently there is a strong tide of opinion in most aboriginal communities to *never* cede, release or surrender their lands or rights, so a treaty on the old model seems unlikely today.[28] [Emphasis in original]

An added complication of determining how much a surrender of aboriginal title is worth, whether past or future, is the collision of value systems regarding land. Whereas 'fair market value', 'highest and best use of land', and other traditional property worth measurements are useful in many contexts, including expropriation, they do not alone capture the value of land to First Nations. In some way, the First Nations' perspective that their land is sacred and plays a vital part in their creation stories will have to be reconciled. Negotiators must also consider the fact that in surrendering land or otherwise diminishing their rights, First Nations will be giving up opportunities to become involved in economic development. The reality that after signing land claims agreement, many First Nations will no longer be able to resist future resource and land development in their vicinity, and will no longer be asked to be part of the consultation or resource-sharing process, should be recognized. As well, the important fact that the Crown will be gaining certainty of resource access decisions by way of removing the costs of compensation for future infringement should be considered and evaluated.

However the reconciliations and valuations are ultimately made, it is clear that the *Delgamuukw* decision will have tremendous impact on land claim settlements, particularly as they relate to title lands. Old policies and approaches will no longer work. The following passage, taken from a 1995 draft Provincial Government discussion paper on the Province's approach to land and resource aspects of treaty negotiations, illustrates the need to re-evaluate policies and strategies:

Compensation for First Nations

Some First Nations have indicated that they will seek compensation based on a calculation of damages arising from past use and alienation of the lands and resources within their traditional territories. *The Province will not calculate the cash component of treaties on this basis, and Provincial negotiators will not have a mandate to enter into discussions on such calculations.*[29] [Emphasis added]

Conclusion

The Federal and Provincial Governments do have options for reducing their risks of future liability for compensation to aboriginal nations. Averting such risks will mean mounting a concerted effort directed at meeting the fiduciary duty to First Nations, including "sharing the wealth" by involving aboriginal people in the economic benefits of the land and its resources. In many cases, this inclusion can be accomplished by government with little cost and should, where aboriginal-private industry tensions and economic uncertainty are high, stimulate economic activity and government revenues. The issue then becomes not one of law or economics, but of political will.

Notes

1 H. Foster, "Aboriginal Title and the Provincial Obligation to Respect it: Is *Delgamuukw* v. *British Columbia* 'Invented Law'?" (1998), 56 *The Advocate* 221-231 at 222.
2 See also H. Slade and P. Pearlman, "Why Settle Aboriginal Land Rights? Exploring the Legal Issues of Litigation and Negotiation" in Roslyn Kunin, ed., *Prospering Together: The Economic Impact of the Aboriginal Title Settlements in B.C.*, (Vancouver: Laurier Institution, 1998) 45.
3 *Delgamuukw* at 266.
4 *Delgamuukw* at 265-266.
5 See Madame Justice Wilson's judgment in *Frame* v. *Smith* (1987), 42 D.L.R. (4th) 81 (S.C.C.).
6 *Delgamuukw* at 265.
7 [1984] 2 S.C.R. 335.
8 *Ibid.*, at 360-362.
9 *Delgamuukw* at 265-266.
10 *Re: Dalgleish* (1910), 15 B.C.R. 217 (B.C.S.C.).
11 Royal Commission on Aboriginal Peoples, *Report of the Royal Commission on Aboriginal Peoples*—Vol. 2 (Ottawa: Canadian Communication Group, 1996) at 631.
12 *Delgamuukw* at 248.
13 *Blueberry River Indian Band* v. *Canada* (1995), 130 D.L.R. (4th) 193.
14 R.S.C. 1985, c. I-7.
15 *Delgamuukw* at 245.
16 *Delgamuukw* at 264-265.
17 *Delgamuukw* at 265.
18 [1996] 3 S.C.R. 101 at 131.
19 *Ibid.* at 131.
20 *Ibid.* at 132.
21 R.S.B.C. 1996, c. 119.
22 [1998] B.C.J. No. 178.
23 *Ibid.* at paragraph 43.
24 R.S.B.C. 1996, c. 157.
25 S.O. 1996, c. 25.
26 R.S.B.C. 1996, c. 266.
27 [1995] F.C.J. No. 1202.
28 J. Woodward, "Damages for Infringement Evaluation and Title" in the *Continuing Legal Education Society of B.C.—Aboriginal Title Update* (CLE: Vancouver, 1998) at 4.1.02.
29 Government of British Columbia, "Draft Provincial Approach to Lands and Resources Component of Treaty Negotiations," April 25, 1995, at page 10.

Potential Impact
on Forestry

Robert C. Strother

Since the release of the decision of the Supreme Court of Canada in *Delgamuukw*, there has been significant uncertainty, speculation and controversy concerning the potential impact of the decision on vested private-sector interests, including forest tenures. The First Nations Summit has interpreted the decision as stating that First Nations "have aboriginal title in our territories," and have called on Canada and British Columbia to "put an immediate freeze on any further alienation of land resources within the province" until province-wide interim measures agreements have been negotiated.[1] Is this truly the implication of *Delgamuukw* for forest companies in British Columbia?

In this paper, I will address the following questions:

- What does the decision say about aboriginal title?

- How can aboriginal title be proven?

- Is aboriginal title absolute?

- What degree of consultation with First Nations is required?

- Do First Nations have a veto over development on their traditional lands?

Note will be found on page 458.

- How will this work in practice in the forest sector?

- Will First Nations be able to obtain injunctions to stop development?

What Does the Decision Say about Aboriginal Title?

Before attempting to explain what the decision will mean for the forest industry, it may be helpful to review what the decision actually says. The first point of importance is that unlike most judicial decisions, this decision does not actually decide the case that was before the Court. Instead, the Court sent the Gitksan-Wet'suwet'en land claim back to the trial court for a new trial. The Court did not decide whether the Gitksan-Wet'suwet'en, in fact, have aboriginal title to the land they claim. What the Court did was to explain the law in relation to aboriginal title, and it is these comments rather than any actual decision in the *Delgamuukw* case that have importance for both First Nations and resource companies seeking to understand the nature of these rights and how their interact with the forest tenure rights. Unfortunately, for every question the Court has answered in this judgment, a number of new questions arise.

The Court began by explaining that aboriginal title was different from aboriginal rights. Aboriginal rights are rights to do something (such as hunt, trap or fish) which was done by the aboriginal group at the time of contact with Europeans. Aboriginal rights may or may not be connected to the use of land. Prior to the decision of the Supreme Court of Canada, it was generally believed by the non-First Nations side that aboriginal title and aboriginal rights were intermingled concepts, and that any land rights of a First Nation were tied up in the exercise of the traditional aboriginal pursuits. Other uses of the land by non-First Nations interests would be permitted to the extent that they were not incompatible with the exercise of the aboriginal rights.

The Supreme Court of Canada decision, for the first time, separated the concepts of aboriginal rights and aboriginal title. The Court explained that aboriginal *title* is a right to the land itself. The Court explained that where a First Nation has aboriginal title, it has the right to exclusive use and occupation of the land. It is not restricted in its uses to traditional uses. The First Nation may use the land for any purpose, including purposes not available in the traditional aboriginal society, so long as those uses are not incompatible with the traditional uses that the aboriginal group exercised in its traditional society.

It is not the case that each First Nation necessarily has aboriginal title over its entire traditional territory. The Court explained that the rights of First Nations "follow along a spectrum with respect to their degree of connection with the land." At one end are aboriginal rights which have no particular connection with land but which were integral to the distinctive culture of the aboriginal group claiming that right. An example might be the right to speak one's language. In the middle of the spectrum are rights which may be related to specific land, but which fall short of the test for aboriginal title. An example might be the right to hunt on a particular tract of land, where the aboriginal group in question did not exercise that degree of exclusive use and occupation to support a claim for aboriginal title. Finally, at the other end of the spectrum, there is aboriginal title, which confers a right to the land itself.

It appears that the Court contemplates that different aboriginal groups will have different types of rights, depending upon their own particular circumstances and history. For example, one aboriginal group may have site-specific hunting rights without any rights to the land itself, whereas another group may have aboriginal title based on exclusive occupation through hunting. The difference in rights that flow from this distinction appears to be considerable, but to identify this distinction for operational purposes may be quite difficult.

Thus, the assertion of the First Nations Summit that the Supreme Court has decided that First Nations have aboriginal title to their traditional territories needs to be qualified. Some First Nations may have aboriginal title to their traditional territory, but this entitlement will have to be established on a case-by-case basis. That aboriginal title cannot be taken for granted may be seen from the failure of the court to declare that the Gitksan-Wet'suwet'en have aboriginal title over their territory, even after 15 years of litigation and huge evidentiary record.

How Can Aboriginal Title Be Proven?

To establish aboriginal title, an aboriginal group must show that it had exclusive use and occupation of the land in question at the time British sovereignty was declared over that land. For British Columbia, that date is generally taken to be 1846, the date of the Oregon Treaty. Some degree of continuity of connection with the land must be shown. What constitutes occupation for the purposes of this test is likely to give rise to much academic writing and potential litigation in the coming years.

A major part of the judgment examines the use of aboriginal oral history to establish occupation. The Court concluded that oral history must be given "independent weight" and "placed on an equal footing" with historical documents.

As a practical matter, it cannot be known whether a particular aboriginal group has aboriginal title in a particular tract of land (as opposed to aboriginal *rights* on that territory) unless that group establishes such an entitlement in court which, given the history of the *Delgamuukw* litigation, is not a very practical scenario.

Is Aboriginal Title Absolute?

It is clear that aboriginal title, like aboriginal rights, is not absolute. Aboriginal title may be infringed by either the Provincial or the Federal Crown if the infringement meets the test of justification developed in the *Sparrow* case and refined in *Delgamuukw*. Aboriginal title may not, however, be extinguished, other than through surrender by the aboriginal group in question.

The Court sets out a series of tests to determine whether infringement of aboriginal title can be justified. First, the infringement of aboriginal title must be in furtherance of a legislative objective that is compelling and substantial. The Court specifically stated that the development of forestry, as well as mining, hydroelectric power, agriculture and the general economic development of the interior of British Columbia, are the kinds of objectives that meet this test and in principle can justify the infringement of aboriginal title.

The second test for justification relates to the Crown's fiduciary obligations to First Nations and has several components. There must be adequate consultation with the affected First Nation before aboriginal title can be infringed. In most cases, compensation will be required, because of what the Court describes as the "inescapably economic aspect" of aboriginal title. The Court does not discuss the basis on which the amount of compensation is to be assessed but states that the amount of compensation payable will vary with the nature of the aboriginal title affected and the nature and severity of the infringement. Finally, the Court indicates that in many cases, some priority will be required to reduce economic barriers to participation by the aboriginal group.

If these tests of justification are met, the Crown (federal or provincial) may lawfully infringe aboriginal title.

What Degree of Consultation Is Required?

The Court places consultation, like the rights themselves, on a spectrum. There is no single answer as to what degree of consultation will be required to infringe aboriginal title. It will depend on the circumstances.

At one end of the consultation spectrum, when the interference is relatively minor, the obligation will be to discuss the proposed activity in a good faith effort to substantially address the concerns of the aboriginal peoples. In the middle (and what the Court contemplated as "in most cases"), something that is "significantly deeper than mere consultation" will be required. At the other end of the spectrum, the Court stated that some cases will require the full consent of the First Nation, particularly when provinces enact hunting and fishing regulations in relation to aboriginal lands.

The nature of consultation that is generally required has been the subject of a more recent judgment of the British Columbia Supreme Court concerning the development of the Huckleberry Mine near Houston, B.C. In a judgment released January 29, 1998, the Chief Justice of the Supreme Court held that the consultation process leading to the mine approval certification had been deficient in failing to provide the affected First Nations with data sufficient to enable them to make a reasonable assessment of the impact of the mine on wildlife in their traditional territories. He did not strike down the approval certificate, but ordered further consultation on this issue.

In reaching his decision, the Chief Justice made some interesting observations on the consultation process that suggest a standard of reasonableness and good faith on the part of both governments and First Nations. For example, he pointed out that it would not be open for First Nations to remain silent throughout the consultation process and later try to derail a project by complaining about inadequate information or inadequate consultation. Similarly, First Nations demands for information must meet a standard of reasonableness measured by generally accepted professional, scientific and commercial practices and standards. As well, it would not be open for aboriginal groups to complain if they refuse to be consulted in an effective forum created in good faith for such consultation.

It seems likely that the precise nature of the consultation required will be developed in future case law as different circumstances are addressed. At this point, it cannot be said there is one standard of consultation that must be met, other than to state that it must be meaningful, timely and made in a good faith effort to address legitimate concerns of affected First Nations.

Do First Nations Have a Veto over Development on Their Traditional Lands?

There is nothing in the *Delgamuukw* decision that supports the assertion that consent of First Nations is always required before forestry operations can take place on what might be characterized as aboriginal lands. Indeed, the concept of justifiable infringement is inconsistent with a right of veto.

The Court does state, however, that there will be cases where the consent of a First Nation holding aboriginal title over particular land will be necessary before a particular form of infringement can be characterized as justifiable. The implication of the judgment is that such cases will be limited to circumstances where the proposed infringement prevents aboriginal people from engaging in specific activities, rather than circumstances where the proposed activity simply interferes with the exclusive nature of the First Nation's rights.

The Court does not state whether, in those cases where aboriginal consent is required, there are any limitations on the ability of the aboriginal group to withhold consent (as, for example, in many commercial agreements where consent is required but may not be unreasonably withheld). These matters must presumably be left for another day.

How Will This Work in Practice in the Forest Sector?

One of the difficulties in assessing the practical implications of this judgment is that in setting out in general terms the legal principles which apply, the Court was not faced with the practical difficulty of applying those principles to an actual situation. Most of the difficult questions have been left to be decided in other cases, presumably by trial judges in British Columbia when they are faced with a specific problem with immediate economic implications.

The "spectrum" approach to all the difficult problems, whether the nature of the rights held, the degree of consultation required to infringe or the amount of compensation required to be paid, means that no one can be sure in any given situation precisely what rights an affected First Nation has. Presumably, the Court took this approach to encourage governments and First Nations to resolve these issues through the treaty negotiation process rather than in rights litigation. But in the meantime, it will be necessary for the provincial government in particular to work out a protocol for approaching these issues in a practical way. It is likely that much of the focus of this approach will be on the nature and scope of the consultation that is undertaken with affected First Nations before forestry operations take place.

The government will first have to consider what sort of rights should be assumed to exist in the proposed cutblock or licence area. Does the First Nation (which will undoubtedly be asserting aboriginal title) actually have aboriginal title, or does the aboriginal group have site-specific hunting rights short of title, or something else or no special rights at all? The Court has given some guidance as to how these difficult issues may be established in a courtroom but not much assistance for a District Manager trying to determine the circumstances in which a cutting permit may lawfully be given. There will inevitably be a great temptation to slow down an already cumbersome approval process.

Unless the treaty process can be considerably accelerated (not a very likely scenario), the uncertainty about what precise rights each First Nation has is likely to continue for some time. A practical approach for the government may be to assume that a local First Nation has aboriginal rights that may amount to title, without assuming they *do* amount to title or attempting to resolve that issue in the field. Consultation is certainly required to infringe aboriginal title and is probably required to infringe aboriginal rights, so the safest course for the government would be to consult fully in all cases.

In the absence of certainty that the aboriginal rights amount to title, it would, however, require an unusual factual scenario to justify the government in insisting upon aboriginal consent before cutting permits can be granted. Even if there were certainty that the aboriginal interest amounted to title, it would be a small number of cases where consent would be required.

What the government must consider is what impact the proposed activity will have on the relevant aboriginal group, and, if that impact is material, whether there are practical ways to mitigate the impact. If the impact will be material, and there are no practical ways to mitigate the impact, it may be necessary to consider whether the activity can be justified on a scenario of aboriginal title.

Will First Nations Be Able to Obtain Injunctions to Stop Development?

The ability of First Nations to obtain injunctions to stop development on their traditional territory does not appear to be greatly changed by the *Delgamuukw* decision. Injunctions are very fact-dependent, and the ability of a First Nation to go to court to obtain an injunction before establishing the precise nature of its own rights will depend on the specifics of the activity and its effect on the aboriginal people, as it did prior to the decision.

One additional nuance that will undoubtedly be developed in any injunction applications is the significance of compensation as part of the justification for infringement of aboriginal title. Under conventional injunction law, if the loss can be adequately compensated for in damages, an injunction will not be granted. The Supreme Court appears to contemplate that in cases in which the other justification tests are met, the existence of compensation will provide the basis for legitimizing the infringement, even when the rights amount to aboriginal title. That is not to say that injunctions can never be obtained—it will depend very much on the impact of the proposed activity on the aboriginal people. But it does appear that the judgment in *Delgamuukw* provides arguments that can be used to oppose as well as advance injunction applications.

Thus, the practical effect of *Delgamuukw* remains to be seen. In each case, three questions are likely to arise:

- What is the (likely) nature of the aboriginal interest?
- Will the proposed activity infringe that interest?
- Can the infringement be justified?

Note

1 For example, the First Nations Summit, in their "Statement to Minister Stewart and Minister Cashore regarding *Delgamuukw* Decision," January 30, 1998, made the assertion that "the Supreme Court has now confirmed what First Nations have said all along—we have aboriginal title to our territories."

Potential Impact
on Mining

Ken Sumanik

Introduction

The potential impacts of *Delgamuukw* on the mining industry are conjectural: they depend ultimately on who owns the land and to what extent the owners and prospective users are able to agree on terms and conditions of use. In the interim, mineral tenure holders and mining developers are expected to engage in "meaningful consultation" with aboriginal peoples as a pre-requisite to "work," while the ownership questions are being argued in our courts. This uncertainty has increased the currently high levels of risk to exploration and development.

Mining Is a Risky Business

The study of risk measurement in the mining industry is made difficult by diverse influences. Some are technical, some human, and some political—each study is unique. Between 1927 and 1967, Cominco explored more than 1,000 properties in Canada. Of these, only 78 were of sufficient interest to warrant a major exploration program. Sixty were found to contain insufficient ore to justify production; 18 were brought into production, but of these, 11 were not sufficiently profitable to permit recovery of the original investment. Only seven of the original

---

Notes will be found on page 465.

1,000 properties became profitable mines.[1] During that 40-year period, the company spent more than $300 million in its search for new mines.

Technical risks have now been overtaken by human and political risks. These commonly include security of mineral tenure, access to land, excessive regulations, taxation, mineral commodity prices, and energy and labour costs. Much has been written about the impacts of these factors on the industry. National, provincial and territorial associations and independent members have expressed their concerns to governments, but to little or no avail. This ambivalence towards the industry varies from one jurisdiction to another, depending on its relative economic importance.

Two significant risk factors have emerged over the past decade: aboriginal land claims, and the creation of more parks and wilderness areas.[2] Results of a Fraser Institute survey sent to 174 senior and junior mining companies identified aboriginal land claims and new parks and wilderness area designations as major concerns; 92 percent and 89 percent of respondents respectively. This conclusive evidence dispelled previous doubt that aboriginal issues were not a paramount concern of exploration companies planning to work in B.C.

Protected Areas and Parks and Wilderness Area Designations in B.C.

The *Parks '90-Wilderness '90* initiative was a government campaign by the provincial Ministries of Environment, Land and Parks, and Forests to convince British Columbians that their provincial park and wilderness systems had to be expanded. This led to an increase in Land and Resource Management Planning (LRMPs) and the creation of a Commission of Resources and Environment (CORE), which directed land-use planning by multi-stakeholder groups in the regions of Vancouver Island, Cariboo-Chilcotin, and Kootenay-Boundary. The objective of this "Protected Area Strategy for British Columbia" was to increase the area of provincial parks and wilderness, from 6 to 12 percent and to re-zone land use on the remaining 88 percent. CORE is no longer operational but LRMPs continue, albeit "without prejudice" to aboriginal land claims.

Most of central and southern British Columbia is covered by LRMPs that have either been completed, or are nearing completion. Only the northernmost regions of British Columbia outside the boundaries of Tatshenshini and Muskwa-Kechika Parks, remain "unplanned," but when the process is completed, more than 12 percent of British Columbia will be designated as Parks and Protected Areas (PAs). Mineral exploration and mining is prohibited in Parks and PAs. A significant percentage of the areas not designated as Parks and Protected Areas are being zoned as Special Management Areas. Although exploration and development are allowed in those areas, they have onerous operational constraints that preclude effective exploration and development. They are considered by industry as "Parks-in-Waiting."

Aboriginal Issues

Aboriginal issues, particularly those involving land claims, have emerged recently as a significant factor in mineral exploration and mining developments in Canada generally, but in British Columbia particularly. Unlike other provinces and territories, land claims were not negotiated with most B.C. aboriginal groups, except for several treaties covering small areas of land on southern Vancouver Island. However, negotiations were officially started in 1993 with the establishment of the Treaty Commission, a tripartite organization including Canada, British Columbia, and the First Nations Summit (FNS), representing about 70 percent of B.C. aboriginal peoples. Together, they are actively involved in treaty negotiations. Since its inception, the Treaty Commission has accepted 51 Statements of Intent from First Nations to negotiate treaties.[3] The Nisga'a land claim which commenced before the Treaty Commission was formed, has been negotiated and a final agreement has been signed by Canada, British Columbia, and the Nisga'a. Other aboriginal groups not negotiating treaties are affiliated with the Union of B.C. Indian Chiefs.

Frustrated by a treaty process that was either too slow or failed to protect their interests, some aboriginal people in B.C. resorted to acts of civil disobedience. Prominent in B.C. were the Duffy lake, Adams River and Green Mountain road blockades and the Gustafson Lake confrontation. Conflicts have also arisen between some aboriginal groups and resource developers and governments in other provinces, where land claims have been settled for many decades.

In the Yukon and Northwest Territories, where land claims are nearing completion or have been settled recently, mineral exploration and mining development is relatively static or decreasing. Inhabitants of Nunavut, established in 1992, have stated repeatedly that their "territory is open for business." Despite a significant diamond discovery at Lac de Gras northeast of Yellowknife and several important satellite discoveries, prospectors and developers are not flocking to Nunavut. Land north of latitude-60 is resource-deficient except for minerals, yet many inhabitants accept mining reluctantly.

Delgamuukw

On December 11, 1997, the Supreme Court of Canada (SCC) rendered a decision on *Delgamuukw*, a claim by the Gitksan and Wet'suwet'en to 58,000 square kilometers of west-central B.C. The decision culminated

13 years of litigation, which began in the Supreme Court of B.C., went to the B.C. Court of Appeal, and finally the Supreme Court of Canada. The Court has recommended a re-trial but this option rests with the Gitksan and Wet'suwet'en. Presumably, the Supreme Court decision is now one of the principal reasons for B.C.'s sagging mining and mineral exploration industries. But other factors that reflect the industries' cyclical nature must also be considered before assigning any or all responsibility for our present economic plight to the Supreme Court and to aboriginal people.

B.C. Staking Activity and Exploration Expenditures

The number of mineral claims staked each year is a consistent measure of exploration activity. A record of mineral claims staked annually in B.C. is presented in Figure 1.

It depicts the cyclical nature of exploration and development. Combining exploration expenditures annually with the number of mineral claim units staked, Figure 2[5] is a reliable indicator of investment and economic activity. Two discrete cycles are evident from 1960 to 1998. Although the greatest variation is coincident with changing governments and government policies, other factors also contribute to the variation but are not as apparent.

A list of events from 1980 to 1998 that eventually affected exploration and development is presented to supplement data .

Figure 1: Mineral Tenure Recorded (as Reported by Year)

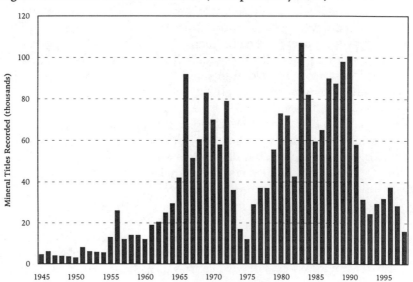

From the mid-1970s to 1990, B.C. had a relatively stable regulatory environment which enabled mineral resource exploration and development to flourish.

Chronology of Events: 1980 to 1998

1980–1990   A decade of consistent rules and regulations; access to land

1982–1983   Windy Craggy discovered by Falconbridge; development started later by Geddes Resources

1984   Gitksan-Wet'suwet'en (Delgamuukw) case begins, Supreme Court of B.C.

1985–1989   Flow-Thru' share period; beneficial to exploration

1990   Discovery of Mt. Milligan, Eskay Ck. and Red Mountain Parks '90 - Wilderness '90; LRMPs begin
Duffy Lake Road Blockade

Figure 2: BC Staking Activity and Exploration Expenditures

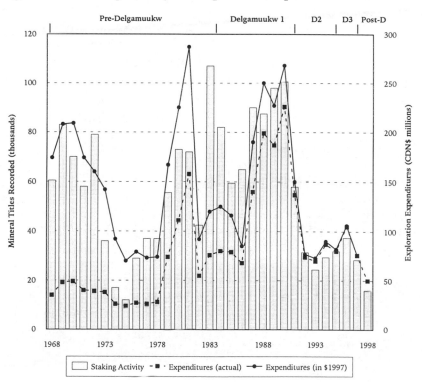

1991	NDP elected; Delgamuukw, (BCSC) decision; Delgamuukw 2, BC Court of Appeal begins
1992	Commission on Resources and Environment started
1993	Tatshenshini Park created; Windy Craggy Project terminated
	Delgamuukw2, BC Court of Appeal decision; negotiations attempted as an alternative to litigation
1994	Negotiations fail; Delgamuukw 3 SCC action commences Tatshenshini designated a World Heritage Site
1995	Cheslatta lawsuit, Re: Huckleberry Mine approval
	Green Mountain road, Adams River Bridge and Gustafsen Lake conflict
	NDP re-elected
1996	CORE planning completed; LRMPs continue
1997	Muskwa-Kechika Park created; Delgamuukw3, SCC decision
1998	Post Delgamuukw "How to Cope and Prosper Workshops"
	Statement to Ministers Stewart and Cashore from the First Nations Summit (FNS) stating that aboriginal title is on "an equal footing with the Crown's title"
	Rejection of referral process by the Shuswap Nation
	Tsay Keh Dene vs The Ministries of Environment, Land and Parks and Forests, Re: S. Kemess Mine approval
	Takla Lake Indian Band v. Attorney General of Canada, Government of B.C. and Royal Oak Mines Ltd., Re: S. Kemess Mine approval

These events have had a negative impact on mineral exploration and development in B.C. Only when ownership (i.e. aboriginal title) and access to land issues are resolved and a stable regulatory order re-implemented, will there be a return to normal staking and spending.

The industry continues to work with aboriginal groups in many jurisdictions and is fully committed to improving relationships. Cooperation and understanding by governments, aboriginal groups and industry is a pre-requisite to investment for future exploration and development.

Notes

1 J. R. Hoskins, 1982. "Mineral Industry Costs," Northwest Mining Association, p. 241.
2 L. Jones and F. Arman, 1997. The Fraser Institute Survey of "Mining Companies Operating in Canada," pp. 21-22.
3 BC Treaty Commission Annual Report, 1998, p. 2.
4 Mining Review, 1995, p. 18.
5 British Columbia's Mineral Exploration Review and Natural Resources Canada (1968-1998).

8   All Still Here and All Looking Ahead

The Public Opinion Landscape

DARRELL BRICKER

Excerpts from a luncheon keynote speech and slide presentation delivered on 27 May 1999 at the Delgamuukw conference.

What I'd like to discuss is the public opinion landscape and Canadians' views and attitudes regarding aboriginal issues. One thing that people do have, relative to issues involving natives or aboriginal people, are opinions. Some of them better informed than others; some of them are more legally driven. One of the most interesting aspects of looking at these opinions is that they represent what I would call the antiseptic light of public opinion. They really do show you what the art of the possible is in terms of communicating to the public and talking to the public about some of these issues. You are going to find as we go through these data that while sometimes we would *hope* that the Canadian public has very well-informed opinions about these issues, quite frankly they don't. A lot of what [follows] are impressions or views that people have that have been derived from their own personal experiences—mostly what they have read in the newspaper, heard through the media, or possibly picked up from a friend or a relative in a casual conversation.

Public opinion on this issue is very malleable because it is not based on a lot of factual information. As we go through the legal machinations in places like British Columbia, people come more in contact with the realities of [issues] such as the *Nisga'a* treaty and the *Delgamuukw* decision. This [presentation] might show you the possibilities that open when people come into contact with these issues in their day-to-day-life. Right now, the unfortunate thing is that it could go either way, depending on how people work through these issues and how they communicate them. I'll show you how there is potential to build a coalition in support of a more affirmative agenda on native issues, and I'll show you the potential pitfalls for trying to build that agenda. Currently, it is a very controversial issue—and one in which public opinion should be considered.

Figure 1   Methodology

- Interviews by telephone—April 1st-9th, 1998
- Randomly selected Canadian adults
- Sample

	N	Error
Canada	**2,550**	+/– 1.9%
British Columbia	800	+/– 3.5%
Alberta	300	+/– 5.7%
Saskatchewan & Manitoba	300	+/– 5.7%
Ontario	400	+/– 4.9%
Quebec	400	+/– 4.9%
Atlantic provinces	150	+/– 8.0%
North	200	+/– 6.9%

- Data weighted to reflect actual Canadian population figures for 1996 Census.

This 1998 study was the most comprehensive survey I have ever conducted specifically on aboriginal issues. When I talk about aboriginal issues I'm not saying that we were speaking to aboriginal people directly, although they were part of the random sample and are represented to their level in the Canadian population generally. In telephone interviews, 2,550 randomly selected Canadians were asked what they thought about aboriginal issues. Anyone who knows anything about public opinion research would know that is a very large sample, with a statistical margin of error of plus or minus 1.9 percent.

Given that most pyrotechnics on this issue these days are in one particular jurisdiction in Canada, that being British Columbia, we did a very large oversample. In other words, we sampled more people in B.C. than we would normally sample for a proportionate nationwide survey because we really wanted to look at B.C. by itself, outside of the Canadian population. The data, though, are all weighted back to reflect the actual proportion of the B.C. population within the Canadian population. That's a very long-winded way of saying: "This is Canada."

I am going to discuss context. By context, I mean what Canadians think about aboriginal people, the situation of aboriginal people today in Canada. Are they making progress? Are they better off or worse off than they were in the past? And when people look at the most important issues facing native Canadians today, what do they see them as being?

The next subject is obviously a very controversial issue: self-government, and what Canadians thing about some propositions relative to self-government. Next, are land claims. And finally, segmentation— a rather fancy word but one that is absolutely critical to understanding the public opinion environment on aboriginal issues. The survey will show you how the Canadian public segments out on this issue, so you can get some sense of how a coalition could be built or how it could be fractured, based on some of the basic tenants of public opinion.

Context

Figure 2—How Well Informed Are You about Native Issues?

Only 13 percent of Canadians say that they are well informed about native issues. Only 13 percent. The highest in terms of self-information—people who know the most about or identify themselves as knowing a lot about native issues—are people living in the Yukon and Northwest Territories. Obviously, we are dealing with a larger percentage of the native population and there's a lot of interaction between people. But looking at places where we see the most populous groups in the Canadian population, for example Ontario, it is 12 percent, a pretty low number. So, in the biggest jurisdiction in the country, very few people know about native issues, or self-identify as knowing about native issues. Not surprising. When you talk to people, for example in Toronto, about native issues, they really don't know what you are talking about. They think of native issues as being out somewhere else, in some remote place. They don't see them as something that is present in their own lives. The place that this has changed rather dramatically over the space of the last year has been British Columbia, where people have become a lot more informed about this issue—some of them positively, many more of them negatively. (Although B.C. was only 15 percent at the time of the survey, that number, at minimum, has probably doubled.)

Figure 2   How Well Informed Are You about Native Issues?
"Well Informed" 6/7 on 7 pt. scale (N= 2,550)

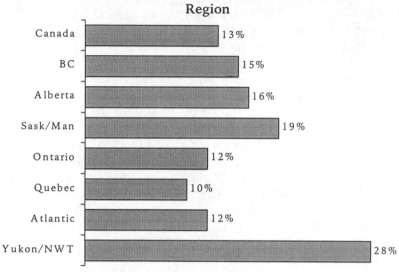

Region

- Canada — 13%
- BC — 15%
- Alberta — 16%
- Sask/Man — 19%
- Ontario — 12%
- Quebec — 10%
- Atlantic — 12%
- Yukon/NWT — 28%

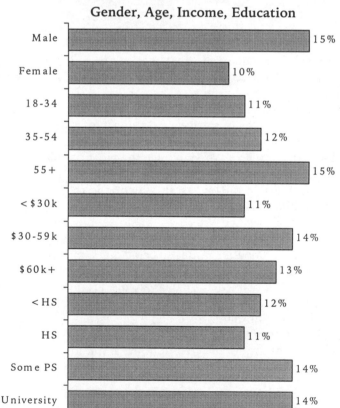

Gender, Age, Income, Education

- Male — 15%
- Female — 10%
- 18-34 — 11%
- 35-54 — 12%
- 55+ — 15%
- <$30k — 11%
- $30-59k — 14%
- $60k+ — 13%
- <HS — 12%
- HS — 11%
- Some PS — 14%
- University — 14%

Figure 3—Overall Situation of Aboriginal Peoples over the Past 10 Years

The question: When you take a look over the last 10 years, do you think things are improving, or they are getting worse, for natives? What you find is 41 percent of the population say the situation has improved for natives, and 22 percent say that it has worsened. One of the overall things that is going to come out of this presentation is that there really is some positive momentum behind the native agenda right now. People are thinking that things are moving in the right direction, as we're talking about land claims, about self-government, about resolving some of these issues. They do think that there is a step in the right direction.

Figure 3   Overall Situation of Aboriginal Peoples over the Past 10 Years (N = 2,550)

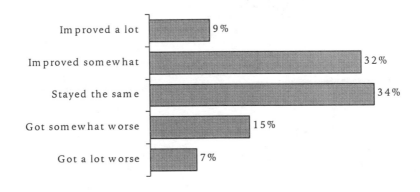

Figure 4—Personal Sympathy with Aboriginal Concerns

The question: What about your own personal sympathy about native issues? Would you say you have become more sympathetic, less sympathetic, or is it really just about the same? Thirty-five percent of the population says that over the last little while they have become more sympathetic. Only 15 percent say they have become less sympathetic. If I were doing this for a political party, I would say you have a rating of plus-20. In other words, when you take the people who are less sympathetic from the people who are more sympathetic, you are headed in the right direction there too. In terms of the overall level of belief that things are getting better for natives, people see that. And in terms of their own views about natives, they seem to be getting more sympathetic. At least they identify themselves as doing that.

Figure 4   **Personal Sympathy with Aboriginal Concerns**
(N = 2,550)

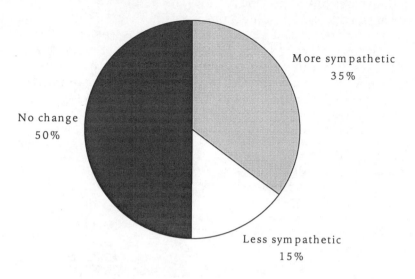

Figure 5—Most Important Issues Facing Canada's Aboriginals Today

These slides are very interesting, given the subject matter of this conference and the content of the discussion about native issues over the space of the last 10 years. The open-ended question is: when you think of issues confronting the native population in Canada these days, what would you say is the most important issue facing them today? Data collected since 1990, when we first conducted this survey at the time of the Oka crisis, show that what is really emerging as the number one issue facing the native community has nothing to do with self-government or land claims. [Instead], when you ask Canadians what they see facing aboriginal people today, the number one issue involve social pathologies. Alcoholism and drug abuse. Unemployment and racism. Now that's a sobering thought, given that some of these things that we're talking about have at best a tangential relationship to solving any of these problems.

You can continue down the list. Unemployment at 15 percent. What you find is that the political, or power, aspects of this have declined, and the social policy aspects have really increased over the space of the last 10 years.

Figure 5   Most Important Issues Facing Canada's Aboriginals
Today; Open-ended, Volunteered responses (N = 2,550)

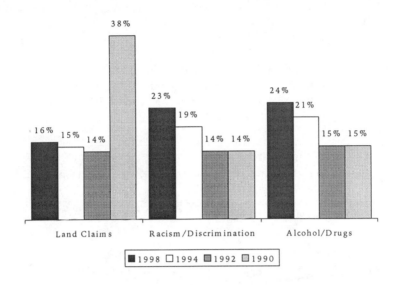

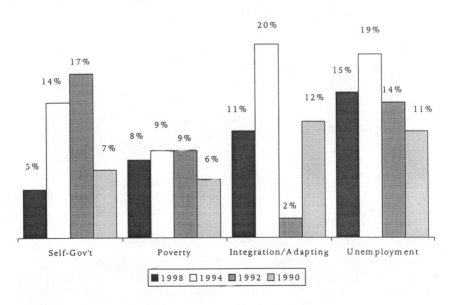

Note: Totals to more than 100%; up to *two* responses accepted

Figure 6—Perceptions and Attitudes about Aboriginal People, Life and Culture

When you ask people about what really gets them upset on the native agenda, it doesn't tend to be things like self-government and land claims. It tends to be things like, why do we have Third-World conditions in this country? Why do we have higher than average infant death rates in these populations? Why do I see what I see on the streets of downtown Edmonton, Saskatoon and Winnipeg? That's what Canadians are worried about, that's what they want to see solved. This legal stuff is all very interesting, but unless it leads to some of those solutions, people are not that interested.

Figure 6   Perceptions and Attitudes about Aboriginal People, Life and Culture; based on a 7-point scale (Agree 6, 7)

Figure 7—Standard of Living versus Average Canadian

Are natives better or worse off than the average Canadian? Sixty-three percent say that the native standard of living is worse than the average Canadian standard is. And that's universal across the country. That's what the public wants to deal with.

Figure 7 Standard of Living versus Average Canadian

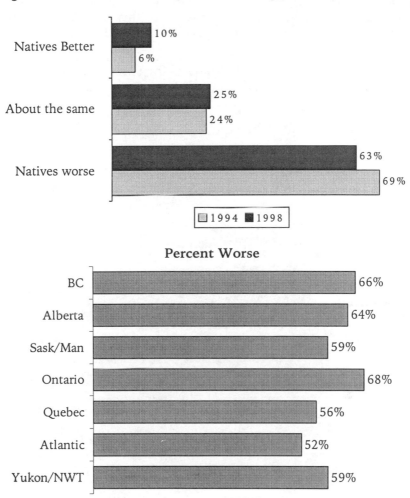

Percent Worse

Figure 8—Young Aboriginals Chances for Success in Life Compared to Young Canadians

Probably the most shocking number that I saw on this survey, not that I'm easily shocked, [involve opinions on] young aboriginal chances for success in life. Compared to young Canadians, many more think that the life chances of young aboriginals are very much disadvantaged than are the life chances of non-aboriginal Canadians in this country. The hope here, if anything, is that we'll be able to do something about this problem. Because when they talk about the linkage of social pathologies and life chances, they are talking about this group of young natives, and about trying to do something to salvage their lives.

Figure 8   Young Aboriginals Chances for Success in Life Compared to Young Canadians (N= 2,550)

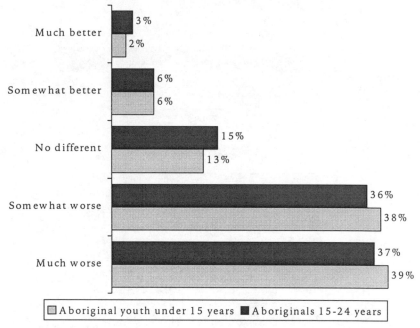

Note: Split sample. Each scenario presented to 1,275 respondents.

Figure 9—Awareness of Specific Aboriginal Issues

The question: Have you ever heard of the following things related to the aboriginal agenda? Remember that this is back in April of 1998. The federal government's apology to native Canadians: 71 percent had heard of that. Now remember, you've got a lot of yea-saying going on here. You don't know how many actually have, but you know that it's higher than for the ones that are lower in the bars here. The Royal Commission on Aboriginal Issues: 54 percent. Nisga'a: at 53 percent, obviously much higher in British Columbia. The creation of Nunavut was only 35 percent. The gathering strength initiative by the federal government, and *Delgamuukw*: 21 percent. Half of these people are lying. Why? [Because] what does it have to do with what they are worried about, which is solving those social problems?

Figure 9   Awareness of Specific Aboriginal Issues (% aware)

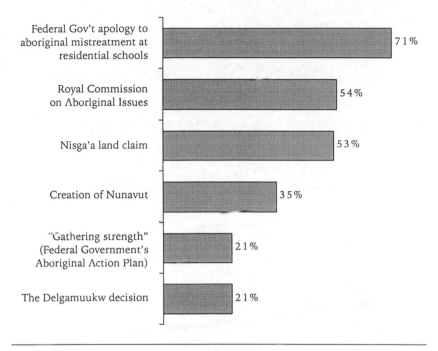

Self-Government

Figure 10—Perspective on the Concept of Aboriginal Self-Government

We asked this question back in September 1990 and again in April 1998: When you look at self-government, do natives have inherent right to self-government? Do they have a delegatable right? Or do they have no right to self-government? The majority, 62 percent of the population, says that at least some right to self-government exists within the native community. (What I would love to see someday is somebody doing a survey of aboriginal peoples on these issues. I haven't seen one that I thought was credible yet. It's the Mount Everest of doing social research in Canada—really doing an accurate survey of opinions, not just demography, but opinions of aboriginal Canadians themselves on some of these issues.) When you ask them about the inherent right that exists, they answer: No—and this is where you get the Canadian population and the aboriginal population to assert—it's a conditional right. Only 26 percent of the population actually believe that there is an inherent, non-conditional right to self-government.

The next level is for delegatable: 36 percent. And then finally, no right to self-government at all: 36 percent, a very significant minority.

Figure 10 Overall Perspective on the Concept of Aboriginal Self-Government (September 1990 to April 1998)

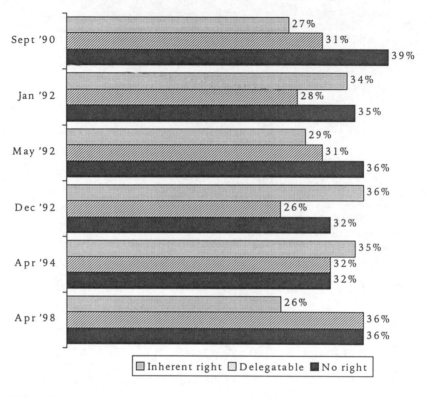

Figure 11—Nature of Self-Government

Again, we have been asking this question since January 1992, so we have five iteration of these data. What are Canadians looking at, consistent with their view of sort of a delegated power—a separate nation within a nation? No, it's not. Only 27 percent—although that's up dramatically—believe that it is. Is it like a provincial government? 28 percent of the population accept that. Or is it more like a municipality? 40 percent agree with that. Based on the number of focus groups that I've done on these issues, I can tell you that Canadians get very conservative, very fast, on these issues, when you move beyond the powers of a municipal government.

Figure 11 Nature of Self-Government

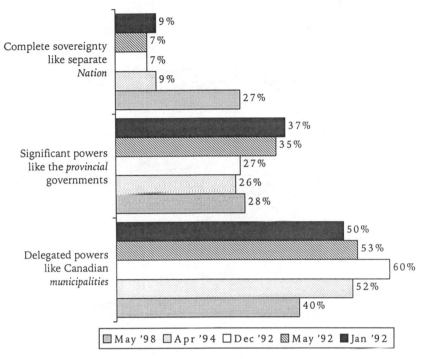

Complete sovereignty like separate *Nation*
- 9%
- 7%
- 7%
- 9%
- 27%

Significant powers like the *provincial* governments
- 37%
- 35%
- 27%
- 26%
- 28%

Delegated powers like Canadian *municipalities*
- 50%
- 53%
- 60%
- 52%
- 40%

☒May '98 ☑Apr '94 ☐Dec '92 ☒May '92 ■Jan '92

Figure 12—Canadians' Expectations for Self-Government

The question: What do you think aboriginal self-government will mean for the overall standard of living for aboriginal people? Fifty-five percent say that it's going to improve. Stay the same: in the mid-20s. Get worse: 18 percent. Now that's not exactly a stunning endorsement in terms of affecting the things that people want to have affected, is it?

Is it going to improve the standard of living? The Canadian population is basically split on that. They don't necessarily see the linkage between self-government and actually improving the day-to-day lives of the aboriginal peoples that they are worried about.

Figure 12 Canadians' Expectations for Self-Government— April 1994 to April 1998 (N = 2,550)

"What do you think aboriginal self-government will mean for the overall standard of living for Aboriginal peoples?"

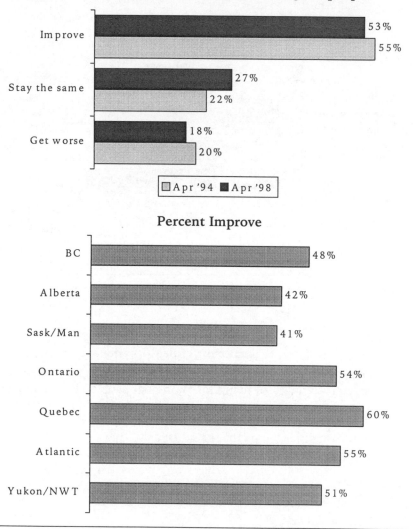

Figure 13—Canadians' Feelings about Aboriginal Self-Government

This is on a scale of 1 to 7, where 1 is strongly disagree and 7 is strongly agree. These are the people who gave 6 or 7 to these various responses.

The government should not be responsible for covering any financial problems aboriginal self-government may get into: 49 percent of the population agree with that. Based on all the research I've done on this, people believe that if you are going to govern yourself, you have to govern yourself. In other words, don't be coming back to us all the time asking for money. There has to be some finality to this.

Aboriginal peoples are fully capable of governing themselves competently: 40 percent of the population strongly agree with that point. So, yeah, you can do it, is basically what they are saying.

Even with self-government, the federal government should be responsible for ensuring that quality services are maintained by aboriginal governments: 38 percent agree with that. Basically, what they are telling us is similar to the way that they peruse and are responsible for the services that provincial governments provide to their citizens. The federal government has a similar role to play with aboriginal governments.

Government efforts have failed badly, so aboriginal people should take control of their own affairs: 27 percent of the population strongly agree with that. I would say that that is under-representing that opinion. People really do believe an awful lot when you talk about self-government: i.e. they can't do any worse than we have done.

Figure 13 Canadians' Feelings about Aboriginal Self-Government —Percent Agree (score 6 or 7) (N = 2,550)

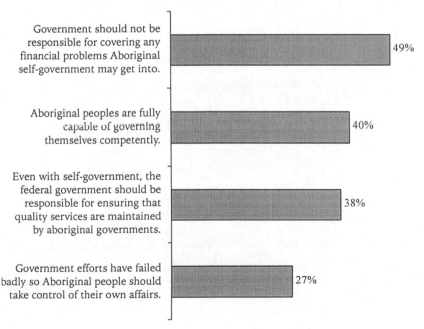

Figure 14—Tracking Canadians' Views on the Overall Legitimacy of Native Land Claims

How legitimate are land claims? No legitimate land claims, no compensation: 19 percent of the population agree with that. So, in other words, to make the argument that there is no such thing as a legitimate land claim doesn't wash in Canada. Some legitimate land claims are worthy of some compensation. Better than half support that. The last one is that all the claims are legitimate, they deserve full compensation. About a quarter of the population agrees with that. What you see from this is that people do want to talk about it. They believe that there is a basis to make these claims.

Figure 14 Tracking Canadians' Views on the Overall Legitimacy of Native Land Claims

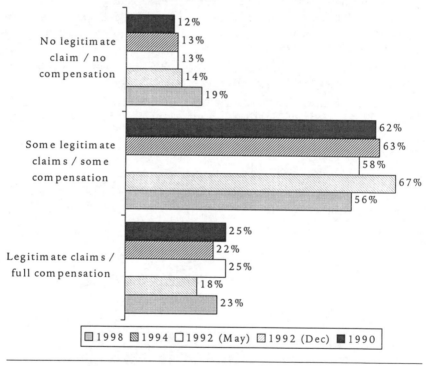

Figure 15—Preferred Approach for Addressing Aboriginal Land Claims

And how do they want to deal with it? Negotiate, don't litigate. This is again consistent: 62 percent of the population say have a treaty negotiation process; 34 percent say let the courts decide.

You see the story beginning to develop here?

Figure 15   Preferred Approach for Addressing Aboriginal Land Claims

Do nothing 1%   Other 3%

Let courts decide 34%

Treaty negotiation process 62%

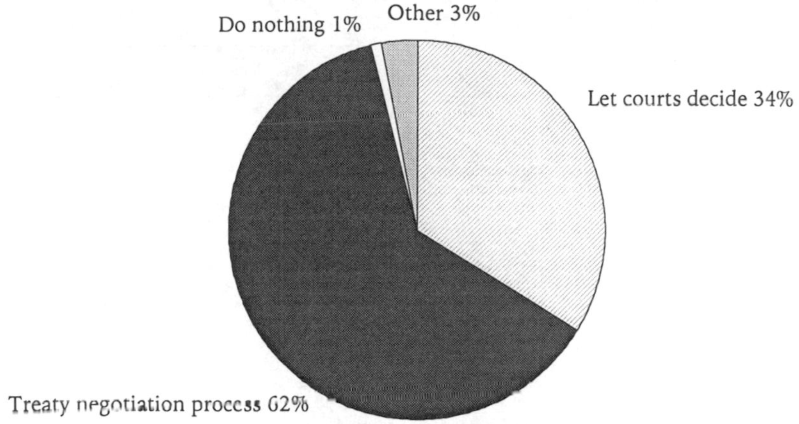

Figure 16—Possible Impacts of Aboriginal Land Claims

This is the percentage of the population that strongly agrees, so this is 6 or 7 on a 7-point scale, where 1 is strongly disagree with this statement; 7 is strongly agree. The first is after treaty's signed, same rights for all: 73 percent agree with that. This is one of the things that the aboriginal negotiators and other people are going to have to realize as part of the aboriginal community: if you are going to negotiate a self-government agreement, or you are going to negotiate something that's supposed to settle this in terms of land claims, it has got to settle it. And you know what? To a certain extent, it means that you'll have a very difficult time trying to sell the concept. Even though we say different doesn't always mean that it's unequal, Canadians have a hard time with that. Principally what we have seen over the space of the last 15 to 20 years in Canada is that the concept of equality has become very ingrained in the Canadian psyche. That's why the government of Quebec has such a hard time talking about distinct society status for people in the province of Quebec. Canadians don't buy that. So if it is a similar sort of approach to aboriginal self-government, you've got some problems.

Will there be reduced confrontations and protests? Yes, they should go down: 39 percent. Settle land claims to give aboriginals sound financial basis for the future: 37 percent agree with that. But in comparison to this other point, everything else pales. The one in B.C. that we asked, just focusing on treaties helping businesses in B.C., only 17 percent strongly agree with that point. In British Columbia, treaty negotiations and settlement are not necessarily linked to economic progress.

Figure 16 Possible Impacts of Aboriginal Land Claims
Percent Agree 6/7 on 7 point scale

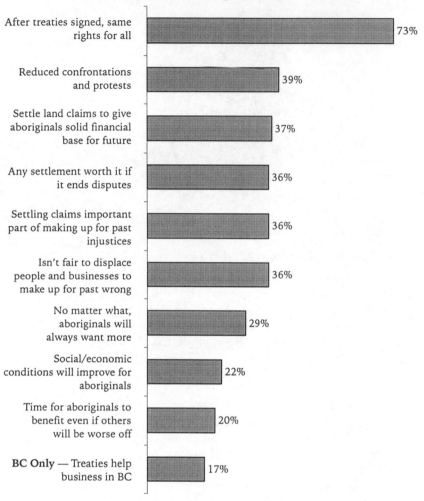

After treaties signed, same rights for all	73%
Reduced confrontations and protests	39%
Settle land claims to give aboriginals solid financial base for future	37%
Any settlement worth it if it ends disputes	36%
Settling claims important part of making up for past injustices	36%
Isn't fair to displace people and businesses to make up for past wrong	36%
No matter what, aboriginals will always want more	29%
Social/economic conditions will improve for aboriginals	22%
Time for aboriginals to benefit even if others will be worse off	20%
BC Only — Treaties help business in BC	17%

Figures 17 to 19—Reasonability Regarding Land Claims Negotiation of Position on Land Claims by Region Regarding Land Claims Negotiations (BC Only)

Who's being more fair and reasonable here? In April 1998, the feds have a 10-point lead over the aboriginals. I didn't think I'd see that. This is becoming a lot more controversial as time goes on. Actually, when you go into the individual provinces, the provinces rank further ahead than the federal government. Interestingly enough, it becomes more controversial in B.C., where it's more competitive. The problem in B.C. is that this is all beginning to shake out, and people are starting to feel this in their day-to-day lives. For example, what's happening in Musqueam right now is really bad for this. I don't care about all the legal arguments, about who is right and who is wrong, but the impression of the public is: is this turnabout fair play? In other words, is this what we can expect under native self-government? Is this what we can expect in terms of attitude from the native community when they have their chance to govern? And the answer coming back is: now I am more uncomfortable.

So again, looking across the country, and looking at who is more reasonable, the only place where the natives actually lead is in Ontario where this issue matters about the least. In B.C. it's not going very well.

Figure 17 Reasonability Regarding Land Claims Negotiations (Percent reasonable)

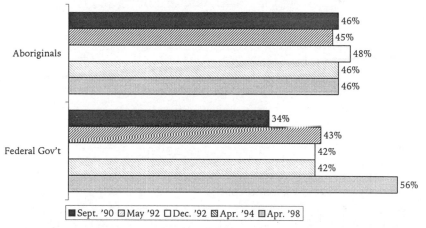

Aboriginals — 46%, 45%, 48%, 46%, 46%

Federal Gov't — 34%, 43%, 42%, 42%, 56%

■Sept. '90 ☐May '92 ☐Dec. '92 ☒Apr. '94 ☐Apr. '98

Figure 18 Reasonability Regarding Land Claims Negotiations (BC Only)

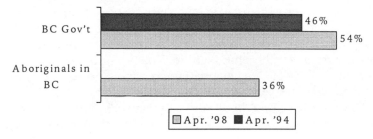

BC Gov't — 46%, 54%

Aboriginals in BC — 36%

☐Apr. '98 ■Apr. '94

Figure 19 Reasonability of Position on Land Claims by Region

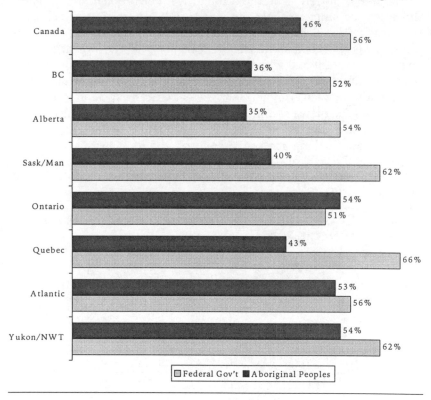

Federal Gov't ■ Aboriginal Peoples

*Figure 20—A Pyschographic Segmentation of the Canadian
    Population on Aboriginal Issues*

Psychographic segmentation is basically cluster analysis. All of you
who took Statistics 270 in Political Science know what I'm talking
about. In this instance, what cluster analysis does is take the responses
from 2,550 people and, based on how they answered those questions,
break them into certain groups that are logically consistent. I'll give you
an example of this. Imagine, for example, we took 2,550 people and put
them in a room, and asked them to find the people who they were most
comfortable talking to about aboriginal issues and assimilate with
them in the corner, and become a group. That's essentially what the
computer does. It puts people together in like-mindsets. In other
words, people who are very supportive, against people who are very
against. Then you have everybody who is in between. The reason that
you do this type of analysis is that you are not going to find the average

Canadian on this issue. There is no average Canadian. It is all levels of extreme, one way or the other. And that is similar to, I guess, the old statistical joke about means, and the problem with arithmetic means whenever you are doing it. That's not your statistical average. If your head is in the freezer and your feet are in the furnace, your middle is absolutely perfect. There are no people who are absolutely perfect here. It is a matter of fairly inconsistent and extreme opinions all over the place. So what I try to do, using the computer, is to actually sort these people into groups.

On aboriginal issues this is really, really important because there is an opportunity here to build a coalition in support of aboriginal issues, and there is an opportunity for coalition to fall apart. This shows how those coalitions are made up, and how one would go about building a coalition.

For example, I would usually do this for a political candidate. Tell them how to build the percentage of the vote that they have to win in order to win an election. And I want to take it from five groups: the committed advocates; the ambivalent patrons; fair-minded pragmatists; skeptical opponents; and confident hard-liners.

Figure 20 A Pyschographic Segmentation of the Canadian Population on Aboriginal Issues

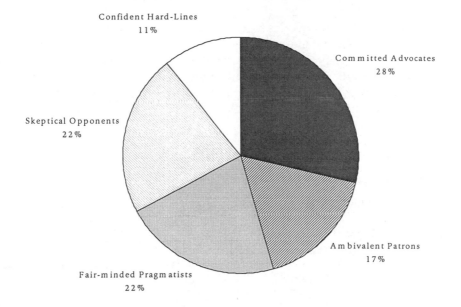

Figure 21 Committed Advocates (29%)

- Strongest supporters of aboriginals
- Immediate justice
- Accept special status, self-government, land claims
- Increase aboriginal control
- Like Federal Government's affirmative approach but want more
- New Canadians, Ontario, highly educated, Liberal voters

The people who are the most supportive constitute 29 percent of the population. They are the strongest supporters of aboriginals. They believe in immediate justice. Anything that is happening right now on the aboriginal issue, as far as they are concerned, is too slow—we must move quicker. They accept special status. The question I raised before, about 73 percent saying there can't be separate but equal but different, these people don't have a problem with that at all. That's fine as far as they are concerned. So the federal government's line on Nisga'a in B.C., where you don't have to be treated the same to be treated equally, these guys would say absolutely, that's true. Not a problem. They accept special status, self-government, and land claims. They believe there needs to be an increase in aboriginal control over their own lives, and are really very supportive of aboriginal self-government. They like the federal government's affirmative approach, but they want more. They want the government to move more quickly. They tend to be newer Canadians; they tend to be disproportionately in Ontario; they are highly educated; and they are Liberal voters. So, if you are a government that has 100 seats in the province of Ontario, you would really care about what these guys think. They only represent 29 percent of the population though.

Figure 22 Ambivalent Patrons (17%)

- Strong supporters of aboriginals
- Federal Government catalyst for improvement, need to do more
- Worried about impact of redress on non-aboriginals
- Paternalistic—natives not ready yet
- Less informed, younger, Ontario

Ambivalent patrons add another 17 percent. But these people are more conditional. Why are they ambivalent? They are strong supporters of the aboriginal community. In other words, these people are not racist. They are comfortable with aboriginal people and support their cultural, their focus on culture and all that sort of thing . They are very supportive of the federal government's involvement, and very supportive of the federal government pushing. However, they are worried about the impact of redress on non-aboriginals. That's why they are more conditional. It's not just a question of: "We are going to do this because this is what is good for the aboriginal people." They want to know how it is going to affect them too. Although they are more willing to listen, probably more willing to give than some other folks, they tend to be a bit paternalistic. They tend to think that natives may not necessarily be ready yet. They tend to less informed; younger; in Ontario.

So, again, 17 percent plus 29 equals what it equals. The whole coalition, really, for aboriginal self-government is disproportionately in the province of Ontario. Now, I should say that these people are represented all throughout the country. Ontario is just a tendency. It tends to be more than average in the province of Ontario.

Figure 23 Fair-Minded Pragmatists (22%)

- Somewhat assimilationist
- Make a deal to get rid of the "problem"
- do land claims, settle-up, move on—but, be fair to non-natives
- Couldn't do worse than current government
- Quebec, French speaking, middle income, less educated

Fair-minded pragmatists: 22 percent of the population. If you are going to build a coalition that is more than a majority, slightly more than fifty, you have to have these guys, because you move from 46 to 69. These are the people that you have to win, if you are going to communicate on these issues. The solid middle ground. Somewhat assimilationist in their perspective, they want to make a deal to get rid of the problem. In other words, they want to see some finality in this: "Put it aside. We want to do a deal so we can get this behind us. Do land claims, settle up, move on, but be fair to the non-natives." In other words, you just can't do what's good for the native community, you also have to worry about the people who are going to be affected directly by this. Again: "They can't do any worse for themselves than what we've done for them." So a bit of throwing up your hands. They tend to be disproportionately in Quebec; French-speaking; middle-income; less-educated. We haven't got the B.C. group here yet, do we? Although there is a large, large portion of each of these groups in that province too. Those are demographic tendencies.

Figure 24 Skeptical Opponents (28%)

- Question need for action
- Skeptical more than opposed
- Equality driven be fair to non-aboriginals
- Cut them loose, but skeptical of self-government
- Don't want to perpetuate aboriginal dependency
- Ambivalent on self-government, land claims
- Older, French speaking, middle income

Skeptical opponents: again, a fairly sizable group of the population, better than a quarter. They question the need for action at all. Skeptical, more than opposed. To the extent that you tell them that something is going to solve a problem, they want to see some evidence and proof that it is actually going to solve it. So these guys will be worried about the social pathologies and actually having a positive effect on those. Equality-driven: "You have to be fair to non-aboriginals; cut them loose. But they are skeptical about the effect of self-government on those social pathologies that I mentioned before. Don't want to perpetuate aboriginal dependency, ambivalent on self-government, land claims. Older; disproportionately French-speaking; middle-income. Again, these are demographic tendencies. These people also exist in BC and around the country.

Figure 25 Confident Hard-Linders (11%)

- Reject special treatment
- Little sympathy, don't accept responsibility for the past
- Well informed
- Strongly assimilationist

- Government wastes too much time on this
- Too dependent, architects of own problems
- Reject self-government, land claims
- Male, middle-aged, Canadian Born, more affluent, Reform votes

---

And finally, the confident hard-liners: about 11 percent of the population. This is: "No way, we are not going to do this at all. We don't care." Aboriginal agenda is of no interest to me whatsoever. They reject special treatment, and that's what they see this as. Little sympathy, don't accept responsibility for the past. It is interesting when you get into focus groups with people like this. Basically, the line they give you is, "Excuse me, I didn't do anything. Why are you punishing me? That may have been my ancestors, but that was my ancestors, so why are we changing it now? And why am I responsible, and why am I paying for it?" They tend to be very well informed. I am adding the word very because they do tend to be well informed. They tend to know more. When I talk to people in focus groups, these guys tend to be really on the ball. They know what is going on. They have read the material. And they disagree with it. They are strongly assimilationist, and you hear this when you go out in focus groups and talk to these folks: they say, if they just became like us, it would all be fine. Government wastes too much time on this. It is not a priority. They see the natives as too dependent and as architects of their own problems: if the native community has any problems, they did it to themselves. They reject self-government and land claims. They are male; middle-aged; Canadian-born; more affluent—Reform voters.

See what we are dealing with here? We want to build a coalition. Committed advocates, plus ambivalent patrons, plus fair-minded pragmatists, equals majority support. Are you ever going to convince the confident hard-liners to change their minds? I doubt it. Don't waste your time. And do you have to kowtow to the committed advocates? No, because if you kowtow to the committed advocates, the fair-minded pragmatists won't have anything to do with you.

Obviously the place you are shooting for is this 22 percent. These guys are the ones that are the key to this whole debate. They want a certain amount of assimilation; they want to solve the problem; they want to get this thing; they want a deal. And they also believe that rather than holding out a lot of hope for aboriginal self-government, it is now their turn: "They can't do any worse for themselves than we have done for them."

Conclusion

First, there is a general sense among the Canadian population that life for aboriginal people is improving. In other words, there is some positive momentum happening on the aboriginal file. The major issues for the future are not land claims and self-government, they are youth and social policies. Land claims, and especially self-government, are of lesser importance. Of the two, land claims are more important. However, both have tremendous potential for controversy, depending on how they are positioned, and how they are brought to the Canadian population.

Major issues for any settlements are equality—in other words, treating people who are non-aboriginals at least as well as you are treating the people who are benefiting from the settlement; and finality—once we have signed the settlement, it is done. Finally, Canadians get conservative very quickly on this issue, particularly if it violates the tenets of finality and equality.

Questions

Roland Ponguis (Land Rights Director with the Assembly of First Nations) You focussed on what we call the symptoms, the social pathologies. It is funny that Canadians don't make the connection between the two issues, because that is what we call the symptoms of the deprivation of lands and resources, as well as self-government.

Bricker   I think that is a very important point. What it underscores is that there has to be a linkage between land claims, and self-government. The problem is that we don't hear much talk about that. What we hear a lot of talk about is justice. We don't hear a lot of talk about solutions. If I were advising the native community on putting together a communications strategy on this, I would be talking an awful lot about how these settlements lead to solving these problems. But we don't hear enough about that. It's about Constitutions, big government, power. People aren't interested.

Gordon Gibson   These data you indicate come from people who are relatively uninformed. Do you have an instinct as to how the data will shift with increasing information? I understand it depends on the kind of information. With that caveat, can you give us any insights on that?

Bricker   It depends on what jurisdiction you are talking about. I would say that for the short-term in B.C., these data are going to go decidedly negative. Unfortunately, the *Nisga'a* agreement has been linked with a government that is not especially popular right now with the public. I am being very subtle on this. So, the degree to which there is a linkage isn't going to help. But there are also a lot of unanswered questions about *Nisga'a* that a lot of people just try to paper over with platitudes. For example: "You don't have to be treated the same to be treated equally." Well, I'm sorry. You are not going to get anyone to accept that. They don't believe that. That's just a silly thing to say. And to the extent that that is the rhetoric of the people who are trying to sell this—which is sort of like saying to the population, "there, there, you just don't understand"—it is going to fail, in terms of public opinion terms. There has to be a full and frank discussion of what all of this means.

When you talk to people in focus groups about native issues you find that the more information on the table, the better. The fewer platitudes, the better. When people do get the real stuff on the table, they can deal with it. They can discount it depending on the source that it came from, but at least they feel they know the facts. And in fact, when you do focus on the facts, you tend to find that people move to the more affirmative side, because their *suspicions* about what it is about tend to be a lot worse than what it really is about. At least when you talk to them and you let them make a choice. But that is the problem—we tend to deal with the public as being incapable of forming a reasonable opinion on this, based on the facts. When I go out to BC and talk to people about this, I find that you spend the first hour yelling at each other. But after a while, people come to the conclusion that you are going to have to come up with a settlement, or you are going to have the courts impose it. We already know what people think about the courts. And you know what? It is going to be coming from Ottawa rather than from here, which really bothers people.

If anything, I would say to anybody on this: get out there, talk about it, get the facts on the table. [Facts] tend to move people in the right direction.

Gordon Gibson   Well, it seems inconsistent that you say British Columbia is both going to become more knowledgeable and more negative. It contradicts what you said now.

Bricker   It is going to be a two-stage thing. The problem is that they are dealing with things like Musqueam, which is not helping. The more they hear stories like that, the worse this is going to get. To the extent that that is the information people have about the treaties, and that is the information that they are going to have about self-government and aboriginal land claims, British Columbia is going to become very combustible. I am not talking just about a lack of rain here. It is going to be a very, very difficult situation for anybody on this issue, until somebody is prepared to get out there and just lay the straight facts on the table. Stop trying to sell this, and just tell people really what the facts are. And the government of B.C., for example, has really erred on the side of trying to sell this, with its advertising program on television and everything else. It is not done well.

Question   It seems that self-government means that aboriginal communities are going to run their own affairs, at least to some extent, and they are going to be different. How does one address that and get more people on side for that idea, given their strong beliefs in equality?

Bricker   You are asking me to square a circle. It is going to be a very difficult set of circumstances. When we are talking about self-government, it really depends how we are talking about operationalizing self-government. If we are talking about a place that has got its own local community police force with fairly limited powers vis-à-vis the rest of the population—that runs like a municipal government; is able to tax in a fairly limited way like municipal governments are—that is a lot more of an acceptable proposition to the public. When they become more exposed to that, my view is that it should go reasonably well. But the problem is, they don't know. And, when we talk about what government is going to be, for example, in the Nishga territory, nobody really seems to know. They don't know how the people out there are going to be affected by it, and they don't know what kind of precedent *Nisga'a* sets for the rest of the self-government agreements, negotiations, and land claim settlements that are taking place in other jurisdictions. So the problem is that we have got to get some facts on the table here about what it is, and what it isn't. If they negotiated some things that just won't work in terms of public opinion, deal with it. But right now, what we have is a lot of talk about justice and fairness and what's good and what's bad, rather than a focus on what the facts are.

And my personal view of this—I am not supposed to have any, but I will just offer one up—is that the facts will set you free. At the end of the day, if you get the facts on the table, and they are as they are being communicated, then you should be fine.

Fundamental Principles for Treaty Making

Gordon F. Gibson

Introduction

Notwithstanding all of the well-publicized difficulties, it is clear that the business of treaty making with aboriginal tribes will continue in Canada, and especially in British Columbia. For those who are concerned with the course of the current process, there is an obligation to suggest alternate approaches. In discussing this, a few caveats should be noted at the beginning.

First, one should say what treaty-making does *not* achieve. Many people think that treaty making is synonymous with the comprehensive resolution of aboriginal/non-aboriginal issues. *This is simply not true*. Treaties are chiefly of importance to status Indians living on Indian lands. But this is a minority of aboriginals.

Of the approximately 1.1 million Canadians identified by the 1996 Census as of aboriginal ancestry, almost 300,000 no longer self-identified as aboriginals as such. The assumption is that they have made the choice to integrate into the larger society, and apart from special considerations such as occasional cultural contacts or cash entitlements from treaty settlements, which are probably rare for this category, treaties mean little.

Notes will be found on pages 518–519.

Beyond that, of those who *do* continue to self-identify as aboriginals, only about half are, or will be, highly affected by treaties.

Some of these approximately 800,000 self-identifiers were Métis, Inuit, or non-registered Indians. Of the approximately 488,000 registered Indians identified in the 1996 Census, about 54 percent lived off-reserve, mostly in urban settings. Adjusting for known data problems,[1] the off-reserve proportion declines to a bit under 50 percent. While these people may have a legal connection with treaties (by way of ratification voting, for example) by far the major impact of treaties will be within the boundaries of the identified land base. Natives living off their land base and urban natives will continue to live under ordinary provincial laws and receive provincially-delivered[2] services unless they choose to return to the land base. (Such a return, of course, even in the face of fewer opportunities for employment, is one of the hopes of some aboriginal treaty makers.)

An example of this on-reserve/off-reserve disconnect was seen in the ratification vote for the Nisga'a Treaty in the fall of 1998. According to government statistics, some 3,300 Nisga'a should have been eligible to vote. In spite of extensive advertising and other attempts to register people, in spite of the great importance of the vote, and in spite of the special arrangements in the treaty to provide for "urban locals" in Vancouver, Prince Rupert, and Terrace, only about 2,400 persons actually voted. On the reasonable assumption that most of the "missing" 900 were off-reserve, that suggests an off-reserve participation rate in this once-in-a-lifetime event that could rationally be expected to have positive financial consequences for those voting, of only about 50 percent.

More generally, statistics from the somewhat earlier Royal Commission on Aboriginal Peoples (RCAP) suggested that for self-identifying aboriginals[3] overall, only about 35 percent live on-reserve, and of the balance, some 45 percent live in urban areas (very broadly defined) while the other 20 percent are rural.

In short, while treaties, which contemplate reserve-type situations, are extremely important to some aboriginals, that cohort is only something like one-third of the total census-identified aboriginals, and less than one half of the self-identified. Far too little attention is paid to the off-reserve group, and yet aboriginal ghettos are becoming a major issue in western cities such as Winnipeg, Regina and Saskatoon,[4] and very important in Vancouver's Downtown Eastside.

Those left out

It is a shocking truth that while the privation and adjustment problems of reserve Indians arriving in urban settings are often greater than those of foreign immigrants arriving in Canada, the latter have a major financial and institutional support system, while the urban Indians are largely ignored.

Notwithstanding this, *RCAP data show clearly that in terms of jobs, incomes, education, life expectancy, lesser reliance on welfare, lower family violence, and other such indicators, off-reserve Indians and other aboriginals do much better than those on-reserve.* Of course, treaties seek to increase the incentives for Indians to stay on-reserve. That amounts to a clear choice in favour of the one route of the above three that has historically yielded by far the worst socio-economic outcomes (the other two involving greater or lesser contact with the general, off-reserve community).

Equally strange is the near-total indifference of most of the Indian Industry[5] to the estate of the roughly 300,000 people of aboriginal ancestry who no longer self-identify as aboriginals. These are people who appear to have "voted with their feet" in a cultural sense, and become ordinary Canadians. How well are they making out? The best the $58 million Royal Commission could do was to footnote that there is some evidence that these people have "socio-economic characteristics quite similar to Canadians as a whole."

Think about that for a moment. If this is the case, those of aboriginal ancestry who have left the culture (in a self-identification sense) are quite similar to ordinary Canadians in terms of health, suicide, employment, incomes, education, substance-abuse, and so on. What does this suggest? Benign neglect of such an important question is understandable in terms of what turned out to be the Royal Commission's agenda. Still, it is surely not right in human terms that the Commission's researchers were not instructed to follow this question to its logical end.

Treaties as the "flavour of the decade"

The above said, the more glamorous treaty issues are centre stage in British Columbia, and under current thinking of government and aboriginal leaders will increasingly become so across the country. Many may feel, as Pierre Trudeau famously said almost thirty years ago, that it is unconscionable that Canadians should be making treaties among themselves. That remains my personal view in this context.[6]

There are indeed outstanding items to be settled between aboriginals and others, but these issues can and should be seen as simply very important matters of the law of property rights. Remedies (including compensation) should be resolved by negotiation if possible, or some mix of litigation and legislation if need be.

The courts at all levels have consistently expressed a preference for the parties to settle their differences by negotiation, but have not insisted on treaties as the final settlement instrument. However treaties, which are given constitutional recognition and protection under S.35(3) of the

1982 Constitution (as amended in 1984), arguably can give a degree of certainty not available in an ordinary agreement. This is particularly important in British Columbia, given the immense legal uncertainties stemming from the Supreme Court of Canada's 1997 Delgamuukw decision.

The essence of Delgamuukw is that Indian title existed in BC prior to the effective extension of British sovereignty, and continues to exist as a burden on land titles unless properly discharged. Where title still resides in the Crown, the burden must be recognized and dealt with by agreement. When title has been or will be irredeemably infringed (as is permitted for good public purposes, presumably including the grant of fee simple title to private interests), compensation is due.

From the point of view of all concerned, this uncertainty needs to be resolved. From the point of view of *governments*, compensation for past infringement is a very touchy issue, both in terms of overall dollars, and public reaction. Accordingly in British Columbia, both those Indians who are the legitimate inheritors of Delgamuukw rights and governments have an incentive to sort these issues out in a mutually agreeable way. One technique for doing so is to make treaties which, with respect to the subject area of the province, trump the Delgamuukw uncertainties as a result of the constitutional primacy referred to above.

Political realities are also important, and the flavour of the decade is "treaties" as the vehicle for settling outstanding issues. The concept fits well with the "nation-to-nation" perspective accepted by governments in both Ottawa and Victoria (though not by the Official Opposition in either capital). If governments insist on continuing down this path, we need to study the best way of so doing.

Unfortunately, the process followed to date, which has found its first full flowering in the Nisga'a Treaty, has been extremely controversial with the public. That is not good. Quite independent of the merits of the Nisga'a Treaty itself, in a democracy the issue of process is central. Better ways—ways more fully supported by the general public—should be found. Indeed, if the current government of BC is replaced by the Opposition (as the polls indicate will be the strong likelihood at the moment) better ways will *have to be found*, given the Opposition's rejection of much of the current policy.

But those who have difficulty with the approach being taken to treaties at the moment have an obligation to propose a better way. That is the purpose of this essay.

Constraints

As we consider the fundamental principles that should inform a new treaty process, we must remind ourselves that all future actions must be taken in the light of the historical situations we have inherited.

Therefore an "ideal" set of principles, such as those that follow, may require political adaptation to the case at hand. The history and circumstances of every tribe are different; their needs and goals are different. Solutions that vary from this or any other purely principled point of view may well be necessary for agreement. However, policy makers should at least have a place to start, from which point they can make such changes as they believe reality requires.

As a second, somewhat related caveat, some of the principles set out below will be deeply threatening to the practical interests of members of the "Indian Industry." This group has blossomed in the past generation to include many thousands of participants, including members of Indian elites, bureaucrats, members of the aboriginal bar, and a myriad of consultants, who gain their livelihood solely as a result of the existence of legal and other differences between Indians and ordinary Canadians. Without such differences, their present work and/or status would not exist.

It is not surprising, therefore, that these industry participants are overwhelmingly dedicated to maintaining and serving these differences. It is their *raison d'être*. Many of the members of this industry, like any other so closely linked to the well-being of people, want a better world, and are thoroughly and selflessly dedicated to their work. But for most of us who are ordinary human beings, experience teaches that any change which poses a threat to our status and income is invariably and fiercely resisted. The arguments used against change by members of the industry seldom refer to this deeply personal interest, but it is a fact of life.

As the principles to be set out below would, over time, reduce the legal and policy frameworks that sustain differences between Indians and ordinary Canadians (leaving only those differences voluntarily chosen by individuals following their own cultural wishes), one may expect the leadership of the Indian Industry (i.e., those with the greatest stake in the maintenance of difference between Indians and others) to oppose change with vigour and tenacity. This observation does not of itself challenge any given position taken, but rather suggests that all arguments in this field need to be examined with special care.

As a third caveat, and as noted above, the author believes that the concept of treaties between groups of Canadians defined on the basis of their racial and/or cultural heritage is in and of itself objectionable. That said, 132 years of constitutional mistakes (beginning with the singling out of "Indians" in the BNA Act, 1867) and Supreme Court decisions may arguably have left treaties as the easiest option, short of amending the Constitution, which is an even more difficult exercise.

Again, continued litigation might well yield faster answers than the interminable talks we have seen to date, but each side is worried about "rolling the dice." We will almost certainly see further litigation to clarify some legal issues, but negotiation will equally likely be the tool to finish the job of settlement. Thus, to that extent, what follows is a "practical" approach, and the best we can do under the circumstances of history.

Principles and requirements of treaty content

A treaty, as used in the North American aboriginal sense, is an instrument designed to settle past and existing differences, and provide for future relationships. In many ways, questions of *process* are as important as questions of substance. Both will be canvassed here.

Mandating and ratification

Treaties are agreements between two or more collectivities. When collectivities make agreements, it is important that they have the widest possible support. In earlier times in European history, treaties were made by leaders, with little concern for the wishes of their people.

However, the practice on the aboriginal side of the table seems to have always been more consensual. Advance discussion on the aboriginal side today often (though not always)[7] can provide for a well-mandated set of negotiators, a well-informed membership, and a direct voice of each member in ratification once the mandate is actually achieved.[8]

That said, aboriginal mandating typically supports the options held out by the elites, which options always support their own continued hegemony. No mandating in favour of a level playing field for urban Indians outside of elite control, or in favour of individual as opposed to collective rights (cash distributions of all settlement proceeds, for example) will easily get through this sieve.

There is a major lack of aboriginal mandating in one other very important sense. Territorial *overlaps* exist on many of the land claims in British Columbia. The Nisga'a settlement is currently in litigation brought by two neighbouring tribes, claiming an award of their land to the Nisga'a band. Since the foundation of treaty negotiations in British Columbia is based on land claims, the territorial bounds of those claims should be made specific, distinct, and mutually exclusive (unless there is an agreement as to joint tenancy) *before* negotiations are begun.

The lack of such a requirement is a serious flaw in the BC Treaty Commission process.[9] Some aboriginal spokesmen say this requirement for the elimination of overlap is simply an attempt to divide the aboriginal side. The other side of the table should say, reasonably, that in the first place, areas of misunderstanding should be reduced, and second, one should not have to pay for the same thing twice.

There is another technical, but extremely important aspect of mandating from the aboriginal side. To the extent that what is being negotiated is the resolution of Delgamuukw rights, it must be the possessor of those rights who is at the table. Unfortunately, band groupings, or even tribal councils, may not be synonymous with the owners of Delgamuukw rights. A striking example is apparent in the Okanagan, where the Westbank Band is close to an Agreement in Principle, but is almost certainly not the holder of Delgamuukw rights for the area.

As a practical aspect of mandating, it must also be asked whether the aboriginal entity at the table is of sufficient size to have the ongoing capacity to use extensive treaty rights. Even the Nisga'a—one of the larger groupings—certainly do not have anything like the human resources and population density to use a fraction of the stipulated self-government powers which exceed those of even the largest municipality. Some of the bands in negotiation have as few as 400 hundred members, and the largest is under 10,000. Does this make sense?

The mandating practice on the non-aboriginal side of the table is still rooted in earlier times. To be sure, the negotiators have instructions from governments, but none from the people or the people's representatives—i.e., elected MPs or MLAs. Far from seeking mandates from the citizenry, governments[10] in Canada and British Columbia have not even sought negotiating mandates from their legislatures. *This is simply unacceptable in so fundamental an area, and is a direct cause of much of the controversy in British Columbia today.*

For example, the terms and implications of the Nisga'a Treaty came as a great surprise to most British Columbians. Governments went through certain "consultation" motions, but concealed information about negotiating targets, minimized problems, and chose not to highlight questions of principle for public debate. Accordingly, when the final treaty was first unveiled, public opinion was well disposed, but confused. Initial goodwill has soured as the implications sink in. With growing familiarity the public balance of opinion has, as at this writing, turned clearly against the treaty.[11]

While there is room to discuss different forms of ratification in the far larger non-aboriginal public (as distinct from the direct referendum vote available to each Indian person), it is absolutely clear that the mandating process at the beginning must be thorough and unambiguous. Only thus can general public support be gained. The idea is not to hamstring the negotiators in such matters as quantum of land or cash for settlement purposes, but rather to define the principles and the boundaries of discussion. (For example, will the Charter apply fully to Indian organizations through the waiving of S. 25, or not? Is a "Third Order" of government on the table?)

The choice of negotiator is also of great importance. For the aboriginal side of the table, this is a weighty matter, to be much discussed. For the government side, the general practice has been to give the lead to the federal or provincial aboriginal department (Indian and Northern Affairs, or the Ministry of Aboriginal Affairs). This is wrong. These ministries are deeply conflicted.

Federal and provincial aboriginal departments have a fiduciary and/or advocacy relationship for their aboriginal clientele. Thus, they cannot properly at the same time represent the larger public interest. Governments have sought to compensate for this by having mandates flow from Cabinet, but the fact is that Indian matters are seen by most Ministers as misery best left to others, i.e., the responsible departments. Fortunately, the immense financial and political consequences of treaty making will increasingly bring negotiators squarely under the control of the First Minister, or the Finance Minister in the future.

Within the mandating context, it is also important to consider the positions of third parties and local governments. These private and public entities have large and legitimate interests in the negotiations of treaties. Attempts have been made to involve these interests on an ongoing basis, but they have been clearly unsatisfactory. The secrecy that shrouds the real horse-trading and decision-making is the barrier here. Clear public mandating about principles will make these tensions easier to resolve.

Reconciliation

Reconciliation is the fundamental articulated goal[12] of the treaty process, emphasized frequently by the courts. There is a general wish among all Canadians that we should live together in goodwill and harmony. That means it is highly desirable that arrangements be voluntarily accepted by all concerned if reconciliation is to be achieved. It is this very strong wish by the majority of Canadians that gives great bargaining strength to the numerically tiny aboriginal side of the table. Aboriginals must agree, or the deal may not meet the "reconciliation" test.

However this does not imply an aboriginal veto on all future arrangements. In democracies everywhere, majorities reserve the right to eventually impose reasonable ground rules on minorities if that is the only way to resolve urgent and important questions. Even in the face of constitutional difficulties, ways can invariably be found to do this. Thus for example certain outstanding issues in the BC treaty process could be resolved, *in extremis* and lacking agreement, by federal legislation. But minorities have their legal and public relations weapons as well, thus arguing powerfully for agreement.

It is true that court decisions have been very important in enhancing the aboriginal bargaining position, but ultimately public opinion is the strongest force in the balance of power at the bargaining table. Of course, since public opinion in this area is woefully uninformed on the hard issues of winners and losers, and on the controversial enhancement of difference between Canadians rather than a convergence to equality, that opinion is also subject to change and erosion as the treaty process unfolds. Indeed, that is clearly in progress today.

At the end of the day, full reconciliation may not always be possible. There will always be people on each side of the table who believe that even a generally agreed outcome was not the best that could be obtained. But reconciliation remains a worthy goal.

Finality

This is a bottom-line goal for most non-aboriginals, and probably for most aboriginals not a part of the Indian Industry. However, a significant number of the Indian elite draw their status and livelihood from *non*-resolution. Finality is not in their personal interest. They attempt to justify this by an in-principle argument against the traditional treaty words of "cede, release, and surrender" with respect to potential claims not covered by the treaty, and to give the lack of finality institutional life in requirements for ongoing consultations and negotiations and co-management schemes.

On the other hand, "when it's over, it's over" is the intent of ordinary people. This treaty making among Canadians is a very painful, costly business that is bearable only because of the hope that there will be an end to it sometime.

From the aboriginal side, "resolution" has an additional component, specifically, giving constitutional protection to treaties. This is because there are historically unusually favourable negotiating conditions now from the aboriginal perspective, which conditions are unlikely to endure as the public gains a greater understanding of the issues. Therefore, any agreement which could be re-opened later might be attacked and undermined in the future, unless constitutionally protected.

This approach of constitutional protection of treaties, however, has the effect of casting the arrangements in concrete. This, in turn, leads to caution on both sides and a quest for perfection. The "best deal" becomes the enemy of a "good deal"—the latter, of course, far more easily achievable. Indeed, it is in part this "forever" problem that makes agreements so difficult to arrive at.

This "forever" problem also makes it all the more undesirable to try to constitutionalize such continually evolving areas as governance.

Times change, and as will be suggested later, governance should be and remain a delegated (i.e., non-constitutionalized) matter.

Finality is very difficult to achieve. Partly this is because no one can know what a court will say in the future about any form of words, however perfect. More importantly, finality is a threat (both practical and psychological) to a lot of people who have lived their lives focused on grievance and its redress. It is awfully hard to renounce a major basis of one's life, in saying that the issue is finally over.

That said, and all of the difficulties canvassed, without the maximum practical finality there is no point in doing the hard dealing. There must be a payoff in treaties for all parties in interest, or agreements simply will not happen.

Clarity

This requirement may seem obvious, but experience has shown that clarity may be traded off in order to reach agreement by way of papering over hard issues. *The appearance of agreement through clever words when agreement does not in fact exist is a favour to no one* (except those with short-term political interests), and stores up grief to be amplified to the detriment of future leaders and generations.

This is especially important given the recent practice of courts to stretch words beyond any point imagined in long-ago agreements. The BC Court of Appeal decision in Halfway River First Nation v. B.C. is a textbook case in such an exercise, as is *R. v. Marshall* (popularly known as the Atlantic lobster victory of the M'ik Maq) in the Supreme Court of Canada.

Treaty agreements must be excruciatingly clear if they are to achieve their objective.

Equity

The overwhelming majority of Canadians want to be "fair" in terms of quantum of settlement. Unfortunately, this broad area of public generosity does not necessarily overlap with the minimum expectations of Indians, who have been led to believe by a generation of fuzzy-talking politicians that just about anything is possible. These misled expectations may for many citizens escape the bounds of generosity into the land of the ridiculous. But that said, the markers so far laid down by the courts suggest that we are going to be talking about very large sums of money and areas of land.

Additionally, Indians do not see settlements as being in any sense voluntarily "generous." They see them as a matter of right, grudging concessions gained only after a long struggle. Therefore, non-aboriginal

Canadians should not expect any sense of gratitude whatsoever for settlements reached.

Fortunately, there are two mitigating factors for this problem of differing expectations. First, the real-world negotiating experiences of both federal and provincial negotiators in the BC treaty process has educated governments immeasurably as to the magnitude of their problem. Their increasingly harder lines in turn have gradually educated Indian negotiators as to realistic possibilities. Unhappily, both sides are caught in the expectations of their constituencies, who want to pay less on the government side and expect much more on the Indian side. There is no way to square this circle except by lengthy and painful grinding of the immovable object against the irresistible force.

The happier factor is that in economic terms, this question of the quantum of generosity doesn't really matter as much as the huge numbers (in terms of land and cash) would seem to indicate. The political reality is that Canadians generally are determined that a social safety net will be furnished, in quantities as required, to everyone who needs it. This is as true of Indians in need as anyone else. Therefore, a great deal more cash and other resources will have to be dedicated to improving the native condition whatever happens. Huge dollars are inevitably involved. The issue is how best to spend them.

From this point of view, the only question is the timing and manner of payment. Will it be by way of continuing the pattern of endless, soul-destroying welfare, or by a new way of capital payments (in cash and kind) and investment in human resources that establish an ongoing patrimony to displace welfare payments?

As to transfers of land, does it really matter in economic terms whether the government of British Columbia owns a forest and uses the proceeds to subsidize an Indian band, or whether the band owns the forest and takes the profits directly?[13]

Cynics may rightly argue that history teaches us that capital payments or asset transfers to any disadvantaged group are often soon dissipated without enduring effect. However, if, at a minimum, the payments concerned meet the test of reconciliation and finality, so that from that date forward Indians are treated as ordinary Canadians from a social policy standpoint, then that in itself is a development of great value.[14] And of course, capital payments may, in fact, be used to great advantage, depending upon the prudence of the recipients.

Disentanglement

It is a curious reality that notwithstanding the stated wish of Indian bands to get on with their lives under their own control, and the wish of governments to extricate themselves from the myriad problems of the existing situation, treaty solutions arrived at to date or under negotiation tend to provide for a good deal of two-way responsibility and continuing entanglement of one party with the other. For example, the Nisga'a Treaty provides for up to 50 future sets of negotiations or consultations.

To a certain extent this is unavoidable. For example, when a senior level of government provides ongoing funding for a social program purpose, ongoing negotiations, expected program standards, and auditing are required. This is true whether the recipient of the funds is a native government or a municipality or a voluntary agency.

But some of the greatest problem areas are totally avoidable, particularly with respect to resource administration. Provisions for "co-management" of timber, wildlife, and fishery resources are simply a recipe for continuing disagreement and bureaucracy.[15] This is one of those areas where the Indian Industry (on both sides of the table) is set on building in its own continuing importance, rather than working itself out of business.

To the maximum extent possible, treaty arrangements should allow each party to do its ongoing routine business without reference to the other. It does not matter a great deal whether, for example, a given block of wildlife resource or timber is under the control of a tribal council (or any other private owner, or a municipality, for that matter) or the provincial minister. Where it does matter is having it nominally under the control of *both*.

In the same vein but as an even greater problem, the Nisga'a Treaty provision that the government of British Columbia must consult with the Nisga'a government on any future legislation that might affect the subject matter of the treaty is simply too broad, to the point of being ridiculous. No municipality, even the largest, has such an undertaking, nor should much smaller Indian governments.

Equality in Law

Treaties should aim at the long term result of Indians being equal with other Canadians before the law. This is not in any way to deny the existence of aboriginal rights and title which have been discovered (and continue to be found) by the courts. Rather, it is to say that modern treaties should have as one of their invariable objects the conversion of such distinctions into cash or into the same class and kind of property rights (the ownership and control of land and capital, for example) available to all other Canadians.

It must be said at once that this simple long-term goal is revolutionary in terms of existing government policy. *That existing policy is to codify and constitutionalize differences between Indians and other Canadians.*

For reasons argued elsewhere[16] the author believes this policy to be the root source of the current unhappy estate of Indians in Canada, and to be immoral in the broadest sense of the word.

The three following principles are derivatives of this broader one of eventual equality.

Municipal-type government

Senior governments have committed to the concept of a "Third Order of government" for aboriginal peoples without ever defining (even in their own private thinking) what that meant. The Third Order concept is also the bedrock underpinning the recommendations of the Royal Commission on Aboriginal Peoples. However, no court has found any constitutional support for this idea. Indeed, the Appeal Courts of both Ontario and British Columbia have explicitly rejected the concept as being inconsistent with our constitution.

The Appeal Court of BC noted[17] that sovereignty is fully exhausted between the federal and provincial orders of government. There is no more left to go around. Of course, the Supreme Court of Canada may yet invent some different perspective, but for the moment, absent a constitutional amendment,[18] governmental powers for sub-units must be delegated; they are not inherent or sovereign.

There are three theoretical ideas underpinning the demand for a Third Order of government. One is that Indians are different from other Canadians. According to this argument they are somehow more different from the rest of us than are men from women, than old from young, than those of Scots heritage from Chinese, than gay from straight, than left-wing socialist from hard-right capitalist, than religious from atheist, than hermit from Hutterite, and so on. Our ordinary governments in Canada manage to span all of these huge differences quite nicely, but, it is claimed, Indians are so extraordinarily different as to require a Third Order of government. I reject that idea as patent nonsense.

The second theoretical idea is that because the ancestors of modern day Indians were in Canada before the ancestors of most other Canadians, the Indian governance structure that was in place at the time of contact should in some way be re-instituted today. Why this should be is never satisfactorily explained. But governance structures in all societies around the world have changed beyond recognition over the past couple of centuries, mostly for the better. Surely the tests for governance structures for today should be grounded in utility rather than sentiment.

The final idea is that the Third Order is required (so goes the argument) as the indispensable condition for the preservation of aboriginal culture. No such legal discrimination has been necessary to preserve the aforesaid Hutterite culture on the Canadian prairies, nor the culture of the Jewish people around the world in the face of much persecution. Perhaps it is thought by the proponents of this theory that aboriginal cultures are less robust things, but is the preservation of *any* culture at the expense of other citizens (for such things are not cheap in dollars or, in this case, violence to other Canadian ideas such as equality and non-discrimination on the basis of race) a proper object of government? This is a truly fundamental question. I would argue that the preservation of any culture is the responsibility of its adherents, and the role of government is simply to be neutral.

The true, immediate, practical advantage of a Third Order really accrues to the Indian Industry, wherein are found the vast majority of the few Canadians seeing any sense in such an idea. A Third Order identifies elites, preserves them, and gives them status and pay. Priestly elites in the past found this to be usefully the case, and cultural elites are at it here. But is this solution good for the society that has to support it?

Equally, is this Third Order solution good for the very people it is ostensibly designed to serve? As argued elsewhere,[19] it is much more likely to be a bad thing. You do a small group of people no favour by drawing a circle around them and calling them basically different.

There is no greater evidence of this point than to note that existing Indian Act band governments are already a sort of "Third Order" in all important respects save constitutional entrenchment. While providing massive funding, the federal government has at the same time withdrawn so far from interference in the internal affairs of most bands— even to the extent of failing to require proper accounting for funding, according to the Auditor General—that band governments are, to all intents and purposes, already examples of race-based governance of Indians by Indians. To put it mildly, results have not been universally positive in terms of democracy, social outcomes, accountability, or economic development. Would one seriously advocate constitutionalizing this experience?

Now, a very different and more respectable argument is that governmental or other services to people will be more effective if delivered in a culturally sensitive way. This argument has great weight, but such a system does not require a Third Order. As an example, it is one thing, for example, to have some Chinese-speaking public servants delivering services to the tens of thousands of Chinese-speaking people in the Vancouver suburb of Richmond, but quite another to suggest a Chinese Order of government.

I conclude that municipal-type governments used successfully for the governance of small communities all over Canada are far more appropriate than the constitutionalized Third Order kind. There is plenty of room for experimentation, as long as the governmental structure is of a *delegated* nature—i.e., instituted by legislation passed by existing levels of government, and capable of change in the light of actual experience with how things work.

Indeed, even such a governance scheme as that contemplated in the Nisga'a Treaty might well be tried with the consent of the governed, if only to show by experience whether it is or is not as deeply flawed as I think it is. However, any such trial should be an *experiment*, not a constitutionalized Third Order cast in concrete as is the current plan.

The experimental approach also leaves room to try out various solutions to one of the most vexing of questions, namely the right (or not) of non-aboriginals to vote for municipal-type aboriginal governments on the grounds that they live in the area to be thus governed. The approach I prefer is simply extending the franchise to all, in the usual way. A sensitive definition of territory (which in crass political parlance would be called "gerrymandering") can in many cases yield predominately aboriginal areas with aboriginal-dominated local governments. The new territory of Nunavut is one such example, though an extremely costly one.

Of course there are other cases, such as Westbank or Sechelt in BC where (because of extensive residential leasing to non-Indians bringing in band revenue) the aboriginal component of the territory would be swamped.[20] The solution adopted in Nisga'a and evolving in Sechelt and Westbank provides for *no* voting rights (save for advisory organs) for non-natives in local government, and two parallel sets of laws and representation as to Indian and non-Indian, with Indian law designed to has as little an impact as possible on non-Indians.

However, apart from the deservedly bad odour in which they are held around the world, total "separate-but-equal" structures are simply not possible. Local schools and hospitals are attended by everyone (unless we want separate schools and hospitals), and local roads are driven on by everyone. Local commercial law, with Nisga'a paramountcy under the treaty, affects Nisga'a and non-Nisga'a alike. The Nisga'a/Westbank/Sechelt approach has been to provide for some non-Indian advisory input. These are legitimate experiments. But Sechelt, most importantly, is *not constitutionalized*.

Another theoretical approach which will no doubt be explored over the years to come is that of a *trade-off* between powers and representation. In other words, the fewer powers wielded by an Indian government, the less the requirement for non-native representation. Were the powers cut back to simple aboriginal asset management, no non-native representation at all would be called for.

In the end, and with all of the above argument and uncertainty, this is the essential issue: constitutionalized Third Order or not? The issue cannot be finessed. It must be faced. The Third Order solution is not an appropriate part of treaties.

Small Governments, Large Powers

Third Order governments as visualized by the Indian Industry have tremendous powers. On a world scale, these "tremendous powers" are trivial. Yet from the point of view of an Indian subject to a Third Order government, the powers are indeed overwhelming.

Imagine you live in a municipality where the Mayor and Council have an absolute veto over whether you have a house or not, whether your plumbing gets fixed, whether you have access to the transportation pool, whether your child can get a scholarship to university, and whether you have a government job when such jobs are about the only ones available. Imagine that the Mayor and Council can really run the education system rather than the professionals if they so chose. Imagine this same group has total control over business licensing (including paramountcy over *all* federal and provincial powers, which no municipality has) and over property zoning. Imagine all of this with essentially no outside appeal, no matter what might be said.

Imagine, most frighteningly, that most of the money that flows through your community is controlled by politicians.

Imagine further, that the system is set up deliberately to minimize citizen contact with other governments, in terms of services or financial payments and receipts.

Imagine that elections are decided by a few handsful of people voting basically along family lines, the "ins" versus the "outs."

This is what can happen with small governments wielding large powers. This is the fact of government on many reserves today. The unhappy results have absolutely nothing to do with ethnicity or culture. People are people all around the world. Power corrupts. That is why free societies always seek to control power in designing governance systems. We should not be so blind as to ignore the possibility that pervasive treaty-conferred power might not corrupt its aboriginal recipients just as surely as if they were non-aboriginal.

When governments are given power over the people to the extent that those governments can control elections by controlling voters, "democracy" ceases to have meaning.

The model treaties before us today would constitutionalize such powers and cast them in concrete. By contrast, the standard municipal model, well understood throughout British Columbia with its limitations on power and institutionalized checks and balances, makes such a nightmare scenario impossible.

Asset Management

The matter of administering commonly held property is a very different issue. Much of the work of the Third Order of government proposed in the Nisga'a Treaty would relate to asset management, and those aspects of the treaty can be easily preserved.

Administration of Indian community property by organizations controlled exclusively by Indians is nothing different in principle from the many corporations and societies that manage property under ordinary Canadian law. There is no conflict here.

However, Indian asset management entities as set up in the Nisga'a Treaty (or by Band Councils across the country, for that matter) are no ordinary societies or corporations, which are merely instrumental or supplementary to most private property holdings in Canada. Rather, they are holding vehicles for essentially the entire asset base of a community in many cases.

It can be argued, and I do so here, that community ownership of most property is inferior to private ownership of most property, in terms both of husbandry and freedom. Indeed, that is one of the major lessons of the twentieth century, in the economic and political failures of the communist experiments. And in respect of the freedom issue, power over asset management (through the bestowal or withholding of benefits or related jobs) can become just one more route by which a government has the power to control its people and their votes.

Of course, adopting the communal property route as a part of treaty settlements is a judgement to be made by the owners of Indian property and no one else.[21] But other choices should be open, and assessed and chosen by the community, rather than having this single model not just assumed, but actually imposed by treaty. Other Canadians have no right to use their legal power to impose such a model as a matter of law, which is what the Nisga'a Treaty (for example) does.

Individual Empowerment

Are treaties properly seen as settlements with Indian *collectivities* or with Indian *people*—individuals who make up collectivities? This is an immensely important question.

Should all of the fruits of settlement in terms of cash, land, and ongoing financial support accrue to the collectivity and to the control of the elite managers? Or should some portion, large or small, accrue to individuals?

Should the majority of a collectivity be allowed to make a choice about the system for all individuals, or should individuals affected by a treaty settlement have the choice of saying in effect, "I will take my share and get on with my individual life." My view is that individuals should have that latter option.

There is no proposal that will be so strenuously resisted as this one, for it has the potential to dramatically undermine the power of Indian elites and the Indian Industry. The standard defensive argument of the industry is that such a concept will lead to "cultural genocide" (respect for accurate or moderate language is often missing in these debates) by undermining the collectivity. This is nonsense.

Cultures survive according to their usefulness to individuals. They have no merit or entitlement to support beyond that. By analogy, would anyone seriously argue that the government of Canada should control most of the spending in the country so that Canadian culture could be protected, rather than leaving most choice in the hands of individuals? Of course not.

Private property and individual choice are the very bedrock of Canadian society, and indeed, of freedom itself. Certainly any individual has the right to make him or herself "not free" by ceding their property and decision-making to others, but do we have the right to *impose* that on anyone? In structuring treaty benefits to accrue strictly to the collectivity, we do exactly that.

Some will point to the Delgamuukw decision, wherein the Supreme Court opined that aboriginal title is a collective right. They will say that the court leaves us no choice on collective ownership. They forget or ignore the fact that one function of treaties is to *replace* Delgamuukw with a negotiated solution. That solution can contain whatever distribution of property rights the parties may agree upon.

Negotiators for Canada and British Columbia should maintain a policy of structuring treaties to allow individual members of the tribe concerned some major element of choice in terms of how he or she may choose to take the fruits of the settlement.

Quite apart from notions of private property and choice, *this system is also the only one that begins to be fair to urban or "off-lands" Indians.* Under the present system, almost all benefits accrue only to those who choose to reside on the tribal lands. Many people may not wish to do so for whatever reason, including access to employment and urban amenities. An individual entitlement by choice allows such a person access to at least some portion of their notional share of the overall settlement.

Transparency

A final matter of great importance is that of transparency. Nothing is more important to a functioning democracy and true accountability than the public right to know precisely what its governments are up to.

In terms of the accountability of Parliament, while taxpayers currently fund almost all of the activities of Indian governments, court decisions (which Parliament could have overturned but has not) have led to the existing practice whereby the actual use of these public funds by Indian bands is unknown to the public. This is wrong in principle. It is unthinkable that some of the waste and corruption reported from various small Indian governments—reports which may only survey the top of the iceberg—could have reached such an advanced stage were there public, Parliamentary scrutiny of all public funds flowing through Indian governments.

More importantly, as the Auditor General has frequently noted, without such details the general public is prevented from properly assessing the success or failure of existing Indian policy.

Treaty settlements will do nothing to remove this issue from the table. Indeed, the almost $500 million Nisga'a Treaty settlement will not reduce the $30 million per year taxpayer support of band government activities. Quite the contrary: funding will increase by almost 10 percent in order to look after the new costs of the bureaucratic structure set up by the treaty, and the treaty provides that less information than ever will be available to the general taxpayer.

Indeed, Section 2-44 of the Nisga'a Treaty provides that "... information that Nisga'a government provides to Canada or British Columbia in confidence is deemed to be information received or obtained in confidence from another government"—i.e., protected from Freedom of Information laws.

All new treaties should contain a provision that so long as external governments provide more than a certain fraction of Indian government revenues, say 10 percent, the full books should be available to the public.[22] This is, of course, the case with any municipality in BC, with *no* minimum limit. A government is not a private society, like a shopping centre. A government is public property, and so should be its information.

With respect to the Nisga'a Treaty which provides no such comfort, it may be possible to build such a requirement into financing agreements, but it also may be that S.2-44 above would preclude even that protection.

Apart from the legitimate concerns of the general taxpayer, there is a concern with respect to internal Indian government democracy. Without knowing how the funds are being used, tribal citizens cannot assess whether they are being properly spent. Indeed, as frequent newspaper stories attest, with respect to existing band practice, even band members often cannot gain access to the detailed books of account, in spite of material claims of abuse.

Section 11-9(l) of the Nisga'a Treaty says that the Nisga'a constitution must "require a system of financial information comparable to standards generally accepted for governments in Canada." The difficulty is, the financial accountability of federal and provincial governments is not very good, and only works at all because of an active Opposition and press—institutions unlikely to be active in very small governments. The "full, true, and plain disclosure" which governments require of corporations is a far higher standard. That, or the municipal standard is more appropriate for treaties.

As an example of how apparently comforting words (such as those about financial accountability consistent with those of other governments) can have little meaning, one need only look at Section 11-9(k) of the Nisga'a Treaty which requires that "... all Nisga'a citizens are eligible to vote." And indeed they are under the Nisga'a constitution. The problem is that off-lands citizens have a vote worth only (roughly) ten percent the value of an on-lands citizen in electing the Nisga'a legislature. Is this right and proper when the Nisga'a government disposes of a patrimony equally owned by all?

The bottom line is this: where treaties establish Indian governments, they should include very strong Freedom of Information provisions, both for citizens of the Indian government, and for general taxpayers as long as they are significantly funding the Indian government.

Important Other Matters

Contrary to the view many hold, *freedom from taxation* is not a constitutionally recognized aboriginal right. Where it exists, it normally flows from Section 87 of the Indian Act, which obscure provision itself has been stretched beyond recognition by the courts.[23]

Indeed, the taxation exemption in the Indian Act had two intellectual justifications. The first was to insulate Indian lands from local tax seizure. The second was to recognize that since Indians did not have the vote, they should not pay tax. However, when the right of the franchise was restored 40 years ago, the mirror responsibility of paying taxes was ignored. Just as "taxation without representation" is wrong, so is representation without taxation. Responsibility and entitlement are two sides of the same coin.

Modern treaties such as Nisga'a will increasingly pretend that Indians will pay ordinary tax like anyone else. A careful reading of the Nisga'a Treaty will reveal that Indian government (i.e., non-taxable) ownership of almost all assets, and the ability to gift the fruits of these assets to tribal members, will mean that the taxation claim is more political and cosmetic than real. Free or deeply discounted housing and services will end up as tax-free benefits for which ordinary Canadians would have to pay in after-tax dollars.

As a second miscellaneous but important matter, the role of the BC Treaty Commission needs to be re-examined. This supposedly neutral facilitator has clearly had its thumb on one side of the scales. When assessed by its results, the Commission should simply be ended.

Conclusion

Making treaties among Canadians is a very important business. It is essential that the principles to be followed are well articulated, understood, and supported by the general community. That has not been the case to date.

The principles cited above are intended to contribute to that end. There are four over-riding ideas.

The first is the importance of maintaining flexibility as we proceed with experiments in this field so littered with past failures, rather than constitutionalizing solutions before they have been tried and found successful.

The second is ensuring that solutions have general community support, not just in the tribe concerned, but in the province and the country. If such support is missing, the solutions will fail, no matter how theoretically brilliant the construct.

The third is an insistence on the dignity and worth of individuals, with the collectivity being in a subordinate position. Its powers must always be justified by, and only with reference to, service to the individual.

The final idea, which runs through every particular question to be considered, is that of maintaining the maximum possible harmony with the rest of Canadian society. The practical reason is that without a broad consensus on common citizenship values, funding and other relationships will always be at risk in the trials and strains that always come with an uncertain future. To put it plainly, solutions that are not supported by Canadians generally will not in the long run be funded by Canadians generally.

But even more basic than that, Canadian values such as equality, democracy, accountability, the coupling of entitlement with responsibility, tolerance of diversity, mobility rights, and so on, are so fundamental and cherished that it is difficult to see how any relationship *not* based on such things could long or happily endure.

These value references are not mere platitudes. They are genuine issues when one assesses proposals for embedding by treaty small, special-purpose, closed, and culturally homogeneous societies in a large and pluralistic open society.

Notes

1 Counts were not possible or were incomplete on 77 reserves containing perhaps 44,000 people, and another 10,000 or so in prisons were not included. In addition, these figures are difficult to reconcile with the legal status lists maintained by Indian Affairs because of different conceptual bases.

2 In addition to some federal entitlements. The question of who pays—the federal or provincial governments—for provincial services to Indians, remains a large issue.

3 That is, including about 200,000 Métis and about 40,000 Inuit, plus non-registered North American Indians.

4 1996 Census figures give the aboriginal identity population percentages in these three cities as 6.9, 7.1, and 7.5 percent respectively.

5 Defined as those who gain a major share of their income or status as a result of the separate category of "Indian" existing in Canadian law and administrative practice, including bureaucrats, lawyers and other professionals, specialist academics and native leaders; more on this later in this text.

6 Trudeau would probably have conceded, and I certainly do, that our constitution itself constitutes a "treaty among Canadians" in establishing the federal principle and provincial governments. Trudeau's Charter of Rights and Freedoms could equally be so described. A supreme irony is that Section 35 of his 1982 constitutional amendments is the legal underpinning for the treaty process. But Trudeau would have perhaps responded that, all of that said, federalism can only be stretched so far, and that the creation of closed societies in citizenship terms goes farther than the elastic will allow.

7 See the internal dissension of the Caldwell Band, Fraser Institute Public Policy Sources forthcoming, regarding settlement negotiations, and the confusion among memberships of many bands regarding the federal Bill C-49 legislation on land management.

8 It must be noted, however, that mandates are achieved only slowly, and many of the current negotiations at the BC Treaty Commission table are hampered by the snail's pace of the mandate development on the aboriginal side.

9 There have been continually moving goal-posts here. At first, governments took the position that no Agreement in Principle (AIP) stage negotiations would be started without the resolution of overlap issues. This was shifted to allow negotiations, but not actual approval of the AIP. The current claim is that the actual treaty itself will not be signed without overlap resolution, but as Nisga'a demonstrates, even that rule has already been breached.

10 Unless otherwise noted, "governments" include both Canada and BC.

11 Marktrend survey, September 1999.

12 Indian spokespersons often say, however, that the *actual* goal of governments is certainty of land tenure, and that reconciliation is secondary. In this they are no doubt correct.

13 Indeed, from a strictly economic point of view, it can be argued that private ownership of any given forest will probably lead to better management. However, that is not the end of the story. The economic loser in this trans-

action is the provincial taxpayer, while the economic winner is the federal taxpayer, whose subsidy obligation is reduced by the new revenue produced by the former provincial crown lands. As the magnitude of the numbers involved becomes more apparent, the existing cost-sharing arrangements will have to be revisited, to the additional cost of Ottawa.

14 Of course, large capital payments are much harder to justify if the two trade-offs of Indians becoming "ordinary Canadians" and the goal of finality are not available.

15 See again, Halfway River First Nation.

16 See Gordon Gibson, *A Principled Analysis of the Nisga'a Treaty*, Fraser Institute Public Policy Sources No. 27, 1999.

17 In Delgamuukw. The Supreme Court of Canada dodged the issue in its final decision.

18 One of the most serious challenges to the Nisga'a Treaty is that it may be a *de facto* constitutional amendment, through the back door of S.35. This is now before the BC courts and will no doubt be resolved by the Supreme Court of Canada in the end. Until then, every "Third Order" solution that is proposed will be under a legal cloud.

19 *A Principled Analysis of the Nisga'a Treaty* includes a section on the morality (or otherwise) of subjecting one subset of Canadians to a different and arguably oppressive legal regime based strictly on the accident of their birth.

20 This is not the case in the Nisga'a territory, where very few non-Nisga'a live.

21 In this context the repeated emphasis of the Supreme Court of Canada on the collective nature of aboriginal rights is a most perverse doctrine. It is an obstacle that must be gotten around.

22 This applies only to the use of public funds. With respect to the administration of own-source funds, that is a matter of internal democracy. See below.

23 For example, a Federal Court decision recently held that Indians could be "leased" to off-reserve employers and pay no taxes as long as the leasing company had an on-reserve address.

The Road Ahead
Negotiation or Litigation?

PATRICK MONAHAN

The following are excerpts of a presentation by Patrick Monahan, professor of law at Osgoode Hall Law School, York University.

We have explored the details of *Delgamuukw* judgment and many of its implications in specific areas. The purpose of this presentation is to place *Delgamuukw* in a broader context and, in particular, to discuss the question of the extent to which this case will affect the evolving relationships between aboriginal peoples and their government, and governments outside aboriginal communities and Canadian society in general. There are really only two main options post-*Delgamuukw*: negotiation and litigation. At the end of his judgment, Chief Justice [Antonio] Lamer made a plea, almost, to "please settle these cases—don't come back to us again to resolve these cases." What does that entreaty say to us, and what *will* it say to us?

An earlier speaker suggested that the plea from the Chief Justice was, in effect, an admission of failure, an open admission that "well, we [the members of the Supreme Court] really haven't solved these problems." I don't think that is really a fair characterization. It is generally accepted amongst lawyers that, other things being equal, negotiation is clearly preferable to litigation. It is preferable for a lot of reasons. Consensual outcomes are more stable outcomes. They are more legitimate outcomes because all parties accept them. Therefore, they are more durable and more lasting than those outcomes imposed by the court. Litigation is extremely costly—not that negotiation isn't also costly—and the costs include more than the costs of the lawyers involved. In terms of social costs, litigation tends to foster conflict and "all or nothing" solutions. Litigation is also of very limited utility because all it will do is resolve very narrow, discrete issues. It will not provide a comprehensive settlement or resolution of all matters that are in dispute.

The *Delgamuukw* case itself provides a classic illustration of the shortcomings of litigation. The trial began in the British Columbia Supreme Court in May of 1987. The claim itself had been filed three years earlier. We had a 374-day trial that concluded in June 1990. We then had a trial judgment rendered in March 1991 and the Court of Appeal decision in 1993. Finally, the Supreme Court of Canada decision was handed down in December 1997. So we had over a decade between the first day of the trial, which of course was not the day that the claim was filed, until a final judgment from the Supreme Court of Canada.

And what do we know on the basis of *Delgamuukw*? Surprisingly, we don't know very much more than we did at the commencement of the litigation. The Supreme Court *did* say that the claimants had an unextinguished aboriginal right over or in—and I say over or in because I think this is a point that we have to pay attention to—at least some, and potentially all, of the territory that they were claiming. But what exactly is the nature and extent of this right? We do not know because the right may amount to title or ownership (which would be the upper end of the right in question) over some or all of this land. That would mean the right to use and possess the land exclusively, subject to certain limitations that the Chief Justice set out in his judgment. Alternatively, it may merely amount to a non-exclusive right to use certain lands for particular purposes. That would be the lower end of the right. My own view is that if they are forced to decide, the Courts will come down on the upper end of the scale, finding title or ownership, at least with respect to some substantial amount of the land in dispute.

But the Chief Justice was very careful not to rule out the possibility that there could be some lesser right that might be found to exist if you could not establish exclusive possession sufficient to found a claim to title. So that is one area that will require clarification. Moreover, the test of exclusive possession is not very clearly defined in the Chief Justice's judgment. Another open question at the next trial will be the proper treatment of oral histories. I certainly would not want to be the trial judge at this next trial. The trial judge is going to read the Supreme Court's judgment and say: "Now, I am told I am supposed to weigh oral history in the same way as written history. But of course, when I weigh written history, I don't just accept written history at face value. Written history is subject to tests of credibility and testing for validity and so on, so the Supreme Court cannot mean to say that I automatically accept an oral history as correct. If I put oral history on an equal footing with written history I have to have some way of testing it, but how?" I am not sure anyone knows the answer to that question. I certainly don't envy the trial judge who is going to have to step up alone and venture an opinion, and then wait to see what the B.C. Court of Appeal or the Supreme of Court of Canada decides some years later.

So, we don't have a lot of answers from *Delgamuukw*. But maybe the parties themselves will provide the necessary answers by reaching an out-of-court settlement. This is what the Chief Justice was clearly encouraging at the conclusion of his judgment. Unfortunately, this possibility is rather unlikely. In order to understand why, it is necessary to ask a further question, namely, why do people ever litigate?

One possible explanation is simply that litigation is a by-product of the personal failures of the parties. People litigate, according to this view of the world, because they don't understand the real costs of litigation or, even if they do understand the costs, they simply don't care.

This simple answer is not very convincing. It is sometimes a rational choice to choose litigation even though there are significant costs involved. It is rational where the parties calculate that the net benefits of litigation outweigh the net benefits of settlement.

What are the calculations in favour of or against settlement as an option? The first consideration is that the substantive terms of the settlement itself confer a positive benefit because you know you are going to receive what the settlement terms provide. You also have ease of implementation. You know that if the other side accepts it, you are probably going to obtain those benefits, and you know that it is going to be legitimate on an ongoing basis. It is going to provide you with legal certainty in terms of your entitlements, while eliminating negative outcomes that might have occurred if you had gone to court. Because if you do go to court, not only may you not win, but you may lose something that you already have. Of course, the settlement option itself is not cost-free. The cost of settlement is the opportunity of obtaining more by going to court. You give up that opportunity by settling the claim.

Thus the risks and rewards of litigation include the value of the positive result, discounted by the risk that that positive outcome will not be obtained (because you might lose). So you have that discount factor, the potential opportunity discounted by the risk it will not be obtained. You also have the possibility that you could lose something else through litigation, that there will be a negative outcome from the Court's decision. The Court might say: "Not only am I not going to give you what you want, but I am going to take something else away from you that you thought was not even at issue." Now that, of course, is also discounted by the possibility that this negative outcome will not occur. And then there are the direct litigation costs; there's the time, the 10 years it is going to take you; the uncertainty; and the negative impact that litigation is going to have on your ongoing relationships. Certain parties, those with deeper pockets, are better able to bear those costs, and thus may find that they represent a somewhat smaller inducement to settle. On the other hand, business corporations, which are often characterized as having the deepest pockets, are most likely to prefer settlement over litigation for the simple reason that litigation is usually bad for business.

Finally, there is the question of the differences between the parties' relative perceptions of all of these variables. If the parties have a common perception, a common calculation as to the likely outcome, then it is more likely that they will choose a negotiated settlement rather than litigate. This is because both parties will understand which of them is most likely to prevail if the matter actually goes to court and has to be decided by a judge.

Legal uncertainty contributes to the risk that the parties may inaccurately calculate the real risks and rewards of litigation. It increases the danger of one or both parties miscalculating the true risks and rewards of the litigation option as compared to the settlement option. They may mistakenly think they will win big if they go to court, and that might induce them to litigate when they ought to have settled.

Oddly enough, legal uncertainty may in some circumstances actually increase the attractiveness of the settlement option. Someone might say: "Going to court is so uncertain, if we settle we can put all that aside, we can resolve all these issues, and we can immediately eliminate that uncertainty with a stroke of a pen." So we would be wrong to assume that legal uncertainty is automatically correlated with a tendency to litigate. However, the settlement option does assume some minimum, shared legal framework as the basis for negotiations. For example, you have to know who are the right-holders with whom you have to negotiate and settle. If it is not clear who are those right-holders, then you are not going to be able to achieve a settlement. That has been a big problem in the context of cases like *Delgamuukw* because it is often not entirely clear who exactly are the rights-holders.

Let's see how this framework of the relative risks and rewards of litigation versus negotiation applies to *Delgamuukw*. First of all, *Delgamuukw* is not an isolated phenomenon. It is part of an evolving Supreme Court jurisprudence on aboriginal rights. There are two key features of this jurisprudence. The first is what I call *balancing of interests*. The court seeks to find what it perceives to be compromise or middle-ground solutions, rejecting "all-or-nothing" solutions in favour of those that seem to give half a loaf, or at least part of a loaf, to both sides. We have seen this tendency in other areas outside the aboriginal context. For example, in the *Secession Reference*, we see the Supreme Court exhibiting this same aversion to giving a total victory to one side, preferring a middle-ground position. And so the Court creates a duty to negotiate secession following a clear referendum result, an argument that was not ever raised in any of the parties' submissions.

In the *Delgamuukw* context, this same tendency was reflected in the Court's rejection of the argument that aboriginal claims in British Columbia had been extinguished by the assertion of British sovereignty. Acceptance of that argument would have been a categorical exclusion of aboriginal claims. But while that argument was accepted at trial, it certainly wasn't the kind of argument likely to find favour with the Supreme Court. Interestingly enough, the B.C. government itself reversed its own position on that and didn't press the extinguishment argument at the Supreme Court of Canada. But I don't think the Supreme Court of Canada would have accepted the argument in any event.

The second related element in the Supreme Court's aboriginal jurisprudence is a tendency to favour a *case-by-case approach*. Cases are decided on their own facts. Not only does the Court want to avoid all-or-nothing outcomes, it wants to avoid sweeping decisions that will set generalized rules. For example, the Court has refused to indicate thus far whether section 35 includes an inherent right of self-government. My own view is that there is a high likelihood that the Supreme Court of Canada will eventually recognize that section 35 includes an inherent right to self-government. But the Court has thus far refused to make that pronouncement, even though it has had an opportunity to do so in a number of cases. Where it *does* announce general rules, these rules are fact-specific. They are fact-driven, such as the *Van der Peet* test for establishing aboriginal rights, which asks whether a particular activity is integral to this particular community prior to contact with Europeans, not whether certain activities were integral to aboriginal life in general in the pre-contact period.

Now how will these trends influence the tendency of parties to litigate? Ironically, although the Court wants to discourage litigation, this case-by-case approach is clearly going to have the opposite effect, in the short term at least. When every case turns on its own facts, the potential risks and rewards of litigation are very difficult to estimate accurately. Further, if you are entitled to assume that a court will give you at least part of what you are asking for, litigation seems a pretty attractive option. Legal judgment and analysis tend to descend very rapidly into political rhetoric. A lawyer is going to have a very difficult time convincing a determined client that accepting anything less than full satisfaction is the most rational choice in the circumstances.

On the other hand, the calculations over the medium to long term (i.e. 10 to 25 years) are much more favourable to the settlement option. Within the next decade we will have more decided cases, and those cases will tend to flesh out more fully the real risks and rewards of litigation. Lawyers on both sides will, over time, acquire a much more realistic understanding of their likely success in different fact scenarios. Thus, over the medium to long term, we are going to see the emergence of a clear preference for negotiated solutions. But over the next decade, my sense is that the dynamic will very much favour litigation over negotiation and settlement, notwithstanding the best intentions on all sides of the negotiating table. This dynamic in favour of litigation is itself the product of the Supreme Court's own jurisprudence, its privileging of middle-ground positions combined with a case-by-case methodology.

One illustration is the litigation that has been commenced over the *Nisga'a Treaty*. Here we have a situation where the parties have managed to reach a negotiated solution only to find themselves back in court. What is the likely outcome of the challenge to the constitutionality of the treaty that has been filed in the British Columbia courts? If we look at the record in previous cases, we can predict that when the case reaches the Supreme Court of Canada in the year 2006, the Court will try to find a middle-ground solution. Thus, the most likely outcome is for the Court to uphold the treaty in its main essentials, sanctioning the recognition of a third order of government in Canada. But the Court may well also require certain modifications in subsidiary aspects of the treaty by, for example, requiring certain guarantees or special voting rules to protect minority rights (both aboriginal as well as non-aboriginal) in the context of aboriginal self-government. But the main thrust of the treaty, the recognition of the principle of aboriginal self-government as a third order of government, will in all likelihood be accepted. The reason is simply that the courts will not want to have to define self-government rights themselves out of whole cloth. I have already indicated that I believe the courts will accept that section 35 already includes some guarantee of self-government. If this turns out to be right, then the courts will welcome an attempt by the political authorities to define the content of the right. They won't stand in the way for the simple reason that the only other option available would be for the courts themselves to begin attempting to define the context of aboriginal self-government.

What of the other possibility raised, the so-called "legislative solution"? This third possibility (as distinct from the first two of litigation and negotiation/settlement) suggests that the legislature may define, through statute, the extent of aboriginal rights, along with some form of compensation for the limitation of constitutional rights. My own view is that this third option is essentially a non-starter. Its main shortcoming is that it is an imposed solution. It is a solution that says, "We are going to legislate these rights away. We are going to substitute some right of compensation in place of the rights that are guaranteed under the Constitution." And that is precisely the problem. These rights are guaranteed under the Constitution. Federal law cannot override Section 35 of the *Constitution Act*. If I am right—that the courts will say that not only are these rights to title guaranteed but there is a right of self-government already constitutionally guaranteed—then you are not going to have that legislative option. The Court will not accept an imposed solution. It will require there to be a negotiated outcome. Once you have that negotiated outcome, however, as in *Nisga'a*, the Court will ultimately be inclined to accept it.

Whatever the difficulties, that is ultimately the direction and the place in which we are going to end up. But it is going to take us more than a few years to get there. So the next decade will be both interesting and highly litigious.

Questions from the Floor

Mike Scott (MP for Skeena)   I have the dubious distinction of representing the area to which both the *Delgamuukw* and the *Nisga'a* cases pertain. And I have some observations for Mr. Monahan. You say that negotiation is the way to resolve these outstanding issues. You may know that in British Columbia we have had this B.C. treaty process for some seven years now, and it hasn't produced even one treaty. You may also know that the Auditor General was harshly critical of the government last fall when he reported to Parliament saying that, effectively, the negotiations were unfocused, undisciplined, hugely expensive ($9 million to date), and there is no fixed timelines, there are no set goals in terms of concluding any of these negotiations successfully. Almost half of the bands in British Columbia at the present time aren't even in the negotiating process. The *Nisga'a* case is as a prime example of the overlap situation, where neighbouring bands are competing for the same territory. That is a huge issue, and it is now the subject of one of four legal challenges to the *Nisga'a* agreement. So it certainly appears that litigation is going to be with us for a while. Against the backdrop of all this, we have had the *Delgamuukw* decision imposed on us in British Columbia, which has served to greatly undermine the ability of the provincial government to administrate the lands and resources of the province. The area that I live in and that I represent is comprised of many small communities. Virtually all of those communities' primary economy comes from the resource sector. I appreciate [that] aboriginal people in Canada don't want to be a problem. The fact is, right now in British Columbia, that while we may not say that aboriginal people are becoming a problem, this issue is certainly becoming a greater problem all the time. It is creating such economic uncertainty, with no prospect of a resolution in sight, that something has to give. There are four million people living in British Columbia. At some point, those people are going to say, when they are hurt economically to an extent, that this is no longer sufficient, and we have to do something different. The negotiations aren't working, litigation hasn't worked. There has to be some other model that we can follow as a people that is going to be seen to be fair to all, including aboriginal people, but that will allow our resource communities in northern B.C. and other parts of Canada to continue to exist while we work our way through this problem.

Patrick Monahan   Let me say, first of all, that it is always nice to be in the comfort of Toronto or Ottawa and proclaim how things ought to be out in British Columbia. So I welcome the practical comments from Mr. Scott. Some say, "We can't accept this. We can't work with this. This is just totally unacceptable." In other words, what they are suggesting is that there has got to be some way out of this that doesn't involve the *Delgamuukw* model. And my simple comment is, *Delgamuukw* is here. The Supreme Court of Canada has decided. You may think some magic door is going to open, and that we are going to walk through and we are going to say, "oops, we don't have to worry about that any more." But it is not going to happen. In the world of the practical, the reality is that you are going to have accept *Delgamuukw* as your starting point. And I didn't hear an acceptance of that today. I heard a desire to say, "let's go back to some other starting point that doesn't involve *Delgamuukw*." And that, I think, is a non-starter. What *Delgamuukw* essentially says is that we are not going to accept imposed solutions. The Court didn't try to trace out too much more than that. But it said we are not going to accept imposed solutions. Whatever solutions you have, or are going to come to, are going to have to involve buy-in from the aboriginal peoples. And if they don't, then we are not going to accept them.

Now, you say, "Well look at the negotiation process, it has failed, or it hasn't made any headway." I agree to this extent: that it seems we are going to have to have more litigation for some period of time until either we have somewhat more of clear framework, or the parties' perceptions of what the costs and benefits fall more into line with each other. But to say that we don't have to accept this, that we can begin from some other point, just reinforces my own analysis which says we are going to have a lot of litigation in the next few years. And yes, negotiated solutions are going to cost a lot of money. At the end of the day, we have an $880-billion-dollar economy here and we are going to have to take some of that wealth, presumably on a one-time-only basis, and try to settle these claims.

Bill Erasmus   I am kind of in an interesting situation. My wife comes from B.C. and she is Nutaalit, from Vancouver Island. So my children come from two different nations, the Dene Nation and the Nutaalit Nation. And the way we understand that, my children come from two different Nations, they belong in both. Part of the problem of the comprehensive claims policy is that my children have to choose. That is not a starter for us. And that is the problem. See, we are guided by a policy that was designed and imposed by, and now the courts are saying something else. It is an old policy. It was outdated when it came out in 1986, I would venture to say. So, we have to realize that *Delgamuukw* is not going to go away. It is a starting point.

My wife's people never extinguished their lands, or their waters. So it means they have international water rights. It means a whole lot of things that Canada has to come to terms with. And there is nothing to be afraid of. My wife's people are not people to be afraid of. They never extinguished their lands, and I believe they never will. They were never conquered, and I believe they never will be conquered, so what are we talking about? I think we have to talk about recognizing that underlying title belongs to these people. And what is so bad about that? They have always had that title? Somehow, the biggest myth in this country is that these people gave their lands away, or you somehow took them away. You never took them away. You never legislated them away. They have always owned them, and that is what you got to get in your heads. And it's not so bad. It is just like if I get my hockey team from Yellowknife, and we whip your butts, it is okay. It is just a hockey game. I coach hockey. I went into Banff, and we beat the kids from Banff. It is all right, you know? Next year they might come and whip us. But that is part of living. These people are not trying to pull the wool over your eyes. Sure there is frustration. I have dealt with this all my adult life, and I am prepared to continue to deal with it. And if I don't settle it, then my kids will. You know? But we will settle it. So, I think everything is there. I think that is what the previous speaker is saying. He recognizes that we have the inherent right. *Delgamuukw* goes so far as to talk about title. Let's do it. Let's quit dancing around the table.

A Conversation after Dinner

GORDON F. GIBSON AND SATSAN (CHIEF HERB GEORGE)

Excerpts from presentations by Gordon Gibson, columnist and Senior Fellow in Canadian Studies, The Fraser Institute, and Satsan (Chief Herb George) from a conference dinner in May 1999.

Gordon Gibson

I cannot bring to this subject the distinguished lineage of Satsan and the titles he holds. All I can say is that he is still a vigorous young man. I'm an elder. Unfortunately elders don't get much respect in my society.

This is actually my third conversation him, and my second public one. The private one happened after a meeting of the Progressive Democratic Alliance of British Columbia, which was Gordon Wilson's former political party. I was there in my capacity as a *Globe and Mail* columnist. I should describe in passing what a wonderful thing it is to be a political columnist. Your job is to sit in comfort, high up in the bleachers, and watch the politicians stabbing each other and drawing blood. At regular intervals, it is your job to rush onto the field and stab the wounded yourself.

Anyway, at the time of that event, I was not involved in aboriginal writings at all. I have to say that I entered the field in part because of that presentation, which I admired so much. Following the talk, there was a fortuitous event. Satsan was waiting for a cab to go downtown. I happened to have my car there and we had a long, long talk on the way downtown, and I developed a very high regard for him as a leader.

So I have been thinking of these things since, and thinking about why Canadians have been having so much difficulty with aboriginal/non-aboriginal relationships over the years. And I'm almost wondering if it's a bit like Einstein's theory of relativity: that the same events look different to different people, to different observers in different conditions. Einstein found a way to pull those things together. We haven't done that yet.

There are at least two views of native Indians among Canadians. One is that there are 600,000 native individuals in Canada, of 30 million Canadians and six billion people in the world. The other view is that there is a small number of collectivities, and what is important is the collectivity rather than the individual. I want to come back to this as being one of the central questions that all of us have to work with here.

I want to give my paper on how we got to where we are, and then I want to say a little bit about where we might be going, and then we'll hear from Satsan.

The first observation I have to make will be no surprise to the collection of experts and concerned people here, and that is that history is very, very important. Mackenzie King used to say some countries have too much history and not enough geography. I think a great many Indian groups would say they have exactly the same problem. They're looking for more geography. But most Canadians don't understand the history. They don't understand how people were dispossessed across this continent as an act of government policy for a hundred years and more. They don't understand the importance of 1867, when the policy of the British colonial administration with respect to the Indian people was put into the Constitution, and the words, the federal government being responsible for "Indians and lands reserved for the Indians," were added as Section 91.24.

1867 was a time that was racist and sexist. Indians were discriminated against, women were discriminated against, and the Chinese were discriminated against, among others, particularly in my province of British Columbia. The Chinese people and the female people were not put into the Constitution. And 125 years later, their estate has changed remarkably. But for the Indian people, the requirements of our Constitution have not just argued for but *required* a constant institutionalization, a constant reinforcement of the difference between Indian Canadians and the rest of us. With all other people in Canada, and with the exception of language that has been troublesome in its own right, we tended to focus on the things that we have in common rather than the things that divide us. That has been an important part of our history.

In the 1950s, we saw a break with the past. We saw the growth of a sense of guilt, of wrong in the non-aboriginal society that became the spur to action in many areas. We saw the enfranchisement, the phase-out of the residential schools, a lot more money. In 1969, we saw the first serious government reassessment of aboriginal/non-aboriginal relations since Confederation in the Trudeau-Chrétien White Paper, which of course was rejected decisively by the Indian leadership of the time and by their associates and traditionalists. In my opinion, that was an opportunity lost. It was not an assimilationist document but rather an individualistic document. Be that as it may, that's part of history. It was not a central part of the Trudeau government's thrust, and therefore it was abandoned when trouble arose.

Since then, we have backed into the future, with no well-articulated policy. Things have been driven by events, by the media, by the latest academic writing. What has happened is that differences among us have been reinforced and reinforced. This has reached its full flowering in the *Nisga'a* treaty.

So here we are. The usefulness of history is to understand where we've all come from and to underpin the existing patterns or differences, for better or for worse. One must understand history to understand aboriginal rights. Too few Canadians have that understanding. That leads to my second observation. As a result of history and law and the Supreme Court of Canada, some, perhaps most, aboriginal rights are not well understood, at least in concept.

Quantum is another question. *Delgamuukw*, for example, put down very few markers in terms of quantum: what compensation means; how much Indian title there really is in British Columbia; and so on. We may well need more ltigation for that. But the concepts are there. And those defined rights, at least as I analyze it, mostly relate to property. By that I mean the right to use property, to take natural resources, property rights in almost full title, defined treaty rights, rights to compensation for unlawful infringement, which I think we're going to hear a lot more about in the future. These are all constitutionally protected rights under Section 35.

The dollars may be difficult for people to swallow but they should not bother anyone in concept. Even the dollars really fade into the background when you consider the amount of money that is going to have to be spent here anyway. Furthermore, these property-type rights are all clearly heritable, and therefore are clearly specific to individuals, or to collectivities of individuals. A very important question is whether the collectivity or the individual administers these properties and matter of right. But that is a second-order question that is up to the owners of the property to answer.

The third observation I would make, however, is that history may not be the best guide to the future. We must understand history, we must reconcile with history, and those are some of the most difficult parts we're going through now. We have to regard history as a sanctuary and not as a prison. We have to regard it as something we build on, and we must be prepared to transcend history. Talking about the future, we move away from the idea of rights and we move squarely into issues of governance, and the individual and the collective.

How does this interact with *Delgamuukw*? I'll give you cases in British Columbia, two treaties under negotiation. One of them, the *Nisga'a* treaty, would constitutionalize a new governance model. It is highly controversial, mostly because of that governance package. The *Sechelt* treaty is a similar settlement in terms of land, cash, and after giving effect to the semi-urban versus rural characteristic. The *Sechelt* treaty is moving along quietly, relatively quickly, with no controversy. What we have here is a form of government that is municipal-plus, but *delegated* legislation that has been working for 10 years. People are comfortable with it. Governance, I would suggest to you, is going to be the central issue of aboriginal-non-aboriginal discussions over the next few years.

So, we get into the slippery concept of the inherent right to self-government. What does this mean? On the face of it, this is something that is just good and true and beautiful. But without specifics, I would argue, it is a platitude. Clearly, individuals are entitled to their own self-government. "I'm the boss of my own body," my teenage kids say to me when I tell them not to smoke. But that's an individual right. When you get beyond that, where does the inherent right to self-government lie? With people who live in Canada, or people who live in British Columbia, or people who live in Vancouver, or the Catholics living in Vancouver, or the Indo-Canadians living in Richmond, or the Shaughnessy Heights Property Owners' Association? It's much more difficult.

Clearly, the answer is that there are different entitlements to government at these various levels. But how do you draw the lines? All have claims, and the concept can't be discussed really without details, such as whether there is there full consent of the government. What is the scale of the operations? What are the mobility rights and the disincentives to mobility in and out of the area of the government? The federal government clearly has a vision in this regard, which was developed for the *Nisga'a* treaty. That vision is, I'm convinced, to be replicated if they can do it based on one agreement that Indian Affairs Minister [Jane] Stewart made with the Treaty 8 tribal council in northern Alberta. In other parts of the country, that agenda remains unclear.

Now, when you start to talk about governance, I guess the first question involves the law. I am not a lawyer. But is there an aboriginal right to governance? In a Lincolnesque phrase: of aboriginals, by aboriginals, for aboriginals? The courts have not pronounced, but the communal nature of property of aboriginal title requires an administrative mechanism. I would argue that it only requires a society or a cooperative type administrative organization, rather than a full-blown government. What the Supreme Court has in mind, of course, we don't know. The Liberal Party says "yes," but I don't think there's much content in their "yes," with the exception of the actual Indian Affairs department. Most Canadians, I think, are very troubled by the idea. Not by the idea that different Canadians should be different. People are perfectly tolerant nowadays of the Hutterite communities in Alberta, though they weren't a generation ago. And the Hutterites are probably more different from the mainstream Canadians than the people on the Nisga'a lands, for example. It's not a question of difference per se.; it's a question of a different approach, of different entitlements, that instinctively bothers Canadians.

But, the question we have to address is what form of government, consistent with Canadian federalism and with Canadian values, can best meet the needs of the people in Area X? Area X being Indian land. And a number of subsidiary questions arise. Will this government have to do with all of the people in Area X, or only status Indians or aboriginals in Area X? The government of Canada in the *Nisga'a* treaty says only the latter. But if it doesn't include all of the people in Area X, do the powers of the government have to be modified? And perhaps lessened?

A third question: how do we address these issues of government in terms of practical matters, like subsidiarity; costs and efficiency; capacity; human and financial, external controls? There are external controls over most levels of government in Canada. The federal government is controlled by the courts and the constitution; the province is the same; the municipality by the province; and so on. So, how should that work?

We have to worry about democratic accountability of small governments with large powers. This is not a theoretical problem. This is a problem you can see in existence in different parts of the country, whereby an administration of a small government that not only has municipal-type powers, but has the right to grant and withhold housing, employment, perhaps access to higher education. You may get a situation where the elite controls the people, rather than the people controlling the elite. It's a question that has to be answered in each case. And when and if the government is ethnic-based rather than territorially based, what is to be the position of off-reserve or off-lands aboriginals?

In a recent and very important Supreme Court ruling, the *Corbière* case, the Supreme Court said Section 77.1 of the *Indian Act* is not constitutional because it denies the vote to band members off the reserve. The *Nisga'a* solution also discriminates against off-reserve people. The majority of Nisga'a who live off reserve have only about 10 percent of the legislative body's members. Will this be considered good enough? We do not know because the courts haven't pronounced whether or not it is.

The bottom line in all of this is the practical question of designing governmental arrangements to give the best services to citizens with resources that are always limited. Intimately entwined with all of the above is the relationship of the individual and the collective. I pose these philosophical questions without attempting to answer them right now. Indian collectivities, limited membership groups, are inherently closed organizations, like trade unions or co-operatives. All other Canadian governance collectivities are open, in the sense of residence being the qualification, at least a minimum qualification.

So the first philosophical question is this: is a closed society an appropriate unit for general governance? It is clearly an appropriate unit for asset management, or for the administration of lands and so on. Is it right for general governance?

The second question is pretty fundamental: do collectivities have any freestanding value beyond their total value to the individuals that make them up? Some people say "yes," they do. Some say aboriginal culture is, in and of itself, important and something outsiders should be prepared to support. Others say that preservation of this option for future generations is important. I still pose it as a question.

Philosophical question number three: should decision-making capacity in a collective, if that's the way the collective decides it's going, be predominantly individual-based, which calls for such things as private property, and private enterprise, and minimal law and regulation? Or, is it to be predominantly in the hands of the collective elite, however chosen?

Philosophical question number four: the legal and constitutional and discriminatory restraints placed on aboriginal people over the years have fostered, have indeed enforced, a collective arrangement. Is that the right route for the future?

And finally: do outsiders by way of sanctioning, indeed imposing, constitutional and entrenched governance procedures have any right to inflict these procedures as a matter of law on generations yet unborn?

I'm not pretending I have the answer to any of these questions. But I think they are questions that must be asked. Governments up until now have not encouraged debate on fundamental issues of this kind. That is not a favour to anyone, as we're seeing, given the reaction to the *Nisga'a* treaty in my province. The *Nisga'a* treaty, according to polls, is currently supported by 25 percent of British Columbians; opposed by 25 percent; and undecided by 50 percent.

Now, think about this: this is a treaty that should have been a joyous event, a treaty which after 120 years of pretty bad treatment of the Nisga'a people, who persisted over all those years, finally came to what was said to be an honourable arrangement. Why is it that the people of British Columbia have such ambivalence about this deal? And I suggest it comes down to governments having improperly, or inadequately, made sure there was a dialogue among British Columbians and among Canadians on these issues. So I think we all have a job to do. Satsan is a big voice in this dialogue, and a very constructive one. I look forward to what he's going to say.

Satsan (Chief Herb George)

Thank you very much for the opportunity to participate in your conference. I decided I would do something a little different this time: I want to try to put my words into a context of stories. I think that these stories will tell you a lot.

I want to mention that I appreciate the opportunity to sit beside my friend Gordon. When I first met him, it was not under the best of circumstances. I attacked him. [Laughter] He was there trying to get material for his story on the Progressive Democratic Alliance, which had invited me to be a keynote speaker. I noticed him sitting there. I had also been reading his column. I went at him to try to make the point that, 'you know, for the life of me, I can't understand the columns you write because they are based on opinions that you hold about aboriginal issues. And although I read them, and reread them, I still don't get where you're coming from. And maybe we should sit down and talk about that.' We had that opportunity. I was quite surprised, pleasantly surprised, to learn that even though people come to an issue from opposite extremes, when we had an opportunity to sit down, respecting one another and listening to one another, we can arrive at an understanding. We can realize that a lot of the issues that seem to set us apart, we agree to in common. When you get right down to it, the things that we have which create a difference between us aren't all that big, and aren't all that difficult to overcome. I believe that the reason we could have that kind of a relationship is simply because you go in there with an open mind. You go in there willing to listen, willing to change your point of view and the opinion that you hold. I think it takes a lot of courage to do that, and I respect that a lot.

The point I wanted to raise is that if we could take that same kind of energy, that same kind of passion that we brought to the battlefield, to try to find the solution and the resolution, and reconciliation, we could certainly do it. Without question, I believe.

[Holds up an article and quotes from it] *"Fraser's Formula for Prosperity: Small Government with Economic Freedom."* That's my speech tonight. Rather than write one, I thought I'd borrow one *"A new study shows government policy a key growth factor."*

"What's basically needed for success," says Mr. [Michael] Walker, "is a reasonable ability to engage in trade and keep the majority of the income earned. Further than economic rights are fundamental rights. They are a prerequisite for the economic growth, and for broader human development. The least free countries score poorly on United Nations Human Development Index. The most free score highly."

To prepare myself today, I set up a meeting with Indian Affairs—to talk about policy and to get myself into a state of mind of rage. I found something very, very interesting. I didn't get into a rage. I didn't even get upset. Even coming here and listening to the opposition—I call [them] the Last of the Indian Fighters. They are always the same guys. I've come to know a lot of these guys, and I was sitting there talking to [one participant] and realized that, man alive, it wasn't too long ago I wouldn't have given him the time of day. I would have sat over there. But I find that through the opportunity of sitting down, and getting to know one another, that way down deep we're all good people.

But I don't want to talk about the position of *Delgamuukw* itself, or the law, or the Constitution. I spent 24 years of my life working on *Delgamuukw*, and I want to talk about why someone would do such a foolish thing. Why give a fourth of your life away, seeing it's for an endless pursuit.?

The whole point of it goes back to my grandfather's time. My grandfather appeared before the *McKinnon Commission*, in 1911 and 1913 in our area. They came along after the reserves had already been established, and their job was to cut off lands, to reduce the size of the reserves that were originally set up. Our people made representation to the Commission. Our grandfather was there, and he said: "We don't want to talk about reserve lands. Who are you to give us our own land? And who are you to press in these little places and fence us in? You know, we're like animals in a cage when you do that to us. We want to talk about continuing to live on our lands, and how we will share it with you. We don't want to talk about reserves." But unfortunately, that was the case. They were there to talk about reserves, and to put our people on reserves.

Between the time of my grandfather and my young life on a reserve, the spirit of our society has been turned upside down. I believe that I grew up during the worst upheaval our society has ever known. What that was, was the transition between a people who could take care of themselves and a people who are almost wholly dependent upon government transfer arrangements for every aspect of their lives. Those very things that some members of Canadian society get so uptight about—they get free housing, they get free education, they get free health, free this, free everything—without taking into account, or taking the time to educate themselves about how this came about, the devastating effect that it's had on our community, and on our people. Nobody should have to go through that. And I don't think anybody could understand it unless you do.

It was a terrible, terrible thing to grow up in, and to watch. As a result of that, I became a very, very angry person. Very, very angry. I spent all my time in the library of the residential school, reading about South Africa, India, South America, and about different movements for independence and freedom. I learned at an early age that I was not free, that somebody had imprisoned me, and took everything away. They were trying to make me become like my parents who had succumbed to that. And I made a decision, early on, that that will never happen, I will never accept that. Never. And as a result I became very, very angry.

After university, I spent all my time fighting with the profs, arguing. I went to law school, and I spent all my time fighting with the students. And every bloody day there was a line-up to debate with me about aboriginal rights. I got so fed up one day I told them: "Why don't you guys just all f*** off and leave me alone?"

The point of this is that you come from something like that, and through your history you know where you came from, and you know what you had, and you know how you lived. You know what lands are yours, the rights that you have. You know what government that you have. All of a sudden you're on a reserve, and you're forced to govern yourself through the *Indian Act* which, I submit, tried to force on us individual rights. But we as a collective refused to accept that, and we maintain [our collective rights] to this day. Not because we think that it's any better than individual rights, but because that's what we grew up with, that's what we know. That's a part of our history. That's who we are.

Given that, I don't think that anybody else should be so arrogant as to tell us that we should be like them, and that we should adopt those things that they hold dear to them, the values that have, the principles that they have, simply because it's theirs.

Which brings me to my second story.

During *Delgamuukw*, as you can imagine, it was a very, very adversarial relationship between the Wet'suwet'en and the Gitksan and the surrounding municipalities, because they were in court challenging the status quo as a whole, challenging everything. And certainly there was opposition to that, heavy opposition to it. But things change. In one situation in Smithers, I was at a meeting that the Reform Party hijacked and took control of. They were, in my view, misleading the people about the whole notion of self-government, saying that we're going to create independent, sovereign states within Canada. I was only one of two aboriginal people in that building. When I got up to raise a question, I was shouted down. You'll apologize for my language, but I'm going to use it, because this is what was said: "Sit down you f***in' welfare bum … F*** you welfare bum." Just a chorus of it. And I stood up there and I didn't know what to do. I didn't know how to respond. So I started to encourage them. "Come on! Let's go!" I kept getting louder, and they got louder, and louder, and louder, and they realized the foolishness of it all, and settled down to almost silence, like we have right now. And I said: "Good for you. It's good for you to vent and get it off your chest. Because you still have to deal with me. I'm not going away. I'm still going to be here. I'm not afraid of you. It doesn't scare me to come in here to deal with you."

After that there were some questions about governance. I got up again to answer, and this time there was more respect from the people there. When I finished, they were almost going to start to clap, and they realized it, and got a hold of themselves.

[Laughter]

But the problem with that was that there was just a complete misunderstanding. There was no dialogue between us and them. Just total opposition from one side to the other.

So, from that incident we realized that we needed to get out and do some work, promote an understanding between the people who live there, and we started to do that. One evening I was doing some work in Smithers again, in front of a crowd of people, and the issue was governance and the problem with it. The point of view of the person who was questioning me on it was that he couldn't agree that we should govern ourselves with a system that, in his view, was feudal in nature. He characterized our chiefs as feudal lords, because that's all he knows about the feudal system. He doesn't know anything else. I tried to explain to him that that's furthest from the truth, because, in fact, our system is based upon accountability. We never heard of this word democratic until you brought it along. The way it works is this: I am from the Frog Clan, and when my clan is doing our business, the other clans come in and take their seats, and they are the witnesses to the business being done. Everybody knows about it. Everybody participates in it. Before we bring this forward, we have to deal with our own membership, our own clan membership, to reach consensus amongst ourselves. We can't bring this forward on our own as chiefs, because if we do, we'd never survive. You can't be successful because your people won't support you. Often you have to give up your name. And when we bring white people into that, show them the way it works, they are suitable impressed.

I was explaining it to this guy, and he didn't really agree with me, but we talked about the need to educate the greater community. So we thought, well, how can we do that? I suggested to him: "Why don't we use the town council, you know, we have a good relationship with the municipalities, we could get together and utilize the town council chambers and the local community hall, and we could organize from there." And this guy said: "Not a chance. That'll never work." I said: "Why?" He said: "Well, everybody knows they're all corrupt. You elect them, and never hear from them again. They go about, and they just do whatever they want to do. They don't talk to us." And I said: "Well, that's really interesting. What about maybe the regional district?" He said: "Well, they're just as bad. They're elected too, and it's the same thing. They're a bunch of crooks." I said: "Well, why don't they talk to you guys?" He said: "Well that's just the way it's always been. That's the nature of the system. When you elect people, whether it's the municipalities, whether it's provincial government, federal government, regional districts, we never hear from them again. They just can't be trusted." So I said: "Well, that's *really* interesting. Because here you are telling me that you can't agree or support us governing ourselves the way we know how, and that we should adopt your system because it's based upon democratic principles, and now you're telling me that it's corrupt, and that they don't talk to you? That in fact, you don't have a voice? What's democratic about that? I don't think I want that. I don't think that's for us. We'd have a lot of problems with that. Our people won't be left out."

Again, it points to just a total misunderstanding of the reality of the situation, or the truth of the matter. I think the other problem is that people forget that this whole thing is about people. It's about human beings, of which I am one, like you. And we're not seen that way. Somehow or another we're just a pain in the butt. You know, we're a burden to your society, and a burden to the taxpayer. We're just a burden all around. You wish we would just go away. But we're not. We never have, and we never will. We'll always be here, the way we are.

Which brings me to my third story. We had organized in our area to meet with the town councils, realizing that we have got to deal with issue as a community, as the people who live within the Wet'suwet'en territory, of which there are four municipalities. So we set up meetings with the town council, and we started to have a dialogue, a discussion. What can we do to reconcile the differences? In a very, very serious way. At one meeting, we also invited the regional district. I was told by one of the Smithers councillors that I should be very, very careful because there was going to be an individual there who was totally against anything and everything that I was going to have to say about aboriginal rights or title. As a matter of fact he said: "If you can convince him, you can convince anybody."

So I went to this meeting, and we sat down, and we proceeded to have this discussion, and he spent all his time scowling at me. You know, every time I looked up he was scowling at me. We had a break and I finally said to him: "Excuse me, I haven't had the pleasure of meeting you before," and introduced myself to him. He introduced himself to me, then he said: "Your last name is George?" I said: "That's correct." And he said: "Are you any relation to Felix George?" "Yes, he was my grandfather." He said: "We used to go there with my parents every Sunday, and have Sunday dinner with them, and at the time they lived on Holland Lake," which wasn't a reserve incidentally. That's where my grandparents lived; that's where they were from. We started to talk about that, and he talked about the relationship that they had as people. "Oh my God," he said, "what's happened to us? What's happened to me as a human being? What's happened to me that now I can say 'no' to you, when in the past we had a different relationship?"

So we started to discuss that, and we discussed that several times, at different venues in the municipalities, about the fact that at one time there was a relationship that was based upon mutual recognition and respect between the settlers who came and the Wet'suwet'en people who lived there. And remarkably, he became my friend. This weekend, the Cattlemen's Association had a meeting in Smithers, and he called me to invite me to come. We talked about things that are going on, and his whole reason for being now is to find a way to resolve things, as opposed to just sit in opposition.

I think the lesson in that is that if we can get away from the law, emotion of truth, the fact that you don't understand our government so you can't support it, and try to sit down and deal with each other as human beings, we can get somewhere. You can go a long way to resolving the issues that we have, because than they're personal, they're personal to *us*. But as long as we have people who are removed from the community, sitting on one side or the other side of the fence and lobbing grenades at one another, nothing changes for us.

I want to impress upon you that we're talking about human beings, people who have as much right as you do to a healthy economy, and a healthy society. You have no reason why we should be denied that, to use your own words, "on the basis of race." Because that's in fact what has happened, and we need to acknowledge that.

So when I read this article from The Fraser Institute in the [National]Post, I thought it was very interesting that you should have such strong feelings about your right to a healthy economy. And I thought, "well, if they think that's so important to them, than they should be able to realize the importance of that to us as well." We need to start looking at the things that we have in common, as opposed to the things that we disagree on. But I think that in some instances, both things that we disagree on we'll never agree on. That's possible. Possible to die that way, maybe. But I think it's our responsibility for our young people to come along behind us and clean up the mess that we made.

And speaking of young people, when we look at what we wish for our children in the future I bet we have the same wishes, without a doubt. I want those things for my children too. I don't want them to have to spend their lives fighting in the courts so that they can have some measure of this debt, and some ability to exercise fundamental human rights that the rest of the society takes for granted.

In terms of histories, you look forward to clarification from the courts on many, many different issues. I don't think you need to look any further than looking at myself as I stand here for clarification. I'm a Wet'suwet'en person. Whether I can go in the court and convince them or not doesn't remove the fact that I'm still a Wet'suwet'en person, who has a history, who has a language, who has a homeland that he knows.

We have to step back and realize that it's not about the burden of proof—it's about respect. It's about recognition, and of people. It's about a commitment to one another. It's about a spirit of generosity. It's about realizing that we can live and co-exist together, and that we can share from the bounty of the land, and everything that it has to offer us. And if we could look at that from the point of view of our children, in common, I believe we could have that. I look forward to the day that we can.

Just to close on this last point, I had a very difficult time coming here to do the talk. I'm simply sick and tired of it. I think that was why when I was sitting there meeting with Indian Affairs today I just felt no passion in my soul and in my heart for it. I realized that the only people who are going to change it, are people like myself. And if it takes going onto the land and just simply taking possession of it, and taking advantage of the uncertainty that exists to bring about the kind of reconciliation that I think we need, then that's what I'm prepared to do. I've reached the point, I think, I'm very close to it, where I can't in all good conscience get up and try to say that the processes that we have in place to dissolve this issue are good ones. They're not. They leave a lot to be desired. If we have 100 per cent of the title interest in our land base, why are we going to give up 95 percent of it to have a relationship? It doesn't make any sense. Why do we have to give up anything? We're not asking you to give up anything. We're not asking you to adopt our government structures. We're not asking you to live on reserves. We're not asking you to depend on transfer arrangements from us to live. So we've got to look at that in that context. Question yourself about what you ask of us, because the standard that you set is simply too high. It's higher than your own society can bear.

We need some compassion here. We need some understanding. We need some commitment for resolution. That is the solution to our differences and the problem that we have. So I thank you for your attention, and I look forward to a good conversation with you.